Self-build Simplified

By

Barry Sutcliffe

Self-Build is simple,

People make it complicated

Meet "Chips"

You will see Chips popping up regularly throughout the book. Where you see him, he will be either:

Highlighting a personal comment (not necessarily related to the theme of the main text).

Making a point, offering a different point of view, or suggesting an idea that might be useful.

Forward by Valerie Bearne, MCLIP.

(Founder and Chair of the Build a Dream Self Build Association. Founder member of the National and Custom Self Build Association. For many years involved in supporting and advising self builders. Providing information and education on all aspects of self and custom building. Author of 'Self Building; the Internet speaks' and 'Get together and build yourself a house, the essential guide to group self building')

I first met Barry Sutcliffe when I joined the then Association of Self Builders, of which he was a founder member. It was obvious that Barry possesses an encyclopaedic knowledge of building and construction, which he was happy to share whenever needed.

I was delighted to hear that Barry was writing this book and would be reaching an even wider audience in need of basic information and advice to help achieve more and more self and custom built homes. I have long believed that designing and building your own home gives the best quality housing, that suits the occupants, and is more sustainable than any other form of housing. The government agrees, which is why they wish to double the numbers of self or custom built houses in the UK, whilst looking enviously at other countries achieving far greater numbers and percentages.

Barry's conversational approach to the subject makes for an easy read of what can be quite a technical subject. This book is a comprehensive and detailed explanation of the whole process of self building, from having the idea, and seeking a plot, choosing the construction method and materials, identifying and avoiding potential problems, right through to completion and moving in. There is some repetition, but this is to achieve the authors aim of allowing the reader to dip in and out of chapters as needed, for particular aspects of the building process.

A careful study of all the information and explanations contained in this book could save the average self builder several thousands of pounds, achieve better standards, and save a lot of time and hassle. I recommend reading this book from cover to cover, making notes as you go, then returning to all the crucial points to ensure you are not missing anything.

www.badsba.co.uk

Index

PAGE 2	MEET CHIPS	
PAGE 6	INTRODUCTION	
PAGE 23	CHAPTER 1:	SELF-BUILD – IS IT A GOOD IDEA?
PAGE 49	CHAPTER 2:	GETTING STARTED
PAGE 74	CHAPTER 3:	FINANCE & MORTGAGES
PAGE 101	CHAPTER 4:	FINDING A DECENT PLOT OF LAND
PAGE 142	CHAPTER 5:	DESIGNING YOUR NEW HOME
PAGE 173	CHAPTER 6:	GETTING PLANNING PERMISSION
PAGE 201	CHAPTER 7:	HOW WILL WE BUILD THE HOUSE?
PAGE 270	CHAPTER 8:	HOW WILL WE RUN THE PROJECT?
PAGE 299	CHAPTER 9:	HOW MUCH WILL IT COST TO BUILD?
PAGE 350	CHAPTER 10:	GETTING READY TO START BUILDING
PAGE 389	CHAPTER 11:	STARTING ON SITE & FOUNDATIONS
PAGE 424	CHAPTER 12:	BUILDING THE SHELL OF THE HOUSE
PAGE 466	CHAPTER 13:	THE INTERNAL FIT OUT
PAGE 505	CHAPTER 14:	KITCHENS & BATHROOMS
PAGE 524	CHAPTER 15:	EXTERNAL WORKS
PAGE 547	CHAPTER 16:	FINAL CERTIFICATES / MOVING IN / VAT REFUNDS

Before you start to read

To gain maximum benefit from this book I suggest that you do the following:

1. Read the book from cover to cover, preferably before you make any major decisions on if, how and when you are going to take on your own self-build project.
   (*If you have already started work, I recommend you still read from chapter 1. There will almost certainly be information in the early pages that you will find useful later*).
2. As you read, scribble your own notes, highlighting anything you think could be relevant, interesting or important.
3. When you are ready to start your project, read the book again, but this time, just concentrate on a few chapters at a time. As you read, refer to your own comments and notes. Mixing my ideas with your own will almost certainly be the best way to formulate your plans and to create practical, achievable targets.
4. As you move forward with your plans, keep the book close to hand and refer to it before you make *any* important decisions.

As you read, you will notice some repetition. This is to allow the reader to "dip in" to any part of the book and hopefully find all the relevant information.

INTRODUCTION:

PART 1:
Back in the day

Something to ponder:

In the late 1980s (which happens to be when I took on my first selfbuild project), the UK selfbuild industry looked very different from how it looks now. The only people who even considered building their own home in those days, were pretty much divided into two groups. These were:

1) **The brave** (*and sometimes worryingly misguided*) **individual souls and couples** who were prepared to risk all to turn their dreams into reality, by creating a living space for themselves from scratch, that would hopefully be bigger, better and cheaper than the alternative of buying one of the flimsy boxes that were at the time (and still sadly are) forced upon them by the major house builders.
2) **The groups** of (often even more misguided) people who got together to create community selfbuild groups, where everyone would be allocated a plot on a large site, and where theoretically, everyone involved would lend a hand to build not only their own, but also everyone else's houses, over what often turned out to be a frighteningly lengthy period of time.

Both of these types of people (*and I have to align myself with the first group*), usually launched themselves into these potentially massive and financially risky personal ventures without having access to the internet, or any significant levels of useful written information on the subject. Blissfully unaware at the start of the process of how to identify good quality land, how to design a house, how much it costs to build whatever they design, how long it would take, or what problems they may encounter along the way. They often had no knowledge of land costs, planning procedures, project planning, how to manage a building site, bookkeeping, health and safety requirements, structural insurances, warranties or a hundred and one other important matters, any of which, if not attended to professionally and at the right time, could result in the whole thing turning into a complete disaster and with them ending up with no house, no money, kids that hate them and often divorce proceedings pending!

In those days, we didn't have access to the sum of all knowledge via a company (that probably didn't even exist then) called Google and a little box with a screen and a keyboard. There was only one major selfbuild show a year, one or two decent books on the subject, no self-build centre in Swindon, no NaCSBA *(National Custom and Self Build Association)*, no BADSBA Build a dream), no television programmes and channels dedicated to the subject. We didn't have Kevin McCloud, George Clarke or Charlie Luxton to show us what a mess we can make of things if we are left to our own devices, or Melinda Messenger to show us how dodgy UK builders can be and we didn't have one thousand and one companies shouting at us that *"It can all be really easy if you just use our product and ignore all the other rubbish out there"*!

Given that nowadays we obviously have access to far more information, more numerous sources for gathering everything and everyone we need together into one place. When there is far more professional help at hand and with the backing of government policy for our industry, why is it that the selfbuild market is has not been and is still not surging forward, or even growing at any noticeable rate in 2016?

During the 1980s, 1990s and early 2000s, although there are no definitive figures, the estimates are that there were, in some years, getting on for 22,000 selfbuild completions. That is 22,000 potentially misguided, under informed, "wet behind the ears" individuals, couples, families and groups, all having a go, all taking a massive risk, with little knowledge or preparation, without a safety net and often without any ongoing professional backup. But, eventually, no matter how long it had taken and how hard it had been, these people were getting the job done and moving in to their new dream homes.

22,000 completions a year is around twice as many as have managed in any of the past few years up to 2016.

These facts and figures naturally lead us to form the blindingly obvious notion that, for quite a long time, there has been something significantly wrong with our industry. They must also lead to the conclusion that, as the completion figures are still not rising at any noticeable rate, it means that as individuals and groups, we are still not doing it right, we are still not going about the processes in the best way and perhaps most worryingly of all, we are not realising what we are doing wrong.

After looking at the facts and figures associated with our own industry, we would have to admit that, as an industry, we are definitely not learning any of the lessons that we should be learning or changing course to head off in a better direction.

So what are the problems?

There are, to my mind three major problems with the selfbuild industry today.

Problem 1
It is all far too complicated.

I have a number of pet sayings related to our industry. You will find them sprinkled across the pages as you continue read the rest of the book. The one I want to start with is this (the one written on the front cover of this book):

Selfbuild is simple – People make it complicated.

This is the point of the book at which possibly some of the "professionals" in the industry will stop reading. "*The man doesn't know what he is talking about*" they may say, or "*He is a fool and is obviously misinformed*".

A fool I may be, but I am not misinformed.

I have been building houses and other (sometimes substantial) structures for around 35 years. Over that time, as well as working on hospitals, factories, schools, offices, power stations, new roads and various types of commercial buildings, I have completed 5 of my own self builds, numerous large executive homes through my own development company and I have worked on hundreds of new homes on various sites, for both small and large house building companies. If I am sure of one thing after all that time and after seeing the various ways there are to build things, it is that house building *can* and *should* be simple.

If, as many parts of the industry prefer us to think, it is difficult and complicated, then how is it that so many UK commercial house builders, many of whom can't even work out how to use their email systems or spell correctly in their own adverts, can be building tens of thousands of new homes all over the country every year? The answer to that question is that they could not.

Another of the sayings I use (which on this occasion I can't claim sole usage of) is:

> *"Draw me a simple house design on the back of a fag packet and I'll go and build it for you".*

The usual reaction I get when I quote that saying that to potential selfbuilders is one of incredulity, so I had better explain why it is true.

Any commercial house builder worth dealing with, has normally been building homes for at least a few years. There are many building norms, which at least most new homes conform to and anyone with a couple of years or more of house building experience should know them. These people should not need to refer to a manual or drawings to know how proceed. They should all be fully aware of the basics and knowledgeable enough to take on "the fag packet challenge" without any problem.

The house building norms of which I speak include the following (*bear with me here, there is a reason for this list*):

Foundations

- Are generally an average of 900mm deep, 600mm wide for a cavity wall.
- Are a minimum of 225mm depth of usually C30 grade concrete.
- Don't pour the foundations until the building inspector and the warranty company have checked and passed them.
- Make sure when setting out the house that it is "square" (i.e. the corners are at 90 degrees).
- There are usually two skins of blockwork up to damp proof course (dpc) with "semi dry" concrete cavity fill for a cavity wall and one skin of blockwork for a single skin external wall.
- The dpc needs to be set at the right level and should be level within itself to about a 5mm tolerance all around the building.
- Concrete slabs generally need insulation underneath them (100mm is usually ok) and 25mm around the edges. They average 150mm thick for a standard house and lie on a damp-proof membrane (dpm).
- Slabs need to be laid within about a 10mm tolerance in level across their area and should be laid using a vibrating poker to make sure there are no trapped air voids.
- Standard slabs normally have a 65mm – 75mm screed applied to the top of them to give a smooth finished surface.

External walls

- Need to be plumb and the cavities kept clean.
- You should not build brick or blockwork higher than around 1.4m in one day otherwise the joints may squash.
- Vertical dpc is needed at openings.
- Insulation is needed for building regulations.
- Lintels are needed over openings and should have a 150mm seating on to the adjacent walls.
- Room heights are usually around 2.4m
- Downstairs door openings should be at least 2.1m high by 900mm wide (sometimes they are 800mm wide upstairs but 900mm is better).
- Window head heights are generally at 2.1m.
- Window cill heights in kitchens are at 1.05m from the floor to give a 6" upstand behind worktops (which are at around 900mm above floor level), so water can't run on to the cill.

Internal walls

- Are usually either 100mm blockwork or 100mm timber studs
- Sound insulation between rooms is good to have. Fibreglass insulation is good and cheap.
- ½" plasterboard is usual each side of timber internal walls (with more fireproof and better options being available at extra cost), but with timber frames you need timber supports fixed behind the plasterboard wherever you may want to hang anything heavy.
- Finishes are usually wet plaster and skim, dot and dab or dry lining on brick or blockwork walls and a 2mm thick skim or dry lining on plasterboard.

Intermediate floors

- Floor joists can be either hung between the walls, or they can sit in joist hangers, or sit on the walls themselves.
- Floor joist spans have limits depending on their dimensions. Check standard "joist span" tables if no other information is available. There are different types of joists, some can span up to 8m+ without needing extra support along their length.
- Floor boards are usually 18mm or 22mm thick and generally come in 8' x 2' sheets. They can be standard or moisture resistant and there are different types and finishes to choose from. All seem to work ok as long as they are used in the right place. If in doubt, use 22mm moisture resistant boards to be sure.

I think that will do!

You may not have understood everything I just wrote, but I can pretty much guarantee that if you were building houses as a living, if you were any good at your job, you would know all those facts and figures within a couple of years and once you know them - *you know them*. If you look closely at them there is no rocket science in there. Once you have spent a couple of days digging a house foundation, you will remember that it should be 900mm x 600mm, because if it gets any deeper or wider, the site manager will be panicking about the extra concrete he or she is going to have to buy!

If you go to the merchants and buy 18mm standard floor boards and get back to find that the drawings asked for 22mm moisture resistant boards, you'll have to go back and change them and I bet you remember to check next time! In other words, pretty much all the standard, basic building knowledge you need is just that, *standard* and *basic*.

Suffice to say, the "standard stuff" continues throughout the building, whether it relates to materials, processes or the people you need to do all the jobs.

So, the processes required to build a simple house are relatively easy to grasp or learn. That fact suggests that if you were to take on your own selfbuild project, did a bit of research, possibly a bit of training, if you kept it simple and if you had a modicum of help from the professional people who would be involved, you could come up with something pretty good as an end product. Probably significantly superior in quality and lower in price than the offerings of the major housebuilders.

The problem we have however, is that the people who are making their living out of working on your projects, selling you expensive products and services (*which often complicate the proceedings without giving any noticeable benefit*), do not all necessarily want you to know that the process does not have to be complicated and that in fact, you might not need some of *those very people* or their products!

There lies the problem.

We have an industry of a very limited size (around 10,000 units a year) with a massive supply infrastructure behind it, from self build authors (!), estate agents, surveyors, mortgage providers, through architects, warranty and insurance companies, planning specialists, project managers, builders, materials and service providers, to interior and landscape designers, VAT specialists, accountants and Uncle Tom Cobley an' all!

All these people are looking to make a living by selling *you* their wares and if you were to realise that actually you don't really need many of them, they could quickly go out of business. This unfortunately, but inevitably leads to a situation where each and every person who is making a living out of the industry, has to make all efforts to persuade you that you **do** need *them* and *their* product or service and that you need *them* more than you need the other guys that they are competing with.

This is where things start to go pear-shaped.

The people that are selling basically the same product or service under different guises, all have to come up with reasons to convince you why their product or service is the best and that you should not even consider using one of the possibly simpler, cheaper and potentially better alternatives. This can, in turn lead to exaggerated, misleading and / or confusing claims being made, pressure sales techniques being applied and the result of this is all too often that the potential self-builder just ends up getting more and more confused about who or what is actually right and less confident in their own ability to make the right choices. This in turn leads them into doing more and more research to try to find the right answers, which then makes them even more confused and creates a going round in circles effect, which eventually sees them simply disappearing up their own existence and giving up on the whole thing completely!

This situation manifests itself very clearly in the area of the *choice of build method*:

Let's have a quick look at your choices in just *one part* of the building structure, the external walls.

Your choices include:

- Brick & block cavity wall
- Block & block cavity wall plus render
- Block & block plus batten and cladding
- Block & block plus batten, cement board and render
- Timber frame & brick skin
- Timber frame and block plus render
- Timber frame & block plus batten & cladding
- Timber frame & block plus batten, cement board & render
- Timber frame & block plus batten, cement board & brick slips
- SIPS (*structurally insulated panelling system*) as part of a cavity wall, with any of the above timber frame accompanying options
- SIPS as a single skin wall with batten, cement board & render
- SIPS as a single skin wall with batten and cladding
- SIPS as a single skin wall with batten and brick slips
- Closed panel frame as either part of a cavity wall or a single skin wall, with any of the Timber frame *or* SIPS accompanying options
- Oak frame construction with a choice of finishes
- ICF (Insulated Concrete Formwork) with a choice of finishes
- Steel frame construction with a choice of finishes
- Concrete frame construction with a choice of finishes
- Any of the myriad of different types of "Eco" wall systems

Now, add to each item in that list, the different types of insulation which can be used with each of the types of wall construction, in different thicknesses, to give you varying degrees of warmth from basic building regulations compliant" to passive house standard and you will end up tripling or quadrupling the number of external wall construction options available to you.

Confused? You should be!

The worst part of it is that none of those choices are actually right or wrong, your final decision on which to use will usually just all come down to *what you want*, or often more realistically *what you are persuaded to have*, by an architect, builder or good salesman".

And there lies the problem. Most potential self-builders will either research themselves in to oblivion, or end up just taking the advice of one of the people they talk to because they don't have the confidence to do anything else.

Imagine for a moment, how confused you would be if, by trying to be thorough and equip yourself with the level of knowledge you need to compare each of the options listed above, you read every book and magazine article on the subject of *choices for external wall construction*, then visited every selfbuild show, watched every TV programme, downloaded and read every brochure on every product and every option and spoke to as many salesmen as possible? If you did all that you may think that you would be fully briefed and raring to go. In fact, as I said earlier, the opposite would happen, instead of being filled with confidence, you would simply end up completely confused and probably verging on becoming a jabbering wreck, unable to make any decisions on anything in case it turned out to be wrong.

Now that you hopefully see the problem, imagine how things could end up if in this book, I started to list all the options for *every single phase* of the project, from the early stages of working out the best way to design your new home, through warranties, the *main contractor versus project management versus self project managing* arguments and then detailed all the foundation and roof construction choices, right through to all the options available for the interior design and landscaping.

Instead of being a potentially very exciting challenge, the whole concept could very quickly turn into a very scary nightmare and one which you would most likely decide "*Is not for me*".

Your other option, if you still wanted to have some sort of bespoke new home, would be just to give the whole thing over to someone who can look after it all for you (but who will probably not actually give you what you need or want and will end up charging you a fortune).

I have seen this sort of thing happen with potential self-builders *so many* times over the years and it **is** one of the biggest problems we face in the industry.

How do we solve the problem?

We solve the problem by making the whole process simpler. Making sure that people understand that, in fact they don't have to know everything about everything, so that anyone who thinks about taking on a project (i.e. you) only learns *what they need to learn* and, as preparation, only does *what they need to do* and no more.

By the time you have finished reading this book, hopefully you will be totally fired up ready to plough into your own project and you will be aware of exactly what you *need* to learn and do and what you *don't need* to learn and do, to give you the best chance of making sure that your project ends up being one of the successful ones.

Problem 2
We are an industry full of individuals

Ok, so we have to get over the complication of the industry, but what about when we do? How do we actually get going on our projects? Where do we find the land, the finances, the people and all the other stuff we need to pull the whole thing together?

This is the second big problem area with our industry.

Nearly every self-builder has to accept the fact that they are pretty much on their own for the duration of the venture. As I said, there are hardly any local clubs to join, where everyone helps each other (BADSBA, the *Build a Dream Self Build Association* and its sub groups) are the only ones to my knowledge).

In the UK, there is no land finding system which offers a full package which finds, vets and sells plots at reasonable prices. There is no central database of selfbuild designers, planning specialists, project managers, ground workers, brickies etc. Nope, although there are a few companies out there trying to do their best, as far as I know, none of these entities exist (yet) in a professional and widely available format. So unfortunately, it is going to be up to you to get through the whole shooting match, pretty much just by using your own knowledge, experience, skill and initiative. That is a big ask of anyone, but especially if this is your first project and your knowledge of building is minimal or non-existent before you start.

I am reminded of something that happened around 25 years ago, when I was a Selfbuild Project Manager in the North West. I was contacted by a client, who had the land and planning permission, who had not yet started work, but needed to build and finish a 4-bed brick / block detached house in 10 weeks, before he had to move out of the house he was living in. He was then aiming to get married the following Saturday (*he was one of the worryingly misled people who used to just have a go, whom I mentioned at the start of this introduction*).

This guy had hired 2 labourers from an agency to start hand digging his foundations and was at his wits end already. He was basically asking me if I could take over and build the house in less than 10 weeks.

I went to meet him on site and I remember that when I arrived he was standing with a roughly dressed man, next to what was a very small amount of newly hand dug trench, with two guys beavering away with shovels.

As I approached them, I started to hear the conversation between them. It went along the lines of: (My potential client) *"Once we have dug all the holes, how much would you charge me for throwing some pebbles in and stamping on them?"*

Laying aside the myriad of other things he was doing wrong at that moment, roughly translated in to basic technical speak he was actually trying to say: *"Once excavation is complete, how much would you charge me to bring in and lay 150mm of hardcore around the trench, and compact it?"* (By the way, you don't normally lay hardcore in a standard foundation trench, just concrete)

I could almost see in the eyes of the person he was talking to (a ground worker) as he heard those words, a nought being added to the end of the quotation!

The problem here was that that self-builder was on his own. He had no idea how to build a house or how to run any type of construction project above probably putting a barbeque together. He was alone, inexperienced, lacking knowledge and totally ill equipped to do what he was trying to do. He was going to fail.

Although these days the industry is a bit more professional than it was, this sort of thing does still happen. People start a project on their own and then think they have to try to run it right through to the end, on their own, with the obvious consequences that many of them hit major problems along the way and significant numbers of them either fail completely, or are so wounded mentally and financially by the end of the process that they wish they had never started.

So this is another major problem our industry needs to solve.

How do we stop being an industry made up of 10,000 individuals or couples, with no real long term professional back up, often with little or no knowledge of the subject, usually with limited funding and time available to dedicate to the project and who change each year into a completely different set of 10,000 new people, who are in exactly the same position?

The simple answer is that we need to start to join together and use our numbers to give ourselves a bit of punching weight when it comes to attracting the professional people (*and the government*) to give us the support we need to help to start to change the industry.

We might have a while to wait until we get a proper response from the government (who are in 2016 making at least some, albeit it often misguided and ineffective efforts to do something useful). However, there is nothing to stop us at least starting to get our own act together.

This book is intended to empower the individual self-builder to start to think about how to get the right back-up from the right people, at the right time and the right price and then be able to act on their thoughts and move forward with confidence.

Problem 3
We are letting the developers get all the best land at the best prices.

If you read most articles regarding the lack of growth in the selfbuild industry, it seems that the blame is put down to a lack of available good quality and affordable land for individual self-builders to buy.

The reason for this state of affairs is put down to the behaviour of the medium and large scale housing developers. Those nasty, selfish folk have the cheek and the gall to go around buying up all the good land, at trade prices, then they compound this unfairness and go on to make a fortune by selling their poorly designed, poor quality houses at sky high prices to the desperate general public. They won't even agree to give us a few plots on their humungously large developments, despite the government asking them nicely. It's just not fair!

I think this description sums up our industry quite well:

1) We are a very amateurish industry with very little professionalism being shown by either the businesses making money out of it, or the people who are supposed to be leading it.
2) We are actually quite childish in the way we work. If we don't get what we want or need and things don't go the way we want them to, we don't see the reasons for this as being anything to do with us, we just blame anyone else we can and hope that other people will magically appear to fix things for us.
3) Government involvement in trying to promote the industry has backfired because most (**but not all**) of the people they have put in charge of trying to change things are not directly from the industry. Instead many of the people we come across on TV and in magazines are simply professional writers / professional presenters, generally with good communication skills, a pleasant personality and some celebrity status, but with little or no practical or personal experience of the problems that the average self-builder has to face preparing for a project and then actually physically working on one.

Two of the main schemes the government's selfbuild steering group (made up of many of these people) have come up with since 2012 are:

1) To get housing developers to give over land on their developments for selfbuild plots.

Let's be honest, that is not going to happen in any significant manner. We are never going to arrive at a situation where developers spend their money finding, assessing, surveying, buying the land and planning the schemes and then happily hand over plots to self-builders. Three reasons it won't work:

I. It won't be financially viable for the developers.
II. They will not want high quality well finished self builds next to their often cheap and tatty standard houses. They would be shown up for what they are and the developers would not like that.
III. Self-builders won't want to be sharing a development site with developers cheaply built, standard, tacky houses. The type of houses that they are building their own homes to try to get away from!

Another flagship policy being pushed at the moment is to create a whole new sector of the industry which they are calling "Custom Build". This idea came about after a group of "Industry leaders" went off on a "fact finding mission" (Hmmm!) to Holland a few years ago, to see a very large selfbuild and custom build project there. They were all very impressed, took lots of photos and got very excited about the possibility of us starting to do the same thing over here.

Almost immediately, all their attention seemed to turn away from improving the "Self-Build" market and instead they all focussed on creating this fantastic new sector of the market, called: "Custom Build".

The group have since apparently been off on a number of other "*fact finding*" tours around Europe to "*gather more information*".

The problem with this whole idea (*apart from them not inviting me along!*) is that they do things very differently in Europe when it comes to housebuilding. They have a much bigger bespoke section of the market, they have joined up thinking at a national and local level, they keep everything simple and quick with regards to getting new projects going and the population is fully signed up to the way it all works there. Here, we are pretty much at the opposite end of the spectrum when it comes to working together, keeping things simple and house building in general. Unless we see a major rethink of government housing policy, that is unfortunately where we will stay.

We can't expect to do the pretty bits of what they do over there, without having the systems in place on a larger scale to back it up and make it all work.

So, what is Custom Build anyway?

Basically, it usually manifests itself as you (the buyer - *previously known as the self-builder*), becoming involved in a project where you let someone else do all the work, while you sit watching the process from the wings, being allowed to have input in to minor design features and some of the finishes.

The designs are usually all done for you (with you possibly having a choice of a limited number of layouts), the build methods already set and the overall finish of the building already decided.

I wouldn't mind betting that the cost for having one of these custom built "special" houses built, despite what the experts are saying, will nearly always work out to be more expensive than a standard house bought from a developer. Now correct me if I am wrong, but if you are thinking about self-building your own home, I bet you are not planning on leaving 95% of it to someone else or spending more than the market value on doing so.

To my mind, letting someone else do all the donkey work and just watching everything happen from the side-lines is just not self-build. How much personal pride would you have about your own input into the finished article if it was just something that was basically "picked from a shelf" and built by someone else?

Now, having said that I do think there is a place for custom built new homes in the UK.

Other countries have significantly sized custom build housing markets and the quality of their housing in general is far better than ours because of it. We could be in the same position within ten years, if the right policies were put in to place. Those policies are unfortunately however, not the ones that are being put in place at the moment.

There are simple ways to make custom build work over here which would bring it under the heading of *genuine* selfbuild, but let's not confuse an off-the-shelf house with a choice of kitchen units, paint colours, door styles and a few other bits and bobs, with genuine self-build, just to try to make it look like the drive to grow the selfbuild market is working.

So, after that brief, but satisfying rant and departure from the subject of the moment I'll return to the real problem, which is the matter of the developers getting all the good land at trade prices and us being left with the dribs and drabs of mainly poor quality overpriced plots that are left over after they have all had their fill.

It is a real problem and one that needs fixing. It can be fixed. I will show you how to later in the book.

You can fix it by yourselves or you can fix it by joining forces with other people. You just need to know a few tricks and be prepared to commit yourselves to spending the necessary time and effort on making it happen it.

Hopefully once you have read this book you will join the people who have attended my seminars on this topic at the *Grand Designs* and *Homebuilding & Renovating* Shows over the past few years, in being newly enlightened on the subject!

Part 2:
How will this book help you to take on a self-build project of your own?

To briefly recap:

From what you have read thus far, you will now be fully aware that, the way I see it, the selfbuild industry is too complicated.

Anyone taking on a selfbuild project at the moment, whether they are experienced in the industry or not, is entering a scary, lonely, dangerous world, where pretty much everything that happens represents a new, often stressful experience.

Where *every* decision, small or large can have a major effect on the success or failure of the project, where there is a world full of people clamouring at your door, wanting your business and your money and where you are the only person (or people) who will be held responsible, whether the whole thing goes stunningly successfully or completely pear-shaped.

Makes you think, doesn't it?

So, given all that, you would be daft to consider taking on a project without being as prepared as humanly possible, in order to try to ensure that your project is going to be the one that doesn't go pear shaped, so that your project is the one that creates a beautiful new, high quality home, with more living space, at the same time as (hopefully) costing significantly less than a ticky tacky little box would cost from one of the volume housing developers.

So how are you going to get yourself prepared to take on this monumental task?

Let me take a guess at what you think you need to do (these "guesses" are based on literally hundreds of consultations I have had with potential self-builders over the years):

I. **Research, research, research.** At a seminar given by one of the industry leaders in 2014, I heard him tell everyone that they should not even think about starting a selfbuild project until they have done at least 5 years of research.
My comment: Anyone who does 5 years of research will probably never actually take on their own self build. They will be too scared. Minimal, but targeted research, followed by decision making and action is the way to go. This book will hopefully empower you to be able to follow that path.

II. **Watch all the relevant TV programmes, go to the shows, read all the books and magazines, go to the National Self-build and Renovation Centre in Swindon.**
My comment: I agree to an extent, but it is all too easy to get bogged down and overwhelmed by what you see and hear. Go to one or two shows but no more. Read a couple of books, but no more. Look out for the bits and pieces of information that interest you and keep these to one side. **They** *are the right way for YOU to move forward (at least, to start with). Remember, if you are properly prepared, there is no real, definitive right or wrong way to selfbuild, there are just choices that you as individuals will make as you proceed. The problems start to occur if you keep changing your mind (we'll cover this subject in depth later in the book).*

III. **Find an architect you want to work with.**
My comment: This moment is far too early in the process to be thinking about designers. By the time you have finished reading this book you may even find you don't need an architect.

IV. **Design your ideal house.**
My comment: You can't realistically design your house until you find the land you are going to buy.

V. **Start to look at prices of kitchens, bathrooms, electrical fitting and other items for the house.**
My comment: Leave this until much later. You are wasting your time doing this now.

VI. **Look for land, join plot finding companies.**
My comment: By all means start to look at land, but rather than looking for specific plots for yourselves, use this time to get an idea of where you would like to live and what sort of plot you could afford in that area and the different types of plots that are available at different prices. When you have read chapter 4 (Finding land), you may have a different view on the way you are going to find your ideal plot.

VII. **Start getting costs together on materials and labour.**
My comment: This is a reasonably useful way to spend your time, but at this stage just get the basic generic prices of the big stuff. The chances are that you will change your mind on most things as you move forward so all the information you get together now could be wasted.

VIII. **Talk to other people who have either self-built or built extensions etc.**
My comment: Great idea. Try to find out who they used for what and how happy they were with the people they dealt with. We'll also cover this subject in detail later.

You may think that a lot of the comments I have just made were quite negative. They are not really. I simply don't want you wasting time on irrelevant stuff when there are far more constructive and positive things you could be doing with your time.

As I have already said (and will be repeating throughout the book), the biggest trap that potential selfbuilders tend to fall in to is that you think you need to know everything about everything before you start. You don't. You just need to know enough about the important things and you need to know where to look and turn to for everything else.

This is not a Self-build manual, it is a Self-build guide.
There is a major difference.

A Self Build Manual:

If I were writing this as a manual I would be putting my "factual" head on. I would be telling you how to set out foundations, pour concrete, how many bricks are in a square metre, discussing the prices of everything, giving you lots of tables and comparisons to look at etc. That is not what I want to do here and I don't actually think that is what most people reading this will need at the stage that they will usually be in when they are reading a book like this. In any case, there are other books which do that job quite nicely. Mark Brinkley's book "The Housebuilder's Bible" is, to my mind more of a guide / manual, and a good one it is too. It has sold tens of thousands of copies and is full of masses of information on how to build your home successfully. That book does the job it is meant to do very well and I wouldn't even try to go down the same route. This book intends to do something different.

A Self Build Guide:

As a guide, this book aims to:

- **Make you *stop* and think** before you start to stride headlong in to a very major project, that could either see you being very proud of yourselves in a couple of years, or which could end up in tears, with you potentially struggling financially and under stress in your relationships.
- **Start you off at the right place** so that you cover all the bases in the right order, as you move forward. This will help you to see and understand all the positives and negatives of the adventure you are about embark on. By having this clear vision, you may be more than happy to move forward in great leaps, or you may decide that, knowing the implications, *now* may not be the right time for you and your family.
- **Clarify the choices** and highlight the implications of the decisions you will make throughout the project. I won't be telling you what the right choice is, because, as I have said, there generally is no single right or wrong choice in most areas of the selfbuild process. It just usually down to personal preference and budget. What is right for you would be wrong for someone else. What I aim to do is to give you the knowledge you need to make as many right choices for you and your family, as possible.
- **Be a bit technical, but only a bit!** I will be giving you some of the basic technical information on a lot of stuff. The reason for me doing that is not to show you how to build the house, but simply to give you just enough of the information you need to be able to make the choices you need to make.
  My thinking as I write this guide is that if you have to go and get a calculator to work through something I am talking about, I am starting to get too technical!
- **Not to bog you down with detail.** With the best will in the world, unless you are a house builder or a building site manager, a lot of the selfbuild processes are going to be foreign to you, no matter how much research you do. If you try to remember too many facts and figures, you will fail. If you try to know and do too much on your own, your head will explode and you will get nowhere. So I will try to tell you just enough and then hope that you use that knowledge to help the project run as easily and smoothly as possible.

- **Cover all the bases:** I hope that you will find that this guide is something you will want to keep beside you for the whole project. Not just during the build period, but from the very first day you pick it up, whether that is at the *"Is it a good idea?"* stage, or anywhere in advance of that.
  I hope it will furnish you with the answers to the myriad of questions you will have and if it doesn't, it will equip you with the ability to know where to look.

  To use the book as I intend it to be used I would suggest that you read it through completely once as early in the process as possible, then if you think the whole thing is a good idea, get a printed copy (if you are reading it on Kindle or the computer) and read it through again, scribbling on it as you go, making notes for when you are ready to get started properly. Then, when you are ready to move forward, get it back down off the shelf and start to "walk" through it again, letting it guide you on how to make each step, from day 1 to completion.
  I also suggest that you keep it handy to turn to whenever you may get a bit stuck throughout the planning and construction phases.
- **Stop you being taken for a ride.** I mentioned earlier a meeting I had on site with a potential client who had no idea how to talk to, or what to ask a ground worker when he wanted him to come and construct his foundations. That ground worker will have quickly gathered from that conversation that the client had no idea what he was talking about and if he was of a mind, could easily have found ways to swindle the client out of potentially large sums of money.
  I want you, after reading this guide, to know how to deal with everyone you need to deal with during the process and communicate with them in a way that will make them have respect for your ability and knowledge on *whatever* subject you happen to be covering at the time.
- **Give you the confidence in your own ability** and a determination that lets you say to yourself: *"I can do this and I can do this well"*. This should hopefully come naturally, especially if you keep the book nearby to help you when you struggle with anything.

So there we have it. I hope you find the book useful, whether or not it actually leads you into embarking on your own self build project.

If it doesn't and it is the reason why you don't, then in your own case, the book has probably done its job just as well as if you were to take on and successfully complete your project.

My aim in writing the guide has been to empower potential self-builders to "have a go" and in doing so give themselves the best chances of making their project successful and one which they (usually when looking back after finishing it) enjoyed and learned a lot from.

The old saying in the self-build industry was *"Your third one is free"*. That <u>can</u> still be the case if you do everything properly.

So, I wish you all the best and hope that this book goes some way towards helping *you* to *do it properly, professionally* and possibly even to get *your* third one free!

Chapter 1
Self-build: Is it a good idea?

In 2016, the UK is the "poor relation" of self-build:

In many parts of Europe, Canada and America, self-build (or custom build) is "the norm" for new housing development, accounting for up to 80% of all new build homes in some countries. In the UK, as I write, about 8 - 10% of our new homes are genuine self-builds.

I don't know about you, but to me (as I said in the introduction), that suggests that here in the UK we are probably missing a trick! Why would the self-build concept be so popular in other countries, but not here?

1)   The UK planning system is not conducive to helping the self-build sector to grow.

In some countries, the planning system is set up differently. It is simple, coherent and is designed to make the whole process quick and easy for anyone who wants to either take on a self-build or a custom build project of their own.

Here in the UK however, things are very different. Our whole planning system seems purpose- built to be long-winded, complicated and wherever you look across the UK, from one local authority to another, there does not seem to be any sensible levels of standardisation in any of the processes or, more importantly in outcomes. I would not be at all confident of being treated the same by planning departments in two neighbouring authorities, let alone from one end of the country to the other.

For example: Some authorities are now pushing a *pre-planning application* process as the first step in any potential planning application. This is where, once you have found a potentially suitable plot (but preferably *before* you actually buy it), you take your sketched-out design ideas, together with photos of the site and the local area and usually some written notes, to meet with the local planner.

You then sit either side of a table for an hour or so, chatting through your plans and ideas, with the aim of you coming away with a realistic feel of the likelihood of your ideas being approved, should you eventually submit them.

After that meeting, if you approach and prepare for it in the right way and the planner was generally positive, there should be at least a reasonable chance that your proposed ideas will be acceptable, - on the plot you are thinking about buying. The obvious aim is of this meeting is to make sure the plans are given the best possible chance of passing before you submit them!

The pre-planning meeting is basically a sensible idea and one that I think should be rolled out across the country in a standard format. It should also have a standard fee attached to the service. I reckon about £250 would be a fair figure (Ouch! I hear you say, but if they were to receive a reasonable fee for the meeting, the planning officers could then justify giving each potential application a decent amount of time and attention before the full application arrives in to the office and starts to involve a whole host of other people and departments).

If this were how we approached the early stages of the process, then, across the UK, hundreds of thousands of hours of time and many millions of pounds of wasted effort, for all the people who presently get involved in the process at some stage, could be saved. This would happen simply due to the fact that the applications which would most likely be doomed to failure, would rarely make it past the "pre-planning" stage.

Where this potentially good idea is presently falling down, is in the lack of joined-up thinking between local authorities. Some authorities have not even started offering the pre-planning meetings, some offer them as an option if you want to pay a fee of between £50 and £500, some offer them free of charge, some will give you a half hour consultation free but then charge £50 per half hour after that and some are making the meeting compulsory and charging between £250 and £500 for the service.

As I said, to my mind, the £250 fee should be set as standard across the UK and there are three main reasons for me to think this way:

1) Having to pay a significant fee out for such a meeting would make any potential self-builder stop and think about the whole project at an early stage. If you also have to prepare a file full of information for a fairly formal meeting with the planners before you can think about getting the project going, you are more likely to take a more professional approach to the whole process. This is something that is presently often sadly lacking within our industry.
2) Any time spent discussing proposals and potential ideas for such a major project with a truly professional person is, to my mind time well spent.
3) If it costs a few hundred pounds to get yourself to a position where you are fairly confident of success with your planning application and with the project as a whole, then you could have possibly just saved thousands of pounds in design and other fees, together with the many months of work and stress that you may have otherwise encountered if you had just ploughed ahead with your initial ideas, bought the plot, had the plans drawn up and submitted an application which was, from the start, doomed to fail.

What you need to learn from a pre-planning meeting:

If you do get to attend such a meeting (and I think you should make every effort to do so), there are some important areas that you need to cover. You should make every effort to come away with answers to the following questions:

- **Will your initial ideas stand a good chance of being approved?** You need to know this (preferably) before you buy the plot, before you start work on full designs, before you start to incur significant cost and before you get completely immersed into the project.
- **If your ideas may not be approved, what would you need to change to make approval more likely?** It is important to not only be aware of the problems, but also the potential "fixes", so you can go away and change whatever you need to.
- **Is there a possibility that you will simply not get approval for what you need, what you want or what you can afford in that location?** If you come away from the meeting thinking *"We're not going to be able to move this forward without a major fight"* then this is the time to consider other options. Unless you are prepared to commit many months of your time and substantial amounts of your money, it is usually the best option to retire gracefully and find another option somewhere else.

What can you expect the planner to say?

One thing to bear in mind if you do attend a pre-planning meeting is this:

The planner will never say anything along the lines of: *"Yes that application, if you make it, will be approved."* or *"No that application will not be approved"*. The planner would get shot by his or her bosses if they gave that level of clarification at such an early stage. They would also probably find themselves spending half their time in court being sued by disgruntled applicants, who took their advice, but who were eventually turned down!

When you come out of a pre-planning meeting, the words you are hoping to hear would be something like:

"We would not have any major objections to those proposals" or *"They fall within the parameters of the local development plan"*.

If you hear those (or similar) words, as long as you then don't go and change a load of the details that you have just discussed, before submitting the full application, you stand a reasonably good chance of being successful. If, however, you hear the words:

"We, as a Local Authority would have major objections to those proposals", or *"I don't think that proposal would suit the location"*, or *"Those plans would not fall within the parameters of the present Local Development Plan"*, then you should think seriously about binning your initial ideas and starting again.

If you do find yourselves in this situation, where the planner is only offering negative comments about everything you propose, the best thing to do is to have a "Plan B" and move on as swiftly as possible to use your remaining time in the meeting to come at the subject from a different angle, with questions like: "What, in your opinion would be acceptable for a proposed development in that location?"

If you feel that your original ideas are not going to be accepted, and if you get the chance to change the direction of the meeting to cover your plan B ideas, make as many notes as possible on everything that is said. This will enable you, after the meeting, to work out what you would need to come up with and what you would need to change to give yourselves the best chance of getting your application approved. Once you have done that, you'll then be in a position to decide whether what you would actually be *allowed* to build on this plot is something that you would want, that would suit your needs, your wishes and your budget.

I will be looking in much greater detail at the planning processes in later chapters, showing you how to simplify them, speed them up and make them less scary, so I don't want to get bogged down with this aspect of the project here. Suffice to say once you have read the rest of this book, hopefully you will find that all the processes involved, including the planning process, can be much simpler than you may presently think.

2) Information overload

One of the other main reasons that the UK constantly falls behind so many other countries when it comes to self-build completions is because of what I call "information overload".

There is simply too much information floating around, that people feel they have to find, take in, understand and act upon, before they can get a project up and running. As I said in the introduction, this results in many potential selfbuilders spending months, or years glued to the computer screens, reading up on anything and everything related to the subject. Getting more and more confused the more they continue to read about new products, ideas or building methods.

Hopefully by the time you have read this book, you will be less fearful of the whole process and more confident that taking on your own project is realistically doable.

However, before I get into all that, I'd like to spend some time looking at the question:

How much better could the whole self-build process be here in the UK?

From what you have already read in this chapter you will be starting to get the picture that, to my mind, our industry is amateurish, poorly organised, too complicated and it needs fixing.

Just to give you an idea of how it all can (and should) work in the UK, let's look at how things work in other countries.

For this example, I'm concentrating on the USA.

A few years ago, I worked with a local builder to have the house shown above, constructed in Homasassa, North West Florida.

The project was classed as a custom build over there, which is similar in principal to the new concept of the same name, that the government over here in the UK are trying to push (*as opposed to a genuine self-build – see introduction*).

Although the USA and the UK follow the same "in principal" ideas when it comes to what custom build actually is, over there they are simply so far ahead of us in just about every respect that it is, to be honest, quite embarrassing!

In the USA, as it is in many other countries, custom build or self-build is a real option for most homebuyers, with well over half of all new homes in Florida, being built as custom builds / self-builds.

The whole experience over there, from start to finish, was a world away from how it is done here and we need to start to learn from not only the Americans, but also the Canadians and many of the European countries, when it comes to understanding how we need to change things here, if we want to start to catch up.

Here is how it worked for me:

I started the whole process off in 2008, not by indulging in months of research. Instead I simply picked the part of Florida where I wanted to build, then booked myself in to a hotel for a few nights. Then, each day I headed out (*in the sun, in my rental convertible. The things I put up with in the name of research!*) in a different direction, in search of the many developments around the area, earmarked solely for custom build / self-build.

Many of the developments I came across were huge; for example, on the first day I drove into one development which had a main spine road which ran from one end of the development straight through to the other. It had a 40mph speed limit and it took me 10 minutes of steady driving at the 40mph limit to reach the exit at the other end (*which for those of you who have not already worked this out in your head, made it about 6.5 to 7 miles long*). Off that spine road were literally dozens of other roads, heading off in all directions. I followed one of them and drove probably another 3 miles in this new direction before I again reached the limit of the development. I was so stunned by the scale of what I had seen on that first day, that I went back to the hotel and got my map out to look at how far the full site extended. It was basically a circle, which meant that that one single custom build / self-build development covered an area of something like 34 square miles!

To my continued amazement, when I eventually exited this site, I drove around half a mile along a perimeter road and came across a sign for a similar site, which I then accessed almost across the road from the first one!

Over there, the areas earmarked for housing development are called "sub divisions", some of which have been under development for many years and would not expect to be completed for another 15 years or so. Each one of these sub divisions can consist of literally thousands of plots of different sizes, starting from plots of a size that would be about similar to what we call a large plot over here, to plots of 5 – 10 acres each, intended for just one new home and one heck of a garden!

Rather than there being one owner of each sub division, most of the individual plots are owned by people who bought them as an investment when the development started, but often never intended to actually build on them.

The way it works (as far as I can tell from my admittedly limited experience), is that each sub division gets "pre-approved" for housing development when it is originally set up, with guide lines for the type of development that will be acceptable within its boundaries. There are no time limits on how quickly the development has to be completed (*as there are over here with the "start building within 3 years" rule*) and the whole planning application process is very fast and very efficient.

All a potential client needs to do, is to choose a builder, agree a design and a price, then lodge an application that conforms to the overall design concept for the site (*in Florida that often means a building of a maximum of 2 floors in height*). Once that is done, within three to four weeks they can often be able to start building with everything approved!

As I drove around these developments I would pass a row of houses, then a few empty plots, then another house, then some more plots and so on.

Every now and then I would come across a completed house and garden with flags all around the boundary and a builder's marketing sign in the garden. These properties were show homes and were built and owned by the various house builders in the area.

There was usually just one show house from each builder on each sub division, usually on at least a quarter acre of beautifully landscaped plot (*not the row of cramped up together show homes hidden behind some cheap shrubs you see next to the sales office over here*).

The show houses I came across were usually fully furnished and open every day. On enquiring, I found out that most builders, once they opened a new show house, would then keep it open for many years, upgrading as necessary, internally and externally, every few years to keep them looking smart. If you like what you see in one of these show homes and want to see different styles of house by the same builder, you will be directed to other local sub divisions, possibly a few miles away. To my mind this is a far better marketing method than we have here, as by having individual houses dotted round a wide area, each builder gets to be seen by more prospective clients who simply drive by, than if they were all next door to each other in a row, on one site, as they tend to be over here.

Pick a home – *any home*. Pick a plot – *any plot*.

After looking around numerous show homes on various sub divisions, I started to get a good feeling about one particular area, up in the Northwest corner of Florida near a town called Crystal River. The area was pleasant, with lots of new and old buildings displaying traditional American character. It was near to the coast, close to a good selection of retail and leisure amenities with a friendly, laid back population. The main attraction for me however, were the prices of the new homes, which seemed to me to almost unbelievably low. The price was, at that time made even more attractive by the fact that my £1 Sterling bought me $2 USA.

I found myself being drawn to two house designs, which coincidentally were both offered by the same builder. They both offered masses of high quality accommodation on a single floor layout, but they each offered a different layout and both had many attractive features, internally and externally. I would have been more than happy to be living in either house, but I found myself thinking: "Wouldn't it be good if they would allow me to *mix and match* the two designs".

So, between these two home designs, I had found what I wanted, in an area I liked and at an excellent price. Now all I needed was the plot to build one of them on.

As I had been driving round the various sub divisions over the past few days, I had found a number of nice plots which were of interest to me, ranging from a quarter to half an acre and costing around $30,000 - $40,000 (£15,000 - £20,000) each. These plots didn't have big garish (and often unsightly) "For Sale" signs like we do over here, instead on each plot there is simply a small sign, about the size of an A4 sheet of paper, on a short timber peg, with a phone number on it. This is the contact number of the owner or the selling agent (sometimes an individual, sometimes a company).

When you are interested in any particular plot, you call the number and speak directly to the owner or the agent, to ask any questions you may have and enquire about the asking price. Negotiations on the price for buying plots seem generally to be completed over the phone.

Once you are happy with the plot price, your next step is normally to approach one or more builders and start to talk to them about building the house style of your choice on the plot you have found.

How simple is that so far? It is brilliant!

By coincidence, one of my favourite plots of land was also being offered for sale by the builder who was offering the 2 house designs that I was keenest on. This plot was half an acre in size, backing on to a small lake and located on a large development close to a town called Homosassa, just a few miles down the coast from Crystal River.

This was about the point where I started to get excited (and a bit nervous), but after a couple of days spent plucking up courage, I decided to move on to the next stage, which was to make an appointment go to meet with the builder at their head offices to discuss the land, the design, the options for mixing my two favourite designs and the build prices. I rang them and after a general conversation over the phone, they asked me to visit their head office a few miles down the coast to spend a few hours going over my thoughts and ideas and getting to know each other.

On the morning of the meeting I arrived around 10.00am. There is a set procedure for all such meetings, so, over a cup of coffee in reception my guide for the day explained the itinerary, which loosely goes along the following lines:

First stop is the design office. Here you have the opportunity to discuss the layout and build of your new home. You can alter the design of the house style you like, or, as I had hoped, I could mix and match any of the designs in their portfolio. I could even start from scratch and have my own original design created, although apparently, this did not happen very often, as it increased the cost and the reason that people went to a particular builder was because they liked their designs. There was no charge levied for this design consultation.

(Meet "Chips": See front of the book)

Just think about this for a minute:

How much better and simpler would it be if we worked the same way over here as they do in Florida (and many other countries?)

There could be companies who held databases of existing house plans, which could be bought for a couple of hundred pounds or so per set. Each set of plans would be available in a computer file format which allowed designers with standard UK design software to adapt them to suit each client's needs (".dwg is the standard file format).

These plans could then be given to sub-contractors, suppliers, timber frame manufacturers or anyone else who needed them and they could also be used to provide all the information needed to allow a builder, project manager or self-builder to build our new homes.

At the moment, we waste millions of pounds each year needlessly paying designers huge sums of money to basically redesign the same type of houses over and over again, with similar layouts and possibly with a few modifications.

As an example of this, think about the national developers' houses. There is nothing very different between any of them, they are basically all just similar "little boxes made of ticky tacky" (older readers will remember that phrase!), but every developer has their own (often very expensive) designers, knocking out these repetitive designs, with maybe some minor modifications, year after year and charging the buying public millions of pounds to do so.

Ok, self builds are different and they generally have a bit more design appeal and individuality about them, but I am afraid that no one could convince me that if we had a comprehensive database of a couple of thousand house designs available, containing variants of 3, 4 and 5 bed houses over one, two and three floors, that most people would not be able to find a design that they either really liked, or could "knock about a bit" to get it to be just how they wanted it.

Imagine the time and money that would be saved on your own self build project if this were the way things worked over here.

Back to the meeting:

Before arriving at the builder's offices, I had sketched out ideas of what I was looking for in the way of design changes.

After I had been introduced to the designer, we spent 10 minutes discussing my ideas and then he simply set about copying and pasting between the two drawings on his computer, to create my new personalised layout. Checking with me as he did so that he was creating the layout I wanted. I just sat there and watched my new home appear on the screen in front of me. Within an hour of me entering the room it was all finished, checked and approved by me!

The new floor area was calculated and I was told at that stage, what the price of my new design would be.

The builders had worked out a basic price per square foot for each design in their portfolio, so all they had to do was to multiply the size of my new design, by the standard price per square ft for that particular house design, to give a basic price for the house. This price would include their standard finishing specification (which included air con / high spec kitchens (with granite worktops) / high quality bathrooms, carpets / floor tiles etc. Fantastic!

Once the design amendments were complete, I was asked if I was happy with the new layout and the basic price. After a few minor detail changes, I confirmed that I was. At that point the designer contacted a member of the sales staff to take me up to the showroom on the next floor, to move to the next stage of the process. The sales person came down to introduce herself and to show me the way.

The showroom was every self-builder's dream! It was like an Aladdin's Cave, filled with everything you could need or want in your new home. Within these four walls, the builders had brought together samples of pretty much everything that I would need to make choices on, including: bricks, render and cladding types, windows, external doors, roof tiles, kitchens, worktops, bathrooms, internal and external doors, ironmongery, floor and wall tiles, skirting boards, architraves, paint colours, even carpets and underlay!

The sales person would be staying with me for the rest of the day, so after a few minutes discussing her proposed itinerary, we then spent a very pleasant few hours slowly moving around the room, studying and choosing all my shiny new things. We even stopped for a (free) lunch in a special little seating area, where we sat and discussed the choices made so far.

Every time I made a new choice it was entered onto a software package on a computer that the sales person carried around with us. If my choice cost more or less than the basic spec that I had already agreed, the computer would immediately calculate its cost and make the necessary amendment to the final price. One of the nice aspects of this process was that, where I would have expected every change of specification to cost me more money, in fact there were many choices which actually reduced the final price.

Once I had completed my tour around the room and made all my choices, we sat down and went through everything again. I confirmed that I was happy with my choices and the price changes.

I was then taken up to the finance department on the next floor up, where I was shown how each one would affect the final price.

Once this process was complete, I was asked again if I was happy with everything. If I was, I could continue to the contract stage and if I wasn't, I could take the figures and drawings away with me to look them over.

As it happened I was happy and I agreed to pay the deposit (I was only planning on being in Florida for 2 weeks, so couldn't hang about!)

I paid a 1% deposit and was immediately given the contact details of my Project Manager. This person would oversee every detail of the full build (pretty much the role a site foreman plays over here) and he would be my single point of contact from that day until I moved in.

As soon as the deposit was paid, I was given a start date on site and a **moving in date**! – How amazing is that and **how much could we learn** *over here* **from how they do it** *over there*?

This builder didn't have to go off for a pre-planning meeting or bat the ideas back and too for a couple of months with the planning office, or fight over ridge heights, rights of light, parking spaces or any other such rubbish! I didn't need to hire an architect to represent me and I didn't need to pay thousands of pounds to get my designs finalised and my planning permission drawings prepared. From me deciding on the plot and design that I liked, it was all done and dusted in basically one meeting.

By the way, astonished as I was at the efficiency of the system, the cost of the house itself was even more of a shock! The price for this very large 4 bed custom built home (4,900 sq ft in area), with triple garage, huge rooms with 10' high feature ceilings, air conditioning, marble floors to some rooms, high quality carpets to the rest, granite worktops, a large Jacuzzi, in half an acre of grounds, fully lawned and with an automatic irrigation system installed, came to around $280,000, or at the time (in 2009), around £140,000 (not including the plot).

Why is all this possible over there and not over here?

1. Because housing development policy in Florida is to make plenty of land available for everyone who wants a new home built
2. With plenty of available land, the price for that land naturally reduces, which reduces the cost of the full build.
3. They have a much simpler planning system, which encourages this type of build and minimises the time scales.
4. The professional fees (architects etc.) are reduced to pretty much zero by having the designs done in house, by the builder and with the builder also sticking with selling basically the same styles of houses (with minor amendments) for many years.
5. All the products needed to build the houses are sourced from a small number of commercial (as opposed to retail) suppliers and they are generally just bought off the shelf, with minimal input from salesmen (who would all want commission on what they sell). This brings the material prices down significantly.
6. Houses are built quickly and efficiently, with each individual contract run by a project manager. The sites are also well organised. This is something we really need to grasp over here. Project Management is the way to go in our industry if

we want to improve the speed of build, the quality of the finished product and if at the same time, we want to reduce build costs.

The construction of my new home started on the day it was programmed to start and was completed when the builder said it would be completed. There were no unforeseen extras to be paid, no excuses as to why people had not turned up when they should have done. The job was simply executed and completed professionally and to a high standard.

During the build process, I was welcome to visit the site at any time. If I wanted to discuss anything with the Project Manager I would ring him and either go through my points on the phone, or we would send emails to each other.

The more I got to know the way the housing market works in Florida; the more impressed I was. The professionalism and the efficiency of the way they approach the whole concept of house building. The high standards of design, which refreshingly to me, seem to be based on simplicity and common sense and the quality of the finished product, are areas which if they were adopted over here, could have a huge impact on the way we live in the UK.

All in all, the whole process of designing and creating my custom built new home was pretty much a stress free and very pleasant experience. After it was completed I found myself wondering:

"Why can't we do that in the UK?"
The answer is: "We could".

How?

We just need some strong, experienced leadership in the industry, some financial backing to get things moving and the motivation to want to bring our house building industry into the 21st century!

We would not be able to adopt the full system as it is used in Florida, here in the UK. We simply don't have the free land available to let massive swathes of it either be allocated for house building, or for it to sit empty for long periods of time.

Hopefully however, as you continue to read the book, you'll see some of my ideas can be used here, we just need industry to get off its backside to bring the rest of them over to start being used too!

Here are some photos of a couple of the rooms in my Florida house, during construction and after completion:

Bedroom and bathroom under construction and complete

Kitchen under construction and complete

Back to Blighty!

So, unfortunately, after seeing an example of *how it should be done* and *how it is done in* many other countries, we have to come right back down to earth when we come back across the Atlantic to good ol' Blighty.

Here in the UK, we are perhaps 15 - 20 years behind most of the leading countries in the way we approach house building in general and self-build specifically. However, I can tell you honestly that I am glad I have built my own home(s) here in the UK over the past 30 years. Although we seem hell bent on making it as hard as possible, from my experience, if you do it right, the positives should still outweigh the benefits.

I can also say that after dealing (in various capacities) with literally hundreds of self-builders over the past 25+ years, most people who approach the project professionally and plan it properly, would probably agree with me on that conclusion, possibly not during the planning and building process, but generally after its all over!

Once the job is complete, most self-builders start to look back with slightly rosier coloured glasses and think "OK, we made a few mistakes, it took longer than we thought, cost more than we could really afford and we endured many a sleepless night, but look at what we have managed to do, **we've actually built our own house!**" Once those thoughts start to sink in, it is often not too long before they get a valuation on the finished house (just out of interest of course), realise that they have made a shed load of profit (on paper at least) and they start to think "Maybe we could do it again sometime!"

I would estimate that if I speak to 100 potential self-builders (especially those under 50), who, before they build, say "This is going to be our long-term home, we are not going to move again once we have built this house", around 50 of them will go on to build a second and possibly even a third over the next few years. At the end of that process, many of them will be well on their way to being mortgage free.

So, overall is self-build a good idea?

The self-build process is not an easy one, some people fail and we see examples on the TV all the time of projects that go over budget, take twice as long as expected and hit major problems. However, the trick is, by approaching and preparing yourselves correctly, *you* can help to make sure that *you* are one of the group of people who:

- Are fully equipped and prepared to take on a project.
- Have the knowledge and ability to fight your way through any problems you encounter.

- Can find all the right people you need and get them to do the right things at the right time too.
- Get the whole thing finished to a high standard and within a reasonable time.
- Are capable of doing all this without giving yourself a heart attack in the process or ending up in the middle of a divorce!

If, by the time you have finished reading this book, you are not convinced that you fall in to that group, I would seriously think about holding on until you do!

Now that I have brought you down to earth with that reality check, I have to say that I honestly think that there are actually very few people who, having access to suitable levels of finance and who are able to find a suitable and suitably priced plot of land, who would not at some stage in their lives be able to take on and successfully complete their own self-build project.

If I am right in that assumption, there is a good chance that you (*the person reading this book*), at some point in time, could be perfectly capable and well prepared enough to do so.

What are the positives and negatives if we don't self-build?

It is worth stopping here for a minute to ask the question:

"If we don't self-build, what are the pros and cons of our other options?"

You will probably fall under one of the following headings for where you presently live:

1. Living in a developer's modern or new house with or without a mortgage.
2. Living in an older property with or without a mortgage.
3. Renting.
4. Living with family.

Taking one at a time, let's look at the positives and negatives of each of those situations:

1. **Living in a developer's modern or new house with or without a mortgage:**

Positives

- It is legally *your own* home (as long as you keep up payments on the mortgage).
- It usually has a structural warranty so you can relax, knowing that if there are any major structural problems, they should be fixed by the developer without costing you anything.
- There are plenty of these houses about, so it's usually easy to find something suitable.
- Developer's new homes often have both practical and financial incentives to buy, which can make the process of moving home easier and also reduce the pressure on your finances for a while after moving.
- The purchase process is often fast and simple (this is usually mainly because the builders want your money in their banks asap so they can build the next lot of houses).
- It's a nice feeling to walk into a new home built for you by someone else, clean painted walls, no damp and everything (theoretically) working properly.

Negatives

The UK has a very poor reputation for the size and quality of housing that is produced by the large commercial builders.

Over decades we have got used to:

- Our houses and gardens getting smaller and smaller.

- Houses being squeezed tight up against each other.
- Our garages not being big enough to fit a family car in and then to be able to open its doors.
- Poor internal room layouts with odd shaped rooms crammed in to try to get an extra bedroom into the design.
- Living rooms that only have room for a 2-seater settee and one chair.
- Supposedly double bedrooms that don't have room for you to pass the end of the bed once it is in position.
- Single bedrooms that take a bed, a bedside cabinet and nothing else.
- Radiators positioned where we need to put our furniture.
- Creaky floors.
- Walls that look like they have been plastered by a monkey.
- Cracks appearing in walls soon after you move in.
- The cheapest possible internal doors.
- Not being able to hang anything heavy on the walls (usually applies to cheaply built timber frames and parts of standard brick / block built houses).
- Hearing people "whisper" in the next room or through the floor.
- High heating bills because of minimal insulation.
- Poor quality decoration and finishing in general.
- Builders not coming back to fix things when they should.

(This list could go on, but I'll stop there).

2. Living in an older property with or without a mortgage

Positives

- It is legally your own home (subject to paying off the mortgage).
- There are plenty of them about so it's easy to find something suitable.
- They are often better built than the newer developer's homes.
- Room sizes are often more generous than new builds.
- You don't usually hear as much noise "room to room" or "floor to floor".
- Finishes are often better.
- Gardens are usually larger.

Negatives

- Higher maintenance bills.
- High heating bills because of low levels of insulation.
- Problems of all sorts occur more often (both structural and non-structural).
- Normally there is no structural warranty left on the building so there are risks of major remedial costs being incurred if structural problems start to occur.
- Often draughty.
- Creaky floors.
- Cracks appearing in walls.
- Could need extensive redecoration.

3. Renting

Positives

- After the first agreed rental period (normally 6 months), your tenure is flexible so you can move as often as you like.
- You can often find a rental property and move in within in couple of weeks.
- They are often part or fully furnished, so you can potentially save money, time and hassle on finding and buying furniture.
- You (theoretically) don't have to worry about maintenance, the landlord should take care of that.
- You can often afford a rented house (in the short term at least) in an ideal location to suit your job of social life.

Negatives

- You are paying the equivalent of a mortgage to someone else.
- You never increase your equity so will never be able to sell up or down size and bank a profit.
- You are restricted on what you can do with the decoration / fixtures and fittings / garden etc.
- You are at risk of being asked to leave with just a couple of months' notice, no matter how long you have lived there (unless you agree a long-term contract).
- Landlords may not keep up with the maintenance and repairs and you suffer when things start to go wrong with the property.
- While you rent, you will never experience the feeling that "This house is mine".

4. Living with family

Positives:

- Normally cheaper

Negatives

- Everything else! - Get out quick!

And what are the positives and negatives if we were to take on a self-build?

Positives

- Self-building can provide you with your own, well built, unique home.
- You (and usually your family) will have helped to create this building, using your own determination, your own skills and often literally your own sweat and blood! Once all the pressure is off and you are settled in, you will normally (and rightfully) be enormously proud of what you have managed to achieve. You can also be pretty sure that *no-one else* has a house that will be exactly the same.
- If you plan and build it efficiently and carefully, the build costs can be significantly lower than you would pay for a poorer quality developer's house, whilst the quality and the end value are normally considerably higher.
- A self-builder can normally build up equity far faster than someone buying a developer's house. It is still just about possible for your third house to be free if you follow a few rules, build quickly and as long as everything goes fairly smoothly.
- Self-build plots are often considerably larger than developer's plots, offering the potential to build a spacious home and still leave enough plot to give you a garage *which actually allows you to open the car doors when inside it*, driveway, parking areas and good sized gardens.

- Spacious homes usually come with more spacious rooms. You won't often hear self-builders complaining that they can't get a three-seater settee in their living room and you will normally find more generously sized bedrooms and bathrooms. It is also more common to find family rooms and studies in self-build designs.
- Most self-build homes exceed building regulations for insulation and other eco requirements, so when you self-build, you get to control both your carbon footprint and the heating bills!
- You get the chance to design your own interior finishes, along with having an input in to the electrical and lighting design. You also get to choose things like internal doors, skirtings', architraves, paint colours for walls and ceilings, sockets and switch styles, light fittings, ironmongery etc.
- Soundproofing in self-build homes is normally considerably better between rooms and floors than it is in developers' houses. For many people, achieving good levels of internal sound insulation is one of their prime motivators for taking on a self-build project in the first place. You can also easily design different parts of the house to achieve differing levels of soundproofing.
- Underfloor heating is often incorporated in to new self-build homes (it is rare to find it in developers' homes). Underfloor heating can give you a much more pleasant feel inside the house than radiators. It runs at a lower temperature than radiators and the heat comes up gently from the whole of the floor area, so you don't get cold spots in rooms or areas where your radiators mainly heat your furniture. When used in conjunction with solar panels, underfloor heating could also potentially give you pretty much free heating for the whole house.
- Creaky floors are far less common in self build homes. You'll often find that even the show homes presented by the developers have creaking floors within a few months of them opening. (Note: There are easy ways to stop this from happening and I will go through these in a later chapter).
- You can add those luxury touches that you have always wanted: solar panels, ground or air source heating, wet rooms, hot tubs, posh kitchens, built in cinema and hifi, multiple TV and BT points, intelligent home features for computers, heating, lighting, security, garden irrigation and grey water systems, etc. There are literally hundreds of these luxury, eco and / or practical extras that you can build in to your design.
- A self-build house will usually have 10-year warranty, just the same as a standard developer's house. However, because the standard of construction on a self-build house will normally far exceed that offered by the developers, the chance of anyone ever having to claim against a self-build structural warranty policy will be much slimmer.

Negatives

- The self-build process can be stressful.
- There is always a (slim) chance that your project may fail.
- They can take a long time, especially if you do not plan properly or are not as well organised as you should be.
- You need to do some intense research and planning, both before you start and during the construction period.
- You and your family may have to rough it for while during the building process.
- You learn as you progress and you may make (sometimes costly) mistakes.
- A high proportion of self builds go over budget. This is usually due to not enough of a financial buffer being built in to cope with unexpected costs during the initial planning stage.

When is a good time to self-build?

As with most things, when it comes to choosing the best time to self-build there are some times that are better than others. As I have said earlier, pretty much everyone should be able to pick a good time to self-build at some stage during their lifetime.

To help you to decide whether or not that time for you is *now*, here are some "good times" and some "not so good" times to self-build:

Good times to start

- **When you are young:** Young working couples are often ideally positioned to take on a self-build project, as they usually have fewer family, practical, locational and financial ties and commitments. They can be generating reasonable levels of income, but be without the restrictions that a family can bring. At the same time, they have the energy, drive and the free time available to commit themselves to such a major project for a couple of years if necessary.
Mortgage lenders tend to see this group of people in a fairly positive light, especially if they have a decent deposit and some interest and / or working link or background related to either DIY or the wider building industry.
- **When your kids reach their late teens:** Trying to take on a major self-build project between when you are young and when the kids reach their teens can add many more layers of complication to the process. I am not saying don't build while the kids are growing up, but you will need to give everything a lot more thought before you make the decision to start. (I'll look at this subject in more depth later).
- **When you are sure that both your finances and job security are *secure* and *stable*:** Self-builders tend to push themselves to the limit financially, so they can get the best possible new home at the end of the process. The last thing you want to happen, half way through the build, is to find yourself jobless and having to scrimp and save to get the project finished.
- **When you are in a strong and stable relationship:** Have no doubt that even the simplest and smoothest running self-build project will put stress on relationships. If you are taking on the project as a couple or family, it is very important that you make sure you are singing from the same hymn sheet before you start and that you have a plan in place to make sure that you will be able to deal with the significant array of pressures that will be landing on your shoulders, from day 1 to completion.
- **When you are retiring:** At this stage of life you will have possibly paid off your mortgage, have some savings and be living in a house that is now too large for you. You will also possibly find yourselves with a lot more free time. This could be a good time to consider selling up, downsizing and potentially using the freed-up funds to get stuck into a new and exciting project that will keep you active (mentally and physically), busy and interested for a number of years.
- **Coming out of a recession:** At the end of a recession there is a good chance that land will be somewhat more plentiful and cheap. Builders could well still be short of work and will tend to quote more competitively and suppliers could be hanging on to their very existence by a slim thread. Who benefits from all that? Anyone brave enough to say, "Well that's the recession over now, I'll take a punt and get building". Just make sure you do your research so you are sure that the recession **is** over and that you are not just in a positive blip halfway through!
- **During a recession – maybe!** Depending on how secure your income and general financial situation are, it can sometimes actually be a good idea to consider building *during* a recession for the same reasons that it might be a good idea to build at the end of a recession: More cheap land and labour and good materials prices. My only proviso here, is that you should be confident that property prices are not going to plunge too far before the end of the recession. Although you will be getting good prices on everything, you don't really want to be putting all your efforts into building a house which is decreasing in value every day.

Not so good times to start

- **When you have young kids (under 10):** This one probably doesn't need explaining. Young kids soak up most of your time and attention. Trying to keep that commitment, plus possibly a full-time job, can leave precious little time for any sort of social life, let alone taking on such a major project. By the time kids get to the age of around 10 they may have (sometimes) started to be a bit less demanding.
- **Whilst studying or when you have significant social or lifestyle commitments:** Again, this probably doesn't need explaining, but if you already have a busy life, are you going to be able to cope with also taking on a major housebuilding project at the same time?

Is there a best time of year to build?

There seems to be an unwritten rule with self-builders that you shouldn't start to build in the autumn or winter. In my view, this is completely incorrect. In fact, whenever possible, I always aim for a winter start on any projects I undertake. If I can't start in winter, then I'll try to aim for the autumn.

Why? Let's look at *each season* for starting work on building a house:

Spring start:

- **This often the wettest time of the year.** Rain can cause all sorts of problems, including slower, messier setting out and excavation of the foundations.
- **More difficulty moving the excavated spoil around the site** or off site (mud is not easy to move around).
- **Risk of foundation collapse:** Anything from small chunks of soil / mud falling from the side of the trench and having to be hand dug out before concreting, to complete trench failure where a whole side of a trench can give way. Major trench collapse is not only very dangerous, but can also result in a fairly major logistical exercise trying to get an excavator close enough to it to repair the damage once all the rest of the foundations have been excavated.
- **Where trenches have collapsed, there will be more concrete needed for the foundations** coupled with higher costs for labour and plant to carry out the work.
- **Time wasting knock on effects** of all of the above problems can push back the completion date for the project (the longer the job takes to complete the higher the cost will be, see later chapters for the reasons for this).
- **Damage to stored materials:** No matter how well you try to protect the stored materials on site, unless they are in a locked and watertight container, rain and damp can usually find a way of getting to them.
- **Temperatures can still be very low in March / April and even May**, (with frost and snow recently becoming quite commonplace as late as May). Low temperatures can slow down or even stop progress on the building works (e.g. concreting can be held up in very cold conditions and bricks cannot be laid if the air temperature is less than "four degrees and rising").
- **Most self-builders think that spring is a good time to build**, so many jobs are started around this time, which leads to labour being harder to find and more expensive.

Summer start

In my opinion, summer is probably the worst time to start work on a self-build.

- **British summers do not reliably give us a decent amount of good weather**. Look at the last few years where the weather has often tended to be ok from April to June, cold and wet in July and August and not brilliant in September, then we often get a decent October and November.
- **Self-builds are not usually known as being amongst the fastest building projects,** so by starting work any time after June, you could find you still working on your foundations when the autumn arrives (bringing with it most of the same problems you would encounter if you started in spring).
- **Over the summer period, most of us take our main holidays,** making it much harder for anyone trying to find good quality trades people. Couple this with the fact that the people who are available during the summer don't have as much competition when quoting for work. This can often lead to higher prices being charged over this period.
- **The lack of trades people can often mean that you can't get the labour you need** to start on site when you want them to. This can lead to delays in the completion of the project, which in turn can lead to higher costs. It can also cause the people that you do manage to get on site disappearing to other, possibly better paying jobs when they should be with you, as they try to make the most of the labour shortage.

Autumn start

By the time you get to the autumn, most people have had their holidays and have spent too much money, they are thinking about Christmas and now need to start to work hard to top up their bank accounts. This can result in more competitive tendering and a better service.

The following factors also come in to play at this time of year:

- **The weather can still be a problem**, but in my experience over the past 35 years the weather is usually less of a hindrance to progress in the autumn, than it is in spring. Mainly because there is no threat of snow and overall the temperatures tend to be significantly higher.
- **As self-build projects tend to start and run fairly slowly, a project which starts in September / October will often still be constructing the foundations up until at least Christmas**. This results in a lot of the messy underground work being carried out after the worst of the autumn wetness has gone, but while the temperatures are still high enough for bricks to be laid.

Winter start

This is the time of year that most people shy away from starting selfbuild projects, but if you look around the country at all the bigger housing developers, they don't even slow down during this period! Winter is not a season that professional builders fear and in fact, as I said earlier, it is the time of year when given the option, I would always aim to start my own projects.

Here's why:

- **Most trades people tend to take their main holidays during the summer months** which can impact significantly on the availability of good quality tradespeople during that period. Very few, however are sunning themselves during the winter months, so more people are available for work during this time.
- **Although the builders carry on working during the winter, private work tends to dry up**, including self-build (simply because of the myth that it is best to start in summer). This means that there are lots of people looking for smaller amounts of available work. This has an obvious knock-on effect that quotation prices tend to be at their lowest during this time of year.
- **Suppliers have the same problem as trades people.** Less work available to tender for and fewer customers walking through the doors of the building materials suppliers, tends to bring prices down and shorten delivery periods.
- **Rain is seldom a major problem in the winter months**, being replaced by ice more generally during January to March.
- **The biggest enemy to progress during the winter months is the low temperature.** On some of the coldest days, this can result in brick laying being held up and on rare occasions, concreting can be halted. However, this does not generally cause significant delays as, even during most of the coldest days' bricks can be laid during a temperature window between around 9.30am and 3.00pm.
- **In the cold weather foundation trenches are less likely to collapse due to becoming waterlogged over periods of prolonged heavy rain.** A problem that can sometimes end up being very costly during the rest of the year, especially in areas of high rainfall and / or poor quality ground.

Summary:

In this chapter, we are asking the question: "Self-build – Is it a good idea".

We have looked at how the whole concept of house building works in the UK and how much better it is in other countries. It soon becomes clear that a house-building nation, we are years behind the *best of the rest*. At the moment, the self-build / custom build industry lags even further behind.

On scrutinising the way we presently do things here, it is plain to see that our main problems seem to be:

- As an industry, we operate in a very amateurish fashion, from the way we find land, the way we apply planning rules and the way we build. We lack (and have lacked for the past 25 years) professional leadership and we do not have a government that is capable of understanding or fixing the problem.
- We seem totally incapable at present of using joined-up thinking, or of learning the important lessons we need from other, more successful countries, to help us to make thing better. This leaves every potential self-builder having to pretty much fend for themselves from day one right through to completion.
- Every self-builder is on their own, usually taking on their project from an inexperienced and unprepared position, which leaves them far more likely to encounter major problems than it should.
- Due to the above reasons, the whole industry tends to be too daunting, too complicated and too scary to entice large numbers of new self-builders to have a go.

So, to fix the problems we need to:

- Make sure the industry and everyone in it operate at a more professional level.
- We need to start to use joined-up thinking to bring the whole industry together to work as one entity rather than as thousands of individual businesses
- The whole process needs to be simplified.

Having said all that, the advantages offered by self-building, for most people makes it a good option to consider - at least once in a lifetime.

Very few people would fall in to the category of being unsuitable to consider taking on a self-build project at some time.

If you are in a steady job, with a strong relationship or a supportive family around you and as long as you prepare properly, you stand a good chance of completing a successful project.

People who go on to complete three projects can potentially be mortgage free.

I hope that once you finish reading this book, that dream will be a little closer.

Chapter 2
Getting Started

As with any new venture, the start of a self-build project is the time when options are considered, either adopted or discarded, many of the big decisions are made and the course is set.

The decisions that you will make in the very first days of planning your own project are therefore of critical importance. Make the right decisions at this time and the project could be a roaring success. Make the wrong ones and you could be setting the whole thing up to fail spectacularly.

That sounds a bit dramatic, but it is true.

However, daunting as that fact may seem, it is actually not something that you need to lose sleep over, as long as you make sure you go about things the right way (*which I'll hopefully be able to show you throughout this book*).

As I said earlier, the first major rule you need to take on board as you embark on your project is:

"Only learn what you need to learn and do what you need to do. – No more".

(and remember, if you ignore this rule your head will soon melt).

Most potential self-builders tend to work on the notion that, before they can launch in to their projects properly, they need to know everything about everything. They think they need to research for at least a couple years, speak to architects, builders, suppliers, brickies, electricians and everyone else associated with the building process. They think they need to visit every show, read every magazine, complete their house design, plan the whole project and price everything up ready for when they find their land.

This thinking is wrong in **so many ways**! You'll see what I mean as you read on.

By researching every possible option and detail, many people think that they will be clarifying and simplifying things for themselves, when in fact all they will usually be doing is complicating everything and getting themselves totally confused.

In an example shown in the introduction, I listed some of the choices of wall construction available to you for new build housing. I listed around 20 variants for the mainstream basic choices of the main building methods (which was actually nowhere near the total number that would be available), but even if you managed to narrow that number down to a final few favourites you will then have to add back in dozens more variants for things like insulation, cavity widths (empty or full), external finishes, service cavity or no service cavity, wet or dry finishes inside etc.

The options list for the main structure of a house is almost endless. It could take literally *months* of researching, on a full-time basis to get all the information together that you would need and by the time you had studied it all, the chances are that you wouldn't know which way to turn for the best.

If you did manage to wade through all that work in researching options for the external walls and eventually make some sort of sensible choice, think then about the fact that similar numbers of choices and options exist for *nearly every other part of the project. From groundworks to finishes*!

If you can see what I am getting at here, you will also appreciate that if you try to do too much, this is probably not an undertaking that you are ever going to be able to complete successfully unless you managed to get half of your family and neighbourhood helping you, free of charge, - on a full-time basis!

So, how should you go about researching the subject?

This is where the "**Learn what you need to learn and do what you need to do**" rule comes in to play.

Let's look at an example where we are researching the wall construction options:

As with most self-builders, for months or even years before you decide to look seriously into the possibility of taking on a self-build project, you will probably have watched many of the various DIY and building programmes on TV. You will probably have bought the related magazines, possibly have visited one or two of the national shows and checked out various websites for all sorts of products.

What generally happens during these months as you watch, read, visit and study is that, as you see various designs, products, building methods or innovative ideas, you sometimes find yourself thinking: "*I quite like that*".

If that happens, you are already halfway along the road to deciding what choices are right for you and your project.

What is actually happening as you are taking in all the different types of information, is that you are learning about how it all works and finding yourself more attracted to one option than another. You are also automatically mentally bringing together the ideas you see on the TV and the ideas that you have in your head, thinking as you do so: "that could work for us". This is a really big step along the decision making process path and a lot of the time you don't even realise it is happening. You need to be aware of it and you need to respond to it when it does happen.

For example: You may watch a programme about a house being built with straw bales and either think "*What a great idea*" or "*That wouldn't be right for us*". You may read an article on timber frames and be impressed with how it all works. You may see a steel frame house being built in your neighbourhood and be interested in finding out more about it.

Some of the things you see and hear will interest you and some won't. But what is the point of researching all the stuff that doesn't really interest you? Forget it! You are going to have more than enough work to do researching the stuff that does!

Your brain can act as a very efficient automatic filter in this process, helping you to get rid of the unimportant and allowing you to concentrate on the important stuff. Learn to trust it and don't force it down a route it doesn't want to go.

Again, as I mentioned earlier, one *very* important thing to remember is that:

"There are very few *right* and *wrong* choices when it comes to how and what you build. - It just comes down to what you want, what works and what you can afford".

So, bearing that in mind, if you like the idea of timber framed houses, why not just spend your time looking at the options within that product range? Just forget all the other options until and unless you find that either timber frame is not suitable for your type of project or, for whatever reason you go off the timber frame option and become more attracted to something else.

If you like the concept of building with a timber frame, if it works and it is practical for the house style you eventually choose and if you can afford the type of frame you prefer, then that **is** the right choice **for you**.

If your first choice, for whatever reason turns out to be impractical or too expensive, then you just go back and pick up on your second favourite option and see if that works any better. – Simple!

Ok, not quite *that* simple, because sometimes it may be a while before you become aware that your first choice might not work in practice. However, once you know something doesn't work, you also usually know why it doesn't work, so when you come to make another choice, you will be in a better position to make the right one.

Using this method of research, you could reduce the time, the stress and the confusion of making all the major decisions from periods of many months, possibly to just a few days, or even hours.

What you will also usually find is that, because you haven't confused yourself with all the non-relevant choices and because you are aware that there are no real wrong or right choices, as long as they work and you can afford them, you will find it much easier to fine tune your thoughts when it comes to things like insulation thicknesses and types, cavities or no cavities, internal and external finishes etc.

This system of filtering out the flotsam and jetsam is critically important if you are going to be able to make positive and steady progress through the project planning stages, in anything like a reasonable time and with minimal stress and confusion.

What do we need to research?

As a general rule, you really just need to concentrate on the big things then, as long as you then go through the processes in the right way, the small things often take care of themselves.

The big things include:

1. **Being fully aware of your financial situation before you start.** Your finances need to be sound, your credit rating good, you should have no worries about the security of your employment situation and you should at least have temporary (but preferably permanent) access to a significant source of emergency funds, just in case they are needed at any stage. You also need to find out if you are going to be able to borrow enough to buy land in the area you would like to build in and then have sufficient left to build the sort of house you would wish to. We will cover this subject in more detail later.

2. **Deciding where you would like to live** and then finding out what the plot availability and prices are like in that area. The online property sites are a good tool to use for this exercise. Give yourself as much flexibility as possible regarding the areas where you would be happy to live. Self-build plots are not in plentiful supply and prices vary wildly for the same types of plots, sometimes within a few miles of each other. The more flexible you are with your choice of location, the more chance you will have of finding something at a price which leaves the maximum possible pot of money left for designing and building the house itself. When you are considering location, always remember to include all the important factors in your decision-making process. Things like schooling for the children, family and friends, work location, leisure, shopping facilities, transport links, resale values in the area etc. The reputation of the area is worth investigating too. Just talking to people who live there will often be a very enlightening experience. Call at the local pubs and have a chat with the landlord, local shops or the library and you will often find people willing to tell you all.
   I will be showing you how to find and potentially get hold of plots at much cheaper prices than the average in Chapter 4: "Finding Land".

3. **Working out what your new home needs to offer in the way of accommodation.** How many bedrooms do you need? What room sizes would you like throughout the house? How many bathrooms? Do you need an office, family room, utility room, large garden, large garage, parking for multiple cars etc?
   At this stage of the project, I always suggest that you spend a bit of time visiting and looking at the size of the accommodation offered by some of the commercial developers. By standing in a room in a show house, you should be able to say things like: "*We'd need this to be bigger. Maybe 3ft longer and 2ft wider*". By looking at the room sizes on the sales particulars, you will then be able to get an idea of target room sizes for your own home.
   Once you have compiled a list of ideal room sizes, you will be able to get an idea of the size of house you will be hoping to be able to build.

   Obviously, the basic room sizes don't include things like the halls, stairs and landing nor the wall thicknesses. You will need to add these in when you are starting your proper house designs, but what you are doing here, is just getting some basic information on your accommodation requirements so we can calculate our "best guess" costs for the project a bit later on.

It is actually a useful exercise at this stage to start to look at house styles that you like. Now is not the time to be making any final decisions on exactly what you want the house to look like. That will come once you have found your plot and can see what style of properties are in the local area. Your project will usually need to be seen to *"enhance the local neighbourhood"*, so you need to know what the neighbourhood consists of before you can get very far down this route.

We will cover the subject of house design in Chapter 5: "Designing your new home".

4. **Choosing your build method** This tends to be the subject that causes most consternation with potential self-builders. Deciding on how your home is going to be built, is seen as one of the really important decisions and to an extent it is. However, *again*, just remember what I said earlier: *"There are very few right and wrong choices when it comes to how and what you build. It just comes down to what you want, what works and what you can afford"*. In other words, if after a bit of research, you find yourself being drawn to one build method over another, then the chances are that that is the right choice <u>*for you*</u>. You don't need to spend the next 6 months just making sure by looking at every possible alternative. If you like it and it works for your project and you can afford it, then choose and plan to use it!

    If, at any time during the project planning period, you find something else that you prefer, or works better and is possibly cheaper, then use that instead. Your final decision on the build method does not usually need to be made until 3 – 4 months before you actually start building, so there is simply no need to make any final decisions at this stage (see Chapter 7: "How will we build the house?" for more detail on this subject).

5. **Deciding how the project will be managed** This is one of the most important decisions you will make and it needs to be given a good bit of thought to make sure you make the right choice. This is one of the few decisions that, if you don't get right, can be a job stopper.

    Here are your main choices for managing the project:

➤ **Self Project Manage**: This choice will involve you in pretty much every aspect of the planning, the design and the build, from day 1 to completion. To consider taking on the role of project manager for a venture such as this, you need:

- **A lot of time available** to be able to dedicate yourself to the venture from start to finish.
- **At least some experience of the building industry**. Being a good DIYer is sometimes ok, but preferably you should also have worked on a building site of some description, for a reasonable period of time. You are going to be asked a lot of technical questions throughout the build period. If you don't have sufficient knowledge and experience of how a building site works and how a house is built, you can quickly find yourself giving the wrong answers to those questions, sometimes with potentially seriously negative consequences on the project as a whole.
- **Good organisational skills**. Building a house is not difficult, but whoever is in charge needs to be aware of what needs doing and when, who does it and how long it will take. You can glean some of these skills by study, but you will still need to be able to put them into practice every day on site, so you need to have a natural ability to organise. Every time you make a mistake on a self-build (or any construction) project it will normally cost you both money and time.
- **To be able to cope with stress**. No matter how well your project is set up and runs, there will always be a significant element of stress attached to trying to manage a fairly major construction project. If you struggle with the pressure and you find yourself losing sleep, worrying about what is going on around you, you will quickly wear yourself out. If that happens, both the project and your family life can suffer significantly.
- **Good financial and time awareness**. It is a fact that every day that you are on site, your total build cost will increase, whether or not you actually do anything that day. Things like borrowing costs, scaffold, plant, tool hire, security fencing, health and safety equipment and many items all have a cost per day to be on your site, some of them fairly significant. For example, your scaffold hire charges may include the first six weeks in the quoted price, but then cost you a few hundred pounds a week from then on. If the scaffold ends up staying on site for an extra

six months because of lack of progress, it could add literally thousands of pounds extra to the total cost of the project. Again, study can help you to be aware of time related cost factors, but a good level of personal financial awareness is really needed too.
- **An awareness of health and safety requirements for this type of project.** Be aware that if there is an accident on site these days, if the site supervisor (in this case you), is found to be guilty of health and safety breaches, they can be *personally* prosecuted. This can lead to large fines or even a jail sentence.

➢ **Using an architect to supervise the construction** This is not one of my favoured options. Many architects who draw up plans for self-build projects will also offer to supervise or project manage the construction, usually for a considerable fee. Many self-builders are happy to choose this option, as they feel that they will have a professional person looking after the whole process, which to an extent is true. However, when you look in to how this system usually works, it is sometimes perhaps not as attractive an option as it may first appear.

When an architect offers to supervise the construction, what they often actually mean is that they will give the whole project over to a main contractor, whom they work with and then keep a watching eye over what goes on on-site during the build period. This will often be coupled with you using their own architects certificate as the structural warranty for the finished property.

There are two main weaknesses with this system: 1) You will be paying a high price to employ a main contractor to build the complete property. There are much cheaper options and 2) Some mortgage lenders are not too keen on lending to projects using an architects certificate.

So, if you are considering using an architect to supervise the project, with or without an architects certificate, you need to be sure you ask all the right questions and be fully aware of the financial and warranty implications before you start (see later chapters).

➢ **Using a professional project manager:** Wherever and whenever it is possible, this is the option that I tend to recommend to most potential self-builders, unless they have good levels of organisational skills and experience and a strong knowledge of the construction processes involved in building a new home.
- The problem is that presently in the UK, good self-build project managers are in very short supply. There are a few companies dotted around the UK which are offering this service and probably a couple of hundred individuals who have set up in business as self-build project managers, so you may think this is an option that is still worth pursuing.

   The way this system works is that you initially approach a project manager to discuss your requirements.
   - You can be thinking of asking them to provide a full management package from start to finish, or you may want to keep some control of the running of the site yourself and just get them to do the bits you can't.
   - Most project managers will be open to negotiation as to how much input they provide. All they need to do is to make sure you have the finances available to take on such a project and be happy that they will be fairly paid for whatever work they take on for you. Most project managers will be working on multiple sites at any one time, so they don't need to take a full salary from one job. This means that they can be flexible in the way they charge you for their input.
   - Maybe you will pay them by the number of hours they are on site, or maybe so much a month for whatever they need to do, or maybe a fixed price for a full management package. One or more of these options will normally enable you to get whatever level of cover you need, to either take *your* place on site, or at least, to back up your own input (*should you wish to stay involved in the day to day running of the site*).
   - One good project manager should be able to look after half a dozen single self build projects as long as they are all generally in the same geographical location (possibly within around 30 miles of each other). The project manager is directly employed by the client (you) and their job is to give you the best service they can. Their target will be to get your project finished on time, to a high quality and within budget. A good project manager

will potentially be able to make savings in the overall building costs, simply by knowing where to go for the best quality / best value labour, plant and materials (*we will be looking at this subject in more detail in Chapter 8: "How will we run the project?"*).

➢ **Using a main contractor** This tends to be the most expensive way to run a self-build project. There are many reasons for this, but suffice to say at this stage that the cost of using a main contractor over a project manager or over project managing your own project can be as much as 40%, especially if you use them in conjunction with an architects' supervision package.

Main contractors will look after the whole project for you, taking on all the work involved in finding and ordering the materials, labour, plant etc. They will make sure that the warranty inspections are done, and keep the site up to the required health and safety standards (see chapter 8). If they are VAT registered, they can save you paying VAT upfront, to reclaim later, which can (theoretically) keep your overheads down

6. **Deciding on your level of eco credentials:** We are all much more aware of our impact on the planet these days and that awareness has clearly shown itself by the shift in the way self-builders approach their projects. Passive houses are getting more and more common and one of the main motivators, even on a low budget self-build project is to achieve a well-insulated home with low fuel bills.

   How far you go along the route of ecological ethics will depend as much on your budget as on your intended lifestyle, so it is important that you look into this area of the build to see where you sit, what you would like to achieve and what you can afford.

   Be careful here though. I am coming across more and more potential self-builders for whom there is only one driving force for taking on a project and that is: "To build a passive house". Unfortunately, especially when they are early on in the planning process, when I ask them what they think a passive house is, they don't actually know.

   There are many stages between a poorly insulated house and a passive house. The ideal trick is to get yourself to the stage where you can be as "green" as possible, without risking the success of your project by spending too much money on energy saving and not enough on the house itself.

   We will be covering this subject in later chapters, but just be aware that this is a subject that can drag you in and not let you go! It can become so much of an addiction to have the target of creating a zero-carbon home that the other important aspects of the project get side-lined or forgotten.

   Yet again, - remember the quote from earlier: "*Only learn what you need to learn and do what you need to do. No more*". Apply this to your eco research and you should hopefully be able to keep yourself under control.

7. **Investigate your choices when it comes to structural warranties / building regulations packages and site "all risks" contractors' insurance.**

Those 7 topic areas are where you should be targeting the lion's share of your research time. If you get those bits right, then a lot of the rest will usually drop into place in its own time, without too much prompting from you.

How much will it all cost?

One big question for this sort of major venture will always be: "Can we afford it?"

Unfortunately, at this early stage, it is just about impossible to give anything like an accurate answer to the question. At this stage, you don't know how much your land is likely to cost, what sort of size of house and design you will be looking for, what construction methods you will be using, what the labour costs in your area are going to be, or how long it is all going to take.

Not until you start to make some of the decisions we have looked at in this chapter, will you be able to start to come up with even *very approximate* figures for likely costs.

One of the most common questions I am asked when I am working as a self-build expert at the various shows is: "*How much would it cost to build a standard 4 bed detached house?*" My answer is always the same "I'm sorry but that is an impossible question to answer without a lot more information".

This is a significant problem within the UK self-build industry. People want and need to know how much their dream home will cost them before they start the project, so they can decide if they can afford it, but it is not possible to work that cost out until much further in to the project.

The best way we have to get around the problem at the moment is to stick our thumbs in the air and make our best guess! Ok, maybe we can be a bit more scientific than that, but in reality, until we get our act together and approach things more like they do in other countries, in reality that is pretty much all we can do!

As an example of the problems this uncertainty can bring, I can recall how I must have spoken to dozens of potential self-builders who turn up to a consultation at one of the self-build shows, having already bought a plot of land and who already have a full set of (fully paid for) working drawings for (say) a large 3000+ sq ft, 5 or 6 bed house (often with all sorts of expensive features).

They tell me they need to hand the whole thing over to a main contractor to build because they are not confident enough to manage it themselves. We talk and I then find out that, even at this late stage they really have no idea of the likely cost of building the house which they have designed and which is on the drawings that they have in front of them! When I eventually ask what their budget is for the build, they tell me it is something daft like £150,000 (*when a more realistic price for a 3000 sq ft house built by a main contractor is over £350,000*)!

How does this very dangerous situation arise?

These people probably set out with a budget of something like £250,000 for the full project, land and build. They then start to carry out some research and perhaps read a magazine article entitled "Readers project" which usually shows a beautiful looking house and happy self-builders with smiling faces. The title will read something like: "Mr and Mrs Smith have built this 6 bedroomed mansion for tuppence in 10 weeks"!
Then they may read other similar articles which also present a totally misleading picture of how it all works and slowly but surely, they formulate their own idea of how much it is going to cost them to build a similar 6-bedroom mansion.
What they are not aware of, and the magazine article doesn't make this clear, is that the costs listed are often nowhere near being either comprehensive or accurate. If you read some of these sorts of magazine articles, at the end you will often see a list of the costs. It will consist of around 10 – 15 major items, but when someone like me looks at it, I straight away see that there are usually lots of glaring omissions. These omissions could sometimes be expected to almost double the real cost of the project (*things like legal costs for buying the land, borrowing costs, alternative living accommodation while they build their new home, warranties, site insurance, site set up costs, fencing and security, health and safety equipment, site clearance / demolition of existing structures, the new van they bought for the project, scaffolding, skips for taking all the waste off site. The list could go on and on. Also, often these people will have taken at least a couple of years to complete their homes because they have physically done a lot of the work themselves to save on labour costs*).

Once they have read a few these sorts of articles, the people now sitting in front of me at the self-build show (understandably) naturally think they could do the same as the smiling people in the magazine article. So without doing any proper research, they simply go ahead and buy a nice plot of land for £120,000 (plus £5,000 legal and other fees), thinking: "According to what we have read, that will leave us plenty for the build".

They then think that the next stage is to hire an architect to prepare their designs and drawings, without even being aware of the other design options available. What they often end up with, a couple of months later, is a set of drawings for a huge great house of around 3000 sq ft, with all sorts of expensive features, thinking as they look at them, that they will still be well under budget when it comes to building what they have designed.

Unfortunately, fairly soon, reality starts to set in:

The architect sends them an invoice for £10,000 for the initial house design, all the 3D renderings and the full working drawings.

This now leaves them with £115,000 from their original budget (after buying the land and incurring associated legal costs).

They then apply for planning permission and building regulations approval and are told by the planning office that they have to undertake a number of surveys and submit various reports as part of the application. They can't do this work themselves so they ask the architect to do it.

The planning and building regulations application ends up costing them £5,000, leaving them £110,000.

They then realise that they need both a structural warranty and a building regulations certificate, along with site insurance before they can start work. Cost, possibly around £10,000 for the full package.

As they have no knowledge of the workings of the building industry, they then start to look for a main contractor to take on their project, remaining in blissful ignorance of the fact that the people in the magazine article did the project management and a lot of the physical work themselves. Unfortunately, although they don't know it yet, to get a main contractor to take on and build a self-build house costs anywhere between £130 - £180 / sq ft, which, for their design will equate to around £390,000 - £540,000 for the full build cost.

When they get the main contractors quote, after blaming each other for being so stupid, they panic and the thing they do after that, is what they should have done in the first place: They think of the best way to get some professional advice and help!

That is how they end up sitting in front of me at the Grand Designs shows! Unfortunately, about a year too late to save their present project.

Are they daft?

These people are not stupid (in fact most self-builders are very intelligent people), they have simply not spent enough time at the start of the project, getting all their skittles in to rows. Instead, they have just headed off, unprepared (apart from reading a few misleading articles), with fingers crossed, in the direction they think they should be headed, hoping that everything will turn out ok.

I don't like doing it, but on these occasions, I sometimes have to say: "I'm sorry, but your figures just don't add up. This is simply not going to work".

When this sort of thing happens, the "dream bubble" is burst, these people will have wasted thousands of pounds on architects, legal and planning fees, they will have got themselves excited about living in this big, beautiful house and suddenly, after having the shock of getting the quotation from the builder, they are told by someone like me that the project is, unfortunately a non-starter.

This is the point at which many self-builders will simply give up and this sort of scenario is unfortunately all too commonplace within this industry.

The saddest part of all that is that it does not need to happen.

Usually I can help people to re think their project and possibly find a way to save it, but I always find myself thinking: "Why has this happened – again?"

So, the moral of this story is that **you** need to make sure you don't suffer the same fate as these unfortunate folks. **You** need research correctly, *learn what you need to learn* and *do what you need to do* before you go leaping in to the unknown".

So how do you make sure you don't make the same mistakes?

There are two stages to pricing up your self-build project:

1) "Your best guess" at the very early stages.
2) Proper pricing later on (see Chapter 9: How much will it cost? – *But don't read that chapter yet!*).

In this chapter we will look at how to make your *best guess*:

Use your initial research: Earlier in this chapter we looked the seven main areas of research that you need to undertake as the first part of planning your project. You can now use this information to give you a reasonable stab at guessing a rough cost for the full project.

This is how to do it:

- **The first area of research** involves getting a clear picture of your financial situation. You need to list the details of your available cash, the amount that you would possibly be able to borrow from a mortgage lender (taking your earnings in to account) and any other finances that you may be able to lay your hands on, if either you wish to, or if they are needed.
  Once you have compiled all the relevant figures, you should have an idea of what you are going to be able to afford for the full build.
  You are going to need a deposit towards the cost of the land of anything from 5% to 30% depending on a number of factors (that you will learn about from the individual lenders). You will need cash to cover this deposit.
  Self build mortgage companies will sometimes lend up to 100% of the total cost of the project, so have a look at which companies are offering self-build mortgages and what their offers and rates are like.
  When you are splitting up your budget between "land and build", a very rough guide would be to allow 50% for each. This varies dramatically from area to area, but for now it will help you with the process of formulating your best guess.

  Because we are trying to make a very rough estimate of the total cost of the project, it is very important at this stage that you allow a significant cash buffer to absorb all the inaccuracies which are bound to be included in whatever figures you end up with. I would suggest a buffer of around 25% would be realistic.

  So how does all that come together?

  Say you are a couple, earning £25,000 each per annum, your total gross income is £50,000.
  Lenders will vary on the amount they will lend as multiples of income, but somewhere between 3x and 4x your joint income is usually a reasonable figure to be working on.
  For simplicity, here we will say that you could therefore possibly borrow up to £200,000 for the land and the build combined.

  For this example, we will assume you have £25,000 in savings and a further £25,000 locked away in investments or somewhere else that you could cash in if you needed to.

So, taking all those figures together we potentially have a total "funding pot" of £250,000

Theoretically that allows you £125,000 for the plot and £125,000 for the build.

Now bring in the buffer at 25% (*this actually works out at £62,500, but for simplicity let's call it £60,000 for this example*). Take £60,000 away from £250,000 and you are left with a **total target budget** of £190,000

You now have £95,000 as a target price for the plot and £95,000 as a target price for the build. However, you are comfortable in the fact that you theoretically have another £60,000 that you could pull in if things go a bit pear shaped (this is obviously dependent on the lender allowing you to borrow £200,000).

Let's stick with those figures for now.

- **The second area of research** was to look at areas where you would like to live and then find out how much an average plot sells for in that area. From the information you glean from your searches online, you should be able to give yourself an idea of a range of prices that would get you a plot in any of your chosen areas. Say, for this example that plots of the sort that would suit you, are selling for between £80,000 and £120,000. If that were the case, you would be fairly comfortable that your £95,000 budget (including your £20,000 cash) would cover the likely purchase price of a reasonable plot. *So we are still financially ok so far.*

- **The third area of research** was to work out what sort of size and type of accommodation you will need. As part of your research you will have come up with some ideas of room sizes, but when you are trying to work out build prices, you need to know the approximate floor area of the whole house (including walls thicknesses). There are two fairly easy ways you can do this: 1) Get some existing house plans of a developer's house that you like, or download plans from the internet and use those floor areas to get some approximate build costs. 2) Draw up some rough plans of a layout that would suit you and work out your floor areas from those drawing. We look at designing and drawing up house plans in Chapter 5: "Designing your new home".

- **The fourth area of research** was to think about your method of building (brick and block / timber frame / SIPS etc.) We won't be using your results from that research to formulate your best guess build price as there are too many variables. For the exercise we are undertaking here, we will be assuming you are using one of the standard build methods rather than one of the specialist or less common build methods. If you have already decided to use one of the more specialised build methods, or if you are hoping to do a lot of the work yourself, you will need to either add to, or subtract from your financial buffers in your pricing calculations to allow for variables in likely costs. Adding maybe an extra 10% for more expensive build methods and deducting the same if you are planning on having more physical and practical input yourselves.

- **The fifth area of research** was to decide on how you intend to manage the project. This is where, taking the information we are correlating, we can start to focus on getting closer to our best guess price for your project. There is a full chapter dedicated to your choices for site management later, but I am going to pull some of the figures out from it to use for what we need to do here.

    When I present seminars and talk to potential self-builders at the shows, I use a set of figures for build costs "per square foot" (and per square metre) for each of the site management options.

    As you read through this book I will be showing you potential ways to cuts your development costs down dramatically (in some cases by up to 50%), however I won't be using those lower figures here as you would need to be fully "up to speed" on everything you are going to learn as you read the rest of the book, before you can realistically hope to achieve the figures I will be talking about later. Instead, for now and for what we are doing here, I will stick with using the industry averages for our calculations.

(Please note: These figures have not been scientifically calculated, they are figures which I have compiled over many years of building homes myself, by researching the build costs of many of the self-builders I have met and by taking on board what other industry professionals quote).

Here is a rough guide to how the build costs per sq ft pan out on most self builds, depending on your choice of how you set up the project management:

Project manage everything yourself: Usually between £90 - £110 sq ft (£968 - £1183 / sq m)

Hire a project manager: Usually between £110 - £130 (£1183 - £1398 / sq m)

Main contractor: Usually between £130 - £180+ / sq ft (£1398 - £1936 / sq m)

The next thing to do is to take your (external) square footage for the floor area (known as the footprint and multiply it by the price per square foot for your initial sketch designs (*or the plans that you have found somewhere else which would give you the sort of house you would want and need*).

This will give you a rough idea of the total build cost (for this example, *I am going to assume you are using the project manager option and I'll assume we are talking about a modest 1000 sq ft house*)

The calculation should look something like this:

Floor area: 1000 sq ft x Build cost (@ £110 - £130 per square foot)

1000 sq ft x £110 = £110,000

1000 sq ft x £130 = £130,000

"Best guess" guide price for the build of a 1000 sq ft,

Project Managed house = £110,000 - £130,000

So, from that calculation you can immediately see that if you spend £130,000 on your build, you will be well over your target price of £95,000 that you worked out earlier, for the build.

The good news is that at least you are now starting to take some control over what is happening.

Now you that you have some rough figures, you can start to work with them, to find ways to bring the overall cost back towards the target figures.

Ok, where are we up to so far?
- We have confronted the fact that self-builders tend to do too much unnecessary research.
- We have listed the most important areas to research.
- We have seen how easy it is to fall into the trap of starting your project before you are properly prepared
- We have worked out how to get a rough idea of the likely development costs.

That is most of the important stuff that we needed to cover in this chapter, however there are lots of other bits and pieces of information and advice that I can give you, that will not only help you to carry out your research, but will also start to increase your knowledge base on the subject as a whole. We will go through some of them now to complete this chapter (*we will also be revisiting a lot of them in more detail later in the book*).

Things to think about before you start.

1) **Do we need an architect?**

   Not necessarily. You have various options, most of which would be most likely to cost you less money.

   At the planning stage, drawings only need to be fairly basic in nature. You don't need full working drawings to make an application and you would be daft to spend lots of money on full working drawings for a project until you know that your scheme has been approved.
   The drawings you will usually need for planning are (*all to certain required scales and usually printed on to A3 paper*): *plans of each floor / elevations of each side of the house / sections through the house / plot plan / location plan / other bits and pieces as may be required by the individual planning departments.*

   These documents are not normally difficult to create, in fact, if you download some house design software and spend a bit of time learning how to use it, there is a good chance that you would be able to create your own planning drawings, or at least design something that you could then take to a designer to quickly and cheaply draw up a set which *would* be suitable for the planning application.

   If and when you do need a designer of some sort, to prepare more detailed drawings, you *can* use a fully chartered architect if you wish, but you don't need to.

   Here is another one of my sayings:

   Planning Permission deals with "What it looks like"
   Building Regulations deal with "Will it stand up?"

2) **Working drawings** are only *sometimes* needed on site once you have actually started work (*but not always, often your basic plans are enough to build the house from as long as the guys doing the building know what they are doing*).

3) **Building Regulations approval** is not needed until up to a few days before you start work on site (*although it is better to get them a bit sooner than that, in case there is anything in them that you need to take note of, that affects the first few days on site*).

   It may be difficult for you to believe, especially if you have never built a house, but I have never used a working drawing on a single house building project in over 30 years of building new homes. This is simply because (as I said earlier), decent tradesmen all know their stuff. They are all pretty much fully aware of everything that you normally find on working drawings for a simple 4 bed detached house. They don't need to be told.

   Ok, if you are constructing a particularly unusual or difficult feature, or a very complicated house, then working drawings may be required. When I work on the big commercial building sites, we sometimes have literally hundreds of working drawings issued to us, however, most self build houses are usually quite simple and if you have the right people working with you, they will just get on with it without having to constantly refer to "pretty pictures".

   What you do need to prepare however, as part of your building regulations application, is a full set of specifications. These give the builders all the technical information they need to ensure that the house conforms to the latest building regulation requirements. They are normally produced onto a few sheets of A4 or A3 paper and they cover everything from foundations to electrical and plumbing installations, service connections etc.

The best time to prepare and submit the building regulations information is a few weeks before you start work, when you have made all your big decisions and everything is pretty much settled. You don't usually need *any* building regulations information to form part of a planning application.

So, it stands to reason, that because you only usually need a fairly basic set of drawings to apply for planning permission, you will usually find *(in all but the most complicated of house designs)*, that anyone who has a knowledge of "residential technical drawing" should be able to prepare exactly what you need without charging you the earth (*I would start to sweat if anyone tried charging me over £1500. Around £600 - £900 would be about right for a simple 4 bed detached house*).

To get a simple self build design drawn up, I usually recommend that people have a look at the classified ads in their local paper. Many publications have a section called "House Plans Drawn", where local draughtsmen advertise for work in designing extensions, garages and simple houses. These people can often be semi-retired architectural technicians, ex planners, or just draughtsmen who make a living doing this sort of stuff, at a reasonable price, for people like you. As long as they can produce reasonable quality drawings of everything you need for your planning application, to scale, they will often be perfectly adequate for what you need. If you approach one of these guys with a complicated project and they didn't think they were up to it, they would tell you. It would be daft of them to try to take on a project they couldn't cope with.

4) **Who prepares the Building Regulations drawings and information?**

   From my experience, it is fairly rare to find an Architect who prepares a set of house designs, to also then prepare the building regulations application. In larger practices, there could be a specialist who looks after this part of the process, however, what often tends to happen is that whoever designs the house for you will work with someone whom they send each set of drawings off to at the appropriate time, for them to prepare the Building Regulations specs. These people are often either specialist companies who do this sort of thing all the time, or Structural Engineers (or there may be a bit of input from both).

   The person drawing up your plans will normally charge you the fee that they are charged by the building regulations engineer, plus a commission for their own input.

   It is fairly rare to find anyone capable of designing a house not to have access to someone who can prepare the building regulation submission.

5) **If we want manage the project ourselves, where can we learn how to?**

   Well, I would obviously say that you have made a good start already by reading this book, but there are other things you can do to prepare yourself:

6) **Enrol on a Self-build Project Management Course:** There are a few of these starting to appear around the country, including a regular one at the National Self Build and Renovation Centre at Swindon. Go to: http://www.buildstore.co.uk/mykindofhome/events/self-build-courses.html Alternatively, do a search for "Self-build project management training courses" and add your own post code to see if there is anything in your area.

7) **Read one or two relevant books:** I would suggest finding something on general "Construction Project Management". A student reference book would be good. I have looked on line and there are plenty of publications that you can download free, some of which would be useful in teaching you the basics.

   By the way, if you read these sorts of books (as I am sure you know by now), don't even attempt to learn *everything* in them. Just look for the bits that are possibly going to be relevant to you and then read lightly. In other words, don't get bogged down in the technical stuff. You only need to get a feel for the subject. You can do that by reading, but unless you attend either a specialist self-build course or a college course, you are never going to reach a stage where you know "everything about everything".

You just need have the right management framework in place (*either you or a professional project manager of some sort*), to be able to make sure that your contractors are doing what they should be doing to a high standard.

Funnily enough, if you have the right people working for you, you will often find that the tradespeople on site are the best people to go and listen to if you want to learn how to run the project and to make sure everyone is doing their job properly.
One thing I have found over the years is that the trade that follows another trade will always be the best one to find the faults of the previous trade!
On a building site, anything that goes wrong is always someone else's fault and most experienced tradespeople are well used to making sure that the client quickly knows that if there is a problem, it was always the fault of "the bloke before us".
To be able to do that, without making fools of themselves, they need to have a good knowledge of not only the building process, but also the fine detail of construction method. The good tradespeople learn this over years on site and then are able to use it to pass the blame on to someone else when there is a problem.
For you to take advantage of the people who have this dubious skill, you just need to learn to separate the good tradespeople, whom you can believe, from the ones who are just full of "bull" and who are always looking to cover their own backs. It doesn't usually take long to do that.

8) **When do we need structural warranties and site insurance?**

   In theory, you only need them both when you start work on site. However, if you own a piece of land that could be accessed by the public and that could present any sort of hazard (even to trespassers), it is worth making sure you have your site insurance in place as soon as possible to cover you against potential claims from anyone entering the site and getting injured or causing damage.

9) **Who will be responsible for day to day health and safety on site?**

   I am not going to be able to go in to detail in this book about all the health and safety responsibilities involved in running a building site, partly because they are changing all the time and partly they are too complicated for me to try to cover in anything but a separate publication.

   There are already numerous books out there and tons of information on line that will help you learn about this subject. Be aware though, that it is the responsibility of the self-builder to ensure that their own site conforms to the legal health and safety requirements. If it doesn't, you could be personally liable to prosecution. You should also always check that anyone working on your site carries suitable "cards" (SMSTS / CSCS / First aid) and insurance policies. Make sure you see the cards and copies of policy documents before you allow them access to work. (We will cover this in more detail later).

10) **When do we need to find the contractors and sub-contractors?**

    You don't need to worry about starting to look for all the tradespeople you are going to need at this stage. Before you start spending time doing that, you need to find your plot, buy it and get your house designed. Only then can you start to talk sensibly to any main contractor, project manager or sub-contractor. The first thing any of those people will ask you is "can you send us some drawings". Without them they are completely in the dark. So put this one on the back-burner for now. By the time you have finished reading the book you should know exactly when and how to approach all the people you are going to need.

11) When will we need to connect the services to the site?

There is no real "best" time to do this.

If you are planning on bringing a caravan to site to live in you will usually need at least water, drainage and electricity to be connected at an early stage.

Water will be needed on site throughout the build period, so if you don't connect the water at the start of the project, you will need to do one of the following: 1) Bring in a hired water bowser. 2) Hire a "stand pipe" from the local water authority, which allows you to draw water from the water mains. 3) Bring a number of water "butts" (usually old oil drums) to keep on site, which you will need to keep filling (*often by bringing water from home to site every day, in half a dozen 25 litre containers*) throughout the duration of the project.

When I start new housing sites, if they are single self-builds and I am not going to be living on site, I tend to connect the water at the start of the job and the rest of the services when they are needed (once the "second" fixes are being completed inside the house). That way there is less chance of them being damaged during the early stages of the construction process.

Tradespeople tend to bring their own generators with them, so a mains electricity supply is not often a pivotal requirement.

12) Should we incorporate as many of the new eco products as possible?

Possibly use some of the best products and services, but just tread carefully. The eco housing industry in the UK is really in its infancy. It is growing, but it is still just learning its art and it will be changing just as quickly and just as dramatically over the next few years, as it has for the past few years.

Look at solar panels as an example: Just a few years ago the solar energy market suddenly went into a massive growth period when the government started to offer incentives for private householders to pay out very considerable sums of money to have solar panels fitted to their homes. Installation costs could sometimes be as much as £20,000+, but tens of thousands of people across the UK stumped up the cash and invested. Then, over time, the government changed the way it viewed the subject and reduced the incentives and the idea went a bit out of fashion. The benefits of "going solar" were found not to be as dramatic as many people originally thought they were going to be, and slowly the market settled back down to being just another one of the eco options for new housing.

What the massive boom in the solar industry did do however, was to increase the investment put in to research for the product. Everyone was trying to bring the next big upgrade out to win more of the market share. The result of this is that today, only a few years after the market reached its peak, many of the products bought during that period, when compared to the new products available, are now already out of date and inefficient. You can also now get a better system than the one that cost £20,000 a few years ago, for about a quarter of the price.

The problem with the situation as it has evolved, is the fact that tens of thousands of UK families will now be lumbered with a product that they will still be paying for, possibly for another 10 – 15 years, which they will not be getting the benefits from that someone who buys the latest product today will get for a fraction of the price.

This pattern runs through many of the products throughout the UK's eco construction industry. A product that may seem a great idea today, may not stand the test of time and end up being almost obsolete in a few years.

There are two types of thinking when it comes to "green building". You can take either *"the active route"* or *"the passive route"*. The active route is where you spend money to buy "stuff" to help you to be "green". This includes things like solar panels, ground source and air source heating etc. The passive route is when you design and build your home so that it doesn't much use energy in the first place, using design techniques that don't necessarily cost any extra money and with copious amounts of insulation!

I strongly believe that the passive route is the best way to go.

13) Where will we live while we build?

Now, at this early stage is a good time to be thinking about where you will live when you physically start your project.

There is a perceived notion that living in a caravan on site is the cheapest option, but that is not necessarily true.

A caravan on site is a good idea if there are two (or maximum three) of you in an appropriately large caravan and if you are planning on building pretty quickly. It is not such a good idea if you have two or three kids, are building some distance from their present schools and are planning on your project taking 6 months+, or if it will be running through a winter, or if you only have a tine caravan.

It is a good idea to be aware at this early stage of the basic benefits and drawbacks linked with where you live while you build so, in brief:

- Caravans can be fine if they are big enough so that you have room to move, have your own private sleeping space and are not climbing over each other all the time.
- They can be fine if they have a shower or bath and full cooking facilities, can be kept warm, are plumbed in to running water and connected to the mains drains.
- They can help you to provide ongoing security for the site while you build.
- The cost of having a caravan on site will equal the sum of the following:
    The cost of buying or hiring it + the delivery and setting up cost + the connection costs for the plumbing and drainage + the disconnection costs when you have finished with it + the depreciation when you come to sell it + the removal costs and any liability for council tax.
  If you buy a new caravan it will probably drop in value by up to a few thousand pounds while you own it. If you buy a 10-year-old one you should not lose much when you sell it.
  It would be reasonable to expect the overall cost of buying / setting up / living in and removing a caravan to be somewhere in the region of £3,000 - £6,000 if you use it for less than a year. After that, the depreciation could increase this figure.
- Renting somewhere (preferably furnished or part furnished), close to where you are building is often a good choice, especially if you are planning on building and moving in quickly (in less than 6 months). You will have all the creature comforts available that will help to keep the family happy and you simply *move in and move out* when you are ready. When you add up the costs of buying, setting up, living in and getting rid of a caravan, paying rent for a house for 6 months can work out cheaper. Bear in mind though any additional costs of storage for your furniture.
- If you can get bridging finance it is possible that you may be able to stay in your present home whilst you build your new one. Bridging finance is not available to everyone, but if staying put while you build is an attractive idea to you, it may be worth doing a bit of research into whether it would work for you.
- Overall, given the choice and having experienced all three options, I would always try to stay where I am presently living whilst I build, if possible as a first option. Rent as a second option. Live in a caravan as a third option. I would put all my efforts in to getting the new house built as quickly as possible, so that my living costs do not start to eat in to my build budget too much.

Whichever option you choose, make sure you include any cost over and above your present living cost as a "cost of build". Many self-builders quietly ignore these sorts of costs when they compile their costings and then wonder why their money is disappearing faster than they expected. A very important point to remember is that:

If a cost is incurred because you are building a new home that you would not otherwise incur, then it is a <u>cost of build</u> and should be accounted for as such. Don't try to convince yourself otherwise.

14) **Don't assume the whole family are on board and don't start until you are sure they are.**

    Many self-builds hit problems that are nothing to do with the plot or the build. Family disputes during the project can be just as stressful as the build itself. Both adults and kids need to be singing from the same hymn sheet if you are going to consider taking on a major housebuilding project. Ignore this advice at your peril!

15) **Plan ahead, but not too far.**

    I have lost count of the number of self-builders I have spoken to who have not even found a plot of land, but have their new kitchens stored away somewhere ready to be installed into their new home (well, they got a really good deal and they couldn't resist it!). The chances are that when they get round to designing their kitchen, the one they have will not suit or fit the room they want it to go in to.

    The same situation crops up time after time with self-builders. Not surprisingly they sometimes get a bit carried away with the whole thing and, not being used to the construction industry, try to do too many things at the same time, often the wrong time.

    This book will show you how to take care of the important stuff as well as the not so important stuff in the right way and at the right time.

16) **Don't expect anyone who is selling anything to give you an unbiased answer to questions about their product or service.**

    I spend a lot of time in client consultations listening to people who have been taken in by sales people who have painted rather a too glossy picture of whatever they are selling. Then when the product is bought, the customer ends up being disappointed and feeling that that they have been ripped off. This is unfortunately especially relevant to the eco market at the moment, where there are a lot of new products competing for a limited amount of business. It is unfortunately a symptom of the fact that our industry is small and is set up in an amateurish manner, which offers very few checks on claims made by product manufacturers.

    The only real way to protect yourself from this happening to you, is to always try to check out any facts and figures before parting with your cash and never part with large sums of money unless you are 100% happy with everything you are paying for.

17) **Don't blindly believe the views of local builders or trades people you may talk to when it comes to deciding on what build method to use.**

    Everyone in the house building industry has their own pet favourite way to build. Unless you plan on canvassing a significant number of people for their opinion on, say the "timber frame versus brick & block" argument, you cannot be sure that you will not just be hearing outdated, biased answers from folk who possibly stand to benefit from you choosing one option over another.

The same applies when taking advice from family members who may have a link of some sort to the building industry. Just because they are family doesn't make them oracles on the whole subject of building.

Taking bad advice, especially early on in the project can potentially do great damage to the outcome, by setting you off in the wrong direction and causing you to make some dodgy decisions which will come back to bite you. Don't expect a brickie to be able to give you an accurate answer to questions on joinery (or vice versa) and always check out any advice you get from anyone before taking it on board.

Chapter 3
Finance & Mortgages

Introduction:

One of the aims of this book is to guide you into doing things, not only simply and efficiently but also in the right order. For that reason, I had to give some thought as to where to position this chapter on finance.

There are two ways of looking at the best time to sort out the finance for your project:

I. **Sort the mortgage out earlier:** you may think that there is no point in looking for land unless you know that you are going to be able to afford to pay what you have to pay to get the right plot, wherever and whenever you find it.
    To be able to know this figure, you need to have all your personal financial figures calculated so that you know *1) how much you can afford to borrow* and *2) what sort of deposit you will need to have available to put towards the plot*.
    You may also feel that there is also no point in looking for land unless you are sure that you would have enough money to actually build the house you want on it, once you have bought it.
    If this is the way you think, then this chapter is in the right place in the book for you.

II. **Sort the mortgage out later:** Alternatively, you may be of the opinion that there is no point in doing all the work involved in getting a mortgage sorted unless you have something you want to buy.
    You may think that arranging a mortgage is probably going to be quite a big job and you may have to pay a load of fees that you will lose if you don't go ahead with the project.
    Then there is the thought that you may never find the right plot, your circumstances may change and / or the mortgage product you apply for may be withdrawn during the time that you are searching for a plot.
    There is also the chance that you may simply go off the whole idea before you get to the stage when you need a mortgage.
    If this is the way you think, then this chapter would be better placed by swapping it with the next chapter "Finding land".

Which way is best?

Neither of the above options is wrong, they both have their merits. However, I finally decided to put the finance chapter here, because I think that knowing how much you are going to have available to spend as you look for your plot is very important, probably more important than saving the money you may need to spend to get your personal financial status fully clarified.

What would the point be of searching for land for a few months, possibly discarding some of the lower priced options, until you find your ideal plot, in the ideal location, only to be told that your finances won't stretch to allow you to be able to actually buy it?

With the scarcity of good quality land across the UK, the chances are that once you realise you can't afford your first choice, your other options will have been sold.

So, in order to get yourself in to a position where you are ready and able to make a formal bid for the plot you would like to buy, if and when you find it, in my opinion, you need to do whatever you need to do **now** to get the mortgage and your general financial situation sorted, so that as you search, you will only be looking at what you know you can afford.

To get to that position, these days you may not actually need to spend any money on mortgage applications or admin fees, and it need not take you much time.

If you go on line and search "self-build mortgages", you will not only find websites with lots of information on how they work, you will also find a variety of products available, specifically designed for such projects. Have a good look through the choices and you should find on a number of them, little tools called "mortgage calculators". If you are happy to provide some basic personal information, you will usually be able to use these to get a set of figures telling you:

- How much you can borrow
- The maximum percentage of the land cost that the lender will provide
- The maximum percentage of the build "cost" or "value" that the lender will provide *(these can be very different figures, see below)*
- The interest rate
- The type of products and the lending periods available for this type of mortgage

Once you have this information and these figures in front of you, you can then think about what sort of deposit you are going to be able to put down on the plot. Once you have worked out your available deposit, it is a simple task to work out what you can borrow, for example:

Imagine if your calculated borrowing limit is £200,000, and you have around £20,000 in cash as a deposit. This gives you a total of £220,000 to spend.

Say the lender will lend 80% of the value of the land plus 80% of either the full cost or the value of the build.

A quick calculation tells you that if you find a plot for up to £100,000, you could theoretically borrow £80,000 and put down your full £20,000 cash as a deposit. That, theoretically leaves you a maximum of £120,000 available to spend on the build. However, it is not quite that simple.

What you can actually borrow depends on whether the mortgage company lends on the "cost" or the "value" of the build.

Lending on cost

As the name suggests, the lender will lend an amount based on a percentage of what the job has cost at each stage. This is usually calculated at four or five intervals during the build period and it is up to the borrower to provide a professional "cash flow forecast" for the build and a full accounting of everything during each stage of the build, to prove to the lender the actual build cost.

The payments will usually be made at the end of each stage, so you would need to have money available to start the build and get it up to the first stage payment point.

If your mortgage lender uses this system, it will affect how your deposit is used towards funding the project. Instead of being able to use your full deposit towards the purchase of the land, you will have to earmark part of it for your contribution towards the build costs for the first stage.

In the example we are using here (80% lending on land / 80% on build), you would need to provide 20% the plot price plus 20% of the build cost.

If the lender is lending on cost, this will therefore negatively affect how much you can pay for the plot as your £20,000 now has to be split into two parts, part towards the land and part towards the build.

The effect of this type of mortgage on your project, would therefore be to limit what you could pay for the plot to a much lower amount than I have shown in the example above.

In the example, your maximum plot purchase price would be more like £50,000, with you providing 20% deposit (£10,000) and borrowing 80% maximum funding (£40,000).

This would then leave you just £10,000 of your cash for funding the build, which, if the lender, again only covered 80% of the build costs, would also only allow you to borrow £40,000 to build the house.

Ok, it is not quite as bad as that, but I have given you that stark example just to show you how the system works. In reality, the lenders know that the value of the build will generally be far higher than the cost of building it, so what this type of mortgage actually tends to do is to offer higher percentage figures for its lending against both the plot and the build.

So, if using this type of mortgage you could borrow 90%, or even 100% of land cost and build costs, all of sudden the figures look very different:

Say you can borrow up to 90% of the land and build costs, you can now buy land costing £100,000 and only need to find £10,000 for the deposit (borrowing £90,000). This would then leave you £10,000 of your deposit money to put towards the build costs, which would also then allow you to borrow £90,000. This would give you a total borrowing of £180,000 against the total land and build cost of £200,000.

(Note: This is still £20,000 less than you could theoretically borrow based on your personal financial situation (which is a maximum of £220,000), so still limits what you could spend on the project).

The figures get better again if you can secure 100% funding (this is fairly rare but worth searching for if you need it).

Lending on value

Using the same general figures of the lender lending up to 80%, but basing our calculations on a mortgage which lends on "value" (i.e. 80% of land and 80% of **value**) you will see that things work slightly differently.

The land part of the equation will usually work the same as the previous example.

This would mean at 80% borrowing you would still be limited to a £50,000 plot because you would still need to keep some money to start the build.

The lending for the build will then be worked out based on the *anticipated end value of the finished house*.

In other words, you would be able to borrow 80% of the **full expected sale price**, <u>less what you have borrowed already for the land</u>, to build the house.

With this system, obviously the higher the end value of the house, the more money you can get to build it (up to your borrowing limit), so, say the end value was expected to be £300,000, 80% of that is £240,000.

That figure is above your borrowing limit, but on those figures, you should be able to borrow up to your full borrowing limit of £220,000.

However, you still need to be able to build the first stage with your own money.

If your mortgage pays out in 5 stage payments (which is quite common) they will normally be something along the line of:

Payment 1: Land
Payment 2: Foundations complete
Payment 3: Shell up and roof on
Payment 4: Plastered out
Payment 5: Complete

The way the payments for each stage are calculated, would be for the mortgage company to send a valuer (normally linked to a local estate agent) to site to value the property at each of the 4 build stages. The valuer would have had a set of drawings and would therefore be able to value the finished property before it was built, comparing it with other existing local properties.

Each time a stage was completed, the valuer would simply come and check that the work has been done. He / she then puts a realistic value on how much the property would sell for, if it were put up for sale at that time (in other words, part built).

So, say the final value of the completed property was expected to be £300,000, the valuer may put the following vales on it at each stage (including the value of the land):

Valuation 1:	Land	£50,000
Valuation 2:	Foundations complete	£125,000
Valuation 3:	Shell up and roof on	£200,000
Valuation 4:	Plastered out	£250,000
Valuation 5:	Complete	£300,000

Now, imagine you start work on the foundations and, for this example you have designed a very simple house. The cost for those foundations could be around (for the sake of simplicity) £10,000.

To pay the cost of the building the foundations, you can simply use the £10,000 that you have got left from your own £20,000 cash (after paying £10,000 as the deposit on the land).

(Note: in reality you will also try to use credit accounts where possible and set up a "30 days after invoice" payment system with the sub-contractors to help your cash flow, - but we won't go in to that just now, let's just keep it as simple as possible).

In this case, the following scenario could potentially be something like what would happen:

Payment 1: Land   Value £50,000   Stage payment (@80%) **£40,000**

Payment 2: Foundations complete   Value £125,000   Stage payment (@80%) £100,000
Less the land payment already made (£40,000) = **£60,000** paid to you.

Payment 3: Shell up and roof on   Value £200,000   Stage payment (@80%) £160,000
Less the two previous payments (£40,000 + £60,000) = **£60,000** paid to you.

Payment 4: Plastered out   Value £250,000   Stage payment (@80%) £200,000
Less the three previous payments (£40,000 + £60,000 + £60,000) = **£40,000** paid to you

Payment 5: Complete   Value £300,000   Final payment (Max borrowing limit of £220,000) = £20,000

In reality, you may be able to negotiate the actual lending figures with the lender to help out your cash flows, in order to allow you to be able to borrow more for the land.

Just go and talk to them at the right time to see what is the best package they can put together to suit your circumstances.

The important thing to learn from this chapter so far is to:

Check out all your borrowing options. Don't assume that all mortgages are the same.

Why aren't there more self-build mortgages available?

I think it is worth relating something to you here that happened back in 2011.

Early that year, I was asked to become a member of the Coalition Government's *"Self Build Working Group"*, under the leadership of Grant Shapps (then Housing Minister).

This was, theoretically a collection of the *"heads of the industry"* who were called to meet together regularly in London over a period of a few months, with the aim of finding ways to improve and grow the self-build market across the UK.

The target for the group was to try to ensure that, in ten years or so, the UK self-build market should be able to compete with the commercial housing developers as a viable option to anyone wanting to own their own homes. It also had the aim of trying to achieve the sorts of figures found in some other European countries where "self-build" and "custom build" projects account for up to 80% of all new residential building projects.

At the first meeting of the group, Grant Shapps made the introductions and asked for an open discussion on the weaknesses in the industry at that time.

About ten minutes in to the meeting, a representative from the financial side of the industry, was asked:

>"Why do you think are there not more self-build mortgages available in the UK?"

His answer was:

>"**UK lenders generally look at our self-build industry as being amateurish, complicated and cumbersome, with the outcome of this thinking being that in times when funds to lend are scarce** (as they were at the time), **they would rather lend to people in the mainstream mortgage market, where the process is much simpler and the borrowers are usually a better financial bet**".

So, at least in 2011, "*Amateurish, complicated and cumbersome*" was how we as an industry were viewed by the lenders! How do you like that? And do you know what? I totally agreed with what that guy said!

I was the person who responded to the comment at the meeting, saying something like:

>"**Well if that is the case, then surely one of the *main aims* of this group over the next few months has to be to change the industry so that it is less amateurish and complicated, so hopefully then it will be seen as being less cumbersome and more lenders will want to lend to us**".

What the lenders meant by "cumbersome" was that they have to put a lot of research, development work, time and financial investment in to be able to create a new self-build mortgage product to launch into the market.

At that time the housing market as a whole was pretty much "on stop" due to the recession and although the self-build market did not suffer quite the same catastrophic failure over that period, the numbers of self-build starts did reduce significantly from its already low numbers of fewer than 10,000 per annum. The prospect therefore, of a lender putting all the effort needed in to creating new products for what was always a small market and now was even smaller, was pretty minimal.

Over that period, the self-build industry shrunk down to a point where it started to resemble less of a mainstream market and more of a niche.

I attended a number of the working group meetings over the following months and the resultant (disappointing) "*Report with recommendations*" was published in 2012.

I have to admit that while I was involved with the group, that it began to become clear to me just why the industry was in the mess:

To my mind, this was the main reason:

>**There was a crippling, top end lack of leadership, experience, management skills and vision.**

The saddest part of it is that, here in 2017, after all the work was that done during that time, the industry still finds itself in pretty much the same situation now, as it was then.

The problem is not necessarily the people who were in charge of trying to lead the industry at the time. The main problems were that it was, (and still is) an industry that was basically "*small and insignificant*" by nature, made up of a few thousand "itinerant" individuals or couples who are often only around for a couple of years while they complete their own projects and then disappear. People who often have no knowledge or experience of either this industry, or of the building industry as a whole.

The nature of what the industry actually was, meant that there *was* and *is* no real long term leadership, no proper funding for either research or growth, no cohesion, no long-term plan and no-one around who would be in a position to change that situation to any noticeable extent.

Once I started to realise the state we were in as an industry, trying to find a way to fix the problems became one of the main drivers that led me to write this book.

Having already worked within the industry for more than a couple of decades previously, I was already fully aware of all of its weaknesses, however, hearing how the numbers of completions had fallen since the 1970's from over 22,000 per annum to less than 10,000 in 2010 made me start to think that something needs to be done. So the idea began to evolve that if I could start to show people how to approach the whole subject in a more professional manner from day one, maybe, just maybe, the industry would start to be seen in a better light, not only by the lenders, but also by the government, the manufacturers of the products and, perhaps most importantly, by the general public.

So, back to financial matters

Another bit of history

It was the way of things about 50 years ago, that if you wanted to buy a house, you had either to have enough cash to do so, or you took out a mortgage. It was a simple as that.

Then came along this slightly strange group of people who wanted to do something a bit different. They wanted to have a go at designing and building their own homes.

The idea was quite slow to take off, but over time, as the national housing developers started to give their customers less and less, whilst charging more and more, larger numbers of people from across the UK realised that this self-building lark was quite a good idea and started to join in.

In the early days, there was very little help available, either in the form of professional advice or mortgages, with individual builders having to have the cash before they could build, or they borrowed from their families or had to get bridging loans to pay for building their new homes whilst they still lived in their old homes.

Only a couple of brave lenders initially got involved in providing mortgages in stages (of two or three payments) to help these people with the cash flows they needed to turn their dreams in to reality.

By the sixties, the whole movement had gained enough momentum to attract the attention of the mortgage companies who started to recognise this new market as potentially having a strong future and the self-build mortgage (or stage mortgage) as we know it came into being.

The availability of these mortgages meant that the self-build market could now grow without financial constraint and anyone who could afford to contribute some funds as a cash deposit, could now think about having a go.

Banks would often still be happy to set up bridging loans to work in conjunction with the stage mortgages if the borrower didn't have much cash available for deposits and / or the initial site works, as long as they had value in property they already owned that could be used as security.

As the numbers of self-builders grew, so the lenders reacted to demand and created new and better mortgage products, until in the eighties, when I first became involved in the industry, lenders were rather throwing money at self builders and letting them have a go, whether or not they had any previous experience of building.

The number of self-build completions increased year on year up to a peak of around 22,000 a year in the mid-eighties. Land was relatively cheap and reasonably plentiful, there were plenty of tradespeople around to do the work and everything looked very rosy.

The lenders weren't worried about losing too much money if some of the projects went pear-shaped, because they had realised that if a person or family built their own home, in general they could be expected to make around 30% - 35% profit on the build, which in simple terms means that the cost of the land, plus the build was around 35% less than the value of the completed home. They saw this 35% figure as providing a good buffer against the occasional cases of incompetence and error, so they just basically lent to anyone who asked for a mortgage.

If necessary, they would multiply their income by 5 or more to get to the figures that the self-builder wanted to borrow, or even allow people to self-certify their income without any questions being asked, which meant that theoretically, I could apply for a stupidly high mortgage, and to get the money all I had to do was to sign a piece of paper saying that I was earning a million pounds a fortnight as a self-employed spoon bender!

I was lucky enough to benefit from this generosity by the lenders on my first couple of houses, for one of which I seem to remember I managed to get a mortgage of 100% of the land plus 100% of the build costs based on me self certifying my income.

I would have to admit that without such free access to funds, I would probably not have been able to get a house building business going and would probably be doing something very different from what I am doing today, so overall I am not complaining.

It's actually a bit scary when you think back on it: how stupid were the lenders? Gambling on the continuing rise in property values to keep everything afloat. It was this sort of irresponsible lending in that period that helped to spark the 2008 recession.

So, there in a nutshell is the reason for the rapid growth if the self-build industry from the 70's to the early 2000s: Reasonably priced land, very generous stage mortgage products and bridging loans, coupled with a very simple industry, where there was no internet and very little help available of any sort. In those days, you just decided you wanted to build your own home and got on with it.

All of a sudden in 2007 / 2008 things changed. We found ourselves heading in to a recession. Property prices and values stagnated or started to fall, and suddenly, what had been a very lucrative sector of the market started to get much less attractive to lenders.

Some of the projects that would previously have been guaranteed to be successful found themselves struggling. Self-builders were losing their jobs during the build process and were finding it harder to complete them and or afford the sky-high mortgage repayments on their excessively high mortgages. It all started to turn into a bit of a mess.

This experience scared the lenders, and very soon everything related to finance and the self-build industry changed dramatically. Many mortgage companies simply pulled out of the market completely and the ones who stayed in, tightened up their lending criteria to such an extent that you basically had to prove to them that you didn't really need to borrow any money before they would even consider lending to you!

It must be seen as a good thing that, due to the recession, the lenders finally started to look more closely at what had been going on for the past 15 years and what they found caused them to impose a major shakeup in the way they funded self build.

One important change they made was to introduce a much more stringent application process.

By 2010, the lenders who had stuck with the market through the worst of the recession and who were still around, had introduced a new system, where instead of an applicant simply stating that they wanted a self-build mortgage because they wanted to build their own house, they had to start to prove to the lenders that they stood a good chance of running and completing the project successfully.

To prove that you were a good financial bet, it became a requirement that before you would be offered a self-build stage mortgage you went through almost an interview process, where the lenders wanted to find out everything about your financial situation, your building experience, how you were planning on setting the project up and who was going to look after the building work (you or a main contractor).

They also wanted to be sure that you understood the build costs and had a plan for how long it was all going to take.

Each applicant would be required to provide a comprehensive list of costs for each section of work and draw up a programme (a timescale graph) for the building works.

This was a good thing for the industry and I am glad it happened. What this change of thinking and procedure meant to the individual self-builder was that, instead of just ploughing on into a project with fingers crossed, hoping that it would all come together in the end, potential self-builders were now having to give real and serious thought to the whole process before they would be able to start.

Overall, although I think that these changes set the industry up so it was ready to move forward in a much more professional manner, in reality, at least temporarily, it had a major negative effect. What it achieved in the short to medium term was a significant slowdown in the growth of the industry (over and above the one caused by the recession itself). People started to realize that if they wanted to take on one of these major construction projects they were not only going to have to do a lot of preparatory work, they were also going to have to prove to a lender that their preparatory work and their plan for the whole project was professional and financially viable. How would Mr and Mrs Joe Public, with no previous building experience, manage to pull off that trick?

In reality, in many cases, they simply could not. This meant that thousands of potential self-builders each year, once they realised the difficult nature of taking on such a project, simply gave up on the idea.

The obvious knock-on effect of both the new levels of professionalism, together with the overall scarcity of self-build mortgages was to further reduce the potential numbers of self-build completion numbers per year. These figures had already been hit hard by the recession and had fallen by around 50% from their heights of 23,000+ per year in the early 2000's.

When I use the term "potential" self-build completion numbers, what I mean is the number of extra self-builders who could have been taking on their own project over and above the official numbers quoted in government figures. In fact, the self-build industry did not fare too badly during the recession. Completion numbers levelled out at the same sorts of low numbers that had been achieved just before the recession, but the market did not implode in the way that the commercial housebuilding market did over those 4- 5 years. The changes made to the levels of professionalism that the lenders required simply got rid of (for want of a better word) the chaff, the people who would have just launched in to the whole project unprepared and ill equipped and who would have been most likely to fail. As I say, these changes, overall were therefore a good thing.

Funding your project today:

I am going to look a little more closely here at how you go about securing a self-build mortgage these days

The self-build market is still small, and it is still not of major interest to the lenders. For that reason, there are still not a huge number of stage mortgages available and the ones that are available don't tend to be very competitive, when compared to what is now available in the wider house buying market.

The setup is still pretty much the same as it has been over the past 6 years, with the borrower needing to prove that they are a good bet to lend to. The success or failure of the project usually depends on the people who are borrowing the money, so the lenders want to be sure that those people know both: a) what they are doing and b) How to run the project successfully.

To find out about what mortgage products are available, simply search "self-build mortgages" on the internet or look in the self build magazines and you will see all the main offerings. It is worth spending a bit of time looking at the options before contacting anyone directly.

If you look at the details of each mortgage you will find that, whilst they all offer basically the same product, they can be set up in subtly different ways, including:

- Varying lending percentage limits on land and build.
- Varying payment stage points (these are the points during the build which, when reached, trigger a valuation and a stage payment to you).
- Varying interest rates.
- Varying application and admin fees.
- Varying conditions on repayment terms and penalties for early repayment.
- Varying options to change the type of mortgage to a standard mortgage once the build is finished and "signed off".

There are two main types of mortgage product:

Payment in arrears: This means that you have to have the funds available to get the project to each of the payments stage points. The valuer then comes to check your progress and the agreed funds for that stage are then released. That money is then supposed to get you through to the next stage payment point.

A fee is normally charged for each valuation (check with your lender if this is the case)

Payments up front: This is a fairly rare product. As I write this I only know one company who provide it: "Buildstore Mortgage Services" (the accelerator mortgage). However, as the general housing market picks up, there may be new products arriving on the market at any time so it is worth doing a bit of research.

At the time of writing, this mortgage provides up to around 90% of the funds ***up front*** for you to buy the land and start the build (this figure may change by the time you read this). This means that you may only need to find a relatively small deposit and you can think about going for it.

Whichever type of product you choose to apply for, you will need to provide a lot of information as part of the application process and, as I said earlier, you will probably need to attend an interview before the loan is agreed.

Here is a typical example of how the interview process will normally work:

Mortgage Application Interview

Once you get past the initial enquiry stage and you want to move your application forward, you will often be asked to go into a local branch to attend an interview with the person who deals with this type of mortgage.

If you have a choice of branches to go to for this interview, ask which one deals with the most self-build business and who is the most experienced advisor available to discuss the subject of their self-build mortgage products.

I have found in the past that if you go to some of the local small branches who rarely come across applications for this type of mortgage, you just find a general mortgage advisor who has done a short course on the subject of self-build at head office, so they can answer general questions and fill the forms in. However, if you ask any difficult questions, they often won't know the answers and will have to get on the phone or email someone from another office who is more likely to be able to help. You can often find yourself during this type of meeting spending most of your time staring at the advisor as they speak on the phone to someone who actually knows what they are talking about and then listening to them trying to remember everything they have just been told (and usually failing abysmally).

You are better trying to get straight to the "horse's mouth" to save time and to be able to bat ideas and thoughts back and to with them, in order to get the best deal.

When you attend the interview, it is very important that you approach it professionally. You are basically trying to show these people that you can take on and successfully completing such a major project. So, don't turn up in a pair of shorts and tee shirt, with no paperwork, having done no preparation.

You might not think it but the advisors these days will be studying you closely, so that they can get a clear picture of your personality, your skills, your strengths and your weaknesses. If they don't do this properly, then offer you a mortgage and it fails, these people will be dragged across hot coals by their bosses!

Here is how you should prepare for the meeting:

- Print out a list of relevant questions (*don't worry, by the time you have read this book you will know exactly what questions you want answering*). This will show them that you are taking the whole things seriously and that, in fact you are also interviewing them!

Good questions to ask include:

➤ What are the maximum lending percentages?
➤ What are the maximum "salary multipliers" on their self-build mortgages?
➤ What are the interest rates on their self-build products?
➤ When are the stage payments made?
➤ What are the application fees?
➤ How long does their stage mortgage take to set up?
➤ Are there any early repayment penalties?
➤ What structural warranties will they accept?
➤ Can the mortgage be changed to a standard mortgage on completion (normally at lower rates)?
➤ Who will be carrying out the valuations?
➤ How much notice do they need for valuation visits?
➤ Is there any charge for the valuation?
➤ How long after the valuation is the stage payment released?
➤ Can you apply for "interim valuations" if your cash flows are under pressure?

- Get as much visual detail together as possible related to what you want to build. If you are not at the stage where you have your plot, then use "generic" information such as plans and pictures of a similar house.
- Prepare some reasonably detailed cost estimates and try to show that you have acquired a knowledge of the availability of trades and suppliers in the area where you intend to build
- Get some likely cost figures for plot prices in your chosen area(s). DO NOT tell the interviewer that you are hoping to buy land without planning permission and apply later (*unless you are doing so on something like an "Option agreement" - see Chapter 4 for details*).
- If you have a plot which has planning already granted, take the "planning approval" documents, along with any conditions that are attached.

- Show proof that you have the required deposits and have also built a good "financial buffer" into the budget to absorb any unexpected problems (allow about 15% of the build cost as a minimum figure).
- Take any proof you have of your previous building experience, your building related skills and your building related qualifications.
- Take this book (and other similar documents you have gathered together) to show what research you have been doing.
- Take some sort of proof of house values for the local area. If you can find something similar to what you hope to build, within a short distance of your site, this will give them a fairly accurate guide as to what your property is likely to be worth on completion (*this is to give them an idea of how secure their lending will be against local market values*).
- Take your income and expenditure details. If you are self-employed, three years' accounts will often be required (*if you don't have three years, just take whatever you have*).
- Take bank statements or proof of savings to show what level of private funding you have access to help your cash flow during the build process.
- Take a "Construction programme" showing the build target times and dates (*see Chapter 7 for how to create one of these*).
- Rack your brains for anything else relevant that might create the right impression with the interviewer.

Costings:

One of the important things to take with you to this meeting are the costings.

As I just mentioned, you don't necessarily have to have a plot at this stage to come up with some costings, you can just pick a design and size of house that you would be happy to and could afford to build and use one of two methods to get some reasonably likely build costs:

1) If you have no full plans to take measurements and costings from, use the "best guess" method which I described earlier.
2) If you have plans with measurements on them, try to get as many likely costs for those plans as possible and make educated guesses (by doing some research), on any cost areas that the drawings themselves do not cover (things like: warranties, insurances, site cabins, health and safety requirements, scaffolding, paths, driveways, landscaping, service connections etc. (You should know how to get rough ideas of all these costs by the time you have finished reading this guide).

Spend a reasonable amount of time preparing the costs. The process of getting all the information you need together will provide an excellent learning method for you to start getting a feel of the whole project and you will be able to use what you learn, together with the information you gather, when you start work on the project itself.

In a couple of pages, you will see a sample costings sheet with sample costs. Taking a set of figures like this to the meeting (*but not this exact set!*) will score you a whole load of browny points with the lender. The list is not fully inclusive. There could be many items which you would be including in your project that may not be listed below, but at least this will head you in the right direction as you prepare your own costs.

You will see on the costing sheet that I have included a lot of items that you might not presently think should be included as build costs. Things like travelling to a self-build show, Solicitors fees, mortgage application fees and so on. <u>Don't fool yourselves by ignoring them on your own costing sheets. They are real build costs and they should be included.</u>

Repeating what I have already said, and will say again throughout the book: The fact is that if money is, has been, or will be spent on this project that comes out of your pocket, that you would not have spent otherwise, then that **should be** classed as a build cost. Every penny spent on the project will have to come from somewhere. Either from a lender or from you. Either way, if you are spending it on something related to the project you can't then spend it again on a holiday or car. So, if is related to the project, <u>**IT IS**</u> a build cost. Sorry, it just is!

Basically, at the moment, most people who take on a project, not knowing any better, just make up the rules as they go along and don't include a lot of the costs that should be included. On larger projects, this could easily leave them tens of thousands of pounds away from ending up with the right cost figures for the overall project and may also leave them wondering why they are short of money when they don't seem to have overspent according to their own records!

Why is this so important?

- Because these build cost estimates that you compile are what your borrowing is based on.
- Because if you get them wrong you could run out of money before you reach the end of the project.
- Because people coming after you might ask you how much your project cost, then end up using your figures and making all the same mistakes that you did!

If we can get everyone who builds their own home to recognize the fact that any "build related cost" really <u>is</u> a build cost. Then, if we can also persuade the people who publish figures for build costs in magazines and books, hopefully, slowly but surely, everyone carrying out research for their projects would soon learn how to get the costings prepared properly. Then, after a bit of time, there might not be a whole bunch of people going round thinking they can build mansions for tuppence, because they saw some figures in a magazine!

The costs included in the costings sheet do not need to be totally accurate at this stage. Everyone who has ever taken on even a small building project is aware that initial cost estimates very rarely work out to be accurate. Just look at some of the major building works we have seen on TV over the past few years. How often have you heard a news item reporting that "The project is on time and budget" (apart from the millennium stadium)? It is far more common to hear that projects have run *hugely* over the initial estimates (*most of which were compiled by highly paid professional estimators. If they can't get it right, how can you as a self-builder, with limited knowledge and experience of the subject, be expected to do better?*)

So, the lender is looking more for "process" than "accuracy". They want to see that you are aware of all the individual bits that go together to make up the whole project and they want to see that you understand what the likely costs are going to be.

On the next page is a sample costing list (*I have plucked some of the figures out of the air, and they are all generally higher than I would expect to be paying when I follow my own building rules, the ones that you will be learning as you read on through the book. However, for now they will give you a basic idea of how a costing sheet works*).

Warning: *Don't be tempted to copy the list on the next page onto a spreadsheet and just juggle the figures about until they look like they are your own. You will probably be asked questions about your spreadsheet to check that you have not done just that! If you get caught out, you could be turned down on the basis of providing misleading information and unprofessionalism in your approach.*

(See next page)

COST AREA	DESCRIPTION	QUANT	UNIT COST	TOTAL
INITIAL COSTS	RESEARCH / TRAVEL / SHOWS ETC	1	£500.00	£500.00
INITIAL DESIGNS	PRELIM SKETCHES FROM DESIGNER	1	£350.00	£350.00
SITE INVESTIGATION	TRIAL DIG / SURVEY / LAB TESTS	1	£850.00	£850.00
FULL PLANNING DRAWINGS		1	£900.00	£900.00
PLANNING APPLICATION FEE		1	£380.00	£380.00
SOLICITORS FEES	INCLUDING SEARCHES ETC	1	£1,500.00	£1,500.00
QUANTITY SURVEYING / ESTIMATING	PREPARATION OF PRICING DOCUMENTS	1	£500.00	£500.00
MORTGAGE APPLICATION FEES	INCLUDING VALUATION FEE	1	£600.00	£600.00
SITE INSURANCE	ALL RISKS SELF-BUILD INSURANCE	1	£550.00	£550.00
WARRANTY	10 YEAR STRUCTURAL GUARANTEE	1	£2,750.00	£2,750.00
SITE FENCING / GATES	BUY PANELS AND ANCILLARY MATERIALS	1	£3,500.00	£3,500.00
SITE SECURITY	ASSUME BASIC CCTV SYSTEM	1	£350.00	£350.00
SITE CABINS / LOCKUPS	ASSUME 6 MONTH HIRE + DELIV & PICK UP	1	£800.00	£800.00
TEMPORARY SERVICES	FOR SITE POWER / WATER / ELEC (MAT + LAB)	1	£750.00	£750.00
PERMANENT SERVICE CONNECTIONS	DRAINS / GAS / ELEC / TELECOM / WATER	1	£2,600.00	£2,600.00
BORROWING COSTS DURING BUILD	6 MONTHS MORTGAGE REPAYMENTS	1	£3,000.00	£3,000.00
SITE STRIP	REMOVE TOPSOIL / STORE ON SITE - LAB & PLANT	1	£500 / DAY	£500.00
FORM UP STORAGE AREA	150MM HARDCORE TO STORAGE AREA LAB, PL & MAT	1	£1,500.00	£1,500.00
FORM UP DRIVEWAY HARDCORE	PLACE 300MM HARDCORE TO DRIVE LAB, PL & MAT	1	£1,750.00	£1,750.00
SETTING OUT HOUSE	SITE ENGINEER	1	£400 / DAY	£400.00
EXCAVATE FOUNDATIONS	ASSUME STRIP FOOTING LAB & PL	2	£500 / DAY	£1,000.00
LAY STRIP FOOTINGS	ASSUME 900MM WIDE X 225MM DEEP LAB, PL & MA	1	£2,850.00	£2,850.00
BUILD FOUNDATIONS TO DPC	BLOCKWORK AND CAVITY FILL LAB, PL & MAT	1	£5,600.00	£5,600.00
FORM UP SLAB AND POUR	ASSUME 150MM SLAB ON 100MM INSULATION	1	£4,500.00	£4,500.00
SCREED SUPPLY AND LAY	100SQ M OF 65MM CONCRETE REINFORCED SCREED	1	£3,300.00	£3,300.00
DRAINAGE INSTALLATION	ASSUME 900MM DEEP MAX TO BUILDING REGS	1	£3,700.00	£3,700.00
GROUND SOURCE HEATING	INCLUDING ALL EXCAVATION WORKS	1	£11,000.00	£11,000.00
TIMBER FRAME KIT (INC ROOF)	SUPPLY AND ERECT	1	£36,000.00	£36,000.00
BRICKS AND ASSOCIATED MATERIALS	ALLOW £350 / 1000 FOR BRICKS @16,000 BRICKS	1	£8,500.00	£8,500.00
BRICKLAYERS (LABOUR)	ALLOW £350 / 1000 PLUS DAYWORK ITEMS	1	£6,500.00	£6,500.00
BRICKLAYERS PLANT	LARGE MIXER @ 3 MONTHS	1	£900.00	£900.00
SCAFFOLD	ASSUME A 4 MONTH HIRE PERIOD	1	£5,500.00	£5,500.00
FELT BATTEN & TILE ROOF (LAB + MAT)	ASSUME USING "COMPOSITE SLATE" TILES	1	£7,200.00	£7,200.00
WINDOWS / EXT DOORS	TIMBER PRE FINISHED SUPPLY AND FIT		£7,800.00	£7,800.00
BI FOLD DOORS		1	£3,500.00	£3,500.00
INSULATION TO WALLS	FIBREGLASS 200MM SUPPLY & FIT	1	£2,950.00	£2,950.00
INSULATION TO ATTIC		1	£1,100.00	£1,100.00
ELECTRICAL INSTALLATION	SUPPLY AND FIX	1	£7,500.00	£7,500.00
PLUMBING INSTALLATION	SUPPLY AND FIX	1	£8,500.00	£8,500.00
JOINERY CARCASSING LAB & MAT	1ST / 2ND / FINAL FIXES	1	£10,500.00	£10,500.00
PLATERBOARDING / PLASTERING	LAB & MAT	1	£5,250.00	£5,250.00
COVINGS	LAB & MAT	1	£1,850.00	£1,850.00
ALARM SYSTEM	SUPPLY AND FIT	1	£750.00	£750.00
BUILT IN CINEMA SYSTEM	WIRING AND EQUIPMENT	1	£3,700.00	£3,700.00
LIGHTING	SPECIALIST AND FEATURE LIGHTING		£1,800.00	£1,800.00
KITCHEN SUPPLY & FIT	INCLUDING UTILITY ROOM AND ALL APPLIANCES		£11,000.00	£11,000.00
BATHROOMS SUPPLY AND FIT	INCLUDING SHOWER ROOMS AND W.C	3	£2,500.00	£7,500.00
WALL TILING SUPPLY AND FIX	BATHROOMS / KITCHEN / UTIL / W.C	1	£2,750.00	£2,750.00
DECORATING LAB & MAT	INTERNAL AND EXTERNAL	1	£5,500.00	£5,500.00
FLOOR TILING SUPPLY AND FIX		1	£1,200.00	£1,200.00
VINYL FLOORING		1	£600.00	£600.00
OTHER FLOOR COVERINGS		1	£2,000.00	£2,000.00
EPS CERTIFICATE		1	£280.00	£280.00
AIRTIGHNESS TEST		1	£325.00	£325.00
DRIVEWAY	BRICK PAVED	1	£5,200.00	£5,200.00
FOOTPATHS AROUND HOUSE	GOLDEN GRAVEL	1	£850.00	£850.00
GATES AND FENCING	WROUGHT IRON	1	£3,750.00	£3,750.00
LANDSCAPING	TURF, TOPSOIL AND PLANTING BEDS	1	£2,500.00	£2,500.00
SNAGGING & REMEDIALS		1	£500.00	£500.00
			SUB TOTAL	£219,735.00
FINANCIAL "BUFFER"	10% OF BUILD COSTS			£20,000.00
			TOTAL	£249,735
EXPECTED VAT REFUND	SELF BUILD VAT SCHEME			£8,000.00
			NET COST	£241,735.00

Your own money

Three of the questions you are likely to be asked at your meeting with the mortgage advisor include:

1) How much of your own money do you have available to fill the shortfall in the mortgage amount and the full build cost?
2) Will this be adequate at each stage of the mortgage to keep your cash flow positive? If not, do you have access to other funds to help you over the financially pressurised periods?
3) What financial buffers have you built in to your figures to ensure that you are prepared for unforeseen costs?

To be able to answer these questions you will probably need to provide more facts and figures to show that you have given adequate attention to the financial planning side of the project. They will be looking for things like: bank statements / savings account statements / money owing to you / guaranteed income figures and letters of intent from anyone who is prepared to lend you money to assist you with the project (these sources could include family members, friends, the bank, credit companies etc.).

Once you have done your financial research and planning and once you have had your meeting with the lenders, you should be in a good position to know whether the proposed project is a goer or not.

IMPORTANT: Until you reach this stage you would be unwise to commit yourself to buying land or paying for anything related to the project.

Plan to use trade accounts where possible:

Trade accounts are a very useful tool to allow you to maximize the capabilities of your available project cash flow.

Self-builders are notorious for getting into trouble over the project cash flows. Reasons for this include:

- The lack of financial planning that most self-builders get involved in prior to starting work.
- The misleading figures published in books and magazines which miss many of the *real* build costs.
- Unforeseen costs which crop up as the project proceeds.
- "Changes of mind" on designs, materials and finishes made during the project.

Because having a positive cash flow is such an important part of any self-build project, it is important to try to set everything up, to enable you to keep your money in the bank for as long as possible, whenever possible. Trade accounts can help you to do just that.

Self-builders are very popular with builders' merchants, contractors, sub-contractors and many other types of suppliers. Why? Because self-builders are generally planning on spending large amounts of money over fairly short periods. They also normally have a reasonably reliable source of funding (*the stage mortgage*), for at least most of the duration of the project (*people wanting to be paid towards the end are the ones who sometimes suffer from the client having run out of cash*).

What you need to do is to realise that you, as a self-builder are in a strong position financially when you approach suppliers and tradespeople and you need to use that strength to get trade accounts opened with suppliers and to get payment terms agreed with everyone else.

What are the benefits of having trade accounts?

Some of the major builders' merchants now have specialist departments set up, just for self-build projects. These companies tend to offer you pretty good packages to entice you to buy lots of their products. They will often include benefits like:

- **A 30-day credit account.** These accounts are extremely useful because of the way they work. Statements are calculated on the last day of each month and sent out on the first day of the next month. The customer then has until the final day of *that month* to clear the debt, before the merchant starts to chase them for payment. In reality, this means that you can order something on the first day of a new month and not have to pay for it until the last day of the *following* month (around 60 days later). There is generally no credit charge levied on the money owing, so you basically get interest free borrowing for up to 60 days. This is an invaluable financial tool to use as much as you can whilst you build and you should get as many trade accounts opened as possible.
- **Your own dedicated sales person** who you can contact directly at any time.
- **Trade discounts on all products,** which give you the same prices as the local builders for everything the merchant sells.
- **A free costing service:** If you provide the merchant with a set of drawings and specifications, they will often provide you with a full list of discounted costs for everything you need that they stock. Be aware that some merchants will charge you a fee for this service but will then normally give you the fee back once you have spent a few hundred pounds on your account.
- **Free advice:** You will often have the contact details of the manager as well as the sales rep so that if you need any advice, you have someone to ring who might be able to help you. These people are working around building sites every day, so tend to have good levels of knowledge on a range of subjects (always make sure you double-check their advice before following it though, just in case).

Note: Be aware: What you will normally find with these accounts and with your "free" list of prices for everything you need, is that with each merchant, some things are cheap and some not so cheap, but that prices vary for the same thing, quite dramatically between merchants.
The cleverer merchants will offer you very good prices on the things they know you will need early on in the project. The reason they do this is that they know that, at the start of the project, you will probably go to a number of merchants and get them all to give you their prices for what you need and then order the cheapest items from each.

However, they also know that self-builders are usually very busy people and after the first few weeks of shopping around for the best prices for everything they need, most of them will eventually get into a buying habit and go to the one they normally use. So, by giving you good prices early on they can often get you to be an automatically returning customer.

Clever eh?

How to get the best prices:

There are a couple of tricks you can use yourself to make sure you are getting the best rates on everything:

1) Tell each merchant you approach that you are going to give a set of drawings to them and every other merchant in your local area and you do not intend to become an automatically returning customer, but that you will in fact be ordering the products which are at the lowest price from wherever you need to, throughout the project. That way each merchant will have to give attention to making sure each price on their price list is competitive, rather than just giving you a couple of good offers to get your interest.
2) Actually <u>do</u> spend time shopping around for each item. To do this you need to keep all your pricing notes from every supplier to hand, so that when you need, say plasterboards, you can check the lowest price quoted, then ring a different supplier and tell them that *so and so* down the road is selling plasterboards for £x and that he needs to beat that price if he wants the deal. This works quite well and can save you a lot of money on some orders.

What limits will you be allowed on your trade accounts?

The way this often works, is that you will need to make a few cash purchases before you are given a credit account. Once the account is opened it will have a limit set depending on your expected spend each month. Obviously, the suppliers would like you to spend a lot of money with them so the limit will normally be set at a number of thousands. Between three and five thousand pounds seems to be about the norm.

As long as you pay off the account each month, this limit will normally remain the same for the duration of your project. If you fall behind on payments the account could either be closed or your credit limit reduced.

If you find yourselves going over the maximum spend you are allowed each month, just go in to the branch, see the manager and ask if the limit can be raised. Tell them that you want to carry on using them for your purchases, but if you have to start paying cash instead of using the account, you will have to start using your accounts at other merchants and suppliers, even if you have to pay a bit more for the goods.

How to make the most of credit accounts:

The way to gain the most benefits from having various credit accounts is to try to use them to help you to make sure you never run out of cash during the build. The way to do this is to make sure that the stage payments from your mortgage company are coming in quickly. To make that happen, you need to build quickly and get to each payment stage in the shortest time possible after receiving the previous payment.

What happens with many self build projects is that they start off without being particularly well organised and without any major consideration given to a target timescale to get everything finished. This leads to the project potentially meandering through from start to finish rather than being driven to meet targets and this is the reason that self-build projects often take up to a year or more to complete.

The knock-on effect of this lengthy build period is that the cash flow starts to get stretched. Here are examples of bad organisation and good organisation to show you how they can affect your project cash flow:

Bad organisation:

Week 1: You start work on clearing the site ready to start work on the foundations. You have £20,000 in cash (from whatever source) to get the project up to the next payment stage.

You don't have a definite timescale target for this work and you have not yet decided on who is getting the contract for the groundworks.

You get a digger and a dumper truck in and clear the site in 2 days which costs £1,500. You are now ready to excavate and you have now chosen your ground worker, however he is busy on another job and can't get to you for 2 weeks.

You have spent £1,500 to date.

Week 3: The ground works start and go well. The house is set out, foundations are dug and the simple strip footing is poured in 3 days. The ground worker goes off site to allow the foundation blockwork to be constructed by the brickies up to the slab level.

You, however, did not talk detailed timescales to the ground worker and did not expect to get the concrete poured so quickly, so you have not arranged for the brickies, the bricks or any of the other materials and equipment to come to site to be ready for them.

The brickies will not be finished on the job they are on until a week on Monday so nothing is going to happen on site until then.

Week 5: The ground workers want paying £10,000 for their work to date. The timber frame manufacturer wants a 15% deposit on the timber frame (£4,500), so that leaves you £5,500. You have to pay £5,000 cash for the bricks / blocks and other materials because you have not yet had an account opened at the merchants.

You have now spent £21,000 and are in a negative cash flow situation. You have had to put £1,000 on your credit card.

The brickies start work and things go well. They complete the work to slab level in 10 days, so now the ground worker can return to prepare and pour the slab. However, you didn't book them until too late and they are working on another job until next Tuesday.

The brickies want paying "a week in hand" and they give you an invoice for £1,500 for their first week's work. Out comes the credit card again and you are £2,500 in negative cash flow.

Week 7: The slab is complete (taking 3 days) and at the end of this week you are now able to request the first of your stage payment.

The brickies have had another £1,500 from your credit card and the timber frame company is waiting for their "pre-delivery" payment of 30% of the frame cost (£9,000) which you can't pay until your first stage payment comes in, but the timber frame supplier won't book your delivery and erection until they get this payment.

You are now in £4,000 negative cash flow and still owe £9,000 (for the frame) which is now going to mean that the frame will be significantly delayed.

You book the valuer, who comes a couple of days later and he approves the stage payment, but says it will take between a week and two weeks to get the admin sorted and the payment out to you.

The job has to stop until the money is in your bank.

Week 9: You get your first stage payment in of £50,000. You pay off your credit cards (£4,000) and you pay the pre-delivery payment of £9,000 to the timber frame supplier. The ground worker has now also given you his invoice for the slab (£8,000), so after paying everyone off, you are now left with just £28,000 to get you to the next stage payment (which is once the roof is on and covered). But it is now going to be a further 3 weeks before the frame arrives and another 3 weeks before is it up and roofed in so you can claim your next payment.

That takes you to week 15 before you can claim your next payment and possibly week 17 before the money is in your bank. That £28,000 is going to have to be spread *very thinly* before then.

You are getting very stressed already!

Good organisation:

Week 1: You have £20,000 to get you to the first stage payment point. You have planned well, chosen all your sub-contractors for the early parts of the project and given everyone a project programme.

You have purposely placed three small orders (£1,000 total) with the builder's merchants for materials that you will need because they have told you that once you have made three purchases they will open your account with a £5,000 credit limit.

You have given the jobs of site clearance and concreting the foundations to the same ground worker and he starts work. Things go well and the strip footing is poured on day 5. This date ties in with the programme and you have already arranged for the brickies to start the following Monday.

You have ordered the brick, blocks and other materials on your account to arrive first thing Monday morning so the brickies can get straight on once they have set the brickwork lines out on the foundations.

As things are going well, you pay the timber frame deposit of £4,500 to get work started in the factory. You have a delivery confirmed for the beginning of week 5 of the project. You have spent £5,500 so far.

Week 2: Brickies arrive and the work goes well. The blockwork to slab level is completed in 10 days, finishing at the end of week 3. You have still spent just £5,500 of your cash.

Week 3: You need to pay the 30% pre-delivery payment for the frame (£9,000) so you do. And you need to pay the brickies their first week in hand payment (£1,500).

You have now spent £16,000 of your cash but not had to use your credit cards. The ground workers come back and construct the slab.

Week 4: The slab takes 3 days and, knowing that beforehand, you organised the valuer to come on day 3 as the slab is being poured (Wednesday). He says it will take a week to ten days to get the payment authorised and sent out. You pay the brickies their second week in hand payment of £1,500. You have now spent £17,500 of your cash.

Week 5: The frame arrives on Monday. The first stage payment of £50,000 comes in at the end of this week. This tops your cash flow funds up to £52,500.

Your frame is going well. It will be complete and you will be ready for the next payment by the end of week 9. You have a significant amount of money in the bank and you will plan to get the valuer in as the frame is being completed. This means that you should get your next stage payment in by either late in week 10 or early in week 11.

You are not stressed and are actually enjoying the job!

These are slightly simplistic examples of how it would work, but they are "like for like" so are comparable to each other, if not completely comparable to "real life".

It is easy to see that the second example will give you a much faster completion time for your project and that by building quickly and being well organised, both your cash flow and your personal stress levels will benefit hugely.

The effect of the build method on the build speed

Looking at the examples above brings in to play the question of how you are going to build the house. What method of construction will give you everything you need in terms of quality, eco credentials, cost and in this case, most importantly, speed?

We will be looking at the different build methods in Chapter 7 but it is very important that you remember to consider your cash flow for the project, when you decide on which method is best for you.

How to manage your trade accounts

I touched earlier on ways in which you can benefit from the way that trade accounts are set up. For example, by making use of up to 60 days' interest free credit on your purchases. Here is a little more detail about how these accounts generally work which you may find useful when money gets tight:

When you have a trade account, you will receive a monthly statement which will contain three main figures.

"Current amount due"

"One month overdue"

"Two months overdue"

The "current amount due" means the amount of money due to be paid by the end of the month that the statement is issued in. Because the statement is normally generated on the first day of each month what that means is that supplies bought on the first day of the previous month do not have to be paid for 60 days. That's great, but it is also important to know what happens after that.

As I mentioned earlier, self-builders tend to hit cash flow problems during their projects, but most especially towards the end. As cash gets tighter, sometimes you might not have received the funds from the lender to be able to pay off the account at the end of the 30-day period as detailed in the "current amount due" box.

The fact is, that the accounts departments at the merchants are normally quite used to this situation arising and they don't panic when it does. What tends to happen (in my experience) is that unless the merchant is having a clamp down on late paying customers, you will generally hear nothing during the next month, so if you pay up by the end of that month, as long as you have not reached your credit limit, you will usually be able to carry on using your account.

The *following month* is usually when things start to change. What will usually happen that you will try to order something by phone and will be told that *"Your account is on stop"*. What that means is that it has basically been frozen until you pay off at least the "one month overdue" amount, and possibly the full amount (depending on the way the merchant works).

If you do happen to reach this point because your finances are being stretched, you now need to take action in order to stop your account from being cancelled and action taken against you for non-payment. If you make an appointment to see the manager and explain why you haven't paid and that you are very close to your next stage payment date, or will have funds coming in from elsewhere shortly, they are normally fairly relaxed and may even allow you to carry on using the account (with the thought that if you don't get the materials needed to reach that stage payment point, they might not get any of the money owed to them).

Basically, the best way to use accounts is, when you have the money to pay them, promptly do so. This builds up a good financial relationship between you. The longer that relationship continues, generally the more leeway they will give you if and when you hit cash flow problems.

Chapter 4:
Finding a decent plot of land

Let's start by dispelling a myth:

There is a perceived notion in the UK self-build industry that the reason for the year on year fall (or at least lack of significant growth) in numbers of self-build completions over the past ten years or so has been related to a lack of available land. I totally disagree with this thinking for three reasons:

1. Most of the people who lead the industry and think this, tend to live in the South East, where single building plots coming onto the open market are pretty rare and when they do appear, they are very expensive. These people can be forgiven for thinking that land is scarce everywhere, but in fact there are plenty of building plots to be found in most areas of the rest of the UK.
2. The big builders, medium sized builders, and even small builders all seem to manage to find enough building land to keep their businesses going. How many new developments by the commercial house builders have you seen started in the past couple of years in your area or in other areas as you have been travelling around? If self-builders started to get their act together so they could get hold of some of these larger sites, there could *immediately* be thousands more plots available to us across the UK.
3. I personally have access to all the daily planning applications data for the UK and although I only choose to access the data for a small geographical area, I would guess, based on what I get coming through, that there are probably at least a number of hundreds (possibly thousands) of planning applications for new housing, renovations and refurbishments being made around the country every week, some of them for "multiple units". That suggests that a significant number of thousands of plots will be approved for housing each year.
I have also just checked one of the on-line plot finding web sites, which at the time of writing are listing just under 8,500 plots for sale. That is just on one website. There are numerous similar websites and there are also thousands of estate agents across the country, many of whom have at least one or two plots on their books. This suggests that across the country there are probably presently at least 30,000+ building plots available, with more coming through every day.

Compare these numbers of either "available" plots or "potentially" available plots to the 11,000 – 12,000 or so self-build completions that we are achieving each year and it begs the question:

Land shortage? What land shortage?

There is plenty of building land available, self-builders just don't get to see most of it

As can be seen by the figures for the present availability of plots across the UK, the fact is that there is plenty of land either already in, or coming through the system, but for one reason and another, commercial developers seem to be doing quite nicely thank you, as they regularly get the cream of what is available, while self-builders get the crumbs (basically, the stuff the builders don't want).

The most worrying part of this fairly obvious situation is that neither the government (*who profess to being keen to expand the self-build and custom build markets across the UK*) or the leaders of our industry seem to be able to grasp this fact. Instead, they continue to blame *a lack of land, overpriced land, poor planning rules and not enough self-build mortgage products* for the sorry state of the industry.

If they don't see the problem, how are they going to fix it?

So where does the problem lie?

Unfortunately, a lot of the problem boils down to the fact that (as I have said before), we are an amateurish industry. We don't think or act in a joined-up manner. It is everyone for themselves and most of the people who become involved in the industry are, almost by definition, lacking high levels of knowledge, skills and experience when it comes to housing development.

The disparate nature of the industry, combined with poor quality leadership and very little sensible help from the government has meant that things have not really changed for the better over the past 20 years and unless there is a shift of thinking and approach, things will probably be pretty much the same in another 20 years.

Who is to blame?

In my opinion, believe it or not, one of the main reasons why we are falling short of our potential as an industry is because of the growth of the DIY TV culture, along with "the cult of celebrity that we all seem so besotted with.

To make any business or industry work there needs to be a strong product (which "self-build" no doubt is), good market potential (which self-build no doubt has) and strong leadership.

Leaders need to be people who have a good knowledge and experience of the subject and / or product, together with high quality entrepreneurial skills, problem solving skills and a knowledge of how the finances should work. Our industry is desperately lacking on pretty much all of these fronts!

Unfortunately, rather than the government getting a team of people together who have the practical skills and knowledge to be able to drive the industry forward, there presently seems to be a movement towards celebrities and people with good personalities being seen as the answer to our problems with the perceived thinking apparently being:

> "They are on telly so they must know what they are talking about"

Think about it: are most of the people we generally see on TV these days the people we would trust to run businesses or major industries for us? Nope!

Please do not think that I am trying to degrade the efforts, skills or abilities of our TV stars, but I just think that it should be horses for courses. The people we generally see on TV programmes related to the DIY or self-build industry tend to be specialists in one or more subjects within the industry. Some of them have no real relationship at all to this industry, but are, in fact more linked with media or publishing or other professions and have simply migrated to appear on TV because of their ability to present or to communicate well with the target audiences.

The people we see on TV are probably great people to know and will no doubt be good at what they do, but I have yet to look at any of the TV presenters and think to myself: "Now there is a leader for the self-build industry if ever there was one" (the person I think comes closest to making me think that is Tommy Walsh by the way. Kevin Mc Cloud also has a high level of knowledge and is involved in new development, so has some good, hands-on experience. There are also one or two others who might make a decent "fist of it", given the chance).

So, who is to blame for putting the wrong people to the forefront of our industry? Well it is a mix of both our so-called leaders and the government.

As I said in an earlier chapter, in 2011 / 2012, I was involved with the Coalition Government's Self-Build Working Group (which was basically a room full of people who were tasked with finding ways to improve and grow the industry).

I was invited to join the group and I accepted, then just before the first meeting I was sent a list of the people who were going to form the group. After looking through the list, I wrote to the guy organising the whole thing, saying basically that I was sorry, but I would not be attending the group as I could already see that it was going to be a waste of time.

The problem was that the government people involved in organising the whole thing had sat down, talked amongst themselves and tried to think of the best people to invite. Then, as governments tend to do they just went for the people at the top of the various sectors within the industry, thinking that they would know all about everything to do with their sector. This gave us a room full of people who were very well skilled figureheads of their specialist subjects, but very few of whom had any hands-on experience of how the nuts and bolts of this industry works, what it's problems are, how they have arisen, or how to fix them.

Here are some of the people in attendance (I admit I am cherry-picking a bit, but I am making a general point):

Team Leader, Housing Supply Division, Scottish Government / Policy Advisor, Building Societies Association Chair / Confederation of Cooperative Housing Policy Manager / Head of Mortgage Policy, Building Societies Association / Chair of Self Build Working Group's Finance sub-group / Chair Community Self Build Agency Principal Valuer / Property Service, Swindon Borough Council Director / DTZ CEO, Buildstore Policy and Strategy Manager / Homes and Communities Agency Development and Performance Manager / Swindon Council Managing Director / National Self Build and Renovation Centre Asset Transfer Unit Independent Consultant / Senior Lecturer, Institute for Urban Affairs / Northampton University Director / Hanse Haus Germany Network Co-Ordinator / National CLT Supervisory Board Head of Product and Publishing / Homes and Communities Agency Director / Ecomotive Technical Director / Head of Production Management and Pricing, Nationwide / Barclays Bank Housing Supply Division
JTP Cities Managing Director / Strategic Housing Officer, Cherwell District Council Director / Accord Housing Association Limited

Spot the problem?

Although some of these people and some of the others in attendance were going to be able to contribute to a certain extent, where are the people who, day-to-day deal with matters that affect individual self-builders and who would have any idea of the workings of the self-build industry?

People like:

- *Self-builders themselves, including at least two people from each of the following groups: 1) People who are at present planning their first project 2) People who have previously built one or more self-build homes 3) People who have project managed a project themselves 4) People who have used a professional Project Manager 5) People who have used a main contractor 6) People who have used a "Turnkey" package 7) People whose projects failed.*
- *Self-build Project Managers.*
- *House designers who work directly with individual self-builders.*
- *Estimators who directly deal with self-builders as part of their day to day jobs.*
- *Building Society Account Managers who personally deal with administering self-build mortgages.*
- *Individual planning officers who personally deal with self-build applications regularly.*
- *"Bespoke" house builders who have been working with self-builders and custom builders for years.*
- *People who directly deal with both setting up structural warranties and administering them.*
- *People with a knowledge of how self-build insurance is set up and works.*
- *A hands-on health and safety representative.*
- *A manager of at least one builders' merchant who deals daily with self-builders.*
- *A financial specialist with personal self-build experience who could offer ideas on how individuals and the industry could be better funded and how those funds could be best used.*

As chairman and basically the new leader of the industry, the group appointed an "award ceremony organiser" who was also an ex-publisher of a building related magazine and who had built one self-build project of his own. Nice guy (and was he going to turn down such an invitation? Nope!) But, was he the right guy to know, understand and solve the problems, at all the different levels of the industry, whilst at the same time leading and innovating it? I am not sure and the fact that since 2012 nothing particularly dramatic or particularly noticeable has happened or is happening (apart from the right to build legislation), there is a good chance he wasn't!

Ok, I'll stop there, I am sure you get the message. In other words, the group was (to my mind) a waste of time.

In the end, I attended the group because I thought it better to be in than out and at least I managed to get my say at a few of the meetings. Unfortunately, what I said generally met with glazed eyes belonging to people who hadn't got the slightest clue of the message I was trying to get over.

(By the way, at the time of updating this book in 2017: there is now a new Chairman, Michael Holmes, who seems to be getting to grips with some of the issues at last. Let's keep our fingers crossed).

Back to finding land:

Let's start with the ideas that did come out of the working group:

Here are the main ideas that the leaders of the industry came up with to improve the flow of land to the self-build market for the past few years and are still doing so today

(By the way: As I said at the start of the book, I have touched on this before, but you will find that I will be repeating several things throughout the book, so that you can dip in to small sections and still hopefully get the information they need on a subject).

Trying to make the large commercial house builders give over a small number of plots on each new site to self-build. This is doomed to failure for 2 reasons:

- ➢ Major house builders don't want high quality, highly specified and attractive self-build homes next to their small, poor quality overpriced homes. We would just show their offerings up for what they are: little boxes made of ticky tacky!
- ➢ Self-builders wouldn't want to drive through estates of poorly built, cramped together, small developers houses to get to their own much nicer homes. Their values could also be negatively affected by them being in the vicinity of the lower quality housing stock.
- **Trying to get more custom Build projects going** While there is nothing wrong with this as an idea, it is not genuine self-build and it is never going to change the self-build industry. It can add a new sector of the industry called "The Custom Build Industry", but most genuine self-builders don't want houses that are simply "customized". They want their own individual, unique home that has been designed and built to suit them and their requirements.
Custom build projects have been going for decades in the UK. I have even built a few myself, but they have never taken off to become a large-scale sector of the industry, because they are quite difficult to get going as multi plot developments and they are quite complicated and difficult to run once they do get going. As I said earlier, I _do_ think there is a place in the market for this sort of development, but the way it is being approached at the moment is not the right way and unless this changes, it will take many years to make a small amount of progress. Overall, there is room in the self-build industry for some of these projects, but they will always be the exception rather than the rule and they need organising properly.

- **Putting local authorities under pressure to make plots available for self-build.** Again, this is fine as principle and everything that helps, helps but it is just another sticking plaster solution which does not deal with the route problems. Also, simply because this solution involves dealing with local authorities, it is bound to be wrapped up in all sorts of protracted administrative procedures, red tape, conditions and restrictions. The prices of the plots will reflect this and probably be set towards the higher end of the spectrum (come on councils, prove me wrong!)
There was also talk of the government trying to force councils to make at least two plots available for self-build in each and every village across the UK every year. I sincerely hope that this is not going to happen, mainly because it is just nonsense!

  Imagine the chaos if every tiny rural village had to make 2 plots available every year! It would cause riots! Partly from the people campaigning against their village being spoilt and partly from the people in the village who then come along saying "Well they got Planning Permission on their land, so I want the same on mine!" (*This would happen "sure as eggs is eggs" because of a thing called precedent. If planning permission is given on a piece of land anywhere, then a precedent that says that this particular area is suitable for building, is set. This in turn opens the planning authority up to the real possibility of many other people applying for approval for similar properties nearby*).

- **Trying to get us to copy the Europeans and build vast sprawling estates full of dozens, or hundreds of different designs and (often clashing) styles of home, including self-build apartment blocks.** I actually quite like the principal of this idea (if it were done properly), but I am not sure the UK is ready for it yet. It would be great if we were, but I think we need to get the basics of the industry sorted before we attempt this sort of thing.

Unfortunately, for better or worse, we are in the UK and at this present time we (or at least most of us) like a certain style of housing development. We expect harmony of design, we like a driveway of our own, a front and a back garden where possible and a fence to give us our bit of privacy (the feeling that this is our castle). We may eventually change and be happy to go European but I don't think it will be for quite a while yet!

Where does all this leave us?

So, this is where we are at the moment: plenty of land, not everywhere, but in most places. Not enough understanding of the problems and a lack of useful and practical ideas coming from the industry leadership. The most worrying part of all this is that, unless something changes dramatically, the same problems that are with us now will be with us in another 20 years' time. If that remains the case, then people like YOU are going to struggle to get your project up and running and the industry will continue to either tread water or shrink.

How do we start to change things for the better?

For a start, we need to understand why there is a problem with sourcing good quality, reasonably priced land in the first place.

Here are some of the present problems:

1. **Although there is plenty of land around, there is a lack of good quality land coming in to the self-build / open market at the right price.** Good land tends to get snapped up at a much earlier stage, often before it has actually been awarded planning permission. Even if an Estate Agent gets hold of a decent plot, they will normally already have a list of local builders whom they do a lot of business with, who are waiting in the wings to buy it. This generally means that only the poorer quality, the expensive and the difficult plots usually get to the shop window where they may be seen by self-builders.
2. **Many of the agents selling the land do not come across building plots very often and do not know how to value them.** This is particularly common with the smaller agents. Some of the large agents have land departments where the staff are more used to valuing and are therefore more likely to set the price at somewhere around the correct figure.
3. **Because of the lack of knowledge with regard to valuing land, the land that is available is often overpriced.**
4. **Getting to find out about good plots before the builders nip in and snap them up has not been easy for new to the game, potential self-builders.**
5. **It is often hard to work out how much to offer for a piece of land.**
6. **Self-builders are scared of taking on difficult sites** simply because they wouldn't know what to do with them, even though they can be some of the best value plots around.

Ok, those are the negatives, but let's get on to talking about different ways that you *can* find land:

The main routes to finding land in the UK are presently:

- **Register your interest with Estate Agents:** This route will rarely bear fruit unless you are prepared to constantly nag each agent you register with (at least a couple of times a week), so that they eventually get so fed up of you chasing them, that they might actually remember to ring you when a new plot comes in. The problem you have with estate agents is that many of them have regular customers, who buy land and / or property from them all the time. These people give them very quick sales without them having to spend money on marketing. If you are hoping to persuade them to contact you before they contact their regulars, you must *really* make them want to get you off their backs! Don't be rude or aggressive, just be persistent.
- **Register with the property and land finding websites and regularly check the property papers.** There is nothing wrong with this option apart from the fact that some of the web sites have got a bit of a reputation

for not removing plots particularly quickly from their databases once they have been sold (the reason, it is rumoured, is that it looks better if they have lots of plots listed). I have personally come across examples of this, where I have found what looks like a decent plot, only to find, when I open its file, is that it is already sold. Some land websites also advertise in magazines. The weakness of this policy is that there will usually be a natural delay from when the plot details are sent to the publishers, to when they are in print and in the shops. This could result in it being one to two months after the property details are sent to the magazine before you actually read about them. This could obviously then mean that the best plots have already been sold before you get to see them. If you use these companies, it is best to go on line to do so.

- **Attend property auctions.** I have never recommended this option, although quite a number of people (builders mainly) do use property auctions to acquire land. The land sold in this manner has often been through the normal selling channels and has not sold. The reasons for that could be that it is a problematic plot, or have some sort of development restriction which makes it unattractive to most people. The positive side of buying at auction is that if you have cash to spend, you might get a bargain.

  The big thing to be aware of when you attend an auction is that once you bid for a plot you are committing yourself to buying it if your bid is accepted. It is up to you to do due diligence before you go to the auction, to find out the pros and cons of buying it and to have the funds available.

  If you buy a plot through the normal channels, your solicitor (who is normally far more experienced in these matters than you will be) has a few weeks to find any problem areas before you commit yourself to buying the land.

- **Buy land with a house already on it, demolish the house and start again:** This can be a very expensive way to get a building plot. You may buy a derelict house for a lower price than for a house in good order, but you will seldom be able to buy land with a house of any description on it for the same price as an empty plot. Taking this option, you could easily end up paying possibly twice as much as you should do to get a piece of clear land ready to build on, but it does give you more options when searching.

So those are the main options generally available to potential self-builders at the moment.
I will now introduce you to what I see as the way forward for the industry when it comes to buying land. I call it:

THE INSIDER'S TRICK TO FINDING GOOD QUALITY LAND

(INVESTORS AND LAND OWNERS: THERE IS A MASSIVE OPPORTUNITY FOR YOU HERE. YOU COULD EARN EXCELLENT PROFITS BY USING THIS SYSTEM, AT THE SAME TIME AS HELPING SELF-BUILDERS TO ACCESS MORE PLOTS AT REASONABLE PRICES. IF YOU WANT TO KNOW MORE, GET IN TOUCH)

I have been using a system for finding land for around 20 years. I didn't invent it, the commercial house building sector has been using it for a lot longer than that. All I did was borrow the principals of one of the main methods used by builders of all sizes, to buy land for commercial housing developments and found a way to make the same system work for me as a self-builder (and self-build consultant). It was actually quite easy.

It has worked for me over the years and I have been telling people about it who come to see me on the "Ask the Experts" stands at the self-build shows, but now, with the publication of this book, I have the chance to spread the word hopefully to a wider audience.

How does it work?

You must have seen a local builder building a single house or a couple of houses in your area when you have been looking for a decent plot in that same area.

You may have asked yourself the question: "How are they getting hold of those plots and why hasn't that land been found by us?"

Even in the South East, where plots are about as common as rocking horse muck, many local builders will have sourced the land and are happily building their new homes as you read this book, using a similar technique to the one I use and which you are about to find out about.

The system:

Everyone who applies for planning permission for housing in the UK has to make an official application.

The data from all of these applications goes on to a large database. It is then sold on to professional marketing companies who then break it down into geographical areas and sell it to developers, builders, window manufacturers, conservatory manufacturers (and so on), often for quite significant fees.

Every day, details of new planning applications registered the previous day will be forwarded by e mail to all the clients of these marketing companies.

The data that is sold usually includes all the contact information for the owner, the architect and the agent (if one is used). It also includes the address of the site, the type of planning applied for and the number of properties. It will also often give access to the drawings for the house designs, site plans, progress summaries and other useful information.

What then happens is that, within a few days of applying for planning permission, the applicants start to receive mailshots from local builders, window companies etc. All of them vying for any potential work that might be created if the application is successful. One of the most commonly received letters by the applicant (or their agent), will be from the sharpest of the housing developers, who will be asking if they intend to sell the land if the application is approved and if so, could they (the developer) be considered as potential buyers?

If the applicant is planning on selling the land, a process of negotiation can then start between the applicant (and / or their agents) and possibly a number of other potential buyers (usually small or large scale housing developers).

As the planning process continues, so do the sales discussions, to an extent where, quite often, by the time planning has actually been granted, there is a contract in place for the sale of the land to one of the developers. The name for this type of contract is an option agreement. It basically agrees the sale of the land, at the agreed price, subject to the approval of the planning consent (*this agreement can also be used in other ways – see later for details*).

So, if the application is approved, the sale and purchase go ahead straight away and the developer can get on with developing. It is very simple really!

Actually it is much better than that, and this next bit is why this method of acquiring land should be adopted by the self-build industry:

The price the developer usually pays will be <u>significantly lower</u> than any self-builder would normally expect to pay for the same plot, <u>sometime less than half</u> the price, especially if there are multiple plots on the site.

Imagine if we, as self-builders could start to access this way of buying land. We can, I already do!

If you think about it, what the people who use this method are doing, is using the tools at their disposal to get themselves to the front of the que. At the same time, by moving in to what I would call the commercial end of the house building industry, they are simply getting wholesale or trade prices, just as they would do for buying materials at the builder's merchant.

How do you, as private individuals get the same access to plots at the same time as the builders?

Every planning application made, can be accessed by the general public. Some local authorities have kept up with the times and publish them all on-line, some others are a still abit behind and still keep paper copies in their offices.

To access the planning applications in your chosen areas, start by going to:
http://www.planningportal.gov.uk/inyourarea/

At the time of writing, you should see a page something like this:

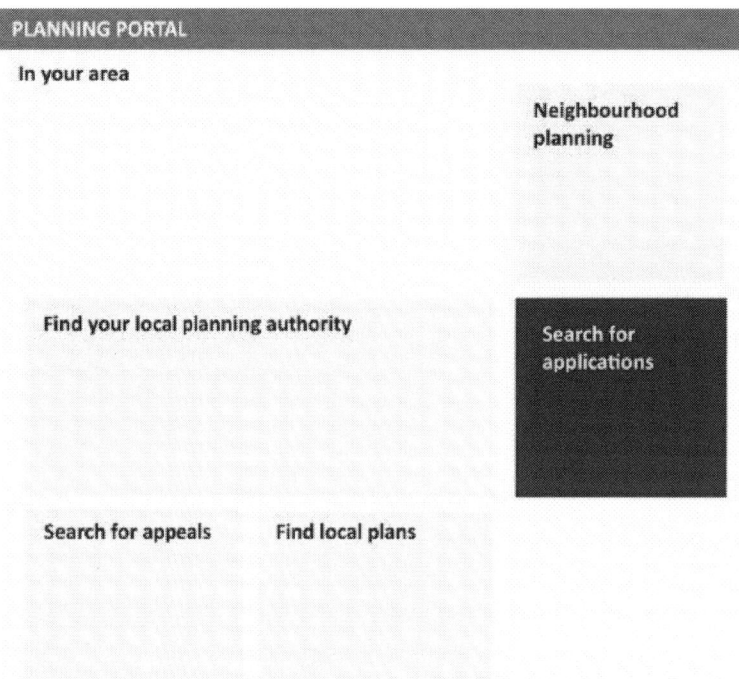

This is the one of the Government's Planning Portal's main pages.

On the right-hand side in the second box down you will see: "Search for applications" (I have highlighted it in a darker shade). Click on this link and you will be taken to a page that includes the following link:

Find your local planning Authority (LPA)

Click the link and you will be taken to another page which allows you to specify either the name of the LPA, your place of interest, or postcode of the Local Authority you wish to access.

Now enter the search criteria for a location of your choice and go to their page.

You then need to look for the planning and appeals register.

Depending on whether or not there is button giving you this choice, you will now head off down one of two routes:

1) If there is no button it probably means they have not got round to putting all their applications online yet. If this is the case, you will need to contact the authority and ask if they have a paper set of planning applications at their offices. If so, you can go and look through them all (as far back in time as they have them for) and make notes on any building plot applications that may interest you.
2) If there is a button, go to the planning application register section and work your way through to the individual applications. You can now browse as many applications as you like and again, make notes to take away with you.

If this is either your first visit to the offices or your first time on the website, I would suggest that, if you have the time, you go back through maybe 6 months of applications, starting with the most recent.

As you look through the individual files, what you are looking at is exactly the same information that is accessed by the data selling companies and sold on for large fees. However, you are now accessing that information free of charge.

The reason for starting your search from around 6 months ago is that this a common length of time for anything but the simplest applications to take to be determined, once it has been batted back and forth between the client, the architect and the planners. If the application is over 8 weeks old, there is a chance that a decision may have been made on it, but this is a far less common event than it is meant to be (believe me!)

If the application has had a successful outcome and the owners want to sell it, *now* could just possibly be the perfect time for them to receive a contact from you!

The next stage:

It is worth making note of applications varying from 1 to maybe 5 or 6 plots as these types of sites could possibly be split down by the owners and sold individually, especially if they realise that this could be the most lucrative method of disposal for them (*or you could get a few other people together to buy all of them – see later for details*).

You now need to start making contact.

If I have a choice of contacts, I would always opt for contacting the owner rather than the agent. Why? Well, if you contact the owner, you are getting straight through to the person who will make the decision on when, if and to whom to sell the land. If you contact the Architect or agent there is a possibility that they will already have people in mind to whom they would like to sell the land to and they may put you at the back of the queue.

How to make contact

Your initial contact is very important. It either sets you up as being someone worthwhile talking to, should they wish to sell the land, or someone to steer clear of!

Let's start with you contacting the owner:

If you write a letter to the owner, the best way to approach it is to try to make friends with them and not to be someone who just sees them as a potential source of land. Remember, they will be getting contacts of varying types from commercial builders and other companies, basically saying "How much for the land mate?"

Quite often, the smaller areas of land that go in for planning permission are located next door to the owners, so what happens to it after it receives planning permission will affect their lives directly. They possibly won't like the idea of a faceless builder coming along and throwing up cheap poorly designed houses for sale to anyone who is willing to pay the money.

If you want to create a good impression, if possible, write your letter by hand, but before you do, try to get time to actually go and see the plot and see if it is suitable. If you do this, when you write, you could be saying things along the lines of:

- *"We saw your details in the Planning Office files and immediately wanted to see the plot, so we drove out and had a look. When we saw it, we realised it was just perfect for us".*
- *"If you were to consider selling the land and if you would allow us to bid for it, we would make sure we kept the new design in keeping with the neighbours and the area".*
- *"If you are planning on selling the land, when the time comes, perhaps we could come over to meet you to talk about our ideas for what we would like to build, so we can get to know you and see how you feel about our thoughts".*

All those sorts of approaches are going to relax a seller far more than a cold commercial contact from a builder. If they like you, they may be far more likely to sell to you (at possibly a lower price) than they would to a builder.

If you are contacting the architect or agent:

You need to be a lot more formal with your contact. Try something along the lines of:

- *"I am writing in regard to Planning Application Number ******, and understand that you are dealing with this application".*
- *"I am an individual who is seeking to purchase a good quality plot in that area on which to develop a new property".*
- *"Could you please let me know if the owner is considering selling the land should it be successful in gaining Planning Permission?".*

It may take some time before you get a positive response.

One thing to bear in mind is that this is not a quick fix. It is not a short cut to getting a good cheap plot of land. It is simply a system that puts you on a level playing field with the big boys. It gives you potential access to all the information about building plots, **before** they **actually become** building plots and it puts **you** in control of sourcing your land, rather than you having to wait until left-over plots appear at the estate agents or on the internet.

You may need to do a lot of research, visiting numerous LPAs, trawling through many applications, making notes, writing letters, chasing up possible leads etc. The process could last for many weeks or possibly months and you may get a number of knock-backs, BUT using this method, <u>you</u> are in charge, you are not depending on someone else to bring land to your attention and you are far more likely to find what you are looking for than if you just follow the pack.

Note: If you see the initials "TPS" on an application it means that the applicant is registered with the Telephone Protection Service and you must not call them. Use another form of contact.

Now let's move on to the next stage:

So, we have covered the basics of how you can access more building land than you have been able to up until now. However, that is just a starting point if we are going to get the industry moving in the right direction.

Now you are aware of your ability to find out about land, just like the developers do, we need to take this a stage further and find ways for you to be able to start to pay the *prices* for land that the developers pay.

When I work as Self-Build Expert at the shows, I talk to many people about just this subject and it is interesting to see how they receive the ideas that I am now going to move on to. I can usually see the excitement building in their eyes as they start to realise that what I say is actually doable.

When anyone comes to ask me how they can find decent land at a good price, one of the first things I say to them is: *"When you are ready, consider placing an advert in your local paper under "Building plots for sale" / "Land for sale" or similar headings. If there seems to be no suitable heading available, advertise under "Property for sale", you should quickly grab people's attention even there".*

The advert should read along the lines of:

Wanted
People interested in self-build, to join with us
to purchase multiple plots of land at reduced prices.
CONTACT NUMBER

That's it! You don't need to say anything else. Anyone who reads that advert who is thinking about self-building is going to be interested in talking to you. You just need to have your story *and a scheme* ready.

What you need to have done before you put the ad in the paper is to get yourself a plan of attack.

How you set things up is up to you. There is no right or wrong way to do it, but if it is to work, you need to achieve the following:

1. You need to find a number of likeminded people who would be happy to work with you on accessing and eventually purchasing between you, a parcel of land for up to as many plots (with planning permission) as you can find purchasers with money!
2. These people need to be able to move quickly, if and when you find something suitable, so they need to be able to get mortgages (pre-approved if possible) and have cash available towards deposits, legal fees and other costs associated with buying land.
3. You need to find out from everyone what they would like to build, should you find suitable land. It is no good linking with someone who wants a £1,000,000 plus plot for a 20 bedroomed mansion, when your total budget is £250,000 and you will be looking to pay £100,000 max for a plot for a 4 bed house. The word likeminded means *in all* respects.
4. You need someone who has the time and the organisational abilities to pull all this together. This may be you, one of your family, one of the other interested people, or you could consider hiring between you a planning specialist or a project manager to work with you and give you the professional assistance you will (all) need to get the project off the ground.
5. You need to get a legal framework together. A commercial solicitor who specializes in residential projects is the person you need for this.

If and when you get a group of people together (*you could always start with numbers of parties as low as two and bring others in as you move forward*), you need to set some ground rules, so that everyone knows where they are and what the plan is. This could be along the lines of:

- We are looking for building plots in the ****** area, or within 20 miles of that location.
- We will consider serviced or un-serviced plots (you can always get the services installed yourselves).
- The property types should fall in a range from 2000 to 3500 sq ft / detached.
- We would need agreement on a theme for the design of the houses before making offers. We would use the services of a designer, paid for jointly, to work with us to create this. This is necessary to ensure that there are minimal or no design conflicts between buyers at the design stage.
- Each buyer will buy their own plot and design and construct their own property. This project is not intended to be a "community" development. Trades found and hired by one party will not be poached until they have left the employ of their original customer.

- All road, service, drainage, infrastructure, communal design, section 106 agreements and any other costs which can be seen to be classed as communal costs will be shared equally by every party (unless agreed otherwise by all parties). If there is a doubt about what is classed as a communal cost, there will be conditions set in the legal agreement between the parties to suggest remedial action.

I am sure you get the picture! I am not a solicitor and I don't want you writing to me saying "I used your notes and there was mayhem!" get this bit of the project professionally looked after.

Get started:

So, now you have access to multiple plots of land, you potentially also have a group of people who have the wherewithal to join with you to buy multiple plots, so what next?

All of you, get out looking for something suitable! Whenever anyone finds anything that they think the other parties will be interested in, they simply get a message to them to go and have a look. The process will either take its own life after that, or no one will be interested and you will all keep looking.

Once you find a potentially suitable area of land (with planning permission) or with planning pending and you get a posse" of people interested, you need to move quickly. Good land doesn't stick around for long.

You need to have all the basic agreements (listed above) already agreed, so you are all singing off the same hymn sheet. You need to find out who is seriously interested, and you need to formulate an offer.

One thing I would like to mention here, is that, to my mind, you should try to shy away from any groups of self-builders getting together to build all their houses communally, unless it is being professionally organised by either a specialist company or a project manager.

Over the years, I have heard so many tales about how these community projects can go spectacularly wrong and how people end up being sued, fighting at site meetings and hating their new neighbours by the time the project is finished.

Think about it: Maybe there are 10 of you wanting houses, built pretty much at the same time once the land is acquired. That would mean either an extremely large groundworks company coming along who could bring 10 teams of men in (this would be highly unlikely to happen), or a smaller ground works company would be hired, and there would have to be an "order of works", with one house being done at a time. Someone would inevitably be last in line and may end up waiting months for their project to even start. The same goes for every trade right the way through the project.

I think you would be far better advised to use the buying power of a group of people to get the land at cheap prices, but then all do your own thing, at your own pace, in your own way when it comes to actually building the houses. Find your own groundworkers, brickies and everyone else you need and when you have finished with them, if someone else wants to hire them, fair enough. But your new neighbours are not going to hold you up by continually pinching your workforce from you when you need them on your site!

Having said that, Valerie Bearne, who wrote the forward to this book, has a different view on this subject, so if you would like to read another opinion, have a look at "Get together and build yourself a house – The essential guide to group self-building".

Back to the plot: - This is where it gets interesting:

What you have now done, by getting a group of people together, all of whom have funds available, is that you have moved yourselves away from being self-builders and you have temporarily, for the purposes of buying land, become developers.

As developers, you should now to be looking to buy land at *developers'* prices. That could mean saving as much as 50% - 60% of the price you would pay as an individual self-builder for a simple single self-build plot.

Here is an example how that works, with figures taken from one of the main property and rental internet sites:

I did a land search of an area in South Wales where plots are in reasonably good supply. In a circle covering a 5-mile radius, decent single self-build plot sells for between £70,000 and £175,000, depending on whether you want to be in the posh end or the not so posh end.

Here is an idea of what was available when I made the search. I was looking at both single and "multi-plot" sites *(I will, for simplicity use the full asking price of the land to base my figures on, however it is unusual to pay full price in all but the most popular areas of the country)*:

Example 1:   Land for 8 detached houses & 4 pairs of semi-detached + 1 block of 4 flats.

Asking price £600,000

A fairly pleasant area of mixed value properties *(it is common to have a mixed value of houses in one area in Wales)*.

Breaking this down to sensible figures:

8 Detached at **£45,000** each = £360,000

4 pairs of semis (8 properties) @ **£45,000** per pair (or £22,500 per semi) = £190,000

1 Block of 4 flats @ **£50,000** (or £12,500 per flat)

Total £600,000.

Example 2:   Land for 4 detached houses close to a mid-range new commercial housing development.

Asking price £180,000 (equating to £45,000 per plot).

Example 3:   Large, good quality single building plot at the posh end

Asking price: £150,000.

Example 4:   11 serviced self-build plots on one site, to be sold individually. Pleasant, countryside area, planning permission lapsed (so buyers need to re-apply).

Asking price £80,000 - £100,000 each.

A quick study of the examples above show that if I have the money available to be able to buy the larger areas of land in this general area, I can be looking at paying around £45,000 per plot, however if I am looking to buy a single plot, I will be looking at around at least twice that figure as an average.

Obviously, this is only a snapshot example and the figures will be different wherever you are live in the UK, but the principle works anywhere.

Builders could simply not afford to pay self-build plot prices. Their overheads are too high and they would go out of business. So builders need to be paying *significantly* less than even the most astute self-builder could even *hope* to be paying, before they could even consider buying land to build and sell property commercially.

Q: What if it is just me buying one plot of land using this system rather than a group of us?

The more people the better for this system to work to its best potential, but it can work for single plot buyers.

By using the planning register to get access to the people who are applying for planning permission, you are at least getting to see the plots at the same time that the builders and developers see them, so, in theory you are in the same position as them when it comes to making offers.

Here are two ways in which that could work for you:

1) **Beat them at their own game:**

    You have more buying power than the developers when it comes to the single plots. If you find a single plot in the planning register and like it, you might contact the owner to ask if you could be considered to make an offer when they come to sell it. If you are doing this, you can be sure that every local builder who likes to do, or can only afford to do single house developments, is doing the same.

    Now, say the owner of the plot doesn't know much about the building industry or how the value of land varies depending who is buying it and just wants to sell it as soon as they get planning permission. Here is what the situation could look like:

    The self-build value of that plot could be around £150,000. If so, the trade value would probably be £75,000 - £100,000.

    The builder needs to get that plot for around £90,000 because of his overheads and his need to make a quick profit by selling it once it is finished. If he has to pay more than £90,000 he is in a bit of trouble and could struggle to make the levels of profit he needs once it is sold.

    If you had found this plot on the internet, you would probably be prepared to pay up to the normal self-build price of £150,000 for it.

    So, imagine you and the builder in a bidding battle: If after all the negotiations, the builder ended up having to offer £110,000 to get hold of the plot, he would be £20,000 over budget before he even started building and would already be losing out significantly on where he needs to be financially. If even something small then went wrong during the build, he could really find himself struggling to make money.

    If you ended up having to pay £110,000, you would be quids in, £40,000 up on the deal in fact!

    So, you have the power in this situation to outbid most commercial developers and still be very happy with the price you would be paying for your plot.

2) **Buy one get one free"** Lets stick with the same figures. Say you have £150,000 to spend and you see two unserviced plots which are in the middle of the planning process which it turns out the owner would sell for £150,000 if planning is approved.
    Let's say that these plots would sell for £100,000 each if they were sold as Individual serviced plots, but the present owner can't either be bothered or can't afford to do the work to turn them in to serviced plots.
    If a developer were to buy them both, he would have to bring in the services. This will cost him extra, over and above the purchase price.
    You would normally have to bring in services to a single plot wherever you bought it, so you are in the same sort of positon as the developer.
    So, how about you buying both plots for £150,000, then selling the second plot for £100,000 as a serviced plot? If it cost you £10,000 to bring in the services, that is £5,000 per plot, so you would net £95,000 for the sale of the second plot.

    This would mean that you have now only paid £55,000 (net) for your own plot. - Result!

I hope the message I have been trying to communicate over the past few pages will now be becoming clear.

Finding and buying land is a bit of a game. The more guile you show and the more you think about different ways to go about doing it, the better the potential outcome can be for you.

What I am trying to do in this chapter, is to give you ideas and thoughts about how you can learn to play the game to your advantage. If you can do so successfully, the benefits could be significant. If you go into any of these processes unprepared, there is a chance that you could catch a cold.

Just make sure you don't rush in to anything and always bring in professional help if and when you need to, to stop you doing anything daft!

The next stage:

How much should we pay for a building plot, whichever way we find or buy it?

Ok, so now you have a potential plot in mind. It may have come through one of the traditional methods or you may have found it through the planning application registry process.

Either way you now need to work out how much that plot is worth <u>to you</u>.

In the good old days, there used to be a formula for the value of land. You would pay roughly the same for the land as for the build:

TOTAL COST: LAND 45% + BUILD 45% + CONTINGENCIES 10%

This calculation would be based on the money available for the project, so if you had £200,000 in total to spend, you would be looking for land at a maximum of £90,000, leaving you £90,000 for the build and £20,000 for contingencies.

Sadly, about 15 years ago that started to change. I realised this around 12 years ago when I made an offer on a piece of land suitable for 6 houses in South Wales.

The sale was being conducted by what is called the sealed bid method, which basically means that all interested buyers have to make a bid by a *certain time* on a *certain day* in a sealed envelope. After which all the envelopes are opened and the highest bid is taken (subject to it reaching a reserve figure set by the seller).

On this sort of sale, a guide price is given by the agent to avoid low offers being made. On this particular piece of land, I think the guide price was around £360,000 for 6 plots (£60,000 each).

Up until that time, I had used my own usual method to work out how much to offer. For commercial housing (as opposed to self-build) this roughly worked out (for me, anyway) at around 30% of the finished value for the land, 30% for the build, 25% as a target profit and a 15% for planning, warranties, building regulations, legal costs, agents' fees and a contingency sum. If the property sold quickly and had not had to eat in to the contingency money, I should make around a 30% profit per house.

That method worked fine until the housing boom hit in the nineties and early 2000s and land started to get significantly more valuable by the month!

For the 6 plot development I am talking about here, I had worked out what I thought was going to be the approximate value of the properties when they were finished and from this I calculated what I would be happy to pay per plot.

These figures were something like:

My estimated end value of the properties, based on present local values - £250,000

30% for the land = £75,000 (£450,000 total)

30% for the build = £75,000 (£450,000 total)

25% target profit = £62,500 per house (£375,000 total)

15% fees, contingency etc. = £37,500 per house (225,000 total)

Because I do a lot of the design and development work myself, my overheads are low, so theoretically I should be able to offer the best prices for land.

I put my bid in, thinking I had given a generous offer for the land that no one would beat. I think I offered around £450,000 for 6 plots (£75,000 each), which was £90,000 above the guide price, so I thought to myself "This is mine!"

My bid failed.

As I knew the owner of the estate agent dealing with the sale, I rang him the day my offer was rejected to ask how much the winning bid had been for. He said he could not tell me the accurate figure at that time, but it was considerably more than my offer (he did say it was well over £100,000 more, probably getting on for **£100,000** per plot). I was completely taken aback! How could this be? Who would offer so much more than the plot was (as I thought) commercially worth?

It took me a while to work out, but when I eventually did, it changed the way I bid for land from then on.

At that time house values were rising quickly, so 6 months after the builders had bought the land, it could be worth 10% more than it was when they bought it.

What they had probably done was this:

- They had ignored the guide price.
- They had worked out a likely value for the finished houses around 6 – 12 months in the future (say £280,000), giving an estimated income from the project of £1,680,000. This was something I had never done in the past.
- They had then decided what profit they needed to make from the job in total (say £300,000 minimum)
- They had then taken off the total target build cost (say £600,000)
- They had then reduced their allowances for fees, contingencies etc. and accepted that their profits could be reduced if anything major went wrong, on the basis that if they didn't get the land in the first place they wouldn't make *any profit* at all. So maybe they reduced this amount from £225,000 to, say £150,000.

Their calculations would now look something like this:

Potential income £1,680,000 - £300,000 (profit) - £600,000 (build) - £150,000 (fees etc.) = max £630,000 available for the land

This would leave them with a maximum amount they could bid for the land of up to £630,000 (£105,000 per plot) and that is pretty much what they did!

What they had done, is realised that the land buying market was getting much more competitive and they had decided to turn the traditional equation for buying land upside down, to make sure they got land to build their new homes on. So, instead of starting with what they thought the land should be worth, they started from the end value and worked backwards, giving themselves *the value of the land* **to them** based on an **end value**, rather than the usual calculation methods.

So, the land value for commercial housebuilding slowly changed to look something like this:

> **MAXIMUM OFFER PRICE ON LAND**
> **=**
> **SELLING VALUE WHEN COMPLETE**
> **MINUS**
> **PROFIT & OTHER COSTS**
> **MINUS**
> **BUILD COSTS**

It would be my recommendation that when you are buying land, that you work more from this basis than the old method, especially if you live in areas of high demand. You need to work out, not *How much is it worth on the open market?* But *How much is it worth **to you**?*

Obviously, as self-builders you are not as worried about the profit element as commercial builders are, but you should still be aiming to achieve levels of 20% - 30% equity over cost levels in order to make the project worth all your effort, time input and stress.

There are plenty of ways to keep the price down for the build (which we will be looking at later) and I have already shown you how to start to find and buy land at much lower prices, but that does not change the fact that you need to know the how the basic principal of how to work out the maximum amounts you can spend on the land.

So, let's see how that works in practice on a single self-build plot:

For this example, we will assume you have a total budget of £350,000

Earlier in the book, you will have seen some sample figures for build costs and we also looked at working out a best guess for the likely build cost of your own project.

To save you looking back, here they are again:

Project manage everything yourself: Usually between £90 - £120 sq ft (£968 - £1183 / sq m)

Hire a project manager: Usually between £110 - £130 (£1183 - £1398 / sq m)

Main contractor: Usually between £130 - £180+ / sq ft (£1398 - £1936 / sq

We have also covered the subject of how to get an idea of what sort of size of house you would be looking to build. Let's say you end want a 4 bed house at £2,000 sq ft.

What you need to do now is find out how much that house would sell for, once it has been completed, on the plot you are thinking of buying. The quickest and easiest way to do that these days is to go on line and have a look through the property selling web sites.

Let's assume, after doing some research, that you estimate that the end value of your new home would be around £450,000. This gives you a starting point to work out how much to offer for a suitable plot in that area.

Going back to the build cost figures, you will now need to decide which management option you would most likely go for. Let's say that you decide to project manage everything yourself.

The guide cost I have given you, which is at least something to start with, says that the likely total cost of your project could fall between £90 per sq ft to £120 per sq ft, so the next step is to make your best guess at where your build costs might end up within that range of figures. Are you looking to go high spec, mid spec or low spec? Let's assume you are going mid spec.

If we follow these figures, a self-project managed build at (say) £105 per sq ft for a 2000 sq ft house would cost in the region of £210,000 to build.

If you now deduct £210,000 from your budget of £350,000 you are left with £140,000. This needs to cover the price of the land and your contingency amount.

If you are allowing a 10% contingency on the whole budget, you would need to leave £35,000 for that.

With these figures, your max budget for the land is between £105,000. Pay any more and you are already eating in to your contingency.

When you find a piece of land you like:

- If the asking price is within your budget range, you are ok.
- If the asking price is more than your budget, you need to go back to the drawing board.

We have already looked at ways to reduce the cost of buying the land, so it is possible that, if you follow my suggestions, £105,000 could get you exactly what you need, but if not, we are also going to be looking later at ways to bring your design and build costs down significantly (to where they should actually be). The lower your build costs, the more flexibility you will have on what you can pay for your land.

If you do need to go back to the drawing board, what do you need to consider?

1. **Your available budget:** can you find any more money from anywhere?
2. **The size of the house:** are you going to have to consider a smaller house to try to keep within your budget?
3. **The build speed / method:** the speed of build directly affects the cost, so if you have chosen a slow construction method, maybe you need to have another look at this choice (see Chapter 7 for more detail)
4. **Find lower cost geographical areas for buying land:** plot prices can vary hugely within a few miles of each other. You may need to be a bit more flexible on the actual location of your project

Other things to bear in mind when looking for and buying a building plot:

Negotiating sale prices:

Once you have worked out the maximum amount you can safely spend on your plot and have found something suitable, you need to decide on your opening gambit as an offer to the vendor.

It is always tempting, once you have found a plot you like, to make an offer of the asking price to make sure you don't lose it. That is a perfectly sensible thing to do in some circumstances (*especially if there is any chance of the land being snapped up quickly by someone else*). Some buyers will happily offer more than the asking price if they think they could get outbid and potentially lose out.

However, before you go committing possibly tens of thousands of pounds extra to your plot purchase price, just stop and work out if you really need to act so quickly.

Here is an example from my own experience when I was a self-build project manager about 20 years ago:

I was employed to find a suitable plot for my client, then design and build the house. My client had a £250,000 budget and we worked out he had around £100,000 - £120,000 for the land.

The first time I drove round his chosen area, I found a very nice plot in a countryside location, with planning permission already granted for sale at £100,000. I contacted the agent to discuss it.

One of my questions to the agent was "How long has it been on the market?" The answer was "9 months". I asked if it had received much interest and it turned out that someone had made an offer a few months earlier but had had to pull out before completing and things had gone quiet since.

This information gave me what I need to report back to the client, who, after visiting the site was keen to make an offer of the asking price. However, I held him back, saying:

"The land is ideal, but I think we may be able to get a bargain if we are a bit clever. There has been interest in the past but not at the moment, so it doesn't appear that we have to panic. Also, because there has been a potential sale which has fallen through and no one else has come rushing in to buy it, the owner might now be wondering if he is asking too much for it. Or he may need the money asap. - So, let's start low and work up if we need to".

The client nervously agreed to take my advice and I suggested that we start at what was really a rather cheeky price of £70,000, just to test the water. We did just that and the offer was accepted with no negotiation!

The client had just saved **£30,000** on the purchase price, simply by me doing a bit of homework and thinking the situation through. That £30,000 could now be spent on the house itself, which should, in turn, increase its value significantly.

So, what I am saying here is: Unless there is real and ongoing interest in any plot you find, don't rush in to make an offer without checking the situation out. Make sure you think it through properly before committing yourselves.

Every £1 you save on the purchase of the land can go towards the build, so don't throw money at the plot needlessly. Do, however, when you do your research, take into account the following:

- The history of the plot.
- The state of the market in general and in that location.
- The asking price (compared to other similar plots in the area).
- Your budget for the land purchase.
- The likelihood of someone else coming in and pinching it from under your nose.

Option agreements (*this is the section referred to earlier in this chapter*)

You may not be familiar with this term, but an option agreement can be a very useful tool if you happen to find land which has not got planning permission, but which you like and you think may get planning approval if you were to apply.

It is the main method I am now using to procure land for the housing development company that I am working with.

I would never recommend that you consider buying land without planning permission, but this system offers a way to secure land which does not currently have planning permission (as opposed to buying it), that then allows you to apply for and hopefully succeed in securing it, *without* all the risk of actually purchasing the plot and then just hope you get planning.

If you buy land without planning permission and pay good money for it, but then have the application and appeal refused, you would probably lose many tens of thousands of pounds on the deal.

How do option agreements work?

Rather than explaining the technical process, it might be easier to give you an example of one of our recent projects.

I found some land which had previously had planning permission for 4 detached houses and had been put up for sale during the recession but had not been sold. The planning permission had expired a few months before I found it.

I liked it, thought it could provide the basis for a good investment and decided to try to secure it for our company. However, I didn't want to risk buying it until I knew that a new planning application would be successful and I didn't want us to pay out for and do all the work involved in a planning application until I knew that if we *did* apply and then if we *did* decide that we wanted it, we would be guaranteed to get it, at a previously agreed price.

I approached the agent, who told me that the owner had lost interest in the land and just wanted to get rid of it. They lived at the opposite end of the country and were elderly.

I asked the agent to forward an offer based on an option agreement deal. This is how this would work:

1. I offered the full asking price for the land (which, because there were 4 plots, was a trade price as detailed earlier).
2. Once a formal agreement were finalised, I would do all the work and apply for a renewal of planning permission on the four plots.
3. If planning permission was approved, I would then market the plots locally and nationally as "Custom built executive new homes".
4. When I made a sale on any plot (exchanged contracts), I would then pay them an agreed price for each plot (so the purchase of the full area of land would be in four parts).
5. The agreement would last for 3 years and if I had not bought the whole of the land within that 3 years, the option agreement would end and the owner could dispose of the land as they wished without repaying any of our costs.

The owners accepted the offer.

In simple terms, that is pretty much all there was to it. I made an offer, the owner accepted it and we were then able to form a very simple legal agreement from which we would both benefit:

- The owner would sell the land that they had not been able to sell for the past 2 years and they received full price for the sale.
- We would secure land to build 4 houses on, at trade price, without having to have the cash to buy it ourselves.

What I had just done was to secure land for the *sole use* of our company, as long as we developed it within the next three years, or at least paid for the four plots within that time.

The cost to us to set all this up would be around £10,000, so if you like, that was our "risk". We risked £10,000 to potentially get a profit on the construction of four new executive homes.

You could do a very similar thing if you use the "planning permission registry" system I detailed earlier.

What you would need to do is to try to get together a group of people who could make the option agreement offer which would allow you to then form an agreement very similar to the ones I do for the business.

Your agreement would have to be set up in a different way legally from how I do within the business, because I still have to sell the plots after the agreement is signed. Whereas you will have buyers already confirmed.

All you are aiming to achieve using this system, is to achieve is a formally agreed *trade* purchase price on a piece of land which does not currently have planning approval.

You then need to be sure that if you achieve planning permission on it, you have a guarantee that you can buy it, within a fixed period of time at that fixed price.

If the planning permission registry and the option agreement systems were to be used properly, together within the UK self-build industry, it could be completely transformed within a few years.

I will be pushing as hard as I can over the next few years to get this system known and widely used. If anyone would like to join me to either get projects going or to promote the idea, please get in touch.

Other things to think about as you look for your ideal plot:

Restricted development:

Often the sales details of building plots are lacking in the information they should contain and are extremely sketchy.

The problem is that, because they rarely get asked to either sell single or multiple building plots, estate agents often don't know what to say about them.

The result of this is that there could be a number of issues that you are not informed about in the sales details, which could come up and bite you later. You need to be able to ask the right questions to the agent so that you don't get caught out later in the process.

One of the most common issues is a thing called restricted development. This is where there are restrictions of one type or another either on the plot or the area (or both), which could limit your ability to create the new home that you really want, on that land.

All of the following would be classed as restricted development and are things that could be missing from the sales particulars. You do, however need to be aware of their potential existence and you need to make sure you ask the seller and / or the planners if any of them are relevant to your chosen sites.

Whether or not the sales details are comprehensive, I would always recommend that before you make any commitment to a plot, you arrange to see the local planning officer for a pre planning meeting (as mentioned previously and detailed in chapter 6).

1) **Building Size**

There may be development restrictions for housing which limit the size of the physical building on the plot. This is often in more sensitive planning areas, where strict controls are in place on over development. If the agent's details are not thorough, you may not release that the lovely large plot you are considering buying to put a large family home only actually has planning approval for a 2 bed cottage, with no chance of getting it changed. Check with the estate agents or whoever is selling and / or your Solicitor before committing yourself to anything.

2) **Appearance**

The same thing sometimes applies to the appearance of the building. It may need to follow a visual theme for the area, so you may be required to stick with a certain design style, specific materials etc.

3) **Number of storeys**

Restrictions on the number of storeys you are allowed to build could be in place. This could severely limit you if the plot is only small and there is a single storey restriction in place so you have to spread out all the rooms you need across one floor.

You can sometimes get away with building a 1.5 or 2.5 storey house (i.e. one floor is located within the roof) on a plot with a one or two storey restriction if you can "disguise" the first floor within the roof space, or add a basement.

4) Roof ridge heights

This might sound as if it is covering the same thing as the previous point, but it is not.

You could have planning consent for a 3-storey building, but it is quite common for the planning consent to include a condition that the top of the roof is not allowed to go above a certain height.

Where ridge heights are an issue, there are a few options to try to solve the problem, including:

- Excavate some ground to allow you to drop the ground floor level lower which will give you more height to play with within the building.
- Build a storey into the roof.
- Build a basement or semi basement.
- Go with a "mono pitched" roof:

5) Building lines

This is quite a commonly found restriction on building plots.

If you find a plot which has houses either side, which all seem to be pretty much in a straight line, there is a good chance that there is a building line restriction in place. Where this occurs, you cannot build anything that protrudes in front of that line.

I have seen many of these where a large plot can have a building line set well back from the front boundary. This can sometimes almost result in the plot being pretty much unusable for housing development. If you come across a lovely plot, with planning for, say one house, which seems to be very cheap, this can often be the main reason for the low price.

6) Orientation

A similar restriction, which can reduce the value of the land would be on its orientation. If you would be forced to face the building in a certain direction, you may find that your outlook from the main rooms is not as pleasant as it would be if the building faced a different direction. This may significantly reduce the appeal of the plot (and also its value) to you.

7) Access / Parking / Turning

Another restriction that can catch you out, is how you need to present the access to the site, the parking within the site boundaries and the ability of vehicles to manoeuvre within the site boundaries.

If the plot is on a busy main road there may be a requirement to be able to take vehicles into and bring them out of the plot in a forward gear. In other words, you are required to be able to turn all vehicles round within the perimeter of the site, to avoid the necessity to back out on to the busy road. Often this type of site will also require extra parking space within its boundaries to minimise the likely need for parking on the roadway itself.

In extreme situations, this may not leave you enough room on the plot to build the sort of house you would want.

There is a possible solution to the turning problem within a site boundary. That is to install a turntable in your driveway so cars can drive onto it and be manually be turned around so they can then drive out in a forward gear (see below).

8) Parking spaces

Parking is a common area of difficulty for larger houses. Generally, the bigger the house, the more parking spaces you will be required to provide within the site boundaries.

There are planning rules which cover the number of parking spaces for standard sized houses, but there doesn't seem to be a hard and fast rule about how many spaces are required for very large houses.

As a rule of thumb, it appears to be that you will need one parking space per bedroom up to a maximum of three cars. However, before you start to design your house and think about where you would like it to be positioned it on the plot, it is a good idea to research the situation regarding parking requirements.

We are now going to move away a bit from restrictions imposed by the planners, towards the things that you need to think about which are related to the plot itself. Things which could potentially cause you either practical or financial problems later in the project.

Service availability / locations:

There are some plots which have no access to services gas / water / electricity / drainage / telecom. There are also plots which will have one or two of the standard services, but not all.

Services availability should always be included in the sales particulars but unfortunately that is not always the case, so you need both to be aware and to check up on the situation regarding all of the services that you would need.

You may be happy to use oil instead of gas, or to dig a well or borehole for water, or even use a generator, but you also need to bear in mind that one day you might want to sell up and move on. If that were to happen, would potential buyers be put off if <u>all</u> of the standard services were not available or connected to the property?

As you start to head into the countryside, there tend to be more and more plots for which services may not be available and if they are, in many cases, the nearest access point to them could be significant distances from the plot boundaries.

The cost to connect to each of the services will usually be directly affected by the distance that the connection point is away from your boundary. If you don't research this matter sufficiently at an early stage, you could expose yourself to the very real risk, later in the project, of receiving some pretty scary quotes for the work involved.

It is worth contacting the service providers in your local area to find out the likely ease or difficulty, including costs or time delays, that you are going to experience with each one of your service connections.

You can either contact the service providers directly, or use one of the specialist companies which pull together all the information on the location and availability of the various services.

If you search on line for: "Dial before you dig" you should find a selection of companies able to provide you with all the information you need. There will be a fee, so shop around to get the best deal.

The same people can normally help you with another matter that needs considering when you are looking at potential building plots:

Existing services running across your plot

This one can sometimes pretty much be a job stopper.

Luckily it is fairly rare to find a plot of land for sale which has been through the planning process which has public drains running through the middle of it that no one seems to be aware of, but it does happen!

Services of all types can cause major problems to all forms of development, so you need to make sure you make yourselves fully aware of anything that could affect the project, which runs either under or over your site.

Ransom strips

These are nasty little critters and can be a nightmare not only for the buyer, but also for the seller of land.

A ransom strip is any piece of land, not owned by the owner of the main area of land, but which provides the only route for access on to that land.

The owner of the main area of land has to have permission from the owner of the ransom strip for anyone to be able to legally travel across it to access the main area of land.

A ransom strip can, in theory, be as little as 1mm wide and it would still provide a legal barrier that stops anyone getting access on to the land.

I have come across these on a few occasions. Once I was looking to buy a very nice piece of land with lovely views, on which I wanted to build a detached home to live in myself. The plot asking price was £30,000, which I thought was quite cheap for what it was.

The selling agent didn't say anything about ransom strips when they gave me the sales brochure, but on the sales particulars I noticed something in the small print saying *"The only access to this land is via a ransom strip across the front boundary. Any negotiations for the purchase of this strip should be held with the owners who can be contacted directly"*. This meant that the owner of the main part of the land would not be getting involved with trying to negotiate for the purchase of the ransom strip.

The strip in question was about 2ft wide right across the front of the plot (about 60ft in length). I rang the agent and asked if anyone had tried to get a price to buy the ransom strip and was told "Yes, but the owners want £30,000 for it" (the same price as the plot!) It turned out that the owner of the ransom strip had fallen out with the owner of the plot and was being difficult, in order to try to stop the land owner making money from the sale of the plot.

Generally, you would expect to pay anything up to third of the value of the plot for a ransom strip (plus the legal costs), so it is not always something that will stop the project.

Visibility splays

Visibility splays are, as the name suggests, the amount of visibility you have from your access, looking either way along the road on which it is located.

It is based on you being sat in a car, coming out of the driveway, where your seating position is a distance (usually 2.4m) behind the front of the car.

The Highways people want to know that when you exit your drive, you can see far enough each way so that you are not a threat to other road users or to pedestrians as you enter or exit your property.

The visibility splay distances requirements vary from 45m if you are in a 20mph zone, to 295m if you are in a 70mph zone.

There is some flexibility however:

A few years ago I applied for planning permission to build a house on a sloping, winding country lane.

As I exited what would be the driveway area, I had a high wall to my right, on my side of the road, which significantly cut down my visibility and a sharp right hand bend to my left, which meant that I could only see 25 – 30 metres in that direction.

Theoretically this could mean that I would not get the planning approval, but I did.

The Highways department visited the site and took the opinion that, due to the nature of the road and my position on it, the traffic coming either way would not be travelling at more than around 20mph and would easily have room to brake if they saw me exiting or entering my drive. They did not see this reduced visibility as presenting a safety problem.

Difficult / Sloping sites

Most people get scared off as soon as they see a site which appears to be difficult. I am the opposite, I get drawn to them! – Why?

Well, for a few reasons:

- The asking price is normally significantly lower.
- The owners are also more likely to take an even lower bid than the asking price (because they are relieved to find someone who has the nerve to take it on as a project).
- The location can often be better (sloping sites can include nice views).
- I don't need to be a specialist myself in building on difficult sites, there are plenty of specialists around who can look after all the technical details. All I have to do is find them and contact them, tell them what I want and let them get on with it. Because the plot price is usually much lower than an easy, flat site, there is usually a decent amount of money still in the budget after buying the plot itself to cover this extra cost.

As an example, to prove that difficult sites can be doable, here are a couple of photos of what could justifiably be given that title. The photos were taken of a development that I completed a few years ago in South Wales.

The site was a sloping field about 240m long and up to 80m deep, with slopes varying in steepness across its length. I had to design houses which had one more storey at the back than they had at the front.

I was lucky and found an excavation project going on locally where the contractor was having to pay to tip every load of earth he excavated at a local tip. I agreed not to charge him a tipping fee if he brought the excavated materials to me and formed up the site as I needed him to. The whole of the rear gardens for all of the properties was made up of this excavated material, compacted and finished off with topsoil.

Make sure that any "spoil" (excavated material) that is brought in to your site is checked for chemicals / invasive weeds etc. by the haulier. Get confirmation in writing from whoever is delivering it, that it is "clean".

My general advice on difficult or sloping sites would be to weigh up the pros and cons before you think about committing yourself. Compare the price with other similar sized plots locally that would be simpler to develop. Think about bringing on board a project manager with experience of this type of work. Talk to groundworkers and other specialists that you may need and try to get a ball park idea of the likely costs, together with the likely time scales that would be involved in sorting the site out.

Always keep in mind that the end value of the project needs to make the extra work worthwhile doing and that your cash flow needs to be able to stand the strain of the extra expense at the start of the project, - then decide if you are brave enough to take it on.

Difficult sites will always present more of a risk on your first self-build project, but if you already have one or two under your belt, then taking on something a bit out of the ordinary could be quite exciting!

Site surveys / ground level surveys

It is always a wise move to carry out a site survey and to check out the ground conditions before you pay any money out for a building plot.

There can be all sorts of hidden problems underneath a building plot that could be very expensive to fix: poor or contaminated ground / running sand / old shallow mineshafts / rock / drains / old bedsteads etc. It is actually fairly rare for a project not to have one or two "built-in problems"

Whenever I talk to clients about build costs, I always say "*I can't give you a fixed price for work underground until we see what is there, however, once we get out of the ground it is a lot easier to give definite prices as things tend to be measurable and don't tend to be open so much to forced change.*

That's how it should be on every site, but unfortunately it isn't. Contractors will often just give clients a price for basic foundations within their quote, then when it comes to signing contracts, in the small print it will state something like:

> "*Foundations are priced for a standard 900m x 600mm excavation and a 225mm strip footing. Extra work will be charged at £50 / hr for labour, £80 / hr for an excavator*"

The rates for extra work are often significantly higher than the standard day rate for both men and machinery.

Be vigilant for this sort of thing happening.

You also need to be on the lookout for the tricks of the trade, where sometimes the ground worker won't even mention anything about extras in his quote, but instead will just suddenly hit you with a hefty invoice for unscheduled works underground.

So, what I am saying here is that if you get a _ground_ investigation done (different from a level survey), you will minimise the risk of unexpected costs later. The time to carry out the survey is after the offer to purchase the plot has been accepted, just after the process has gone to the solicitors, but before you make the final payment to the vendor. You need to be in a position where, if you found a problem that was going to be too expensive to fix, you could still pull out of the deal, without having invested too much into the project at that time.

You will need to ask permission from the land owner to go on site to do the survey. You will also need to find a surveyor to do the work. Just search "land surveyors" on the internet and add your post code and you will normally find someone suitable.

Most surveyors work by satellite these days and the process is quick and easy. They should provide you with a survey drawing, with all the information that you will need to include on your planning application (ask the people you talk to if this is what they do. If not, use someone else).

If the land is flat, then a measurement survey, a few trial holes and a topographical survey may suffice (*level and layout*), plus some offsite research into the history of the plot.

The cost for a survey can be anywhere from £500 to £3,000 for a single plot, depending on its complexity, however it is more common for it to be towards the lower end of that range than the higher end.

If, after having the survey done, you find problems that were not mentioned in the sales particulars, but which are going to have a significant cost impact, then you have every right to approach the owner, saying: "The development is going to cost a lot more than we expected because of the ground problems, so we are going to have to reduce our offer to take the cost difference in to account".

When this happens, the sellers are more likely to take a lower offer, because you have already been prepared to spend money on the survey, so you are seen as a definite buyer. In any case, if they lose you, the next people who come along and show interest in the plot will probably encounter exactly the same problems and will also probably want to offer the lower price.

Legal evils

In my view, Solicitors and Conveyancers as part of the land buying process, are a necessary evil and are usually a pain in the butt, causing needless stress and anxiety where there often need not be any.

However, unfortunately, the fact remains that they are necessary.

If you were to buy land without using a good quality legal representative, you would be opening yourself up to all sorts of dangers that you just don't even want to think about. You need to be sure that when you buy a plot of land, what you are buying is going to give you the opportunity to build the house you desire at a cost that is reasonable and to allow you one day to sell it, preferably at a decent profit. Therefore, you need to be aware of any and all potential problems before you buy, whether they be legal, planning practical or financial.

Solicitors are notoriously slow at getting conveyancing works done, so don't be afraid of giving them a time target to meet and hassling them regularly to see what progress has been made. Often, they have a high pile of work on their desk and the people who shout the loudest are the people who get brought to the top of the pile!

CHAPTER 5
DESIGNING YOUR NEW HOME

I am going to be a bit controversial (again) and try to dispel another myth that has existed in the self-build industry for many years.

You do not necessarily need to take on a qualified architect. Not as your first action, and possibly not at all.

Ok, now I have upset a lot of fine, professional people, I'd better explain myself!

It may appear from that statement that I have a chip on my shoulders about Architects and possibly designers of all types, I don't, in fact I nearly became an architect, but the 7-year long course put me off.

The problem with architects within the self-build industry is partly to do with the nature of the industry and partly to do with the way they operate within it.

Over the past 20 years, the self-build industry has become far too dependent on Architects as the "main ingredient" needed for any decent self-build project. That is simply not how it should be and not how it needs to be. So, let's start by looking at what an Architect is and what their role is, or should be within a standard self-build project.

What is an architect?

The word architect is widely misunderstood by many self-builders. They think it describes a person who will run the project from beginning to end, finding and surveying the land, designing the house, getting the planning permission, applying for building regulations, organising everything to do with the building process, advising the clients throughout, making sure everything is done and finished properly and to a high quality, taking care of the landscaping design, making sure that the project stays within budget and providing all the required warranties and insurances.

This is not the case (and I think that any decent architect would agree with me there).

To explain this, I need to start at the beginning and break the process down:

- Architects do not normally get involved in the land finding or land purchase process.
- To design a house, you need a house designer, someone who can design a house! You do not necessarily need an architect. What is the difference between an architect and a house designer? Up to £100 / hr sometimes!
- Architects can sometimes get involved in the planning application process if the client so wishes, but often this is something that the client would be able to take on themselves, with just a low level of back up from a designer or architect.
- Architects do not usually prepare the building regulations specifications, they normally work with structural engineers or surveyors who (once the client is happy with the design), they hand their drawings to for them to carry out this work.
- Although architects may offer a project management service, this is rarely a fully comprehensive package. It usually comprises of them taking on a main contractor to carry out all the building works, which they then supervise. The level of this supervision can vary from a once a fortnight visits to site, to a daily input of one

sort or another. It is very rare for an architect, however, to offer a true project management service (of the type that I will be describing in Chapter 8). It is not something they would usually want to get involved in.

- Again, although architects are usually very intelligent, highly trained people, their actual on site experience is often limited. They are therefore not always the best people to ask all the practical and technical questions which come up on site almost from minute to minute. So, for practical site advice, hiring a project manager or a site foreman would possibly be a better option to consider.
- Architects will rarely be on site long enough or often enough to be able to adequately supervise the quality control or safety aspects of the project. A project manager or a site foreman is usually the better option for this sort of work.
- The landscaping design on this sort of project would normally either be done by the client if it is simple, or by a professional landscape designer" / landscape architect rather than the same person who designs the building itself.
- Architects will vary rarely get directly involved in cost control. If this is something that is required because the project is too large and complicated financially for the client to look after it themselves, hiring an accountant or bookkeeper is normally the better option.
- Architects can provide warranties, but make sure that your lender is happy to lend on an architects certificate before you sign anyone up. Some lenders are not keen on architects certificates because of the way they are set up. Standard structural warranties usually have a definite 10 year lifespan, where architects certificates do not always have a specific timescale attached to them. Great! You may think, but there are other loopholes and problems with this type of warranty which sometimes (but not always) mean it is quite difficult to claim against.
- Architects don't usually get involved with sorting out general insurances on a self-build project

In other words:

Architects design buildings. That is what they are good at, that is what they do!

I have a great deal of respect for architects. The good ones can design magnificent, complicated, prestigious buildings that are a credit to their profession. My problem comes when self-builders, who are often tight on funds, automatically assume that the first thing they should do when they consider taking on a project is to go and hire an architect, when in reality they could often look after their own projects or find other more practical and cost effective solutions. I think that architects should be fair and if they don't think the project warranties their level of skill (and cost), then they should recommend other options.

I think I also need to add here that in my role as self-build expert at some of the live shows like "Grand Designs Live" and "The Homebuilding and Renovating Show", one of the most common comments I hear from people who have hired an architect is not about the cost, the main problem is that many architects simply won't let the client have the house they want.

Architects usually have strong ideas on what a design in a particular place should look like and they will sometimes simply overrule a client's wishes, on the basis that they are the experts and the client should listen to them. I have to repeatedly tell self-builders who come to me, after becoming totally frustrated at constantly being told "**No!**", that their architect is employed by them and they, as clients have the right to have their house designed as they wish it to be. They need to remember that when it is all finished, it is going to be their home, not the architect's.

I have been involved in a recent example of this:

A self-builder approached me to ask if I could help him. He had a plot of land with outline planning permission and had hired an architect to prepare the full designs. The client had a very tight budget and wanted a simple, cheap to build design, however his architect had firm ideas about what he thought should be designed for the plot. He came up with a house that was much larger than the client wished, he positioned it in a different position on the site from where the client had wanted it, and faced it in a different direction to where the client wanted it to face.

The client protested but was told that this is how this site should be developed and that if the client wanted this architect to continue working on the project he must see sense and agree with what the architect's was doing.

The planning application went in and was refused, because the planners thought the house was orientated in the wrong direction and was of the wrong style for the location. The architect then appealed the decision (with the client paying the cost) and was turned down again.

This whole process took about 9 months to complete and at the end of it the client was no further forward than when he started, but with a design bill to pay for a few thousand pounds and having had to pay all the planning application costs. He also had a design which, even if it had been granted planning approval, would be too expensive for him to build.

The client called me in after parting company with the architect. I met with him and he told me what had been happening.

My first thoughts on seeing the drawings and the site were to agree with the planners. The plot was elevated and the orientation of the building in the present design had it looking over a fairly tatty back garden and a not very attractive village. If the building was turned anticlockwise by about 45 degrees, it would look straight out on to countryside and a mountain in the distance! I could also see that the house was far too large to be completed within the client's budget.

I quickly knocked up a couple of sketches for what I thought might fit the bill and showed how this new design would sit on the site. The client was elated! This was exactly what he had wanted in the first place. I suggested that a new meeting with the planning officer should be arranged and that I would go along to it with the client.

We went to the meeting and within half an hour the planner was saying to us: "I am going on holiday in 10 weeks, but if you could get that drawn up and in to me in the next 2 weeks, I think I could possibly have it passed before I go away".

Planners are not usually able to be so definite, but on this occasion, he was able to say this because of the fact that an application had already been made and he knew the reasons for refusal, which, as it happens, pretty much all revolved around the architect forcing his opinions (which in this case happed to be wrong) on the client.

This sort of thing does not happen on every project, or even regularly and not all architects will force their opinion on their clients, but it is something that I have encountered so many times over the years that I thought it should be highlighted in this book, so that you, the reader can be aware of the potential problems that could be waiting for you in this area and, once you have finished reading this book, hopefully know how to deal with them.

So who do we need to design our new home and how do we go about actually doing it?

To be fair to the many architects who work within this industry, there is a place for them, their knowledge and their skill set, but there are also other options available which are sometimes more suitable.

Let's start with looking at when it is wise to consider taking on a fully-fledged architect:

- If your project has a build budget of over £400,000.
- If the layout or design is very complicated, on numerous levels, or needs to comply with tight visual restrictions.
- If design flair and originality is more important to you than practicality and design cost.
- If you want lots of realistic 3D renderings of the internal and external aspect of the building and the plot
- If you are happy to incur potentially a significant number of thousands of pounds in design fees.

- If you don't have much confidence and feel that you need someone professional who is going to be with you from start to finish, just to give you the confidence you need to take the project on in the first place.
- If there is no lower cost alternative available to give you what you want and need in the way of design.

In reality, the build cost for the majority of UK self-build projects is significantly under £400,000, so the situation for most potential self-builders is that they need to have their houses designed and they want to try to run their projects as professionally as possible, but they don't have limitless amounts of money to do everything they need to do. They are therefore always looking for the most cost effective ways to do just that.

So, with that in mind, let's start to look at the alternative ways to get your new dream home designed and ready for sending in for planning approval.

Just before we move on, I will just add the following:

- *I would have to say that in fairness there are architects who **do** listen to their clients, who design exactly what they are asked to design and who charge a set fee, agreed up front.*
- *I would advise that you never agree to pay architects fees based on a percentage of the build costs. The RIBA (Royal Institute of British architects) allow this, but is a payment system weighted heavily against the client.*
- *The RIBA encourages architects to keep the copyright to their designs, even if the design is wholly the clients design. – No good if you want to have control of your own design, especially if, for whatever reason, you and your architect go your separate ways before you get to build the house.*

As we go in to the design processes in this chapter, don't get confused between planning permission and building regulations. They are completely different things, dealt with by completely different departments of the Local Authority, or even by independent companies.

*I will be covering them both in more detail in Chapter 6, but for now we are just looking at the design of the house itself. Just always remember that planning permission is mainly to do with how a house looks and the visual and practical impact it has on its surroundings. In other words, **"What does it look like?"** Building Regulations is all about **"Will it stand up?"***

In an earlier chapter, I quoted one of my sayings along the lines of:

"If you draw me a house layout on the back of a fag packet, I could go and build it for you"

House design and building houses can be and actually should be fairly simple.

I have worked on many commercial building projects over my career that would not be classed as simple, but wherever possible, if we want to build our new homes cost effectively, quickly and efficiently, we should keep everything as simple as possible. Especially in these days of the increasing importance of eco Building and low carbon footprints, as pretty much a standard requirement for all new building works.

Another of my sayings is:

"Self-build is simple - People make it complicated"

When it comes to building a house, there are standard, low cost ways to do it. Whether we choose to build in brick and block, timber frame, straw bale or whatever other method we may choose, there are a number of building methods that all builders naturally tend to adopt and that designers tend to design to.

Some of these methods are statutory, some flexible and they will all be affected by personal choice, site conditions, location and budget.

Here are a few of the standard features of a house build that will automatically be taken in to account by the designer when creating a house design:

- Basic, standard foundation trenches are 900mm deep, 600mm wide and the foundation of the house is usually a strip footing of concrete 225mm thick. That's it! Unless there are other influencing factors, that's your foundation sorted!
- Floor slabs are normally concrete on top of a damp-proof membrane (plastic sheet) on top of insulation, which lies on top of hardcore.
- External walls in the UK are usually cavity walls of made up of brick (or block and render) on the outside, a cavity and either block / insulation, or an insulated timber panel of some description on the inside. The internal face of the wall will then be finished with a plaster or dry lined finish.
  There is now another up and coming option where we do away with the cavities and have a single skin external wall (this is how many German and Scandinavian houses are built). Either way the wall construction is both fairly simple and standard.
- Ceiling heights are normally 2.4m or 2.44m (8').
- Floor joists are normally made of planks of timber (or one of a couple of choices of a timber or timber and steel based alternative). The planks vary in length and thickness depending on how wide the distance is that they have to span. There are standard tables to tell you what joists you need for what spans.
- Roof construction in the UK normally utilises standard prefabricated roof trusses. These are designed by the manufacturer from layout drawings sent to them. They bring them to site and joiners normally put them together. The roof is then covered with felt, batten and tiles.
- Windows and doors come in standard sizes, or you can have them made bespoke, so you just order the window and doors that match the drawings.

There, you now have a house!

Ok, that is getting a bit simplistic, but what I am saying here is that you don't usually need 7 years of training and the letters "RIBA" after your name to be able to design and build a simple house!

So, what are your other options if you don't use an Architect?

You can design *your* *own* home.

What? I hear many of you gasp!

Basically, if you can use (or learn to use) a scale rule and you get yourself some A3 paper, or if you download "Google Sketch-Up", you can usually design a simple house layout yourself. It *really is* that easy. However, you probably won't be able to prepare drawings that are good enough to put in as part of your planning application.

Later in this chapter I will be showing you how to design a simple house, accurately and sensibly, to scale, in sketch form. If you then feel confident enough to have a go at designing the initial layout of your own new home, when the time is right, you could end up saving yourself a lot of time and money.

What I won't be trying to in this book is to suggest that you then go on to produce a full set of detailed drawings. If this is all new to you, you are still going to need some professional design assistance to complete that part of the design process. So, given that there will still be work to do, what you will then need is to find someone who (preferably) lives fairly locally to you who, for a reasonable fee, can turn your initial sketch ideas into something that can be used for the preparation of both the planning permission and building regulations applications, plus the site working drawings and the tender documents.

Here's how I would go about finding and choosing the right person:

Simple houses

If the house is a simple 3, 4 or 5 bed detached house on a simple plot, someone like a design technician should be ideally suited to the task. These are normally people who are not fully qualified as architects and they may not have the artistic design flair that rchitects have, but they will usually work in the building design industry, either in housing or in commercial construction. They will normally be fully computer design literate and will be able to knock up most house design drawings without any problem and would be able to produce everything that you need for your planning application.

Quite often you will find such people in the classified ads columns of your local paper under headings like "*House Plans Drawn*". Sometimes the people you come across will be semi-retired or even retired and they just offer this service to keep busy and keep their hand in.

One benefit you will often find by using these types of people will be that not only are they perfectly capable of understanding your wishes and converting them into professional drawings, they will also work in a far more relaxed manner and usually be more receptive to listening to your ideas rather than forcing their own on to you.

You can expect these sorts of people to charge anything between £15 to £50 per hr, which could be up to £100+ cheaper per hr than using an architect to do the same thing. Often a full set of planning drawings, taken from your initial sketches could cost you as little as £400 - £500 (depending on where you are located in the UK).

More complicated but not highly technically demanding design work

If your design is likely to be a bit more complicated, you may wish to move up the design chain a bit and go for someone like an architectural technician. These people tend to be more qualified than the design technicians, will often be working on more complex projects and may have completed some sort of formal house design training. You will often find these people working either full time from home or as part of a specialist design company.

Architectural technicians tend to be significantly more expensive than the (often) part time "House plans drawn" guys, but they are not usually set up in the elaborate manner that fully qualified architects often are, so will normally be significantly cheaper than them, coming in at somewhere around £35 - £75 per hr.

How to design your home

We are now going to look at simple ways to design a house.

If you can use what you learn here to enable you to knock up a few sketches of what you would like with respect to the external shape and the room layouts of your house, you will then be able to take those sketches to your chosen designer to turn into fully detailed drawings. If you manage to do so, the benefits to you, your wallet and your project could be significant:

- You will be able to control the design process to make sure you get what you want and not what is forced in you by a pushy designer.
- You can build in any quirky bits you like without first having to explain your ideas to someone else.
- You will normally get these sketches done far faster than a designer, so you will save valuable time on the project as a whole.
- You will almost certainly save money, often a considerable amount of money!
- You will have the feeling that you are really self-building. What better way to create your own home than by starting with a blank piece of paper (or computer screen) in front of you and coming up with your own unique design?
- Your designer will be able to complete his part of the process faster (and at lower cost) because he/she doesn't need to spend weeks sending ideas and sketches through to you for approval before they can move

on with the design. Good designers (who are not just after making as much money as they can out of you) usually prefer it if you can bring some initial design ideas to the table, because doing so saves them having to question you at length and/or guess what you are hoping to achieve.

VERY IMPORTANT

Before we start looking at the house design itself, I think it is very important that you are aware of some basic rules of design.

Knowing these rules could help you to create a simple but efficient and very cost effective house to build. Once you know these rules you will be able to use or ignore them as you wish, but it is important that you know them in the first place.

I use these rules in every design I draw up and whenever those designs are converted in to real buildings, I regularly achieve very low build costs.

I am hoping that you will be able to do the same.

Look at the 2 simple shapes below and imagine they are the basic shape of a house.

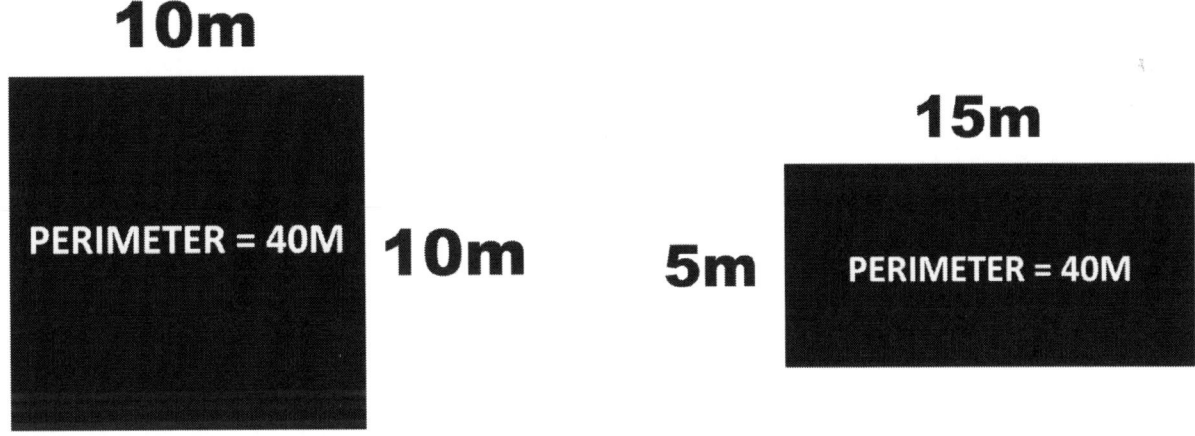

You will notice that both of the shapes have a perimeter of 40 metres. That would mean that to build either of the 2 designs you would need to build 40 metres of external walls. In simple terms, that would suggest that the cost to build either simple shape would be about the same.

Now look at the difference in the floor area they enclose:

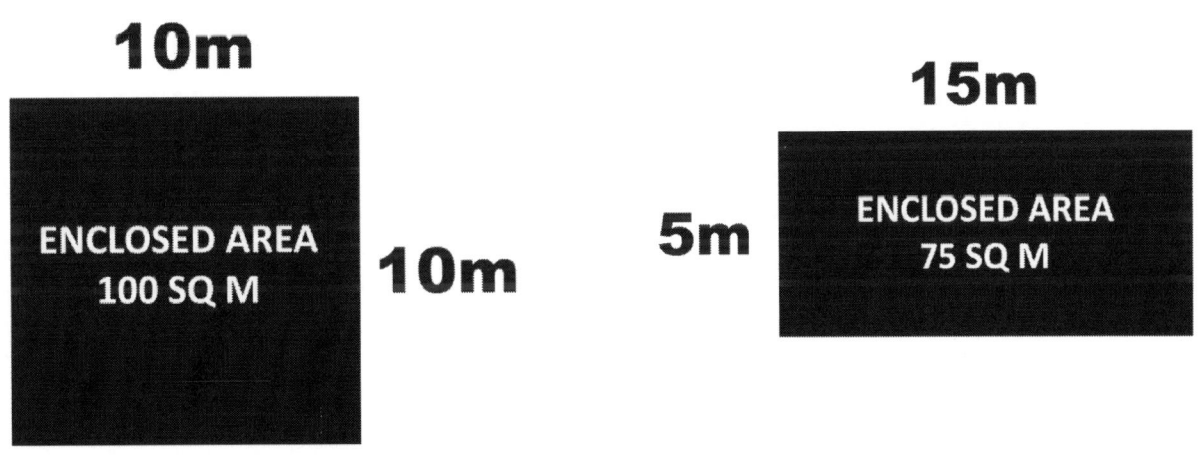

The square shape encloses 100 sq m, whilst the rectangular shape only encloses 75 sq m. In other words, the rectangular shape encloses 25 sq m less floor area than the square shape, for basically the same build cost. Over 2 floors that would equate to **50 sq m** of floor area difference between the two buildings **for about the same build cost!**

What does that mean to you living in the house?

50 sq m would equate to you getting 4 good sized rooms more in the square shape than in the rectangular shape,

FREE OF CHARGE.

Not only would you get the extra rooms free of charge, but by having all that extra accommodation within the building, you would also increase its completed value up to 35%.

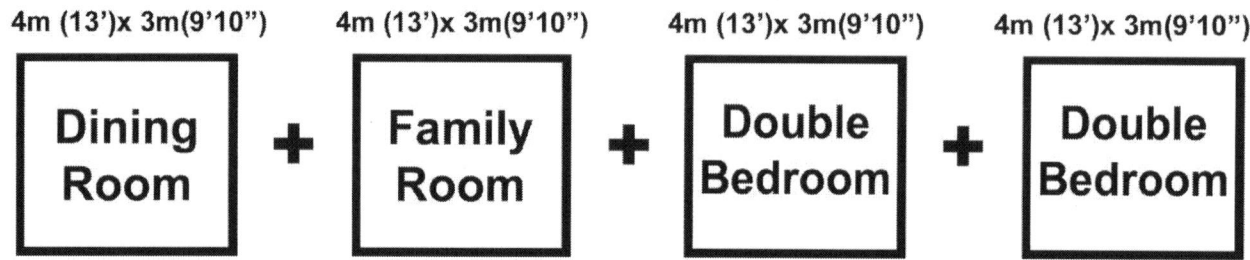

RULE 1

"SQUARE IS THE MOST EFFICIENT SHAPE TO BUILD. ANY VARIATION FROM A SQUARE WILL REDUCE THE EFFICIENCY OF THE DESIGN"

From this simple example, you now already know that if you design your house based on a square shape, you are creating a property that gives you the most efficient use of the space inside the external walls.

I am not saying you should always build square houses, but armed with this little piece of knowledge, if your budget is fairly tight (which is the case for most self-builders), you are now in a position to design your new home to give you the maximum possible floor area for every pound you spend.

Your plot size, shape and contours may force you to vary the design from the basic square shape, but, no matter how far you are forced to move away from the square shape, you will now still probably find yourselves trying to follow the <u>general principal</u> of what you have just learned, as closely as possible.

Now look at the two shapes on the next page:

(*The second shape is popular with self-builders*):

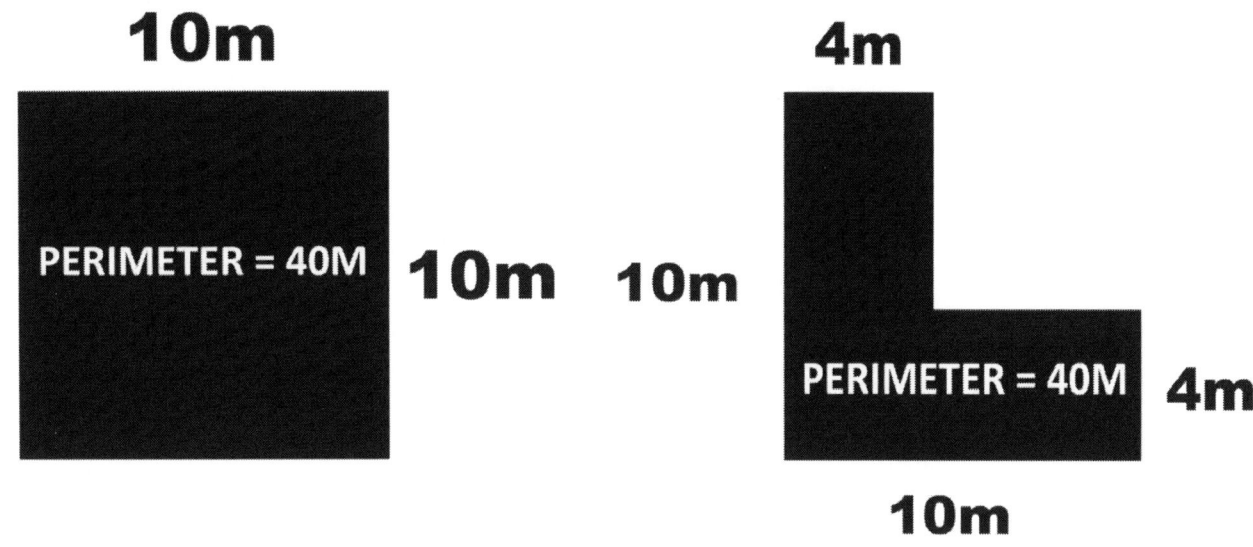

Both shapes still have the 40m perimeter, but by taking the corner out of the second shape, look at the effect on the floor area:

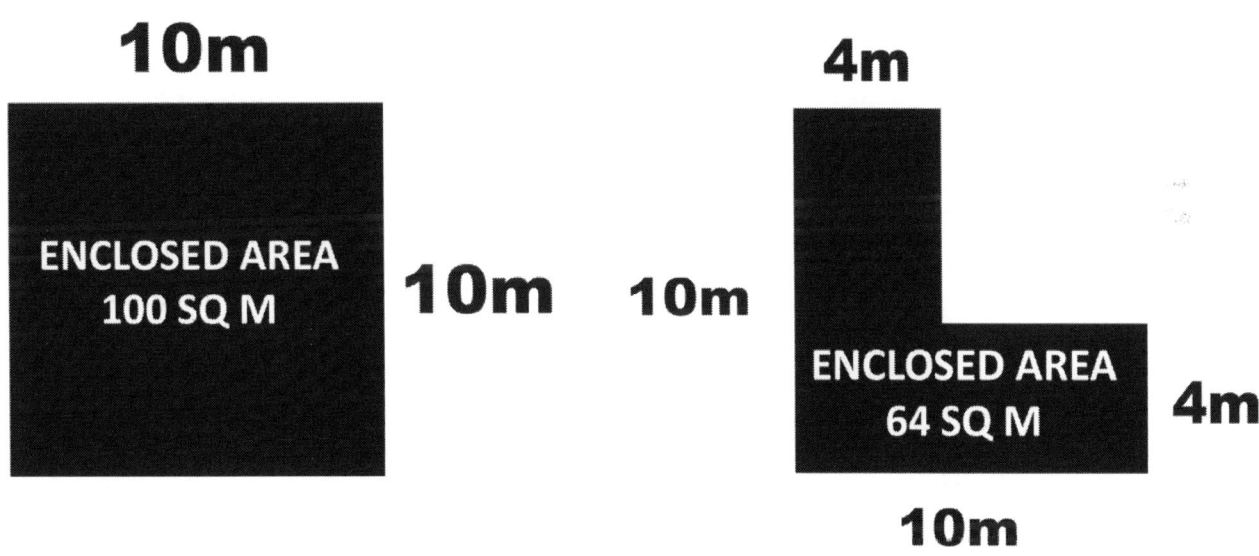

The square shape now has 36 sq m more enclosed space than the "L" shape.

By adding just 2 corners to the basic square shape, you have reduced the enclosed area by even more than in the first example.
You have now lost 72 sq m of internal room space over 2 floors.
That equates to 6 good sized rooms:

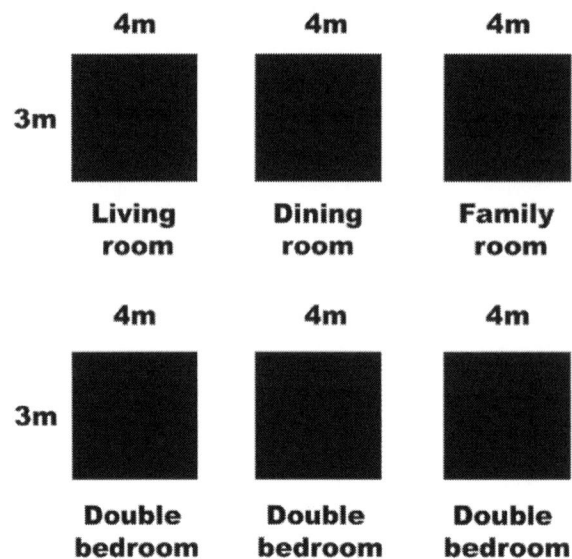

Those extra rooms could increase the value of your home by up to 50%, so:

RULE 2: CORNERS ADD COST
The effects of the design on the roof shape, usefulness and cost:

By adding corners and moving away from a basic square shape, you also bring other "knock-on" effects into play. Look at the two roof shapes of these two images:

This design shows a very simple "up and down" roof. It will be simple and cheap to manufacture, quick and cheap to install and will give you the option of opening up the roof space for another living area, containing possibly 2 extra bedrooms and an extra bathroom, for minimal extra cost (due to the roof structure and covering already being budgeted for). This potential extra living space could further increase the value of the completed property over and above the figures already suggested above.

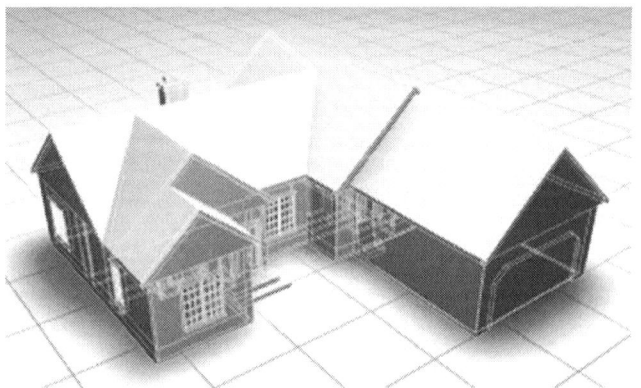

This design, because of the complicated floor plan, will have a very complicated roof which be expensive to manufacture, slow and expensive to install and will not have much potential of using the roof space to create extra low cost accommodation.

The effects of the design on the foundations

Compare these two designs:

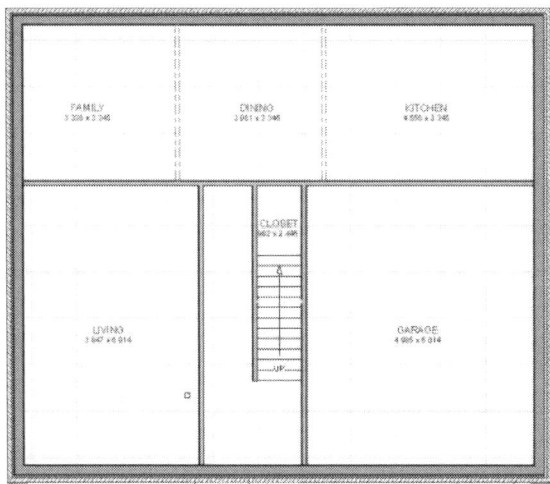

*(**Note:** I have purposely exaggerated the irregularity of the second shape to make a point. It would be fairly uncommon to find such a convoluted shape for a house design, but this sort of thing does exist).*

The foundations for the simply designed house could be set out and dug out in a morning and the foundation concrete poured in the afternoon. The cost to construct these foundations would be about as low as it would be possible to achieve with any design. Any problems found underground would be minimised due to the minimal intrusiveness of the foundations in to the ground.

The foundations shown in the complicated design would take probably five to six times as long to excavate and pour as the first design.

If the ground workers encountered any problems, this time could easily double, creating significant extra cost and knocking the build programme back by weeks.

Further minimise foundations: *Just a quick but important note about load bearing / non loadbearing walls:*

If you have a timber wall that is not carrying any load (i.e. no floor boards above or load from the roof), it generally does not need to have a foundation underneath it. Knowing this fact and making sure your designer is aware of it could save you a lot of time and money in the construction of your foundations, especially if you hit problems in the ground.

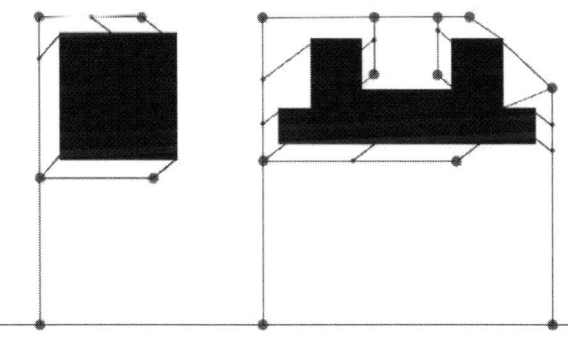

The effects of the design on the drainage:

Here are two house designs with the drainage layout shown, one simple and one complicated:

The simple drainage design on the left will be much faster, cheaper and easier to install than the complicated design on the right. The drain routes will also be less prone to encountering obstructions or other problems underground.

The effects of the design on the scaffolding:

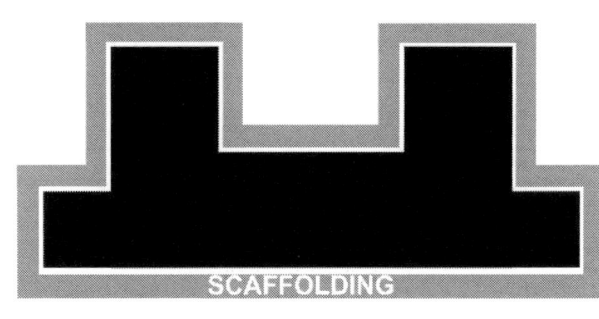

The two shapes above both have the same floor area.
The grey areas around the two shapes above represent the scaffolding required.
When you hire scaffolding, the quote normally includes the erection, the dismantling and a six week hire period.
After the first six weeks, you usually have to pay an extra hire fee for each week it remains on site.
I calculated the amount of scaffolding needed for the two jobs and estimated the length of time it would be required on site.

According to my estimates:

- The complicated design would need around **1.5 times** the physical amount of scaffold compared to the simple design.
- Based on figures given to me by a local scaffolder, the cost for each scaffold for the initial six-week hire would be:
    - Around £5500 for the simple design
    - Around £8500 for the complicated design
- The complicated design would need scaffold for possibly 6 months or more in total, compared to 4 months for the simple design.
- The cost per week after the first six weeks would be around £200 for the simple design and £300 for the complicated design.

The total cost for scaffolding for the two designs (if everything goes to plan on both) would be around £9500 for the simple design and around £14,500 for the complicated design.

I won't take this process any further. I think I have made my point that the further you drift away from a basic square shape and the more complicated you make the design, the higher your build costs will be and the differences in those build costs could mean the difference between your project succeeding or failing, either because you ran out of money during the project, or because you realised that you could not afford to start it in the first place.

OK, let's do some house designing

The first thing I always recommend that you do when starting to design a house is to get some ideas together of the sort of thing you are hoping to come up with at the end of the process, in terms of size, shape, style, number of bedrooms, room sizes, external finishes etc.

It can be a real advantage to the design process if, when you are sitting down to design your own home, you already have some sort of picture in your mind of something that has appealed to you. This could be a developer's house, a design you have seen in a magazine, on a TV programme, in a book of house plans, on the internet, anywhere really, just something to set you off in the right direction.

You might not realise it, but if you have read this book from page 1, you are probably now significantly better equipped to set about designing you own home than you were before you picked the book up.

Do we design on paper on or the computer?

Either. If you have a drawing board and technical drawing equipment, there is nothing stopping you from doing the whole thing on paper if you don't have, or don't understand how computer design packages work.

The only downside with designing on paper is that, these days you will usually need to be using e mail to send contract information, including the drawings around to various people, so if you don't design on the computer you will probably need to be able to scan your finished drawings in to the computer, which may require you to buy an A3 scanner (from £50+ on Amazon), or you can pay to have it scanned.

If you want to use the computer for the design work, you will need to choose a suitable package. As I said earlier, Google Sketchup is one of a number of either free or low-cost aids that could be ideal to assist you to design your first house.

Your choice between paper or computer will normally just come down to how computer literate you are. I tend to use both. I have a computer package and have taught myself how to use it, however, although I can knock a house plan up in no time, I am not too good when it comes to working with the landscaping tools. So, I tend to use my computer for the design of the actual building (because it is the fastest and most accurate way of doing it), then print that out and put it on my drawing board to add all the landscaping details. I then scan it back in to the computer to add all the required text using Photoshop. That may sound complicated but it works for me, an enthusiastic amateur!

I am going to start by designing your home on paper. The reason for this is that by understanding a bit more about the process of designing a house on paper, you might find it easier to use the software packages.

Equipment

You will need to get the following equipment together *(most decent stationery retailers will stock most of these items)*:

- An A3 pad of tracing type paper (so you can see through from page to page and easily copy a layout from one page to another).
- A scale rule (at least 30cm long).
- A set square about 10" or 12" in size.
- A hard pencil (3H or 4H).
- A good quality rubber.
- Good quality ink drawing pens with the following gauge nibs: 0.1 / 0.3 / 0.5 (DO *NOT use a biro as they tend to blot*).
- An A3 drawing board (Amazon do some good value drawing boards).
- Compasses (small and large).
- Stencils with letters and numbers (about 4mm high for lower case and 6mm high for upper case).

Have a few practices with this equipment before you start to try to work on any designs, just get the hang of how the set square works and get to know how to use the scale rule enough so that you get the measurements right on the drawings, at least *most* of the time!

For a standard house plan you will normally use a 1:50 scale. This should allow a decent sized house to fit on to an A3 sheet of paper.

Use the pencils for everything you draw until you are 100% happy with the design. Once you ink it in it is hard to make amendments and when you do they tend to make the drawing look a bit tatty. If you do make a mistake when inking, use a razor blade or a Stanley knife blade to gently and carefully scratch the ink away, then rub over the area with the rubber to re-smooth the surface. If you redraw over this area, the ink will tend to run into the scratches you have made with the blade.

If you are going to be drawing on paper, I suggest that after you have read the next section (which takes you through designing a house), you then have a go at drawing something similar on your A3 paper. This will give you a bit of practice before you start to work on your own designs.

Getting started:

By the time you design your house, you should already either have bought your plot or be in the process of buying it. There is no benefit in designing a house if you don't know what sort of plot it is going to sit on. If you design the house before you have identified the building plot, the chances are you'll end up "binning" your first design and starting again when you do actually find the plot.

We will start by thinking about the plot: For this exercise, we will assume that we have a simple flat plot measuring 20m across by 30m deep.

When you choose where to situate a house on a building plot you need to take account of everything around you; the shape of the plot, access, orientation (south / east / north / west), drainage, neighbours, slopes, hazards and anything else that could potentially affect either the build or the way you can use the finished house. You don't want to be staring in to neighbours living room windows. You might like privacy, you might have to work to a building line, the site might be sloping or a drain may be running through it. At this stage it is good to make yourself aware of everything there is to know about your plot.

We will assume, for this example that there are no particular problems to worry about.

When you think about the position of the house, you need to consider access to and around it, so it is usual to position it with at least a 3-foot footpath down either side. You may want to include a long driveway down the side of the house to give access to the back garden, or maybe your drive will all be at the front of the house.

The next diagram shows a sensible position for a house on our simple flat plot (*the final position of your building will, usually at least depend on those obstructions and other surrounding features as mentioned above*).

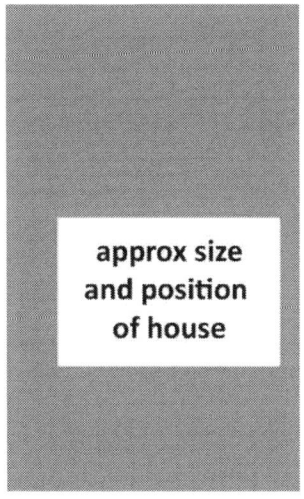

At 20m wide this plot is of a fairly generous size and we have no obstructions hindering the position on site, so I have decided to opt for a side driveway to the left at 3m wide and I will also allow for the path on the right to be 1.2m wide. This leaves us with a maximum width for the house of 15.8m

To get things going, I have started with assuming that the house will be around 9m deep (*this can change as required later*) and the front wall will sit around 7m back from the front boundary (*so we can park a car in front of the house if we want to*). If this works ok we would then be left with around a 14m deep back garden which is ok, not huge, but ok.

So now, just by using the plot itself to guide our first decisions on the design, we have come up with our first ideas for what sort of house we should be able to build.

You will probably notice that the measurements I have chosen for this sample house are not going to give us a square shaped house, so at the moment, this is not going to be the most efficient and cost effective house to build. However, as long as I am aware of that, I can either bring the shape back towards being a square as I continue with the design, or I can accept that for this site, this shape is the best option. It might cost a bit more to build per square foot, but at least I am aware of that fact as I move forward and I am still in control of trying to include as many of the other cost saving design features as possible.

Now we can start working on the house itself.

We have initially come up with a simple house template measuring 15.8m wide (max) and 9m deep (approx). That would give us a house with a footprint (*overall building area, measuring externally*) of 142.2 sq m and an *internal* floor area of somewhere around 128 sq m per floor, or 256 sq m (2750 sq ft) over 2 floors (*as a comparison, bog standard developers 4 bed detached houses usually come in at about 1100 sq ft in total over the 2 floors*). In other words, we can fit a pretty decent sized house on this plot as long as there is nothing on, or around the site that would significantly restrict the design.

What do we need from the house?

You now need to consider your requirements from the finished design in terms of room types and sizes.

I suggest that you start by listing all the rooms you are hoping to include, together with ideal sizes for each room. You should already have gathered some information together during your preparatory research to help you to prepare this list.

I will go with a 4 bed, 2 bath design incorporating the following rooms and approximate ideal sizes:

Room	Size
Living room	6m x 4m
Dining room	4m x 4m
Family room	3m x 4m
Kitchen	5m x 3.5m
Utility room	3m x 1.5m
Hall	To suit
W.C	1m x 2m
Bed 1	5m x 4m
Bed 2	3m x 4m
Bed 2	3m x 4m
Bed 4	3m x 3m
Bathroom	3m x 2.5m
En-Suite	To suit
Garage	6.5m x 3.5m

Starting to draw:

There are guide measurements and sizes for a number of the items that go into a house design that are fairly standard across the industry. Although none are them is hard and fast rule, you should know a few of them if you want your design sketches to be accurate and usable by a designer later on, when it is time to draw up your planning permission drawings.

When you are drawing to a small scale (*which you will be if you use 1:50 as suggested earlier*), you won't be able to be totally accurate with your measurements, but just do your best. As long as your drawings make sense and are at least reasonably accurate, your designer will be able to use them later on to prepare your planning permission drawings for submission.

The sizes and measurements listed below are not necessarily standard, or used in every house design by every designer, but they will be fine for what we are doing here.

They include:

Wall thickness: External walls 300mm / Internal walls 100mm
External door opening widths: 900mm wide (for disability access)
Internal door opening widths: 800mm standard, 900mm for disability access (*I suggest making all internal doors at least 900mm wide, they look better and are more practical*).
Straight stairs: 2.70m long, minimum 850mm wide (I tend to go for wider stairs, they look grander!).
Hallways / landings: Minimum 900mm wide
Kitchen worktops: 600mm wide
Baths: 1700mm long x 700mm wide
Sinks: 500mm wide x 400mm deep
Toilets: 600mm deep x 450mm wide
Shower enclosures: 750mm x 750mm / 800mm x 800mm / 900mm x 900mm / 1200 x any of the other widths.
Windows: Lintel height 2.1m above finished floor level. Standard window widths: 630mm / 1050mm / 1200mm / 1350mm / 1500mm / 1800mm / 2100mm / 2336mm. – Standard window heights: 900mm / 1050mm / 1200mm / 1350mm
French doors / Patio doors: Lintel height 2.1m x Standard widths: 1500mm / 1800mm / 2400mm.

Probably the most important measurements from those listed above will be the wall thicknesses. I would say that 9 out of 10 of sketch drawings that potential self-builders bring for me to look at

during the shows and as clients, show just a single line for each of the walls of the house. Without a wall width, and without it being drawn to scale, any sketch drawn this way is useless. What happens, pretty much without fail, is that as I start to look at any layouts drawn without wall widths, I can see that they simply wouldn't work practically.

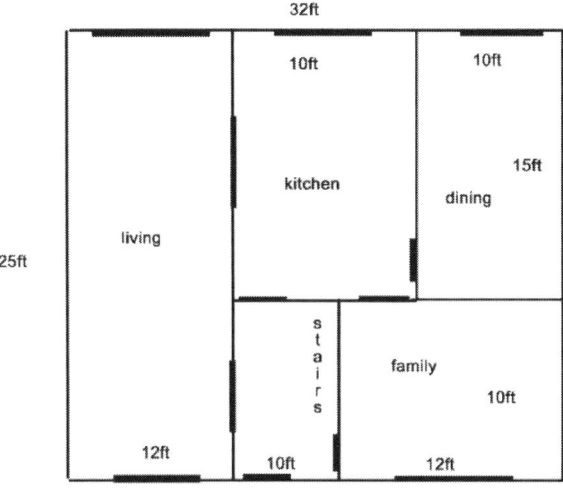

Here is a typical sketch house design as it is often presented to me by potential self-builders who have never done any technical drawing before (see if you can spot the errors):

Errors:

I. The width of the house is 32', but if you add the widths of the living room, dining room and kitchen together, they total 32', so there is no room for the 2'8" of external and internal wall thicknesses.
II. The same applies if you add up the measurements for the living room, the hall and the family room.
III. The dining room is 10' wide (plus a 4" internal wall). The family room is 12' wide. A door is shown between the family room and the kitchen, but in reality, there is only 1'8" of space to fit it in to (doors need to be around 3' wide).
IV. If the living room and family room are both 12' wide, when you allow for the wall widths, the hall can only be 7'4" wide. This would make this area very long, narrow and dark towards the kitchen door.
V. The family room is 10' wide. There is a door shown from the hall in to the family room. This needs to be 3' wide, leaving 7' of hall wall for the stairs to sit against. Straight stairs usually need to be a minimum of 2.7m (9') long, so they would not fit here.
VI. The living room is out of proportion. It is like a corridor. It either needs to be shorter or wider.
VII. There is no back door, utility room or downstairs w.c.
VIII. The front door is not centred on the front of the house, so could make the design look a bit unbalanced.

You can probably now appreciate the importance of both drawing to scale and of including wall widths in all your sketches, so I think we are ready to put pencil to paper.

Designing a house:

For every new design I create, I start by drawing a basic shape for the building.

We will use the building measurements that we derived from the plot size (15.8m wide x 9m deep). The squares you can see in the background of each drawing represent 1 sq metre.

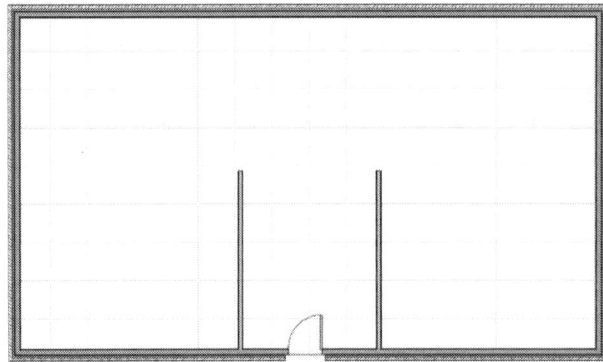

Firstly, I position the front door where I would like it to go. Let's say that it is going to go front centre (so the appearance of the front of the house, will be, at least fairly symmetrical and balanced.

By positioning the front door, I naturally locate the hallway *(the front door more often than not opens into a hallway)*.

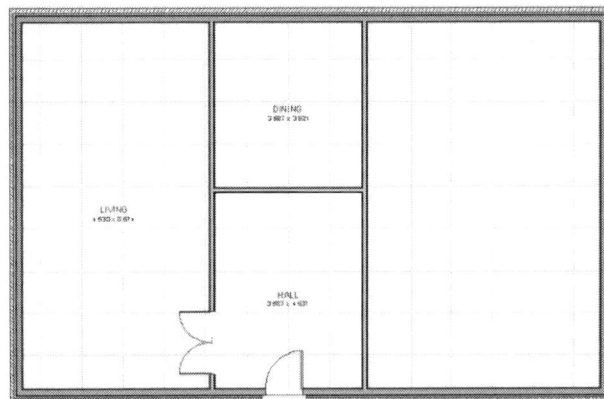

I have shown the front door and hallway walls on the first image. As there is plenty of room to play with, I have made the hall about 3.5m wide for now.

Next, I decided to position the living room next to the hall and to its left. The ideal room size list has this room as being about 6m x 4m, but at the moment, with the house shape I have, I have nearly 6m of width available which might actually make it a bit *too* wide, so for now I have made it about 4.3m *(to do this, I have brought the left side external wall in a bit)*.

The depth of the house makes this room around 8.4m long. Although this is quite long, I am ok with it at the moment. We will see what happens as we go along with the rest of the layout.

In larger houses, it is always good to have a living room next to a dining room if possible (for entertaining), so next I have drawn the dining room at the rear of the house behind the hall.

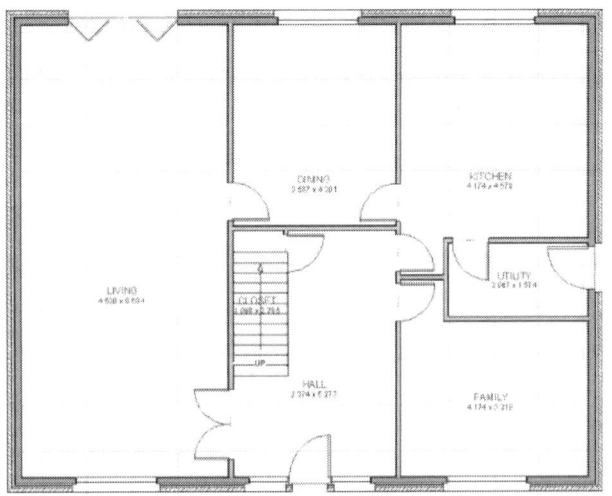

What I have designed so far has left me with an area to the right hand side of the plan into which I need to fit the remaining main ground floor rooms *(kitchen / utility room / family room)*, so I now drop them in to this space, with the utility next to the kitchen, a door out from it to the garden and the family room next to the hall at the front of the house.

These rooms, like the living room, seem a bit wide to me, so I bring the right side external wall in a bit. This is now starting to bring the house in to more of a square shape than it was originally.

I am now only left with the W.C and the staircase to position. The hall is always a good place for the W.C (*as it is normally fairly central*) and is the obvious place for the stairs, so I put the stairs on the left side of the hall and tuck the W.C underneath the staircase.

That is all the downstairs rooms and the stairs in place, but I now need to check that I am happy with the room sizes before I move on. If I want to change anything I can now simply juggle with the wall positions until I come up with the layout and room sizes that I am happy with.

This will then give me the completed ground floor layout.

All the rooms are of good sizes, are in good positions with the dining room next to the kitchen *and* the living room (*good for entertai*ning). The family room is away from the living room (*so different types of activities in these rooms should not affect each other*).

Now that I have something that I am fairly happy with for the ground floor, I will copy the external walls to a new, otherwise blank plan to start designing the first floor. The only other thing I need to show on the first floor plan is the staircase, so that gets drawn first.

I decide to put a bedroom to the left of the stairs so I need to show a wall going up to divide the stairs from the bedroom.

The bedroom would need a door, so I put one in, starting from the top of the stairs.

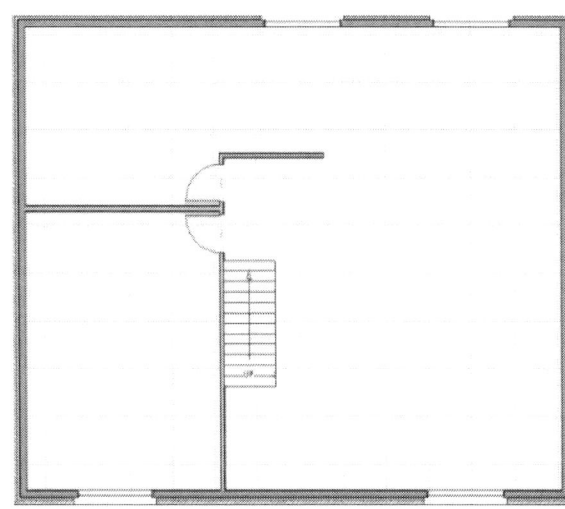

This made a good sized bedroom to the front left of the plan, so I then placed a wall to separate that bedroom from the remaining space to the rear of the plan.

This gave me two rooms on the left side of the building, the second room would probably now become another bedroom.

That second bedroom needs a door too, so I drew that coming off the landing next to the door for the first bedroom.

I finished this phase of the plan off by placing another wall to form what would be the landing and a smaller room at the back centre of the house. I will decide what room this is shortly.

Next, I formed the other landing wall running parallel with the right side of the staircase, making sure I was giving a decent amount of width to walk past the stairwell (about 1.0m – 1.2m is fine).

By extending this wall both to the front and the rear wall of the house, it naturally formed a second wall for the smaller room as well as the remaining bedroom walls.

Because of its size and where it is within the plan, at the moment the smaller room seems destined to be a bathroom.

The wish list is now just for 2 more bedrooms and an en-suite to the main bedroom.

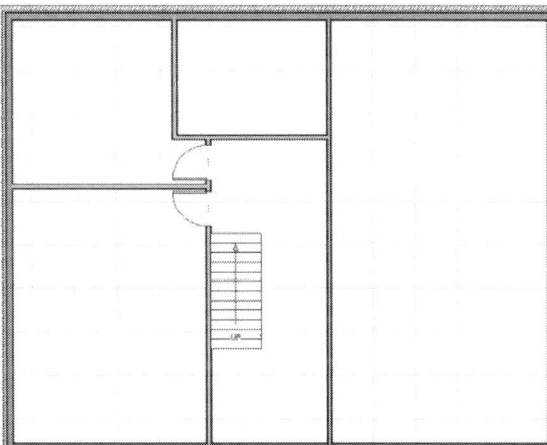

The obvious place for the En-suite to the main bedroom would be at the front centre where there is a bathroom sized space just waiting to be filled! I will consider making a feature window to this room as it is top front centre of the house. Maybe an arched or leaded window would look nice here.

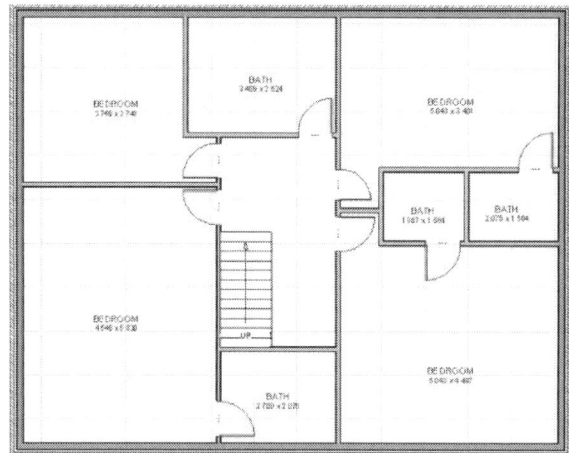

When I put a wall into the remaining area on the right-hand side of the plan, the last 2 bedrooms appeared. They seemed quite large, so I decided to add an extra couple of En-suite bathrooms between the two bedrooms (*if I were designing this house for a client I would simply show them these rooms and give them the chance to keep them or remove them*).

I added doors to each of the remaining rooms and that left us pretty much done!

I have not at this stage drawn in any windows. I normally do this once I have drawn the elevations so that I can draw each side of the building and see what the windows and other features will make the outside look like as I go along. This is something we are not going to do here because it would make things too complicated at this stage.

If you are designing on a computer software package, as you design the software will normally be working out all the room heights as you go along, this makes producing elevations extremely simple.

If you find that you are able to produce elevations, you might also be able to work out how to draw in all your windows and doors, which would be even more useful when the time comes for you to take your ideas to your designer, but for this exercise we have gone as far as we need to.

So, there it is! – We now have a perfectly respectable house design including all the rooms we had hoped to get in to it and they are all pretty good sizes too.

From this point I would normally leave the design for at least a few hours then come back to it and see if I can notice anything I don't like. If so, I simple play about with the drawing until I am happy.

Remember this:

When designing your own home, there is no real right or wrong.
It is all down to your own personal choice, what will suit the plot and what you can afford.

Your own house will probably end up looking very different from the layout I have come up with here, but what I am trying to show you with this example is that if you start at beginning and work sensibly and methodically, one room at a time, after a bit of practice you should be able to come up with a decent enough layout that suits what you want and need from your new home and that you could at least take with you to show a designer, who would then be able to find any errors and fix them. The design could then be drawn up professionally, ready for a planning permission submission.

By you doing for your own project what I have just done in this example, you could save yourselves weeks of time and potentially thousands of pounds in design costs (depending on whom you use as your designer).

Homework!

Having now read through how to come up with a design for a house, I suggest that you spend some time either on the computer or on the drawing board, having a go at coming up with your own designs. As you do so, you will find yourself understanding more of how the design process works. Try different shapes: square, long and narrow, narrow but deep and even try a shape with a couple of corners in it.

Every new design you come up with will help towards making sure that when you do this for real, you'll stand the best chance of getting what you want, what you need and what you can afford.

Now I have a basic design, can I work out an accurate build cost yet?

Nope! I am afraid not. You'll need to wait until we get to Chapter 9 before you are going to get anything like accurate build costs. For now, you are going to have to stick with the best guess figures we pulled together earlier in the book.

The good news is that if you have taken on board what I have been saying throughout this book so far, the chances are that you are going to be building your new home for considerably less money than you would have done had you not picked the book up in the first place.

Twice as big doesn't mean twice as expensive!

The final bit of "technical" advice I want to cover in this chapter is the way build costs rise with increased building size.

Most self-builders (and indeed most builders) seem to work on a "straight line graph" when it comes to build costs. It doesn't take much thinking about to say that: "If the building is twice as big it will cost twice as much", but in fact that is not the case.

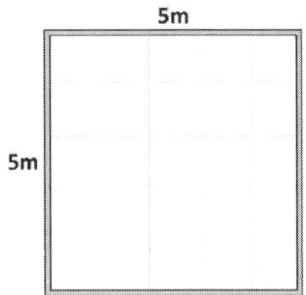
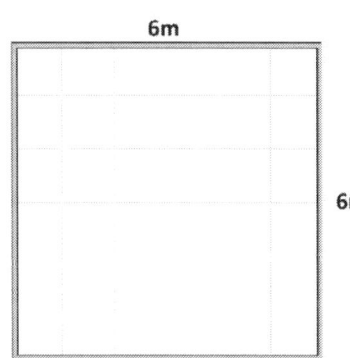

To the left are two examples of the same shape, one larger than the other.

Assume, for this example that the shapes represent a completely open plan basic house design:

Start with the first plan:
It has a floor area of 25 sq m

It has 20m of walls surrounding it.
Say the room is 2.5m high
Say each square metre of wall costs £100 to build.
The cost to construct the walls for the first plan to a height of 2.5m is £5,000.
That equates to **£200** of wall cost for each sq m of floor area (£5000 divided by 25).

Now take the second plan:
It has a floor area of 36 sq m
It has 24m of walls around it
Say the room is 2.5m high
Say each square metre of wall costs £100
The cost to construct the walls in that room is £6000
That equates to **£166.66** of wall cost for each sq m of floor area (6000 divided by 36)
If the walls had cost the same to build per square metre in both examples, the second plan would have cost £2880, whereas, in fact it only costs £2400.

*If I take this same example a stage further and use a floor plan that has sides of 10m, the total cost of the walls would be **£10,000** and the wall cost for each square metre of floor area would reduce to just **£100**, or **half** the cost when compared to the first example.*

How does that work?

When you increase the floor area to twice the size, you do not necessarily increase the amount of materials used by 2. That is because (especially if you are using an efficient design shape like a square) you are basically just enclosing a lot more air within the shape.

In reality, as is shown by the example above, you only need to use a fairly small amount of extra building material to do so. It just comes down to maths!

This might make you pull a confused face as you try to work out why that happens. It just does and it is something that you can take advantage of now that you know about it!

In the real world what this means is that if you just make a room or a house bigger by moving a wall that already exists on the plan, it does not necessarily have to have a major impact on the build cost. Knowing this fact could

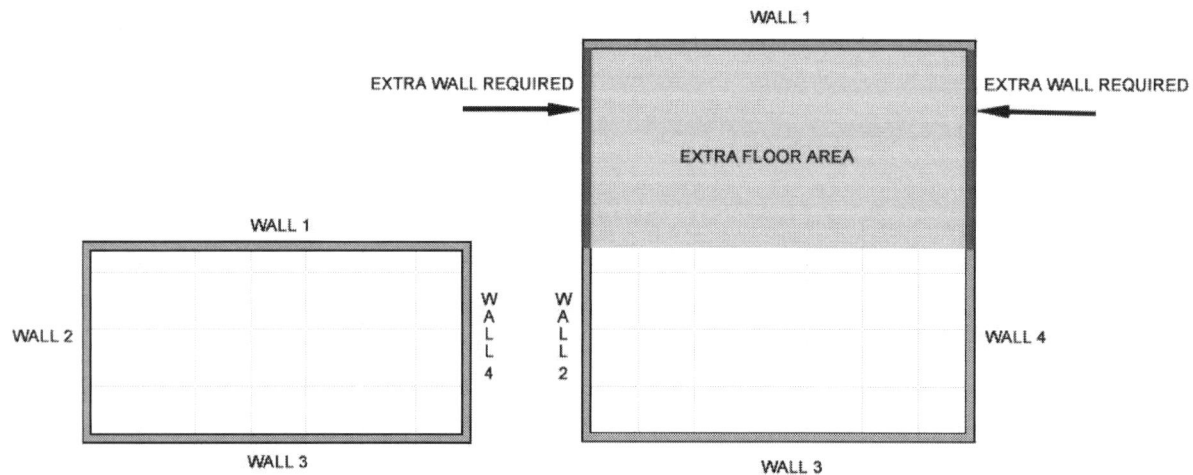

now come in handy if, say you ended up with a fairly rectangular house and wanted to square it up a bit. You could end up with bigger, better shaped rooms without having to worry about a significant rise in build cost.

Look at the two examples of floor areas above. The floor area to the right is twice as large as the floor area to the left (giving about 25 sq m more space within the walls). The wall numbered 1, 2, 3 and 4 are all the same on both drawings (totalling 21m in length), so the cost to build them will be the same for both shapes.

The only extra walls needed to surround twice the floor area of the example on the left are shown in red and total just 7m in length.

The same principals apply wherever you use them around the house for the walls, and it also works in a similar way on the floor and ceilings.

So, now you have another cost cutting" tool in your tool box! Not only can you design for the maximum use of the floor area by keeping everything simple and squarish, you now know that by making your house larger, you don't necessarily increase the costs by a great amount.

Bring these two facts together and you are potentially starting to save some serious money!

Chapter 6
Getting Planning Permission

Before I start to talk about the best ways to achieve planning permission on your own projects, I am just going to spend a bit of time looking at some of the myths around the subject.

In my experience, if you ask most potential self-builders (and even some of the industries so-called experts) about the subject of planning permission, they don't often have a true grasp of how things really are when it comes to questions like:

- What is it?
- Why do we need it?
- What are the different types and what rights does each type give you?
- How do we go about getting it?
- How long does it take?
- Who applies for it? Do they need an architect for this?
- How much does it cost?
- How long does it last for?
- What happens if an application fails?
- Should we think about buying land without planning or with only a short time left on a permission?
- How do Building Regulations tie in with planning permission?
- If someone builds a log cabin or has a static caravan on their land, do they still need planning permission?
- Does planning permission tie in with structural warranties or site insurance?
- At what stage of our project will we need to think about applying for planning permission?

We are going to cover all of those questions in this chapter, but I will start with the last one:

At what stage of our project do we need to think about planning permission?

Now! That is why this chapter is positioned where it is in the book, after: "*Finding land*", and after "*Designing your new home*", but (fairly obviously) before "*Starting to build*".

However, I have to pull back a bit here and explain something:

The truth is that, in reality, as part of an ongoing live self-build project, planning permission is something that needs to be given a great deal of attention **before** you buy any land (if you need to buy land) and **before** you design your house.

However, it is situated here in the book because at this stage, I am hoping that if this is your first read-through of the book, you have not already launched in to your project and that you are reading this in order to learn how to do it before you actually do so! (With me so far?)

I have touched on some of the issues related to planning as needed in the first few chapters, but there are two main reasons why the *main* planning permission chapter is here.

1. Assuming this *is* your first read-through the book, at this stage, as you are hopefully just researching. You should not be thinking too seriously about buying your plot just yet. You may be looking around, but not buying one.

If you already own land with planning (full or outline), that is fine, but don't think about buying anything until you are fully prepared, both practically and financially and are able and willing to commit yourself to the project for as long as it takes.
2. In the process of self-building, "full planning permission cannot be achieved without you first getting a set of design drawings prepared, so it is common sense to put this chapter *after* the design chapter.

If you think I am waffling on a bit here, I am sorry, but I have written what I just have for a reason. I want you to be clear about the way this whole process needs to be carried out.

As I have said more than once already, there is no real right or wrong way to do much of what is involved in taking on and completing your own self-build project, but there are good and not so good ways to go about it. I am just trying to make sure that you go about what you need to do in a good way!

What is planning permission?

Most people know that we need planning permission to allow us to build new homes, extensions etc. but there is a lot of confusion about what it actually is and that is one of the reasons why there is such a long list of questions at the beginning of the chapter.

Planning permission is a fairly simple, but very important part of the development of land. It is generally feared by those who don't know much about it and helpful to those who know how to take advantage of it.

Planning Permission exists to protect the country from being spoilt by bad buildings being placed where they shouldn't really be. It makes sure that what is built is reasonable (*in size, style, appearance, quality*) and that it suits its location. It prevents too much building in any particular area. It makes sure that a wide range of local issues are taken into account before any new building project can proceed. It also takes account of government policy at all times.

There are a number of different types of planning permissions, but there are only 3 that directly affect self-builders who build new homes (which is the area of the industry we are dealing with in this book):

1. Outline
2. Full
3. Reserved matters (or detailed)

If you have land which does not have a valid full or detailed planning permission on it when you *start work* on the building, you may have to pull down whatever you build. So, you need to make sure you have consent and that it is *still valid* on the day you start construction work.

The value of land that has planning permission is usually dramatically higher than land which does not have it. Land can go from being pretty much worthless to being worth £millions, overnight, just by its owner getting a piece of paper which says on it: "Application approved". For this reason, there is a massive industry across the UK which is solely geared up to turn land *without* planning permission in to land *with* planning permission.

Some of the people you will be dealing with as self-builders make a very good living by being part of that lucrative process and you need to make sure you do not let anyone take advantage of your lack of knowledge and inexperience within the building industry, in order to make themselves large amounts of money at your expense.

Why do we need planning permission?

Imagine you built a lovely Cotswold cottage on your picturesque half acre rural building plot, with beautiful view over local hills.

Now imagine a couple of years later a gang of groundworkers appear right in front of your house (between you and the views), and start to excavate the foundations for 200 developers' "little boxes".

Within a couple of months, instead of looking over the rolling hills, you are now looking straight at the back of a row of 3 storeys high, boring, cheaply built boxes. Wouldn't you have wanted to have some say in whether or not those houses were allowed to be built right in front of you?

How about if your favourite place to go walking in the countryside, somewhere that had been a local beauty spot, attracting tourists, was suddenly stripped of all its trees and developed for more little boxes?

When we decide to build a house and start to think about what we would like to put on the plot, we don't tend to give a lot of attention to our neighbours or the location in general. We just want to get on with putting our dream house on our plot!

Someone needs to be in charge to be able to say: *Hang on a minute, that building looks terrible there! It just doesn't suit what is around it and there is no mains drainage. What are you going to do with all your waste water? And the access is on a tight bend onto a road with fast moving traffic. It is downright dangerous!"* This is NOT a good idea!

Here is an example I produced on the computer to show what I mean. – It needs no description!

That's why we need planners!

OK, planners may be a pain, they may seem to be power hungry and sometimes arrogant. They may take an age to make a decision and they may keep asking you for more information, but at the end of the day, they are protecting not only your neighbours, but also you! They will be making sure that any decision they make on your application not only suits the location as it is today, but also protects the area and its inhabitants from poor quality development happening there in the future.

This has been the way the system works for many years and to my mind, overall, it is a good thing that it does.

What do the different types of planning permission mean?

Outline planning permission: basically means that the principal of development of one sort or another has been agreed for that particular piece of land. It can either be a fairly broad *"Outline planning for residential development"*, or it can be more specific, such as *"Outline planning for a 4 bed detached house and detached garage"*.

This is usually the lowest cost and quickest way to apply, as you don't normally need to provide much detail with your application. It is useful if you want to find out whether or not a piece of land would be granted planning so you can either then consider buying and developing it yourself or, if you already own it, selling it on for profit.

I would not recommend that as self-builders, you ever buy land which does not have at least a few months of an outline planning approval left on it and you should never apply for planning on a piece of land owned by someone else unless you get an option agreement in place. This will allow you to buy that land within an agreed period at an agreed price, allow you to try for planning, then, if you are successful, buy it, or if you are not successful, leave it. This way, your maximum risk, if you fail, would entail just losing the cost of making the application and your time.

Once you have outline planning permission, you still cannot build on the land until it has either full planning permission or reserved matters. Outline planning is only saying "Yes, this land is suitable for development".

Full / reserved matters planning permission: before you can start developing new property on a piece of land, you need to secure either *full planning permission* or *reserved matter planning permission*.

If the land does not already have planning permission, you can go for at least *full planning* which requires you to provide all the basic details of the project.

If the land already has outline planning granted, you can apply for either full planning or reserved matters. It is common in this situation (depending on how much information has been supplied to secure the outline planning) to apply for reserved matters, which acknowledges that you have outline permission already granted and deals more with the smaller details like external finishes to the building and landscaping etc.

How do we go about applying for planning permission?

The application process is actually quite simple and if you are prepared to spend a bit of time going through the forms and getting the information together, there is normally no reason why you should not be able to prepare and submit an application yourself, without having to use (and pay) and architect or some other professional.

It used to be a real pain in the neck making an application because everything had to be done six times over! You were required to send in six sets of application forms, plus six sets of everything else associated with it. It used to take me ages to get the package together and then I'd need a forklift to carry the paperwork to the planning office!

Nowadays, most planning departments have got online application systems up and running, so it is a lot easier, but if yours doesn't you may still have to go through what I used to do.

Although I will list below all the basic information you will be required to provide as part of your initial application, I am not going to go in to detail about every other document you might or might not be required to provide as part of the application process. The reason for this is that pretty much every application made, on every piece of land across the UK will include some sort of variation from the norm, so I could end up compiling lengthy (boring) lists full of things that you might never need to know about.

Once you start the process of preparing the documents and as you read the accompanying notes that come with the application forms, you should quickly become aware of all the documentation you will need to provide for *your* initial submission, however, it is fairly rare that the documents submitted initially will provide everything the planners will require in order to make their decision.

What normally happens is that the application will go in and get registered (*this can take a few days*), then, over the next few weeks you will start to receive contacts from the planners asking you for further information of varying sorts. You need to try provide whatever they ask for as quickly and as professionally as possible to avoid your application process dragging on for months.

Here is a list of the basic documentation which normally makes up the initial "Full" planning application package:

- Plans of any building already on the site

- Plans, elevations and sections of the new building(s)
- Existing and proposed site plan
- Sections through the site
- Location plans
- Details of some of the materials you want to use (bricks / render / roof tiles and occasionally some other bits and pieces)
- Details of any trees you intend to remove (or in some cases lop)
- A Design and access statement.

As I mentioned above, this may not necessarily be a comprehensive list. The actual requirement will vary from site to site and authority to authority. To be sure that you are aware of everything you will need to include in your submission, here is a link to the government's planning portal that will take you to a PDF file telling you all about making a planning application. It also has links which will allow you to find your way to the website for your own local planning department, where you should be able to find a reasonably definitive list of everything you will need to provide.

You can also use this as a starting point to guide you around the government's planning portal" to learn more about the planning process and how it works:

www.planningportal.gov.uk/uploads/1app/1app_guidance_note_england_en.pdf

How long does it take to get planning approval?

Simple applications are supposed to be "done and dusted within 8 weeks. In fact, the government Planning Portal states the following:

"Most planning applications are decided within eight weeks, unless they are unusually large or complex - in which case the time limit is extended to 13 weeks".

However, my reaction to that statement, from my own personal experience would have to be: **What a load of poppycock!**

In the thirty or so years that I have been dealing with applying for planning permissions, I don't think I have ever managed to hit the 8-week mark.

So why is that?

There are a number of reasons:

1. The eight weeks starts after the application has been registered. Registration can take from a week to three or four weeks depending on whether you have submitted all the right documents and information and how busy the administration department of the planning office is.
2. Councils are notorious for being inefficient when it comes to getting anything processed and completed on time. There is too much red tape and it only takes something small to happen to throw everything completely off track. So, if someone is off sick you could suffer by no one else picking up their work.
3. There can be 101 things that the planner comes up with during the planning process that can hold it up. Unfortunately, these things tend to come in one after the other, rather than all at the same time, so weeks can just disappear while you answer one query or solve one problem, only to be landed with another one the following week. Sometimes these problems involve you in getting professionals to site or writing reports, so as you can well imagine, 8 weeks is not a long time if the planners find more than one or two problems that need any significant work doing before they can be responded to.

4. Not all the departments involved get do their jobs in the timescales that they are asked to. The planners have to consult with various departments within the council about each application and those departments theoretically have a certain amount of time to respond. Unfortunately, it only takes one or two of them not to come back when they should to have a knock-on effect on the whole application.
5. Planning committees only sit every few weeks, so if the decision is not going to be made under delegated powers, but instead has to go to the full planning committee, if you miss one meeting by a day, you could then have to wait a month for the next one. Even then the committee could ask that the decision be deferred until the next meeting so they can go to visit the site before making their decisions.

I have actually had an example of an application that has dragged on and on, recently:

I applied for planning for three executive homes on land our company owns, at the end of April 2015.

The admin department did not get the application registered until the end of May (they were just *busy*) and the notices did not go out to the various departments until 2nd June.

Although the basic premise for approval had already been agreed at a pre-planning meeting, there were a few minor problems which were picked up by the various departments as the weeks went on. Highways were concerned about visibility splays, the Arboriculturalist (tree specialist) was concerned about the roots of trees with preservation orders on them, the wildlife people found a badger hole near the site and we had to carry out a survey to see if it was still being used (it wasn't). The nimby neighbours didn't want the development (NIMBY's), the drainage people wanted more details of how we would drain both the surface water and foul water. We had to prepare a report to say that the site was not suitable for affordable homes and then when they got round to agreeing with us, we had to get a contract drawn up to say that if we did not start the development within 12 months, they could re-assess that decision.

The application was originally intended to be what is called a delegated application, which basically means it is straightforward and the planning officer is pretty much free to make his / her decision without having to go to the full planning committee with it.

However, right at the end of the process on our project, the neighbours were still complaining that permission should not be granted. In fact, they persuaded a ward councillor" to request that the application should go before the full committee after all.

They actually waited until **the same day** that the planner had emailed us to say he had, that morning recommended it for approval, to ask that it went to committee. This apparently is something they can do if they wish!

This action meant that there was a final delay of 3 weeks from when the planner basically said "yes" until the next full planning committee meeting, which was held on 22nd December, nearly eight, months after the application first went in!

So, as you can see the 8-week guidance that is offered by the Planning Portal may just be *a little bit optimistic* in some, if not most cases.

Despite all that, as applicants, what you need to be aware of is that the planning process <u>itself</u> is quite simple and relatively cheap.

If you are well organised and have prepared properly, there is no real reason why you should not be able to submit your own application and save yourself the cost of paying someone else to do it for you. However, you also need to be aware of the importance of chasing, cajoling and responding quickly to anything that occurs during the process that could slow down the final decision date. That way you will at least minimise the chances of delays and problems occurring.

To prepare yourself for this, you need to have a good look at the Planning Portal and try to get a feel of how the whole process works (there is plenty of information on the site and elsewhere to help you), then, when the application is actually sent in, you need to start to push, nag and hassle everyone to get their bits of the process completed in the time that they have been allotted and not let them run over this time, without being chased by you, unless they have a very good reason for doing so.

Also, when problems occur, you need to act quickly to solve them. So, for example, during this recent application, in an email we were asked for a badger survey to be carried out. I immediately phoned all the people in the area who could carry out the surveys, until I found one who was fully qualified and who could come to site within a couple of days. Even then it was over a week after the survey was carried out before we had the report to send off to the planner.

The planning process can be extremely frustrating, and it is more so because if you get planning on land, its value skyrockets. So, you are not only waiting to find out if you will be allowed to build what you want, but you are also waiting to find out if you are going to be considerably better or worse off financially than you were at the beginning of the process!

Who is best to apply for planning permission? Will an architect or planning specialist be worth hiring to make sure it goes through?

I may be going to upset a few architects and planning specialists (again), but I think it important for you to know the facts on how this all works.

I also have to reiterate here that I have nothing against architects or, for that matter planning specialists, and at the right time, doing the right job, I have been, am and would be more than happy to work with them both on larger commercial and housing projects. However, when it comes to self-build, I think they can sometimes be an asset and sometimes a liability. Funnily enough, which they are often does not depend on how knowledgeable and experienced they are, but rather the way they go about doing their jobs.

I'll explain that statement by running you through two fictional scenarios, with the first one giving you an example of how it could all go wrong and the second one showing you how you could try to make sure it doesn't (both of these examples assume that you now own a plot of land).

How it could go wrong

If you take on an architect to prepare your drawings and apply for planning permission on your behalf, you are usually hiring someone who has a good reputation, who has experience and is seen as being good at their job (and who will probably be costing you quite a lot of money). However, quite justifiably, because of all those positive things that they have done, they are probably quite proud of their reputation and they want to make sure they maintain it.

What happens when someone is proud of what they have achieved and is keen to carry on building up that reputation, is that they tend to think they are right a lot of the time. If they bring that attitude to your "little" self-build project, along with a bit of a superiority complex, it can cause problems. I have seen this scenario countless times.

You may have spent weeks or months deciding what sort and what size of house you would like to build and you may well be quite content with your choices. Then the architect arrives, looks at your plot, looks at your drawings and simply says "No!".

As soon as they see the plot, the architect's professional minds tend to kick into gear and within a very short time they may well come up with a completely different scheme to what you had envisaged. This is where the problems start.

You are excited and pleased to have someone professional on board, so you listen to them and you nod your head, and say "Yes, I see" when you think you should, as they describe what they actually see as being "right" for your house design and your plot. Then they go away and you start to think to yourself: "I'm sure their ideas would be very nice, but they are not really what we wanted". However, you are in awe of these people and you dare not say anything to upset them in case they turn tail and leave you high and dry. So you let them continue with their scheme, you pay them and the drawings come through, along with lots of nice 3D renderings and an invoice for £4,000. You gulp, but decide to stick with it and pay it anyway.

Once the designs are reluctantly (although you wouldn't dare say so) agreed, the architect says "Right let's go for planning", so you do. He quotes you a further £3,000 for taking the application through the planning process and sends everything in to the planning office.

After 3 months, the application fails and the Architect is not happy: "How can they refuse it? There was nothing wrong with it. – Right, - we are going to appeal! It will cost you another £2,000 for me to help you through the appeal"

The appeal process fails and after 6 months, you are left back at square one, rather less well-off financially than you were when you started.

(*You probably recognise that scenario from me recounting my own experience earlier*).

How could that have gone better?

To start with, now you have been reading this book, I hope you would be prepared to have a go at coming up with your some of you own design sketches before you consider taking on a professional designer.

Once you have these sketches you can go (yourself, without any professional backup) to meet with the planners for a pre-planning meeting. As we discussed earlier in the book, this is a meeting that you may have to pay for, but at which you can sit down with the planning officer who would look after your application, to have a fairly informal chat.

You will take your sketches with you along with any other relevant information you can think of. As we touched on earlier, the idea is for you to come out of that meeting with a good idea of whether or not your design ideas would be acceptable to the local planning department. If they look and sound a bit sceptical about what you have come up with, just be prepared to change tack and to ask them what they *would* like to see being built on your plot.

At this stage, if you already own the land, you should already be well aware of the principle of development for the plot. It should, by now at least have outline planning for a development of the sort of property that you are envisaging (if it hasn't you would not have been well advised to buy), so let's assume for this example that you know the plot is suitable for a 4 bed detached house but you are just trying to find out what style and size you are going to be allowed to build.

However you get there, by the end of the pre-planning meeting, you should be coming out with a pretty good idea of how your designs need to be presented in order for them to be passed.

Now would be a good time to get a designer involved.

As we touched on earlier, you can choose anyone who can knock up a set of scaled planning drawings, from a draughtsperson through architectural technicians, all the way up to a fully-fledged architect, depending on how much you want to pay. But whichever you choose, just go in to this new relationship with the thought in your own head that "*This is our project. We are in charge*" and be ready to stand your ground if you happen to get an overbearing designer, wants you to change everything you have done, to conform to their much more professional ideas.

What could and should happen then, is that they prepare all the drawings you will need and you then make the application for planning permission. You fill in all the forms and if you are missing any information that you can't get together yourself, you go can simply go back to them to ask them for a specific bit of help.

When you make a planning application, you have a choice as to who you want to be the main contact for the application, should the planner need to get hold of someone. Unless, for whatever reason, you think you can't take on this responsibility, you should always make _yourself_ the main contact. What you don't want is for your designer to be the main contact, do all the negotiating and have full control on decisions made concerning _your_ application. YOU should be the one to make those decisions, using the designer and anyone else you need to help you if and when required. If you put yourself down as the main contact, all that will happen is that any correspondence related to the application will come through you. That means that you will always be fully aware of what is happening with the application and you will control who needs to do what in response to any contacts or requests made by the planning office.

By following the path set out above, you should, within a couple of months (possibly more if it is a complicated application), be getting to a point where you are pretty confident that you have done everything that the planners want you to do order for them to be able to pass the application.

Hopefully now, you have reduced the chance of the application being refused to almost nil and you are simply waiting for the approval notice to arrive.

By taking control of your own design and application process, you could find that you have saved time, money, worry and stress and that you have given yourselves the best chance of success.

Putting yourself as the main contact does not stop you from using the designer, or any other professional (including planning specialists) as much or as little as you wish, it simply puts you in control of the final decision making processes.

How much does it cost?

One of the misconceptions about obtaining planning permission is that it costs a lot of money. It can, but it doesn't necessarily have to.

Everything we cover in this book is designed to show you ways to do things correctly, but at the same time only spend what you need to and not more. However, to make everything work properly you do need to be honest with yourself and make sure that when you are working out the cost of anything, you include everything relevant or related.

So, to put the cost of making planning applications into a simple formula, including all relevant and related costs, here is a rough guide to the likely cost breakdown for a single full planning application:

I. Purchase of your own drawing equipment or design software packages: £100
II. Any site surveys needed: From £0 - £1,000+
III. Initial sketches: £0 - £500
IV. Pre-planning meeting: £0 - £250
V. Preparing the planning drawings, either yourself or hiring a design professional to prepare drawings: £0 - £10,000
VI. Preparing & printing drawings: £50 - £300
VII. Gathering maps, other plans and whatever other information may be required as part of the application: £50 - £250

VIII. Planning application fee: I did a quick check when I was writing this chapter for application fees. For 1 house, for a standard full planning application in England and Wales. the fees were: England £385 / Wales £380, Here is a link to the fee calculator so you can check if this is still the case:
http://www.planningportal.gov.uk/planning/usefultools/#feecalculator

You can quickly see from these figures that there is a low-cost route through the application process and a pretty high cost route too!

The low-cost route involves you taking control of the process and doing what you are able to. That cost will then increase depending on how much input you need from other people to get all the information together and the application made. The cost range, taking the above figures as a rough guide, could be around:

Low cost: £585   High cost: £12,785

Quite a difference isn't there?

Where your own project ends up within that range will depend on how much you can, or wish to do yourself.

How long does Planning Permission last for?

Generally planning permission lasts for five years from the date it is approved. If you have applied for outline planning permission, from the date it is approved, you will then need to further apply for full planning permission" or reserved matters within three years, before you can start to build. If you don't apply for either of those within three years you start to hit problems which mean that if you still want to build, you have to go back to get the application extended to then allow you to submit the full or reserved matters application.

I don't know why they make this so complicated, but unfortunately they do.

Here is a link for you to read exactly what the official planning guidance is on this subject:

http://www.planningportal.gov.uk/general/faq/faqapplydecision

For you to comply with the planning rules, you need to be seen to have *started work* within the planning period (*in other words, within the five years, as long as you got the full or reserved matters within the 3 years for an outline approval or within three years anyway if you went straight for full planning or reserved matters*).

There are tricks that both developers and self-builders use if they are not quite ready to commence the full project, whereby they start work on the building within the three years to show that they have complied with the planning approval requirements.

What starting work actually means is not particularly clear. The general thinking is that if you have constructed at least part of the property's foundation, you are seen to have started work. Possibly clearing the driveway and laying some hardcore or erecting a fence around the perimeter would probably not be acceptable evidence of having started.

My own view on this is that if you are buying land to build on, you should be making sure that when you buy it, you are able to then continue straight on with the project. Anything other than an immediate start, or at most a few months delay would usually point to something going wrong, or you not being properly prepared for the project in the first place.

What if your planning application is refused?

If your planning application fails, the planning authority must provide you with written reasons why that has happened. From that point you have a couple of options.

I. **Negotiate:** If you are not sure why the decision has gone against you, you can get in touch with the planner and / or the other staff who were involved in the decision and try to find out why.

It may be that it failed because of a something fairly minor or something that you could change (*this should not have happened if you had kept in regular touch with the planning officer throughout the application process*).

If there appears to be something that you can and are willing to change to help the application pass, you may then be able to re-apply with your modified plans, free of charge, within 12 months of the original decision.

II. **Appeal:** If negotiation does not look like it is going to change anything but you still think the authority's decision is wrong, your next option is to appeal to the First Secretary of State. You have six months from the date of the decision letter in which to do this.

There is no fee attached to this process, but you need to be aware that getting your designer and possibly a planning expert involved in the process, could prove to be fairly costly. The process is also usually pretty slow. If, following the appeal the original decision is overturned, you then have the right to claim expenses, based on what the financial implications of the turning down of the original application have had on you. This could involve you in trying to claim for loss of profit, mortgage payments, architect and other professional fees etc. Because the planning committee is fully aware of the potential of a claim against them, they take the vote on each application very seriously.

Believe it or not the planners work to the rule that:

All applications must be viewed as being suitable for approval unless there are sufficient reasons provided as to why approval should not be granted

That will probably come as a bit of a surprise to you, as it did to me when I first read it!

Should we think about buying land without planning or with only a short time left on a permission?

Buying land without planning permission

As a general rule, never buy land that does not have a live planning permission on it, if your intention is to build on it, *unless* you have either an option agreement (as we discussed previously) in place, or some other financial protection package attached to it, that gives you the confidence that you are not going to lose a chunk of money if things don't work out as you hoped.

The fact is, that when you are awarded planning permission on land, its value multiplies dramatically, so why would anyone in their right mind sell you a piece of land which does not have planning permission on it for £20,000, when they are confident that if they were to apply for themselves they would get approval and increase the land's value tenfold? They simply wouldn't!

The only times that you may consider buying land without planning and without some sort of option agreement or financial protection in place, would be if you were thinking of it as a longer-term investment. This could be, for example if you are fairly confident that there is going to be some change to the local planning policy which would, at some time in the medium or longer term future, bring the land within an area designated for new housing.

Even then, I would still be dubious about paying out for basically a field and sitting with my fingers crossed, possibly for years, hoping that one day it will magically turn in to a building plot. I would much rather invest my money into something that will make me a good return in the short term!

Buying land with a short time remaining on the permission:

It all depends on how well advanced you are with planning the project as a whole and how confident you are in being at least able to be seen to have started under the "3-year rule".

Here are a couple of scenarios to give you some ideas on how it could all work:

1) **Finding land with a few months of outline planning permission remaining:** If you were to find a nice plot which had, say 9 months of an outline planning permission" left on it before it hits the 3-year marker, you will know that you still need to obtain full planning permission before you can build anything.

   In this case the action I would suggest would be to make an offer and start a negotiation, but at the same time contact the planning office and ask for a meeting with the local planner to discuss the site. This meeting should be treated as a pre-planning meeting (which we have covered previously).

   The result you would be looking to achieve at this meeting would be along the following lines:
   - The planner does not see any problem with granting an extension of time on the existing application, to give you time to buy it and get the full application in before it lapses
   - If you wished to construct a different style of building (*which you would need to show examples of*), to that which is presently covered by the outline planning permission, the proposal would still fall within the local development plan parameters and the planners would not expect any major objections to it.

   If you could get yourself into either of those positions, you should be fairly safe to continue with your purchase negotiations, whilst, at the same time starting to gear things up so that you could move to get the reserved matters application in and start work within the 3 years, just so that you are minimizing your risk of passing the 3 years marker and then, for whatever reason finding yourselves unable to extend the approval.

2) **Finding land with a few months of full planning permission remaining before the 3 years was up:** You would be in pretty much the same situation if the land has full planning on it, but now, for the moment at least, you would not need to apply for a further planning permission before you could start to build.

   In this situation, as long as you were happy with the design, position and size of the house, you could simply plan to get started on the foundations as soon as you completed on the purchase of the plot (which should be within the three years). If you were confident of being able to do that, there should not be any major problem. All you would need to be aware of is that, if the purchase took a while and left you with only a few weeks after the completion of the purchase until the 3-year period runs out, you may still have a problem because you would still need to get the building regulations, structural warranty and site insurances all sorted before you started work. Anything less than three months from buying the land to actually starting work on site, after buying the land is getting a bit tight.

   There could be one solution to this situation: You could negotiate with the present owners to allow you to do some work on the foundations before you actually buy the land. There would be some risk attached to this idea, as they could decide to pull out of the sale and sell it for more money to someone else. However, if both parties were being sensible, you should be able to agree a deal where you get a simple agreement drawn up and witnessed by a solicitor, giving you permission to do the work and obliging the seller to sell the land to you at the agreed price, within an agreed time (*in other words you would be setting up a very simple, slightly different form of option agreement*).

It is always worth trying to play the best hand you have in any situation and here is no exception.

*If I were looking at land which had been granted planning of one form or another, but had not then either been sold or had the building work started, I would be thinking to myself "There has been something going on here, or **not** going on, as the case may be. The owners may, for whatever reason, have just neglected to move things forward. Either way there may be a bargain to be had".*

*I would be looking to use the fact that there is only a short amount of time left on the planning approval to give me the confidence to say something like: "**Because there is not much time left on the planning approval, I would be taking a significant risk by buying it**" (hoping this might enable me to negotiate a healthy discount!)*

How do Building Regulations tie in with Planning Permission?

I'll just repeat here what I have already said a couple of times:

Planning permission deals with "What does it look like?"

Building regulations deals with "Will it stand up?"

As I have said, it is not always quite that simple, but if you just remember that quote, you won't be far off.

When you lodge a planning application, you are asking the planners to approve all the visual aspects of the building. Its size, it location on the plot and the setting.

The planners then have a standard set of procedures to go through that they have to adhere to for every single planning application. These procedures aim to make sure that what is built is going to be suitable for its location.

Its location, however does encompass and bring into focus a few slightly more technical issues which have less to do with its visual aspect, but more to do with health and safety and the new building's effect on the community and the local area in general.

Included in this list of issues are things like:

- Is the site safe to access and exit from both a traffic and pedestrian point of view?
- Can both people and vehicle drivers see sufficiently far from the entrance to be safely aware of any traffic coming towards them?
- What is the level of traffic passing the entrance and how does this vary from time to time during the day and night?
- Does the adjoining road have any history of traffic incidents?
- Will the driveway length, width and slope suit people with disabilities?
- How will the new property be drained (foul and surface water)?
- Are there any environmental issues that need to be considered?
- Is there any wildlife that needs to be protected?
- Are there any trees that need to be protected, both during the construction period and after completion of the building?
- Is there any likelihood of flooding within or across the site boundaries, either today or in the future?
- Does the development fit in with the local housing development plan?
- Does the development put any unsustainable pressure on the local community in respect of schools, hospitals, extra traffic movement, parking etc?
- Will the council's refuse collectors be able to access the waste bins without travelling excessive distances from the carriageway?
- Does approving planning for this application create a "precedent" that will result in other applications being lodged in the future which could problems for the council?
- Is there access for a fire fighting vehicle and can the fire hose reach the building?

This is not a comprehensive list, but as you can see from it there are a lot of issues to be considered in any planning application before it is either approved or refused. Nothing in the above is actually *directly* associated with the building regulations application, although some of the areas do overlap a bit.

One area where the planning permission is changing and will continue to change is with regard to climate change, with eco factors becoming more and more important as part of the viability of new development of any sorts of building.

At the moment, it tends to be local authorities that make their own decisions on the levels of eco friendliness that they want new developments in their area to achieve, so you might find yourself having to provide more details of the eco credentials of the development as part of the planning permission. Where this is the case, the planning and building regs will overlap more, because as part of the building regs application you will need to prove whatever you claim with respect to your eco credentials, before your application is approved.

As an example of where planning and building regs can overlap, in a recent application I made, there was a lot of landscaping to be carried out on a long shared entrance drive. This part of the development included building retaining walls, cutting away an existing sloping bank and creating turning areas for general traffic, deliveries and fire engines. The landscaping also had to create a natural visual barrier between our development and a number of existing houses adjacent to the site.

As part of the planning application I had to provide details of the landscaping, the turning areas and the retaining walls, as the planners needed to be confident that the creating of the landscaping was not going to cause any risk of the sloping bank collapsing, or of it negatively affecting the rights of the adjoining properties.

At one stage, the planners did ask for full calculations for all the retaining walls (which had not at that stage even been designed), but I managed to persuade them to allow us to submit the calculations along with building regs application after the planning was granted, but before work started, as there would be a high cost in designing and preparing the calculations for the walls (which would be a complete waste of money if the planning application was refused).

Building Regulations, as the quote says deals mainly with "Will it stand up?

So, for the building regs application you need to show what methods and materials you intend to use to construct the foundations, drainage system, the structure itself, the roof etc. You will also need to provide proof of any engineering calculations, to prove that the materials and methods used will provide a finished building that complies with the latest building regulation requirements for structural stability, insulation values, disability access and a number of other matters.

Why do self-builders confuse planning permission and building regs?

Unfortunately, one of the two main reasons for the ongoing confusion between planning permission and building regulations is that it helps to get work for a lot of people within the industry.

I have lost count of the number of potential self-builders I have spoken to over the years who think that they need to prove to the planning office that everything in their design will be structurally sound, well insulated and will comply to a lot of the requirements that are actually covered by the building regulations.

I even get strange, disbelieving looks when I explain what I have just been clarifying in this section. I often see the faith in me of the people I am talking to, dissipating by the second when I tell them they don't need to get their building regulations application in until just before they start work. I can see them wondering to themselves: *"Has the guy lost the plot! How could he even think that?"*

So, assuming I do retain some reasonable levels of sanity, the way I see it, is that the two main reasons for the confusion are:

i. Architects, designers and many people involved in marketing products can stand to gain if they get any sort of business off the back of a potential self-builders paying out for extra design work, advice, surveys etc. *before* the planning application goes in.

        Think about it: If they get the work before the planning application goes in *and then the application fails*, they will still have had the order for the work and have been paid for providing it, despite the fact that the project may not go any further and it was not actually needed.

ii. Self-builders just find it very difficult to process the thought that they can apply to have a significantly sized building built on a piece of land and not have to prove to anyone that it will pass all the requirements for insulation, structural stability etc. It just doesn't compute to a lot of people.

        What these folks just need to understand is the fact that they <u>will</u> have to prove those things before they are allowed to build anything, but they then need to consider: *"Why would we want to pay out potentially thousands of pounds to prove that a building complies with a load of technical requirements when there is a good chance it may never be built?"*

        Surely the sensible way to do this is to find out you are going to be permitted to be built, *before* you have to spend potentially large, but unnecessary sums of money on proving the technical stuff?

If we build a log cabin or have a static caravan on their land, do we need planning permission?

Before I start to write this section I need to write a disclaimer!

As I have said before, there are many areas of confusion within the self-build industry and this is probably one of the areas which creates more confusion than many of the rest.

What I am going to write below is a mixture of my opinion, and bits and pieces I have brought together, to try to get at least something like a reasonable stance on the subject.

Do not take anything said here as gospel. Planning laws vary from area to area across the country and even if something is ok to do in one place, it might not be ok in another.

So, having cleared that up, here are my thoughts:

If you want to avoid the need to have planning permission for a log cabin or static caravan, they must be classed as temporary buildings.

To be classed as a temporary building, a log cabin must have <u>no permanent</u> hard standing, concrete foundations, or any permanent groundworks (including drainage) that cannot easily be removed.

Log cabins come under different headings:

- **Permanent structures,** normally built mainly using wood, but on a solid foundation with all the services connected, just like a brick building.
- **Less permanent structures** with no concrete foundations, assembled on site and raised off the floor on a timber or metal frame. The finished structure can also be dismantled and removed from the site, leaving no evidence of it having been there.
- **A log cabin on wheels** (or basically a timber built static caravan).

It would appear that planning permission is not needed for a log cabin if it is on the same site as an existing house as long as:

- The property is not in designated area such as an area of outstanding natural beauty, National Park or similar category.
- The property on which it is situated does not form part a listed building site.
- The outbuilding is not forward of the principle elevation of an existing house.

- The cabin will not be above 4m in height.
- Total area covered by buildings will not exceed half of the garden of an existing house.
- The cabin is not to be used commercially (a home office is usually acceptable if it does not detract from the main use of the property).
- The cabin is not to be used as a dwelling.
- There are no other covenants that prevent you from exercising permitted developments rights.
- The maximum height of the eaves of the building will be limited to 2500 mm.
- The height of the building must not exceed 2500 mm within 2 metres of a boundary.
- All buildings with a veranda, balcony or raised platform will need permission.

There seem to be different rules for siting log cabins and static caravans within the grounds of an existing property than there are for siting them on an empty plot.

- You do not appear to need planning approval to live in a mobile home on the site where you are carrying out building work, as long as one of the family members is involved in the construction or management of the project on a full-time basis.
- Each case is individual and different councils may have conflicting requirements. For a completely new build, i.e. no house has been there before, some councils would require planning approval. For this situation, it is advisable to include the mobile home in your initial planning application, it will not cost any extra to add and is highly unlikely to affect the planning approval decision for your house.

Can we live in a static caravan on a plot permanently?

According to the "10 Year Rule" (in the Town and Country Planning Act 1990), if you can provide proof to the council that your static caravan has been situated in its current position for more than ten years, it is generally too late for the council to initiate proceedings against it.

You would need to show proof such as invoices for associated work, evidence of a postal address such as a utility bill, transportation, and sworn statements by people who have known the site during the ten years. This proof can be used in the application for a certificate that establishes the use as lawful. Once this is given, the site can then be used for a static caravan, including replacements.

Does planning permission tie in with structural warranties or site Insurance?

No, they are completely different, but important things. We will deal with structural warranties and site insurances later.

Additional general information:

To finish off this chapter I am going to run through a couple more general bits and pieces that you may find useful:

Planning drawings:

Just to show you how simple it can be to produce a set of drawings suitable for submitting for planning, here are some I recently used as part of a Planning Application.

I created these plans after teaching myself how to use a simple software package. I am nowhere near being fluent or an expert. However, the beauty of these packages is that once you learn the basics, the computer does a lot of the work for you.

I completed the design in a few hours and once that was done I could simply get the software to compute all the elevations and sections, so all in all, to get the full package together of the basic, scaled drawings probably together took me around two days.

The more time consuming part of the process was made up of:

- Filling the planning forms in and gathering the information together that they asked for.
- Getting the site plans designed (*this was a complicated job on this project but is usually quite simple on a single self-build*).
- Printing six copies of each document for the submission of the application.
- Checking that everything was included in the final package before submitting it (*if it isn't you could lose a couple of weeks' progress as nothing would be registered until the admin department are satisfied that they have everything*).

Using the CAD software:

For this project, firstly I designed the layout using a scale of 1:50 as that seems to be the one which generally works best for getting a standard sized house on to an A3 piece of paper.

To start, I needed to set a few simple parameters for the design:

- The width and makeup of the external walls
- The width and makeup of the internal walls
- The room heights (normally around 8' or 2440mm but higher if you want them to be. 2440 is the standard size of an imperial sized plasterboard, so sticking with this height saves cutting and wasting boards)
- Door widths (internal and external) I set them all at 900mm.

Once I had all the basics set up, I drew the ground floor plan, using trial and error until I was happy with it. I then copied that plan by clicking add floor, then choosing the parameters for how the new floor should appear (I said: "Copy floor below"). This was going to be the first floor.

On this new floor, I removed most of the walls and just left the staircase, then designed the bedrooms (*it is always handy to try to keep one or two ground / first floor walls above each other to add stability and strength to the house structure*).

Once the first-floor layout was complete, I repeated the "add new floor" process to get a second floor.

When all the floor layouts were complete and I was happy with them, I added the external measurements and some text with a few clicks of the mouse then, one by one, again with just a few clicks, pulled up the elevations of each external wall and the cross sections through the house (these are required for part of the planning submission) then printed each drawing off.

It was then a simple exercise to print the drawings off, to scale, on my A3 printer (you will need an A3 printer to be able to print an average sized house out at a scale of 1:50).

On the next couple of pages are a few of the drawings produced for this application. There are some missing, but the ones that are shown should give you an idea of how even someone with no real training or knowledge of designing a house on a computer can come up with something reasonable:

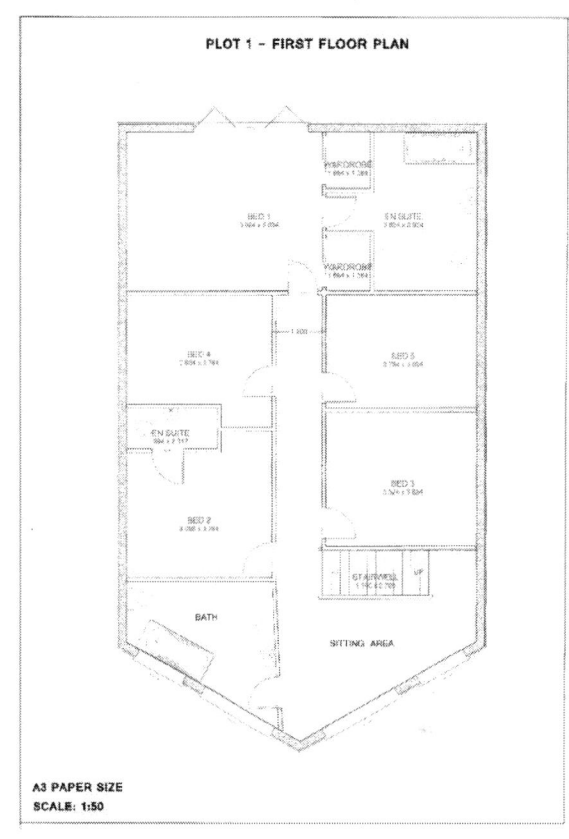

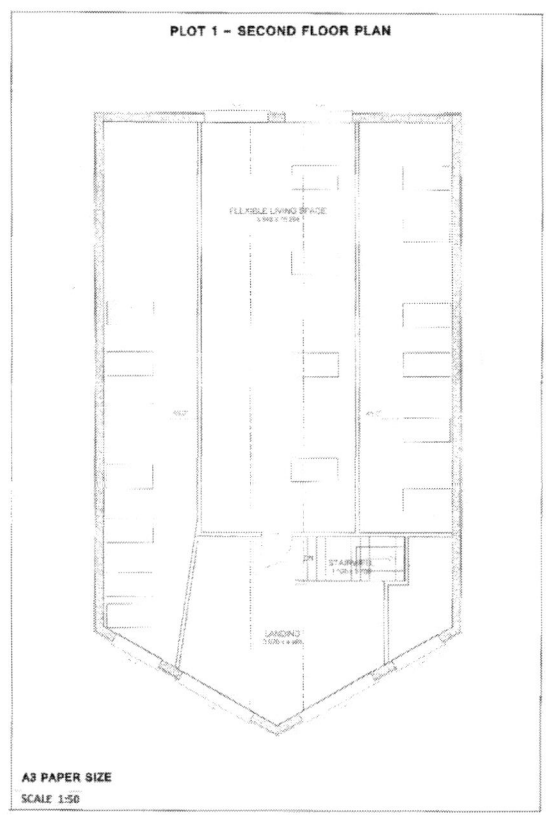

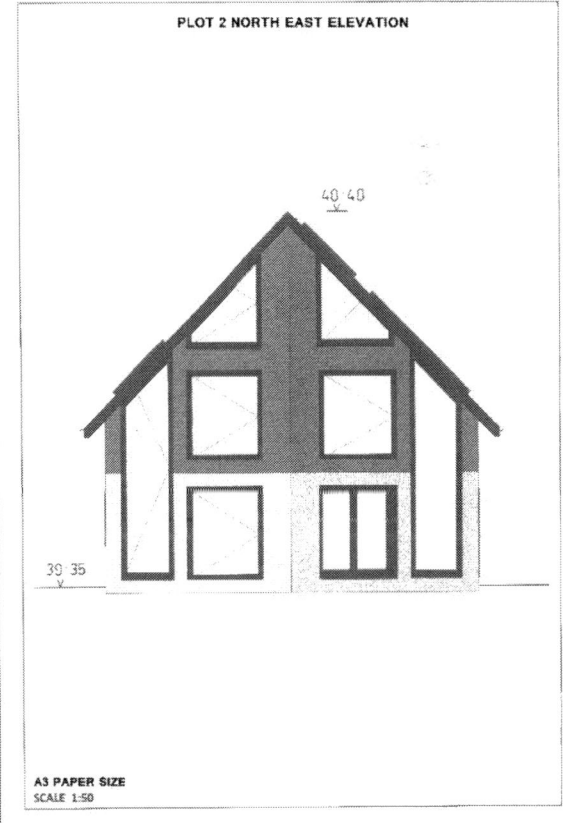

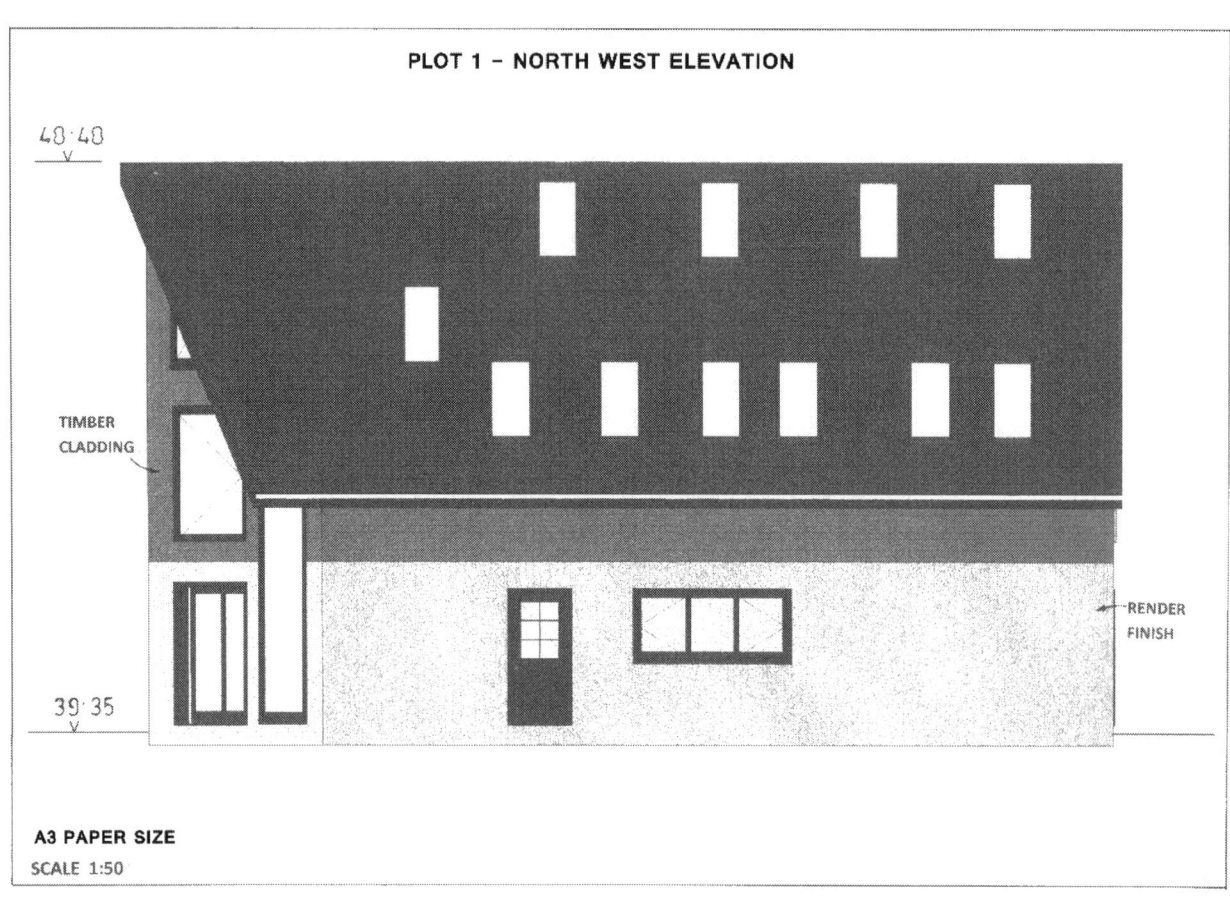
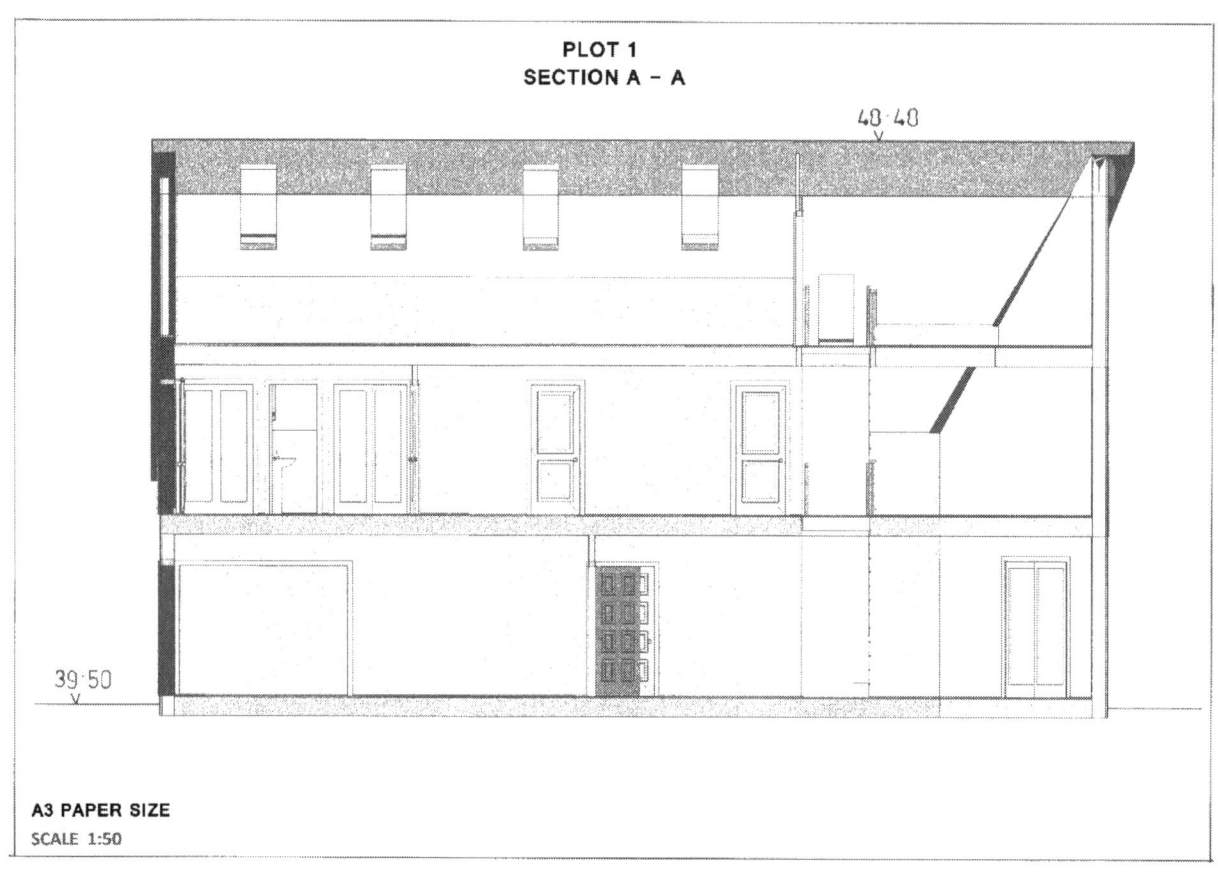

These drawings (along with the rest of the information requested) were sent off to the planning department and the planners were perfectly happy with them.

I have made numerous applications over a number of years for different local authorities and never had any problems with them coming back asking for more technical details (*that's not to say they all went straight through to approval without a hitch, they didn't! I often had meetings about changing some aspect of the appearance, the siting on the plot, the access, the drainage etc. but no requests for more technical information to prove the adequacy of the structural stability of the house itself*).

The only time you may find that you are asked for extra information or drawings would be where you are making a complicated or sensitive application that needs a lot of visual description to clarify your exact intentions to the planners.

Design and access statement

This is a fairly recent addition to the planning permission application which may not be around for long (check with your local planning office and / or the Planning Portal to see if you still need this before you pay someone to write it).

If you do need to include one of these statements as part of your planning application, you will, most likely need to get some professional help to put the report together. Planning specialists, Architects and many house designers will be able to help you to prepare it and if they can't, they will normally know someone who can.

Here is what the Planning Portal has to say about a design and access statement:

A design and access (DAS) statement is a short report accompanying and supporting a planning application. It is required for many types of planning application, both full and outline, but there are exemptions.

A DAS should explain the design principles and concepts that have been applied to particular aspects of the proposal – these are the amount, layout, scale, landscaping and appearance of the development.

Design and access statements are documents that explain the design thinking behind a planning application. For example, they should show that the person applying for permission (the applicant) has thought carefully about how everyone, including disabled people, older people and very young children, will be able to use the places they want to build.

Demonstrating how the local context has influenced the design is also an important element. This should be discussed in relation to the scheme as a whole.

The requirement for the access component of the statement relates only to 'access to the development' and therefore should explain how the design ensures that all users will have equal and convenient access to it.

For most straightforward planning applications, the DAS may only need to be a page long, for more complex applications, more detail is likely to be necessary.

The Government has produced guidance on what a DAS should contain and its role in the decision-making process.

For further information go to:
https://www.gov.uk/government/uploads/system/uploads/attachment_data/file/7727/1505220.pdf

(If this link disappears from the internet, just search "Design and Access Statement guidance" and you should quickly be able to pull up the relevant information).

Chapter 7
How will we build the house?

Introduction:

Well, here we are at one of the two biggest decision points in the process of building your own home: How are we going to build the thing? (The other one being the decision to start the project in the first place).

Now is the time, not only to consider the standard *Traditional build v Timber Frame* argument, but you also need to at least be aware of some of the other "build options" open to you.

It is also the time to make a decision on whether you are going to project manage the whole thing yourself, *bring in* a project manager, pass the building work over to a main contractor, or come up with another management option.

Your decisions now will set up the rest of the project and will have a direct bearing on your budget, your stress levels, the time it takes to complete the project and your quality of life, both during the building process and after you move into your new home.

You therefore need to consider all your options carefully.

I do have to admit at the outset that I have strong opinions on which building system you should use and the how your project should be managed. I favour pairing the closed panel timber frame system (which we will look at later) with hiring in a professional project manager as being the best overall combined package to give you a fast, professional, economical build, which reduces the stress levels involved for you and your family and could get you in to your new home, in probably as short a time as would be practically possible, considering that, at the end of the day, you are (usually) not professional builders and self-build projects (with the best will in the world), don't tend to be amongst the best and most efficiently organised construction projects!

I have personal reasons for my choice of the closed panel system as being the best choice as the build method for most self-build projects. The main one is that is that is that, after 25+ years of involvement in self-build and being constantly frustrated during that time at how slow and inefficiently run most self-build projects are, I decided that it was time I started to do something about it.

So, in 2011, to test my own theories about the best way to build, I set up my own closed panel timber frame, manufacturing company, making a product that was a bit different.

I am not going to mention the company name here for 2 reasons: 1) Because this book is not intended to be an advert promoting one make of product over another and 2) After realising that my investor / business partner was, shall we say not quite what I thought he was, I decided that I could not remain as part of the company, so I left in April 2014 and unfortunately I now have to look elsewhere, to try to find something similar to what turned out to be the brilliant product (though I say so myself), that I was manufacturing only three years ago!

So, although I do have favourites (don't we all?) I will do my best to present an unbiased picture of each of your choices throughout this chapter, to allow you to make up your own minds. (No, honestly, I will!)

Before I get stuck into comparing your options, I think it is worthwhile to briefly run through another bit of my own site experience. Not only related to self-build but also to commercial house building.

By doing so, I think it will help you to see why I have come to the conclusions that I have. I fully understand that other people will have alternative views which are just as strong and if anyone reading this wants to drop me a *short article expounding the benefits of what they see as the best building systems, I will try to update the book asap to incorporate some differing views.*

My own house building experience

I built my first self-build house about 30 years ago in North Wales, on a nice plot overlooking the Wirral Estuary.

At the time, I had not really heard much about timber frame or any of the other options that were available. I seem to remember at the time that ICF (Insulated Concrete Formwork) was just being introduced, but really there was only one way that I thought about building my first house, the traditional way.

For the shell of the building I used 2 skins of 4" insulating concrete blocks with 2 coats of render on the outside, which was then painted with 2 coats of good quality external render paint.

Insulation values in those days were quite a low priority, so we didn't use any sort of extra insulation over and above the fact that the blocks used to build the shell were classed as insulation blocks. To keep warm, we just kept the heating on!

The blockwork construction meant that the shell went up relatively quickly (*six bricks are the same size as one block, so blockwork walls are much faster to build*). The roof went straight on after the blockwork, so, because the shell went up quite quickly, we had a covered roof over our heads about 2.5 months after starting work, so could make a start on the internal works.

Apart from the foundations, which were very troublesome, the rest of the building process presented no real problems and on the whole the experience was a positive one.

Here is an old photo of the house (*as you can probably see I had not learnt a lot about health and safety at that time*).

We completed the build in 6 months and lived in the house for 2 years before the bug got hold of us again and we decided to have another go! Just around that time, a building plot came up for sale in my home village in Cheshire, so we went for it.

My wife and I had both enjoyed the experience of creating our new home so much that we discussed the idea that I might think about a change of career, from working as a sub contract site manager, and instead set myself up as a self-build consultant / project manager". A few months later this is exactly what I did.

I then worked for a few years on various self-build projects for individual clients. All the houses I built during this period were constructed with a brick and block external shell (traditional construction) and a mixture of blockwork and timber internal walls.

Generally, all these houses were very similar to build once you became aware of a few basic rules, and having had a number of years working on large commercial building and civil engineering projects, I found the process of house building pretty simple and straightforward (in fact these houses were so simple to build that it was around this time I started to use the phrase: *"You draw it on the back of a fag packet and I'll build it!"*

Each house would take about 6 months on average to build and clients always seemed to be happy with their new homes

A few things used to annoy me with traditional construction:

- The slow rate of build.
- Their dependence on the weather.
- Because of the length of time taken to build, there were often problems keeping the labour force turning up every day.
- Usually, by the time the roof went on the whole house was soaking wet internally and this took literally months to dry out.
- There were literally thousands of individual types of materials, fixtures and fittings to be ordered and it was almost a full-time job keeping up with measuring, pricing and ordering the materials just for one house, to be delivered to site in the right quantities and on time, so that they were available to be incorporated into the build.
Some materials turned out either to be hard to get hold of, or were on long delivery times. This could cause delays in progress, which would then have knock-on effects further along the line.
- Openings for windows and doors were often built slightly out or square and walls built out of plumb by a small amount. Not enough to cause a structural problem, but enough to make window fitting a struggle, or to have door linings (which have to be installed completely plumb), showing up the slight none plumbness of the walls, resulting in us having to do some clever jiggery pokery to get them to look right!
- After plastering, for the next 6 – 12 months, cracks would start to appear as the whole house dried out. These were normally in locations where there was a large area of wall with no corners and also between the corners of the downstairs and upstairs windows (*cracks always appear where it is easiest for them, so between windows often gives them the shortest route to travel*).
I would end up filling cracks in walls for months or having clients wondering if their house was falling down when they saw these cracks appearing! When a crack is filled it then needs painting. Unfortunately, often there would be none of the original paint left and we would have to buy more (which you could guarantee was *not quite* the same shade as the original).
- The upstairs walls were always built of timber with standard plasterboard either side in the houses I worked on and because of this, were not particularly soundproof.

Apart from those snags the houses were fine. They were good and solid and a standard four bed detached was easy to build in around 6 months (*possibly 8 if you hit problems*). Here are a couple of photos of the sort of thing I was building at that time:

During the early nineties, believe it or not I had started writing the first draft of this book (*it only took me twenty odd years to finish and publish!*) and in the process of talking to potential publishers, I met a self-build author called Bob Matthews.

Bob had already written and published his own self-build book (Practical House Building) and was keen, like me, to try to help make the industry a bit simpler and a bit more professional, so that more people would be attracted to the idea of building their own home.

Bob had had an idea to form an "Association", by getting together a few likeminded people who had specialist knowledge of different parts of the industry.

Within a couple of years, Bob, me and half a dozen others had founded the original "Association of Self Builders" (now succeeded by "NaCSBA" – *The National Custom and Self Build Association*).

As I got more involved with the association, I found myself talking to a lot of people from different sectors of the industry and as I did so, I started to come across this new-fangled timber frame system being considered as an option to traditional build by more and more people.

To start with, I was very anti the idea of a wooden house. How could it ever take the place of a good, solid brick and block built house? It would probably blow down in a heavy gale!

My anti timber stance was made even stronger by the fact that a few years earlier I had been renting a house which happened to be one of the ones that helped to give the product the poor reputation it suffered for years.

Although the house was only a few years old, it felt very flimsy and poorly constructed. You could hear people whispering through the walls and it was very cold. To top it all, on the gable wall, there were lots of horizontal cracks appearing along the brickwork joints, which turned out to be the visible signs of a significant structural problem.

What was happening was that the wall ties had been fixed with cheap screws which were rusting and breaking, leaving the wall ties unattached to the timber frame part of the wall! This, meant that there was nothing holding the brickwork skin to the timber frame, so when there was a strong wind, the buffeting of the gusts was basically sucking and blowing the wall, making it move in and out from the timber frame, which in turn was causing the brickwork to crack at the easiest place it could find to do so, the joints.

The experience of living in that house, was enough to set me against the whole timber frame industry. In fact, I was so sure of the strength of my position, that a few years later, at one of the AGMs of the Association of Self Builders, I invited the MD of a large timber frame manufacturing company to debate with me the subject: *"Traditional Construction versus Timber Frame as a housebuilding method"*. After the debate, I was quite proud of the fact that most people listening considered my argument to have won.

However, much to my dismay, my being anti timber frame didn't seem to stop it from quickly becoming more and more popular. At that time, I couldn't understand why.

A few years later I moved from the North West of England to South Wales and took on another self-build project.

By this time, I had learnt a lot more about the system from working with the Association. I was constantly advising people who were thinking about starting projects, in the middle of projects, or who had hit problems and needed help. A significant number of these people were building with timber frame and to my surprise, most of the things they said about the product turned out to be positive. If a project was struggling, it was normally the timber frame that was the bright spot. This, over time had persuaded me to think slightly differently about the whole concept of timber frame and self-build.

As my day job, I had been pushing on with being a self-build project manager whilst I lived in the North West and planned to keep that career going in South Wales. However now that I had been seeing the increased interest in timber frame and wasn't quite as anti the whole concept as I had been a few years earlier, I started to think it might be a good idea if I tried one out for myself, as my first building project in South Wales. That would allow me to speak from experience when I talked to members of the Association and also to my own clients.

Once I had found a nice plot of land, I shopped around for timber frame companies who appeared to offer a good quality product at a reasonable price and settled on a company in Mid Wales. I was actually quite pleased with the quote for providing and erecting the frame, as everything I was reading (usually from the brick and block side of the industry) had been saying that timber frame was a lot more expensive to build with than brick and block.

I accepted the quote and started to plan to build what was a fairly large 5 bed house, utilising a 4" timber frame with a brick skin to the outside. Here is that house:

The foundations were completed in about 2 weeks (which was about normal for one of my projects) then the frame came and went up in just 2 weeks. The roof took another week or so to get ready to cover so, from the start of the building works on site to being roofed in and weatherproof only took 5 weeks.

Price and speed of construction were the first notable difference between the traditional and timber frame systems and I was quite impressed. I would have normally expected the house to take around 10 – 12 weeks to get to the same stage using a brick and block traditional construction.

I soon realised that the next benefit of the timber frame was that, as soon as the roof was covered we could get on with all the internal works, starting with the first fix joinery, electrical and plumbing works. These installations were proceeding at the same time as the brickwork was being built around the outside of the frame, so basically, we were now doubling the speed of progress when compared to a traditional build.

The full build was finished in about 12 – 13 weeks, about half the time it would take me to build the same house in brick and block, which was pretty quick, especially as I had not been particularly pushing for a fast build. I had really just wanted to see how the system performed and learn as much as possible about its strengths and weaknesses along the way.

In Chapter 3 (Finance), I talked about how a fast build can help your cash flow and reduce your build costs. Using this method of construction for the first time, immediately made me aware that, despite what I had previously thought, timber frame actually has a lot of inherent advantages over the traditional build method. Not only was it much quicker to build, I started to see that if I did it right and did it quickly, it could potentially reduce my overall build costs, possibly by quite a significant amount.

Having used myself as a guinea pig for this project and because we moved into the house, I was able, for the next couple of years, to monitor how the building performed with regard to problems cropping up and things like general soundproofing, creaky floors, warmth, overall "feel" (i.e. did the house feel solid of flimsy?), settlement & drying out cracks appearing etc.

To our surprise, we found that the number of problems and overall negatives to do with the building were actually considerably fewer than they usually were for a traditional house. It was warmer than our previous self-build, quieter (*which might have just been me learning to build better houses as I went along*) and strangely, living inside the house actually felt more natural. I am not sure why that was, maybe it was the increased amounts of natural materials that had been used in the construction of the building (if you have ever been inside and walked round a log cabin you may understand what I am talking about).

Don't get too worried when I talk about shrinkage cracks. They are not normally signs of any structural problem; they are usually just the depth of the plaster, which shrinks as it dries out over a number of months.

You can tell if it is a drying out crack by putting a knife blade or something sharp in to the crack and seeing how far in it goes. If it goes much further than half an inch or so, you may have a more serious problem, but that very rarely happens on new houses.

Over the time I had been building with brick and block, I had constantly bemoaned the work this involved me in for the first few months after moving in. I would have to keep filling the cracks in (with standard filler), rubbing them down and repainting them. The difference between the first six months living in a traditional house and living in a timber frame was that there were no noticeable shrinkage cracks *at all* in the timber frame.

I would have to say that as a living experience, given the choice between the two types of build, I would go for the timber option every time, **if it is built correctly and to a decent spec!** (*see later in this chapter and also later chapters to learn how to pull those particular tricks off*).

So, my first timber frame experience had been a very positive one over all.

"Come on! There must be some negatives to timber building with frames!"

There are, and in fact there are quite a few of them, so to balance out the positives and to be seen to be giving different build methods a fair hearing, I'd better chip in here with the downsides of building with timber frame:

Problem 1). Rain while you build. In Wales and Scotland, it rains a lot. In England, not quite so much, but heavy, constant rain whilst a timber frame is going up can potentially cause problems that will manifest themselves in the months and years to come.

On my first timber frame project, it rained a lot while the frame was being erected and so by the time the roof was covered, the whole of the frame was soaking wet inside and out.

When timber gets wet it expands. Not by much, but enough. Then when it dries it shrinks back to its original size. We'll come to the effects of that in a minute.

The first job, once the roof is covered is to install the insulation into the (possibly) soaking wet timber frames. The insulation often used is fibreglass, which is a product that will happily soak up any moisture around it until it becomes like a soggy sponge (which then makes it both heavy and pretty useless as an insulator). The fact that this can happen, opens up the possibility of the insulation in your wet timber frame eventually "sagging" and leaving areas (generally at the top of the panel) with no insulation and resulting in the insulation values of whole panel being severely reduced.

Problem 2). Trapping the first problem in. Once the insulation is fitted in to the frame, generally the first fix works commence. These include the electrical and alarm wiring, the plumbing pipes, any "in wall" drainage that is required and from time to time, other bits and pieces like surround sound wiring etc.

Once that job is done, the *internal* face of the *external* panels are covered with a vapour barrier (which is basically normally a plastic sheet). Unfortunately, as its name suggest, the vapour barrier stops any moisture from passing from one side of it to the other, which means that any remaining moisture *inside* the wall is pretty much stuck there until it either finds another way out, or naturally dries out over a long period of time. This could potentially cause mould or other damp related problems to occur within the frame and even when it has fully dried out, the constitution of the insulation will have changed so that it now does not perform anything like as well as it was designed to.

There are a few ways to cure this problem. One is to use the more expensive, but higher performing expanded foam insulation (which do not absorb water like fibreglass does), or, alternatively, make things so that the water can't get in to the frame in the first place (see later).

Problem 3). As I said a couple of paragraphs ago, when timber gets wet it expands. Once the house is protected from the weather it will then, over a period of months, slowly dry out and contract back to its original size. In doing so it can sometimes have a tendency to warp. This drying out process can potentially cause small gaps to open up between timbers joints and start to create cracks and creaks around the house. I hate creaky houses!

This is not generally a structural problem and there are fixes which can reduce, or even cut out the creaks altogether. These are:

1) To make sure adequate fixings are used in the erection of the frames and that every nail is driven well and truly home.

2) Screw and glue all the floor boards to the joists.

Problem 4). Noisy walls that can't carry the weight of anything heavy fixed to them: This is one of the most obvious drawbacks of using a standard, sometimes fairly flimsy timber frame with a plasterboard finish (which is the way most UK builders do it).

- **How many houses have you been in which have cheaply built internal walls which won't take the weight of anything more than a lightweight picture frame without needing special fixings?** With most timber frames, what happens is that the builder will fix things called noggins within the timber panels, wherever there is a chance that something heavy will need to be hung. A noggin is simply a timber panel, usually made of OSB (orientated strand board), which is fixed between the timber studs that make up the panel's framework.

  They will be used for example, where you will need to fix kitchen wall units, extractor fans, shelves, coat hangers, radiators, wall mounted TV's etc. Fixing noggins allows the walls to take the extra weight without fear of damage (within reason) to the surface finish of the walls in those locations. However, noggins do not future proof the house for anything heavy you want to fix to a wall where they are not fitted, after you move in.

- **How many houses have you been in where you can hear every noise made in the room next door?** Thin wall panels with thin, poorly fitted plasterboard are the standard construction for the developer's (and some self-builders) internal walls. They are rubbish! They are what give the UK the worst of its generally bad reputation as housebuilders, but we still use them!

These two problems are really annoying, but are actually very simple to cure, without the need to spend a lot of extra cash.

Many self-builders are not aware of the fact that when you build a house, you can use different types of materials in different combinations for the same job, to give you vastly differing end results.

This is most definitely the case with internal timber framed walls. We will look in more detail at types of wall construction later in this chapter and you will see how much better things can be without any real extra effort or significant cost.

Ok, so those are the main problems with timber frame. Overall, they are much quicker to build than traditionally constructed houses, can be much warmer and can be built at a lower cost if you know how to do them properly.

That was the conclusion I came to after I finished my first self-build house all those years ago, and after I had lived in it for a couple of years. It is still my view today, 25 or so years later.

After I came to that conclusion, I also made the decision that I would not build any more traditional construction houses and instead would move over to timber frame, not only for my own houses, but I would also recommend the same for all my future clients.

I continued to build using timber frames for the next 15 years or so without any other noticeable problems occurring (right up, in fact until the recession hit in 2009 when the banks got nervous about funding the house building market as a whole and took away the funding for my housing development company, which meant that I had to basically shut up shop for a while).

I found the timber frame system to be a major benefit when I became a housing developer. The biggest plus to me as a developer was that I hardly ever had any call-backs to deal with problems once the new owners had moved into their new homes. Using timber frame in the way I did, simply made the whole process of building houses faster, cheaper, more flexible and *just generally better*!

In the mid 2000s I built a house in Florida (as detailed earlier in the book) and I learned a lot. The whole housebuilding industry there is just so much better than it is here. Better organised, more professional and the houses they build are better designed and better built. The same applies to a lot of the European countries.

I started to realise over time that here in the UK we are so far behind the curve when it comes to housebuilding that it is almost laughable.

As this realisation came to me, I started to pay more attention to how some of the European countries had already taken what I now see as the next step in the evolution of house building. More and more housebuilders in, for example Germany and the Scandinavian countries, were moving over to using a closed panel system (sometimes called *offsite construction*), or derivatives of it.

Closed panel timber frames, as the name suggests are a hybrid building system based on a standard timber frame, but with far more work being done in the factory rather than on site. I'll go into detail on this system later in this chapter, but as you are already aware from earlier, this system is now the way I think that the industry *as a whole* should be building houses.

After I had researched all the closed panel options and after the banks had pretty much closed my housing development company down in 2009 by cutting off its funding, in 2011 I decided the time was right to move from timber frame to closed panel as my main construction method for housing. However, as the housing market was just about dead at that time and because I could not build any houses without any buyers or any money, I decided to try to get funding to create my own closed panel timber frame product.

This was going to be a product that:

- Suited the UK market (both commercial and self-build).
- UK house buyers would understand and like.
- Gave a high quality, warm, sustainable, low carbon, quiet, creak free (hopefully!), low cost, finished product.

I designed the system, drew up a business plan and secured funding to set the company up in 2012 by taking on an investor who said he was a financial director, who would come and run the financial side of the business, as well as providing the funding we needed to get the whole thing set up.

At this point I can only say that the way the system was welcomed by the people who knew about it was incredibly positive. Pretty much everyone who heard about it wanted it. When people compared it to anything else they could choose, it was a no-brainer to go for this product. It solved all the problems found with timber frames, its quality was undeniable, the speed of build was incredibly fast, it helped commercial builders to build at lower costs and complete more houses per year, so therefore make better profits.

For self-builders, it made the process much simpler, faster and potentially significantly cheaper and it gave them a high quality finished home.

Building regulations inspectors loved it too! One quote from the inspector on one job went along the lines of *"If all houses were built this way, our job would be a hell of a lot easier!"*

Unfortunately, what happened over the next months and years, just as interest was starting to turn into new business, was that I found out that I had gone in to business with someone I should not have done! Unfortunately, this person was not the financial director he had claimed to be and he was slowly financially ruining the business. I tried to get him to step down but he had no intention of doing so, so after a tumultuous couple of years I eventually simply had to leave the company early in 2014. This was all the more frustrating as I left just after I had secured significant further funding from another investor, money which was earmarked for considerably expanding the company and for getting it established within the UK offsite construction" market.

So, there we are, a brief history of my journey to where I stand now, with regard to how I think we should be building houses in the UK.

Now I will, in a *totally unbiased* manner *(Hmmm!)* run you through the main choices for the alternative build methods that you can adopt for your own project. I may repeat a few things that I have already said in this and previous chapters, but I want this to be a stand-alone section that you can read and re-read until you decide which is going to be the best option for you and your family, so I need to cover all the main points here.

House Building methods

1) Traditional Build (or *Brick & Block* or *Block and Block* construction")

This is the construction method that we are all familiar with: "Good solid houses" are built this way and have been for as long as most of us can remember. This is true, some of the time!

Let's look back thirty years or so to how houses were built then:

During the seventies and eighties, insulation in housing was given very little thought. Standard wall construction was usually built as shown here:

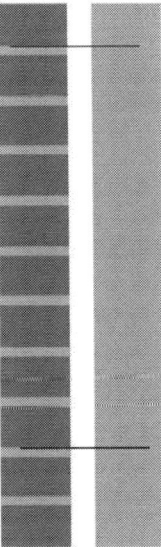

Pre 1970's
Wall 10" wide
2" Cavity
4" Concrete block
No insulation

On the outside would be a brick, with a 2" cavity separating the brick from a 4" concrete block, which formed the internal skin.

This internal skin was then plastered with 2 coats, the first being a cement render and the second a thin, finishing coat just 2mm thick, called the skim coat.

This internal wall construction was usually in blockwork (at least downstairs). This, together with the external walls construction, is what gives that solid feel to the house, the feel we older folk grew up with. Its strength meant we could hang cupboards or anything else we wanted to on the walls.

As time passed, it started to become usual to build at least some of the upstairs internal walls out of timber so that they were lighter. By being lighter they didn't need to have support all the way down to the foundations, which in turn meant that they did not have to sit on top of the downstairs walls. This meant that the first floor could be laid out differently to the ground floor Up until then, it was common practice to find the upstairs layout almost exactly the same as the downstairs layout, with all the upstairs walls built in blockwork.

The houses of that time were good and solid, but very cold. They needed constant heating during the winter months, but that was not a major problem because energy was relatively cheap, so people just used a mixture of extra clothing and whatever heating system they had to keep themselves warm.

As the norm of building all walls in blockwork or brick started to change, and the upstairs walls were basically built out of simple timber framed panels, with a plasterboard each side, people started to complain, saying that the walls were too flimsy and not soundproof.

If you think about it, that change from block to timber walls and the resultant reducing of the levels of soundproofing within the building was the cause of the first complaint levied against timber frames being used as a part of the house building process, so in fact the timber frame problem actually began before modern day timber frames even became widely known or used (I say modern day because timber frames have been used in the UK for over 1000 years, they were just a bit more chunky in those days than they are now!)

We now come forward a few years to the time when insulation started to become something that the building regulations people were paying more attention to. Things were changing. Land prices were increasing rapidly. We were starting to talk about how we were using the planets resources up at too fast a rate and energy prices were starting to nudge upwards.

As these events occurred, the building regulations people started to realise that they would have to start taking these concerns in to account and the regulations started to change in favour of more insulation in the external walls, under the floor slabs and in the roof. Double glazing also became the norm in new homes.

Taking this on board, housebuilders started to re-think the way they built the external walls of their houses. They wanted to keep construction costs as cheap as possible, so they liked the idea of using fibreglass as an insulating material, because it was cheap to buy and easy to use.

The thinking on standard wall construction then started to change a bit, with a move made to widen the cavities (and thus the overall width of the wall) and fix the fibreglass insulation to the blockwork internal skin, with the width of the cavity itself reducing to anything from 1" upwards. This led to walls looking like the one shown here:

1970's & 1980's
Wall 11" wide
3" cavity
4" Concrete block
2" insulation

One of the other products that started to become more popular at the time was the lightweight concrete insulating block, which was used to replace the solid blocks for the internal skins of the external walls, offering better insulation values, but at about twice the price per block.

Building regulations continued to be upgraded over the coming years and developers were set higher targets in terms of insulation values for every part of the house. One of the ways to achieve the higher levels of insulation in the walls, was to further widen the cavity and increase the thickness of the insulation. The other common method was to use a 6" insulating block in place of the 4" standard block which had been widely used until then.

One phase the walls went through, was to be built without *any* air cavity, with the insulation forming a "full fill" across the cavity width (this is something which has been coming back in to fashion over the past few years as traditional build struggles to meet the insulation requirement of the latest building regs).

After a few more years the building regs people decided that the full cavity was not really a good idea, as it cancelled out two of the benefits that installing a cavity had offered in the first place, which were 1): To keep moisture from passing through to the wall to the inside of the building and 2) To offer a natural thermal break to the structure of the wall (*so why has it been making a comeback? I ask myself!*)

The construction of external walls in housing continued at the same sort of specifications, sometimes with a cavity and sometimes without, until around 2005 when global warming really started to hit the headlines and when both scientists' and politicians' minds turned to finding ways to save the planet.

1990's & 2000's
Wall 12" wide
2" cavity
6" lightweight concrete block
2" insulation

So, when we built houses, it was seen that more insulation was going to be one of the obvious next steps to take.

Full cavities became ok again (before going out of fashion <u>again</u> a while later) as an option to allow builders to increase the insulation at the same time as trying to keep the wall widths down as much as possible. Wide cavities soon became commonplace. I remember seeing cavities of 125mm wide in some new houses, with 100mm of insulation fitted and a 25mm open cavity.

Now, to my mind, this started to become less of a cavity wall and more of two single walls held together by bits of wire (the cavity ties). I started to get concerned over the structural stability of some of these walls, especially with the ways the major housebuilders seemed to throw them up in no time flat.

There were five natural by-products of this constant drive to increase insulation values in new homes:

1) The walls carried on getting wider and wider (whilst the room sizes in the building got smaller and smaller).
2) They became harder and slower to build.
3) There was more waste generated, which had to be taken off site and often ended up at tips of one sort or another.
4) The carbon footprint for building the walls increased as more and more deliveries to site were needed to provide the larger amounts of *everything* needed to build the walls.
5) They became much more expensive to build.

The higher cost probably had the biggest effect on the industry, as it also coincided around that time, with the significant and continuing increase in land prices. These two factors meant that the main house builders had to find ways to either get higher prices for the same houses (which was difficult with all the competition in the industry), or get more houses onto the same area of land.

The way they got around this problem (or so they thought), was to start to shrink the size of new houses so they could squeeze more units to an acre onto their sites.

Wider walls and smaller houses obviously meant smaller rooms, which is exactly what we have been getting for the past 20 years or so, with the problem getting worse and worse as time goes on.

The funny thing is that, if what I said in Chapter 5 is true, the shrinking of the size of the houses is not the way to save money.

(I showed how the cost of a building does not increase as a straight-line graph as the floor area increases. If you are simply adding or subtracting mainly air the cost difference is minimal. The best ways to save money in the build cost are:

1) Build quickly (and well). If you build good houses, more people want to buy them and your profits will increase because of the increased number of sales per year, rather than trying to squeeze more money out of each sale by cheating the customer.

2) Reduce the wall thickness back down to what they used to be, by better designing the way the wall is constructed and the way it insulates the home.

Coming up to date:

As we all well know, the drive to save the planet has not slowed down, and indeed is now becoming an important part of our everyday lives. The drive to save energy, build sustainably and to create lower carbon footprints is now an on-going quest and every year the building regulations are getting more and more stringent in these respects.

To build the shell of your house in brick and block, to anything like a good level of insulation, you are now looking at walls up to 16" thick. Over the two external walls that equates to 32" of total external wall width. It used to be 20" for the two walls in the seventies.

So, there is the first part of our honest look at traditional brick and block construction in housing and it does not paint a particularly rosy picture. The real thing to think about it, is that, unless there is some radical new thinking on this type of construction, the same factors that we have just been looking at which are making this process slow, inefficient and expensive *now*, will only get worse as time goes on.

However, unfortunately, the problems do not end there.

Traditional brick and block construction really struggles with airtightness.

For those who are unfamiliar with this term, houses now have to be very airtight. I am not a fan of this new type of regulation.

As a new house is completed, it has to undergo an air pressure test, which is becoming nearly as important in the eyes of the building regulations department as the levels of insulation in the building.

To achieve a decent standard of airtightness in a house you need to stop the air from leaking out anywhere. The test aims to see how much air can escape from the new building by pressurizing the whole structure and then recording how quickly it returns to normal pressure as air escapes from it. The test involves you having to seal or tape up every hole in the building (air vents, extractor hoods, chimneys, letter box, trickle vents etc.), before the testing. Your score is based on how slowly the pressure reduces once the building is theoretically airtight.

In my opinion, the daft thing about this test and the thing that makes it a waste of time, is that after the test has been completed, you then go around and take off all the tape you have put over everything vaguely resembling a route out for the air, so now the air can continue to escape to its heart's content!

I do wonder how much money will be saved in heating bills per year from the tiniest of tiny trickles of air that could potentially find their way under a skirting board, or some other part of the wall surface and through a badly filled joint, into the cavity and beyond!

Compare any savings to the cost of having the test done and the loss of productivity on site by everyone having to stop work and get out of the house for the time it takes to seal it up, test it and unseal it!

I also tend to think that this test is less designed to save money on airtightness and more to make builders build better (which in itself is not a bad thing), by scaring them into making sure that they think about each part of the build process as they work, just in case whatever they do wrong causes them to fail the air test, leaving them with the problem of trying to find the leaks and fix them.

Back to brick and block versus the air test:

Brick and block construction by its very nature is not good at making leakless structures. Blocks are rough textured, so are bricks. Gaps in joints are commonplace and reveals (openings for windows and doors) are often not quite plumb, so the window and door frames don't fit well to the openings. Each one of these construction weaknesses allows air and heat to escape from the building.

As things are now, we are having to build to more and more strict regulations of all types, before our houses will be awarded a building regulations completion certificate.

By 2020, as I understand it, the aim is to be producing pretty much carbon neutral new homes.

I simply don't think traditional brick and block construction is going to be able to reach that goal, whatever people do to try to change it to make it do so.

How sustainable is brick and block as a build method?

Unfortunately, "Not very" has to be the answer, for the following reasons:

- The basic materials (bricks and blocks) are not classed as sustainable.
- Brick and blocks require a lot of carbon creating activities to manufacture, deliver and construct the walls with them.
- They are not particularly recyclable.
- By being slow to construct, the whole building process takes a long time to complete, which means that carbon creating activities are going on, both offsite and on site, a lot longer than they need to.
- They are not good insulators.
- They are not particularly airtight.
- They create a lot of waste which often has to be collected and tipped (two more carbon creating activities).

How does the overall cost of building brick and block houses compare with the alternatives?

Again, unfortunately, not very well.

This is where we get in to the argument of "Which is the cheapest way to build?" This argument has been going on for many years and no-one has come up with a definitive answer. Why?

Because there are too many variables.

In some industries, it is easy to compare like for like when it comes to the products it produces. However, in the housebuilding industry it is very difficult to make an accurate.

Even two identical houses built next door to each other could have significantly differing build costs due to different sets of problems brought about by the condition of the plot, the drainage, the services, and many other factors. As far as I know, no one has ever tried to do a like for like comparison between two identical houses, one of traditional build and one of timber frame construction. Even if they had, the results would not necessarily be relevant to a different style or design of house.

As we have not yet covered some of the subjects which deal with how costs are affected by many different factors, I can't really go in to detail yet, on why this method of build has probably become one of the most expensive ways to build a house of all the main systems. At the moment, all I will say is "It just has". As you carry on reading, the reasons why should become clear.

How does building with brick and block compare with the alternatives for speed of build?

I am afraid to have to say that the answer is "Not very well" again. In fact, it is probably the slowest way to build a house of all the mainstream building methods.

Conclusions on traditional construction

- A good solid method of construction, giving strong houses, with good sound insulation between all rooms that are divided by blockwork (as opposed to timber) walls.
- It is easy to hang heavy objects on the block walls without having to use special fixings.
- It gives a solid feel to the completed house.
- It is not a good insulator and it is now starting to suffer from that weakness by having to continually evolve to try to keep up with thermal insulation and airtightness requirements for new build housing.
- The thermal and airtightness weaknesses will continue to make it a more expensive and less viable option year on year into the foreseeable future. At some stage it will become economically unviable as a build method.

- It is the slowest of the commonly used house building systems.
- It is not a sustainable building method.
- The build process is more vulnerable to the weather than some other systems.

2) Timber frame

Timber frame should have wiped the floor with the competition in the UK thirty years ago. It failed to do so.

Why? Well, as usual, we Brits made a pig's ear of it!

There are a number of stories knocking around about how timber frame got a bad reputation. The one that rings true to me is the one I personally experienced and talked about earlier, where there was nothing wrong with the frame itself, but the developers erecting the frames during the seventies were using screws that could rust - and they did, leaving the external brickwork skin of the wall trying to escape from the timber frame itself.

The bad press that came after the problem was made public, knocked timber frame as a product, back by probably ten years or more. It has still not fully recovered.

To be fair and not to put all the blame on the original problem, a lot of the UK's commercial house building industry has also done its best to make things worse for itself, by building timber framed homes from the skinniest, cheapest materials they can get their hands on, with more of an emphasis on speed and profit than on quality.

The use of cheap materials, thin internal walls and the poor workmanship that went into throwing up many of the developers' timber framed homes, meant that many people who either lived in (or even visited) one have always been quickly struck by how flimsy, poorly finished, noisy and creaky they are.

The use of low quality materials, together with shoddy workmanship resulted in a poor quality living experience for the people who either bought or rented these houses and once word of this got round, the reputation of what can actually be an excellent product (if it is designed and constructed properly) was so badly damaged that it never fully recovered.

Developers continue to use timber frames today and in fact I would say that I see a lot more new timber framed houses going up these days than I did 10 to 15 years ago. However, the ones I do see, still seem to be trying to get away with using all the cheapest materials possible, just aiming to scrape through the process of conforming to building regs by the skin of their teeth.

Self-builders have (sort of) saved the day for timber frames in the UK. They tend to approach the whole building process differently. They are not usually looking to build as cheaply as possible. They are more likely to want the best. They are not trying to scrape through building regs, they want to sail majestically through with their chest puffed out with pride!

So what that has meant is that timber frames built by self-builders have actually generally been well built, to high specifications and in an eco-friendly way. More like the other countries where timber frame is and has been done properly for many years (countries like Canada, America, Germany, Sweden, Norway etc.).

So what else has gone wrong?

- In the UK, we tend to make fairly small timber frame panels (up to around 8' long x 8' high) in the factory and bring them to site on fairly small flatbed trucks. The fact that the panels are only small and fairly light has meant that a couple of chippies can either to carry them onto site between them, or bring them from the wagon to the building with a forklift and then manhandle them into position.

This is fine in itself but the industry has never taken advantage of the fact that this product could easily be made in very large panels which, with the use of a telehandler or crane on site, could speed up the erection time and reduce the overall build time very significantly.

- Developers have not insulated the buildings, either thermally or acoustically as well as they should have. This has led to the growing (and deserved) "noisy, cold house" reputation that has attached itself to the product in the eyes of the general public.
- We have not addressed one of the public's worries that timber is a fire risk. Of course it is, but the alternative homes built by *"traditional construction"* methods still usually use timber for all of the following components: *floor joists, floor boards, upstairs (and some downstairs) walls, roof trusses, internal doors, architraves, skirting boards, kitchen units, stairs, handrails and windows.*

    The main problem with fires in houses has never mainly been caused by the timber in the structure, it has been more to do with the stuff we have been filling the rooms up with, not being fireproof. Things like settees and chairs, tables, drawer units, wardrobes, cabinets, soft furnishings, blankets, carpets, vinyl flooring etc. Gloss paint is also oil based and flammable.

    The fact is, that timber frames are covered with plasterboard. Plasterboard is a fireproofing material and building regulations requirements demand that the plasterboard or some other materials will protect the frame in the case of fire, long enough for the occupants to exit the building, just as they would be able to in traditionally built houses.

    What the timber frame suppliers need to start doing is to tell people how fireproof their product is, rather than keeping quiet on the subject. They could also start to use cement board instead of plasterboards for the external walls (cement boards are far more fire resistant than plasterboards).

- The industry has never (until recently) properly highlighted the benefits of timber frame with regard to sustainability, recyclability, airtightness, warmth, speed of build, strength etc. They need to do so.
- No one has ever come up with definitive and accurate figures to prove what like for like costs are between timber frame and traditional build, taking in to account not only physical costs, but also related and resultant costs (such as the fact that if you build a house twice as fast, you could potentially build twice as many and make two lots of profit over the same period of time).

    If these comparisons had been prepared and published, I bet a pound to a penny that, until recently at least, timber frames would have been seen to be the cheapest way to build new homes, by a pretty large margin.

- Because of the early problems and the continuing rumours about the negative aspects of timber frames, the lenders have never fully been on board to back them as being a high-quality product.

    To be fair, there are now not many lenders who refuse to lend on timber frame, but that is due to a fairly recent change of heart, now that we are all taking much more interest in sustainability. Up until a few years ago, perhaps only one in two or three mortgage companies would be happy to lend to self-builders if they were proposing to build using any sort of timber system.

- The general house buying public have never been shown the advantages of timber frames. Developers that build using traditional build methods obviously would not want their buyers to know the advantages of a different system to the one they use, so they have kept quiet on the subject and the timber frame industry has never had a strong enough voice for them to be listened to by the masses. So the status quo has continued for many years and it is only the push for sustainability that is slowly bringing about a change in the way the public perceive timber frames, as possibly being a viable alternative product for the construction of their new homes.

Some basic facts about timber framed housing:

1) Timber frame in the UK is not a new thing. As I said earlier, there are timber frames dotted around the country that are over 1000 years old and still standing up quite happily!

They pre-date what we now refer to as traditional construction" (brick and block cavity walls) by a number of hundreds of years.

2) What we call timber frames are actually *modern* timber frames, which are computer designed and engineered so that they don't use as much timber to do the same job as the old style frames.

3) It is not the outside skin of a cavity wall that does the loadbearing work to carry the roof, it is the inside skin. The outside skin (normally the brickwork) is usually almost completely cosmetic. It takes little or no load at all. So in traditional build, the carrying work would be done by the blockwork internal skin and with timber frame it is actually the timber frame that carries the weight of the intermediate floors, all the superimposed loads (e.g. you and your furniture) and the weight of the roof. (this sort of blows the argument of "I want a brick built house because it is good and strong" out of the water!)

4) Timber frames are better than traditional build when it comes to making changes to the structure, either for *extending* or r*epairing*. For example: I recently saw the aftermath of a car crash where a car drove into the corner of a fairly new, traditionally built house. It completely smashed through the bottom 3' of both the brickwork outer skin and the blockwork inner skin of the wall. The shock from the impact on the structure as a whole, could well have cracked the joints of many courses of both brick and blockwork for a good distance along both the front and sides of the house, potentially going up all the way to the roof.

The biggest problem in this case will not have been with the brickwork outer skin of the wall, but with the blockwork inner skin, the one taking the weight of the roof and the first floor of the building.

As it was, the residents had to be moved out for 2 – 3 months. The structure had to be supported internally while investigations took place into the extent of the damage and outside, barriers were erected to protect the public just in case the whole wall collapsed.

As I looked at the damage I thought to myself: "If that had been a timber frame, only two panels would have been affected. We would have removed the damaged area of brickwork, propped the ceiling inside the room at that corner of the house with metal / timber props, cut out the damaged parts of the timber panels, checked the walls around the general area for any signs of cracking, replaced the damaged parts of the panels, then made good the brickwork on the outside. We would probably have done the work in three to four days without even having to move the residents out!"

A brief history of the modern timber frame:

In the 70s, when modern timber frames first started to be seen as a cost-effective alternative to brickwork and blockwork by the commercial house builders, both the external and the internal wall panels were generally constructed from 4" x 2" softwood timber studs. The external walls would be clad with a 9mm thick "OSB" board (orientated strand board) for strength and rigidity and there would be 4" of fibreglass insulation installed into the spaces between the studs of the timber frame panels.

The norm would be to have a 2" – 3" empty cavity and the outside skin of the wall would be constructed with either bricks or blocks (blockwork walls would then be finished with a cement render and masonry paint) to give the traditional finished appearance that we are used to seeing.

1970's - 2000's
Wall 10" wide
2" Cavity
4" frame
4" insulation

These timber frame walls, "like for like" will usually have been significantly warmer than the equivalent thickness wall built traditionally because of the inclusion of the 4" of insulation, but this level of insulation still falls a long way short of helping to achieve a house that could be classed as being well insulated or eco (believe it or not, some developers are still getting away with using these minimal levels of insulation in their new homes today).

On the outside of the frame is a paper-like covering called *breather paper*. This protects the timber panels from the weather until the cladding, whether that be brick, block, timber or cement board and render is complete (see image below).

Strips of nylon banding are stapled to the breather paper to indicate where the timber studs are positioned behind the OSB boarding (look closely at the image to see this banding), so that the external cladding can be fixed to what is the strongest part of the frame structure.

On the inside of the external wall frames (*not* the internal wall frames) is fixed a vapour barrier. This stops vapour from the inside of the building getting in to the timber frame structure. This construction generally helps timber frames to achieve significantly better levels of insulation and airtightness than traditional build, which can lead to lower fuel bills.

Timber frame panels come in lengths of anything from 2' up to 10' or even 12' lengths, with the maximum length being dictated by how they are going to be transported from the delivery wagon to their location in the building. If they are going to be carried by a couple of chippies they need to be quite light, in which case then the maximum length which would be safe to carry would be about 8'. If, however there is a forklift available on site, then they could be made up to around 12' in length.

Before the frame arrives, the scaffold is fully erected around all but one side of the foundations, leaving one side open to allow the panels to be brought in and distributed around the floor area, ready to be finally positioned and fixed. Which side of the scaffold is left open will normally be decided on site, depending on which direction the panels will be coming from as they are unloaded from the delivery wagon (this is normally the front).

It is usually a 2-man job to position and fix a panel and each panel will normally take about 10 to 15 minutes to position, check for plumb, fix to the floor and also fix to the panel adjacent to it.

To erect the ground floor panels for a standard 4 bed detached 2 storey house would normally take 2 – 3 days for 2 men, including all the unloading and depending on the weather.

Once the frame is up to first floor joist level, the missing side of scaffold is built to enclose the whole building.

At the same time, the first-floor joists can be cut, set and fixed, followed by the floor boarding.

My personal recommendation for a standard timber frame intermediate floor (first / second floor etc.) is that you consider using 22mm (not 18mm) moisture resistant, plastic coated chip board flooring. These boards normally come in 8' x 2' sheets. The moisture resistance means they tend to stand up to the rain better than cheaper options whilst the shell is being built. The extra 4mm of thickness helps with soundproofing, feels more solid and is less likely to creak. The cost of these boards is also pretty reasonable.

I would also suggest that, to minimize and possible negate altogether the chance of creaky floors becoming a problem, that you consider both screwing and gluing the boards to the joists. Chippies will tend to want to use a nail gun to nail the boards down, using ringshank nails. These are ok, but I have found in the past that if the boards contain a lot of moisture, once the house is complete, they can shrink. This can lead to a tiny bit of the nail sticking up from the surface of the board, which allows the board to move up and down slightly when it is stood on. This is what causes the creaks. You could theoretically go round at a later date and hit all the nails in further with a hammer, so they would not allow the boards to move, but by the time the boards have shrunk, the chances are that you will have fitted carpets or floor boards and filled the room with furniture, making getting at all the nails quite problematic.

Using screws will normally reduce or even cut out completely any movement of the boards. The glue will act as a belt and braces measure.

If your chippie argues against this method with you, ask him how he will guarantee that after he has fixed the floor that there will be no creaks and squeaks when the floor dries out.

Once the joists and floor boards are set and fixed and the scaffolding has been completed, the first-floor timber frame panels can be brought up, positioned and fixed, to take the shell up to wall plate level (I am assuming for this example that we are building a standard 2 storey house with a simple roof).

Loading, setting and fixing the first-floor panels will usually take a day or so longer than the ground floor due to the extra work in getting the panels from the ground floor up to the first floor (*however you may decide at this point to invest in hiring a telehandler or a crane to do this job and then follow straight on with the roof trusses, again using the crane to position them*).

The roof of a simple 2 storey, 4 bed detached timber framed house will normally be constructed using standard trusses, attic trusses, or built as what is known as a hand cut roof (I will look at roof construction in Chapter 12).

Once the roof is on, the timber frame is pretty much completed. If you are using a stage mortgage, once you have felted and battened the roof, ready for tiling, you can usually book the valuer to come and sign off this section of the project, which will normally mean that you'll get your next stage payment in the bank within a few days.

If we compare traditional build with timber frame on a like-for-like basis, from floor slab to weather tight, it will normally be seen that the timber frames option will be completed in around 25% - 35% of the time taken to complete the same amount of work traditionally.

Once the roof is on the inside work can start. This will be going on at the same time as the cladding (whether brick or block & render / timber cladding / cement board & render etc.)

Some people would say that it is a bit of a cheat to say that timber frames are so much faster than traditional building because the frame is only half the job. Once the frame is up, there is still a lot more work to do to complete the shell of the house, because you still have to build or fix whatever outside finish you are using (brick / block / cladding etc.).

I disagree: However you build a house, it is the finish date of the completed job that dictates how fast or slow the build method is. With a timber frame, once the frame is up, you can get straight on with working inside the building at the same time as finishing the outside. This significantly speeds up the project overall.

Conclusions on timber frame construction:

- It gives a faster, more sustainable build than traditional build, which if done right can significantly outperform traditional construction, at potentially a lower cost.
- Timber frame has missed a trick with marketing itself. The poor reputation it gained from the early problems it encountered when it started to become widely used has never really gone away.
- It is much easier to achieve higher levels of insulation and airtightness with timber frame than with brick and block houses.
- People are still slightly afraid of it as a product when it comes to strength, noise, fire resistance and longevity. This could easily be remedied.
- It is easy to achieve high levels of soundproofing in a timber framed house.
- Although it gives a faster build than traditional construction, it is still not particularly fast.
- It can suffer from the results of too much bad weather during construction, by the timber expanding when wet and then drying out later, causing minor, irritating problems.
- Some types of insulation that are used in the frame can also be ruined if they get wet.
- The builder needs to decide where heavy objects will need to be supported within the building and strengthen the walls at those locations before plaster boarding. This means that the building is not particularly future proof if other heavy objects need to be fixed to walls after the build has been completed.
- It is more flexible in terms of design than brick and block and more forgiving of mistakes during construction. If you miss a window out, just cut a hole, build in a lintel, frame the hole out and you have your window opening! This would be a big, slow, expensive job with traditionally built houses.
- The majority of lenders are fine with timber frames these days, as are the insurance companies.
- I like the feel of living in a timber framed house better than living in a traditionally built home. I think it feels healthier.
- For self-builders it offers the advantage of having a big chunk of your new home coming on the back of a wagon at a reasonable price and going up without much, if any input from you during the process.
- By having the shell of the house manufactured in a factory and erected on site there is less likelihood of errors occurring during the build (things missing or in the wrong place).
- The self-build market is the best place for timber frame. Commercial builders tend to build it too cheaply and quickly and it struggles to offer a satisfactory end product when that is the case.
- Given a choice between timber frame and traditional build, having used both options on many occasions, I would opt for timber frame every time.
- I think that as a product competing in the housebuilding market with some of the new offsite manufactured products, it is now found to be wanting in some areas, including quality, strength, noise, speed of build, airtightness, insulation, fire resistance and other potential problems down the line. To compete it would have to reinvent itself and be marketed much better.

3) SIPS panels (structurally insulated panelling system):

This is one of the new kids on the block in the UK, but is a product that has been around for quite a while in other countries. In the UK, it has not yet really taken off in England and Wales but is becoming popular in Scotland.

The SIPS system as a whole, offers some noticeable advantages over both traditional construction and standard timber frame build, but it also has a few minor, in built drawbacks.

As a product it is possibly the simplest in terms of manufacture, being made up of 2 sheets of OSB board (oriented strand board) and rigid foam insulation, all glued together to create a very strong, highly insulated, lightweight panel. The thickness of the panel is limited only by the available thicknesses of the rigid foam insulation boards, which means that both strength and insulation values are pretty flexible depending on the budget available.

One big difference between SIPS and standard timber frame relates to the thermal insulation values achieved within the external wall panels. Timber framed buildings usually opt for fibreglass insulation in the external wall panels. Fibreglass is not nearly as good as rigid foam as a thermal insulator, so like-for-like in terms of panel thickness, SIPS will give you a significantly warmer house.

Depending on the budget available, SIPS, as a system can be used for the construction of passive house homes (passive house basically means that the building needs little or no energy to achieve a comfortable internal temperature year-round).

Technical:

SIPS, as a building method is classed as one of the modern methods of construction and thus, unsurprisingly has a bit more technology incorporated into its design and manufacture. We don't need to go into all the details of how it is made or its performance figures here. Suffice to say, it is strong, it is warm, it is quick and it is fairly reasonably priced.

What I do just want to touch on related to the technical side of the product, are a few of the advantages it offers, including:

- **Speed of build:** When compared "like-for-like" to a standard self-build and if you can get hold of large panels, SIPS will usually give you one of the quickest ways to go from slab to weathertight (and often your all-important next stage payment).
  To install the large SIPS panels, you will need a crane, so it stands to reason that if you are using a mechanical lifting device which is moving large panels straight from the delivery wagon to the location where they will be fixed, the shell of the house is going to be completed pretty quickly.
  If you do a quick search on SIPS house building videos on you tube, you will see some very impressive example of how these houses can go up in next to no time.
  A perfectly attainable slab to weathertight build time for a simple 4 bed detached house could be around 3 – 5 days. Once it is up you also need to remember that the insulation is already fitted (whereas with standard timber frame the insulation has to be fitted on site later).
- **Reduced cold bridging:** rigid foam is a good insulator, timber is not. Cold bridging is where part of a wall allows heat to escape from the inside to the outside due to poor insulation within its structure. In a standard timber frame, the timber studs that form part of frame itself are the weakness in terms of cold bridging. SIPS do not use timber studs; the rigid foam runs continuously both horizontally and vertically around each floor of the building. So, in terms of reducing cold bridging a SIPS wall will be the far better option.

True as this may be, it is not the end of the story. When we are talking about external walls and cold bridging, we also need to think about the overall performance of the wall in terms of thermal insulation. To do this we need to look at the u-value of the wall as a whole.

The u-value represents the heat retaining qualities of the wall and it takes in to consideration all contributing factors, including cold bridging. The lower the u-value the better are the heat retaining qualities of the wall.

The way I see it is that it is more important to have a lower u-value for the wall overall, as a finished job, than having less cold bridging in some parts of it. So what I do is look at the wall as a full package and consider: How much will it cost to build this wall so that it achieves the u-value I am looking for whilst keeping the costs down?" In other words, if you are considering using SIPS, remember to compare not only the cold bridging statistics, but also the overall u-vales and the difference in the supply and erect costs for the various wall panel products available.

- **SIPS panel sizes:** As usual some of "us Brits" aren't really up to speed when it comes to making the most of new technology and this is often the case when it comes to SIPS manufacture.

  SIPS panels can be made in very large sizes. Large sizes mean fewer joints, better airtightness, a faster build and potentially a lower overall build cost.

  Unfortunately, a lot of SIPS manufacturers in the UK don't have the facilities to manufacture the large SIPS panels and instead stick to between 8' x 4' or 8' x 8' as their standard panel size.

  Basically, apart from less cold bridging and better overall insulation values, this means that they are pretty much reverting to the standard timber frame way of building the shell of the house, bit by bit, carrying the panels to their positions by hand, plumbing up each one and fixing each one to the next. This is most definitely not even coming close to making the most of the potential of the product.

  Luckily there are some UK companies who do have the facilities to manufacture larger panels (you need a gantry crane and long tables to make them on in the factory). If you can find one of these companies they should be able to provide you with a kit that will go up far quicker, be better performing with regard to airtightness and thermal insulation, give a better quality overall finished job and potentially be cheaper (due to less work being needed to erect the kit on site).

  If you can find such a company, you will also potentially be able to make the most of one of the biggest advantages of the SIPS system:

- **The SIPS roof:** One of the biggest selling point for the SIPS system to my mind, is the fact that the strength of the panels allows them to be used to create completely open roof spaces (with no roof trusses filling up the space and making it unusable for anything but storing boxes and the artificial Christmas tree!)

  The way this works is that the panels simply span from the wall plate (the top of the external wall) to the ridge of the roof, leaving the roof space underneath the panels almost completely empty (there may be the need for a small support wall or purlin, depending on the length of the slope of the roof).

  This gives every SIPS system user the potential to get an extra floor in their house at almost no extra cost. In real terms that one fact can theoretically turn a 2000 sq ft, 2 storey, 4 bed house into a 3000 sq ft, 3 storey, 5 or 6 bed house, for around the same build cost.

If you are considering having a SIPS roof, it will almost certainly mean that you will need to use a crane for the erection of the frame, whether or not you are getting the smaller or larger wall panels.

So now that you know about the SIPS roof, when you are considering the design of your house, you can start to think about making the most of the free space in the roof that it will give you as part of your design

Additionally, if you think about that for a minute, that extra floor area in the roof could potentially increase the value of your house by up to 30%.

Good eh?

- **Floor cassettes:** Another benefit that some SIPS manufacturers can offer is the floor cassette. Instead of cutting and setting each joist individually on site, if a crane is going to be used, you could ask the manufacturers if they can supply floor cassettes as part of the overall frame kit. This could can save more time and money and reduce site generated waste (thus lowering the carbon footprint for the build).
- **More efficient scaffolding:** With a SIPS build where a crane is being used to erect the kit, it is not usually necessary to leave one side of the scaffolding open to allow the panels to be brought in and positioned (as is usually the case with small panel SIPS and standard timber frame construction). Instead the whole of the scaffolding can usually be completely erected before the kit arrives on site.
  This can have the advantage of to ensuring that progress is not held up whilst you wait (sometime for days) for the scaffolders to get back to your site whenever they are needed, to alter or extend the existing scaffold. This can not only give both time and cost saving on the overall project programme, but it can also often result in the scaffolding remaining safer for longer due to the fact that it is not constantly being altered as the building work progresses.
- **Potentially higher levels of airtightness:** If you use the SIPS system, but more especially if you use the large panels in both the walls and the roof, you will stand a good chance of getting some very good levels of airtightness in the finished building.

Large panel SIPS have few joints, both in the panels themselves and in terms of the number of joints made by joining the panels together. This can result in the creation of a very airtight finished building. An airtight building will usually give you better u-values and lower heating bills. It is also essential if you want to try to get anywhere near building a passive house.

The negatives points:

- **Cost:** At the moment, because it is still a niche product in most of the UK, SIPS are still tending to be expensive when compared like-for-like with the alternatives. If you can use the large panels, this extra cost could be at least partly negated by the saving in time that you will benefit from in getting the whole job completed sooner.
  (*The other thing to bear in mind related to cost is that if you are getting the third floor free by using SIPS, you are getting a lot more house for your money*).
  The best way to find out if a SIPS quote is competitive is to get other quotes from different products and compare what each of them gives you in terms of what the kit includes, price, speed of build etc.
- **The manufacturing process:** SIPS panels are glued together. The OSB board is glued to the rigid insulation board with a very strong adhesive. It is the bond between the timber and the insulation that gives the panel its strength.
  If that bond were ever to fail, all that would be left would be 2 loose sheets of OSB and a sheet of foam insulation holding the house up! OK, that won't happen, but to make sure it doesn't, the companies making SIPS have to go through rigorous checks to make sure their manufacturing process are of the highest quality. These checks are very expensive and so are the accreditations they need to gain the confidence of potential clients. The cost of all this quality assurance work adds significantly to the selling price of the kits and makes some people a bit nervous about the longevity of the product.
- **Service installation:** With traditional construction all the services (electrical wiring, gas pipes, phone cables etc.) are fixed to the brick or block walls then a plaster finish covers them all over. With a timber frame, there is plenty of room inside the frame to install the services before the plasterboard is fixed. With SIPS, because the panel is solid, there is nowhere for the service cables and pipes to go. This leaves you with two options:

1. **You can install service conduits** into the panel during manufacture, to run the cables and pipes through. To do this you would need to design the full service installation (wiring and pipework) prior to the panels being manufactured. This should not really present any major problem, but if you forget anything and the panel is manufactured and installed before you realise, it is not easy to add extra service runs without taking slices out of the front of the panel, then trying to make them good after the service run was installed. This would not only be a nuisance, but could also potentially weaken the structure of the panel itself.

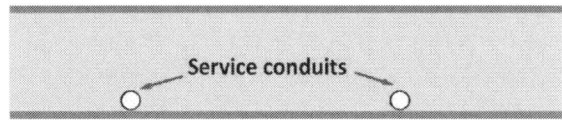

2. **You can add a service void** to the inside skin of the wall. In simple terms a service void is normally created by nailing or screwing lengths of timber batten (usually 2" x 1" or 2" x 2") to the face of the panel. This creates a void which into to which the services are installed. Once that work is complete, a plasterboard is normally fixed across the battens to complete the wall.

   The drawback of adding a service void is that it will reduce the room size by up to 5" in each direction (2 x 2.5") when compared to fitting all the services into the basic wall panel structure. You will also probably need to fit noggins behind the plasterboards as you have to do for standard timber frame.

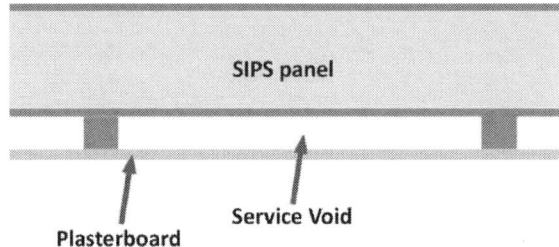

- **Re-sale potential:** In Scotland, there is not much problem when it comes to selling SIPS homes. They are popular and respected as a method of constructing houses. In the rest of the UK however, the story is slightly different. In England, Ireland and Wales, SIPS are still looked at a bit suspiciously. There are not enough of them around for everyone to have heard of them and we always tend get a bit worried about anything new, until it has been around for a long time and has been properly tried and tested.

  I would have to say that I see both sides of this. I think the product is a very good one. I would use it, if only at first on one of my own houses, to see if it as good as it sounds. I would be checking on the value for money that it offers before booking it and I would talk to estate agents to ask what sort of welcome it tends to get from house buyers and lenders, before making my final decision.

  What would put me off is if I could only get hold of small panels (this would be a job stopper for me). I would also be concerned if I ever heard of an example of the glue binding between the OSB and the rigid insulation failing and if I would have trouble selling the finished property at some time in the future.

Finishing treatments with SIPS

SIPS panels are very flexible when it comes to the options for finishing the external walls of the house. They are often used in conjunction with the following external skin treatments.

Facing brick and cavity: This gives a wall which is quite similar in construction to a standard timber frame, when it has a brick external skin. It is also constructed in pretty much the same way, using ties to fix the bricks to the OSB boards (which form part of the SIPS panels). The finished appearance of the house is almost identical to a traditionally built brick and block house.

Block and render: A similar construction method to the one used to clad a standard timber frame with a block finish, using metal ties to fix the block to the OSB boards.

Once the blockwork has been built, it is normally finished with 2 coats of render and a paint finish, giving the look of a traditionally built, rendered house.

Batten, cement board and render: This is an alternative to rendering onto a blockwork external skin.

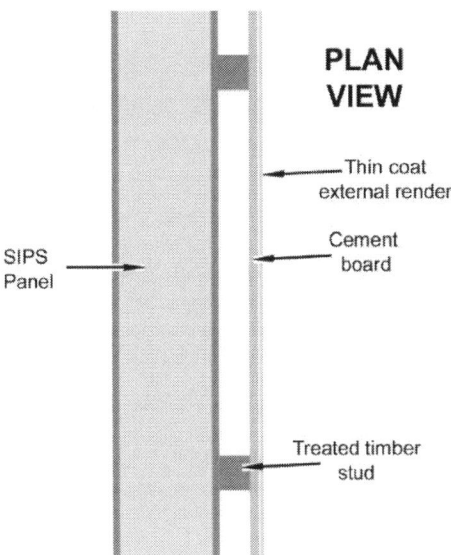

Treated timber battens are fixed to the outside of the SIPS panel and these are, in turn fitted with a cement board covering. A thin coat render (*one of the newer types of render*) is then applied to the face of the cement board to give an appearance almost identical to a traditional render. The render can either be painted or come with a self-coloured finish.

The benefit of using this option of finish with a SIPS construction wall is that it gives a much thinner overall wall construction, which in turn gives more floor space inside the building.

Batten and cladding: As with the batten, cement board and render finish, treated timber battens are fixed to the exterior face of the panel, however with this system, timber, plastic (or a timber / plastic mix), cladding panels or boards are fixed to the timber battens (rather than the cement board, followed by the thin coat render). These panels / boards can be delivered pre finished, which means that once the house is fully clad, the wall needs no decoration and is, to all intents and purposes, complete.

This method of mixing SIPS with a treated batten and pr-finished cladding represents one of the fastest ways to build the shell of your new home and if you accept my claim that speed of build can save money, It could be a very prudent option to consider.

If, however a cladding finish is not acceptable, either to you or to the local planning authority, then the SIPS panels with a batten, cement board and thin coat render could be the next preferred option. Alternatively, you could consider a cement board with brick slips (thin slices of bricks glued to the cement boards and jointed to look like normal brickwork).

Conclusions on SIPS construction:

- SIPS is a fairly new product to the UK and can potentially offer a product that would be good enough to become very popular. However, to my mind it needs to be brought down in price and the larger panel sizes start be offered by all SIPS companies.
- Its main advantage is the free space in the roof, which must give it the edge over many other types of construction, as it gives extra accommodation, almost free of charge, in any house where it is used.
- It is a good product for self-builders to consider, if for no other reason than a very big chunk of your new home comes on the back of a wagon and goes up quickly.
- It is also a good product to consider if you are trying to get a very airtight and well insulated home, possibly heading towards Passive House standard (especially when the large panels are used).
- SIPS have not quite grasped the imagination of the self-build market in England or Wales, but they already very popular in Scotland. SIPS companies just need to sharpen their act a little bit and get their product marketing better so that people don't see them so much as an alternative building product and more of a competitor to traditional construction and standard timber frame.
- They need to allay any fears over any possible breakdown of the bonding of the glue to the insulation and possibly find a way of reducing the need for the service void, whilst allowing extra fittings to be installed simply and quickly.
- It also needs to actively dispel rumour about "racking" "bellying" and "off-gassing". I am not going to go in to detail on these subjects here. As far as I am concerned they are terms which have been bandied about (mainly by competitors) since the product was launched in the UK to try to make buyers nervous, but which I don't think are particularly significant these days. You could to ask the manufacturers about them if you are interested in the overall concept of the product for your own project.

Apart from that as far as I can tell, SIPS is a perfectly good building option.

4) Closed Panel Timber Frame Construction:

Well I did say earlier that although I have manufactured my own version of this product, I would do my best to be unbiased when comparing all the main choices of construction methods available to you. - That is what I have tried to do so far and what I will continue to try to do. Wish me luck!

As you read this chapter, you might think I am trying to persuade you that this product is the best simply because I am trying to get your business. I am not. I don't have the company any more, I left (as I explained earlier) after a disagreement on how things should work, with the financial director.

Not only am I not working for my own company, but neither do I have any proper links with any other company. I have seen a couple of companies who seem to be pretty good, but I am not going to push anyone on you. I'll just tell you what's what and leave the rest to you.

Let's start with a bit about the industry

The closed panel system has, up until recently been mainly provided to the UK by the European countries. UK based closed panel companies have been and continue to be a fairly rare animal to find! That is now starting to change.

We have all watched the TV shows like Grand Designs, where a house kit arrives on the back of a big posh sign written truck from Germany, with insulation, plaster-boards and windows already fitted, sockets and switches already built in, door frames fitted and sometimes even with the external render applied before it left the factory.

These kits usually come accompanied by a group of smartly kitted out tradesmen equipped with all the best tools, who travel over from Germany and stay until the job has been professionally and efficiently completed, creating a new home with minimal waste or fuss, usually in a very short time and to the customer's *complete* satisfaction.

Wouldn't it be nice if all houses were built like that here in the UK?

Theoretically they could be. The problems that stop that from happening at the moment are:

I. We are pretty much always a good few years behind the leading countries when it comes to anything to do with the housing market.
II. Much of the thinking in UK housebuilding is still stuck in traditional brick and block mode.
III. The price of the foreign imports is presently too high when compared to their UK competitors (standard timber frame / SIPS / traditional) for them to be an economically viable option for the majority of self-builders or commercial builders.
IV. We don't have a workforce that is trained up to a sufficiently high standard in this type of construction for us to be able to offer it as a standard option across the UK.

A few years ago, at one of the self-build shows, I was talking to one of the bosses of one of the well-known German closed panel companies and I asked "Why do you always bring your own guys over to build the houses?" he answered "Because we wouldn't trust the Brits *to get it right!*".

OK, he is actually probably right! But hearing those words really annoyed me. The fact that other countries have such a low opinion of our house building industry was one of the main motivations that led me to start up my own closed panel manufacturing company, which would aim to provide a UK based product that could not only match the Germans and Scandinavians in terms of quality and speed of the build process, but at the same time, cost significantly less.

Within three years of making the decision to give it a go, I had developed the product and got a factory up and running. That was the good bit, however as time went on I have to admit that I slowly came to realise that what the German guy said had an alarming air of truth about it!

As we developed the product, I was finding that because of the complexity of the kit and the skill and accuracy that was needed to put it all together correctly, I, or the foreman (who did have the needed skills) had to be watching the rest of the men almost every minute of every day, whether they were in the factory or on site, to make sure that they were doing the job properly, rather than succumbing to the "British Builders Disease" of "Oh that will do!"

Some of the experienced guys on site, generally the older ones, the ones who still take pride in their work, were keen to learn the new skills they needed, but quite often, with the (generally) younger lads, I would constantly be finding laziness creeping in and a general attitude of "I don't really care".

Just getting a full crew of men in the factory or on site every day was hard enough work, with people constantly taking days off for one reason or another, but I also found that even where I hired in fully experienced timber frame erectors to put the kits upon site, they often simply could not get the hang of all the new stuff they had to learn. Most of the timber frame erectors I came across were used to throwing timber frames up for commercial housing *companies and self-builders. They weren't used to working to tolerances of a couple of millimetres (which is what we needed to do). Usually if they got a house up within a couple of inches they were more than happy!*

So, after working with the company for a couple of years, in general, this is the way I see it now: Not only do UK housebuilders try to use the cheapest materials they can find to build the cheapest houses they can, but a high proportion of the UK construction workforce has got so used to not having to try, that no matter how good the product is, unless someone is there constantly making them work to a higher standard, they will often produce a poor quality finished product.

I am not talking here just about closed panel timber frame. I am talking about every form of house building, from traditional build through all the timber based products, to the specialist stuff. The malaise seems to run through the whole industry.

It is a shame that I have to speak about our building industry like this, but there it is.

Having said all that, there is hope. - YOU!

What the house building industry needs to get it into shape is to have higher numbers of customers who will simply not put up with second rate goods or work.

Where do we find most of those sorts of people at the moment? In the self-build marketplace!

If you are like most other potential self-builders, if and when you actually get going on your own project, you will probably be very keen to get a finished product that is both of high quality and good value.

The businesses who supply the self-build industry know this to be a fact and they know that if they want to win your business, they are going to have to up their game from the levels that maybe some other types of customers would be happy with.

So, if you go marching in to a timber frame manufacturer and tell them you are a self-builder, not only will they normally get the best cups and biscuits out for you, they will also tend to make sure that the product they present to you will be the best they can offer. YOU will get the "good gang" joiners making the frame, YOU will get the best gang of frame erectors (you will also tend to pay a slightly higher price, but for "one-off" customers, which is what you are likely to be, that is usually the way of things and is bearable as long as everything is "right").

So now, when we take the reasoning that self-builders will be looking for a good "kit" and a good quality job, - when we look at closed panel timber frame as an option, it stands to reason that you (as a self-builders), stand a good chance of getting the best quality in both materials and labour that the closed panel manufacturing company can offer.

From my experience, the companies which are taking on board the modern methods of construction (including closed panel) tend to be quite ambitious and are positioned at the more professional end of the market, getting a lot of their work by recommendation and reputation. So, by choosing closed panel built in the UK as your build option, as long as you can find a good quality supplier, you will be giving yourself the best chance of getting (what I see as) the best available product and the best people doing the job for you.

You want the quality, but you also need to be just as keen to get the best price too, so make sure you shop around. These companies will be quite happy to deliver a full house kit across the full length of the country, so as long as you are happy that they can also attend to any problems you may encounter with the frame once it has been erected. Don't worry about getting quotes from companies that are situated a few hundred miles away from your site.

OK, that's the end of that temporary diversion from the main topic! Let's get back to the proper stuff.

So, what is a closed panel timber frame system?

Think of a timber frame. Well closed panels are basically *timber frame plus*

As we discussed earlier in this chapter, the external walls of a standard timber frame are made of treated timber studs (normally 6" wide these days) with an OSB board and breather paper to the outside face.

The internal timber frame walls are also made of timber studs but are normally made up of 4" stud frame (sometimes treated) with no OSB board or breather paper fixed. Just studs.

Window and door openings are formed within the studs, with timber lintels above them and the rest of the materials for the kit usually all come loose, to be fixed / fitted on site.

That is normally it, that is a timber frame. That is what is delivered to site and erected.

The roof will usually be constructed using standard roof trusses, which will often come directly from a local roof truss manufacturer.

The difference between standard timber frame and closed panels is that a closed panel frame starts with this basic timber frame, but instead of then taking it to site, it is kept in the factory where much more work is done. This means that when it is erected on site it leaves significantly less work to do to finish the house completely.

This can theoretically lead to closed panel projects being completed in less than half the time of a traditional build and significantly faster than standard timber frame.

The main bonuses though are that they could also potentially actually *save you money* and give you a *better finished job* into the bargain.

What else happens to the standard timber frame in the factory to produce a closed panel?

One of the main advantages of closed is that, if the factory has a gantry or mobile crane, the panels can be made much bigger.

This image above was taken in my old factory and shows an 8' thick (in other words very warm) external wall frame being manufactured.

The length of this panel is probably around 12m (getting on for 40') and its height is the standard room height of 2.44m.

The lads are just turning it over after fitting the OSB (orientated strand board) to the outside of the frame, so that they can start work on the next phase, which is to fit the socket and light switch boxes, conduits to run the electrical cables / radiator pipes in, fit the fibreglass (or rigid foam insulation), the vapour barrier and the internal finishing board (plasterboard or cement board – see below for details).

Once that is all done, what we will have is a wall that is pretty much structurally complete, before it has even left the factory bench.

The image below shows a completed external wall panel.

You can see the finished internal wall board (we didn't use plasterboard, instead we opted for a much higher quality cement board which is much stronger, so it can take heavy weights without needing a supporting board to be fixed behind it. It is also quieter, more fire resistant, water resistant and gives a much more solid feel to the finished houses. You can also see the sockets (which have been covered over with plastic to stop any rain getting in to them whilst the kit is being erected) and you can see that we have lapped the vapour barrier (the green coloured sheeting) over the front of the panel. This is to do two jobs: 1) To help protect the frame from the weather while it is being erected and 2) To lap up and join together with the next panels, both above this one and to the side of it. Lapping and taping the vapour barriers together can help to give a finished product that is *very* airtight (which will help to keep heating bills down).

The finished panel shown above will be lifted off the bench by the gantry crane and be moved to sit on one of the storage racks until it is time to load it onto the delivery wagon.

To complete the wall when it gets to site, the electricians will need to run their cables around the house, fit the fronts to the light switches and sockets and install the radiator piping. Once that is done the internal face can either be skimmed with plaster or dry lined.

Skimming simply involves a plasterer coming in and taping all the joint with a product called scrim tape and applying a 2mm thick coat of skimming plaster to the face of the boards. This layer hides all the plasterboard joints and gives a nice smooth surface, ready for decoration.

Dry lining involves taping all the plasterboard joints with three layers of a special paper tape. This is applied as a two-part mix with a slurry, by a trained taper and jointer, using a clever applicator tool to cover all the joints with what is, in effect a high quality filler paste.

One coat of tape is applied each day for three days and a full 4 bed house can be taped with a single coat applied in a few hours. Once the slurry is fully dry (around 36 hours after the final coat, depending on the air temperature), it is then sanded down to give a smooth surface which completely hides the all the joints and the wall is then smooth and ready for painting or papering.

My preference is to dry line the walls, for a couple of reasons:

1) The finished wall is less likely to show drying out cracks after dry lining than it is after skimming with a thin plaster.
2) Because it goes on quickly, dries quickly and is ready to paint as soon as it has been sanded down. Compared with the time taken for a plasterer to skim a house and wait for it to dry out before painting, dry lining could save up to 3 to 4 weeks of building time.

Here is a plan view of a standard external wall panels, showing both the frame and the other bits that go into it:

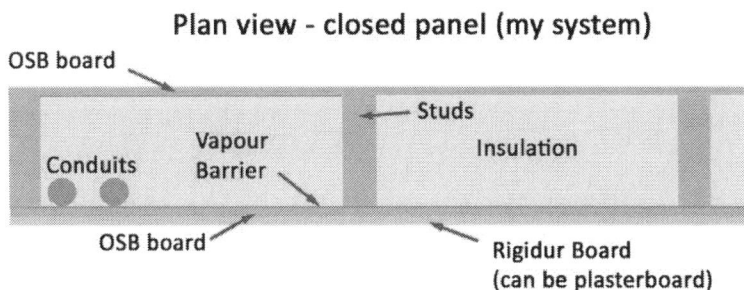

The insulation in this particular panel is fibreglass, which, because it can be squashed enough to allow the conduits to be fitted, fills the whole width of the internal void of the panel.

The insulation can be upgraded to rigid foam insulation which gives a significantly better thermal performance at like-for-like thicknesses. If the rigid foam option is chosen, then the thickness of the board is kept to about an inch less than the void so the services can still be installed within the panel.

One of the advantages this system has over SIPS is that you don't need to add a service strip to run all the cables and pipes in. This not only saves time and a significant amount of money but also reduces the chances of sockets and switches being put in the wrong place.

Also, the fact that you are not adding a 25mm batten and a ½" board to the internal face of each wall to create the service strip also increases the floor area within each room by around 5"+ in each direction. This might not sound a lot, but it could mean the difference between a bed or a settee fitting or not fitting in the room!

Floor cassettes & roof cassettes:

Because a gantry crane is needed in the factory to move the wall panels, the manufacturer also potentially can make floor cassettes and roof cassettes in just the same way that they make wall panels.

All that happens with floor cassettes is that a lot of the work normally done on site is instead done in the factory, in regulated conditions and without anyone being rained on in the process! This tends to give a better quality finished job, saves time on site and (because of economies of scale), saves money in materials, whilst also producing significantly less waste. This in turn helps to reduce the carbon footprint of the building as a whole, during construction, which gives the system a good few extra browny points on the sustainability scale.

Floor cassette construction can use either standard joists, or one of the newer systems (e.g. I-beams or Eco joists). Standard 22mm moisture resistant chipboard is fine, but (as I have mentioned before), I suggest that you ask for this to be glued and screwed to the joists to help to avoid squeaks and creaks once the house is completed.

Roof cassettes can be manufactured using standard treated timber rafters, with OSB fitted top and bottom and insulation installed within the cassette. A ventilation void is built in to make sure that there is no build-up of damp air within the unit.

On the next page, you will see a couple of pictures of 1) a floor cassette and 2) a roof cassette being fitted to a job my old company did in Gloucester.

Floor cassette:

Roof cassette:

Already, you can probably see that this system has progressed a long way from the standard 8' x 8' timber frame panels and I am guessing that, after reading this section so far and after seeing the pictures, you are looking at this product thinking "*This seems to be a pretty good idea*".

It gets better.

To make this product and system work, the panels have to be manufactured to a high standard and very accurately. It may look like a normal timber frame but in fact it is much more of a technical product. It is very heavy and each panel has to be made so that when the crane lowers it in to position, it fits into its allocated space *exactly*. If it is ever more than a couple of millimetres too big or too small we can encounter problems getting the whole thing plumb and airtight, so it is very important that the lads in the factory know that they have to make every panel pretty much perfectly and they have to know how to achieve that objective.

The fact that everything has to be spot-on helps to keep minds focussed (especially after what I said earlier about the quality of available labour in the UK).

If you work in this type of factory, everything you do will be recorded. Every panel you work on will have your name associated with it, so if one of your panels is found not to fit properly on site, you (or you and whoever else worked on that panel with you) will be to be held responsible (unless, of course, the problem is due to a drawing error).

If work has to be slowed down or halted on site to fix a problem that you have created, it will cost both time and money and you will not be very popular! If you have any sense therefore, you are going to do your best to make sure that you don't make mistakes or poor quality panels.

When that happens and when this type of thinking is imposed on a manufacturing process, everyone wins. The manufacturer gets a good reputation and more work, the product becomes more popular and you (the self-builder) gets a better product at a good price.

How much does it cost?

This is a difficult one with this product. Each manufacturer tends to offer a slightly different product and if your kit comes from Europe it will cost a heck of a lot more than if it is made in the UK.

To give you an idea, we used to charge around £44 - £50 / sq ft (around £460 - £520 / sq m) for a standard sized house for the full monty, supplied and erected. This could give you a fighting chance of being in a finished 200 sq ft house (depending on how you go about the rest of the project), for under £100 / sq ft (£1,100 / sq m).

This is *not* the cheapest way to build a house (I can build for significantly less than that figure if I use all the tricks I am telling you about in this book), but with this product, you would be creating a high quality, sustainable, eco home, which is going to provide you with a comfortable, warm, high quality, low running cost lifestyle for as long as you live in it.

Weaknesses with the closed panel timber frame system

- There are not many closed panel timber frame companies operating in the UK, so you may end up having it delivered from a factory situated hundreds of miles away from your project, or having to bring one in from abroad. Neither of these options is ideal, especially if you were to have any problems with the frame in the future and needed adjustments or repairs.
- The cost of the frames themselves is not particularly competitive yet as they are still very much in their infancy as a product in the UK, however the cost savings you can make by being able to build much faster using this system could more than offset the cost of the product itself. Haggle when you get the quote. Most companies have got a bit of play in their figures.
- The maximum size of the panels you can use (and therefore the speed of build) will depend to a certain extent on the geographical location of your site. If you are hidden away up a narrow, winding country lane, you are not going to be able to drive a 40-foot delivery wagon to the site, so the panels may need to be manufactured short enough to go on the back of a small flatbed pickup wagon. Before you order, get the manufacturer to check your site for access (they will need to do this *before they start to design the panels* on the computer).
- Another practical problem is sometimes encountered where the entrance to the site is restricted or where there is insufficient room to site a crane (which is needed throughout the erection process). Again, get this checked out with the manufacturer prior to ordering.
- If it rains whilst the panels are being erected and your manufacturer uses plasterboard for the internal finish, even with protection, there is a risk that some plasterboards could get wet and ruined. Make sure you check around the house before you sign it off after the erection is complete, or better still, get the manufacturer to use cement board instead of plasterboard. They cost more, but are water resistant and give a far superior finished job.
- If your manufacturer doesn't take great care during manufacture, the panels may be made slightly too long, short, high etc. Just a few millimetres of error creates problems for the erection teams, which can cause delays on site. For this reason, you need to use a company with a good reputation for providing a high-quality product.
- Once all your services are installed within the panel and the wall has been finished, it is a bit fiddly to fit extra sockets and switches if they are wanted (this system is not alone here. - It is the same with standard timber frame and SIPS). I recommend that you simply make sure you give the subject plenty of thought before the panels are made and fit plenty of sockets in each room (without pebble dashing the walls with them!)

I am yet to really find any significant practical weaknesses with this system:

- A high quality finished product (as long as you use a good manufacturer / erector).
- Very quick to build.
- As insulated as you want it to be.
- Airtight.
- Strong.
- Quiet.
- Can be competitive on price, but should also save money on the overall build if used as part of a well organised project.
- Flexible in design.
- Sustainable.
- Creates a lower carbon footprint than other most build methods.
- Reduces the chances of mistakes being made on site, because much more work is done in the factory, under supervised and regulated conditions.
- Takes a lot of the stress off the self-builder due to the high percentage of your new house that is included in the kit and all comes to site in big deliveries.

Conclusion on Closed Panel timber frame

So, there we have it: a brief run through the closed panel timber frame building system.

I haven't gone into too much detail and I have only really skimmed the surface. There is a lot more to this product than I have written here.

If you would like to find out more about the system, I would suggest that when you are ready, you should contact a couple of manufacturers and try to arrange factory visits so you can see the product first hand and ask any questions you may have, face to face with the people who actually make it.

You will probably find that each company you talk to will offer a slightly different product. That's fine. There is no right or wrong. But don't be afraid to ask if they can alter their standard spec to suit you (e.g. panel thicknesses, insulation types, board finishes etc.) They can only say "yes" or "no"!

5) ICF - insulated concrete formwork (some people call it insulat*ing* concrete formwork)

This form of construction has been around in the UK for a long time. I remember first seeing a stand for the product at one of the early self-build shows at Alexander Palace in the eighties. As far as I remember, at the time there was only the one company selling the product in the UK.

Over the years, the ICF market has slowly grown, with UK representation now from Germany, North America and Canada.

The marketing people tell us that this form of construction has benefits over some other forms of construction, a claim which in some ways I do agree with.

The product is very different in concept and form to anything we have so far looked at in this chapter and it will attract a certain part of the buying market to it because of the benefits it can offer.

It is quite a technical product, so I won't try to explain all the facts and figures about it. On the next page, I will give you a link to a web site which will tell you more about it and you can then research is as much as you wish. I'll just give you the basics here.

What is it? How does it work?

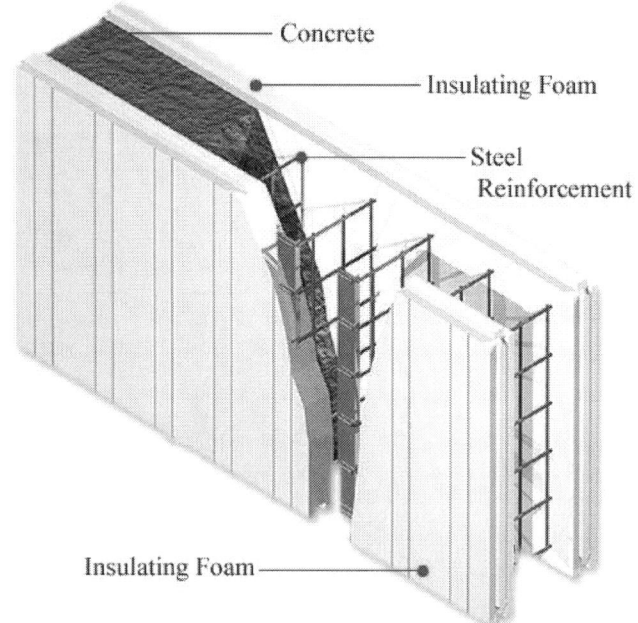

As the name suggests the product itself is basically a shutter system, into which concrete is poured to form a very strong wall which will (theoretically) allow you to achieve pretty fast build times, high insulation values, excellent fire resistance and also gives you a number of other extra benefits not found in the more mainstream construction methods.

The ICF shutters themselves are usually made from expanded polystyrene, either in a monolithic block with large voids inside, or from 2 sheets of polystyrene which are held together with ties.

The blocks are then built like lego, up to a maximum of about 3m in height, to form up the walls, so they can easily cope with the standard 2.4m floor to ceiling height generally used in the UK.

Depending on the type of system you are using and the design of the building, you may also then have to install reinforcing into the void created between the two skins of the wall. You may need to bring in a professional "steel fixer" for this.

Once the shuttering is complete for a section of the building, concrete is poured into the voids (or cavity) using a concrete pump (comprising a long hose running from a pump wagon which transfers the concrete from the delivery wagon to the building). The concrete needs to be supplied in a runny mix so that it finds its way into all the nooks and crannies of the shuttering. Make sure you follow the manufacturers instruction when you pour the concrete (*I remember watching a Grand Designs episode where they poured in too much concrete and the sides of the polystyrene blocks split, letting the concrete flow out. – Nightmare!*)

A poker vibrator is used to help to make sure the concrete gets to everywhere it is supposed to. If the concrete is not installed properly, then the insulations values and / or the structure of the wall could be compromised, due to the fact that there will be empty pockets of air instead of strong concrete.

In this image, you can see the fully filled shutters and hose from the concrete pump.

This link should take you to a you tube video of an ICF wall being poured:
https://www.youtube.com/watch?v=eR1ELGHe944 (if the link doesn't work, just type in "ICF concrete pours" into the you tube search bar and you will get links to a selection of videos).

The structure is completed in stages and theoretically *you* as a self-builder can do the work of building the walls yourself (preferably after attending a training course, usually provided by the supplier, for a couple of days). This hands on option will make this build method an attractive option to some self-builders.

Where you have openings in walls (for windows, doors etc.) you will need to form lintels to take the weight of the structure above it. This is done by installing extra reinforcing bars (to the designer's specification). Anyone who doesn't have a good knowledge of construction (and *this* construction in particular) will need to bring in professionals to make sure this work is done properly. The last thing you want once you have moved in, is for any kind of structural problems to start to show up in the future, due to poor workmanship when you were building the walls.

Because this is still quite a niche product, if you don't have the skill, the confidence or the time to do the block building work yourselves, you may struggle to find local tradesmen who are familiar with the system and who are capable of doing a professional job for you, not many builders have actually heard of ICF, never mind know how to build it!. You may, end up bringing labour in from a good distance away and having to pay for them to stay in your local area while they do their work.

A bit of the technical stuff

I'll just quickly run through some of the basics of the technical side of this product. You can get all this information from the various ICF company web sites, but some of it may be a bit biased, so by reading this you will at least have a bit of a picture in your heads of how it all works so you can ask the right questions:

Internal walls:

Internal walls can be constructed in ICF in just the same way as the external walls are constructed. Alternatively, you can use any of the other building systems, including timber stud work (this second option is significantly cheaper).

If you use ICF, due to the weight of the walls, you will need a foundation under every wall, which can add thousands of pounds to the build cost. If you use timber for the internal walls and if the wall is non-load bearing, you won't need a foundation.

Upstairs internal walls can be built using any build method, but if you choose to use IFC then your first-floor layout (*unless you use supporting steel or concrete beams*), will usually need to be exactly the same as your ground floor, due to the fact that the weight of the first floor walls will need to be transferred directly down to the foundations. This could be very restricting on your upper floor design.

ICF really comes in to its own for the external walls. It is strong, warm and reasonably fast to build. However, these qualities are not so important when it comes to internal walls (especially if they are not load bearing), so I would suggest that a good combination, if you decide to go for an ICF build, would be to use the ICF on the external walls and insulated timber studs for the internal walls (both load bearing and non-load bearing).

Floors

Floors for ICF houses are often constructed using precast beam and block flooring with a screed finish.

People who opt for ICF are usually doing so because they like the idea of a very solid, very strong, soundproof house. A beam and block floor is a good way to help achieve this, but concrete based floors are very heavy, so they don't suit any of the timber construction options that we have discussed in this chapter.

If you want to use a concrete floor construction, then whether you want to or not, you need to consider either ICF or traditional brick / blockwork construction.

With both, the beams simply sit on top of the ground floor walls and the upstairs walls then continue upwards, sitting, in turn on top of the beams.

Here is an image of a beam and block ground floor, with service ducting installed. The blocks simply slot in between the beams and are cut as and where required. A sealer coat of cement mixed with water has been brushed into the blocks to bind the floor together. At some stage during the build process, insulation and a screed will be laid over the whole area to give a warm, smooth and tough floor finish.

One thing to bear in mind with this type of floor is that the application of the screed will usually require all internal work to stop on the project, everything to be moved off the floor, the screed to be laid and then given at least a week to set hard enough to allow people and "objects" onto its finished surface. This whole operation can add around 2 – 3 weeks to the overall build time.

Another option for the floors in ICF buildings is to use standard timber joists. This will be a much faster option than beam and block and usually involves using some form of proprietary joist hangers (which will generally be supplied by your ICF company as part of the kit). The hangers will be connected through the formwork (which needs to be first cut away), into the concrete. (Note: These hangers will need to be positioned very accurately or your joists could be out of true when fitted, resulting in an uneven floor finish).

Roof

Roof construction for ICF tends to be the same as for traditional build, i.e. usually standard roof trusses, attic trusses or a hand cut timber roof.

The option of installing roof cassettes (as can be used in SIPS and closed panel construction) tends not to be a practical or economical option for ICF construction due to the fact that you would be trying to mix and match two different types of specialist systems from two different manufacturers. This is something that should be avoided where possible as, in this industry, trying to get things to join up properly is where many of the headaches occur on site.

You can usually order standard roof trusses or attic trusses from any manufacturer to work with ICF, or you can choose to bring in loose timbers and have the roof hand built by carpenters / joiners.

Constructing the roof for an ICF house is pretty much the same as constructing it for a traditional brick / block house.

Service installation

Services are installed by cutting channels into the polystyrene and running pipes / cables in them. Socket and switch holes will also need to be cut out of the polystyrene. This can be done with a sharp blade (slow and untidy) or by using a special tool, a hot knife, which melts the polystyrene along the line of the cut.

Services through ICF walls need to be given some consideration. If you have things like extract fans from kitchens and bathrooms to the outside, or if you are thinking of installing mechanical ventilation, you really need to include a "void" in the wall when it is being built, otherwise you will have to cut holes for the piping and ducting (which, through solid concrete is not easy!)

Finishes:

Once the main shell and roof has been completed there are a number of finishing options available for the outside face:

- Brick slips (thin slices of brick stuck directly to the polystyrene)
- Tile hung
- Timber clad
- Render

For the inside face the choices seem to be restricted to:

- Plastering
- Drywall (plasterboard stuck to the polystyrene).

You will need to look into each of these options to decide which would be the best for you. The manufacturers should be able to give you advice on the different products available which suit this system.

Strengths and weaknesses of ICF

Strengths

- ICF walls are very strong.
- The construction of the walls themselves is reasonably fast (but, from what I have seen, I wouldn't expect them to be built faster than timber frame, SIPS or closed panel walls).
- Using the ICF system allows the self-builder to do more of the work themselves (after training).
- Where both external and internal walls are constructed with ICF there will be little sound transference between rooms.
- They allow the option of using precast concrete suspended floors, which reduce sound transmittance between floors.
- They can achieve high insulation values and will be very airtight.
- The system is generally considered as a modern method of construction" (MMC) which means it is seen as an innovative way to build by the British Research Establishment.

Weaknesses:

- ICF shuttering is very bulky when delivered to site and it needs to be stored safely and securely until needed, so you will need plenty of storage room somewhere on the site.
- Trying to find qualified and trained people to build the shell professionally can sometimes be difficult.
- The system does not lend itself to a cavity and brick outer skin construction (we Brits do tend to like our cavities!)
- Some people may not be keen on some of the choices of external finishes or the way they are applied.
- The external renders which suit the system can be expensive.
- If internal walls are built in ICF they will all need foundations (extra time and cost).
- If ICF is used upstairs, the walls will usually have to be located directly over the downstairs walls, unless steel or concrete supporting beams are used (reducing design flexibility).
- Concrete is not generally viewed as being a sustainable building material.
- Service installation has to be right first time as alterations could be difficult if they involve cutting through concrete walls.

How should we approach finding out more about ICF?

As this system is a bit different from what most people are familiar with, I would suggest that you look at ways of familiarising yourselves with ICF.

I. Use the internet: Just search *insulated concrete formwork* and spend a bit of time looking around what you find. It would be ideal if you can find your way to case studies or blogs related to ICF projects that have been completed anywhere in the UK.

II. Contact a couple of ICF companies and see if you can arrange a factory visit. As is the case with closed panels, there is a lot of stuff you should know about this system if you want to be able to make an informed judgement on whether or not it will be suitable for you and your project. So talking directly to the people you could be buying it from, is certainly a good idea.

III. Ask ICF companies to let you speak to previous clients. If the product is good and the company is professional, they should be able to give you at least a couple of phone numbers or email address for people they have worked with. You want to know as many of the pros' and con's as possible before you make any decisions on matters as important as this.

IV. Join the "Build a Dream Self Build Association, which can arrange members visits to other member's projects using ICF.

Conclusion on ICF construction

ICF has been around as a product for over 50 years and it has been around for over 25 years in the UK. However, for some reason it has never really taken off as a preferred build method by house builders here.

So far it has remained a niche product and system, mainly used by self-builders, who like the fact that it is strong, a good sound insulator and can make the house very quiet. It is also used by a small number of (low volume) house builders and developers.

Without being an expert on the product, the fact that the ICF industry has not exploded on to the scene, or even grown at any noticeable rate, suggests to me that it is never going to present a serious alternative to either traditional build or timber frame here in the UK. It may suit the housing market in other countries much better, but it just isn't exciting the UK house building market. Why not, I am not sure, but there it is.

I have no real problem with it myself. I do think the marketing guys trying to sell it tend to big it up a bit by saying it is sustainable, fast, flexible and cheap. Two comments on that:

1) We are all getting a bit savvier when it comes to what is sustainable and what is not. Concrete is not generally seen as a sustainable building product when all things are considered, so trying to argue that point could backfire! If all that were really true, then wouldn't everyone be using it by now?

2) It is not as fast as either SIPS or closed panel and I would be surprised if it is as fast as timber frame when you take a timescale from ground floor slab to roofed in as an example to work from.

I have only seen three or four examples of this system being built. As I mentioned earlier, one of those was on Grand Designs on the TV and did not go well! The other two were projects I passed in my local area and neither of them was built in a particularly fast time and the finished product did not look good. One of the houses was up for sale for a couple of years before it sold.

What I would say here though is that, if anyone from the ICF industry would like to contact me to re-educate me on the subject, I would be happy to listen to them and anything I learn in a positive sense, I would happily add to the next edition of this book.

6) Steel-framed construction

I have to come clean here and say that my personal experience of steel framing as a self-build or commercial housing construction method is pretty much non-existent.

I used steel widely when I was working as a site manager on constructing commercial buildings such as factories, schools, hospitals and the like. In fact, it is one of the most commonly used materials in the commercial building sector. But in 30+ years in the house building industry I have never actually worked on a job where steel has been used as the main building method for single self-build property.

That is not to say that it is not used at all for self-build. I have seen examples of it being used by others where it was an ideal choice. I just have not seen that as being the case very often.

During a consultation at the Grand Designs show in London recently, I looked over some initial plans with a couple who had designed a house that was basically a box on legs, with parking underneath. The structure was completely glazed on two sides and was cube-shaped, with a flat roof.

I immediately suggested steel as an ideal building material for the frame, simply because it could answer all the questions that this particular design needed. Steel legs (fireproofed), would be very strong and they could form part of the main structure of the house itself. The flat roof would be easy to construct in steel, with timber joists and plywood boarding used to fill in the gaps. Also, forming the large open glass areas with a steel framing structure should not present a problem.

So, the fact that steel leapt out to me as offering the best solution in this case proves that, in certain circumstances, steel has its place.

I do actually use steel myself in some of my own houses, usually in small amounts for things like lintels where I need something very strong to hold up (for example) an external wall or part of a roof over an open area. What I do find on these occasion, however is that it is very expensive.

Types of steel frame:

There are two main types of "steel frame" used in housing.

When you think of a steel house you probably, like many people tend to think of large steel beams creating a frame as is shown on the next page.

However, in fact, there is another steel system which is used for residential construction. It is called *"light steel framing"* and looks like this:

Whichever type of framing design you choose; you also need to be aware that the steel frame itself only does part of the job of giving you your finished walls. You still have to fill in all the voids that the frame created. This is where it gets a bit more complicated and potentially expensive.

To complete the walls, you would need to use things like insulation boards, bricks, blocks, timber studs, OSB board, concrete etc. You could also consider bringing in some of the more sustainable building materials (like straw, clay blocks etc.)

Because using steel framing as your main build method is quite a complicated thing to do, you will probably need to bring in a design professional to help you to make sure you "get it right". Someone like a steel frame design engineer or an architect (*Yes! I am actually recommending considering hiring an architect!*), someone who has experience in creating building which use a mix of steel and other materials and who can make sure that the design is going to be one which both the building regulations department and the warranty providers are be happy with.

The cost of hiring the architect or designer will obviously increase the overall cost of the build, as will the extra physical work that will go into creating all the structural and visual detailing related to the building the frame, fitting in all the "bits and pieces" and getting it all to fit correctly and look good.

Sustainability / insulation / fire resistance:

Steel is not a particularly good choice if you are concerned with creating a home that will be seen as sustainable. It is a poor insulator so needs other forms of insulation to help the overall building to achieve acceptable u-values.

Steel on its own does not stand up well when exposed to intense heat (e.g. created by a fire), so as well as providing thermal insulation you would need to consider fire protection to all the exposed steel elements of the building.

Conclusion on steel-framing:

As part of the preparation work for writing this book, I did some research into steel framed housing in the UK.

I would have to say that, even after trawling the internet, I failed to come up with much more information than I had already picked up over my years on site. Nothing seems to suggest that it either is, or could become a popular choice for the UK self-build market.

It is expensive, complicated and most of the jobs it does can, often be done by other, more sustainable products (such as eco joists or timber I Beams).

It does tend to come into its own a lot more on multi storey developments like flats, structures with a flat or curved roof or when the building stands on legs.

Here is a link to a site where, if you are considering using steel for your project, you may be able to find out what you need to know.

www.steelconstruction.info/Residential_and_mixed_use_buildings

7) Eco / Passive house

Introduction

Over the past 10 years these two terms have gained more and more importance in all aspects of our lives, perhaps where they are having the most effect is in the way we live in our homes.

We now recycle most of our waste, recycling is big business and our housing market is keen to be seen to be changing to try to present at least a sheen of sustainability.

Here in the UK, we are still trying to work out what eco and passive really mean.

Commercial house builders are now more and more trying to sneak the words eco in to their marketing to give the impression that their houses are better than the standard cheap rubbish we are all used to, but in fact, often the only thing they do differently is to upgrade the wall insulation a bit, maybe even make the houses a bit more airtight, offer a grey water system and stick some solar panels on the roof.

To be fair, those things are all steps in the right direction but they are basically playing at being eco rather than taking it seriously.

So what is an eco or passive house?

This is how a well-known font of all knowledge site (beginning with "Wicki") on the internet describes an eco-house:

*"An Eco house (or eco home) is an environmentally low-impact home designed and built using materials and technology that reduces its **carbon footprint** and lowers its energy needs.*

This includes:
- *Glass that has two or three layers with gas in between to prevent heat loss*
- *Solar panels*
- *Geothermal heating and growing plants on the roof to regulate temperature, quieten the house, and to produce oxygen*
- *A wind turbine for when there is wind, and a battery if not"*

If that is correct, we are not quite there yet!

The same site describes a passive house as

"The term Passive House (Passivhaus in German) refers to a rigorous, voluntary standard for energy efficiency in a building, reducing its ecological footprint. It results in ultra-low energy buildings that require little energy for space heating or cooling".

Nope, we're not there yet either! (*Well 99% of us are not*).

The problem we have at the moment, is that we don't really know how to incorporate the ideas of both eco and passive building in to our new housing stock without build costs doubling or tripling. Most of us think that if you go eco or passive, you have to go the whole hog. You don't.

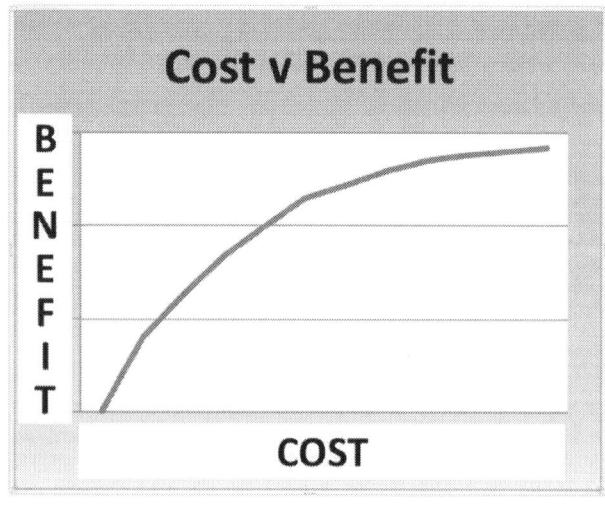

How do we build sustainably, at low cost and with common sense?

One important thing you need to remember when considering the potential eco credentials of your new home is that there is generally a relationship between how much you spend and how much benefit you receive in return. This graph shows the relationship visually:

This is the way it goes:

Starting from a very low level of sustainability / eco performance, to increase your performance significantly does not need to cost you very much money.

Imagine a basic brick and block built house with single glazed windows and with no insulation fitted anywhere. Although we have not built houses that way for a very long time, that is basically the bottom line reference point from which we start.

If you then take that building and change the brick and block to a basic 4" timber frame, add 4" of fibreglass insulation to the walls and the roof, and polystyrene insulation under the floor, you can make a significant difference to the running costs (and the carbon footprint) of the house without making much difference to the cost of the build (it may even work out cheaper with timber frame).

If you want to take a step up from that level, you need to be thinking along the lines of:

- Upgrading the timber frame to 6".
- Swapping the 4" fibreglass insulation to 6" rigid foam insulation in both the walls and the roof.
- Double glazing the windows
- Upgrade the underfloor insulation to rigid foam and make it thicker.
- Making the building more airtight by looking for all the weak points where air could potentially escape and using mastic, tape or other low cost options to reduce air loss through these gaps in the building structure to a minimum.

Those few upgrades to the basic insulation spec would cost maybe three to four thousand pounds extra on a standard four bed 2000 sq ft detached house.

At this stage, most commercial builders would be marketing their houses as "Sustainable / Eco Homes".

To my mind, that would be ok to do. That level of spec is pretty good and would sit nicely on the cost versus benefit graph shown above. Your house is still gaining a good increase in sustainability without having a hefty price tag attached.

To move up to the next level you could be thinking of the following upgrades:

- 8" timber frame with 8" rigid foam in the walls and roof
- Triple glazed windows with argon gas in the cavities
- Solar panels
- Underfloor heating to the ground floor (this links nicely with the solar panels to give you free heating and hot water). *Note: Underfloor heating on the higher floors can cost a lot more than on the ground floor, so I tend to stick with just using it on the one floor.*
- Installing a grey water system

You would be talking about an additional £10,000 on top of the previous upgrades to get to this level, but you could now be secure in the knowledge that you would probably be in the top 10% of UK housing when it came to being sustainable and eco.

This is the point at which I, personally would stop.

If you want to carry on upgrading, you are going to be getting into the area where the following equation starts to apply:

A LOT OF COST = A LITTLE BENEFIT

This is where the equation has changed from a couple of thousand pounds of investment in insulation to drastically reduce your heating bills, saving you hundreds of pounds a year, to where you need to spend £10,000+ to bring in a product or a system which may only save you a couple of hundred pounds a year extra.

Without wishing to complicate things, there are two ways to move towards creating a passive house and they are, confusingly: 1) *The passive way* and 2) *The active way*.

To reduce your energy consumption and carbon footprint the passive way, you do the things you need to, to cut down the consumption in the first place. So passive ways to be eco include: insulation, airtightness, triple glazing, grey water, recycling, water saving devices etc.

Other slightly more complicated ways to achieve the passive type of savings include:

Thermal mass: This is where you use parts of the building as storage radiators. You use the sun's heat to warm up a large mass (usually a concrete or blockwork wall) somewhere in the property, over a long period of time. The heat is then given off over weeks and possibly months into the house. I am not a fan of this method. It restricts the house design and is not controllable.

Solar gain: Solar gain is an effective way to create passive heating as radiation from the sun is predominately short-wave infrared radiation which is able to pass through glazing and heat the inside of the building. The heat that is re-radiated by the heated fabric of the building is long wave radiation and is not able to pass back out through the glazing.

This results in heat warming the inside of the building, giving you free heat. The downside of solar gain is that, again, it is not controllable. It can make the building *too* warm and it restricts design (with thought having to be given to the location, type and size of the windows to make sure they gain maximum benefit from the sun's rays).

I have nothing really against these systems except their controllability and potentially **their cost**.

The active way to a lower carbon footprint and lower energy bills

To reduce your energy consumption and carbon footprint the active way, you need do things to create your own energy. Below are the most common ways to do this.

Mechanical ventilation: This is where you build a system in to the fabric of your house that recycles the heat from the air which would otherwise be vented to the outside and lost. So, kitchen and bathroom vents would be linked to the system. The warm, smelly, moist air would be taken into the system, the heat taken out of it to be sent back into the building and the (now cold) smelly, moist air expelled to the outside of the building.

These systems cost from £1,500 or so and can go up to around £5,000. The savings in heat have to be weighed against installation, running and maintenance costs. However, some people like these systems, saying that they make the house a healthier place to live (it is true that they are good for people who suffer with some types of allergies, but apart from that I am not sure if this could be proved).

I am not particularly a fan of this idea. I would rather just open a window, let a bit of smelly moist air out, then close the window and keep a couple of thousand pounds in my bank!

Ground source heating: This is where you take heat from the ground and use it to produce hot water (and potentially warm air) in the home. This is quite a costly system to install, usually with a price tag of £10,000 - £20,000. You also have running costs of electricity to power the system and maintenance costs.

Air source heating: Takes heat from the air to do the same thing. Again, it is a costly system to install, with a price tag of around £7,000+ and you have the same sorts of maintenance costs as for ground source heating.

Wind power: We are all now familiar with the huge wind turbines scattered across the country. I think they are great! I like the look of them (though many people don't) and I like the concept. I am just not sure turbines work for individual homes. The simple reason being that the cost of installing a wind turbine is going to be very high, but the benefits to your eco credentials are not going to be equally as high. This is probably my least favorite of the active ways to be eco when it comes to housing.

There are many other systems available to help you to save energy by either the passive or active methods. Probably the best way to find out about them all would be to visit one of the shows (Grand Designs, Homebuilding and Renovating etc.) or visit the Self Build Centre at Swindon.

Summary of eco / passive building:

Before I summarize, the only other advice I will give you about this subject is that you need to be aware that there are a heck of a lot of products out there which offer help with the passive or active ways to improve the eco credentials of your home.

Some of them come with a hefty price tag and dubious claims about their potential benefits and efficiencies. Just make sure you do your homework before you commit thousands of pounds to any one of these products or systems. Speak to people who have used them, check the figures and don't be taken in by sales patter.

I tend to stick with the simple, passive, cheap ways to improve the eco credentials of the houses I build. I am a fan of solar panels as long as they are cost effective and efficient (they are getting much better now than they were a few years ago).

You would have to work very hard to get me to pay out £10,000 - £15,000 on any system that didn't then bring me savings of at least £2,000 a year!

To my mind the best way to be eco-friendly is to:

- Insulate well.
- Use triple glazed windows.
- Use energy saving equipment where possible.
- Get an electric car.
- Recycle.
- Use bikes instead of the car when possible.
- ONLY if your budget stretches to it and if you can get a good deal, possibly use *solar power* to run an underfloor heating system and to provide hot water.

If you do all of that you will be as eco-friendly as you need to be.

Chapter 8:
How will we run the project?

There is confusion right across the self-build industry about what the term running your project actually means.

Are you running the project if you are paying for a custom build house where you simply choose your finishes and a few other bits and pieces? Are you running it if you have hired a project manager to look after the whole thing? Is an architect running the project if he / she calls in to site twice a week?

I would say "Yes" to the first two of those and "No" to the third.

Sticking with the first two:

As long as you are having more of an input that you would if you bought a house from one of the commercial house builders, I would tend to think you can class yourself as a self-builder (Or these days, to be politically correct, the government would like you to be called a *custom builder*!).

So, assuming you are proposing to be a self-builder of one description or another, you need to decide how you are going to set the project up. Are you going to run it in a hands-off manner, letting someone else do all the organising and ordering, with you just overseeing the big decisions (as I did when I had a house built in Florida)? Or are you going to want to be fully immersed in the whole thing from start to finish?

Unfortunately, many self-builders, people who don't have the required levels of management skills, knowledge of the subject, or experience of the industry take the second option. They often get a bit too carried away with their own abilities and dive in to the project with their fingers firmly crossed. - They try to do too much and usually end up in trouble.

Some self-builders, on the other hand simply don't have sufficient confidence to take on something so big, where actually, if they set everything up right, they could probably handle it well.

If you have read the whole book from the start to this point, you should now be starting to get a good idea of how much of the management of the job you are capable of doing yourself and be in a good position to consider and make the right decisions on this matter.

Let's have a look now at the six main choices when it comes to running your project:

1. **Do as much as possible yourself** (including the physical work where possible).
2. **Manage the project yourself, but hire in tradespeople to do most or all of the physical work.**
3. **Use a project manager to run the stuff you don't have the confidence to run** (this could be all of the project or a small proportion).
4. **Give the whole project over to a main contractor and just make the big decisions yourselves.**
5. **Use a design and build package, so you don't even have to worry about sorting out the design yourselves.**
6. **Get together with a group of other self-builders and share the work of managing the whole venture.**

I'll go through these options one at a time, but first, here is an important point that you need to be aware of before you make your decision on how best to manage the project:

Where your decision on running the project could trip you up

There is one major thing about building that everyone should remember:

When you are either designing or building a new building of any type, if you make a mistake, anywhere, at any time, which you don't notice quickly enough, then, as you continue working, building, adding to the fabric of the building, the chances are that you will be continually (and potentially dangerously) compounding the mistake without realising it.

The result of you not noticing a mistake in good time can be that you end up paying out literally thousands of pounds further down the line to put it right.

Your decision on how you will run the project needs to take this fact in to account. DO NOT take too much on, if there is a chance that the pressure will potentially cause you to make mistakes that you may not notice. Don't try to fool yourself into thinking that you can do more than you can.

If you do, it will probably end in tears!

That has probably scared you a bit, and it should. However, just take it as something you need to bear in mind and don't let it scare you away from doing what you want. Make sure that before you start, you consider all the relevant factors (both to do with the project and your personal situation) and make sure you are fully prepared, with the right people around you whom you can turn to for help when you need them.

If you do that, there is a good chance that you will be fine.

Here, just to highlight the point, is an example of how things could go pear shaped if you were to try to take on too much.

This example uses a perfectly normal and feasible scenario which could apply to any self-build project:

Let's say that you have decided to do as much of the physical work as possible to save money. You have done all your research and preparation, you have had the site cleared and you are now ready to start on the first job of setting the house out ready to dig the trenches.

There are a few things to think about with the foundations, including a building line on your plot (a line which you must not build in front of – see chapter six). The line runs along the front of all the neighbouring houses,

Part of your initial research covered *how to set out the house*, so you buy the tape measures, the timber pegs, nails and string lines and you are ready and raring to go!

You have never done this sort of thing before, but it can't be that difficult marking out a few corners and digging a hole!

It is raining on the day you do the setting out so you try to get it done as quickly as you can.

You hire a mini excavator, spend a couple of hours learning the controls and you start to dig the trenches. That seems to go fine. You then, over the next few months (doing some of the work yourself but bringing in people when you need them), build the foundations up to floor slab, build the shell of the house, put the roof on, wire it, plumb it, fit the kitchens and bathrooms, decorate and eventually complete all the work on the house itself so it is just about ready for you to move in.

The last job you need to do once the scaffold comes down, it to form up the drive, connect the services and do some tidying up.

One day, while you are working on forming up the drive and you are standing having a quick chat with one of your neighbours, the neighbour notices that the line of your front wall seems to be in front of the line of his front wall.

You never noticed this, because the scaffold has been up for months and it is only when it came down, with the house fully built, that it has become obvious.

Accidentally, when you set the house out, because it was raining and because you were hurrying, you set the face of the blockwork out on the wrong side of your setting out string line and you have now encroached in front of the building line.

The neighbour reports you to the planning office.

You are now in breach of your planning conditions and are at risk of being told to pull the whole lot down.

Ouch!

What went wrong?

It is quite simple really. Your lack of skill, experience and knowledge when you originally set the house out meant that you made a simple mistake and every action that came after it compounded its effect, until it was potentially catastrophic.

You may well defend yourself by saying that it was raining and you were rushing, but try telling that to the planning committee when you are hauled up in front of them a few months down the line!

Just something as simple as you digging the foundation trench on the wrong side of the string line, caused knock on effects which could result in you losing your new lovely new home.

If you had decided not to take on that task yourself, but instead paid a site engineer, or the ground workers to do the job (at a cost of a couple of hundred pounds), there would be far less likelihood of this sort of mistake being made. These people do this stuff every day and would be experienced and knowledgeable enough to look out for things like building line issues. They would also take their time and always carefully double check their work.

So, from this (slightly dramatic) example you can see how easy it would be to catch a cold if you were to try to take on too much yourself, when you don't have the necessary experience, knowledge or professional back-up that would make sure that things were done right.

OK, let's look in more detail at the six main choices for managing the project

I partly covered this subject earlier in the book, so now I will be talking a bit more about the options I have already covered, however I will be repeating some of what I said earlier here as this is the most relevant place for it to be and I am also adding another three choices for running the project.

So, your choices are:

1) Doing as much of the work as you can yourself.

After what I have just written about how easy it is to make mistakes, I have to say that even discussing this option here gives me the shudders!

Over the years, I have seen and heard about so many projects that have gone very wrong when this option has been chosen. I would guess that it is probably responsible for the majority of failed projects in the UK.

Let's go back to the seventies and eighties for a minute. In those long gone days, self-build as an industry was in its infancy, the housing market was (for the most part) getting along fine and everything was rosy.

Self-builders would often decide to take on the whole project themselves, literally digging every hole and building the house themselves from start to finish, often with no previous building experience or knowledge of how it should be done.

As I said in an earlier chapter, in those days it was a lot easier to get hold of self-build finance. Lenders would simply look at the income and expenditure of the applicant and make a decision on whether or not to lend on the basis of their financial situation, using the likely end value of the completed home as the main criterion for their decision as to whether or not to lend.

Unfortunately, because of this very silly way of assessing the viability of a project, over the next few years, what happened all too often, was that once they got going, the self-builders themselves soon found out that *"This house building malarkey is a lot harder and more complicated than we thought it was going to be"*!

Projects would go over budget by huge amounts and take up to 2 or 3 years to complete. Many of them simply didn't get completed at all. The ones that did were often of very poor quality because money had run out and all the finishes (the kitchens, bathrooms, tiling, decorating, flooring etc.) had to be done for "tuppence".

There were also completed houses which didn't even have structural warranties (*because no one told the self-builders they needed one*). Mortgage lenders will not usually lend money to buy modern house that has not been built under warranty, so these houses were pretty much unsellable, so nearly worthless when it came time to try to sell them.

People were going horrendously into debt to get the project finished, but would often have no way to pay the debt off without selling the house, then, to make things worse, even if they did try to sell the house, no one would want it because of the shoddy workmanship that had gone into building it.

After a few years of this stupidity carrying on, the lenders finally realised their mistake in as much as they came to the realisation that they were sometimes lending money to people who didn't really have a clue what they were doing. So, (thankfully) they started to re think their lending policies.

After all the dust settled, things got better and a lot more professional, so that these days if you intend to start a self-build project where you are hoping to take on a lot of the building works yourself, you will need to _prove_ to the lenders that you are capable of completing the project successfully.

Over the past few years, I have sat on various experts' panels at the live shows and listened to people planning on taking on a self-build project who still intend to just do a few short courses (1 day to a week or so in duration) in brickwork, plumbing, electrical installation, joinery etc. and then get on and build their own home.

Well, full marks for enthusiasm but no marks for common sense I am afraid!

If you think about this sensibly you should ask yourself the question:

If house building were that easy, then why do tradespeople have to complete 2 – 4 years of full time training to be qualified and knowledgeable enough to be let loose in to the industry?

Answer: Because it is b***dy difficult and complicated work!

So, an amateur having a go at building their own home either after a few days training (or worse still after *no* training) is simply a recipe for disaster.

Believe me, I have heard many of those disaster stories straight from the horse's mouth!

All in all, (just in case you are still in any doubt) in my opinion, this option **was** and **still is** the riskiest route to building your own home.

Is there any way to make this option work?

If I can't persuade you away from choosing this option, then to give yourself the best chance of making it work, you need to be fully aware of the following points and you need to make sure you have them all fully covered in one way or another before you start.

When you try to run the whole project yourself.

- *Fact:* **You are on your own.** You have no one to tell you when you are doing things wrong or to check your work on a day to day basis.
- *Your action.* Get hold of someone professional that you can go to for advice if and when appropriate or when you are stuck. A project manager, an architect, a construction engineer (with experience of housing) or even

an experienced builder who will agree to advise you and visit the site whenever you need them to. All of these people will probably be hireable on an hourly payment basis.

- *Fact.* **You need to do everything in the right order.** If you have never built before you can't be expected to know all the methods that take the professionals many years to learn.
- *Your action.* Read this book and try to digest all the important factors that may become relevant to your chosen method of build.

  I really hope you haven't just leaped straight past all the early chapters and into the building sections, thinking that you don't need to know about the pre-building processes. Those early chapters will help you not to make the mistakes that, if you do, could land you in big trouble.

  Remember though, that this book is only written on a very general basis and can't cover *all the bases*, so again, having a professional around to guide you at the important stages is quite important.
- *Fact.* **It probably won't be as cheap to build as you think it is going to be.**
- *Your action.* Don't just plough on regardless or you will end up with a half-finished house and no money left. The build could end up taking you many years to complete. Make sure you do all your preparation work properly before starting to spend the big money.
- *Fact.* **You need your family behind you.** This dream of building your own home may seem a great idea to you, but what about your partner and your kids? Will they be happy to lose you to the project every evening, weekend and holiday for the next 2 – 3 years?
- *Your action.* Make sure you have the full backing of all the people who will be affected before you make the decision to go ahead.
- *Fact.* **You can't really expect to hold down a full-time job and build a new house at the same time.** Many people try to bite off more than they can chew in this respect. The fact is that, if you are working till late every evening and weekend on the house, you are not going to be firing on full cylinders at work. You are going to be exhausted and could end up losing your job (and your family into the bargain!)
- *Your action.* Don't even think of trying to build the house yourself if you are working full time. Just don't!
- *Fact.* **You will need building regs, a structural warranty, insurance, plus plumbing and electrical qualifications**, otherwise the finished property will not be sellable to anyone else in the future because the mortgage companies would simply not lend on it.
- *Your action.* Make sure you attend to these matters <u>before</u> you start work.

Conclusion on physically building the house yourself:

All in all, this is not a good option. I can say that in full confidence having seen, listened to and tried to help many people over the years who have tried this route and for one or more reasons have failed (sometimes spectacularly).

To my mind, the maximum involvement you should have in taking on your own self-build project would be to:

2) Self Project Manage:

This is the option I chose for my first project.

At the time I had no experience of building new homes, although I was working as a site manager for a commercial building company, so I did have a head start compared to people with no previous experience of building at all.

I have to say that overall I enjoyed the experience and I honestly think that if you follow the guidelines below and in the rest of this book, as long as you have the time to dedicate to being there when you are needed (in other words, most of the time), as long as you know the difference between a brick and a block and have some basic knowledge of DIY and / or managing teams of people, you should be able to take on the project management of your build.

What you need to do

- **Read this book from cover to cover and then, when you are ready to start, keep referring to it as you go along.** If you are only project managing the build (as opposed to doing a lot of the physical work), as I have said before, you don't need to know *all* the details of *all* the building processes (if you try to get to know everything about everything, two things will probably happen: You will only start building the house when you are eighty-five and 2) Your head will explode).
- **Sort your finances out properly before you start:** I will be giving you advice on costs and cash flows in the next chapter. If you put the ideas and suggestions you will find there into action before you start work, they could save you from, fairly early in the project, finding yourself financially in a sticky situation.
- **Keep the whole building process as simple and fast as possible:** This is what you need to do:

> **Keep the house design as simple as possible** (see the chapter on house design).
> **Give out the sub contract packages in large chunks if possible** (see later chapters for how to do this).
> **Where practical give out the packages as supply and fix contracts.** Suitable packages for this would include: Groundworks / drainage / service connections / scaffolding / windows / electrical / plumbing.
>
> By doing this you pass over a lot of the work and responsibility for getting everything and everyone that is needed to complete the job, to the people who know best how to do it. They will know how to do all the measuring up of what is needed, they will do the ordering (and they will know how much to allow for things like waste / damage etc.). They will provide the right number of people needed to do the work, at the right time and they will look after all the technical stuff that you won't understand.
>
> Your job then will be much simpler and less stressful and you will find you have more time to go out and look for better bargains on the rest of the stuff. Things like: choosing the bricks / roof tiles / kitchens / bathrooms / joinery items / paint / flooring etc.
>
> To make things even easier, for the parts of the job that you do keep control over, try to make use of the people you now have around you to help you to understand how and when to do what.
>
> For example, say you give the brickwork package out to a professional bricklaying gang as a labour only contract, leaving you to get all the materials and hire in whatever plant they need.
>
> What you can then do is, 2 -3 weeks before they are due on site, ask them to give you a list of what they need on site the first day they arrive. They will give you a list, probably something like: *A full load of bricks / blocks / a large mixer / a pallet of cement / 10 tons of sand / 3 boxes of wall ties / a water supply and a 45-gallon water butt / cement admixture / mixing boards.*
>
> By you picking their brains rather than you trying to work out what they will need yourself (and probably either getting it wrong or missing some important item or other), you will then have time to look into pricing and ordering each item to make sure you get everything to site on that first day.

> *One important thing to remember here is that if you are ordering the materials and plant, then if is anything missing, not working, or the wrong things have been ordered and if that means that the men cannot get on with the job, you can usually expect to be charged daywork rates for them to stand around doing nothing while you sort it out. At least if you get them to give you a list of what they want and they make a mistake in what they ask for, then, if they are stopped from working while you sort out their mistake, they won't be able to charge you for their standing time. (Daywork means basically an hourly rate for anything that is not covered by the price for the job which they will have given you in their quotations).*

> **Try to get all contracts with subbies on a price rather than a day rate.** Price work means they get paid for what they do. Day rate (or daywork rate) means they get paid for just turning up. You get a lot more work out of tradespeople who are on a price than on day rates. You don't want to be constantly chasing people to get

jobs done, so having them on a system where they only get paid for what they do is far better than paying them by the hour.

➢ **Try to use readily available materials that you can source locally.** Bricks and roof tiles may have to come from factories a long way from the job, but things like blocks, cement, sand and all the myriad of small items can usually be sourced locally. If you order locally, there is more chance of it arriving on time and in the right quantity. If it doesn't, then you may be able to go and pick stuff up to avoid delays on site.

➢ **Programme the works.** You need to make sure everyone knows when they are needed on site and how long they have to do the work. I will show you how to draw up contract programme later. It is one of your main tools for planning a successful project so make sure you use it.

Also, you need to try to build up what I call a head of steam. This is when you get as much work as possible going on every day as possible, then, once you have managed that, you must do your best not to let the pace drop. It takes a lot of effort to get things running smoothly and efficiently and if you let that pace drop, it will be very hard to pick it back up again.

➢ **React quickly to problems as they occur.** On a new build you can pretty much guarantee that things will go wrong on a regular basis. It is just the nature of the animal. If you don't react quickly to a small problem, it can quickly turn into a major problem, causing long delays, which can end up costing you a lot of money and causing you all sorts of other, often totally unrelated problems.

➢ **Try not to get bogged down by the details:** As a Project Manager there are things you are expected to know and things you don't need to know.

IMPORTANT: I have been a professional project manager for a long time and I still probably don't know even half of the stuff that goes into creating a new house! I would also guess that half of the stuff I have learnt over the past thirty odd years, I have forgotten!

Does that make me a bad project manager? – Nope!

*What my experience has taught me is that **I need to know** certain things and **I don't need to know** other things.*

If you are taking on all of the building works yourself then you really need to know nearly everything about everything (this is an impossible goal to achieve), but as a Project Manager, apart from having good organisational ability, you really only need to know the stuff that you don't get other people to sort out for you.

For example, if I give the electrical installation work out as a supply and fix package, then the things I **need to know** are:

- Where I want my sockets, switches, fuse board and anything else that will be included in the installation.
- That the subcontractor is fully qualified (and that his qualification is acceptable to the lender), has the right insurance to cover his work and has all the information from me that he needs in the form of drawings, specification, building regs docs etc.
- How much I am paying for the installation, when the payments will be due and if I am keeping some form of retention.
- When he is going to start work and when he is due to finish so that the next trade can follow on without delay.
- What warranty comes with the work and how do I get him out in an emergency.

*Things I **don't need to know** are:*

- What thickness cable is required for which type of circuit.
- How to wire up a fuse board.
- What a ring main is.

- *What fuse rating is needed for what circuit.*
- *How to connect to the mains.*
- *How to fix socket and switch boxes into walls.*
- *How earthing works.*
- *A hundred and one other things.*

The same principal applies to all of the other packages that you give out to sub-contractors.

Your job as a project manager" is as an organiser and coordinator, not as holder of all knowledge on every subject.

One of the reasons that the numbers of self-build projects has been on the decline up until very recently is that the main guidance within the industry seems to be saying to potential self-builders "Make sure you research, learn and know everything before you start or it could all turn out to be a disaster". That is basically garbage, so long as you do things properly.

So, just learn what you need to know, relative to your own input into the project, give as much as you can to the experts to look after and leave them to get on with it, then just make sure you know how to check that their work complies with the project specs and that you are happy with it before you pay them.

Conclusion on self-project management.

This is not my preferred option for running a self-build project, especially if you have very little experience of building. However, it may not be a bad choice as long as you follow the guidelines I have given you, prepare everything properly and professionally and don't get complacent.

By project managing the job you could find that the whole thing will actually work out cheaper than if you try to do all the physical work yourselves. This is due to the fact that you will build much faster and save money on borrowing costs, hire charges and many other costs, which accumulate on a day to day basis, even if you don't lift a finger.

3) Using an architect to supervise construction and provide the warranty:

This option is still fairly commonly used. I have mixed feelings about it, but it is definitely a viable and (usually) reasonably sensible option to consider as long as you realise what the implications of using it are.

Often, if you use an architect to design the house and / or take it through the planning process, they will also offer to supervise the construction for you. That's fine, however, what that often entails is you (or them) finding a main contractor to take on all the works and them simply overseeing what the main contractor is doing, then issuing interim certificates at set stages during the construction (so that you can get your stage payments from the mortgage company).

In reality, what this often means is that you are following probably the most expensive route to getting your house built, by using a main contractor (see later for detail) and then adding another layer of management cost (often up to 10% of the project value) on top of that, just for the architect to watch the proceedings and issue a final certificate to cover the structural warranty, at the end.

10% of a £200,000 contract is £20,000. That is a lot of money to find within your budget that could possibly be used elsewhere (compare it to the £3,500 - £4,000 to get a structural warranty from one of the main warranty providers, which do the same job as the architects certificate).

On top of that, I have a couple of other worries about this system.

I. Where a standard structural warranty is for 10 years, in theory an architects certificate has no limit on its duration. My worry is that if the architect retires or dies and / or stops making their payments to their insurance company, will all insurance companies be happy to pay out whenever, forever on that policy? I have never heard of this circumstance being tested but I would be interested to know the answer.

II. With the greatest of respect to architects, they are often brilliant at their own jobs (designing buildings), but have sometimes not got a great deal of site experience which enables them to closely monitor the quality of the work being produced by the people on site.

I have had personal experience of this a few times, where an architect is supervising a project and calls to site once every couple of weeks. They get out of their car, go and have a chat to the foreman and a quick walk around the job, get back in their car and drive off back to the office to send an invoice to the client for a few hundred pounds for their time!

III. If I have the choice of paying for an architect to supervise the project or a professional warranty provider, I would want to know as much detail as possible about either choice.

Warranty companies will give you the full details of everything that is covered, what is not, when you have to do what to make sure they are happy to provide your final certificate. They will also give you a dedicated professional inspector who can call to site any time and who is trained to make sure that the practical works on site are being carried out to a high standard.

If you can find an architect who will do exactly the same for you at the same sort of price, then great. If they can't offer that full service and package at the right price, then I would be seriously considering the other warranty options.

4) Use a professional project manager (PPM):

This is, to my thinking, the best management option for self-building. It is the way it is done in many other countries and there are many good reasons why that is the case.

The problem is that, as usual the UK is slow on the uptake when it comes to new ideas and we have not yet fully embraced PPMs as a viable option in the self-build industry.

On reading some of the other self-build books, I have noticed that some self-build authors just seem to pass briefly over the subject of PPM as if it were just another choice with equal importance to choosing a pattern for the wallpaper! It is not.

A good PPM could save you literally tens of thousands of pounds on the build cost (compared with some of the other management options). They can find all your sub-contractors, get better prices for you on materials and labour, get the whole thing built and finished far faster, reduce the number of errors, give you a better quality finished product and take all the stress of the build away from you.

I actually think that if we could standardise the use of PPM it could be a major boost for the industry, which if set up properly, could potentially increase our self-build completion numbers to match those of some other countries, where up to 60% - 70% of all new housing is either self-build or custom build.

What is a professional project manager?

PPMs are often ex site managers from either the commercial house building or the commercial buildings sectors of the industry, who have moved over to looking after individual projects for clients. They often have many years of site experience and bring with them good quality contacts for subcontractors and suppliers.

Alternatively, they can be builders, ex-housing developers who may have semi-retired but who want to keep themselves active, or even self-builders who have built a few of their own homes over the years and have enjoyed the experience enough to want to do more of it.

The PPM is usually employed directly by the self-builder (the client) to look after their project, either fully, or in part, depending on how much input the clients themselves wish to have.

They are usually paid on 1) an hourly rate, 2) a price for the job, or 3) so much a month.

Because they are directly employed by the client, they act for them in everything they do.

What do they do?

Every project manager will approach the job slightly differently.

As yet, because this is a fairly new thing in the UK, there is no norm, no PPM standard procedure manual, so to give you an idea how the system works in general, as I was a self-build project manager for some years, I'll take you through how I worked.

The first thing I would do after being contacted by a potential client, was to meet with them (normally at their house), where we would talk through their proposed project to find out exactly what they may need from me.

Usually it was the case that they would have a limited budget, very little experience of building and they would be looking for me to run the whole thing from day 1 to completion.

I would normally agree a fee for the managing the full project (with an option for them to complete the last stage of the final finishing themselves of they were confident enough) and if they were happy with my quote, I would draw up a simple contract for them to sign.

My first tasks would normally then normally be:

- Check the drawings for errors and discrepancies.
- Mark up on a drawing with them, where they wanted all their sockets, switches, radiators etc.
- Check that they had their finances sorted properly and that their cash flows would be ok to so that there would be money available to pay bills throughout the build period.
- Make sure that planning permissions, planning conditions, structural warranties, building regs and, site insurances were all taken care of.
- Open accounts at Builders Merchants and other suppliers (in the client's name).
- Agree timetables for the works, with a target completion date.
- Visit the plot, checking for potential problems and how would be best to set out the storage areas, the cabins, W.C etc. to make sure that stored items didn't get in the way of other things happening, or risk getting damaged by vehicles moving around the site.

My job from then on was to work on their behalf to get the project organised, started and completed to a set budget and timescale.

I would then contact local sub-contractors for each part of the project, then draw up "packages" for them to quote on (based on the contract drawings) and get them to submit tenders.

I would go through all the tenders with the clients, showing them the plusses and minuses of each, to allow us to decide who we preferred to take on the job. This would (normally, but not always) either be the lowest cost quote or, if we preferred someone else whose quote was more expensive, we would try to get them to lower their price to an acceptable level, so we could use them.

I would do the same with sourcing all the materials. Using my contacts and negotiating skills, I would play one supplier off against another to get the best possible prices for the client. These prices would usually be significantly lower than the client would have paid if they had gone to the same supplier themselves, simply because I knew the suppliers and did regular business with them.

Using my contacts, experience and negotiating skills, the savings I would make for the client on an average contract could easily reach a number of thousands of pounds (*and often cover the fee I charged for taking me on in the first place*).

I would draw up a week by week contract programme, which would then be adhered to as closely as possible.

Each subcontractor would be given a copy of this programme with their tender documents and a target start and finish date would be agreed.

I would then be responsible for everything that happened on site from day one to completion, including record keeping, health and safety, problem solving etc. With me meeting with the clients every two weeks or so to update them on progress and go through anything that needed their attention (this would not stop them coming to sire every day if they wanted to look round, tidy up, check things and just generally feel part of the process).

If the client wanted changes, whatever they were, it was my responsibility to action them and work out any extra cost or time implications that they might trigger.

My job also involved advising clients when I thought they themselves were making any mistakes, either practically or financially.

In reality, what I did was to take all of the pressure from the client and run the project as a professional building site.

At the end of the project I would get the final certificates organised from the warranty providers and building regs departments and help the client to do the paperwork for their VAT refund.

Over all, in general, I would say with confidence that my charges for project managing the job would normally be cancelled out by the money I saved the client through:

- Finishing the job quickly
- Stopping errors and bad decisions being made during the project
- Getting better prices from warranty providers, insurance companies, subcontractors and suppliers.

However, I reckon that the main benefit for the client was that the pressure of taking on such a big task was taken from them, which meant that they could sit back, relax and watch their dream home being built.

They could still have as much or as little input as they wished, but with the knowledge that, whether they were there or not, all the work was being carried out and supervised by professional people, who knew what they were doing and that anything that went wrong, "Barry would sort out".

Now, wouldn't you like that for your project?

Check before you hire any project manager:

I would strongly advise that before you hire a PPM, you make sure that they are genuinely and sufficiently experienced and knowledgeable to take on the task. The easiest way to do this is by asking for a CV and for details of their previous work history.

There are, unfortunately a number of people who claim to be PPMs who are actually just self-builders who have very little experience of the construction industry, but who had a go at their own house, enjoyed it and decided to make it their career, sometimes without any sort of formal building management, health and safety or any other type of training. (Note: These people may actually be perfectly capable of carrying out the work, but you should check their credentials before they start working on your project).

Conclusion on professional project management (PPM):

I strongly feel that this is the way forward for self-build in the UK.

It is the standard method for bespoke house building in many countries where self-build accounts for up to 70% of all new builds. That fact alone suggests that it is probably the best and most efficient choice.

Lenders prefer projects which have PPMs as their investment is seen as being more secure.

Building regs and warranty providers are happier because there is a knowledgeable and experience person in charge of making the hour to hour decisions that need making on site

The client gets a high quality finished home in a reasonable time and being more likely to come in on budget.

Now the negative news on PPM:

There are presently not a lot of us around!

The best way to find one would be to search "self-build project managers" on the internet, along with your post code and see what it comes up with.

Also, check Yell.com, the self-build publications and try to visit the self-build shows nearest to you, where you will sometimes find a couple of stands taken by PPMs looking for new work.

5) Use a main contractor

A main contractor is someone who takes on the whole project from start to finish (you might be more used to using the term *builder*, but they are basically the same thing).

This is usually one of the most expensive ways to self-build, so it suits a certain type of client and a certain type of situation.

Main contractors can come into their own where someone wants a high quality, bespoke new home building from start to finish, as quickly as possible and with as little input from them (the client) as possible. These people are happy to hand the whole thing over to someone else and then basically wait for the keys to be handed to them (really this is not genuine self-build, it is more custom build, which is becoming more popular now and is actually what I am doing day to day, as my proper job!)

If we are comparing like for like, a main contractor offers pretty much the same sort of service as a professional project manager, the difference being that a whereas a PPM is there to make sure the client gets what they want at the best price and always has the client's interests at the centre of their actions, a main contractor usually simply gives a price for doing a specifically agreed amount of work and gets on with it with as little contact with the client as possible.

The big difference here (apart from the cost) is the level of input into the proceedings that the self-builder either *gets* or *doesn't get* depending on which choice is made.

Where a PPM will happily make any changes the client wishes, if a main contractor is used and if the client wants anything that was included in the original contract, to be altered, it is usually seen as an amendment, which will usually have a price tag attached and sometimes quite a lot of paperwork to sort out before the change is made.

Finding a decent main contractor (builder):

When you apply for Planning Permission there is a good chance that you will get quite a lot of junk mail for a few weeks. This is because (as we discussed earlier) there are systems in place which spread the news of your application across the building industry, allowing anyone who wants to try to sell you their wares, to send you their sales leaflets and brochures.

Along with all this flotsam and jetsam, there will usually be a few contacts from some local builders asking if they can tender for the work. I suppose the good thing about these people contacting you is that it shows they are well organised and keen (which is always a useful sign when looking for a main contractor).

If you don't get any of these leads, then you will find plenty of main contractors listed in all the online trade directories.

If you have seen these directories, you will be aware that they are now, at last, trying their best to present a more professional image by including unbiased references as part of each set of contact details.

Before you make any phone calls, I would recommend that you make the most of this facility and read as many references as you can on each company you may feel inclined to contact. That way, straightaway you can directly address any issues that are brought up in those references when you speak to the company for the first time. If you are not happy with their responses to these concerns at this stage they are probably not worth bothering with.

As you set about searching for a suitable main contractor, look for the ones who **specifically state** *that they are geared up for self-build. This will usually mean that they have the full range of tradesmen available either in house or whom they regularly work with on the larger projects. A high proportion of builders will not be able to cope with a project as large as a whole house and would not be able to easily get hold of all the people they want, of the quality you need. This could potentially result in your project suffering by you having given the work to someone who was not really up to the job.*

Where possible, try to concentrate on the professional looking companies. The ones with a good website and where the text and details on the website also present a professional and an up to date image. As you look at the various websites, if you look closely at the text, you will sometimes find poor grammar, a poor level of the use of English and other minor details which just say *"We're not actually very professional"*. If they can't even get their shop window" looking good, then how much hope is there that their product will be of a high standard?

Many builders will claim that they can do all sorts of types of work, but in fact, when you look a bit closer, they are just "Jim and Bob" with their 15-year-old Ford Escort van and a cement mixer, who will have a go at anything you point them at!

When you look at any type of advertising, wherever it is, you need to be looking for wording like:

- Self-build specialists
- 20 years' house building experience
- All aspects of house building undertaken (including full new builds)
- NHBC / Gas Safe / NICEIC registered (or similar)
- References available
- All work fully guaranteed
- No obligation quotes

You should not have much problem in finding at least a handful of suitable main contractors, wherever you live in the country.

Ideally you should contact between six to ten companies to start with and quickly whittle that number down to about four to six companies after an initial phone call or site meeting, before you start to send out tender documents.

Sorting the wheat from the chaff:

It is always best to meet contractors face to face. It is too easy for people to hide behind a phone and paint a rosy picture of what is sometimes a pretty shoddy outfit. So get a representative from each company you contact to come to meet with you, either at your present home, or on site, or both.

By the time you meet, make sure you have read as much of this book as possible, preferably more than once. Doing so will help to furnish you with the gist of what you need to discuss.

If you can show a reasonable level of knowledge and intelligence to these people, they are far less likely to try to pull the wool over your eyes.

Here is a quick example of how you can present the right or wrong impression:

Many years ago, I was renovating a house and got a knock on the door from one of the door to door companies who offer to re-lay tatty tarmacadam driveways.

Mine needed doing, so I let him do his standard sales talk, along the lines of: "Your drive is in a heck of a mess, we're in the area and can come in and get it all fixed up for you".

I let him finish his sales patter, then came back at him with some very simple but relevant and important questions:

"So what depth of macadam will you be laying? Can I call a couple of previous customers for references? Where is your office? Are you members of any Trade Associations?

The guy blustered his way through trying to answer the questions, but basically proving that he only needed to be wearing a pair of cowboy boots and hat to make it any clearer what sort of contractor he actually was.

After going a bit red in the face, he said he would get back to me with references, contacts and the rest of the information and then quickly disappeared, never to be seen again!

So, just remember:

You don't need to be an expert to catch out the charlatans, you just need to make them think you are!

So, back to the plot:

Now you have the company representative sitting in front of you in your living room (they will probably be the owner, the MD or the project manager for a job of this size). You now need to find out whether or not these people are going to be the right choice for you to trust your project to.

The first pointers you will get revolves around their appearance, presentation and body language.

- Are they confident?
- Do they have files, photos and other paperwork with them to show you what they have done previously?
- Are they keen to talk about their other projects locally and will they give you phone numbers for clients or offer to show you a job in progress? (Sometimes not offering phone numbers is not necessarily a negative sign, as ex-clients often don't want to be hassled with constant calls from people asking about a job that was completed a couple of years ago. However, a visit to see a current or recent job should not be too much to expect).
- Do they sound like they know what they are talking about and do they seem to have a good level of technical knowledge?
- Are they affable? Do you think you would get on with them over the months that you would need to be regularly in contact with them?
- Are they pushy, or are they just happy to learn more about your project without heading straight into "How much it will cost and when can we start?"
- Do they have a waiting list of jobs they have already signed up, or could they "Start on Monday"? If they don't appear to be very busy there might be a good reason for that. I like to hear them say things such as: "We are booked up until the end of next month, but, at the moment, we could potentially book this job for the month after if we get a decision shortly".
- Can they convince you that they have sufficient levels of manpower (either directly employed or subcontracter) to cope withal the work and not leave you in the lurch while the men from your site are taken off to work on another job?

 *One of the biggest problems I hear about when I do the expert consultations is that main contractors often take on too much work.*

They will have access to a number of tradespeople for each task and part of their job is to juggle the way they use those people between the jobs they are working on.

What often happens is that a new job starts on time and then makes good progress for the first few days or weeks. Then, all of a sudden some or all of the workmen start to disappear for days at a time.

The reason for this is usually that the company has over committed itself and programmed too many jobs to run concurrently. Either that, or a delay on another job has caused problems, which have meant that the men have had to go to another site for a few days.

You will usually find that after these initial meetings with a selection of builders, that you will come away with a shortlist of suitable candidates to tender for the work.

How much will main contractors charge?

Answer: Usually a lot more than it would cost you for most of your other options.

Why?

When you ask a main contractor to tender for work, you are normally looking for a fixed price so that you know as far as it is possible to know at this stage, what the job will cost if they do the work.

For them to be able to give you a fixed price they have to make sure they are going to make a profit. To do so, they usually do some or all of the following:

- Charge full price on all the materials (where, in fact they know that they will buy all the materials at discounted prices). That way they know they will make a profit on the materials supply, even if there is a price rise before they order.
- Add a percentage (around 5%) for waste.
- Add another percentage (around 5%) for damage, loss, theft, breakages.
- Add an amount (maybe 2% - 5%) for "contingencies" such as bad weather / delays due to tradespeople not turning up at the right time / costs they may inadvertently miss when tendering / unforeseen costs / other delays causing extra expense, extra hire costs etc.
- Once they have made all these allowances they then add their profit at maybe 20% - 30% of the total.

The effect of all those additions is that the "fixed price" they give you often includes a large amount of **just in case** money. However, when you accept their tender, you agree to pay **that full amount, *whatever happens*,** even if, in fact the job goes smoothly and they don't incur *any* of those extra costs and if they get good discounts on all the materials.

This form of pricing can result in the client (you in this case), paying up to 20% - 30% over the odds for using their services when compared to using a PPM (where you only *pay for what you get*). On an average 4 bed, 200 sq ft house, this could cost you up to an extra £50,000 over and above what the same building would have cost you using a PPM.

The benefits of taking on a main contractor:

If they are professional and can produce a high quality finished job, they will pretty much take over everything for you. To a greater extent even than the PPM.

They will literally just take their instructions (drawings / specs / building regs etc.) and produce the house within an agreed timeframe. There are very few meetings, very little pressure on you to do anything or provide information or to make decisions. In fact, if you try to get involved in any way, you will usually be politely told to "go away"! You just need to pay their invoices on time.

This set up will suit some people but not others.

Conclusions on using a main contractor:

An expensive and relatively inflexible way to get your new house built.

It will suit people with plenty of money and little spare time who just want a house built for them without the fuss and bother of having to be involved on a day to day basis.

Finding a good quality builder who is not going to keep disappearing for periods during the build period can be hard work, but all you can do is take whatever steps you can to minimise the risk of this happening by doing your part right at the outset, professionally and by asking the right questions of the right people at the right time.

As a viable option for a self-build project, I would put this before doing all the building work yourselves, but after either of the Project Management options I have already covered.

There is, however another option which may drop into the slot between project management and main contractor, which is:

6) Using a Design and Build package

This option is *sort of* a cross between using a PPM and using a main contractor, with some additional bits added on for good measure.

D & B has been around for a long time, but although this is how many homes are built abroad, it has not really taken off as a mainstream option for self-build in the UK. This might be because, as usual, in the UK we are a bit behind the curve with the whole concept of self-build.

In many countries, it simply makes sense that, if you want a new home building, you should be able go to someone who will help you get exactly what you want in terms of size, design and quality, at a reasonable price and in a reasonable time. Someone who does not want to squeeze every penny of profit possible out of you, but instead who concentrates on giving you a good product at a fair price.

In many case, this is what the Design & Build package offers (although be careful on the pricing side, sometimes they can turn out to be quite expensive).

This is *never* going to be the cheapest option (in fact it could well be the most expensive), but depending on what type of package you want, what sort of company you use and where you are located in the country, it might be an option worth thinking about if you have a decent budget to spend, have not got much free time and don't really want to have to go through the process of finding an architect, main contractor and warranty company.

How does it work?

It is actually a simple concept and pretty much does what it says on the tin.

You go to D & B companies at a very early stage and they get fully involved with everything from the initial designs right through to completing the full build and handing over the keys.

It is a bit like buying a self-build from a national house builder who is allowing you to have an input into the design. It is really moving you from being a true self-builder, to being a (politically correct) custom builder.

You will not usually get a VAT refund at the end of the project if you are entering in to a full fixed price contract with a design and build company.

This is an important point to discuss and clear up before you agree to enter a contract with any company.

If project is set up as a self-build, with the D & B company acting simply as project managers, rather than them setting themselves up as designers / main contractors you may stand at least a good chance of getting a few £1,000's back as a VAT refund at the end of the project.

You will usually get the VAT back with any of the options we have discussed in this chapter, except where you have given the work to a main contractor, either directly or via using architect's certificate. The refunded sums can be quite substantial, sometimes reaching figures of over £10,000. Receiving this sort of sum at the end of the building phase of the project can make a big difference to you when it comes to furnishing and equipping your new home.

Some companies may say that they won't be charging you VAT, so you don't need to get it back. That's fine, but just look at the bottom line price to see if that seems to be what is actually happening.

Where do you find design and build companies?

You may find a local company who can offer this service, but the chances are you would need to go with one of the larger national companies.

Conclusion on design and build

It is not going to be cheap, but it may just suit a small number of people. It is probably the least stressful and demanding of the options available in the UK at the moment.

You may have problems finding a design and build company near enough to you for you to be happy that they can run the job properly.

If you have plenty of money and little free time it could possibly be your best option.

7) Join a Community Self Build

I am going to be a bit controversial again here. – But bear with me for a minute!

I think that the Community Build concept which works very well in other countries, is basically "a *disaster waiting to happen*" in the UK as things stand.

This can change, and indeed it must, if this option is to become anything like a viable one.

Unfortunately, at the moment, because we have, by its very nature, an industry that is made up of amateurs, it is a concept fraught with danger.

There have, as far as I am aware, been just a handful of fairly successful community projects in recent years, however the schemes that have been completed would only be attractive to a *very* small number of people and would probably not have been anything approaching successful on anything but a one off, special, development basis.

They would not appeal in the least to the mainstream UK house buying public.

So, where is the problem with these schemes?

What happened a few years ago, is that (as I mentioned in the introduction), members of our Government (accompanied by the leaders of the industry), went off on various fact finding missions to see some of the community self build schemes presently active in other European countries, and they have been seduced by them. To my mind, this is not a good thing to have happened!

These (well meaning) people have come back expounding the virtues of *"How they do it over there"* thinking that they would be able to copy the same template here and create exactly the same sort of developments for main stream self-build developments in the same way that they do it in the Netherlands and some of the other countries that have been visited.

They are simply wrong. At ***this time*** anyway. Maybe in 5 – 10 years this will be a workable concept, but it is not now.

Why am I saying this?

What is happening in the UK is that we are trying to pretend that our self-build industry runs along the same lines as the other European countries, Canada and America.

It doesn't.

Here in the UK our self-build market accounts for less than 10% of all new house builds. In some of those countries the figure is over 70%.

Where we presently have a very disparate, amateur and disorganised small scale self-build sector, these other countries have joined up, professional, well organised and well run large scale self-build industries.

Where they have:

- Reasonably priced plots. Wherever you look.
- A professional procurement system for small and large areas of self-build land.
- A slick and fair planning system which allows self-build to flourish.
- A clear required building standard.
- A well organised, fair and competitively priced supply chain.
- A well organised and joined up industry.

We have

- Overpriced land.
- Complicated and long winded land purchase systems.
- No standard self-build development template in place.
- An "every man for themselves" mentality.
- No professional project management systems in place.
- Overpriced and often inflexible architectural and design practices.
- Slow, and restrictive planning regimes with no standard policy rules and too much personal opinion being responsible for the planning decisions that are made (hence the often-used appeals process).
- Complicated and ever changing building regulations,
- Amateurish supply chains which mostly treat self-builders as easy meat (with some exceptions).
- Differing ideas amongst the professionals on what self-builder are.
- Confusion amongst the public on what self-build is, how easy or difficult it is and what options are open to them.
- A general lack of clarity and conformity to all aspects of the industry, leading to malpractice and over pricing of services and supplies.

Until we are thinking and acting in a similar manner to these other countries, we cannot hope to be able to copy what they are doing and expect that we will be successful.

If we try this now, we will fail.

It will not be the politicians or their advisors who will suffer, it will be the individual members of the public who go along with their ideas, assuming the people in charge know what they are talking about!

Looking to the past for proof.

To put some perspective and detail to these comments let me take you back to the eighties and nineties.

About 25 years ago, I was a co-founder of the original *"Association of Self Builders"* (now re-subsumed as NaCSBA).

As I have mentioned before, the industry was a much simpler place in those days and occasionally we would get to hear about a community self build project starting up.

These projects would involve a number of people getting together and building their own small developments.

Sounds like a good idea. Everyone getting together, helping each other, keeping costs down, buying in bulk, using their own skills and energy etc. Great!

Each group would tend to have at least a couple of ground workers, brickies, joiners, electricians and representation from most of the other required trades, plus possibly a house designer or two thrown in to the mix for good measure.

The problem with that is that these professionals would make up only a small percentage of the total number of people involved in the project. The rest would be teachers, accountants, doctors, factory workers etc. These people often had no idea of anything to do with the building industry before getting involved in their particular community build project.

Someone (often a committee), would try to lead this disparate group and would take responsibility for trying to pull together everyone's ideas, needs and wishes, then relate this wish list to the planners for approval. If they managed to get that sorted successfully (a process which often took years to complete), they then had to agree a build programme that would see some of the group getting into their nice shiny new homes possibly 2 – 3 years before some of the others.

These others however would have to work on the first houses, for up to 3 years whilst living on site in a caravan or elsewhere.

You are probably already sensing that this was (and still is) a not particularly good concept, which neither stands a good chance of running smoothly or ultimately reaching a successful conclusion, unless the group is managed by an experienced professional who has the expertise to avoid the pitfalls.

Sadly, what regularly happened with these projects, is that there would be major disagreements and falling outs amongst different member and factions of the group. There was usually no strong professional project manager around on a fulltime basis (or even to be called when required), who would be able to bring some technical know-how or common sense to the proceedings.

Often the leader was an architect, who, although they had a good knowledge of design, had very little experience of team management, financial management, programming works or many of the other essential practicalities of building a house.

This generally amateurish approach led to various problems on many sites over the years, with stories coming out of happenings like fist fights breaking out across the tables at meetings!

My major concern is that presently in the UK we have not moved on very much from those days and that if we start to go back down that route, trying to turn community build into a mainstream self-build option, we are asking for trouble unless we set up the industry to be ready for it.

On the other hand

Well, now I have annoyed the government and a good section of our self-build elite, I better say something in my defence!

I am actually a big fan of what Walter Segal did for self-build build in the 1970s. I totally agree with the idea of allowing ordinary people to create their own individual homes, simply, cheaply, quickly and possibly, as part of a team.

That concept is what drives me and it has done for many years.

It is why I helped to found and run the Association of Self Builders 25+ years ago. It is why I sat on the Government's Self-Build Working Group in 2011. It is why I regularly attend the self-build shows as their self-build expert and it is why I created my own timber frame based manufacturing company.

It is also why I have written this book.

Walter Segal's concept was revolutionary in the 1970s and it still has relevance today, however I feel that it is now about time we brought it up to date a bit.

What I think we need now are new homes which are:

- Timber based.
- Of simple and economical, but attractive design.
- More spacious than those offered by the big house builders.
- Making use of the roof space as living space as standard.
- Well insulated.
- Airtight.
- Very simple and fast to build.
- Low cost.
- Sustainable.
- Future proof.

That may sound like a tall order but it is not. I am in the throes of trying to make it happen as we speak and I know that it is perfectly feasible!

Conclusion on community self-build

It is potentially a growth part of the industry for the UK, **if** we can get our act together.

However, we Brits have different values to the Europeans when it comes to housing. Any community based schemes need to take that into account.

The concept won't work if the Government and councils try to bully us into accepting this a concept and a style of house building, when it is still literally "foreign" to us.

We need to learn lessons from the Europeans, the Scandinavians, the Americans and the Canadians and adapt their ideas to suit this country.

Chapter 9
How much will it cost to build?

This is the part of the book where we start to get down to the nitty gritty. This is where we start planning for the commencement of the site works, helping you to understand how much the whole thing is likely to cost, so that you can plan your cashflows and make sure that you are able to cover all the expected and unexpected costs and, with a bit of luck, helping you plan properly, so that you don't run out of money part of the way through the build.

Before we start though, I want to recap on what we have covered so far. We need to do this so that you are clear where you should be with your project preparations by the time you reach this point.

Before you start accurate pricing work, you should have:

- Purchased or otherwise obtained your plot.
- Completed your designs.
- Obtained full planning permission.
- Set a target start date for the works on site.

Until you have completed all four of these stages, the cost calculation figures we used in earlier chapters will be all you need to work with.

You simply can't hope to get anything like accurate prices for the build until you have your land, your designs, planning permission and a target start date.

The good news

I am sure that you will be pleased to hear that, if you have been following all the guidelines I have been setting out throughout the book so far, there is a very good chance that you are now going to be able to build your new home at a much lower cost than you probably would have done if you had built it without reading the book.

The ideas on plot finding, designing, organising and building the house, believe it or not, could possibly have reduced your "target" build figures by up to around 30% - 40% from what they might otherwise have been.

You'll remember the best guess figures we used earlier in the book. They ranged from around £90 / sq ft, to over £180 / sq ft. Well, if you are taking on board everything I have been saying, you could now potentially be able to build a 2000 sq ft, simple house from around £60 / sq ft. That would bring the total cost (compared with if you would have otherwise built at £90 / sq ft), down from £180,000 to £120,000. That is one heck of a difference!

By the way, just so you don't start writing to me, that would be a squarish shaped 3 storey house (with no sticky out bits), that you have mostly designed yourself, built on a flat plot with no ground problems, a short drive and easy service connections.

It would be built with a standard 6" timber frame (or closed panel), with fibreglass insulation with a cement board and render or clad exterior, Marley modern (or similar) roof tiles, power floated slab, plaster boarded and taped walls, PVCu windows, standard kitchen and bathroom equipment, mid-range priced floor and wall tiles, short macadam driveway and self-project managed.

If I were building that house, I would hope you be nudging the price down to about £50 / sq ft, but I have been doing it for a long time. Still, if you hit £60 / sq ft and save up to £60,000 compared with what it might have cost you before you picked up this book, you will have done well.

Pricing:

I am going to repeat something that I have spoken about earlier:

One of the most important principals to remember when it comes pricing your project is that:

EVERY £1 THAT GOES OUT OF YOUR POCKET FOR SOMETHING WHICH IS IN _ANY WAY_ RELATED TO THE PROJECT IS A "PROJECT COST".

THAT INCLUDES _EVERYTHING_!

(From buying this book to paying the removal guys to move you in!)

So, to record the cost of the job properly, from day one, you need to:

- Keep every receipt in any way related to the job, from day 1, when you first make your decision to go for it (and don't fool yourself that buying this book or filling the car with petrol to go and look for plots is not a project cost! If you would not have otherwise spend the money, it **is** a project cost!)
- Set up a cost spreadsheet for the project (see later).
- Regularly (at least once a week) write up your cost outgoings (doing this at the start of the job gets you in to the right habit and helps you to keep up once things start to move quickly).

If you ignore what I have just said, the chances are that at some stage during the project, you will start to find black holes appearing in your bank balance, leaving you less money to spend than you thought you should have, simply because you have not kept good accounts.

I fully realise that figures might not be your favourite thing and thinking about keeping accounts is probably not something that excites you (self-builders are normally more practical people they are bookkeepers, so even the thought of doing what I have just said may send shudders down your back), but believe me, I have been there and bought the tee-shirt and I know how important that part of the project is. I am not exaggerating when I say that keeping good financial records can mean the difference between a successful or a failed project.

As I said at the start of the book, this is not intended to be a technical manual, it is a guide. So, as this is the case, in this chapter I will not be going into detail of everything you need to price during the job. Every job is different and the book would be twice as thick as it is if I tried to do that.

Also, some writers will give guide prices for individual items and overall costs for labour, plant and materials. I am not going to.

Why?

Because, in reality, prices for pretty much everything associated with a new build project can vary dramatically (*depending on factors like location / time of year / site conditions / level of specification etc.*) so using a guessing or average cost system, which people might then take and use for their own projects, could potentially and unintentionally be very misleading. It could therefore be very dangerous to the financial viability of your project.

What I am going to do however is try to help you to simplify the decision making and pricing process so that you can come up with your own figures without breaking into too much of a sweat. That way, hopefully you won't end up getting overwhelmed by the whole thing.

Just as an example of how prices can vary on this sort of job, here are a couple of quick examples:

1) On a recent project I needed to use a basic all-purpose silicone mastic (the stuff you would pay around £4.00 - £5.00 a tube for at B & Q). I needed quite a lot if it (probably about 60 – 80 tubes) to seal the timber frame for airtightness. I usually pay around £2.20 / tube at a small merchant in South Wales, but found a local merchant near the job in Gloucester, selling it for £1.25. So between buying it from the DIY shop at up to £5 / tube and buying it from the local merchant, there was potentially around a 400% (up to £300) difference in price, just for that one small item.

2) Brick prices can vary widely. If you choose a particular brick which is only made in Scotland, that brick may be priced at £400 / 1000 if it is delivered on large articulated vehicles, to a site within 50 miles of where it is made. So, if you lived near to the manufacturer and, say you need 18,000 bricks for your project, the total cost would be £7,200 to get right number of bricks delivered to site.

    However, if your project is in Penzance, Cornwall and say, for example that you live up a winding country lane, which only small delivery vehicles can access, those same bricks will now have travel maybe 500 miles or so and have to be delivered in smaller loads (to get around the bends).

    If that were to be the case, the price for getting the same number of that same brick to site could be nearer to £800 / 1000 (or £14,400 in total). If you still went ahead and bought them, you could end up paying £7,200 more than you would have done if you lived in Scotland.

You will find, once you get going, that similar things to these examples happen all the time and you need to be both aware of them and prepared for them.

So:

Don't take anyone else's figures in to account when pricing your own project. You need to prepare your all own costings!

Different management choices = different pricing strategies

The pricing processes for any self-build project will vary significantly depending on which management route you have chosen.

In this section, I will take each management option one at a time, (using the same headings that we looked at in chapter 8) and I will give you some guidelines on how to get all the prices you need together for each option.

The management options were:

1. Do as much as possible yourself.
2. Manage the project yourself, but hire in tradespeople to do most or all of the work.
3. Use a project manager.
4. Give the whole project over to a main contractor.
5. Use a Design and Build package.
6. Get together with a group of other self-builders and share the work of managing the whole venture.

1) Pricing the project when you do most of the building work yourself

As you would expect, doing everything yourself includes being responsible for working out all the prices for the labour, plant and materials.

This is not going to be an easy or quick task, especially if (unless you have a good knowledge of the construction industry), you have no real idea what a lot of the items are.

To help you to get a feeling for what you need to include in a comprehensive pricing document for a job like this, I am going to list below many of the standard material and plant hire items, together with the different trades that you would usually need for an average 4 bed detached house.

The list is not comprehensive, you will still need to think your way through your own project to see what and who else you may need for your particular job.

The idea is that my list will simply act as an aide memoir for you as you initially plan and then as you move forward.

Materials

If you copy the items on the lists below which are relevant to your job, onto a spreadsheet (along with your own additions), you will then be able to print it out and give blank copies to all the local builders merchants (and other suppliers) to get them to do the hard work of pricing up the individual items for you (usually free of charge).

Tell each merchant that you are building a new house and that if they want any of the business, they will need to give you their best prices. Add that you won't be ringing round all the merchants every time you need something, to see if you can barter them down in price any further (you will be *far* too busy), so they need to put their best price on the written quote in the first place.

Tell them also that you will be giving the same list to their local competitors and that you will go with the cheapest option.

This is important (I mentioned this earlier in the book, but it is worth repeating here):

Often a merchant will give you a few good prices as loss leaders to try to get you into the habit of using them as your automatic choice, but then, after a while, they will start to charge much higher prices for the other items, in the hope that you won't be comparing them with anyone else.

*They need to know that you intend to be **very** choosy on who you order from, from day one until **everything is completed**, just to make sure they stay on their toes.*

Once you get each of the prices of the main items that I have listed (plus your own additions), you also need to consider all the ancillary items. This can be a fiddly and laborious job if you try to work out how much of everything you need. However, there is a way to cheat a bit.

Rather than trying to price up *every* screw, nail, nut and bolt on the whole job, for many of these smaller items which are not going to affect your budget significantly, you can simply make an allowance for them by adding somewhere between 5% and 20% of the total cost of the main item. It might take a bit of research for you to work out how much to add, but you would have to do that anyway if you priced everything up and the pain will be considerably less if you do it this way.

For example:

After looking through the brochures you choose your internal doors and after getting a few quotes in you find that you will be paying £85 each.

So:

Internal doors: Price quoted £85 / each (15 needed)

Ancillary items will be: Hinges / handles / latches

(Common sense says that these items will be more than a fiver but less than the cost of the door. – I would check some prices on line then end up allowing around £17 per door)

Bricks: Price quoted (say) £350 / 1000. (14,000 needed)
Ancillary items: mortar admixture / wall ties / damp proof course / cavity trays / cavity closer.
(I would not include sand, cement, lintels or special bricks for this item as they are all significant items themselves and deserve to be priced separately).

After again checking the internet for some ideas, I would end up allowing around 20% for these items (which equals £70 per 1000 bricks or around £1000 in total).

As long as you cover all the big items and make sure you at least pick up on all the significant smaller items related to them and make a reasonable allowance, this method should stand you in good stead for getting reasonably accurate figures for all your materials, whilst also freeing up some of your time to get on with other stuff.

Materials contingencies:

Once you have calculated each of the item costs, it is then sensible to add a contingency to the *total* amount (something in the region of 10% - 15% is normal) to cover omissions and errors in your pricing.

What will happen is that, with the best will in the world, unless you are used to working out prices and are involved in the building industry in a management capacity, even with research, you will overestimate some of the ancillaries and under estimate others. The contingency will help to absorb these errors.

If you are very accurate in your pricing and later in the job realise that you haven't used up your contingencies, you can simply re-budget for your finishes, increasing your allowances on the things you want and need.

I have never yet heard of any self-builder who has had trouble spending and spare money on their project!

Plant

Use the plant lists (below) in the same way as you use the materials lists. Prepare a blank spreadsheet of items you are going to need (using my lists and your own additions), along with a note on how long you are likely to need each of them for, to a few plant hire outlets.

Tell them that you are going to be building a house and that you could be a good customer for the next few months.

Ask them to price up the individual items (you can usually ignore the list prices. Most, if not all hire shops have the ability to juggle the prices for individual clients).

Labour

The labour lists are probably not going to be as important to you as they will be for some of the other management options because the management option we are discussing at the moment is where you are going to be doing a lot of the work yourself (possibly assisted by family or friends).

Bear in mind however, that if you are borrowing money you will need to build the house to industry standards and everything you do will have to be approved both by the building inspector and the warranty inspector (that basically means that things like the electrical and plumbing installations have to be either installed or signed of" by a professionally registered, electrician or plumber. If they are not, you might not get your warranty completion certificate. If that were to happen, it would pretty much render the property unsellable at any time in the future).

So, even if you are hoping to do nearly all the physical work yourself, ***don't*** scrimp financially on the important things, just to keep a few more pounds in your pocket. Doing so could cost you dearly later on.

The following rule applies to materials, plant and labour:

It is always better to overestimate the costs and have a bit of money left over than to underestimate and not be able to complete the job.

So, here is the list of the big ticket items that normally go in to building a new home:

LABOUR / MATERIALS / PLANT GENERALLY REQUIRED FOR A STANDARD 4 BED DETACHED HOUSE ON A GOOD QUALITY, LEVEL BUILDING SITE:

There are a lot of items in all three of these sections that you won't need, but seeing them here will hopefully remind you to at least give each one of them some thought.

I. **MATERIALS:**

- temporary security fencing (buy or hire)
- concrete for blinding the foundations
- reinforcing for concrete foundations
- possibly shuttering to foundations
- blockwork to dpc
- concrete common bricks for foundations
- hardcore for slab formation
- screed under damp proof membrane
- under slab insulation
- damp-proof membrane
- concrete to slab
- possibly reinforcing to slab
- possibly pre cast (suspended) floors
- possibly timber ground floor joists
- possibly beam and block flooring
- above slab insulation
- finishing screed to top of slab
- possibly facing bricks for main house
- possibly timber battens and external render boards (if thin coat rendering externally)
- possibly timber battens and timber cladding (if cladding externally)
- cement
- sand
- possibly 4" or 6" lightweight blocks for external walls (if building traditionally)
- possibly blocks for internal walls
- possibly timber studs for internal walls
- cavity insulation for external walls (50mm - 200mm depending on your specification)
- possibly sound insulation for internal walls (usually fibreglass)
- cavity lintels
- cavity trays
- quoins
- fire stop for cavities
- other special bricks
- rendering materials - sand / cement etc.
- first / second floor joists
- floor boards
- inter-floor sound insulation
- stairs
- stair handrails / newels etc.
- possibly trusses (attic or standard) including bays and annexes
- possibly timber for a "hand cut" roof
- loft insulation
- loft access ladder
- loft boarding
- roofing felt & battens
- roof lights / sun tubes

- roof tiles
- chimney liners and pot
- lead flashing
- timber to form dormers
- fascias / soffits / barge boards / ventilation strips
- external balcony (decking / fence / finishings)
- windows / external doors
- bi-fold doors
- mechanical ventilation
- possibly vapour barrier (if timber frame)
- plasterboards or cement boards for internal walls
- possibly sand and cement (if plastering)
- possibly dry lining materials
- plaster
- skim
- electrical installation *(discuss with three or more electrical wholesalers)*
- plumbing installation *(discuss with three or more plumbers' merchants)*
- boiler (may be included in plumbers' package)
- cinema sound / automated house installation
- telecom installation
- tv network wiring
- radiators
- boiler
- underfloor heating (*speak to three or more plumbers merchants*)
- solar panels
- ground source heating (*speak to three or more suppliers*)
- air source heating (*speak to three or more suppliers*)
- stove & fireplace
- possibly air conditioning
- bathrooms / en suites
- ground floor w.c
- kitchen units and appliances
- utility units and appliances
- internal doors
- skirtings and architraves
- covings
- fitted wardrobes
- paint / stain / varnish / wallpaper
- wall tiling
- floor tiling
- vinyl flooring
- laminate flooring
- carpets
- alarm system
- porch (various items)
- driveway finishes

- turf
- fencing
- garden walls
- gates
- landscaping
- turf
- patio slabs
- pathways
- steps
- drainage (probably requires specialist measuring for these materials)
- possibly concrete for covering drainage system (usually in shallow areas)
- main service conduits / ducting

Once you have gone through the list above you should also then go through the drawings and the building regulations specification with a fine-tooth comb to make sure you haven't missed anything else important.

II. PLANT

You will need to decide whether it is better to buy or rent some of these items. Sometimes renting for more than a few weeks works out more expensive than buying.

- cabin / canteen
- lock-up
- site w.c (with hot running water)
- hot drinking water / handwashing boiler (health and safety requirement)
- security fencing / bases / interlocking brackets. (sometimes cheaper to buy)
- hand tools / shovels / picks etc.
- excavator
- dumper
- fork lift
- setting out equipment
- generator
- compactor (whacker plate)
- concrete pump (possibly for foundations and maybe slab)
- vibrator poker for foundations and slab
- petrol disc cutter
- power float (if using a power floated slab instead of screed)
- vibrating concrete tamper (for levelling concrete slab) – often a plank will suffice
- mixer – small mixers are usually inadequate. – a large (bulk) mixer will normally be required
- scaffolding (main building)
- mobile tower scaffold
- ladders (sometimes cheaper to buy)
- hoist
- possibly an elevator (for bricks and roof tiles) try to get the supplier to send roof tiles on a wagon with a hydraulic crane to load direct to the roof). this is expensive so try to use other alternatives
- fall bags (to cushion fall from height)
- temporary lighting
- waste skips
- plaster mixer
- nail gun
- screw gun

- router
- electrical testing equipment
- drain testing equipment
- drain rods

III. labour / professional services:
- site insurance
- warranty company
- structural engineer (for building regs preparation or structural calcs)
- building regs inspector
- epc (energy performance certificate) supplier
- sustainable energy specialists
- designer (architect / architectural technician / house designer)
- arboriculturalist (tree specialist)
- bio diversity specialist
- garden / landscape designer
- wildlife specialists (eg: bat / badger / newt surveys)
- site engineer
- general labourer
- groundworkers
- steel fixers
- power floaters
- screeders
- drain layers
- brick layers
- scaffolders
- carcassing / first fix carpenters
- roofer tilers
- window fitters
- stair / handrail manufacturers
- second / final fix carpenters
- electricians
- plumbers
- plasterers
- dry liners
- balcony specialist
- interior designers
- intelligent home specialists
- alarm specialists
- tilers
- decorators
- kitchen fitters
- floor laying specialists (laminate / vinyl / carpet
- air testing specialists
- landscape designer

Once you have gone through the list above you should also then check the drawings and the building regulations specification with a fine tooth combe to make sure you haven't missed anything else important.

You are probably already realising that pricing up this sort of project is quite a major job, especially if you are planning on doing as much of the work yourself as possible. It could take you a few weeks or more to complete all the pricing activities. It is very important however, that you do not just gloss over this section of the project in order to get on to the more interesting stuff.

That stuff may be more interesting. This stuff is probably more important!

The trick is, wherever possible, to get other people to a lot of the pricing work for you.

Why not let people who will make the profit from selling or hiring you the goods or services do as much of the work as possible:

Get them to work out as many of the prices as possible. Make *them* work for the sale!

Alternatively, to save you a lot of time, you could invest in hiring a quantity surveyor, who can work out all your quantities and costs for you. You can then use this information when you go out to tender as part of your tender package.

Using the costing figures:

Once you have these figures entered onto a spread sheet, you will not only be in a far better position to be able to keep control of the project from a financial point of view, but also, if you give a copy to a potential mortgage lender, they will know that you are approaching the project professionally and although they are not too keen these days on people trying to do all the work themselves, they might just think you are capable of pulling it off.

The cost spreadsheet you have now created is probably one of the most important tools to make sure that your project succeeds (that and the project programme, which we will look at later).

These are not lists to be prepared then put away in a drawer. They should be out on your table and looked almost every day.

If you use them properly they will warn you if or when things are starting to go wrong and give the you the opportunity to put them right before it gets too late.

2) Pricing the project to manage it yourself but hiring in tradespeople.

You will no doubt be pleased to know that, if you step away from trying to do everything yourself, pricing up the job should be a lot faster and simpler.

The truth of it is that the people who try to do most of the building works themselves will probably not end up paying much less than you do to get the house built (don't tell them though, they won't believe you anyway if you do!)

The chances are, that you have a full time job, possibly a family, a fairly busy life and you are intending on trying to fit in the self-build project around everything else you do. That's fine as long as you have made sure that you are properly prepared.

Managing the project is quite a major, time consuming and pressurised task, especially if you don't have a lot of experience of the building industry. There are many potential pit falls awaiting you and the trick is to try to immunise yourself against those risks, at the same time as making your workload as light as possible.

Here are some ideas on how to set things up if you want to be more of a hands-off project manager, letting others do most of the physical work.

I am going to be assuming that you are using a timber based structure. This is because to cover all the different types of construction would make this chapter far too long. However, this does not mean that if you choose a different method, you are not going to be able to use these figures as the basis for your costings. You'll just have a slightly different list when it is all done.

As you are probably fully aware after reading previous chapters, I think self-builders should generally choose the timber structure, but if you do use a different build method, just try to stick as closely as possible to the principles I am going to set out here and you should be fine.

Divide the project up into big packages:

Having been running building sites of one type or another for over 30 years, I am a big fan, where possible, of:

- Splitting the project down into a smallish number of big chunks.
- Letting *other people* do as much of *my job* as possible.
- Leaving myself to concentrate on the stuff I can do best.

If you are project managing, but are not actually planning on doing much of the work yourself, a good way to do that is to divide the project up as follows:

Package 1)   Design / planning / building regs specifications:

It is fairly common to give this these three tasks out as a single package.

Most types of house designers (whether they be architects, architectural technicians or just guys who design houses) will usually be able to cope with looking after all these particular matters for you.

All you need to do is:

- Do as much of the design work as you can, before handing it over to someone you have to pay.
- Make sure you shop around before choosing who you go with.
- Try to get some sort of fixed price for the work (or at least a fixed price for a basic package and then an hourly rate after that.
- Get a timescale for how long they envisage it will take to get the designs completed and through planning.
- Get a payment system agreed.
- Find out what information they need from you and get it to them as quickly as possible when they ask for it.

By giving these three items out as a single package, for this section of the job you will just be left with sorting out the warranty, the insurance and the building regs site visits (this is different from the building regs spec and involves organising the site visits during the build, in order to get the various stages approved by an inspector, who can then issue a building regs completion certificate).

Package 2)   Groundworks / foundations / slab / drainage / service connections / external works

For clarity, this involves all the following work (preferably as supply and fix) and possibly some other stuff relevant to your own job:

- Site clearance.

- Site set up (including security fencing).
- Temporary driveway (usually just laying hardcore where the permanent drive will be).
- Set up storage / welfare area.
- Setting out.
- Foundations.
- External walls to dpc.
- Ground floor slab.
- Drainage.
- Service connections (maybe part done at the start and completed at the end of the job).
- Preparation of site for scaffolding.
- Permanent drive and footpaths (at the end of the job).
- Levelling out landscaping ready for turfing etc.
- Possibly fencing.

There are literally thousands of individual bits that go into completing this list and if you are not an expert on the subjects of groundworks and drainage, then giving the whole lot out to one groundworks company will save you a lot of time and work.

You will need to give every tenderer a full set of relevant drawings and building regs as part of the tendering package.

Agree a 5% retention on each payment for this section of work (*take 5% off the invoice amount and keep it for 6 months to cover having to put anything right that they do wrong*).

If there are any problems found later in the job they could be expensive to fix, so keeping a small cash buffer is a sensible thing to do just in case the ground workers, for whatever reason won't or can't complete the work.

Package 3) Shell of the building (not including brickwork)

As we are using a timber structure for this example, this would involve:

- Deciding which timber option to go for (timber frame / SIPS / Closed panel)
- Contacting at least 4 (preferably 6 or more) companies, to compare how they work and their prices.
- Go and visit the factory and make sure you are happy with what they do and how they do it.
- Find out from them the tolerances they need the foundations and slab built to, then make sure the ground workers know what these are and that they actually build to them.
- Get a timescale for delivery (in writing if possible).
- Find out what their payment structure is and make sure you can comply with it.
- Get all the information to them that they require as quickly as possible when they need it.
- Keep checking on them after ordering, to make sure they are on programme, letting them know if you have any difficulties or delays which could affect their delivery date.
- Make sure they visit the site a couple of days' site before delivery to check that they are happy with everything (so they can't blame you if the delivery and crane arrive, and if for some reason they can't get on with the job).
- Make sure the scaffold is up as they want it before they arrive on site and organise for it to be altered whenever required as the frame goes up.
- If the shell package includes the external and internal walls, floors, roof structure, windows, external doors and anything else needed to make the building water and weathertight, that is great and saves you more work

(SIPS and closed panel systems are best for this). If it doesn't, then you will still have to sort those items out yourself.

If you go for one of the timber options, you will get between 25% to around 40% of your house coming to site in one package, theoretically at trade price. This route will also offer a far simpler and faster way for you to get your costing figures and other tender packages prepared.

If you go along the timber route, just make sure you check all the different specifications of the different companies.

Pretty much all timber frame / SIPS / closed panel companies design their products slightly differently from each other. Some include items that others don't and prices vary massively, so when you make your final decision on who to give the package to, you need to be happy that you have a full understanding of what you are getting.

To help this process, in your tender package, make sure you ask for a full, detailed specification of everything they "Supply and do". If you are not sure about anything, go and see them to discuss their quote before you sign anything.

If you choose to build traditionally in brickwork / blockwork, or if you chose some of the more unusual build methods, there could be literally hundreds of individual components that you will need to source and order. This could put more pressure on you than you can cope with.

Give each tenderer a full set of relevant drawings and a set of building regs specifications.

You won't be able to have a 5% retention on this package.

Package 4) Brickwork / stonework / rendering / cladding:

This is for the wrapping of the timber building shell.

Some houses will be designed with a mixture of two or more materials. If so it just means you will need to do twice as much work in finding and contacting four or more of each trade.

Once you have found the people who are going to price the work up, you need to do the following:

- Meet them all to see what you think of them and so you can compare them with each other. Try to get some contacts so you can check out work they have completed recently.
- Give them a tender package made up of all the relevant drawings, the building regs spec and what they are pricing for (this may involve other ancillary works such as garden walls, retaining walls garages etc.).
- Find out how, when and how often they would want paying. Tell them that you work on a retention basis, keeping 5% of each invoice payment for 6 months. Find out what their day rate is and when it would come in to play (a day rate is an hourly rate that is paid for anything they do that is not included in their original tender).
- Find out when they could start, how long they think it would take them to complete the work and what they would be needing from you. Try to get some sort of written document from them with the completion date. Better still get them to agree a completion date and a penalty if they don't hit that date (*good luck with that though!*)
- Compare prices and maybe try to barter them down a bit.
- Make your choice. Let the unsuccessful ones know and agree a start date with the chosen company.
- Keep in regular contact with them from that time on to make sure they are not falling behind with other work and to let them know if anything changes on your project which could affect them.

I would recommend that you keep responsibility for buying some of the materials: bricks / cladding / rendering materials / sand / cement / admixture.

Make sure that your chosen contractors come to check everything the day before they start so they can't turn up and say *"That's not how we need it, we'll have to leave site and charge you until it is put right"*.

Package 5) Scaffolding

For this sort of job, you need professional scaffolding in place. A lot of self-builders will try to save money by using the lightweight towers and moving them around the site as they are needed. Nine times out of ten this simply won't work. You need proper scaffold, supplied and erected by professional scaffolders.

Scaffolding is normally provided to this sort of job on a supply and erect basis and the price quoted will usually include for three or four visits to site (to alter the scaffold as and when required) and a 6-week hire period.

After those first six weeks, it usually changes to a *weekly* cost. This weekly payment can be up to a few hundred pounds, depending on the size of the job, so make sure you know how much it is (this ongoing weekly charge can sometimes add thousands of pounds to the cost of the job and is another reason why you should be planning to build as quickly as possible by considering using SIPS or closed panels).

Ask the scaffolders to make sure they allow in their price for an adequate number of hop ups. These are small lifts up around the roof area which get smaller as they go up the slope of the roof (don't worry, they'll know what you mean when you discuss the matter).

Also tell them what method you are using to build the shell. There are different ways to set the scaffold out depending on whether you are using traditional build / timber frame / SIPS or closed panel construction.

Check how and when they want paying and make sure you are confident that you can comply with the payment stages.

Finally, find out how much notice the scaffolders need to come to site to make the alterations and make sure you give them as much notice as you can when you need them back.

(Note: you won't be able to apply the 5% retention to this package)

Package 6) Windows / external doors

If the windows and doors are not included as part of your timber frame / SIPS / closed panel package, you will need to source them yourself.

I normally try to get windows and external doors (including bi-folds) on a supply and fix basis, this is a lot easier and less likely to lead to problems occurring during fixing.

Fixing windows and doors into new homes is usually a fairly quick process, taking on average a day for a full set, for a standard 4 bed detached house. Obviously if you are going for the more specialist products this can change, with prices, delivery times and fitting times all increasing dramatically.

With windows, as with everything else, try to get at least 4 quotes (preferably 6) for the job and don't think you have to go for the well-known manufacturers. Some local window manufacturers can offer very good products, a good service and a low price. Just make sure they are established businesses which are likely to still be around in 5 years, just in case you have any problems and need to claim on the warranty.

Always try to visit the factory so you can meet the boss and see how they are set up. Also, take note of how busy they are. A quiet factory may not have much work on because they are not very good!

Give each supplier a set of accurate drawings and a building regs specification (which will contain information about the requirements of the windows and doors in terms of insulation values and quality).

Make sure all measurements are double checked before they start to make anything. They need to know the opening size and **then deduct 10mm from the width and the height** (as a fitting tolerance) to work out the exact size of the windows.

If you want to do a bit of homework on prices, have a look on the internet and see if you can find one of the DIY stores who have their window and door prices listed. If they do, your "like for like" prices for supplying a full house of windows and doors from a trade supplier should work out around the same price, but with the trade supplier including fitting in the package (in other words, they should end up about 20% cheaper from the trade supplier).

The chances are that you won't be able to apply the 5% retention to this package.

Package 7) Roof finishing

There are many types of roof finish, all with dramatically varying price tags attached. The cheapest type of roofing will usually be a large concrete roof tile sitting on 2" x 1" treated roofing batten, on standard new residential build quality roofing felt.

Roof tile options:

Marley Modern roof tile: The cost for a Marley Modern concrete tile (or similar by other manufacturers) is around £0.75 - £1.30 each and you need roughly 10 per sq metre (£7.50 - £13 / sq m total).

Labour & fixing prices for these tiles are as cheap as they will get.

Natural slate roof tile

The cost for a **natural slate** roof tile is from around £3 to £6 each and you will need between 10 and 15 per square metre (£30 - £90 / sq m total). Labour and fixing prices are expensive as these tiles need special fixings.

Handmade clay tiles

The cost for a **hand-made clay tile** is around £0.70 - £1.20 each and you will need around 50 – 65 per square metre (£35 - £78 / sq m total). Labour and fixing prices are very expensive as there are up to 7x more tiles per sq metre than a standard concrete tile. Small tiles also need more roofing batten and fixings.

Overall, supply and fix of this option could cost around 5x the price of supply and fix of the Marley Modern and significantly more expensive than natural slate.

If you have time to do some shopping around, you may want to get the roof tiling package as labour only so you can play suppliers off against each other (something a supply and fit company will rarely do).

Whoever you talk to, ask them if they have a delivery truck with a hydraulic crane on the back. If so, rather than the delivery vehicle offloading packs of tiles on to the ground and the roofers carrying them all up the ladders a few at a time, the delivery vehicle should be able to pick up full packs or even full pallets of tiles and place them directly on to a roof platform (that they would bring with them). The roofers can then simply spread the tiles around the roof. This could save a lot of time and money.

If you do manage to get hold of a hiab, make sure you tell the roofers so they can adjust their price downwards accordingly.

For the tendering package, if you do go down the route of supply and fix, you need to make sure you request the tenders to include:

"All labour plant and materials required to complete the work to building regulations standards, including, but not limited to the supplying and fixing of: Roofing felt, treated battens, tiles, all fixings, fascias, soffits, barge boards, dormer cheeks, associated lead work to roof".

Some roofers won't fit the fascias, soffits, bargeboards, dormer cheeks or leadwork, they will just want to do the tiling. If that is the case, but you want to use them anyway, then the rest of the package can usually be given to the joiners or the joiners and the plumbers (with any leadwork being done by the plumbers).

Send every tenderer a set of relevant drawings and a building regs specification as part of the tendering package.

Try to keep the 5% retention on this package.

Package 8) Electrical installation

I would almost always recommend that this package is given out a supply and fix. There are simply too many bits and pieces involved in a full electrical installation for anyone except a professional to be able to know how much of what is going to be needed.

If you were to try to provide the materials for this section of work, I can almost guarantee that you would end up paying large sums of money in "standing time" for the men on site, while you ran around trying to find all the bits that are missing, which are stopping them working.

The electrical contractors will also probably get better prices on the materials than you would be able to.

Regarding the tendering package for this section of the job, you need to include a set of building regulation specs and all relevant drawings, fully marked up with everything you want in each room and outside the house.

You should prepare these drawings to make sure you get *everything* you want, *where* you want it. I suggest that you put plenty of sockets in (approx 3 x double sockets per room as an average). You will also need to include items such as:

- Entry point for mains
- Wall sockets (I suggest using all double sockets, - they are cheap and two sockets are better than one!)
- Floor sockets (for kitchen islands etc.)
- Light switches
- Ceiling lighting points
- Wall lighting points
- Fuse board (close to entry point for the mains)
- Ventilation fans & switches
- TV points (including Sky)
- Telecom points
- Cooker point
- Central heating circuits and thermostats
- Mains wired smoke detectors
- Cinema sound wiring
- Outside lighting
- Outside power points
- Automatic house wiring
- Alarm control panel and sensors
- Earthing points (if you don't know what these are don't worry, just add them to the spec and request the electricians to include them as required)
- Power for remote controlled garage door
- Power for electrically controlled gates
- Wiring to solar / ground source / air source heating.

Here are some symbols I use to show the main items on the electrical s (there is no hard and fast rule about how you show the individual items as long as you identify on the drawings somewhere what each symbol means):

X XX = Single socket / Double socket
⅄ = Light switch
○ = Ceiling light
⋇ = Wall light
BT = Telecom point
TV = TV point
---------- = line of wiring from a switch to a lighting point
| FB | = Consumer unit (Fuse box)

You need to make sure you have all the details marked up as accurately as possible onto the drawings, because the electrician will use these same drawings to install the electrical system.

If you make any errors or omissions with the marking up of the drawings, it could cost you time and money moving stuff about or adding things you forgot.

Preparing the drawings is not a particularly simple or quick task, especially if you are trying to do it when you don't have much knowledge of the subject, however it can be made a bit easier if you do the following:

i. Ask the contractor to request from you, any missing information before they submit their quote (this puts the onus on them to make sure they are happy that they are including for everything in their prices). Tell them that you are happy to meet with them to make sure they have all the required information.

ii. Include in your introduction to the tender documents that they are to quote for:
"All labour, plant and materials to complete the installation works to building regs standards". Add that all installation work should be fully tested, certified and warrantied.

That way, if you miss anything important, they should pick it up.

Always ask for proof of an insurance policy to cover their work and for proof of qualifications for them to be able to carry out the works.

Apply the 5% retention to this package.

Package 9) Plumbing and heating installation

As with the electrics, I would strongly recommend giving this out as a supply and fix package. The only possible proviso might be that I would source the boiler if I wanted anything special (otherwise just ask them to recommend a suitable boiler and see what they come up with. They will have to calculate the heat and hot water requirements for the house, based on the drawings, which is quite a complicated thing to do, so you are best letting them recommend the boiler once they have done that calculation)

As usual send out a full set of building regulation specs and relevant drawings, this time marked up with things like:

- Mains entry point
- Boiler position (either state which boiler you want or ask them to recommend one)
- Radiators (I normally just draw a think black line). Try to keep them below windows and out of the way of furniture.
- Sink positions
- W.C positions
- Washing machine location
- Dishwasher location
- Bath / shower locations
- Wet rooms
- Outside taps
- If using underfloor heating, mark where the manifolds will be positioned.

If you don't have a scanner, just draw and write on the drawings as appropriate, then copy the marked up drawings to give to each of the tenderers.

If you can scan the drawing and use a software package to allow you to add shapes and text this will allow you to

a) Present the drawing more professionally.

b) Print as many copies as you like and make alterations simply and quickly.

Plumbers can often offer other plumbing related services as well as the standard plumbing / heating system installation. Things such as underfloor heating, leadwork and other related bits and pieces. When you first approach them, ask what services they offer and then, if you choose to, you can include those in the tender package.

Apply the 5% retention to this package.

Package 10)   Joinery

You have more options when you decide how to set this package up, especially when you are using a timber based shell for the house itself.

There are a lot of timber items which need to be included in a new home, so the joiner is not necessarily always going to be able to measure up accurately what they will need in the way of materials (big joinery outfits normally can, one man bands often can't).

To accurately itemise all timber items in a building, you would usually need either a quantity surveyor or a computer CAD package that spits out the quantities at the same time as the initial design work is done. You could ask your designer if they could provide you with a set of quantities for all the joinery works, but even that doesn't really tend to work with this section of the job.

Usually, I find that the easiest way to set the joinery package up, is to give it out as a "labour, plant and all fixings" package, with you sourcing the main materials. However, you set it up so that the joiners work with you to make sure they have what they need, when they need it, in the way of timber supplied to site.

Most decent joinery companies will be able to work out the labour and plant requirements for the job and they will simply make an allowance for fixings, but measuring all the timber for the job is usually just too complicated for them.

So, by you working together, all you need to do is to approach the ordering of the timber in small chunks, bit by bit, with them letting you know what they will need in the first delivery (for when they initially arrive on site), then working with you, on a day-to-day basis, to make sure that everything else is ordered and delivered ready for when they need it.

The way to do this is for you to get together with one of the joiners a couple of weeks before they start work. At this meeting you should talk through and list what they will be doing on site during the first phase of their work. Your job will then be to make sure that everything on their list is on site the day before they start.

Once they get going, they then need to keep in regular touch with you and give you at least a week's notice to enable you to find and order everything else in good time.

Their work will normally include some or all of the following:

- Fixing joists / floor boards (not timber with timber frame – timber floor boards are usually part of the package).
- Stud walls (not if using timber frame).
- Roof trusses / bracing / fascias / soffits / bargeboards.
- Bay or porch canopy roofing.
- Window fitting (if not bought as supply and fix).
- First fix (door linings / stairs / noggins in walls / boxing ins for pipes / window cill boards etc.)
- Second fix (hanging doors / stair handrails / architraves / skirtings / more boxing ins / bath panels / shelving to airing cupboard /etc.).
- Final fix (ironmongery / snagging etc.)
- Kitchen / utility room fitting.

The drawings, specification and building regs will normally give them enough information to format a basic tender, but, before you send the tenders out, have a think through everything to see if there is anything you need to add, like fitted wardrobes, vanity units etc.

Good quality, professional joinery companies will usually be able to offer a range of services from carcassing the shell of the house, to final finishing works. The more they can do, the less work there will be for you in trying to find other people to do what they can't.

The 5% retention should be applied if possible to this package to cover faulty workmanship, but if you are supplying the materials, you may have a fight on your hands to prove that problems which occur are due to poor workmanship (their fault) and not faulty goods (your fault).

Package 11) Plastering / drylining / taping and jointing

All three of these trades give you basically the same service. They apply the finish to the internal and / or external walls of the house. They just do it in different ways:

Plasterers

These are the trade that most people are familiar with. For internal walls, they will coat bare block walls with a coat of cement render. Once that coat is set they will return again and apply a finishing coat of "skim" (usually the pink stuff we are all used to seeing in new houses).

If the internal walls are built in timber stud, the plasterers will usually fix the plasterboards and apply a skim finishing coat.

They will normally work as labour and plant only, so you would need to sort out all their materials, including:

- Sand
- Cement
- Bagged plaster
- Plasterboards (usually square edged – the supplier will know what you mean when you order them)
- Scrim tape
- Plaster beads
- Skim beads
- Covings
- Admixture
- Plasterboard nails / screws

Dry liners

Dry lining is the system a lot of the house builders use when they are building traditionally (brick and block). It is also called dot and dab.

Basically the plasterboards (square edge) are stuck on to the blockwork walls with adhesive, then the joints are covered over with a self-adhesive scrim tape and finally, they are given a smooth skimmed finish.

Dry liners will usually stick the plasterboards to the walls and you will provide the "skim" (in 25kg bags). They will usually, however often bring their own adhesive, jointing tape and tools etc. (Check with them to make sure).

You would need to supply any covings etc. (some dry liners will not be able to fix covings, - ask them when you meet or talk to them. If they can't, you may need to bring in someone else who can).

Tapers & jointers

You will have supplied the boards and had them fixed, usually by the joiners (order taper edge boards for this system, not square edge boards), but you won't need the skim this time (it is not used with this system).

The tapers will normally bring all the additional materials and tools that they need, but some of them may ask you to provide the adhesive (make sure they give you the name of the product they generally use).

Their price will usually be for labour, taping, fixing materials and plant.

This is a very simple, quick system that gives a dry finish, ready for painting within a few days of it being applied, so can speed up the job significantly.

Basically, between one and three layers of tape area applied to the joints / corners / angles of the boards. Each layer of tape is wider than the previous layer (with the first coat being about 50mm wide and if three layers are used, the last coat will be up to 100mm wide.

The first layer of tape is applied and given a thin coat of filler over the top of it, sometimes using a special applicator tool on a long handle (to do both tasks at once and to get up to the high places). Once set (usually after 24 hours), a second and then a third coat are applied, each followed by a coat of filler (again, with 24 hours between coats). The filler should be applied so that it levels out the recesses formed by the taper-edge plasterboards, to give a level surface across the width and height of the whole wall. Once the filler has fully set, it is sanded to give a completely smooth surface, ready for decorating.

Renderers:

Rendering usually refers to the external finish of the house. You render over blockwork to create a finish that can then be painted with masonry paint to give the final finish to the outside of the property.

This is a slightly more involved process for materials ordering and it is usually best if you do the ordering, taking instructions from the rendering gang as to "how much of what" they will need and when.

You will need to make sure the scaffold it safe to work on and that the platforms are set at the right height to allow the rendering gang to reach all areas of the walls.

You will then usually need to make sure the following materials are all ordered and delivered ready to start on site:

Sand: Usually 1 ton bags.

Cement: (buy it by the pallet load, with maybe a part pallet for the last load).

Admixture: Buy it in 25 litre containers.

Render beads: For forming up straight corners and angles.

Bellmouth beads: For running around the bottom edge of the render to give a nice straight line and a lip for the rain to run off.

For a standard, simple single house project, you won't normally need to supply a full set of drawings to each tenderer, but a set of building regs specs should be sent if there is anything relevant on them.

By the time you are ready to talk to any of these trades, you will usually have the shell of the house up and the roof on, so you can just arrange to meet on site and show them round. If they are only pricing the job on a per sq metre basis they will usually just estimate the size of the job, how long it will take and then set their price per sq m on what they see as they walk round.

Make sure you get all quotes in writing (they will tend just to tell you the price verbally, so you need to get that price in a bit more of an official form).

Try to get some sort of definitive timescale from them for doing the work and ask if there are any special conditions they need. You will find that some will say that they need the house empty (without other trades people in) and clean but some will be happy to work around others.

The 5% retention is not critical with this package, but if you can get them to agree to it, go for it, just in case.

Package 12)   Wall and floor tiling

This is normally a fairly simple package to give out.

Even though you might get some good prices on tiles, you will usually struggle to get anything like the prices that the professionals pay for the adhesives, grouts and all the ancillary bits and pieces, so you are usually best leaving the supply of everything but the tiles, to them.

You will need to supply them with a specification to show what you want and where. This will detail what areas of what rooms you want them to tile, for example:

Kitchen walls: Between wall units and worktops. 100mm sq bumpy white tiles

Kitchen floors: Full kitchen floor area. 300mm sq plain faced tiles.

Utility walls: Between wall units and worktops. 100mm sq bumpy white tiles

Utility floor: Full utility floor area: 300mm sq plain faced tiles

And so on.

It will also help if you actually mark the walls to clearly show where the tiling is to go (especially useful if you are not on site all the time to answer any questions).

Tile prices: Bear in mind that smaller tiles will usually cost a lot more per sq m than larger tiles, both to buy and to fix.

Also, be aware that the very large tiles can also cause problems if the wall or floor is not exactly plumb, straight and level. Because of the size of the tiles, when any sort of light source shines on them, they will naturally highlight any of these discrepancies

They are also more prone to cracking due to minor structural movement within the house.

Bear in mind that if you buy unsealed tiles (i.e. tiles without any sort of glazed finish), you will usually need to seal them before grouting, to stop the surface of the tile from getting stained (sealing will add a few pounds per sq m to the overall cost).

If you shop around, you can usually pick up some fairly nice tiles for around £15 - £20 / sq m.

Tilers will normally charge per sq metre for floor and wall tiling (including adhesive). This could be anywhere between £12 and £25 / sq m. If there is any specialist detailing work to do, they may charge you a day rate of around £20 - £25 / hr.

Make sure that whatever you are supplying is on site the day before it is needed.

Get all quotes on paper (just so they can't accidently forget what they said when you originally met) and try to keep the 5%, just in case there are problems with tiles cracking or grout falling out after they have finished.

Package 13)   Decoration

This is usually another fairly easy package to deal with. You don't normally need to send them any drawings, but check the building regs spec to see if there is anything specific on there that relates to painting and decorating and if so, send them a copy of the notes. They won't normally bother with giving you a price per sq m but instead will just give you a price for the job.

Decorators can usually work either labour only or supply and fix. I would normally tend towards the labour-only option so I can shop around and choose my own paints and colours and ask for discounts at the wholesalers (if you ask the decorators to provide all the materials, you may find they charge you full price).

If everything is going to be magnolia or white it may be better to let them get their own paint, but it is always worth asking what they will charge you for 10 litre tubs of good quality matt / silk emulsion / gloss etc. and see how their prices compare to what you pay for the same thing

Make sure you let them know if you are using different colours in each room as this will affect the time it takes to do the job and their price will probably increase.

If you are supplying the paints, make sure you have enough of each colour paint on site the day they start so they don't start charging you standing time. Find out how much an hour they charge if there is anything they need to do, which is not covered by the price for the job.

Most decorators will want to do three coat work to the walls, with the first coat being a sealer coat (or mist coat). I do things a bit differently by doing away with the first coat and instead, use a very thick paint called obliterating paint to do the job of both the first and second coats. This saves a lot of time in both labour and materials (if you go for this, make sure they know when they tender, so they can reduce their quote accordingly).

The 5% retention is not that important for this package, but again, if you can get it, do so, just in case.

Of course, the other option you have here is to take on all the painting and decorating work yourself. It's one of the sections that, as long as you take your time and use good quality materials, you can normally produce a reasonable quality job and save a few thousand pounds in labour cost.

Don't try it though, unless you think you can produce a high quality finished job. Remember that the decoration is the first thing you see when you walk in to a room. If you make a mess of it, it can really have an effect on the finished quality of the whole project and can even reduce its value when and if you ever want to sell the house.

Package 14) Carpets / other flooring

Again, a simple package to deal with. You buy the carpets or whatever is being laid and get carpet / floor layers to give you a price for the labour and all the other bits and bobs they will need (just make sure they know they are providing all the ancillary items so they don't assume that you are).

You don't usually need to send any drawings or specs out for this part of the job, just meet the people on site and walk round the rooms to show them the scope of the job.

You will normally be given a price per square metre for laying carpets and other flooring. If you can get that in writing it will give you a bit of peace of mind, but I have never come across someone who has changed the quoted price after they have done this sort of job (unless there were problems that slowed them up significantly, which are fairly rare when it comes to laying carpets and flooring)

It is doubtful that any floor layer would agree to the 5% retention.

A lot of self-builders tend to ignore carpets and floor coverings when it comes to pricing up the project. Don't fall in to that trap!

With some carpets, laminates and real wood flooring costing up around £30 / sq metre (plus underlay and fitting etc.) the total cost for your floor coverings in a reasonable sized house can run

in to a number of thousands of pounds. That money needs to be found within you overall build budget.

Package 15) Driveway

You have lots of different choices for driveway finishes, but they all usually need the same input from you when pricing.

Whenever I come to this section, I will just decide on the type of finish I want and contact local companies who specialise in laying that particular product, send them a site plan and ask them to quote for the full installation. – Labour, plant and ancillary items" Just make sure you know what ancillary items they have included for and what you may still need to bring in).

I will normally have provided a hardcore base ready for them to lay the driveway surface directly on to (the ground workers are usually best suited to this task).

Setting it up like this this, leaves you free to shop around for prices on the product you want to use (paving / macadam etc.) without having to worry about all the ancillary bits and pieces you may need to complete the works.

There may be some variance between companies when it comes to what you provide and what they provide, so the way to deal with this, is to make sure you have a note pad and pen with you when you meet each tenderer. Make notes on everything you discuss and agree, then at the end of the meeting, ask them if you have covered everything they would need to start work if they get the job.

Once you have decided to whom you are going to give the job, write up the notes from the meeting you had with them and email them a copy, asking them to acknowledge receipt and agreement.

By sending them this document, you will be covering yourself against them coming back asking for things that you did not originally agree and for additional money for new items that were missed at the original meeting.

Get a day rate figure from them, just in case there is any extra work.

Try to keep the 5% on this package just in case any problems become apparent with the drive over the next few months (settlement being the most common).

Package 16) Landscaping

Many self-builders don't get round to giving out this package. The reasons for this are usually:

- The finances of a self-build, more often than not, get very stretched towards the end and you might simply find there is no money left
- It is quite often useful to be able to stand in the new building and get the feel of how the new building sits within the plot before making your mind up about what you are going to do with the landscaping. Once you have got rid of all the builders, you may not want to be bringing more of them back later for the landscaping. A lot of self-builders will do this work themselves over the next few months, once they get settled

This is not a critical package as part of the basic self-build project, but it is nice to get it done, if for no other reasons than to get the place looking nice and so that you aren't trudging mud and muck into your nice new, clean house for months after you move in.

You can get your VAT refund before the landscaping is done as long as you comply with the building regs regarding access and drainage and any related planning conditions, but you won't then be able to claim for any of the "claimable" materials you buy for the landscaping.

It is always a good idea to build an allowance for the landscaping in to your overall budget, but if you do find you are running out of money for whatever reason, you can always put this job on hold and use the money to get other work done, which will help get the house structurally completed in order for you to get your completion certificates and be able to move in.

Whenever you are ready to start this section of the project, you have two choices: 1) Do it yourselves or 2) Get the professionals in.

If you take option 2) I would suggest simply getting three or four different companies round for a meeting to discuss your ideas and to get some idea of likely costs.

The landscapers would normally come up with some basic design ideas, based on the drawings you will have sent them. Once they have done this, if you are happy to do so, you can use them as a basis to move forward, towards getting a fixed price for the whole job.

Professional landscaping companies will normally price to supply everything (unless there is anything you specifically want to supply) and will include for all labour and plant.

Payment will normally be in agreed stages (don't pay anything up front unless it is for some special item that needs ordering early).

The 5% retention is a good idea for this package, especially if there is any structural work involved such as walls, paths, retaining walls etc.

Package 17+) Any other specialists

These could include basement construction, home automation, ground or air source heating, swimming pools etc.

Using what you have learned from preparing all the other packages, you will need to decide which route is most appropriate for any other, more specialist packages which remain to sort out.

Just keep the general principals in mind of:

- Send *all* the relevant information. You don't want anyone coming back to you later saying "You didn't tell us about that".
- Try to cover everything involved in that package in your paper work and negotiations and try to make sure there is no wriggle room for them to come back asking for more money.
- Get everything written down and where possible, agreed by the signature of the person tendering.
- Agree a day rate with everyone working on any package
- Try to get the 5% retention agreed on the contract

Preparing tenders and contracts:

For most of the packages listed above, you will need to prepare a tender package (which will also form part of the contract with each sub-contractor).

A tender package normally includes:

- **A full set of the relevant drawings** (not necessarily a full set of *all* drawings).
- **A specification of the work they are being asked to price** (you need to list everything you want them to do and reference it to the drawings).
- **A copy of the building regulations for the project** (this ensures that they have the information available to them to allow them to price the work up in accordance with the relevant regulations.
- **A contract.** You will need to supply this (I'll give you some ideas shortly).
- **A programme of the works** (see later chapter on how to create this).

- **A covering letter** introducing the tendering package to them.
- **Any other details they may need to be able to accurately price the works.**

This may sound like a lot of work to get everything together, but once you have gathered the basic information together for one package, you send similar stuff out to each sub-contractor.

The contract:

Below is a sample contract I have drawn up to give you some ideas that you may wish to use to help you to prepare your own contracts. I have designed this one for the groundworks package, but, as I say, the basics are the same for each section of the job.

Important note: This sample contract is intended as a guide only and its inclusion here does not imply its legal correctness. Always get anything legal checked out by a Solicitor. It may cost you a couple of hundred pounds to do so, but it could save you £1,000's in the long run.

(Note: You can also source contracts documents from the Joint Contract Tribunal (JCT), RIBA and DIY Doctor, for a fee).

TENDER DOCUMENTS AND CONTRACT FOR GROUNDWORKS AT:
PLOT 1, ANY ROAD, ANY TOWN.

Please find enclosed 2 copies of each of the contract documents which include the following drawings and other information in order to allow you to price for works at the above address:

- location plan
- site plan showing the storage compound and routes for the gas, water electrical and telecom main service route from the boundary to the house
- north, east, south and west elevations
- ground floor plan
- first floor plan
- drainage plan
- foundation plan
- specification of the works included in your package
- a copy of the building regulations for this project
- a programme of the works including a target start date for your section of the works

One copy of the documents is for you to keep for your information. The other is to be returned to us with your quotation. Please initial each page / drawing to confirm that you have noted and agree with its content.

Please check all drawings thoroughly as they should include all the relevant information you require to complete your section of the works.

If there is any information missing that is required for you to price or complete your section of the works, please notify us as soon as possible. If you do not notify us of any missing information we will assume that this package includes everything you need.

Once you have checked all the documents can you please initial the bottom right hand corner of each page of each document, to confirm that you have received it, that you have checked it and are happy that you can complete the works with the information it contains.

If there are any special requirements that you will need us to satisfy as part of your works on this contract, please state these in detail in your quotation.

Please return one full set of documents to us with your quotation.

Quotation:

Please quote for all labour, plant and materials for the following works **(all work is to conform fully to all of the contract documents)**:

- Strip topsoil to the area shown on the site plan and deposit on site.
- Supply, lay and compact 6" hardcore to driveway area and storage compound.
- Set out the property to a tolerance of + / - 3mm (this is required for the timber frame).
- Excavate foundations.
- Lay foundations and complete all construction work up to the completion of the ground floor slab. The square of the building should be within + / - 3mm and the level of the top of the brickwork at DPC level should be within =/- 2mm in 3m with a maximum tolerance of = / - 3mm
- Excavate, lay and backfill the full drainage system including making connections to mains.
- Lay gas, water, electricity and telecom services from the property to the boundary.
- Remove all your waste and debris from the site at completion.

Payments:

- Please give full details of how you would prefer payments for the works to be made. A payment schedule must be agreed in writing before any sub-contractor starts work on site.
- Please note that a 5% retention will be held by the client on all payments for a period of 6 months from the payment due date. This sum will be released after 6 months' subject to it not having been used to correct errors or omissions in the related works.
- Please indicate your hourly rates for the following items (these may be needed should there be any cause to alter the contract documents by adding additional items of work or altering the existing details):
    - Site engineer
    - Labourer
    - Joiner
    - Bricklayer
    - Drain layer
    - Ground worker
    - Excavator
    - Dumper
    - Vibrator poker
    - Concrete pump
    - Vibrating tamper
    - Power float

Changes to contract documents:

- No changes should be made to the works described in the contract document without written consent from the client (this can be in the form of a text or an email in circumstances which require a quick decision).
- No works that would involve extra charges being incurred by the client will be undertaken without written consent (again, this can be in the form of a text or email in circumstances that require a prompt decision to be made by the client).
- No payment will be made by the client for works carried out without their explicit written confirmation.

Notice to start work

- Please confirm that at the time of tendering, you are able to start work on the date indicated on the programme of the works.
- Please confirm that you will give at least 3 weeks' notice before the start of the works if you are unable to adhere to the target start date.
- If we (the clients) are not able to meet the target start date, we will give you at least 3 weeks' notice and an estimate of the delay. Please confirm that you are happy with this arrangement.

Insurance, health and safety

- Please confirm that your company carries up to date all risks insurance to cover your presence on site and please supply a copy of your policy.
- Please confirm that all your site staff have the required levels of qualifications and training relevant to their duties on site with regard to health and safety.
- We (the clients) will provide all site welfare facilities with regard to health and safety.

Responsibility for loss / damage

- We (the clients) accept no responsibility for loss or damage to goods, plant or stock left on site unattended.
- We (the clients) will provide a steel lock up cabin for general use, but accept no responsibility for items lost or stolen.

Contract documents:

- If you do not agree with any item contained in the contract documents or feel there are errors or omissions, please detail your concerns in writing.
- This document forms part of the tender package and also forms the contract between the client and the sub-contractor. By initialling each page, you are indicating that you are happy with the content.

Please initial each page of all tender documents and sign and date here to confirm agreement with this document.

A similar document should form the front few pages of your tender document. You will then need to add everything else to the package (listed previously) and send two copies to each tenderer (one for them to return, initialled with their quotation and one for them to keep).

Summary on tender packages

What I have just done with the tender package as a whole and with the contract specifically is to pass over a lot of the hard work to each of the sub-contractors.

In the *sample contract* you will see that I have asked them to quote for "Labour, plant and materials" (in other words: Everything). So now all I have to do is to compare all the quotes, ask any questions I still have, accept one of them, do the bits I said I would do, give them a start date and let them get on with it.

That doesn't work for all the packages, but where it is an option, because it saves me a lot of work, it is usually one I take up.

By the way: trying to save money by providing materials and plant for the subbies, actually often costs you more money in the long run than if you let them get everything themselves.

Although you might get better individual prices for one or two of the items you will need, by shopping around, you will generally find that trying to get everything, in the right amounts, at the right time is a difficult task when you are not used to it.

For example: If you take on the responsibility of providing all the plant for the brickies and the mixer doesn't turn up in time for them to start work, you could find yourself with 4 or more men standing on site doing nothing and charging you around £100+ an hour daywork rates until you sort the problem out. – Ouch!

When is it worth you considering providing materials or plant for the job?

On a reasonably big job (which a self-build is), what you might do with some of the sub-contract packages, to save money, is to consider taking responsibility for supplying some of the materials and / or plant, for example:

Concrete

If a sub-contractor prices up the concrete on their tender document, they will usually measure up how much they think they will need and allow an average price per cubic metre. They will then add an additional amount of money on for waste and other bits and pieces. You will then pay the full price that they quote, whether or not they actually get a better price on the concrete and whether or not there is any waste.

If you decide to keep control of that particular item, you can shop around all the concrete suppliers (which can sometimes vary locally by up to 20%) and you will have the additional benefit that you will only pay for what you get, so if there is no waste, you won't pay for any waste!

(What I have just said does have to be tempered with that previous paragraph. If the concrete turns up 2 hours late and you ordered it, you may get clobbered by having to pay standing time for the men).

What you need to do as you prepare each tender package is think about each bit of it and decide what you want them to do and what you want to do yourself, remembering all the time that you have a finite amount of time to do all your bits in and around running your existing home, working and giving time to your family.

Summary on pricing when you project manage everything yourselves

You will no doubt by now be thinking "This is going to be pretty complicated and hard work". Well it is, but it might not actually be as bad as it may seem. You'll find that once you get going on one or two of the packages, that you will be able to copy and paste some of the information into the rest of the packages. Also, once you get the knack of preparing the packages, it will all become a lot simpler in your mind. Yes, it's a bit of a bind having to do it, but once it is done you'll be in a much better position to make sure that you set the job up properly.

3) Pricing when using a professional project manager

If you have read the earlier chapters, you will be aware that this would be the management option I would recommend for any self-build project. It is not always the cheapest, but overall, I think it is the best.

A project manager can do pretty much all of the management work you could and they can sometimes do what you can't. They are employed by you, to give you the best job they can, at the best price, in a reasonable time scale.

They are paid either on an hourly rate, or (preferably) they should offer the option of working on a fixed price for the project.

From a pricing and management point of view, this should take the pressure completely away from you and usually includes them taking on some or all of:

- All pricing works (labour / materials / plant).

- Tendering and payment terms agreements.
- Contract negotiations.
- Contract preparation.
- Materials delivery reconciliation.
- Bookkeeping.
- Submitting regular reports to you on the financial position of the project.
- Warning you if there are any foreseeable financial problems likely to occur.
- Recommendations on how to re-organise your finances and the job, if you need to free up more funds.

It is quite likely that, should you decide to use the services of a project manager, they could actually pretty much pay for themselves, by virtue of the fact that they will probably already have all the right contacts in all the right places.

The chances are that they will also complete the project in a significantly shorter time than you could hope to do if you run it yourself. This could potentially save you thousands of pounds in interest payments on your borrowing, as well as making substantial savings on your day to day expenses (for living somewhere else while the house is built), plus other expenses like scaffold hire, cabin hire, plant hire etc.

How much should you pay a project manager?

If you are building in traditional brick and block or if you are using one of the more unusual building methods, the project could take quite a while to complete. So, if the project manager were to be employed for the whole time until the job was finished (up to a year depending on the complexity of the job), they could prove to be quite a costly commodity.

However, to run a single house project for a professional project manager would not usually be a full-time job. A good project manager should be able to run up to six projects at the same time, depending how complex they are and whether or not they are in the same general geographical area.

So, you would not expect to be paying anything like a full-time salary to any project manager who would, say, be doing all the admin work, but only be coming to site two or three times a week for a couple of hours each time. May be a third of a reasonable full time salary for the time they are involved with the project would be about right (allowing for the extra time and work they have to do before the job actually starts on site).

To give yourself a rough way to work out what you should be paying as a management fee for a simple four bed house, try this:

- Allow at least couple of thousand pounds (maybe four thousand at the most) for the initial set-up of the project (in other words the measuring, pricing, tendering, programming, dealing with warranties and insurances etc.)
- Estimate your target project duration (read the earlier chapters for help with this)
- Work out when you might be happy to take over running of the project (part-way through / never) and come up with a rough estimate for how many weeks in to the project that should be.
- Work on the project manager being on site for 6 – 8 hours a week, with 3 – 5 hours travelling time and a further 4 – 6 hours on the admin work.
- Estimate (or find out) the going hourly rate for a project manager in your area (anywhere between £20 - £35 / hr would be expected)
- Work the figures through to give you an estimate of what you should be looking to pay the project manager in total.

So, as an example, let's say the estimated fees for a simple four bed house could be:

£3,500 (for setting everything up). plus 20 hours a week @ £25 / hour for 16 weeks = £11,500

So, you now have a guide figure to work from: £11,500 would basically cover your PM for around 5 months. One month doing all the preparation work, plus four months on site.

However, taking in to account the fact that a good PPM will be able to run three to four projects simultaneously, £2,300 a month for what is a minor part time job for them would actually be pretty good money!

A good PPM would look to make between £3,000 and £4,000 a month in total. If they can run 3 jobs simultaneously, they need, say £1,300 from each (if they can run 4 jobs they need around £1,000 a month from each).

If you are planning on hiring them for around 5 months in total, using these figures, you would be looking to pay between £5,000 and £6,500 in total.

Using both sets of figures you now have a sensible price range that you can use as a guide to negotiate with potential PPMs. In this example if you ended up settling at £7,500 - £8,500 for the full job, I think that would be a fairly satisfactory outcome.

Once you agree a fee, you can then set up a payment system: Weekly / monthly or (my preferred option) at the end of each build stage (this tends to keep them focussed on getting progress because they know they won't get paid until they get to a certain point.

If you were planning on keeping them on until (say) the plastering were completed, the payment stages would normally be something like:

1: After all preparation works are completed
2: After foundations are complete
3: When the shell is up
4: When the first fixes are finished
5: When the house is plastered.

You need to make sure you get any project manager tied in to a contract. If they are professional, they should have their own draft contract, which they will go through with you, amend to suit your project and expect you to sign. It is always worth taking these documents to a solicitor to make sure there are no weaknesses in them that could cause you problems further down the line.

So, that's it! If you use a PPM, the setting up of the project should be faster and far less stressful for you, the job should run more smoothly and quickly and the whole thing should be a much more enjoyable experience for you. Before I move on, I'll just mention (again) that if I were a self-builder setting up a project, who didn't have a lot of experience of the building industry, the best possible combination of method and management to go for, to my thinking, would be:

"A project managed contract using a closed panel timber frame system for the build".

"Nuff said!"

4) Give the whole project over to a main contractor

Apart from choosing to try to do everything yourselves, this is my *next least favoured option*!

However, if you can afford it, are short on free time, and can't find a decent PPM, but really want to take on a self-build project then this might be your only option.

Strangely enough, the main contractor option is the way that most self-builders think is the automatic way to set up a project, so at the moment, a good proportion of all self-build projects will presently end up going down this route.

Don't get me wrong, if it is set up right and if you get a good main contractor, the job can go really smoothly and quickly, It's just so bl***y expensive!

Let's take a quick look at the likely costs for each management option using the figures I quoted in the earlier chapters:

- **Managing the project yourself:** At £90 / sq ft, a 2000 sq ft house could cost you £180,000
- **Using a project manager:** At £110 / sq ft, the same house could cost £220,000
- **Using a main contractor:** At £130 / sq ft, the same house could cost £260,000

So, using these figures as an example, there could be an **£80,000** difference in the cost of building your new home.

Why?

This is usually the way it works using a main contractor (*we did start to cover this earlier*).

- You send them your drawings and they send you a quote for all the work.
- After possibly some negotiation, you agree a (sort of) fixed price (by the way, I don't think I have ever heard of a fixed price self-build contract actually staying fixed. There are always too many loop holes in the tender and the contract which favour the contractor for that to happen).
- You agree a stage payment system with them (usually after foundations / once the shell is complete / after plastering and finished), with any extras being charged at the stage payment point after they were incurred or agreed.

That sounds fine in theory, but the problem is with the way main contractors usually price the job in the first place. It is usually so full of holes that it is basically useless.

I get very frustrated at the number of companies who will send a basic 1 or 2-page quotation for a major project such as a new self-build (and believe me that is a regular occurrence!)

Such a quotation will normally include a few lines thanking you for requesting the quote and the contractor telling you that: "It gives them pleasure to price the full works at £???,???", with payments being due at "so and so" stages, adding that they look forward to working with you! – That is it! - No detail of what you are getting for your money, how long it will take, when and why they could or would be claiming for extras.

This type of quote is just basically a waste of paper and if ever I get anything like that it goes straight in the bin (ok, if I am feeling generous, I might then contact them again and ask them to quote properly, but more likely I won't bother!)

Why is that type of quote useless?

If you look back at all the work involved in going out to tender if you are going to project manage the job yourself, you will hopefully understand that the pricing up of a job is a complex and involved task involving a lot of time and effort. If you don't put in that time and effort, the price you come up with will probably be nowhere near correct.

Many builders can't or are not prepared to devote that sort of time (and expense) to every quote, so what they will do is simply measure the square footage of the building and multiply that figure by so much per sq ft (or metre) to give them their basic price for the job.

However, because that price is so wishy washy they then start adding other amounts in to make sure they don't price too low.

Things like:

- 5% for waste
- 5% for damage
- 5% for theft

- 5% for lost time due to poor weather
- 5% for and other contingencies

Once they have added in those figures, they will then add their profit at (usually) around 20% - 30%.

By doing this they know that they are pretty well covered. If the job didn't go well and they were to use up all those "5%" amounts, they would still get their 30% profit. If the job went well and they didn't have to spend the contingency money, they might make over 50% profit on the job.

Great for them, not so good for you (*because you end up paying **all** those contingency figures whether or not they actually happen!*)

99% of these fixed price contracts will also have a load of extras payable for things that may go wrong that are not the fault of the contractor. Things like extra excavation for the footings, extra concrete in the foundation, price rises in materials etc. You will also usually find that you will pay full price for any extras when the contractor might actually get a significant discount on them (with them buying at trade prices).

So, when you start to think about all that, you can see how this option can end up being very expensive.

How do you reduce the prices and extras for the main contractor option?

It is possible to get a bit of control over what the main contractors will be able to charge you and the way to do this is for you to ensure that each contractor that quotes, is quoting based on a **full and comprehensive** (*fuller and more comprehensive than you would probably be able to knock together*) tender document that you will provide for them, as part of the tender package.

To make this work, you would usually need to get a quantity surveyor or estimator to prepare the tender documents. The documents, as a full package, should try to ensure that there is either little or no wriggle room for them to keep coming back asking for more money.

It needs to cover things like:

- Have they taken all their pricing information from the contract drawings and building regulations specification?
- Have they allowed for the initial site strip (the clearing of the site ready for the job to start)?
- Have they included for preparing a temporary driveway and storage area?
- Have they allowed for providing welfare facilities?
- What depth have they allowed for excavating the foundation?
- What are their rates (labour and materials) if they go over what they have allowed for the foundations or slab formation?
- Have they included for the drainage, drainage connections, service trenches, service connections, temporary water and electricity supply connections?
- What sort of floor slab have they priced for?
- What sort of build? Traditional, timber frame (etc.)?
- How long have they included for the scaffold to be on the job? – Would there be an extra charge if it were on site for longer?
- How much / 1000 have they allowed for facing bricks?
- What type of windows / doors (internal and external) have they allowed for?
- What type of roof tiles have they priced for?
- What is the specification on the staircase?

- What have they allowed for the kitchens / bathrooms / utility rooms etc?
- What have they allowed for ironmongery / skirtings / architraves / covings to ceilings etc.
- What allowance have they for the purchase of tiles (floor and wall)
- What will the floor finishes be to each room?
- Can you choose individual paint colours to each room? – What sort of paints have they included for?
- Have they allowed for any external works or landscaping?

This list is nowhere near comprehensive, but gives you an idea of most of the major items you need to make sure you cover (your quantity surveyor or estimator should make sure you have included everything in the tender package before it goes out).

As I said earlier. you should send every tenderer 2 copies of the pricing documents and every company tendering for the work should be asked to initial each page of the tender document, sign at the end and return the initialled and signed copy to you (this ensures that they can't come back in the future and say "I didn't see that bit" or "You didn't send me that document").

Sadly, what you will find with this method of tendering is that a good proportion of builders simply won't bother quoting or returning the tender. It is just too much like hard work for them! For that reason, you need to send the documents out to at least six, (preferably more) contractors and then hopefully you'll get three or four completed quotes back.

By setting up the tendering / pricing process up professionally, you will stand the best chance of both getting better quotes and minimising the number of extras you will be asked to pay.

On the downside, once you have paid for the tender documents to be prepared and you have had the quotes back, you will still usually end up paying up to 30% more to get the job completed than you would do either project managing it yourselves or getting a professional project manager to do it for you.

5) Pricing using a design and build package

From a pricing point of view, this is probably the easiest and least stressful of the lot.

When you take on a design and build (D&B) company, in theory, they should be looking after pretty much every aspect of the build, from the initial designs right through to completion.

Using a D&B package is a bit similar to using a main contractor, but where you step away from the process if you decide to hand it over to a main contractor rather than manage it yourself, you will be further away if you hand the whole thing over to a D&B company. They will look after pretty much everything for you.

That's great if you can afford it and if all you want is to have your own house built on your own land and if all you want to do is to pretty much just say "yes" or "no" to a load of questions you will be asked along the way.

How do I see this option? Well as a bonafide self-builder, it does seem to me to be cheating a bit! It is getting towards being a very similar package to custom build, but you would probably have a bit more choice throughout the process with D&B than you would have with custom build.

From a cost point of view it is probably even more expensive than using a main contractor, due to the way the package is personalised to each client.

With a D&B project, you tend to have a team of professional people working with you all the way through the project, all of whom need paying. This will include your own designer, possibly a planning specialist, a quantity surveyor, project manager, possibly a site foreman etc. In theory that sounds like it is all going to cost an absolute fortune, but that doesn't necessarily have to be the case.

With D&B, rather than you contracting different people and companies to do each of the bits, it all tends to be done in house. In other words, everyone is employed by the D&B company and most people are on salaries rather than running their own businesses. The effect of this is to make everything run a bit more smoothly and professionally and possibly a bit more cost effectively.

This professional approach usually runs through the builders who, if they are not directly employed, will usually at least get most of their work from this one source. This should, again in theory, make the whole main contractor process much slicker, which in turn, should result in lower prices being charged by the contractors (although you may not see the benefit of that lower cost due to the higher costs in other areas).

So it is a bit of swings and roundabouts when it comes to costing with a D&B company and overall, if I had to make a guess, I would say that the cost of the job should end up within a few percent up or down, of what it would if you used a main contractor, but more likely up.

If that is the case, due to the fact that D&B makes your life simpler, it might not be a bad option, if you can afford it and want to keep as hands off as possible.

Before you make any decision on whether or not to use this option, you do need to try to firm up the prices as far as possible, so ask a few questions:

1. At what stage would you get some sort of fixed price and what are the costs (and the timescales) to get to that stage?
2. How much does the designer / the designs cost?
3. Are the designers paid by the hour?
4. How do they work out the price for taking the application through planning?
5. What do they do about warranties and insurances?
6. Do they use a main contractor or a project manager?
7. How much choice do you have on the fitting out of the house? How do they work out their prices for this part of the project?
8. Can you take over before completion to save money if you want to?
9. Do / can they do the landscaping / driveways etc?
10. Can they give you an overall guide price for previous work on a house similar to yours?
11. How is the payment system set up? (Will this tie in with your mortgage stage payments?)
12. Do you get cost reports during the build?
13. If the build is going over budget (for whatever reason), what would they do to try to pull it back?
14. Can you speak to previous clients?

D&B is not something which has yet taken off in the UK. It is much more popular in other countries where things are set up far more professionally than they are here. Unless we change the way we view the self-build market here, I can't really see it ever becoming a viable option for a lot of people, simply because of the cost. Nice idea though!

6) Get together with other self-builders (community build)

Unfortunately, I am not going to be able to offer you much detailed advice on this option regarding pricing in this book, partly because I have never been personally involved in one of these projects, but also partly because these sorts of projects all tend to be set up in very different ways, so the pricing will work differently from project to project.

On most projects of this type, a professional quantity surveyor or estimator would be taken on to do the pricing. This sort of work is usually outside the skill range of the people who get involved (having all the costs professionally calculated and kept control of would, on its own, normally add quite a large cost to the overall project, but which is split between the participants).

These types of projects normally consist of a group of people, usually led by a project manager or foreman, using their own skills in order to build a number of houses, all helping each other along the way.

The thinking amongst fans of this process is that, by grouping together, they will achieve economies of scale. That is definitely true of buying the land (as we discussed in earlier chapters), but I am far from convinced that the same applies to materials (see below).

Neither am I sure that it will be an efficient way to run a job from a health and safety point of view, partly because of the length of time that the project could potentially run for, with the requirement for full health and safety cover for the *whole site* for the *full* run time of the job and also because some of the responsibility for health and safety is bound to fall to the individual plot owners (which could be a recipe for disaster if some or all of the owners have little previous experience of building).

One of the other arguments put forward by people wanting to build this way is that, theoretically it should be cheap for labour (because many of the people involved work for free). Here again, that is not necessarily the case.

Why? Well, for a start, you normally need to get some sort of professional team to run the project, coordinate the various owners and trades people and to keep everything under control (a very difficult task from what I have heard).

The fact is that, as with D&B, there are relatively few existing companies or experienced construction individuals who could take on such a project. This could result in the project taking on an architect to try to run things.

Doing so could bring numerous disadvantages, including the following financial downsides:

- You will tend pay the architect high hourly rates (up to £150 / hr) for their input over possibly a long period of time. This cost will have to be split between the individual house builders.
- Architects are not known for their cost consciousness and as such, could be specifying all sorts of expensive and complicated features which may sound eco-friendly and a good idea at the time, but in fact turn out to be useless, expensive white elephants.
- Architects do not usually have much site management training, so may not be particularly efficient in organising the works efficiently from a cost or time saving point of view. If this is the case, they may want to bring in a foreman to look after the practical side of the works, which would add another layer of cost.
- There will be a lot of differing opinions from the various people involved in the project on what should be used with regard to materials, build methods and / or design styles. This could result in decisions being made which cost each builder more than if they were in control of the decision making processes themselves.

Other factors also need to be taken into consideration from a financial point of view, such as:

- The development of the *whole site* will need to be included in the build cost for each house. This means that each builder will have to pay their bit for roadways, kerbs, paths, mains drains, street lighting, mains services, section 106 agreements and numerous other things which could add significantly to the basic cost of the build of the individual houses. If you build one simple house on a simple plot, you usually don't need to worry about things like major development design works, adoptable roadways, street lighting, drainage systems, services infrastructure etc. You just get on with building your own house! With bigger sites all the infrastructure works can account for a significant percentage of the overall cost of the job.

- Buying in bulk might not necessarily actually happen, or if it does, it may not create many savings.
    1. With everyone involved possibly choosing different bricks, roof tiles, kitchens, bathrooms from different suppliers there is a chance that real bulk buying simply will not happen.
    2. The difference between bulk buying and buying at trade prices is not necessarily very great, possibly 10% - 15% max if you are lucky, sometimes the merchants pretty much give their best prices to anyone who buys from them regularly, including the small builders who want a pack of bricks here and 20 bags of cement there.

All in all, I am not a fan of this option from any angle. However, as a part of the industry that has been around for many years, I am open to having my mind changed. So, if anyone has any facts and figures to prove me wrong, please let me know and I will add your comments in the next update to this book.

Chapter 10
Getting ready to start building

In this chapter I will concentrating on important things that *every* self builder should know about before starting work on site (no matter which management option is going to be used for the actual building works).

Some of what I am going to be going through here won't be as important to you if you are handing everything over to someone else to run. However, it is always useful to have at least a basic knowledge of what is going on, just in case the people you use are not doing their jobs properly.

A word of warning! - Please don't take the information you will read in this chapter and then start trying to lay the law down with any of the sub-contractors about how they should do their job, based on what you have read in these few pages.

*All I am doing here is making you aware of how things **can be done** and giving you a bit of the guidance that I think you will find useful.*

Different people work in different ways, so if your project manager doesn't follow exactly what I have detailed below, don't go steaming in telling him / her that they don't know what they are doing. – If you do, you could soon find out what a 2' spirit level feels like lodged up your left nostril!

Planning to start - What needs thinking about?

1) Your health and safety responsibilities as owner / builder

When I think back to how we regarded health and safety when I started work on site in the 1970s, I am actually quite surprised that I am still here to tell the tale!

Safety was seen by most people as a side issue and there were very few people in authority who were around on a regular basis to make sure that building sites were *at least* fairly safe places to be.

I remember on a big contract where I was the site engineer and we had a surprise inspection from the health and safety people. I had to walk the inspector around the site. When I heard that the inspector had turned up and was in the office, I quickly sent one of the lads off to make sure everyone was wearing their hard hats (we did at least provide them, although getting anyone to wear them was another matter)! I duly started to escort the inspector around the site and we soon came across "Tiny" (our nickname), a big rotund, jolly Irish labourer. Tiny had been working on site for many years and had no time for all this health and safety rubbish. As myself and the inspector approached Tiny, he was standing in a trench which came about up to his waist with his shovel in his hand. On his head, he had put a shiny metal bucket with the handle acting as a chin strap. He just stood there and smiled at us both as we walked past!

These days, Tiny would probably have been sent packing straight away for having such a glib attitude towards health and safety. At the very least he would have been marched in to the office and given an official written warning, but what happened then was that the inspector simply smiled back and walked straight past!

OK, he probably knew that the guy was taking the mickey, but these days things have been tightened up so much, both practically and legally, that if the inspector had seen Tiny, or anyone else messing about like that on a building site, he would have no hesitation in taking action against him.

Overall, these improvements in health and safety have been a great asset to the industry. Far fewer people are injured or killed now than there used to be (which is most definitely how it should be). It is just not as much fun anymore!

Anyway, back to the matter in hand, *your* **self-build and** *your* **health and safety obligations and responsibilities:**

As the legal owner of the plot (the building site), no matter who does the building works, as the owner, there is a good chance that if there is an accident, you could be held legally responsible, even if you were not on site and if you personally had nothing to do with it.

These days there is a huge industry made up of professional blamers whose job it is to find out who was responsible for injuring their clients and getting as much compensation from them as possible. You can actually go to prison if you are found to be negligent or responsible for another person's injury or death, either on a building site or anywhere else. So, you need to be aware of what you need to do, what you need to know and where your own responsibilities lie, so you can take the actions you need to, in order to cover yourself.

As an example of how it works now: If you have a scaffold on site (which you probably will have), that scaffold needs to be maintained in a safe condition *for every minute of every hour of every day*. Unfortunately, what happens with scaffold it that it tends to get altered by the guys on site.

It may be that the joiners need to pass something large from the ground up to a higher level, so they take up some boards, move some supports and make a nice big hole to pass the item through. Once they have done so, one of them may just throw the scaffold planks back across the opening, not thinking to replace the supports (which are what give the boards the strength to be able to take the weight of men and materials). A hod carrier then walks across that section of scaffold with a heavy hod full of bricks, a planks snaps and he falls through, seriously injuring himself.

Who is responsible for that situation? The guy who took the scaffold boards off? All the people who were around at the time who didn't think to put the supports back? The hod carrier? Or you?

Unfortunately for you, if you had not handed over **all** official responsibility for checking and maintaining the scaffold (*and sometimes even if you had*) to someone like a site foreman, the blame could be landed at *your* door.

Why? Because if you are seen to be the person who is in overall charge of that site. **You** will be responsible for providing a safe environment for anyone and everyone to be able to work in, **always**.

Doesn't sound fair does it? – If someone else makes a mistake that you are made to pay for? Well if you look a bit closer, it actually does make sense.

If building sites were allowed to run without having someone around who has a sufficient level of health and safety knowledge, it can almost be guaranteed that on every site there would be accidents, some serious, some not so serious. But building sites are very dangerous places and accidents would be bound to happen.

When an accident occurs it is usually someone's fault. Something has gone wrong, someone has been injured and blame needs to be placed in order for lessons to be learned and in order to try to make sure that the same thing doesn't happen again.

If you (as site owner and "developer") have made someone on site (who is suitably qualified), officially responsible for all health and safety matters, at all times, then you would have been seen (in management terms) to have taken the right steps to try to ensure that the safety risk on your site is being professionally managed. If, however, you have just decided to take on that responsibility yourself when you are not adequately qualified to do so, you would, in legal terms be guilty of "negligence", *whether* there was actually an accident of some type on the site and you could theoretically be prosecuted, even if nothing went wrong.

These days, all site operatives have to have what is called a CSCS (Construction Skills Certificate Scheme) card before they can work on any type of building site. To get the card they have to go to a local test centre and take a multiple-choice test. If they pass, this card confirms that they have proved that they have attained a reasonable level of site safety awareness.

The person running the site has to have a higher level of safety knowledge and expertise. Whether you are going to run the job, or whether you have a project manager or foreman taking that responsibility, whoever would be legally seen to be in charge needs to have a different card. This is called an SMSTS (Site Management Safety Training Scheme) card. Getting one of these cards involves taking a 5-day course with an examination at the end.

The only way to build your defence for any occasions when something goes wrong on site, is by being seen to have done everything you should reasonably do to safeguard against such things happening.

So, taking scaffolding as an example, here is what needs to happen:

- Check all the credentials of the scaffolding company before you take them on. Do they have full insurance? Are all their employees fully trained and qualified? Do they have good quality equipment? Don't even *think* of allowing your site to be run on a *cash in hand – Chuck me some boards up mate*, basis!
- The tender documents need to be clear about how you expect the scaffolding company to erect and maintain the scaffold in good order. Include wording saying that the scaffolder needs to regularly make sure the scaffold complies with all health and safety requirements and requesting the erector to "*Check on the condition of the scaffold on a regular basis*".
- Put up a sign in the site cabin asking anyone who notices any safety risk on site, to report it to you (or the person in charge of safety) immediately. Then if a problem is reported make sure everyone knows that work stops on that particular area of the job, until the problem is properly fixed.
- Don't allow anyone on site to adjust the scaffold because it is in the way. Get the erector (or at least someone who is trained in scaffold erection / safety) to do this.
- Keep your own eyes open whenever you are on site. Some hazards are blatantly obvious (*in the case of scaffolding, this could be things like: handrails missing / gaps in the platform / overhanging boards / ladders not secured etc.*)

In each tender package, you need to state that the tenderer is responsible for their own section of the work with regard to health and safety and for making sure that their actions do not put any other site operative in danger. If there were to be an accident and you are seen to have done as much as you can (on a day-to-day, ongoing basis), to have minimised the risk, you should be ok.

2) Finding existing services under your site

The chances are that somewhere underneath your plot, or within the footpaths or road adjacent to it, that you will find service cables, pipes or drains.

If you start digging, even on your own land and hit one of these, guess who is going to get the repair bill? You!

Unfortunately for us, it is not the responsibility of the service provider to find out that you are building a house on a particular plot somewhere in the UK, or to let everyone who applies for planning permission know that they have cables or pipes in the vicinity. Neither is it the responsibility of the ground workers to know where everything is. Just as with health and safety, the responsibility lies with **you** to find out the what and where and then take steps to make sure that you do not cause any damage to whatever it is, wherever it is.

This is a very important part of the procedure, that you should take very seriously on every project if it involves an element of digging. If you don't do your research properly and end up hitting (say) a broadband cable, you could be hit with a repair bill for thousands of pounds. So, not only would your job probably have to stop, it could mess up your build budget big time and you may even be prosecuted.

Hit a gas main and "Boom"!

Luckily there are easy ways to find out what, if anything is hidden away under your plot

What I do before each project is make an internet search on "dial before you dig". This will bring up a selection of companies who, for a fee, will find out from all the utility providers if they have any equipment in the vicinity of your site. You can then contact any of them that do, to ask what measures you will need to take to protect whichever type of service it is.

Alternatively, if you want to try to save a bit of money (but not time), you can contact all the service providers in your area individually and directly yourselves. When you get through, ask to be put through to the "dial before you dig" section (even if that is not what they officially call it, they will know what you mean).

Do not underestimate the importance of making sure you do this before you start digging any holes on a site (even trial holes before you buy the plot). It is a very serious matter.

3) Warranties

Before you start work on site you need to have in place a structural Warranty. This will cover the completed property against structural defects, usually for 10 years.

If you don't have a structural warranty on a new home, mortgage lenders will not be interested in lending on it, either to you, or to anyone who may want to buy it in the future.

Different companies offer slightly different policies, but basically if, during the guarantee period, it is found that any part of the structure has been built with a defect, the idea is that the warranty company will fix it. The word "structural" means exactly that. This is not a warranty for the washing machine or for a leaky radiator, it is all to do with the building structure itself.

It is worth checking how the individual companies work. If there is a problem, do they fix it immediately or do they want to find out whose fault it is and then try to get them to fix it first? If possible, I would always want to use a company that will fix the problem first.

Don't get structural warranties and building regulations mixed up. They are completely different things. The structural warranty is completely separate from the building regulations approval (see building regs later), but you need them both.

There are a number of structural warranty providers to choose from and they all offer similar products at around the same sort of price.

The chances of you actually suffering with a structural defect within 10 years are fairly slim. It is normally the other stuff, the fixings and fittings that cause most of the problems on new homes.

Here are some of the main providers I found when I searched recently:

www.selfbuild.uk.com/Structural-Warranty.aspx

www.buildingwarranties.com/

www.premierguarantee.co.uk/about-us/

www.selfbuildit.co.uk/structural_warranty.htm

www.buildstore.co.uk/finance/build-care-structural-warranty.html

www.jhai.co.uk

There are also another couple of options when it comes to structural warranties which I'll mention separately.

Architects certificate

This does pretty much the same thing as a standard structural warranty, but it is put in place by your architect, who offers the cover using their own specialised commercial insurance policy.

Some mortgage lenders are not too keen on this type of warranty for a number of reasons (I went through these earlier, but they are worth repeating here):

1. It usually has no strict 10-year limit, so in theory could last for ever (great for you, the owner, but not so good for the insurance company who get a claim made on a property after 100 years!)
2. If the architect stops paying for the policy, there could potentially be disputes about the insurance company paying out to anyone covered by it (get this checked yourself if you are thinking about using one).
3. Some lenders prefer to have a person who is a trained and experienced "Inspector of the building construction process" looking after the stage inspections, rather than an architect (they sometimes feel that architects, although very clever people, are not trained to pick up practical errors, omissions and potential problems in the construction process on site).

Architects will often build the warranty in to a package, with what they call "Project Management" or "Construction Supervision". Just be a bit careful here, that they are not simply charging you a few thousand pounds to come to site every few weeks just to have a quick chat and head off home. If they say they are project managing, ask them what they will be doing and would that mean that you don't need another project manager to do all the ordering and running of the job day to day *(I bet I know what the answer to that question will be!)*

LABC Warranty:

This is a structural warranty provided by the Local Authority Building Control department. In theory, it has the advantage of bringing together the building regulations inspections and the warranty inspections so that they are both under the same roof. However, when I checked at the start of 2016, it is still not working quite like that. It appeared, when I spoke to them, that they have set the system up so that the warranty is provided by, a separate structural warranty provider (but with a name that makes it sound like it is actually the building regulations department providing it. However, the building regs inspections and final certificate are still provided by the local authority, who are a completely entity.

Warranty inspection stages

It is very important that your warranty is in place before you start the building work. The first inspection is on the foundations before you pour the concrete and this is one of the most important inspection stages. If you don't get this stage inspected by both the warranty and building regs guys, it could nullify the rest of the warranty.

On a simple self-build project, you could be ready to pour the foundation concrete after just 2 or 3 days onsite. So, what you need to do is to give the warranty company at least a week's notice of starting on site and then also give them at least 3 days' notice of when you think you are going to need the first inspection carrying out.

Once they have visited the site for the first time, they will normally be able to visit for an inspection within a couple of days of you notifying them, but check with them how much notice they will need. You don't want to be ready for an inspection then have to stop work for a few days because the inspector was too busy to visit when you needed them.

The normal inspection stages for a self-build project are (check these before you start):

1. Prior to concreting the foundations.
2. Prior to concreting the slab.
3. Prior to covering the roof.
4. Prior to plastering.

5. Before backfilling drains.
6. After backfilling when a test will be required to be carried out on the drainage system).
7. At completion.

At each stage, after the inspection, you should get written notice that your project has passed that inspection. If it doesn't, then you should get a written notice telling you what needs doing before it can be re-inspected and passed.

When the house is complete, you will get a completion certificate, which will usually trigger your final payment from your mortgage lender.

4) Building regulations

Just as you need to have the warranty in place before you start work, you also need to have building regulations approval of all the drawings and specifications.

The drawings will usually be the same ones you used to get the planning permission (although you may be asked for more detail on complicated designs or specialist items). Your designer will usually be able to give you all the information that will be required for the building regulations application. Often, they will actually make the building regulations application as part of their design package. If there are any queries, they can deal with them without having to involve you.

You need to ensure that the building regulations are submitted for approval at least 1 – 2 weeks before you start work, because, as before they can send anyone out to inspect work done they have to check all the drawings and the calculations to make sure that the designer has not made any mistakes.

Building regs are different in one respect to warranties. Once you have building regs approval, you have it, it doesn't last ten years, it is just a one off thing that you need before you start.

As with the warranty providers, you will need to give the inspectors as much notice as you can when you are going to need them for an inspection. They will generally be called out at the same stages.

Also, as with the warranty, at each stage, you should get a notice to confirm that your project has passed the inspection, or one to tell you that it hasn't, detailing what you need to do to fix the problem. Without this, just like the warranty, you have no proof that the inspection has taken place.

When job is finished, you will get a completion certificate. You can then use this to help you claim your VAT refund, if applicable.

5) Where will you live? Family organisation / schools / holidays / transport.

I don't really need to go into detail here, we looked at this subject in the early chapters so you should already have a plan in place for how you are going to organise your family and personal situation whilst you build your new home. Now is the time you need to be putting all those plans into action, so that they are all sorted out before you start work on site.

As a brief re-cap:

- If you are planning on living on site temporarily, you need to find a mobile home, get it delivered, wired and plumbed in (including connecting the drainage).
- If you are renting you need to find the right place and make the move before you start work. Try to get a six-month rental contract if you are hoping to get the new house built quickly (six months is usually the shortest rental contract you can get).

- If you are staying in your present home have you got the finances sorted in the way of bridging loans or mortgages?
- Do you need to get any plans in place regarding schools?

Just make sure you think through your family, personal and financial situation well before you start work, to stop problems creeping up on you later, when you need to be concentrating on building your new home.

6) Compliance with planning conditions:

When you received your planning approval notice, the chances are that there will have been some conditions attached to it. Some of these might require action from you before you start work on site.

You need to make sure you comply with all the conditions otherwise you could find yourself in trouble.

Conditions could include:

- **Access safety.** If your plot is adjacent to a main road, there may be conditions to make sure that the visibility splays in either direction ensures that both traffic and pedestrians are not put at risk.
- **Tree preservation orders.** You may need to set up protection around any trees which have TPOs on them. This could involve getting an arboriculturalist to prepare a report on the trees and their roots. This could then mean that you have to protect both from damage, during the time you build and once the house is occupied.
- **If you have any protected wildlife** living on site, you may have to bring a specialist in to give you advice on what you need to do. This may be so you don't affect them negatively, especially during the breeding season, or you may even need to move them from your site to another location (*this would only be done at certain times of year, so needs plenty of "planning ahead" to make sure your planned start date is not affected*).
- **Ground problems:** You may be required to carry out a ground survey before you start. This could be in areas where the ground is known be poor or contaminated or have some other problem. Really, this should all have been taken care of before you bought the plot, but if there is anything left to do, make sure you get it done in plenty of time so it doesn't hold you back.

When you get your planning permission documents, have a good look at the conditions and start to think about what their implications are on the project. Then plan ahead to make sure that you comply with them all without causing problems or delays to the main part of the project, which is building the house.

7) Target start and completion dates

I strongly recommend that before you start, you set yourselves some timeline targets. If you don't do this and, instead just let it all happen in its own time, it can end up taking literally years to build a single house. I have seen and heard of so many examples of this. If you have read the earlier chapters of this book, you should be fully aware that if you let the project drag on longer than you need to, your costs will increase. You will also probably be putting up with lots of inconveniences in your day to day life, all associated with the build.

You need to get focused and organised. As I have said previously, on a big project like this, you need to build up a head of steam and keep pushing and pushing, right through to the end. If you lose your momentum, it is very hard to pick it up again.

I have heard about many projects that have taken 2 years+ to complete, when they could easily have been finished in 6 months, simply because the self-builders didn't get themselves properly sorted out, revved up and raring to go, - making sure they did everything they need to do to maintain that momentum.

This is probably going to be a very busy and possibly stressful period of your life and you want to try to reach the other end of the process as soon as possible, then you can enjoy the fruits of your labours.

There is nothing more pleasing than to be sitting in your new home, knowing that you did things right. There is nothing more depressing than seeing your dream home sitting there half completed for months because you haven't!

Remember that you will probably be making a monthly mortgage payment on whatever money you are borrowing, starting from as soon as you have bought the land. Self-build mortgage rates tend to be higher than standard mortgage rates, which means that you will be eating in to your build budget every month, just to pay for your borrowing.

Usually, once you have completed the build you can transfer the borrowing to a standard mortgage at better rates. That in itself should be enough of an incentive to get things moving quickly.

So, in one sentence:

"From the day you start to borrow money for your self-build project, you should be thinking about a target date for the day you will be moving in".

8) Programming the works

I have mentioned this bit of the book a couple of times in earlier chapters. I have mentioned it because it is, to my mind, one of the important bits of the project.

If you are taking on a main contractor or a project manager, they will normally draw up the programme for the works, but if you are taking on the management yourself, you are going to have to do it.

Bearing in mind what I have just said about getting a head of steam up and setting target dates, when you are looking after your own project, this is probably the most important tool you will have to hand to help you to succeed in doing that.

A programme (or contract programme to give it its official title) is something you should be looking at every day, starting from a couple of months before the job actually starts and continuing right through to the day you move in to your new home.

As well as being your main tool for getting things done, the programme will also form part of the tender packages that you will send out to the sub-contractors. It is very important on a significantly sized building project that everyone is singing from the same hymn sheet. The programme is the hymn sheet!

Drawing up a workable programme is not a particularly quick or easy thing to do. To do it properly, you really need a certain level of knowledge of what is involved in each part of the job. Unfortunately, by the very nature of the beast, self-build tends to attract people who often have little or no knowledge of the industry.

There is, however, a way to cheat! If you don't have the knowledge and skill to be able to work out how long each section of the job will take, why not let the people who do know, tell you?

We have touched on getting prices for the job in previous chapters. The only reason I mention that here, is that as part of the tendering process, you will ask each sub-contractor to tell you how long they need to complete their section of the works. Once you have all the tenders back, you can then use the timescales that each trade has given you, to help you to draw up the programme.

On the next couple of pages, you will find two sample programmes. The first one is for a traditional brick and block built house and the second is for a closed panel timber frame build.

I am going to show you the basic way to set about this task, assuming you don't have access to project planning software. However, if you want to make the job easier and quicker for yourselves,

there are now a number of project Management software packages that take a lot of the hard work out of preparing the programme.

Just search online for project programming software and you will find some pretty good systems on offer which cost between £100 and £200 for a year's subscription. Possibly a good investment, especially if you are trying to run a family and hold down a full-time job while you take on your project, providing you are capable of using such software.

The way the programmes are created is as follows:

1. Open a spreadsheet (or a new project in your specialist software).
2. Give yourself a target number of weeks which you think is a reasonable length of time for the job to take. If you are planning a very quick job, say 10 weeks, you may decide to format the programme in days rather than weeks. Otherwise, put numbers corresponding to the weeks, at the top on line one (shrink or widen the columns so that you can print the finished programme out on either an A4 or A3 sheet of paper (depending on what printer you have).
3. Down the left-hand side, list all the main activities. You can copy the ones I have on the two examples, but also think of anything else that you may have on your own project that doesn't appear in the samples.
4. Either using your own knowledge and experience, or the estimates that you have received from the people who have tendered for the work, using one cell to represent each week and starting with week one (usually either part or all of week one will be "set up site"), start to fill in the cells for each trade, working your way across the programme.

    As you do this you need to think as practically as your own knowledge and experience will allow you to do, to work out the order in which the works need to be done. You will see, for example on the first programme, that I have put the first three activities to run concurrently. That is because while someone is setting up the cabins and security fencing etc. someone else can be stripping off the topsoil, after which I would hope to get a site engineer started on setting the house out so the same machine which stripped the top-soil can get on with excavating the foundations.

    You will also have to consider if there needs to be any phasing of the works. Will you have to build the main shape of the house before you can come back to build annexes or other features? Will you have to put up and take down scaffolding more than once as part of that phasing?

This is where your skill at design and the thought you put in to how the house will be built starts to become apparent. If you designed a simple house, with four corners and a gabled roof, you should find that the programme runs nice and smoothly. If you have built in lots of what I call sticky out bits, this is where they could start to come back to bite you in the bum (they will then continue to do so by costing your more when you get to building the house itself!)

5. You will see that on some items I have included a float (in a lighter colour). This is the time during which you have the chance to reorganise the work if the job is not quite running to schedule. It is where carrying on with one job will not hinder the next. So, for example, if the electricians have not quite finished, but the decorators are due to start, you can get the electricians to at least free up a few rooms for the decorators to get started in while they finish off their bits and pieces elsewhere.

    The same applies to all the trades. You just need to think the process through.

    See programmes on the following pages.

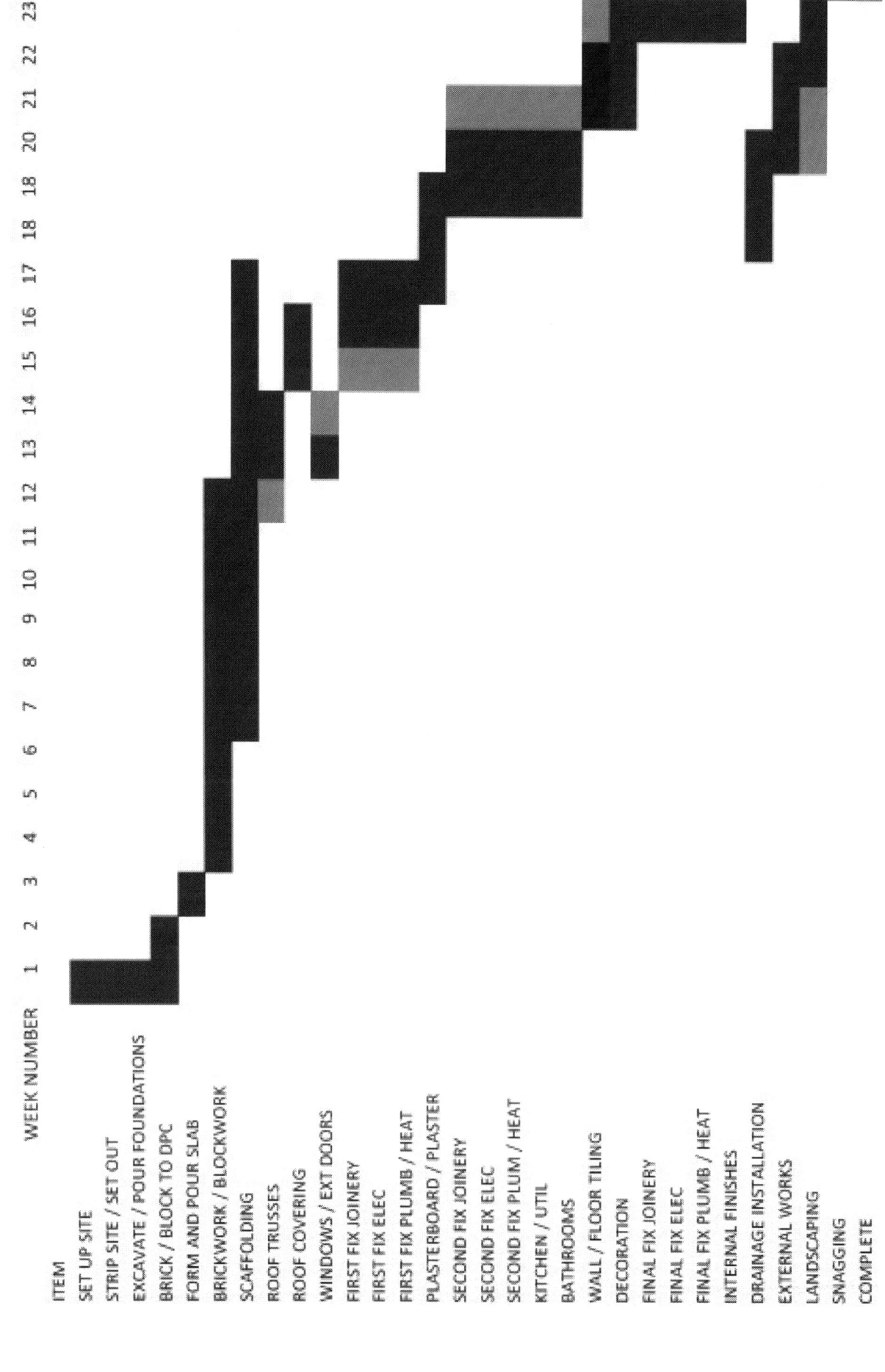

PROGRAMME OF WORKS - closed panel build with cassette floors and roof.

Both of those programmes are based on building a simple 4 bed detached house of around 1800 sq ft.

Although I have used a closed panel system for the second programme, I would probably use the same sort of time scales for SIPS, possibly adding a few weeks if the programme were to be for a standard timber frame. However, if this is your first project and you do not have either very much, if any experience in the construction industry, then you may wish to add a few weeks to my timescales.

What you will often find as you prepare a programme for a job is that *it* actually guides *you* on the timescales rather than the other way around.

You may have given yourself a 12-week target date, but as you try to fit in all the trade estimates for each part of the job, you simply find that they don't fit into 12 weeks. When this happens, go with the longer time scale. It is pointless trying to squeeze the jobs in to timescales which are not realistic. You can organise well and get more tradespeople in to work on each job, but sometimes it just has to take as long as it takes!

However, having said that, believe it or not, both of those programmes have a fair amount of flexibility in them where time could potentially be saved.

- For both programmes, I have assumed the bricklayers are what is called a "2 and 1 gang" which is 2 bricklayers and 1 labourer. Their completion time could be speeded up by getting extra brickies in and changing to a "3 and 1", a "3 and 2" or a "4 and 2" gang.
- I have assumed 2 joiners would be working on the project. Their completion could be speeded up by adding extra joiners.
- I have assumed that the roof tiles will be the small clay tiles which take a while to lay. If a large concrete tile such as a Marley Modern and more roofers were to be brought in, a week could potentially be taken off the build time.
- The programme is divided into weeks, however a particular task could complete early during the final week of its allowed time on the programme and, if you are well organised and realise in time that this is going to happen, you could be pulling the next job forward to start earlier (*note: drawing up a daily programme will help you to notice things like this*).
- For the decoration, an extra painter would speed things up.

All in all, if everything went smoothly and you got everything organised properly it should theoretically be possible for even an inexperienced self-builder to knock 3 weeks or more off each programme, bringing the traditional build down to 21 weeks and the closed panel build down to 10 weeks.

9) Only do what you need to do, when you need to do it

Many self-builders make the mistake of getting all excited, fired up and they go flying in to a new project, with all guns blazing on day one and try to do everything, "everywhere" all at the same time.

Slow it down to speed it up! Rushing around trying to do too many things at the same time, trying to have the house finished in no time flat, is simply going to fail every time and is probably just going to bring on a heart attack! You will probably make mistakes and end up having to put errors right, losing time (and money) in the process.

You should always bear in mind the following when planning your building works

> Do what you need to, how it should be done, when you need to do it. And do it just once.

If you are going to manage the project yourself, you will have a lot of work to do.

If you are not careful this workload can quickly become overwhelming, especially if you are trying to hold down a full or part time job at the same time.

So, what you need to do, is to break things down where possible, into bite sized chunks. If you do this and you remove that 100mph or bust mentality, you should find that everything slots together a lot better and a lot more smoothly, without you getting too stressed out into the bargain.

For example:

One of the most common errors that self-builders make in my experience is ordering / buying stuff too soon. Kitchens and bathrooms are the main culprits for this!

Think about it. There is really very little point, 2 months before you have even started work on site, going out and ordering or buying your kitchen! The same applies to the bathroom suites, internal doors, architraves, flooring, wall tiling and a whole host of other items.

What will happen is that the supplier will want paying asap for the items and although they may store them for you for a few weeks, they will usually soon start nagging you to take delivery. Where are you going to store this stuff for the next 6 – 12 months?

Also remember that when you buy something with a guarantee, once you take delivery, the guarantee is running. If you take a long time finishing your build, you could find that by the time you actually get to move in, the guarantees are out of date and you then have to pay to put anything right that should, by rights, have been paid for by the supplier.

Another example: Why spend many valuable hours early in the project talking to decorators about colour schemes and types of paints when all they actually need to do is turn up with their paint brushes and paint?

In the early stages of the project, you need to spend your time thinking about, planning and getting the stuff done that needs doing then and in the next 2 – 3 months. By all means, find and choose your painters early on (even before you start if you wish), but then just contact and talk to the different trades and companies when you need to.

For most people involved in building a house, 4 weeks should be enough for them to get your job organised and get themselves to site, but for the more important things like the foundations, the frame, the brickwork etc. if you get everything and everyone organised around 8 weeks before you need them and then keep in touch with them regularly, that should generally be all the planning ahead you need to do once you have done all your initial planning and organising (prior to physically starting on site).

Just think sensibly about each item and each trade, keep in touch with everyone with a quick phone call or email every couple of weeks and use the programme every day to make and keep yourself aware of your priorities.

Going back to ordering kitchens and bathrooms too soon. I know it is tempting to do the nice bits of the job rather than the hard work bits, so you would probably rather be choosing your kitchen and bathrooms than talking to bricklayers. However, in most cases, if you impulse buy things too early, you will find that once you get going on the actual building works, you will naturally keep coming across bargains, simply because of the fact that you will be visiting the builders' merchants and many other suppliers on a regular, if not daily basis. The chances are that with all the different places you are going to be visiting, you will find better bargains by giving yourself more time to look.

10) Sort out your cash flow

This can be a real job stopper if you don't get it right!

I have been dealing with self-builders on many levels for many years, I also watch Grand Designs! If there is one common denominator on just about every self-build project, it is that money either gets very short, or runs out altogether before the end of the job. If you are not prepared for this, it can (fairly obviously) cause you major problems.

The chances are that by the time you actually start building, you will have already spent a significant portion of your budget. You will probably have bought your plot, paid all the associated survey and legal fees. You will have hired a designer of some description, paid for all the planning costs, including all the reports that are required on most types of new build projects these days (things like wildlife / bat / badger surveys, tree reports, traffic surveys, design and access statements) and also section 106 agreement.

You may, by now have hired in a quantity surveyor or an estimator to help you to prepare your tender and contract documents, bought a decent A3 printer, ink and spent hundreds of pounds in fuel costs, running around getting everything organised.

There may additionally be specialist items needed for the build itself, which have to be ordered well in advance and which needed either paying in full upfront, or at least required a hefty deposit.

Add to those costs your monthly mortgage payments for the borrowing to buy the land, possibly the purchase and siting of a caravan on site, a generator, maybe drainage connections and the provision of a water connection, building regs, site insurance, warranties and you will soon realise that, before you actually start to build, you have bitten a pretty sizable chunk out of your available funds.

So, bearing all that in mind, before you get started on site you need to work out:

- Your total budget.
- How much you have spent in total to date.
- How much you have left.
- How and when that money is going to become available (savings / stage payments etc.)
- Do you have a sufficient financial buffer that can be used if and when necessary? If so, how much is it and how easily accessible is it?

Unfortunately, what often happens with self-builders is that when they first think about taking on a project they do a simple sum:

"How much money have we got to spend? - Ok, using that figure, how much have we got for the plot and how much have we got for the build?"

The weakness with that equation is that although the two main costs, the land and the build, are taken into account, the ancillary costs (such as the ones I have just listed) are either forgotten about or ignored.

However, unfortunately, just because they are not taken account of doesn't mean that they go away. They are still real costs which either have been paid or are going to need paying at some stage. These forgotten costs are what can often scupper the whole project.

If you don't get a good grip of all the relevant figures, by the time you get half way through the foundations, your cashflow could be struggling soon after.

That might sound a bit dramatic (*how would we run out of money so soon in to the build?*) Easy:

One of the earliest jobs, the foundations, are actually the most likely part of the whole build to muck up all your financial planning and put you under cashflow pressure.

As a quick example of how things could potentially go awry (we looked at a similar example earlier, but this is important, so I want to look at the subject again here).

Days 1 - 3: You clear the site and set up the cabins, fencing etc.

Day 4: You set out the foundations and start digging, hoping to be pouring concrete by day 6. As you dig, you find that the ground is getting wetter and poorer in quality the deeper you go, so by the time you get to the normal foundation depth the base of the dig is not suitable for bearing the weight of the house. You contact the building inspector and he says that you'll have to go deeper until you find something more solid.

Days 5 – 12: You find yourselves having to excavate twice as much earth out as you expected to and then will either have to fill the whole foundation back up with concrete or build extra blockwork up from the foundations to the floor slab level. Then, to add insult to injury you realise that you have got nowhere to lose the extra excavated materials, so you have to hire in a dozen or so 20 ton wagons to take it away to a tip, at £180 a load!

Ouch!

The outcome of the extra depth dig ends up losing you a week in progress and £10,000+ in extra payments to the ground workers, the extra concrete and getting rid of the excess earth.

Your total build budget was only £100,000 to begin with, so now here you are, a week in to the project with all your cashflow figures well and truly messed up!

Planning to avoid cash flow problems

One of the main tools that self-builders tend to use to get out of tight financial spots, is to go back to the mortgage lender and ask for additional, interim stage payments.

Many lenders will accommodate such requests but they don't like them (they are one of the reasons that this type of mortgage is not more widely available, they are often too troublesome to administer because of the amateurishness of the way the whole industry works).

The problem with requesting extra stage payments during the project is that every time that happens, you are simply robbing Peter to pay Paul. You are just moving the problem on to another part of the job. So instead of going cash critical in week 2, you just go cash critical in week 22! Either way you run out of money before the job is finished.

So, what you need to do to reduce the need to have to run back to the lenders or to keep having to raid your financial buffer, is to make sure that, from before you start work on site, you have a *pretty damned good idea* of exactly where you are financially with the project as a whole.

As I mentioned in an earlier chapter, one important tool you should try to have in your financial toolbox is the trade account. You will probably know what these are even if you have never used them. I'll briefly recap:

Basically, if you have a trade account, whatever you buy during each month (up to your credit limit) is simply recorded on your account. You don't actually pay for anything you buy when you buy it. Then, at the end of each month, your account statement is totalled and sent out to you for payment. You are asked to clear it within thirty days.

If your balance is below your credit limit, you will still be able to buy more stuff during the next month, even if you have not paid off the previous month's account. If you don't clear your previous month's account by the requested date, you will usually receive a reminder letter and be told that unless you make the payment within 14 days or so, your account will be put *on stop* until you do. Your account won't usually be closed because of late payments, just suspended.

This is a brilliant way to help you to get through the project without having to go back to the lenders for more money. Before you start work on site, try to get accounts opened with as many of the people you are going to be buying or hiring from (concrete suppliers / builders merchants / plant hire companies etc.) and make sure you make full use of those accounts during the build period.

Another little trick is when you apply for your mortgage, to check the stage payments arrangements to see a) how many there are, and b) when they are. The more stage payments you are going to receive, the easier your cash flow will be. Ideally you need as much of the money as possible at the early stages as possible to cover all your start-up costs, plus any forward ordering you may have to do. Having your payments weighted towards the early stages will also help you to cover those unexpected costs, like the one I used in the example (above). (Have a look at the Buildstore accelerator mortgage).

Another major tool you can plan to use to help your cash flow, as we have discussed a few times already, is to build quickly.

You are, by now, fully aware how building quickly can reduce your overall costs, but another very useful side effect of building quickly is that your cashflow should improve.

It is common sense really. If you build the house quickly, you will have shorter times between agreed payment stages, so you will be getting more funds coming in over a shorter period. If you tie this in with using trade accounts (which can give you up to 8 weeks to pay for goods), you will often have received the stage payment before you have had to pay for the goods you needed to use to reach it!

This sort of financial juggling can ease the cash flow pressure on the project significantly.

Think about this possible scenario:

- You design a simple house that is going to be quick to build
- You use a closed panel frame to further speed up your build, giving you a 14-week total build time
- You set the mortgage up so that you will be receiving 5 stage payments during the build

This scenario would be bringing you a stage payment roughly every 2 - 3 weeks! So the likelihood of you running out of money, as long as you have planned and costed the job properly and as long as you don't hit any costly problems during the build, should be pretty much completely negated.

Finally, to act as another financial safety buffer, try to get a decent overdraft facility agreed with your bank before you start work. Doing this before the job starts will show the bank manager that you are planning ahead. If you go to the bank in panic during the job, basically "begging" for help, the manager may get a bit nervous and be less likely to help you out, just in case the job goes pear shaped and you can't pay the money back.

Sorting out the cash flow doesn't have to be a difficult job, but it is a very important part of the project planning. Make sure you give it the time you need to in order to get it set up properly.

11) Choosing and ordering materials (before you start work on site)

On most building projects, there will be some materials that you will need to get organised and ordered before you start work on site. You need to make sure you have identified what these are and taken care of them, to save yourself from running around like a headless chicken once you get started.

Your planning and building regulation conditions will usually require you to have confirmed the following choices of materials before you start work:

- Foundations
- Bricks, render or cladding
- Insulation
- Roof Tiles
- Window / external door materials and style
- Internal wall construction
- Drainage
- Landscaping details
- Various other stuff

Any of these items may need to be given thought and possibly ordered prior to you starting work.

On top of that, as soon as you do start, you will need to think about other materials such as:

- Concrete
- Blocks
- Possibly reinforcing steel
- Hardcore
- Drainage
- Special bricks (for when you have detailing such as angled bay windows, plinths etc.)
- Quoins

If you are managing the job yourself and are therefore responsible for ordering items which are going to be needed in the first 2- 4 weeks, you need to make sure that you have done everything you need to have done, at least 2 – 3 weeks before you start, to ensure that everything you need is going to be arriving when it is needed. If you don't, you could get a shock. Some bricks are on 16-week delivery times, things like quoins, special bricks, special lintels, some types of insulation etc. can also be on long delivery times.

As I said in an earlier chapter, the situation you really need to avoid is for your bricklayers to come to site, raring to go, only to find that some of the materials haven't arrived, or worse still, even been ordered!

Getting everything ordered that you will need in the early stages shouldn't really be a big job. If you are not sure about what you will need, talk to your subbies. They will usually be happy to give you lists of what they need and how often they are then likely to need the stocks replenishing.

12) Contingencies. Practical and Financial

We have touched on this a few times over the previous chapters. It is something many self-builders ignore when setting up their finances for the job, but they do so at their peril.

When you start any major building project you need to create buffers (contingencies), for both the financial and practical parts of the job. If you don't set up adequate practical buffers, the result is usually delay, but it could be, in some cases, that the project fails.

Financial contingencies could be needed to cover unexpected things like:

- Extra expenses incurred underground
- Theft.
- Damage.
- Price increases.
- Under estimating of costs by you, your builder or your project manager.
- Overruns on time, leading to extra hire costs (scaffolding can cost thousands extra on long overruns on brickwork / roof / roof covering).
- Your own choices (you might see a kitchen you love for £5,000 more than your original budget).
- 101 other things!

You also need to remember that although you (as a builder of a new property) should get your VAT refunded, you have got to buy everything first and pay the VAT before you can reclaim it in one lump at the end of the job.

A lot of self-builders calculate the total cost of the build as a net figure (i.e. after the VAT refund), but forget to allow possibly the £5,000 - £10,000 of cash which will need to be paid out to buy the goods in the first place, before the refund comes back in much later.

With the flush of optimism that accompanies the start of most self-build projects, people also often neglect the fact that building jobs very rarely come in under budget.

I always say a minimum of around 10% should be allowed on your basic budget for financial contingencies. This can be in the form of a sum put away somewhere, or possibly an overdraft facility.

Practical contingencies

No-one likes to think of the negative aspects of a project before they start, but if there is one thing that can be guaranteed, it is that there will be some. Possibly little ones, possibly big! You need to be ready for both.

For example:

- What would happen if you became ill during the building work or if you had an accident that stopped you from being able to carry on doing what you had planned to do?
- If any of the sub-contractors let you down would you have alternatives to bring in who could take over?
- What would happen if, when you came to order the bricks you found that they were on a 4-month delivery period and you wanted to start in 6 weeks?
- What if bad weather means that the time you took off work to get everything up and running, has all been used up and the job is hardly under way?

These and similar situations arise regularly on self-build contracts and although they are not normally of a critical nature, they can often cause significant problems with the day to day running of the job. If they are not anticipated and dealt with quickly, they can end up costing you significant time and money.

I am not suggesting here that you spend a lot of time trying to double-think every aspect of the project, but it is useful to be aware that things could go wrong, so whatever your plan A is, it is useful if, at the back of your mind you are always thinking: "What is our plan B for that bit of the job?"

Any negative scenarios that you can predict and make contingencies for, could potentially save you time and money at some stage during the project.

13) Getting contractors / sub-contractors tied into a programme (timescale)

You should by now have completed the tendering stage of the project and be pretty much sorted with who you intend to use for the various parts of the job.

Now you need to get them all lined up to start work when you need them.

Prior to any work starting on site, the best tool to use for organising both labour and materials ordering is the contract programme. Each sub-contractor should have had a copy of the contract programme with the tender documents, so should be aware of the general timescale and the provisional start date. Thus, when you are ready, all you should need to do is speak to them to confirm that they will have the manpower, plant and materials available for when you need them (and also to be finished by when you need them to be finished. – This is just as important).

Once you have everyone provisionally booked, you need to keep in touch with them regularly to make sure they are still available. Construction is a very difficult activity to plan ahead. Weather, supplies and other problems are constantly causing you to re-think and re-organise, so giving each sub-contractor a call every fortnight or so, to check if they are still ok for the start date, is a prudent thing to do.

By the way: Don't just ask them to contact you if they have any problems with the start date and expect that they will. The chances are they won't!

Unfortunately, most contractors plan ahead only in very short terms, so if they were to get delayed on a job, it probably wouldn't even occur to most of them to let the following client know. However, if <u>you</u> ring <u>them</u>, you can at least remind them you are there and focus their minds!

14) Measuring quantities for ordering:

If you are going to be running the job, you will need to work out how much of each type of material that you are going to require during the project. This can be quite a time-consuming job. If you are not experienced either in the industry or with ordering construction materials, you should try to do some delegation.

There are a couple of ways to order materials, but however you do it, just remember to add a small percentage on for waste / loss / breakages. You need to do this for just about everything from start to the finish (except, obviously, the big-ticket items such as kitchens, bathrooms etc.).

A reasonable amount to add on for waste and damage is around 5%, but, to avoid having lots of stuff left over at the end of the job, you will need to use your own judgement to work out how much extra to add to the order for each item.

Here are the two main ways to approach the materials ordering if you are managing the job yourself:

1) Ordering everything yourself:

Here are a few examples of how to order some of the big-ticket items:

- If you are ordering bricks, and you are going to make sure they are well stacked, on a good surface away from mud and easily transportable to their required location around the building, you will probably end up wasting very few. However, brickies will be cutting a lot of bricks (houses are not usually designed for brick sizes so lots of bricks need cutting and the left-over bits are usually wasted).
I would normally suggest adding 5% to the net measurement when ordering bricks. However, if you are a bit clever, you will wait until you are ordering the last load before making your final calculation. At that stage, it is a lot easier to work out what has been built and what is left to build. Then if you subtract the number of bricks left on site on the day you do the measure, from the total amount you need for the whole job, you should be left with quite an accurate total for the numbers of bricks you are going to need to finish, then just add the 5% on to that number, rather than adding it at the start to the total amount needed for the whole job.
- If you are ordering cement for the main brickwork, you are best just ordering it by the pallet load and then asking the brickies to let you know 2 days before they need some more, so you can reorder whatever they need to finish the work. The same theory applies here, buy full pallets while everything is being built, but towards the end of the job, start to ask how much the lads think they will be needing to finish, then order smaller amounts to try to reduce potential waste when everything is completed.
- Cavity insulation will usually be bought by the pack, or roll. You will usually get the best prices if you buy in bulk from a specialist, or better still, direct from a wholesaler (as opposed to a retailer). If you have somewhere safe to store it all, and you can make sure that the packs aren't left open in the rain, or strewn around the site, you should be able to fairly accurately measure the amount you will need and get that ordered to come in one big delivery (without allowing for waste). If you are a bit short at the end of the job, just get what you then need from the local builder's merchants.

The same sort of thinking applies to all material items.

2) Delegating the measuring work:

- **Let the suppliers do the work:** If you want to make life a bit easier for yourselves, wherever possible try to give the job of measuring all the materials over to the people who are selling them to you. As I said in an earlier chapter, the way I usually do it, is to give a set of drawings and the building regs specification to three or four builders merchants and ask them to give me total prices for anything they would like to be considered for supplying. That way you get them to do all the work, not only to measure everything up, but also to price it as well.

  Most builders' merchants will have someone employed, either in each branch or in head office just to do this job. They have to do it for the bigger builders, and as a self-builder, you could be taking a significant amount of business to them, so let them do a bit of work to earn their money!

- **Use a professional estimator:** This will cost you anything from a few hundred pounds to a couple of thousand. It is not an option I have used (being very reluctant to pay for things that I could get free), but if it is a very big or complicated job that needs special attention, or if, for whatever reason, you can't get the merchants to do your pricing for you, then in some circumstances this may be an option to consider.

- **Use your designer's software:** These days, with most designers using specialist software to design houses, it is worth you asking your designer to provide you with a set of quantities for everything you are going to need. Some of the design packages will calculate everything down to the last screw!

  If this is the case then the designer should give you these quantities either free of charge, or just for a few pounds. Why? Because all it usually takes to get the computer to spit out all the quantities is to hit print material quantities and *"Bob's your uncle"*!

- **Use estimating software:** If you are handy on the computer and are quick at learning, you may consider using some CAD estimating software. There are a few packages around and you would need to do some research to decide if this is a viable option for you.

  The drawback with this method for you as a self-builder is that you usually won't have the original design software or the designs stored in your own computer. To calculate the materials quantities, the estimating software will need the design information to be able to do its job and unless you have a system that can supply that information in the correct format (normally ".dwg" format), you might have to enter a lot of information yourselves, by hand. This sounds a bit too much like hard work to me, when I can normally try to get the merchants and suppliers to do the job for me!

Whichever way you get your measuring done, just remember that any simple mistake in measuring could potentially end up with you ordering either too much or not enough. Either way, errors can quickly end up costing you a lot of money. So, whether you are doing the measuring yourself or getting others to do it, make sure that, wherever possible, you always double check everything before ordering.

I remember a colleague (Hello "Dave M" if you ever read this!) many years ago when we were doing our site management training, pricing up some hardcore for a tender for a new access road into a steel works.

Instead of allowing £10.80 / ton for hardcore, he hit the decimal point button at the wrong time on his calculator and because he was in a hurry and didn't check his calculations, ended up allowing just £1.08 / ton! There were around 3000 tons needed so he ended up under-pricing the job by around £30,000. Not a good way to impress the boss. It is easily done though, so be careful.

15) Negotiating prices on materials and plant:

(We went through this earlier, but it is a sensible place to recap here).

As a self-builder, embarking on a major project, you will be spending many tens of thousands of pounds on materials and because of this, you are going to be looked upon by the builder's merchants, hire companies and many of the specialist suppliers as gold dust!

These people all know that when a self-builder comes to them before starting a project that they will usually:

- Have plenty of money to spend.
- Want good quality materials (which usually mean higher profit margins).
- Are not usually going to be aware of building materials costs.
- Need large quantities of everything.
- Are not going to be used to negotiating price reductions. So are ripe for the picking! (*OK, not all suppliers are so unscrupulous as to take advantage of that situation, but some do*).

You as a self-builder are their dream customer!

You need to be fully aware of this very strong position that you are in to try to use your buying power to get some significant reductions on prices for material and plant hire.

The best way to do this is to play them off against each other. Don't do this secretively, use the fact that you are doing that to put pressure on them to give you their best possible price by telling each one of them that you are doing so and who they will be competing against.

There is nothing more irritating than, every time you want to order something, spending valuable time on the phone or in builders' merchants' branches, trying to negotiate discounts. Much better to set things up at the start so that they know they need to give you their best price if they want to stand a chance of winning the orders from you.

All you need to do is to give every supplier a full set of the drawings which are relevant to them. Also give them a copy of the building regulations specification (so that they can see the type and standards of materials required). Tell them that they will need to sharpen their pencils" (i.e. give you their best prices) if they want to get your business, then just see what they come up with.

This is also a good time to ask them to open an account for you, preferably with something like a £5,000+ credit limit).

Remember: Watch out for one trick some suppliers use, which is to offer you some loss leaders for some of the basic products (plasterboards / cement etc.) to get your business. They sometimes do this in the knowledge that most people will tend to shop by habit and once they get used to dealing with one supplier, they will go to the same place for most of their business, often without comparing prices with competitors. So, they reckon that all they need to do is to get you to come to them for the first few orders and they will then have you for the duration of the job. Let them know upfront that that is not going to happen!

16) Planning the site set up (including health and safety / security etc.)

Now is the time to be thinking about how you will set the site itself up. This is not a particularly complicated thing to do but requires some consideration as you need to make sure that your site is a safe and efficient place to work.

You also need to give some thought to security.

On the next page you will see a sample site set up for a simple rectangular plot on which is to be built a simple rectangular house.

Although every site will obviously vary in size, shape etc. there is a basic concept of how to set everything up which applies to most sites.

The main things you need to think about are:

1) Security fencing

You should enclose your site with security fencing. Not only to protect against theft, but also to comply with health and safety regulations.

As I mentioned earlier in this chapter, as the owner of the site you need to be seen to be taking whatever actions necessary to ensure the safety of the public. This includes not allowing them access into a dangerous area *(in this case, a building site)*.

So, rather than taking any chances, it is a sensible move to install good quality security fencing to the whole perimeter of the site, with gates and a good quality lock.

You can choose to buy or hire this fencing. If you are planning on the project being completed quickly it may be cheaper to hire. The cost to buy the individual panels may only be around £35 - £40 each compared to around £5 / week to hire, but there are quite a few other bits and pieces you would also need to buy, such as the bases to fix the panels in to and all the jointing clips.

Your other option is to look online for second hand fencing. This could be picked up very cheaply, but often the quality is poor.

It is worth you spending some time working out which of the options will be cheaper for your site.

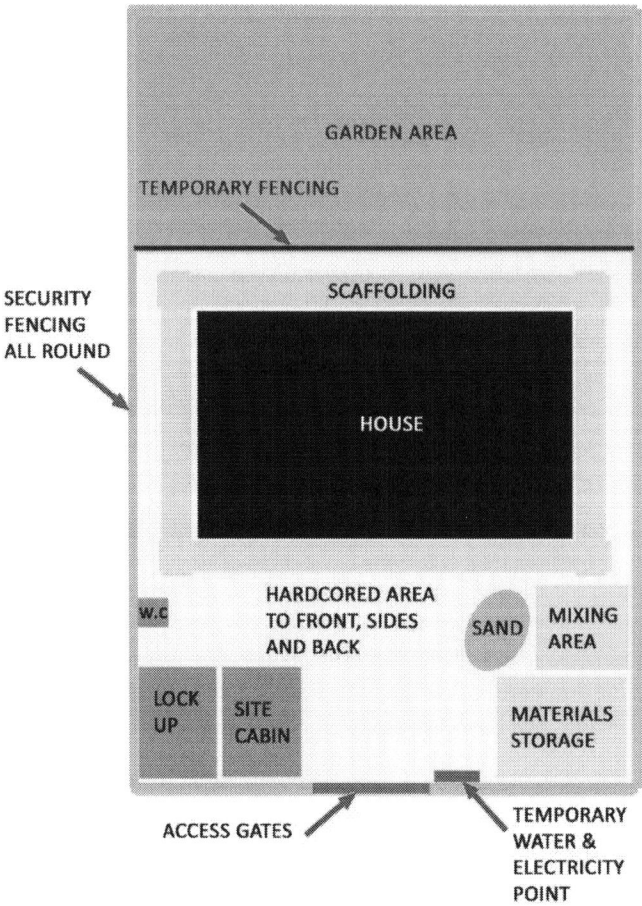

2) Temporary water and electricity point

You will need power and water on site while you build. You can get these by hiring:

- Generators.
- Water bowsers.
- A water stand pipe from the service provider. This supply would come straight off the mains supply in the road. You would use a hose to transfer the water to a water butt on site (You won't usually be able to leave the stand pipe connected permanently, it will just be used to refill the butts and then be disconnected)
- You can also use water butts and refill them yourself using water carriers.

The most efficient option to provide temporary electricity and water supply to the site, is to do it as part of your permanent mains connection (which you will then connect to the house when it is built). Alternatively, you can simply apply to the water authority for a temporary supply to use while you build. Either way, the service provider will probably make your permanent connection on to the mains at the start of the job.

The way a temporary supply works is to give you a point, normally just inside or near to the boundary where the service (water / electricity) enters the site, from which you can run electrical supply leads or water hoses to wherever they are needed.

The service provider will come and make the connection to the mains. For the electricity, this will usually be to a temporary fuse board, which you will normally locate in a secure box or brick housing structure. The water supply will usually be to a lockable box into which a stop tap is fitted on to a board at around 3' off the ground.

If you are eventually going to use the temporary supply pipe as your permanent connection, when you are ready, your ground worker will excavate a trench from the temporary metre box to the entry point position on the house. The service pipes and / or cables are then laid and the trench backfilled. The service can then be permanently connected to the house and the temporary metre box discarded.

3) Site cabins / lock-up / w.c.

These are things that you have to provide on every building site.

You usually need a secure lock up for your valuable materials and plant, a site cabin with hot running water, hand-washing facilities and drying facilities. You will also need a w.c (which is normally hired from and maintained weekly by a local hire company).

4) Hardstandings

It is sensible to provide every new building site with a hardstanding area so that delivery vehicles can be driven in to drop off their goods onto a firm surface that isn't going to turn to mud every time it rains.

Later in the project you will usually need a driveway forming up in hardcore, so if it is practical to do so, some part of the future driveway area is usually the best place for your hardstanding to be constructed (simply because you won't be wasting any stone forming up an area for storage, only to be removing it later to form up garden areas).

The size of your storage area will depend on what type of build you are planning.

A traditional brick and block build will need a lot more storage room than a timber frame build because of the amount of materials you have to have delivered in small quantities in order to build the foundations and shell of the house.

Bear in mind that if you drop packs of bricks onto grass or soil, which then turns to mud in the rain, you could lose dozens, if not hundreds of bricks by them getting covered in mud or soaking wet, making them unsuitable for using to build the house. At £350 to £500 / 1000 to buy, losing bricks in the mud could be expensive and could result in you having to re-order small part loads at the end of the job, which, on top of the bricks you lost, can increase the overall cost of the bricks significantly.

If, for whatever reason, positioning the hardstanding on the future driveway is not practical, you will probably have to stone up areas which will eventually become garden. If this is the case, you will usually be able to rescue at least some of the stone to use in areas such as patios and garden paths. So, it doesn't necessarily all usually have to go to waste at the end of the job. It is just better to put it where it needs to be permanently in the first place.

Around the house, you will usually need to provide a level stone base for the scaffolding to sit on. This stone can later become the base course for pathways around the house, so again it should not be wasted (just make sure that you lay it at the right level so that you don't have to scrape it off later to prepare the area for the footpaths).

5) **Materials storage**

Once you have your hardstandings formed up, you need to think about your materials storage system.

Giving thought to:

- **Access to the materials storage area for delivery vehicles.** Normally the ideal place is somewhere that the wagon can back straight up to and then easily drive out in a forward gear. If that is not possible, then try to position it along the road, so that the goods can be off loaded with a hiab over the security fencing).
- **Physical access to the different materials (i.e. not blocking them in).** You don't want to have to be either climbing over, or moving one type of material to get to another. Think about the order in which you will want to be using everything, then put the stuff you need first in the easiest position to reach.
- **The distance from where the materials are stored to where they are going to be used.** Keep them as close as possible to where they will be needed. Every metre further away from the job means more time spent carrying. Time costs money.
- **The method of transporting the materials to their required location.** Is everything going to be manhandled or put in wheelbarrows? Or will you have a site forklift to move things around? A forklift will allow you to store further away from the job and it will also allow you to load faster (especially at height), but hiring one will be very expensive.
- Always cover materials that are easily damaged. Plastic sheeting is ideal for this. Fix the sheeting down with weights so it doesn't get blown off in the wind.
- Keep pinchable stuff securely locked away in a metal lock-up (timber cabins are easy to break in to).

6) **Mixing area**

Your brickies will need a mixing area. This usually incorporates a large mixer, sand, a pallet of cement and a mixing board (usually a sheet of plywood), with either a water hose or the big 45-gallon metal drums full of water close by.

Bear in mind that:

- The sand delivery vehicle need to be able to back up directly to the location where you need the sand offloading.
- The mixing area should be as close to the working area (the house) as possible to the labourers are not having to carry mortar long distances.
- If you are using water butts to store water in, these are going to have to be kept full. If you have a hose that is fine, the brickies will look after that job themselves. If not, you will need to ensure that water is being provided at the rate it will be needed (often meaning that you need to keep bringing water in in 25 gallon containers from somewhere else).

Coloured mortars: *You will probably want to consider using a colour dye in your mortar for the main brickwork.*

Depending on where you are in the country and depending on the natural colour of the sand in your area, a simple sand / cement mix of mortar can end up giving you a very boring grey / white finished joint colour once it has fully dried out.

There are now many types of dyes you can buy to add to the mortar to give a finished colour that complements the bricks. You can buy them in small bags, large buckets, or you can order it pre-mixed, either as dry sand or as ready to use mortars, which are delivered to site each morning in tubs with water and retarders mixed in to it (to slow down the going off times).

These premixes might be more expensive than adding the dye to the mix on site, but they tend to give a very even colour to the finished job by virtue of the fact that the correct and exact quantities of dye is added to each delivery, which helps to avoid the possibility you ending up with differing shades of joints by putting different amounts in each mix (this can spoil the whole job).

To find premixed mortar suppliers in your area, just do an internet search on "premix mortars" and add your post code.

If you order the premix mortar you won't need the plain sand for the main face brickwork, but you may need it for the underground work and blockwork.

It is much cheaper to get the different types of sand / mortar for the two different parts of the job and you don't really need pretty joints underground. Just make sure the brickies don't get lazy and start using the dyed mortar for the blockwork.

However, remember to use the coloured mortar for anything which is below the DPC, but which **will end up being seen**. *Talk to your brickies to make sure they have this in hand).*

7) Scaffolding

As part of the health and safety measures, you will need to make sure you have professionally erected, safe scaffolding on site for a good proportion of the building programme.

In the old days, you could get away with hiring in the quick-form type scaffold that clips together, and knock up your own scaffolding. This is not really a viable option these days unless, before you start, you go on a scaffold course to learn all about how to put it up and maintain it safely.

Your best bet is to get the scaffold professionally erected and kept in a safe condition, then get rid of it as quickly as possible (building using timber frame, SIPS or closed panels will usually help you to speed up the house build so that you can off hire the scaffold earlier and save money).

The way the scaffold is erected will vary depending on which construction method you use. Be sure to discuss (at the tendering stage) with the scaffolder, how you are building the house (which build method you are using), and also talk to your brickies or timber frame / closed panel erectors to find out from them how they need the scaffold setting up and at what stages they will need it altering.

Have these conversations **before** you agree the price as the requirements of the brickies or timber frame guys may require extra input from the scaffolders over and above what they normally provide.

As a quick guide to what type of scaffold is need for each type of build method, basically:

For traditional build. The scaffold goes up as the building goes up. Usually in about 4 lifts (i.e. 4 platforms), plus some extra lifts up any gables or special features.

For timber frame. Three sides are built before the frame comes to site. The front is usually left open so the frames can be brought in from the delivery wagon. The front is then closed in as the building goes up. Again, lifts for gables may be required.

For closed panels. Because the panels are normally crane lifted into position and the whole thing goes up so quickly that, ideally the scaffold is built complete before the kit arrives (this obviously saves on having to keep getting the scaffolders back for each lift and possibly losing progress whilst waiting for them to arrive).

Just be sure that, whoever is responsible for the scaffold keeps a regular check on it for safety and also remember that you could be held responsible if there is an accident and you are proved to have been negligent.

8) Health and safety / CDM

As we now well know, health and safety is very important on building sites these days. All sites need to be set up in accordance with CDM regulations and if your project involves more than 500 man days of work on site (which a new build house almost certainly will), it has to be registered for CDM regulations (*Construction Design and Management*).

These regulations have to be followed by all parties involved (meaning you, the designers, and everyone on site). It doesn't matter which way, or who project manages the job, it is still up to you to make sure that the CDM regs are in place and followed.

To find out more about the CDM regulations and your obligations under them just do a search on "CDM regulations" and you should quickly find what you need.

As I have mentioned repeatedly, if anything goes wrong on site and someone gets injured, **YOU** as the person in overall charge of the site can be personally prosecuted, and in the worst case, sent to prison and fined, so don't chance it! Just make sure you do whatever you need to do both **before** and **during** the build.

As this is such an important aspect of the build, I am not going to set out what you need to do here. You really need to find out about the current regulations from the proper people. Therefore, as well as researching the overall subject, I also recommend that you go to the following website to get you started on finding out what you need to know:

www.hse.gov.uk/construction/cdm/2015/summary.htm

9) Site insurance:

Just as important as the CDM regulations is site insurance. You have to have a suitable site insurance policy in place before you start work.

A common type of policy is called an "All risks" policy, which should cover you for everything you need on a self-build project (including public liability). Just do a search on *"Self build site insurance"* or *"All risks self-build insurance"* to pull up a selection of companies who can provide a suitable policy.

Before you sign up with anyone, make sure you ask the questions: *"Does your policy cover us adequately for **every aspect** of the build, or do we need to get any further cover?"* and *"Are we covered if someone let us down and breaks a contract agreement, but then tried to sue us"* (as happened to someone I know).

The only time you will not need an insurance policy for the building works would be if you were to give out the **whole project** to a main contractor and have nothing to do with any of the buildings works yourselves. They will then be responsible for looking after all this type of stuff (just make sure they know that they are!)

Very important: Make sure you get a suitable policy in place before you start work on site. – NO excuses!

10) Thinking ahead

It is very easy, when you are getting ready to start work on your project, just to concentrate on getting the tasks and people organized that you will need for the first few weeks. In fact, that is only part of the job.

Just as important, if you want to get up a head of stead and get the job finished as quickly as possible is to also plan the next stages of the job.

Use the project program to see who you are going to need and when and work out who you need to be getting lined up, in plenty of time to make sure you get them to site when you need them.

The main activities to get sorted out before you start work (on top of the obvious ones related to the ground works) are:

- Scaffolders
- Bricklayers
- Timber frame suppliers
- Roof truss manufacturers
- Roofers

Just think through your program and if in doubt, talk to the people you plan on using in order to find out what their situation is and how much notice they will need to be able to start on site with you.

Conclusion

Planning to start is a very important stage of your project. Get this bit right and the rest of the project will benefit from the work you do now. Good planning can save you a lot of time on your build program and potentially save you tens of thousands of pounds on the build costs.

The CDM regulations and site insurance are also both very important aspects of your project, which if you ignore, could in the worst case, land you in prison.

Get this bit right and you can be confident that you have taken all the right steps to make sure that you will be giving yourself the best chance of ending up with a smooth running, safe and successful project.

Chapter 11
Starting on site & foundations

Well, at last here you are. - ready and raring to go!

By now, hopefully you have:

- A healthy bank account which is ready and able to withstand the strains that are going to be loaded upon it over the coming weeks and months.
- Sorted out your accommodation for the duration of the build (if you are planning to live on site, this includes getting your services connected).
- Sorted out your mortgage stage payments system (where relevant) to ensure swift payments into your bank when you reach each payment stage.
- Got your building regulations either passed, or at least submitted and you might have provisionally booked your first inspection.
- Sorted out your warranty.
- Got a site insurance policy in place.
- <u>Notified the Health and Safety executive of your project and submitted your CDM application (where appropriate).</u>
- Opened accounts at builders' merchants and as many other suppliers as possible.
- Sent out tenders and contract documents to trades and suppliers for, preferably all, but at least the first few major sections of the work.
- Got your programme sorted so you know you have given yourself a fighting chance of sticking to it.
- Spoken to at least the first few sub-contractors and provisionally agreed a start date for the ground workers and possibly a sub contract Site Engineer (if you are responsible for the setting out of the foundations).
- Checked on ordering times and prices for the first materials that you are responsible for supplying (remember, you will need to have confirmed and booked delivery dates for anything on long delivery times).
- Ordered your timber frame / SIPS / closed panel frame etc. (if appropriate).
- Sorted out site cabins / lockup / security fencing / temporary water and electricity supplies / any plant hire items you are responsible for and anything else you think of that you may need during the first couple of weeks on site.

If you have taken care of all those matters, then you should be pretty much ready to go.

Starting on site:

I am only going to be able to give you a fairly simple run through what happens when you start on site. Every building site has a different set of circumstances to deal with, when it comes to how it is set up. Your site will be no different. There are, however general guidelines that each site follows and those are what I will be concentrating on here.

We'll start with getting the site set up properly, then move on to setting out and excavating the foundations.

On your first morning on site, the first person you would normally expect to see is the ground worker, who will normally arrive on site between 7.30 and 8.00am. I would expect them to be bringing with them an excavating machine, possibly a dumper, a setting out engineer, labourer(s) and all the other bits and pieces that may be needed.

If they are not providing the setting out engineer, you will need to have organised for him or her to turn up.

There is no hard and fast order in which to do the first few tasks, but, for simplicity, I would suggest that they should normally happen in the following order:

- **Site strip:**

This involves clearing the topsoil, including any vegetable matter, from the building area. Topsoil is normally around 6" deep but can often be deeper (or non-existent).

You will usually need to clear the area of the house itself, plus about 2m extra all around. This will provide an area to give a solid base for the scaffolding to sit on and room for people to safely walk around the scaffolding. You will also usually clear the driveway area and any area where you plan on storing materials, siting cabins etc.

The excavated material is normally stockpiled somewhere out of the way on site for re-use, once the house is finished, to cover the garden areas ready for grass and planting. A good place to stockpile the topsoil is at the back of the plot, however bear in mind that after the house is built you will need to be able to get to it (usually with a medium sized excavating machine), to be able to take it and spread it around the site.

- **Security fencing / cabins**

Once you have reduced the ground level by removing the topsoil, it is sensible to erect your security fencing and gates. You can either hire or buy this (*buying normally works out to be more cost effective and if it is in good condition when you have finished with it, you may even still be able to sell it*).

The security of the site is important, not only to keep your stuff safe *inside*, but also to keep unauthorised people *out*. Remember that if you have not taken sufficient steps to keep people off a building site, if they get in and injure themselves, there is a strong possibility that they could sue you! Unfair (maybe), but a fact nevertheless!

You will need to order enough fencing panels to go right round the perimeter of the site and you will also need:

I. Clips to join the panels together.
II. Feet (which can be made of a rubber material or concrete)
III. Lock and chain (with spare keys or coded padlock).
IV. Safety / keep out signs (you can buy these online)
V. Proprietary gate hinge fittings.

You are also probably going to need to bring in some form of storage and site welfare facilities.

The storage cabin will be for all the materials that you can't or wouldn't leave outside. The welfare facilities are to make sure the workers have got somewhere warm to go and sit, dry their clothes, get a cuppa etc. (the CDM regs will tell you what you need).

You may also want to get hold of a lockable office, somewhere for you to go when you are on site and / or when it is raining (although this is a bit of a luxury and is not needed on most one house sites).

Most of the equipment you need will be available at local plant hire centres, but if you can't find what you need, go on line, type in cabin hire companies" and your postcode and you should get a good list of suppliers.

The cost of hiring these types of cabins is quite cheap, from around £20 a week, however you will also need to pay for the delivery and picking up of the cabins, which can run to around £100 - £150 each way / per cabin.

- **First aid kits etc.**

There will be a few bits and pieces you will need for the welfare cabin (again, see the CDM regs), these include:

- Health and safety signage: You can get this a most plant hire shops.
- Boiler.
- Hand drier / paper towels.
- Heater.
- Clothes drying area.
- Table.
- Chairs.
- Washing facilities.
- Cleaning materials, brushes, cloths etc.
- Mop / bucket.
- Mats.

- **Setting out for the foundations**

As I mentioned, this work will normally be carried out by a qualified site engineer, however the ground workers themselves will often have the experience and knowledge required to set out simple buildings on flat plots (larger groundworks companies will often employ their own site engineer).

I cannot over-emphasise here the importance of getting this bit right. If the setting out is wrong, the consequences can be disastrous. You will remember me talking earlier about accidentally setting out in front of a building line.

The rule is that: You and / or the ground worker and / or the engineer double and triple check everything to do with the initial setting out (with each one of you trying to come at it from a different angle so you don't risk just repeating errors already made).

To set out the house, you normally need:

- A theodolite.
- A dumpy level.
- A 4' or 6' Spirit level.
- String lines.
- A chalk line.
- Timber pegs (2" x 2" x 18").
- Nails (2" wire).
- 2 x 30m tapes measures.
- A sledge hammer.
- A claw hammer.

Your drawings should be have setting out measurements on them, or be of a large enough scale for you to be able to accurately scale from them (at least 1:50).

If there are any critical measurements on the site, you should <u>never</u> scale them from a drawing!

The first job is to set out a baseline. This is a permanent reference line, from which any other point on the job can be re-established if it is lost.

The baseline can be the face of brickwork for one of the walls, or an arbitrary line set out away from the building somewhere where it will not be in danger of being accidentally moved.

For this example, I will assume we are using the face of brickwork of one of the external walls as the base line.

Whoever is taking responsibility for the setting out of the building will need to do this job as it is very important that it is right. *Not* within a couple of inches, but **right** (to within a couple of millimetres)!

I won't go over the mechanics of how to set up a base line here. It is too important a job to allow anyone to do it who doesn't have the full ability to be able to complete the task successfully. So, I am assuming you have got *the right guys for the job* and that they will just get on and do it!

Once the base line is established, you need to be able to re-establish it at any time. To do this the line is extended (either using string lines or a theodolite) in each direction to a position somewhere out of the way of the excavation (so it is out of the area that is going to be constantly driven over by the excavator). Thin nails are then used to accurately locate the extended baseline on to either a timber peg, or (as shown in the photo above) a profile board, made up of two pegs and a piece of timber. It is a good idea to surround the pegs in concrete to help to ensure that they don't easily get knocked out or over.

You now have the base-line for one wall, so you can measure everything out in one direction from that line, however you don't yet have a line to measure from, to position all the walls that are going to be at 90 degrees to the first line. So, as the next job, you need to get that second base line set out. It is good practice to extend the line to a nail in a profile somewhere out of the way.

These base-lines are now going to be used for setting out the whole house and for getting the lines of the digs marked on the ground so that the excavator driver can set him or herself in the right position to dig the trenches.

How this is done
A string line is pulled tight between the nails on two of the profiles forming one of the base lines and either usually sand, lime or marking out spray paint is used to mark a line on the ground directly under the string line, to mark the face of the brickwork.

After me telling you how accurate these lines need to be, you may be wondering how come sand or lime is accurate enough for digging the trenches. Good question!

The reason is that although the string lines will be pretty much exactly where they need to be, the excavator driver can only work to how accurately he or she can manoeuvre the trench digging bucket.

They will normally aim for the middle of the sand / lime line with the outside of the digging tooth on the bucket, and surprisingly they can usually get within an inch or so of the correct line of the wall. However, at this stage the fine levels of accuracy are not quite as important. The lines for the walls themselves are what needs to be spot on. The excavation is just for the concrete of the foundation and the trenches very rarely end up in a perfectly straight line due to all the obstacles that are encountered underground (which can sometimes make a right mess of the trench).

The setting out process is repeated for all the external walls of the house and once they have all been checked for length and square (i.e. making sure the corners are all at exactly 90 degrees), the excavator can then start to excavate the trenches.

The diagram below shows where you should be up to once the setting out has been done, but before you start excavating.

It shows a simple rectangular house on a rectangular plot, with the red line denoting the security fencing and the light grey area highlighting the area of the plot cleared of topsoil. The face of brickwork lines are the face of brickwork lines between the setting out profile which have been positioned out of the way of the excavation.

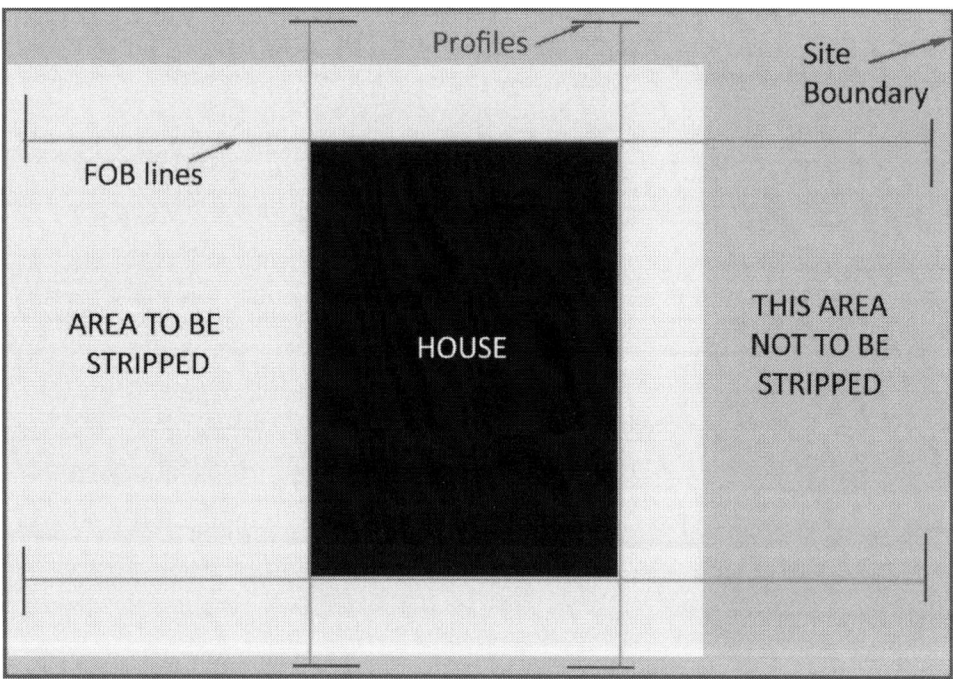

A standard foundation (or "footing") for a cavity wall construction will usually be 900mm deep and 600mm wide (if you are using "single skin" construction, for example with a SIPS or a closed panel, the trench width may be specified to be narrower, which can save time and money on the excavation process).

Going back to what I touched on above, it is quite common for there to be problems when digging the foundations. Poor ground, rain, rocks, old foundations etc. can lead to the sides of the trenches falling in. If they do, they have to be cleaned out before any concrete is poured.

Although the standard depth of the foundation is 900mm, the actual depth will be governed by the quality of the ground. The house needs to sit on something very strong and solid, so the bottom of the trenches need to be very firm before the concrete can be poured.

Once your ground worker is happy that the trench is ready for concrete, you will need to get a) the building inspector and b) the warranty inspector out to check that they are also happy with the trench before you pour any concrete.

The problem you have here, is that you will need to book the inspectors a day or so before you need them, at which time you won't usually be sure exactly when you are going to be ready. The best thing you can do in these situations is to make your best estimate on when you expect to be ready and if, for whatever reason you get held up, make sure you let the inspectors know asap so they don't set off for your site and then find you are not ready for them when they get there.

Below is a photo of the foundation trenches for a brick and block (cavity wall) house I built many years ago. It will give you an idea how the site should look just before you pour the concrete (keen eyed readers will notice that some of the profiles were a bit too close to the trench and are at real risk of getting knocked – If they do the wall could end up in the wrong place. I can't remember how they ended up where they did, but I have to assume that I also set some more profiles further away, just in case!)

In this image, you can just see that a string line is being used to check that the trench has been dug in the right position, ensuring that the face of brickwork line will be in its right place on the foundation once the concrete is poured.

If you look carefully, you will also see a timber "square" lying on the ground near the top left of the excavation. This is something the ground workers will knock together out of timber, to form and exact 90-degree angle. They can then use it to further double check the angles and lines.

This photo also shows how the trenches can collapse before the concrete is poured. Look between the two ground workers and you will see that a chunk of the side of one of the trenches has collapsed. The two lads are going around the whole building cleaning all the loose sand / soil from the bottom of the trench, ready for the building and warranty inspectors to come to check the foundations before concreting.

Since those days, I have learnt a few tricks when it comes to designing foundations. One I mentioned in Chapter 5 (the design chapter), you might find useful whether you are designing your own home, or using a professional designer and is worth repeating here after you have been looking at the photo above:

If a wall is going to be none load bearing (i.e. if a wall is going to be made of a timber stud and is purely dividing two living spaces with nothing sitting on it, such as joists or an upstairs wall), then it usually does not need a foundation underneath it. On a standard 4 bed house this could apply to up to 50% of the internal walls on the ground floor.

Here is how this can work in practice.

The image below is of a house I have recently designed.

On most houses, all the external walls will usually be loadbearing, but the lighter internal walls on the image are made from timber studs and have nothing sitting on them (no floor joists or lintels), so they are classed as non load bearing. The darker coloured internal walls are load bearing (they have all joists spanning between them and the external walls).

I am using a steel support to take the weight of the joists between the living area and the dining area, so this part of the wall (where it says "steel") will not require a foundation.

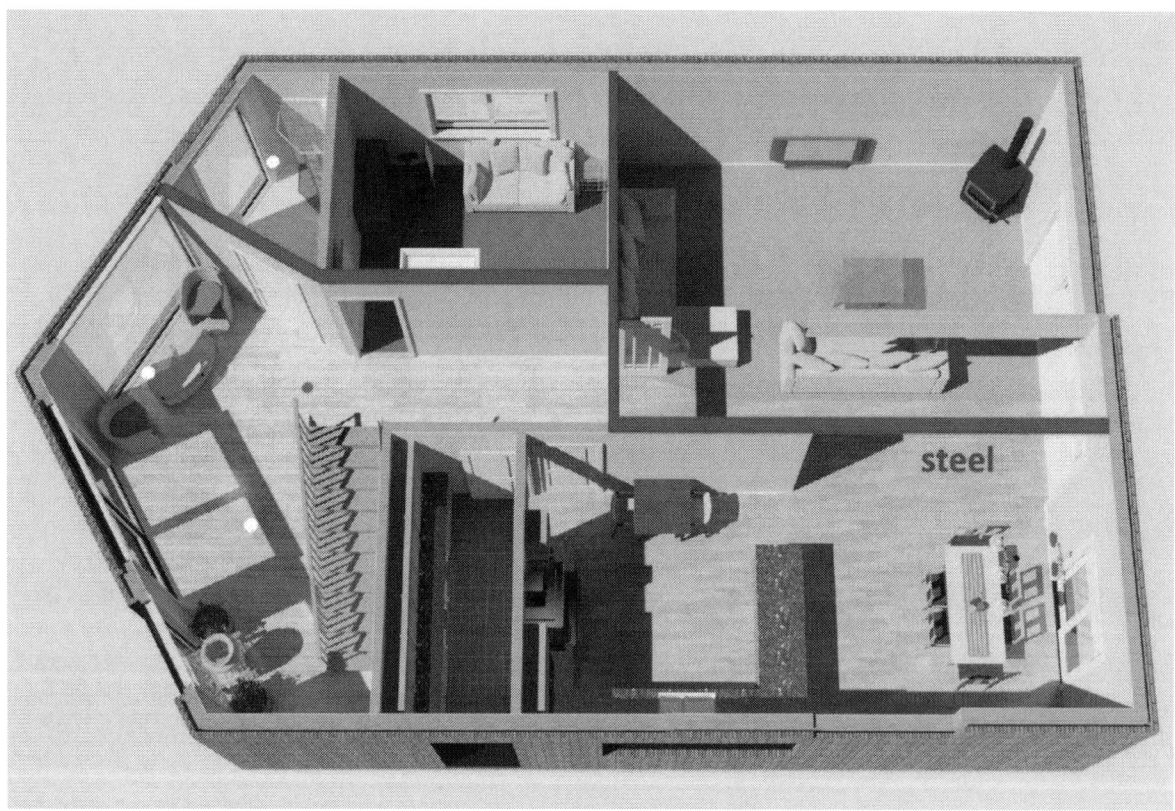

This one bit of information, if you take note of it for when you are designing the house and the foundations, could potentially save you hundreds, if not thousands of pounds on your build costs, especially if you are building on poor ground, which is going to require a lot of work underground.

Be aware that some architects and designers will automatically draw a foundation under every wall. It is just what they do!

So, if when you see your foundation drawings, they show foundations under every wall, just ask your designer if there are (or if there can be) any non loadbearing walls included in the design. They should normally be able to come up with a few.

(By the way, if the wall is to be built of brick or block it **_is_** loadbearing and it needs a foundation).

- **Excavating the foundation**

If you are lucky, your standard trench foundations will end up looking something like this once they are excavated and concreted (for clarity, *the earth is shown around the trench, with a 225mm x 600mm concrete strip at the bottom of the trench*):

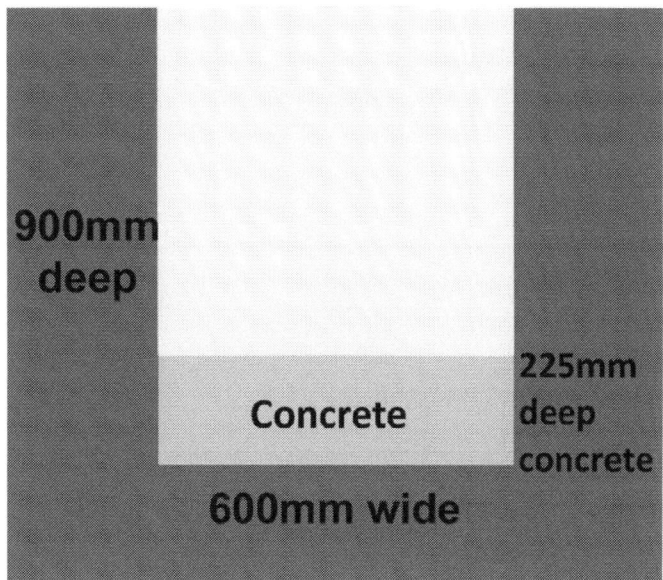

The earth you excavate will normally be stockpiled somewhere out of the way on site.

You can often find uses for this "spoil" (given its proper name) somewhere when you do your landscaping towards the end of the job, but just make sure that your building works are not going to cut off access for an excavator to get to the spoil (otherwise you could find yourself having to move it all by wheelbarrow!)

Something to bear in mind when you excavate soil:

When excavated, soil usually does something called bulking. This basically means that it pretty much doubles in volume as the excavator loosens it and moves it about. So, wherever you are thinking about storing the spoil needs to be able to contain a lot more mass than just the length x width x depth of the dig itself.

Given time to settle and get rained on, the spoil will slowly shrink back down in volume, but if you are moving it off site on wagons when it is freshly dug, you need to be aware that for every wagon you order to take soil to the tip, you will possibly be taking half a wagon of soil and up to half a wagon of air! This can be very costly if you have to pay to tip it (up to £150 - £180 a load these days). This is a very good reason for you to think of innovative ways to keep as much of the excavated materials on-site as possible.

A standard concrete strip footing (as shown above) is made up of a continuous layer of concrete, usually 225mm deep (for a standard cavity wall, narrower for single skin walls).

The top of the concrete is poured to an exact level which is worked out by starting with the floor slab level and working out how far below that level, the top of the concrete foundation needs to be.

As a guide, for a standard foundation:

➢ The trench will normally be 900mm deep from ground level.
➢ The finished floor slab will be 150mm above ground level
➢ The concrete will be 225mm deep

This means that the distance from the top of the concrete foundation to the finished floor level is ideally going to be 825mm (which is an exact multiple of the thickness of a brick course), giving 11 full courses. If this happens on your site, then the brickies won't have to cut bricks to build courses of brickwork up to the exact finished floor level.

To accurately ascertain the correct level of the finished foundation concrete (and thus the finished floor level) all around the house, you (or your *setting out engineer*) will usually need to use a dumpy level to set it to the level shown on the drawings. This is a very important job, which, if you get it wrong could have very serious consequences.

If you get the finished floor level wrong it can potentially have drastic implications on the project, for example:

*Sometimes there is a planning condition attached to an approval that says that the ridge of the roof will be at, or below a maximum set height. If you set the dpc / floor level too high, this could push the ridge height upwards, potentially above the maximum allowed height. This could land you in very big trouble. Be **very** careful!*

The ground worker will normally knock steel pins into the ground around the trench bottom and these pins will then be hammered down to exactly the right level for the top of the concrete, to within a couple of millimetres.

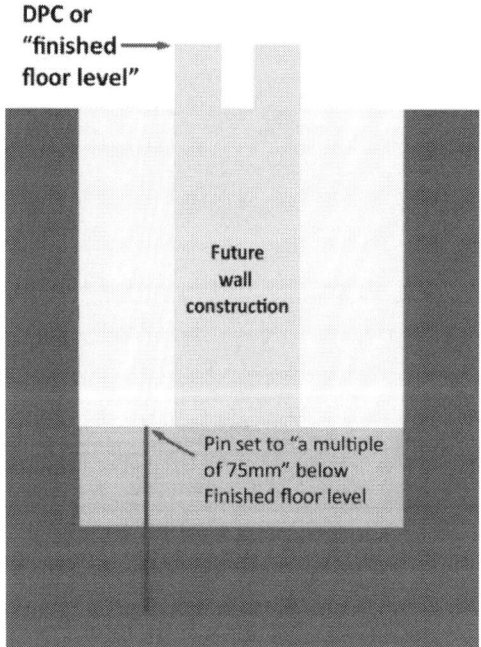

- **Concreting**

Concreting a simple strip foundation is usually pretty straightforward.

You need to measure up the theoretical quantity of concrete required, using the drawings and then allow for any extra depths that you might have had to dig, or any trench sides that have fallen in whilst you have been digging.

Once you know the approximate quantity you'll order the concrete to the specification that is detailed in your approved building regulations. This will normally be a mix called C30 or C35. The figure simply refers to its crushing strength. You need different strengths of concrete for different uses.

Here are things you need to bear in mind when organising and ordering concrete for the foundations:

Access: You will need to get the delivery wagon as close to the trenches as possible (but not so close so that it threatens to collapse the sides of the trench), in order for it to be able to pour the concrete straight in (within 4ft – 6ft max). To do this you need to make sure you have a good solid roadway from the access to the site, right up to where the wagon will need to get to and you will need to be sure that the trench is not going to cave in with the pressure imposed on its sides by the weight of the delivery wagon holding up to 6 cubic metres of concrete.

Getting to the hard to access areas: Quite often the delivery wagon will not be able to move around the dig to all the positions it needs to, in order to be able to pour the concrete straight into the trench. Where this is the case you need to come up with an alternative way to get the concrete to where it needs to be.

Two common solutions to the problem are:

1) Use a dumper to carry the concrete around the building and pour it straight into the trench at the right location.
2) Use wheelbarrows.

The second option will obviously be slow and you need to bear in mind that you will normally get around 40 minutes to empty the concrete from the vehicle. After that you can be liable for paying standing time, which can cost anything up to around £100 / hour.

A third option, which is expensive and should only be used where there is no other option available would be to bring in a concrete pump.

The image above shows such a pump being used on one of my jobs, where the building was down a steep bank and about 20 metres away from the road.

The pump simply sets up in a suitable position and extends a long boom to the location of the pour (in the photo it is being used for a slab, but it can also be used for the trench pours and anything else you need to do).

The delivery vehicles back up to the pump and offload the concrete into a hopper which feeds it directly into the hose which you can see in the photo.

There is another way to get concrete to the hard to access areas and that is to tweak the mix. This always seems to me to be a bit of a cheat, but it works and it complies with the building regulations!

Normally concrete will come as what is called "A 50 slump mix". What this means is that if you were to pour it into a cone shaped receptacle and then turn the receptacle over, slide it off the concrete and watch how much the concrete collapses by. The number of millimetres it collapses by is called its slump.

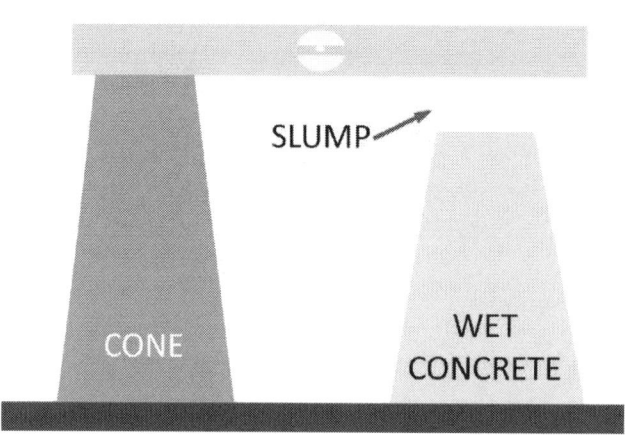

So, if you are struggling to get access to some of the trenches, a further option open to you is to ask the supplier to quote you for a different mix which will give you a thinner / runnier concrete which will basically act more like water and tend to find its own level. A 100 slump will often be runny enough to be encouraged in the right direction by a couple of labourers with shovels and wellies.

To achieve the right level of runniness, the supplier needs to add more water to the mix and also more cement (to keep the strength once it is set). Adding more cement will make the concrete more expensive. However, when compared to the cost of paying to barrow it all across the site and possibly paying £100 or more for standing time, this is an option that could potentially be worth considering.

Laying the concrete You'll normally need at least a couple of people down in the trench to lay the foundations. Once concrete has been poured into the trench, the next job is to get it to the correct level so that the top surface is as close to the level of the top of the steel pins as possible.

This is normally done by shovelling it around as required to get it roughly to the level it needs to be. This job is made easier by using a vibrator poker (see one of these at the left edge of this). The poker basically aggressively vibrates the concrete so that it naturally tends to find its own level, then, once you have got it pretty close to the top of the pins (possibly with a bit more shovelling), you can then tamp it (usually with a piece of timber) to give a nice smooth surface for the bricklayers to work off.

Tamping trenches usually involves getting a piece of 4" x 1" timber, cut to just less than the width of the trench, then using the 1" edge you gently tap the surface of the concrete, moving along the trench as you do so. As you do this, you will find that the action naturally brings some of the water from within the concrete mix to the surface, creating a fairly smooth surface for the bricks to sit on (you can see tamping being done on the slab in the photo showing the concrete pump, a couple of pages ago).

Remember that the joint for a brick should only be 10mm wide and that you will have set the top of the pins so that the distance from the top of the concrete should work out exactly at full course (i.e. a brick plus a 10mm joint).

It is therefore very important that when you have finished tamping the concrete, it is all within a 5mm or so tolerance right around the trench.

The concrete will normally take a day or so to go off (harden), during which time you can be thinking about loading out the blocks ready for building the walls up to DPC level.

In the photo on the previous page, you can see that the trench has slightly collapsed in some places, so this trench is going to use quite a lot more concrete than was actually measured on the drawings.

The delivery vehicle has not had to come far off the roadway to be in the correct position and the ground is made up of compacted sand, so didn't need any stone to be laid to give a firm base to drive onto. However, we were careful not to drive too close to the trench after it had already partly given way. The driver is normally the best judge of where is safe to park.

(Note: Don't let the concrete touch your skin, - it will burn and could put you in hospital!)

- **Different types of foundations:**

There are a number of different types of foundations generally used for housing. Here are a few of the most common:

Strip foundations. This is the standard foundation which, when I have been talking about the house foundations, I have been referring to. It is the simplest of the foundation types and usually the most economical.

For a standard cavity wall, it is usually 225mm deep x 600mm wide and depending on the ground type, a "C30 mix, 50 slump" concrete would generally be a sensible mix to order (check your building regs before you order).

Reinforced strip foundations. These can be required where there is some doubt about the strength of the ground under the foundation trench, or where there is a possibility of shrinkage of the ground around the trench (e.g. in areas of clay).

By installing one or two strips of steel mesh into the standard strip foundation, it becomes much stronger and less liable to be affected by movement or shrinkage. If the ground is very suspect then a more beefy reinforcing may be required by the building and warranty inspectors. Where this is the case, the designer will often have been aware of the poor ground much earlier in the project and will usually have already had the foundation reinforcing designed - and those designs submitted for building regs approval.

If you need mesh, you will usually be able to order it from your local builder's merchants and your ground workers should be able to install it correctly. If you need something more substantial you will normally either get that via your ground worker, or from specialist steel reinforcing companies, usually with steel fixers coming to site to fabricate cages or anything else that is specified to go into the concrete.

Stepped foundation: As the name suggests, this foundation changes level in steps along a sloping piece of ground. The steepness of the slope will dictate the number of steps needed and how close together the steps are.

Stepped foundations are common in hilly areas where level plots are seldom found.

The main thing to bear in mind, if you need to use this method is that you need the steps to be the same depth as a multiple of a brick + bed measurement (i.e.75mm / 150mm / 225mm etc.)

If you are using blockwork (as opposed to bricks) to build up to DPC (which I usually recommended as it is the fastest way to do so), you need to make the steps in multiples of 225mm as this is the depth of a block + bed.

Mass fill foundations: Where you have had to dig down extra depth due to bad ground, or for another reason, it is quicker and safer (and can sometimes be cheaper) to mass fill the trench with concrete, rather than having to send the brickies down in to the trench to build trench blockwork up. Mass filling will replace the need to make the trench safe before the brickies could go down and work in it.

To mark the top level of a mass fill foundation, instead of hammering the steel pins into the bottom of the trench, you would usually hammer them into the side, with the underside of the pin being the top of the concrete level.

Designed foundations: Where the foundations listed above are not suitable for a project, you will usually need to bring in an engineer to help you to design something that is.

This can be the case where you are constructing a basement, or have very poor ground which demands something more than a reinforced strip foundation.

It can also be necessary on some sloping sites where a retaining structure is required to hold back the ground around part of the building.

Once you start to think about bringing in an engineer to design your foundations, your costs are going to increase dramatically, not only because of their fees, but also because there will, by default, be a lot more work on constructing designed foundations than there would be pouring concrete straight in to a trench.

This is a specialist and complex subject and not something that I can adequately cover to any reasonable depth in this book. Suffice to say, if you are considering including a basement as part of your build, or if you are expecting complications with your foundations, then it is well worth you at least talking to an engineer at the earliest opportunity, in order to discuss whether you could potentially require their services. If you think you will then you need to think about your budget and how expensive foundations will affect it.

Piled foundations:

These are used both on sloping sites and where ground conditions are poor.

Put simply, a pile transfers the load of a building down through the weaker layers of the ground, until it reaches a point where it is strong enough to support whatever is going to be built either on it or against it.

There are many different types of piling system available, each of which is suitable for a particular type of project. Again, I am not really able to go in to the details of each type of pile in this book. Only a small percentage of new homes need piling and each case will bring with it its own individual set of problems requiring its own individual set of solutions.

If you need piled foundations, you will also usually need to carry out a ground survey and then find a suitable engineer who can look at the results of the survey in order to design the rest of the foundations to suit the ground conditions and to tie in with whichever piling system you end up using.

The photo above shows a hammered piling system which I used on one of my own projects. This was necessary because the site was a sloping field which I built up to create a flat area for the houses to sit on. There were 24 piles under each house which had to be designed to work in conjunction with a reinforced concrete slab and retaining walls.

Something worth bearing in mind:

All this talking about piling and the different types of foundations may be a bit scary if you don't know much about building, but don't let it put you off.

When this sort of work is required on a site, you tend to be able to purchase the land at a much lower price, with the saving in land cost often more than outweighing the extra cost of the build.

For example: I bought the plots shown above at quite a low cost because of their location on a sloping field.

At the time, I had not had to use piles very much in my career, except for on the large commercial jobs when I was a site engineer in my twenties. My job in those days was setting everything out, so I didn't really get involved in the design side. Therefore I didn't really have much practical knowledge about piling for residential projects, or designing a piling systsem to link up with a reinforced slab. That was not a problem though.

All I did (and all you would need to do) is to bring in the right people and let them do the hard work. You just have to have the money to pay them.

That is exactly what I did. I found good contractors for all of this part of the job and let them all get on with it, reporting to me and liaising with both the building regulations and structural warranty inspectors as they did the job

The important part of this process is to make sure that both the building regs and warranty people are happy with everything from the technical and build quality points of view. So, even though this all looks very complicated, in fact, my own input into this section of the work was fairly minimal and I benefited by getting the land cheaper.

Potential problems with foundations:

There are a number of common problems to watch out for when you are excavating foundations. Here are a few of them:

1. **Poor quality ground.** The inspectors will be looking for a good solid base to the trench before they approve it for concreting.
Some inspectors will jump down into the trench and give them a good stamping on all the way around. Some will poke the ground with a stick to see how solid it feels and some will just walk around the edge of the trench and go by looks.
To avoid the possibility of the trenches failing the inspection, you should pre-check them as you go. Your ground worker should know what will pass the inspection and what won't, but if you want to take charge, just use your own common sense.
Does it look and feel good and solid to you? Are there different types of ground visible around the dig? Can you see tree roots in the trench? Is there existing debris sticking out of the trench? Can you see any signs of running sand or running water? Use your own judgement and speak to the ground workers if you are not sure. None of this is brain surgery!

2. **Trenches caving in as you dig:** This is quite a common occurrence, especially at the wetter times of year, when the ground can get saturated. There is not a lot you can do to remedy the problem itself, without shoring up every trench as you go along (which is not really practical).

The best advice I can give you would be to:
   I. Get the excavation works completed as quickly as possible.
   II. Get the inspectors booked a few days earlier so they come at exactly the time you need them.
   III. Get the concrete poured as quickly as possible (try and do all three of these tasks on the same day if possible).

Once the concrete is in, a collapse in the side of the trench is not as important. Small and medium sized lumps of soil will tend to sit on top of the concrete if the trench collapses, as soon as a couple of hours after it has been poured. The brickies can then usually just clear it out of the way as they work.

3. **Obstructions in the ground: rocks / roots etc.**

   Rocks and large stones are found in many foundations. The problem with them is that they are often positioned half in / half out of the proposed trench and can pull out a huge great chuck of the bank as they are dislodged by the excavating bucket. Again, there is not a lot you can do about them, but if you ask the excavator driver to be careful when he finds them, they may be coaxed out, without too much damage (the driver should be able to sense through the controls when he hits something substantial such as a large rock. He just needs to stay attentive).
   Roots can be a bigger problem. If you find significant roots as you excavate you should let the inspectors know (usually by phone) and let them decide how to deal with them.
   The problem that roots bring with them is that, if they are still live they can continue to grow and theoretically damage the completed foundations. Often, if you can get them all out and they don't go more than a couple of foot deep, you may be ok, but if they are deeper than the foundation excavation then you may be asked to excavate the foundations even deeper than the roots, in order to be able to take the concrete down to a depth where the roots can't get underneath them.
   Old Foundations are quite a common problem, especially in towns and cities. Where you find old foundations, you will need to completely remove them and then take whatever remedial work necessary to prepare the area for the new concrete. Discuss the best course of action with your ground workers and the inspectors.
   Varying ground types in the same foundation: As well as looking for a solid bottom to the trench, inspectors will also be looking for any changes in the makeup of the ground. If, for example you have some rock, some sand, some clay etc. then there is a chance of a thing called differential movement or settlement happening under the foundations over time. This can occur when one part of the bearing ground on which your house sits, moves more, or less than another part, potentially causing settlement in one area and result in cracking in the main structure of the house. I am sure you have all seen settlement cracks on older houses.

   The usual way to solve this problem would be to reinforce the strip foundation so that one part cannot move independently to another. A simple steel mesh reinforcement (as mentioned earlier in this chapter) is normally sufficient for this task, but you need to get the approval of the inspectors for whatever remedy you intend to apply in order to solve the problem, before you actually use it.

4. **Other problems:** You could well come across other problems with the foundation trenches which are not mentioned here. If you do, use the knowledge and experience of your ground workers to try to solve them wherever you can. If they can't solve them, contact the inspectors and get their advice and if they can't help, get an engineer in to sort the problem out.

The rule is: *"If you are not sure, don't guess"*!!

- **Building up to DPC level:**

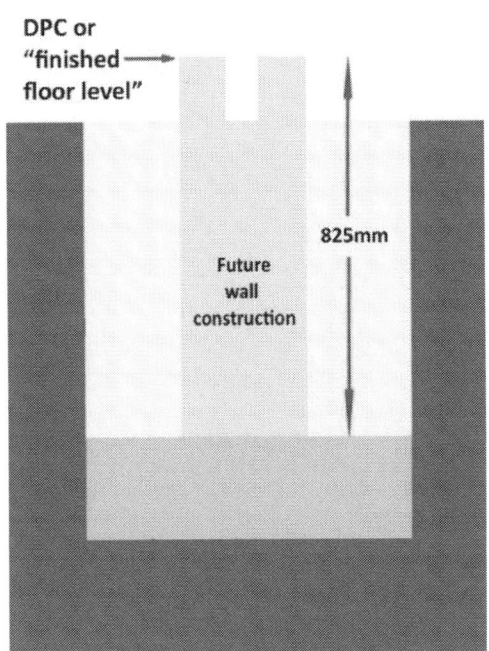

Once you have poured the foundation concrete, the next job is normally to build up the external walls and any internal walls which need foundations, to the DPC (or finished floor) level.

For a standard cavity wall foundation that hasn't hit any problems underground, you should only have 825mm of wall to build in order to reach the DPC level.

The make-up of the wall will depend on the type of construction you have decided to use for the main shell of the building.

❖ **Traditional Build**

If you have chosen a brick and block construction, you will need to build a cavity wall construction underground for it to sit on. This is normally made up of two skins and is normally built in blockwork.

Once the blockwork is completed up to DPC level, you need to fill the cavity up to ground level with concrete cavity fill (a weak mix semi-dry concrete). This is to give strength to the wall once you backfill the earth to each side of it.

With traditional construction, these days, to achieve the higher levels of insulation that the building regulations require, the thickness of the inside skin of the wall is tending to be 150mm (an increase from the standard 100mm wide block used until the past few years).

Again, to help traditional construction meet the insulation requirements, the cavity is also tending to get wider than the 50mm that it used to be. It can now often be set at 75mm, 100mm or even 125mm wide, with the intention of filling it above ground with insulation (rather than leaving it as a cavity).

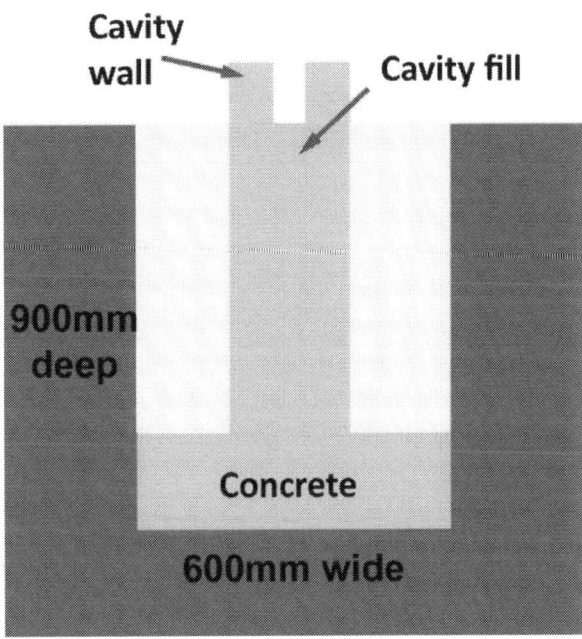

 *The problem I have on the subject of widening of the cavity is not particularly the filling of it with insulation, but the fact that the wider it gets, the less like a cavity wall and the more like two single walls joined together with bits of wire!*
I have not seen any proof to say that the structural strength is compromised by the cavity being wider, but if anyone has any proof one way or the other, maybe you could let me know!

- ❖ **Standard timber frame / closed panel / SIPS:**

All of these building systems do pretty much the same job and they can all be incorporated in to different finished wall constructions such as:

Cavity walls. The foundations for these walls would be built in exactly the same way as for traditional construction.

Single skin cladded or rendered walls. The frame provides the load bearing strength for the building. So, whatever you put on the outside of the frame (cladding, render, brick slips etc.) is usually just cosmetic. It doesn't usually carry any load.

So, as long as the inside skin is strong enough to do its job, the brickwork outer skin of the cavity wall doesn't have to be there for any other purpose than aesthetics.

This means that if you prefer to, you can simply finish the timber frame with timber cladding (or a cement board and render finish) and not have any cavity at all. Just a single wall.

If you go for the single skin option, then, as you don't necessarily need a cavity wall underground, you only need a foundation wide enough to support and spread the load of one wall, rather than two. This can reduce the foundation width to around 450mm – 500mm (from the normal 600mm) and potentially save you time and money.

- ❖ **Block / Block & Render**

This is a similar construction to traditional brick and block, so needs two skins of wall underground.

- ❖ **ICF (insulated concrete formwork) + render**

There are lots of different permutations of this wall style available. If you have decided to go for this build option, you will need to deal directly with your supplier to find out what type of foundation wall you need to build underground.

- • **Constructing the ground floor**

Once you have built your foundation walls up to dpc level, if you have constructed a cavity wall, you will usually need to fill the cavity up to ground level with cavity fill concrete. This is to add strength to the wall structure underground in order for it to be able to withstand the pressure of the ground which will be pushing against it once everything is backfilled.

Cavity fill is basically a weak mix of concrete, normally semi dry (which means it is not runny). It can either be hand mixed (which is a slow job) or you can order it pre-mixed for delivery. The pre-mix will be expensive to buy (because you will only need a small amount and will pay part-load charges), but it can save money over hand mixing by the fact that the job will be done much faster, so you will save money on labour charges. (Note: single skin walls obviously don't need cavity fill as they have no cavity to fill! Again, this saves a job, saves time and money).

Your next job is usually to prepare and construct the ground floor.

This will normally start with you backfilling around the outside of the foundations up to and against the newly built wall, with an excavating machine. The earth you backfill should be of good quality, especially if you are going to be constructing paths around the house later on in the project.

Ideally, if you are going to be constructing paths, drives or patios, you would be advised to backfill around the foundations with stone, compacted every 150mm or so with a vibrating plate. This should give you a solid sub base which will take the weight of whatever is built on top of it, with minimal settlement.

The ground floor will normally have services and drainage which need to be built into / under it. You need to check the drawings and specifications and talk to the guys who are constructing the floor itself, to see what other works need doing at the same time. If you miss anything before you concrete a floor slab it is a major, slow and expensive task to go back and put it right later.

As with the foundation walls, there are numerous ways to construct the ground floor. Here are a few of the main ones:

❖ **Concrete slab**

Firstly, your ground worker should excavate the remaining earth from inside the building as required in order to take the existing ground level down to the formation level. This is the level at which the new construction start. When you do this, make sure there is no vegetation soil still within the building enclosure.

This is normally the kind of routine you will follow for forming up a concrete slab (although every sub-contractor has their own ideas on how best to do it).

I. **Lay and compact the hardcore**

You will usually use an all-in stone, often called scalpings or "2 inch to dust", depending on what part of the country you live in. This is basically a mix of all sizes of stone, from dust up to about 50mm stone.

Using this type of fill should ensure that the base under the concrete is solid, without any air voids within it that could, over time, settle and cause cracking of the slab.

The finished depth of stone is normally at least 300mm, (max about 600mm, depending on what your local buildings regs requirements are). The stone is laid in layers not exceeding 150mm and each layer is well compacted using the same sort of vibrating plate as was used for backfilling around the foundations (or whacker plate as it is more commonly known).

The best tool for forming up the slab itself is a mid-sized excavator with an extending front arm and a 2' – 2'6" bucket. This can pick up significant quantities of stone, reach a good distance across the slab area with the extending arm and a good driver can spread the stone evenly over a wide area.

On a level site stoning up the slab is a quick and easy job, but on a sloping site it is a bit more complex as one end of the slab could require a lot more attention and depth of fill than the other.

As the warranty providers and the building regulations inspector do not tend to like this stone layer going any thicker than 600mm in case of future settlement, if you are building on sloping sites where the chances of that happening are quite high (usually at one end of the building), you will possibly need to consider another form of construction for the ground floor.

Usually some form of suspended floor, which is not affected by the varying depths under the slab is a good option in those circumstances.

Your designer should have been able to work out what floor construction will be best when the initial planning drawings were being prepared and the ground / floor levels were calculated.

II. Under Slab drainage / services

Some people prefer to install these services underneath the hardcore, some on top. I have no particular preference except to say that if the drains and services are underneath the stone, you need to be careful not to dislodge or damage them whilst you lay and compact the stone.

The under-slab drainage and services are exactly what they say they are and normally include foul drainage runs (from bathrooms or toilets in internal rooms) and your water connection (note: The electricity, gas and telecom normally come in through the walls).

If you are going to be installing something like an island unit in the kitchen and you will need an electricity or gas supply going to it, you can install ducting under the floor to run cables or pipes in later. Just make sure you get the positioning right. It is a real pain, when you are fitting the kitchen to find your floor socket in the middle of the floor rather than hidden under a unit! – It can also be a devil of a job to put right as it will usually be set in solid concrete!

Your ground worker will usually know exactly what to do to install everything under the slab, so you shouldn't need to get involved, unless you are ordering the materials for them. If that is the case, you probably won't know exactly what to order (material lists and full specifications for this type of thing are not included on standard drawings), so the best thing to do is to get the ground workers to give you a list of everything they need and let *them* measure up, using the drawings / specifications they received with their tender documents. Just make sure everything is ordered and delivered on time so that there are no delays on site.

As with the floor sockets, make sure you double check the positions of each of the service ducts before you finally concrete the slab. Even if they are out of position by just an inch or so, they can cause problems. They can also sometimes be knocked out of position as the rest of the work is done. However, whatever the reason, if they are not in the right place, they could end up coming up under a wall or be too far away from the corner of a room and need to be moved.

III. Sand Blinding

On top of the stone you usually need to spread a layer of sand, about 2" (50mm) thick. The main job of this layer is to protect the DPM (damp proof membrane) from being damaged or punctured by the stone. The whacker plate can be used here to give a smooth and compacted surface to the sand layer.

IV. DPM / Radon barrier

Thick plastic sheeting is laid over the whole of the slab to stop any damp or gas from coming up through the stone and penetrating the concrete slab.

If there is no risk of radon gas being present in the ground, then a simple plastic sheet does the job. However, if there is the chance of Radon gas being present, a different method and materials are used. You should find out whether Radon is present during the design / planning and building regs process, but it would be good for you to do a bit of research on the subject too.

Your ground workers should know what they are doing here, but just make sure that when they lay one piece of sheeting next to another that they allow a good amount of lap (the exact amount should be noted in your building regs specification – usually 300mm). The joints between each sheet should also be taped with waterproof tape.

The edges of the DPM should be taken up the face of the external wall brickwork and draped over the top of it so that it can lap underneath the DPC (damp proof course) that will be installed as part of the external wall construction, to form a damp-proof seal across the whole of the building.

V. Insulation

There are two options for positioning the insulation under a slab.

Option 1) Under the concrete. If you are going to power float the slab (see later), the best place for the insulation is underneath the concrete and on top of the DPM.

Option 2) Over the concrete. If you are going to use a screed as your floor finish, you will usually install the insulation above the concrete slab so that the warmth from within the building is not potentially heating up 8" or more of concrete underneath the flooring before it reaches the insulation (unless you want it to! Some people like the idea of using a concrete floor as a very big radiator (the technical term is thermal mass) where heat is absorbed over a period of time by the concrete and then released slowly back in to the building (I don't think this is a good idea in this situation. Heat rises, so it will take a lot of heat in the room, over a long period of time before there is any noticeable raise in the temperature of the concrete slab. For screeded floors, I recommend insulating on top of the concrete).

The insulation itself normally comes in the form of large 8' x 4' (2.4m x 1.2m) sheets of polystyrene, between 75mm – 125mm thick.

Bear in mind that up to 15% of the heat loss from a house will be through the floor. The polystyrene insulation is one of the cheapest forms of insulation to buy, so putting extra thicknesses of it under the slab will be cheap and should prove to be a very cost effective exercise when it comes to finding ways to lower your energy bills.

VI. Concrete

Again (as just mentioned), there are the two options here:

Option 1) Power float finish. If you are power floating, the concrete itself it will (usually) have been laid on top of the insulation. The power float will be used to give a very smooth shiny surface to the concrete once it has fully set and your floor finishes are then laid directly on to the concrete.

When power floating, you should always try to get the concrete poured as early as possible in the morning, especially if you are pouring a relatively large slab.

You need the concrete to go off (set) enough for you to be able to walk on it at the earliest time possible so that you can start the process of the power floating.

What will often happen, is that you will pour the concrete during the morning and it will be hard enough to walk on by mid-afternoon (especially during the summer months). One or two men will then stay on after the normal shift has ended, to complete the work and may end up working until late in the evening (so some temporary lighting might be needed).

The job is complete when the power float is simply sliding across a dry, shiny surface with no slurry left to spread out.

Most builders will bring in some halogen lights to light up the slab as it gets darker, however a little trick for getting a better finished surface can be also to use car headlights. The low level of the car headlight (about 18" above the ground) can help to highlight imperfections in the slab as the light will tend to cast shadows from even the slightest ridge or bump. These can then be polished out.

The diagram below shows the makeup of a standard power floated slab. Some people might say that you don't need the sand layer as the polystyrene is not going to be able to puncture the dpm, however, I would always recommend using the sand layer.

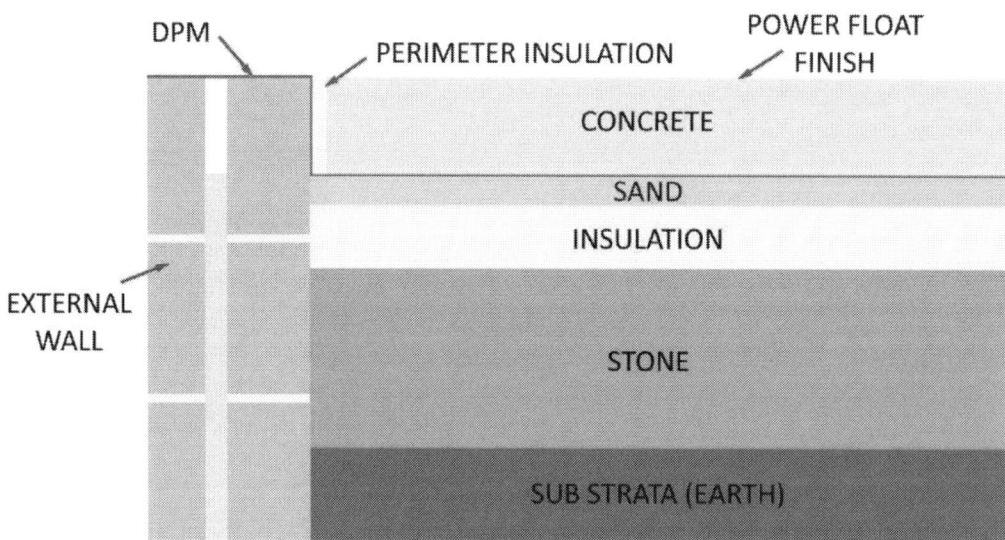

Option 2) Standard concrete slab and screed: If you are planning on using a screed to give the final floor finish, concrete will usually be laid *underneath* the insulation. Where this is this case, the top of the concrete is normally just finished with either a tamped or a trowelled finish. It needs to be flat (with 5mm – 10mm tolerance) but it doesn't need to be particularly smooth, because the screed which will be laid over the top of it later, will create the final finished floor surface.

To my mind, screeding is cheating a bit (and is a costly way of doing so!). The screed is a layer of sand and cement semi dry mix that is trowelled smooth to harden and give the final floor surface, ready for carpets or tiling. The fact that we use it suggests that we are not capable of laying concrete floors well enough or accurately enough for them to do the job the screed ends up having to do.

Screeding is not only an expensive job, it also loses you around a week in progress as it sets very slowly, so no one can go back on to it to carry on working. I always try to find contractors who are happy to use concrete and power float for the floor slab. That way I keep around £3,000 - £4,000 in my pocket and save a week in build time!

Whichever concreting option you take, you will need to install insulation around the perimeter of the building, between the external wall and the concrete slab itself (see diagram above), to avoid losing heat through cold bridging or thermal bridging.

When it comes to laying the concrete slab itself, I strongly suggest that you don't try to mix it yourself, but instead use a pre-mixed concrete brought to site in a wagon. If you try to site mix it, you will end up with areas of the slab going off (setting) before you pour the adjacent section (especially during the summer months). This will affect the strength of the overall slab and the job might even be condemned by the inspectors.

The mix of the concrete will be stipulated on your building regs specification, along with its slump (usually a C30 or C35 mix and a 50mm – 75mm slump).

As with pouring the foundations, try to set things up so you can get the delivery wagons as close to the building as possible so they can use their chute to get to all areas of the building without too much shovelling (this one little action can make the whole job faster and less labour intensive).

If the slab is large, you may need to install expansion joints at certain positions. If they are needed, they should be shown on the drawings and detailed in the building regs.

Use a vibrator poker to make sure the concrete gets into all the corners and around any drainage fittings you may have built in to the slab.

Here is a diagram of a standard screeded concrete floor:

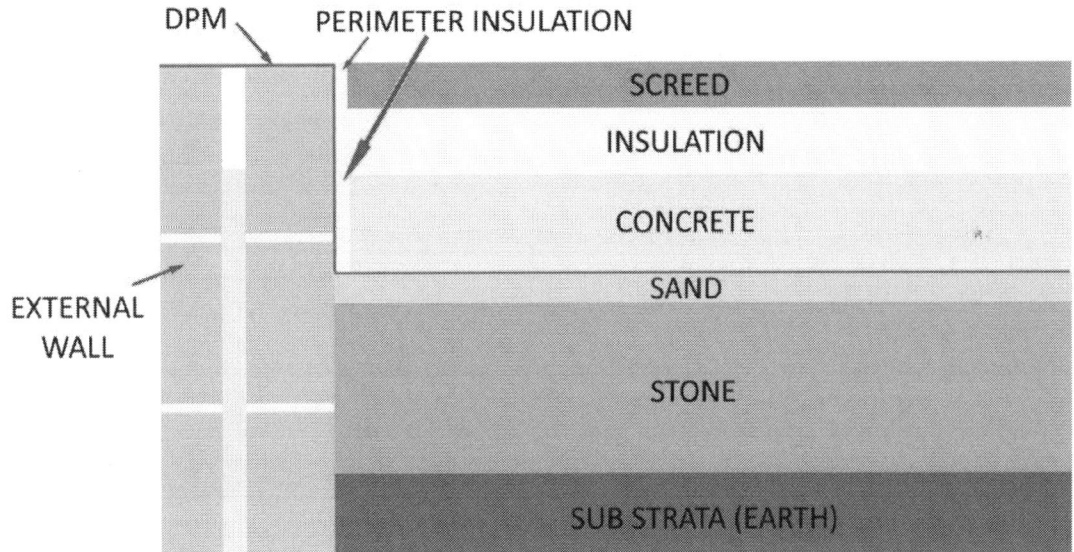

❖ **Beam and block floor**

This type of floor construction is one of the options if you have poor or sloping ground.

The way the system works is that precast reinforced concrete beams are manufactured off site (made to the measurements on the drawings), then brought in and positioned to sit on the external walls (and sometimes on the internal walls) below dpc level. The beams are normally set an exact width apart which allows a standard concrete block to be fitted between them, to form a solid suspended surface which acts as a shutter, ready for insulation to be fitted and a concrete screed to be laid, to create the final floor finish.

Services can be installed under and through the floor as it is being laid, just as with a standard concrete floor.

This image is of a completed beam and block floor. You can see the beams running left to right and the blocks infilling the spaces. The drains have been fitted prior to inserting the blocks and the whole floor has had a cement sand slurry brushed in to the surface.

❖ Suspended timber floor

I quite like this type of construction for the ground floor. It is widely used in other countries and used to be used a lot more in the UK than it is now.

Why do I like it?

- It is quick
- It is a dry process (as opposed to concreting / screeding).
- Amateurs with reasonable wood working skills can lay it if they wish, without having to employ specialists, or bring in wagon loads of concrete and screed, or hire equipment such as whacker plates.
- It doesn't have to set and harden before you can walk and work on it (saving you time and money).
- The insulation can be set directly under the floor board, which is much more efficient when it comes to saving energy, as you don't end up heating the screed or concrete slab as well as the room.
- It is a more sustainable form of construction than concrete.
- I think it has a more pleasant feel than concrete underfoot. Timber floors have natural movement, so they don't feel quite so hard when you walk on them (I like that, although some people don't!)

Downsides? It can creak if you don't lay it properly.

Laying a timber ground floor is pretty much the same as laying the floor joists for the first floor, except that you will also be fitting insulation in between the joists.

The easiest way to fit the insulation is to set 2" x 1" timber battens partway down each joist before it is fitted into the floor. The distance down the joist should be exactly equal to the thickness of the insulation.

I would recommend using up to 200mm of rigid foam insulation rather than polystyrene. This depth of good quality insulation would give you a really warm floor and cut down your energy bills from day one.

Important note: Whenever you use a suspended floor construction, you will need to provide ventilation underneath the floor. This is usually in the form of air bricks built in to the external wall just below dpc level, with ducting allowing the air to travel up from under the floor.

All the details should be on your drawings and in your building regs, but ventilation is a quick and simple job that can often be forgotten as you work on the foundation walls. If you lay the floor without properly installing the ventilation, the inspectors can require you to go back and install it later. This would be a difficult and costly exercise.

- **Using underfloor heating?**

You can pretty much install underfloor heating with any type of ground floor construction. It works well when you use a concrete or beam and block floor with a screed and it can work quite well with a suspended timber floor, but this option is a bit more complicated and costly to lay (look online to find examples of laying underfloor heating on timber floors).

Personally, having used underfloor heating, I would recommend it for self-builders when it is laid in a screed (but would not necessarily recommend it as part of a suspended floor).

It doesn't have to be expensive and it adds a bit of luxury to the finished job. It could also increase the value of your home if and when you come to sell it).

Conclusion

We are now at the end of the first stage of the build.

While you have been working on this stage, as we discussed in earlier chapters, you should also have been preparing for the next stages.

It may seem a bit strange to you that here we are, nearing the end of the book and you are only just starting work. However, this has simply but clearly shown the importance of doing all the preparation works properly.

The fact is that all the work you have been doing prior to starting, is actually pretty much the most important part of the job.

If you have done everything properly so far, *now* will be the time that you start to reap the benefits.

Anyone can build a house, but not many people do it properly. <u>*You and I*</u> are doing it properly!

So, I always look forward to starting work on site because I know that I have, by then done all the hard work and now, as long as I follow my own rules (the ones you have been reading about thus far), I can potentially be looking forward to be moving in to my new home usually in about 10 – 12 weeks from now!

So, get stuck in, build up a head of steam, keep up the pace, concentrate on getting the small details right first time, keep a close eye on your budget, try not to overspend on frivolities and with a bit of luck and a good head wind, you too could hopefully also be moving in to your shiny new home quite soon!

Chapter 12
Building the shell of the house

Introduction

By this stage of the process, you will have chosen the method of construction, so we don't need to go through all the options again in this chapter.

What I am going to do now, is to run through the processes involved in building the shell of the house, using each of the main build methods.

1) Traditional brick / block
2) Timber frame
3) SIPS
4) Closed panel
5) ICF

I'll be approaching each build method from the standpoint of you taking the role of project manager (but not doing any of the building work yourselves). This will allow me to give a general overview of the main processes involved, without me having to go too deeply into the nitty gritty. If I tried to do that, this chapter alone would end up doubling the size of the book and you would probably end up chucking the thing on the fire, after I had bored you rigid with dozens of lists of materials and descriptions of how and where to use each of them!

As I wrote in the introduction, this whole book is concentrating on making you aware of *what you need to know* and *what you don't need to know*. There is no other part of the job like the building of the shell where you could so easily get so bogged down trying to learn every detail, that you could well end up making a complete hash of the whole thing.

Remember:

Let the people who know what they are doing, do what they know how to do!

We will start talking about each of the main build options from the point where the previous chapter ended, with the foundations dug, a concrete slab constructed and all the under-slab services installed.

I am also going to assume you are going to be laying a screed on top of the slab at a later date, as that is the most common way to do it in the UK.

Building the shell

1) Traditional build:

If you chose the traditional build route for the shell of the house, the next 3 – 4 months are going to be the busiest part of the project for you.

As we discussed in an earlier chapter, you might be able to delegate some of the work to people like sales reps for the builders' merchants (letting them work out the quantities you will need for many of the materials), but as project manager it is up to you to make sure that:

I. Everyone arrives on the right day and at the right time.
II. Everything they need is there ready for them.

You will also need to keep on top of the forward ordering of materials so that the various tradespeople don't run out and you end up paying them standing time while you wait for deliveries, or go rushing to the merchants to get what they need in order to get them working again.

So, let's get started at the point where the slab has been poured.

As soon as possible, you now need to get the bricklayers started.

There is a good chance that you will be using the same brickies who built the foundations, to build the main shell of the house. On the other hand, the ground workers may have quoted for all the works underground, in which case you will need to bring a different set of brickies in for the rest of the job.

We'll assume that you are bringing in a different gang.

Some time ago you will have gone through the tendering process and will have had their prices and guide times for completing the work. They should also have told you how many brickies and labourers will be working on your job.

At least couple of weeks before you were due to start on site, you should have made contact with the brickies to make sure they are still going to be free to come and start work when you need them. You should also have sorted out all the ordering of whatever materials and plant you will need to have delivered and ready for them when they arrive.

The size of the bricklaying team is a very important factor in getting the job off to a good start.

For example: If you are building an 1800 sq ft / 4 bed simply designed house, you should aim to get the brickwork and blockwork finished in around 8 – 10 weeks. To do this you will need at least a 2 & 1 gang (this means 2 brickies and 1 labourer). Ideally, if you can get a "4 & 2" gang you should get it finished either on time or early, even if you get a bit of bad weather.

If, on the first morning, the brickie who has said in his tender that he will have the job finished in 8 weeks, turns up on his own, or with just a labourer, you need to get on to him straight away and tell him he will need to find someone else to work with him otherwise he won't be finished in the time he said he would be in his tender and you will fall behind your programme.

If you have managed to include penalty clauses in the contract (where the sub-contractors have to pay a fine if they finish late), you could set your stall out at this early stage, by light-heartedly mentioning the late finishing charges (just to put a bit of pressure on and to show that you are not going to be a pushover).

On a traditional build, in order to get the house finished in a reasonable time, the brickies getting their work done promptly is critical. If they let you down, the knock on effect can easily push your target finishing date back by a number of months. If that happens, your build costs could increase significantly.

What do the brickies need?

The first thing you need to do when organising the materials and plant for the brickies is to remember that this is not a DIY project! This is serious stuff and you need to understand that you are employing professional people, who need to make a living from this work.

I remember my first self-build project where I treated it as a big DIY project and it ended taking me far too long to build as well as costing me a lot more money to build than it should have done.

For example:

I bought a little DIY mixer for £120, thinking that I was being very astute and saving the cost of hiring a mixer in at £20 / week. Buying this bit of plant would also mean that at the end of the job I would get to keep it! Wrong choice! As soon as the brickies saw it they sent me off to get a proper mixer that would be big enough to turn out the mortar mixes at the rate they needed them.

So, I ended up paying for a big mixer *and* a little mixer and the brickies straight away knew that I didn't know what I was doing! So, if they had a mind to, they could probably get away with things that they shouldn't really get away with!

To back this up, the photo below shows a job I did a few years later where I project managed a traditional house being built in ten weeks. We actually had **two** big mixers running full time to keep the brickies going!

So, you need the proper kit for the job. Which means that you will need to organise the following items (this list is not exhaustive, but should cover the main items. Check your spec and drawings and talk to your subbies to make sure you include everything they need).

- **Facing bricks:** To get the best prices, you will usually be best ordering these in full loads of up to 10,000 bricks. That is a lot of bricks and you will need a lot of room to store them. Make sure you have an area designated for them, preferably close to the building (but not in the way of the scaffolding), so the labourers don't have to carry them too far and somewhere where the delivery vehicle can get to, turn around and be able to get out of the site just as easily. Make sure you have had your choice of brick approved by the planners before you order them).
- **Blocks:** Again, to get the best prices, you are best ordering these in full loads. Get them as close to the building as possible and make sure the delivery vehicle has good access and egress.
- **Concrete common bricks:** These are a fairly cheap brick used where the full sized concrete blocks are too large for a particular job and would need to be cut, which would slow the job down and cost you extra money to pay the brickies for cutting them. Buying these one pack at a time should be ok. You don't usually need too many.
- **Special bricks:** This covers things like plinth bricks / angled corner bricks / air bricks / contrasting bricks (for architectural features) etc.

- **Cement:** Check the spec in case you need a special type of cement (possibly because of the ground conditions). I would normally order cement by the pallet load during the early stages of a job, then when you get near the end of the brickwork phase, try to order just enough to finish.
- **Building sand:** You will use this for the blockwork skin of the wall, but possibly not for the brickwork skin (see below). To get the best price and if you have room on site, you will usually be advised to buy this loose in at least 10 ton loads (*this will work out a lot cheaper than buying the 1-ton bags that you see in the builders' yards*). You need to locate the sand pile right next to the mixer, so the labourer can stand by the sand, and shovel it straight in to the mixer.
- **Cavity Insulation:** This will be detailed on your specification. Again, the larger the load, the better chance you have of getting the best prices. However, (especially if you are using the rigid foam insulation) this product can be both bulky and expensive. It is also easy to steal, so you would be advised to store it in a lockable container.
- **Insulation clips:** Where appropriate (to hold the insulation in position).
- **Wall Ties:** Make sure you get the right ones, there are many different types (check your building regulations specification).
- **DPC:** You'll need different types and widths for different locations (again, check the spec to make sure you order the right stuff).
- **Mortar plasticiser:** The brickies use this to make the mortar more workable. It is a liquid, available at all merchants and usually comes in 1 gallon and 5 gallon containers. Get at least 5 gallons to get you going.
- **"Spot" boards:** These are simply squares of plywood (around 2' sq), onto which the brickies: a) empty the mix from the mixer b) put the small amounts of mortar on, next to where they are working.
- **Water:** You'll need either a water butt or a running water supply, positioned right next to the mixer.
- **Cavity Closers:** If applicable. Check the specification.
- **Lintels:** For above doors and windows. Your specification should give you the sizes, makes and ordering codes for these.
- **Possibly dummy door and window frames:** These are sometimes used to build in as the brick and blockwork is forming up the openings. Dummy frames help to ensure that the openings are plumb and square. If they aren't, then the doors and windows might not fit properly. A good brickie tends not to need these, but you are sometimes better safe than sorry. Your joiner might be able to come to site to knock these together for you if you ask nicely!
- **Coloured sand / mortar:** I mentioned that you possibly wouldn't use the building sand for the brickwork. That is because (as we discussed earlier in the book), you will usually probably want to put a colour into the mortar that accentuates the colour of the brick (this is very common on new homes).

Standard mortar colour is usually a boring whitish / grey colour once it dries out and can spoil the look of a wall built with a nice brick, so colouring the joint with a matching or contrasting colour can really make a difference to the look of the finished house.

There are now specialist companies around the country who can supply these coloured mortars in a variety of guises and you will often find that brick merchants will have linked up with such companies and have a brochure or sample board of all the colours in their showroom.

There are three main options when it comes to using mortar dyes, these are:

1) **Powder / liquid additive:** You can use your standard building sand and simply mix in a mortar dye (either in powder or liquid), to each mix that the brickies prepare on site.

    Personally, I don't think this is a good option. If you use even slightly different proportions of the dye in each mix, the mortar, once it has dried out will look very patchy, with different shades all over the house.

A good labourer will make sure they put exactly the right amount of dye in by using some sort of measuring jug, but even then, they might throw a couple more shovels full of sand and extra cement in to the mixer without thinking, which can thin the density of the dye, - which can, in turn alter the shade of the mortar once it has dried. This is a difficult operation to monitor and you are trusting someone who is not usually fully trained to do this job, so in my opinion this is not the best choice.

2) **Ready mixed with sand (or, as it is often called, mortar).** You can buy this in either 1-ton bags or in large loads, either way, it has the dye already mixed in to it. This will come from a specialist supplier and will have been accurately mixed at their plant, with an exact amount of dye used per ton of sand. It will be quite a bit more expensive than standard building sand (or building sand plus liquid or powdered dye), but at least you will know that, as long as the brickies use the right amount of cement in each mix, you should get the same colour dried finish to all the brickwork. (Note: Always remember to get some standard building sand for the blockwork, to save you using the expensive coloured mortar on block walls *which are not going to be seen* when the job is finished).

3) **Ready mixed mortar:** The way this works is that you hire large plastic tubs from the supplier (about 0.25 cu metre), then, whenever you need fresh mortar, the supplier will mix the amount you need at the mixing plant and bring it to site, then fill the tubs using a chute from attached to the delivery vehicle. The mix that comes to site will include the dye, the cement and a retarder that stops it going off at the normal rate. The inclusion of the retarder allows you to use the same tub of mortar for up to a couple of days (as long as you keep it covered with something like a sheet of plywood). This will be the most expensive option if you plan to use coloured mortars, but it saves you having to stockpile the coloured sand.

You will still probably need the mixer and cement etc. for the blockwork but in some circumstances, using the tubs can be a sensible option.

I have often used these premix mortars on the larger commercial jobs and occasionally on self builds. The biggest disadvantage I have found is that if you don't use it all before it starts to go off, it just tends to get left in the tub and sets hard. It is then very difficult to get out, unless you have something like a forklift on site, to turn the tub over in order to remove the block of now solid mortar. You then need to dispose of it, usually in a skip. So, if you don't use the whole mix in the brickwork, you are not only going to be wasting expensive mortar, but you will also be paying to get rid of what's left.

Bricklayers payments / prices:

Before the brickies start work, you should make sure you clarify how they are going to be paid.

On this sort of project, it is normal to pay them on what is called "a price", which means "so much" per thousand bricks laid.

The rates will vary around the country but, at the time of writing in early 2016, they are tending to be somewhere in the range of £350 - £500 / 1000 bricks laid, £9 - £14 / sq m for laying 4" blocks and around £13 - £16 for laying 6" blocks. When you go out to tender you will soon see what the going rate is in your area and it is up to you whether you pay more for someone you think will do a better job.

You will also need to agree how you will measure the work done for calculating each payment. There are some give and take areas that need to be considered:

- Long straight runs are easy money for the brickies.
- It takes longer to build a corner and the sides of a window or door opening than a straight run of brickwork.

- It takes a while to set DPCs (damp proof courses), lintels, fix insulation etc.

So, what tends to be the most common way to agree payments is to *measure through*. This means that you ignore the window and door openings and pay for them as if they were solid brick and blockwork. The extra you pay for the non-existent bricks and blocks will make up for the extra time taken to do the fiddly bits. This also makes the job of measuring up and agreeing quantities for payment much faster and easier as the brickie can easily double check the measure by just measuring the size of the full wall.

One thing you don't want to do *if at all possible* is to pay day rates or daywork for the whole (or even part) of the project. The term is almost a swear word for any professional site manager!

What daywork means to anyone who has been in the business for a few years is:

"Don't worry about coming in on time, don't work too hard, take longer breaks, stop and have a few chats during the day, then pack up and head off home early"!

Avoid daywork like the plague wherever possible (and if anyone insists on it for a full house build, don't use them). It is, however a necessary evil for some parts of the job, where specialist work is needed. So just be careful and be aware that slow brickies will always try to get the jobs on daywork rather than a price.

Payment terms:

You will normally agree to pay the brickies either weekly or fortnightly on a Friday.

Make sure that whatever you do agree, you stick with it. If you don't pay them on time they might not be there the following Monday. That is just how the industry works.

This means you need to make sure you have your cash flow sorted, so that there is always sufficient money in the bank to make these regular payments. For a traditionally built house, this could mean having cash to cover up to 16 (or possibly even more) weekly payments, depending on the size and complexity of the house.

Your mortgage stage payment schedule becomes important here.

There could be quite a long period of time between the stage mortgage payment coming in for the foundations and the next one coming in for the roof (sometimes up to 3 – 4 months on a traditional brick and block house). So, not only will you need to pay the brickies for their work during this time, but you could also need to pay suppliers' invoices, along with paying deposits to order materials for later in the project (such as kitchens / bathrooms etc.)

This cash flow pressure is one of the big drawbacks with traditional build The slowness of the build puts financial pressure on you all the way through the job. The faster the build, the shorter the intervals between stage payments and the more positive your cash flow becomes.

Scaffolding:

On a traditional build, the scaffold goes up with the brick / blockwork. Brickwork and blockwork is built in stages called lifts. Each lift (i.e. a lift of brickwork or a lift of blockwork) forming a cavity wall should be a maximum height of about 1.4m before you back it up (in other words, if you build the brickwork skin of the wall up first, once you reach 1.4m height, you should then build the blockwork skin, in order to ensure that the wall is sufficiently strong to stand up on its own while the mortar sets).

Scaffolding lifts should roughly coincide with the lifts on the wall. In reality, a lift for the scaffolding usually comes in at about 1.8m.

The way this usually works, is that the brickies will build a lift of brickwork and blockwork, then let it go off (set) for a couple of days while they do the same somewhere else on the building. They will then come back and build up the first lift to a height of about 6' (1.8m), which is roughly head height.

The scaffolders will then come back and erect their first lift of scaffolding

Each time the brickies complete another lift, you need to make sure the scaffolders are primed to return to site promptly, to ensure that the brickies are not held up.

You will normally agree (before you start work) with the scaffolding company how many lifts you will need in total and it is always sensible to bring the brickies into that discussion, to make sure they are happy with what you decide.

I would also recommend that you ask the joiners what height they need a scaffold platform setting at for when they construct the roof.
There is often conflict between the brickies and joiners about the level of the top scaffold lift. The problem is that all the different trades tend to have different ways of working, so you need to try to agree a compromise that everyone can work with.
As long as the scaffolding is safe and adequate for the task, there are no hard and fast rules about what heights the platforms should be, however, personally I tend to go with a thing called a foot lift on each job as it tends to make things work better between the brickies and the joiners. Speak to your brickies, joiners and scaffolders to see if this would be the best option for your own job.

If you have a gabled roof or other roof features, you will probably need extra smaller lifts of scaffolding up the sides of the house (getting smaller as they go higher), called hop-ups. These allow access to build the brickwork / blockwork up to the apex of the roof and allow the joiners to work at the highest point of the roof.

Here is a photo of a standard scaffold from a house I built a few years ago.

You can see a hop up on the left gable. From the height of the first lift of scaffolding, I can tell that there will originally have been a foot lift on this job, however it looks like it has been taken away at the request of the rendering contractor (to make his job easier).

You can also see a couple of premix mortar tubs at the front of the house. I am guessing that these have been left there because they are full of set, unused mortar (which we will have had to find a way of getting out of the tubs before the supplier would pick them up empty!)

Also of note on this site is the tight storage area, which has forced me to use the 1 ton bags of building sand (the bag at the front of the plot), rather than getting 10 ton loads of loose sand delivered. This will have added extra cost to the project over all.

(Note: The sharp eyed amongst you will notice a number of health and safety issues with the scaffold in the photo, but the job was just about finished at this time and the scaffold is being stripped, so no one except the scaffolders will be going onto it. Anyway, that's my excuse and I'm sticking to it!).

Building the shell:

Keep your eyes open: As a project manager, you don't need to know everything about what the bricklayers are doing. If they are good sub-contractors, the drawings, specifications and the warranty inspectors should be all that is needed to ensure that they produce a good quality finished structure.

Even if you had a high level of knowledge about bricklaying, you would still not be able to watch every brickie lay every brick, to make sure they are doing it right. Trying to do so would only cause friction in any case. Imagine someone staring constantly over your shoulder as you do whatever job it is that you do, after a while you would probably tell them where to stick their job.

However, having said that, it is always handy to have a basic idea about what your sub-contractors are doing, so you can just occasionally have a quiet word when something doesn't look quite right. Just doing this, using a friendly but firm approach, has the effect of making them think that you *do* know a bit about what they are doing and tends to make them take more care to get the work right first time.

Here are a few things to watch out for:

The brickies will normally start by building two corners up to about 3' high in a pyramid shape. Once this is done they can simply attach their string line to the right course at each corner and "fill in" the rest of the wall, one course at a time, forming up any window and door openings as they go along. As they do so, keep your eyes open for:

- **Plumb walls:** Get a decent spirit level and keep it in the car. Don't go round checking the walls when the brickies are there, but after they have gone home, walk round the building with your level and check that everything is plumb. Often the levels the brickies use get a bit battered on site and sometimes don't read completely accurately. This could result in the walls going out of plumb by as much as an inch or more over the height of one storey of the house. If this happens it can cause all sorts of problems later on, especially with things like fitting the windows, external doors, door linings and architraves.
- **Cavity widths:** Building inspectors like to see cavities staying the same width all the way up the building and can get a bit niggly if they get wider or narrower, even by a few millimetres. I am not quite sure why this is apart from just wanting the walls to be nice and plumb. Structurally the cavities don't really do anything except form a gap (which we now sometimes fill with insulation anyway), so a few millimetres over a 5m height would not usually cause any major problems. In any case, to avoid the inspectors pulling you up, as you are checking the walls for plumb, also just watch the cavity widths.
- **Wall ties sloping down towards the outside of the wall:** The job of the wall tie is to give structural stability to the two skins of the wall and also to stop the passage of moisture from the outside skin of a cavity wall to the inside skin. For this reason, when the brickies bed them into the mortar, they should ensure that there is a slight slope outwards, so that any moisture within the cavity will not be able to travel up the slope to get to the inside skin.
- **Empty cavities:** If mortar gets dropped on to the wall ties as the wall is built, it theoretically gives moisture a bridge to cross the cavity and create damp spots on the inside walls. Keep a check on this by shining a torch down the cavities to make sure all the ties are clean. If they are not, the brickies can normally use a long piece of 2" x 1" batten to chip off any lumps of mortar.
  There is actually a simple way to stop the mortar from falling into the cavity in the first place. It is called a cavity batten and is simply a piece of wood (the same width as the cavity) with string at either end. The batten is kept in the cavity as the wall is built up, with the string lines being used to move it up as the brickwork is built.
  With the batten correctly positioned, any mortar that is dropped simply lands on it and can then be easily removed.
  Building inspectors are usually quite keen on keeping their eyes on the cavities.

- **Wall ties doubled up at openings:** Generally, the spacing for wall ties is 900mm horizontally and 450mm vertically (this is the size of a standard slab of cavity insulation). However, at openings (doors and windows), the vertical spacing reduces to 225mm (i.e. they double up). Brickies can occasionally forget this and keep them at 450mm centres. If the inspectors catch this, they will ask for the error to be remedied, which could mean taking the wall down and starting again.
- **Perpendicular openings:** The brickwork "reveals" (the sides of the window and door openings) need to be perfectly plumb in both directions. If they are out of plumb by just a few millimetres there is a good chance you will have problems with fitting the windows and door frames.
- **Insulation fitted properly:** Fitting cavity insulation is a fiddly job. It needs care to install it correctly and if there is no-one around closely supervising, it is easy just to *accidentally miss a bit*, hoping that no one will notice. Also, these days on traditional build, in order to achieve the minimum required insulation values, you will often need incorporate a 3" or 4" cavity (as opposed to the traditional 2" used previously). The cavity then sometimes has 2" or 3" of solid foam insulation fixed to the inside skin of the wall, leaving a 1" or 2" cavity. The insulation should be fitted neatly, and clipped to the wall ties with manufacturer approved fittings, to hold it in place (tight up to the inside skin). If the fittings (usually plastic clips) are missed, the insulation can, in time, fall across the cavity and form a moisture bridge.

  Look out for this during the building process by again shining a torch down the cavities. If you have built up more than around 1m above where the insulation is loose, it will be a difficult problem to put right, so this is another reason to keep a watchful eye on the cavities after the brickies have gone home in the evenings.
- **Good quality joints:** The brickwork is one of the most important aesthetic features of your house. A good brickie can really give the finished job a real look of quality, however, a bad brickie can leave it looking a real mess and reduce its value by thousands of pounds.

  An integral part of making the brickwork look good is choosing the right joint. The four main choices for finishing the brickwork joints are:

Raked out (or recessed)

Weathered

Bucket handle

Flush

Personally, I find that the best joint to give an attractive finish is raked out. The bricklayers have a special tool to do this job, which gives a quick and very tidy finish to the edges at both the top and bottom of the joint. This is especially useful on textured bricks as it accentuates their edge features.

The only problem with a raked out joint, is that it is not quite as weather resistant as some of the other joints and so is not recommended on very exposed walls. Check with the building inspector to see whether or not this type of joint is suitable for your project.

The weathered joint is quite easy to do, but the bottom edge of the joint can often look a bit tatty with the mortar following the texture and shape of the brick up and down along each course. This is fine on bricks with sharp edges, but not so good on hand made bricks, which can be quite irregular in shape. This is, however, a good joint for exposed walls.

The bucket handle joint can be quite attractive, but takes a level of skill and concentration to finish each joint tidily (again, especially with handmade / irregular shaped bricks). This is a good joint for weather proofing.

The flush joint is the easiest to achieve. It is also weather-proof and probably the most commonly used joint on new homes in the UK.

Other things to watch with the brickwork joints include:

➢ **Regular mortar thicknesses** on each course. Each mortar bed should be 10mm wide.
➢ *Mortar runs* **down the face of the brickwork** (usually caused by rain while the mortar is still wet). You can usually prevent runs by providing hessian sheets for the bricklayers to cover the freshly built walls with whenever it starts raining and before they go home at night.
➢ **Make sure the perps are in line**: The perps are the vertical joints between the bricks. The word perp is short for perpendicular. They should be exactly above each other on every other course. They usually are, but occasionally you'll see brickwork where, possibly because of odd sized bricks, the perps have wandered a bit, which, unless care is taken by the brickies, can make the wall look horrible (see below):

Good perps

Bad perps

- **Make sure openings are in the right places:** This may sound fairly obvious, but it is quite an easy error to make. Errors in setting out can cause major problems later, so just spending half an hour with the drawings and a tape measure, going around each floor as it is built to check door and window positions, is a useful exercise to do.
- **Lintels seated correctly:** The correct seating for a lintel is 150mm (6"). Sometimes this is not possible to achieve (e.g. *across* a 4" / 100mm wall), but in general the inspectors will be looking for at least 150mm seating on each side of any opening (8" one side and 4" the other will not be acceptable).
  Lintels tend to be made to suit standard door and window sizes, so all you need to do is add 300mm (12") to the opening width on the drawings and then order the nearest lintel size (equal to or a bit longer than that measurement).
- **Cavity trays / weep holes:** Cavity trays are fitted above openings and are intended to catch any moisture that may enter the cavity above the opening and fall towards the top of the window or door below it, then to guide it out through a purpose made gap in the external skin (*rather than it potentially dropping on to lintels and finding its way to the inside skin of a cavity wall*).

They can be made from a wide section of DPC, lead or other appropriate materials. Weep holes are simply perp joints which are left empty where there is a cavity tray, to allow any moisture to run through it, to the outside of the building. Weep holes are often forgotten about by the brickies, so keep your eyes open to make sure they go in. The specification will detail where they go and how many you should be creating. You can get preformed plastic weep hole formers if you want to make things look as neat as possible (see image).

Cavity tray:

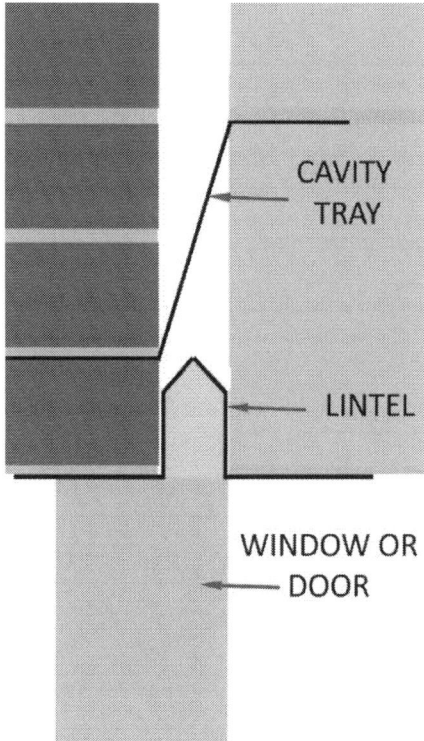

- **Wasted bricks / blocks:** Brickies are notorious for wasting bricks and blocks. If you are paying £500 / £1000 for your bricks, that's 50p each! Blocks could be anywhere between 70p and £2.00 each.
  What will tend to happen is that wasted bricks and blocks will accumulate under the scaffolding, as they get dropped or kicked off the scaffold, by either the brickies or scaffolders (when they come to adjust or clean the scaffold).
  Speak to them at the start of the job and if you see excessive waste happening during the building works, remind them and threaten to charge them for needlessly wasted materials.
  The other main place that bricks and blocks are wasted, is in the storage area.
  If deliveries are simply stacked on the soil without at least being on some stone, plastic sheeting or pallets, when it rains, the soil will turn into mud and can quickly ruin a full layer or two of bricks.
  Also beware of vehicles passing the stacked bricks, which can splash mud onto them. Once you get mud on a brick, it is usually difficult and time consuming to get them clean again. So, always stack bricks (and other similar materials) on pallets and make sure you cover them with plastic sheeting or hessian (fixed down to avoid it being blown away in strong winds).
- **Cleaning out the mixer at the end of each day:** It is easy to forget about cleaning the mixer at the end of each day (especially on Friday!) If this happens, the following morning (or the following Monday), you'll often end up with a big lump of solid mortar inside the drum which needs to be got rid of before you can start work. 5 minutes every evening, rinsing the inside of the drum out is all that is needed to avoid this. The easiest way to clean the mixer is to put a few half bricks in with some water and run it for a few minutes. Empty it out and keep the bricks by the side of the mixer for doing the same thing the following day.
- **Leaving the water running:** This is an annoying habit of some labourers. They will leave a hose filling a water butt and go off to do another job. The butt overflows and the water creates a mud / sand bath in the area

where they do the mixing. This was not too bad when water wasn't metered, but now, leaving a hose running is going to cost you money (as well as making the site muddy and dangerous).

- **Leaving cement uncovered:** You will normally buy cement by the pallet load of around 56 bags. The labourers will uncover it in the morning. They should then cover it at night and whenever it starts raining. Just a little bit of water can ruin a *full pallet* of cement (costing you a lot of money (over £150 for a pallet load) and meaning you have to throw the unused bags in to a skip, which you then have to pay to get taken away.
- **Leaving coloured mortar uncovered:** The coloured dye in mortar can wash out if it gets rained on. Keep it covered at all times.
- **Altering the scaffolding and not saying anything to anyone:** This is a very common occurrence on all building sites and can be extremely dangerous.

    A ladder, a scaffold board, a toe board or hand rail can sometimes get in the way of the men trying to do a particular job and they will often just alter it so that they can carry on. Then, once they have finished what they are doing, they forget to put the scaffold back to how it was.

    This could leave the scaffold in a dangerous condition for anyone else using it.

    Make sure that all the trades know that they are **not to** alter the scaffold without permission and if you are concerned that something on the scaffold might have been altered, always get the scaffolder to call in to check it.

One of the biggest dangers on scaffold is trap ends". This is where the end of a board has been moved from its original position and not replaced, leaving one end which doesn't any longer sit on a support tube.
If someone stands on one of these planks, it can tilt and the person can fall straight through. Keep your eyes open for these traps. Also look out for:

- *Ladders which are not securely tied at the top.*
- *Ladders which are too steep (steeper than 1:4 slope).*
- *Ladders which are in a poor state of repair.*
- *Missing or loose handrails.*
- *Scaffold tube ends sticking out dangerously.*
- *Anything else that simply doesn't look right!*

Following health and safety requirements

Safety is big business on a building site these days. If anyone gets badly injured, there is often legal action taken against the person responsible (As the person who owns the site and whose project it is, this could be **you,** even if you don't have anything to do with the actual day to day running of, or safety on the site).

Check the **CDM** requirements. You are legally bound to follow them, even if your site is not of a size which means that you have to formally register it. Make sure to follow them at all time.

Progressing the brickwork / blockwork:

Part of the job of a project manager is to plan ahead and keep everything moving, by making sure everything and everyone is there at the right time and that everyone knows what they are doing.

With this in mind, while you are getting the brickwork started you should also be thinking about the follow-on activities.

With traditional construction, these normally include:

- Joiners, for setting the joists and erecting the roof trusses. You also need to be agreeing their overall contract package for the on-going works after the shell is up.
- External windows and doors.
- Roof structure.
- Fascias / soffits / barge boards / guttering.
- Felt / batten / roof tiling.
- Electricians.
- Plumbers.

Here are some thoughts on how to deal with each of those tasks:

Joiners

The first real job for joiners on the majority of self-build projects will be to set the first floor joists.

On a traditional build, once the brickies reach the top of the ground floor walls they normally stop for a couple of days to allow the joiners to set the joists.

Joists are usually set on top of the blockwork (but can also be hung in joist hangers between the walls).

You should have a joist layout drawing as part of your building regs submission and the details of the joists themselves should be on your specification.

You will need to get everything ordered, so that all the materials are on site on the day the brickies finish the ground floor walls (if you are not sure of what you need to order, ask the joiners for advice).

If you get everything you need to site and ready, on a simple 4-bed detached house, the joiners should have the joists set in one or two days, after which the brickies can carry straight on with the brick and blockwork to the upper floors (remember to get the scaffold lifts organised too).

One thing you need to avoid if at all possible here, is for the bricklayers to go off and start another job while they wait for you to get the joists sorted. If they are getting stuck into another job, the chances are you will have to wait for them to get to a suitable point in that job before you get them back. This could lose you a couple of weeks or more on your own job.

If the brickwork is reaching joists level towards the end of the week, try to get the joiners to work over the weekend to set the joists. That way the brickies can get straight back to work on your project on the Monday and won't need to go anywhere else.

External windows and doors

There are different ways to approach the fitting of the windows and doors.

1) **Fit as you build:** Taking this option helps to avoid the possibility of the units not fitting in the openings, but if this is the option you take, you need to make sure that you provide adequate protection to the frames so they are not damaged by falling bricks, mortar or other debris.

2) **Fit after the build:** This obviously opens you up to the possibility of the openings being built too small or out of plumb, but negates the risk of the frames being damaged. It is a good idea to get dummy frames made up, which can be built in as the openings are formed. That way the chances of the windows not fitting are considerably reduced. The joiners will normally knock up these frames for you.

It boils down to a personal choice and experience, as to which option you take. Either way make sure you order the windows in plenty of time to ensure delivery when you need them.

To fit windows and external doors to an average 4-bed new home will normally take between one and two days. If you have bi folds, or anything special that has cost a lot of money, I would suggest fitting them once the roof is on and you are sealing in the building, that way there is less likelihood of them getting damaged.

When you order windows and doors, always remember to deduct 10mm off the structural opening size for the size of the windows themselves. If you don't, I can almost guarantee that they won't fit!

*You also need to make sure that this tolerance is only allowed by ONE person (either you or the supplier). It has been known for the joiners to **add 10mm** to the opening sizes for the dummy frames, as well as the manufacturers **taking the 10mm off** the structural size for the windows themselves. If this were to happen, you could end up with a window that is 20mm smaller than the opening.*

I normally make a point of stating on a **written order**, to the manufacturer that I have **not** allowed any tolerance for the window sizes, either on the specification or on site and that the supplier **should therefore deduct 10mm** from the width and height for the manufacture process. By writing this down, it makes it clear who is responsible and it reduces the chance of any error.

Roof Structure:

Trusses: If you are using roof trusses, on a simple, four cornered building, constructing the roof frame is normally quite a simple task.

You will have sent the drawings off to the truss suppliers at the tender stage and you will also have sent the drawings to the joiners as part of their tender package.

Normally the trusses come as a package with pretty much everything they need to construct the roof, except for the fascias, soffits and barge boards. So once you have organised who is doing what and when, you should only really need to sort out providing a few minor items.

The building control and warranty inspectors will need to check the structure before you cover it with felt and batten, so you don't need to know every detail of the roof construction (make sure you book them at least a couple of days before the frame is complete).

If you want to use the attic space for extra rooms or storage, you can swap the standard trusses for attic trusses. These are basically more chunky trusses, manufactured with a large empty space in the middle. Once they are all set in place, the empty spaces form a long open area, which can then be formed into living or storage space.

Attic trusses are more expensive than standard trusses and will usually need a crane to lift them, but to get the benefit of a whole extra floor, in my opinion they are a great idea.

Attic trusses

Traditional or hand cut roof

If you are including living or storage area within the roof, but attic trusses are not suitable, you will usually need to build the structure in situ. This is also known as a hand cut roof.

To build a hand cut roof you need to employ good quality, experienced carpenters. In any hand cut roof you will find that there are a lot of quite complicated cuts, angles and joints to create, so whoever does it needs to know what they are doing and be capable of forming these cuts quickly and accurately.

Ordering materials for this type of roof is going to be a lot more complicated for you as a project manager, as there could potentially be dozens of different components. To help you with this task, you can ask for help from the joiners and / or you can pick the brains of the timber supplier.

If you send a set of drawings to your timber merchant, there is a good chance they will have a quantity surveyor within their ranks who would be able to do the full take off of all the materials required. They may charge you for this service but it will probably be worth paying the charge to avoid over or under ordering.

A hand cut roof is always going to be a slow and costly job, but at the end of the day, by designing this living space within the roof, you are making far more efficient use of the overall space within the building, so as long as it is not prohibitively expensive, it is usually worth the cost, the time and the effort (by the way, before trusses came along, this was the way most residential roofs were built).

Fascias / soffits / bargeboards / guttering

These are the finishing items for the roof structure. The main material choices for the fascias and soffits etc. are treated softwood or plastic.

If you choose softwood, you will need to paint or stain the timber, both before you use it and once it has been fitted, making sure that you re-treat any newly cut ends.

If you choose one of the plastic options (and there are many to choose from), you obviously don't need to treat them before use and they have the advantage that they don't generally need any significant maintenance during their lifetime.

Guttering / downpipes

These are usually plastic, but if you are looking for a more traditional appearance there are some nice cast iron products available. There are even plastic gutters / downpipes, which look like cast iron, but which are priced somewhere between standard plastic and genuine cast iron.

It is a good idea to at least fix the guttering (if not the downpipes) before taking the scaffolding down, rather than trying to fit them whilst standing on ladders later.

You will need to measure up what you need and order everything, ready for either the joiners or the plumbers to fix (I tend to give this job to the joiners where possible, as they are usually already working on the roof structure).

If you are not sure about the exact type and number of fittings you need, just either ask the tradesmen to measure up and give you a list to order, or give the drawings to the supplier to measure.

Felt / battens / roof tiling:

You will have already chosen the roof tiles as part of your full planning application.

I suggest keeping control of the ordering of the roof tiles (rather than give the task to the roofers), as doing so allows you to negotiate on price and shop around. In some cases, however, the roofers will get the best price, if you tell them exactly what products to get prices for.

If you are going to price the roof tiles yourselves, you could still ask the roofers to quote for supplying the felt, batten and fixings. That way they will make sure they have everything they need to start work and you won't be responsible for any under-ordering or delays in deliveries on these materials.

If you do order the roof tiles don't forget to include all the ancillary stuff like ridge tiles and verges. The chances are that you probably won't know what to order or how much of it you'll need so (as usual), it is a good idea to pick the brains of the experts (the merchants) by giving them a set of drawings and simply asking them to price for everything you need. It would also be prudent to get the roofers to check their quotes, to make sure they are happy with everything.

As a project manager, your task for this section of the works is to:

- Make sure the roof has been constructed properly so the inspectors will pass it first time.
- Get the inspectors in at the right time.
- Make sure all materials are there when needed.
- Check that the scaffold is ready for both the joiners and the roof tilers and that it is safe.
- Make sure the roofers turn up on time and stay until the end of their section of the work (or at least that they don't leave site for anything until the building is weathertight).

There is not a lot more you need to get involved in unless you are taking on some of the physical work yourself.

Electricians & plumbers

You will need to keep in touch with the electricians and plumbers whilst the shell of the house is going up to make sure they are organised to start their section of the work as soon as it is ready for them to do so.

I will be looking at all the electrical and plumbing installations in the next chapter.

Mortgage payments with traditional build

Building traditionally, you will normally receive a payment once you have constructed the ground floor slab and your next payment will often be once you reach wall plate level (top of upstairs windows). This can mean you having to last for a number of months between payments (as we discussed earlier). So just make sure that your finances are going to be able to stand the strain!

Conclusion on building the shell of the house traditionally

Using the traditional build method means that there will have been a lot of work for you to do to get the shell of the house up and weathertight, so the chances are that you will have probably found this section of work to be quite stressful.

To reduce the levels of stress, as I have been saying throughout the book, the trick is to always to try to delegate any of the work you can to the experts, especially where you are not 100% sure of what you are doing, or where you don't have the time to learn everything you need to learn.

As you read through the next three options where you are project managing a *timber frame, SIPS* or *closed panel* frame, things are generally going to be a lot easier.

2) Timber Frame:

The timber frame takes the place of the inside skin of the external wall (in other words the blockwork) on a traditional build and it included all the internal walls. It carries the weight of the roof and passes it down to the foundations. The frame package also normally includes the roof trusses.

The brickwork skin of the external wall does not normally do much (if any) of the loadbearing work. It is generally there for aesthetics. In most houses, you could remove the brickwork without having any significant impact on the structural stability of the house.

For a self-builder, one of the benefits of using a timber shell is that by doing so, a large chunk of your house comes in one package, saving you from having to do a lot of the work that you need to do with traditional build.

The first big practical difference between traditional and timber frame construction on site, is that you will usually need to have the scaffold erected on three sides before the frame arrives.

As it was with the traditional build method, before you get the scaffold erected, you should speak to the brickies and the frame company to find out what levels they need the scaffold platforms to be set at.

You will also need to ask the timber frame supplier how far away from the frame the scaffold uprights need to be to allow them to erect the frame and then make sure the brickies can work with that distance (*this distance is quite important and often causes problems if not given the attention it needs*).

As I mentioned, the scaffold needs to go around three sides of the building before the frame is delivered (usually leaving the side nearest to the road open). This is because, although the frame goes up pretty quickly, the individual timber frame panels are usually carried into position by the erectors, so they need access into the building from wherever the delivery vehicle will be parked.

The scaffolders will then need to return to complete the ground floor level of the fourth side once all the panels to each floor are in position.

There is a train of thought that says the scaffolding should go up to all four sides, with just a small gap being left in the front to allow the panels to be carried through. In practice, I tend to think that this would not work as well as it appears to do in theory. However, I have never put the idea to the test, so I could be wrong!

The timber frame package

The timber frame package will usually come with most of the panels up to around 8' long. This panel size allows two men to carry them from the delivery wagon and set them where they need to be in the building.

To get the panels up to the first floor, the erectors will usually slide them up the front of the scaffolding (once it has been erected) and onto the first-floor joists, before moving them around to where they need to be. For more difficult to access jobs, there may be a need to hire a small crane to position the first-floor panels.

The frame package will also usually include the floor joists and floor boards. The joists will vary in size, but the floor boards will normally be a 2' x 8', 18mm or 22mm moisture resistant chipboard flooring board, either with a grey painted finish or with a thin plastic protective sheeting stuck to it, which you will remove at the end of the job.

Different erecting teams will have differing ways of assembling the panels, but generally, once they have completed the ground floor, they will set the joists (some will also lay the floor boards before setting the upstairs walls, others will leave that job until after the building is weathertight), then, once the first floor panels are in place, they will move straight on to setting the roof trusses which, depending on their size and weight may be hand manoeuvred in to place, or may require the use of a crane or forklift.

I recommend that you ask the suppliers to supply the thicker 22mm boards and that you ask the erectors or joiners (whoever ends up doing the job), to glue and screw (preferable) or glue and nail

(not so preferable, but not too bad a job) the floorboards to the joists. I hate creaky floors and I find that is a belt and braces approach to fixing the boards is the best way to keep them to a minimum.

Also, when laying the floor, make sure the chippies leave a 10mm gap all the way around the external wall of the house between the end of the floor board and the wall. This is to allow for expansion. The inspectors will be looking out for it.

Timber frame roof: Timber frame packages normally include for the supply and fit of standard roof trusses or attic trusses. Often the package will also include the fascias, soffits and barge boards (check with the supplier). If this is the case, the work on the roof will just be a natural continuation from the wall panels for the erectors.

If you are project managing, you just need to be in attendance to make sure the scaffold is adjusted as required and to make sure that everything else around the site is as it should be whilst the frame is erected.

Apart from that, if you employ a decent company, you should just be able to watch your house appearing before your eyes!

Timber frame erection times. For a simple 1800 sq ft timber framed house, expect the timber frame to go up in something like the following timescale:

Sole plates (the timbers that set out the shape of the building, normally 4" x 2" or 6" x 2"): 1 day
Ground floor panels: 1 – 2 days
Joists / floor boards: 1 – 2 days
Second floor panels: 1 – 2 days
Roof trusses and bracing: 1- 4 days
Fascias and soffits: 1- 2 days

Bear in mind however, that the work may not be continuous. The scaffold has to be altered between some of the sections of work, so the erectors may have to go off site for up 1 – 3 days while they wait for this work to be carried out (usually at first floor level and again at roof level).

So, for a simple 1800 sq ft house, expect the frame to take between 3 – 4 weeks to completion (ready for felt and batten). Larger houses need not take significantly longer if more erectors are used and if you have the scaffolders organised efficiently.

3) SIPS

SIPS packages in the UK seem to me to be a bit of a hybrid system, with each manufacturer having their own opinions on the best way to supply and erect the kit.

The wall panels will often come to site around the same size as timber frame panels, so the erectors can set them in pretty much the same way that they would erect a timber frame. The jointing and fixing methods will be slightly different and, with SIPS the insulation is already inside the wall. Apart from that, erecting walls with small panels will tend to echo the timber frame process.

However, as we discussed earlier in the book, the SIPS manufacturing process actually lends itself to making larger panels. This means that if your supplier has a gantry crane in their factory, they can potentially manufacture panels up to the length of the delivery vehicle (up to around 12m long). This will obviously mean that a crane will be needed on site to lift and place the panels, but imagine how much faster the frame will go up, when one panel is often the full length of the external or internal wall!

The longer the panels are, the fewer joints there will be. This will not only speed up the job significantly, but will also help to improve the airtightness of the finished building (fewer joints = fewer places for air to get out).

Using longer panels and a crane also allows the supplier to use factory manufactured floor cassettes as part of the kit (rather than setting the joists and floor boards in situ). Floor cassettes, as well as usually offering high levels of accuracy and finish, will also further speed the job up.

SIPS roof: This is one of the big selling points with SIPS panels. The SIPS roof normally comes in large self-supporting units, which give you a completely open space within the finished roof structure. This one bonus of using the SIPS system can be very valuable to you, adding potentially up to 30% - 40% of extra floor area within the building at a fairly similar build cost. The SIPS roof will also be built far faster than a trussed roof or attic trusses, and, once on, immediately gives a weathertight finish without having to first cover the roof with felt and battens.

Scaffolding for SIPS: If the small panels are being used, then the same sort of scaffolding as used for the timber frame kit, will normally be adequate for the SIPS frame, however, if the larger panels, floor cassettes and roof cassettes are being used, then the full scaffold really needs to be built before the kit arrives (on all four sides, including hop ups).

You simply won't have time to get the scaffold altered whilst the kit is going up and if everything is not ready for the erectors you could find yourselves paying standing time for the men and hired-in plant (including a crane) at between £500 and £1200 / day, depending on where you are in the country.

Erection times: SIPS frames are usually erected faster than timber frames and very much faster than traditional build.

SIPS erection times: For a simple 1800 sq ft SIPS frame, expect something along the following timescales:

Sole plates: 1 day
Ground floor: 1-2 days
Joists / floor boards: 1-2 days
Second floor: 1-2 days
Roof trusses and bracing: 1-2 days
Fascias and soffits: 1-2 days

So, you could expect a SIPS frame to be complete and weathertight in around 2 weeks, saving around 1 week in erection time compared to a similar timber frame. The further benefit of the SIPS kit over the timber frame is that the insulation will already be installed throughout the building.

Your major tasks at this stage of the project will be (once the scaffolding is sorted and general condition of the site is as it should be), getting everything organised for the brickies, roofers and the follow-on works.

Sounds easy, doesn't it? Well hopefully it should be.

Brickwork for timber frame or SIPS:

If you go for a brick or blockwork external skin to go with your timber frame or SIPS kit, the process will be fairly similar to how you would do it when you are using traditional build except that:

- You are only going to be building one skin of the wall instead of both skins, so the process will be faster.
- If the weather is decent and as long as there are no other major problems, for a simple 1800 sq ft house, rather than taking 8 – 10 weeks to build the shell of the house using brick / blockwork, it should take 5 – 6 weeks with a SIPS kit. There is also an additional advantage that, if the brickies, for whatever reason, let you down, the effect will not usually be as dramatic with a SIPS build as it would be with a traditional build because the frame is already up, the roof is on and you can get on with other activities inside the building while you sort the brickies out.
- You won't need to order any blocks or concrete common bricks or sand for the inside skin of the wall.
- You won't need to order insulation or all the ancillary bits and pieces if you use the SIPS panels, but you will need to order those items for the timber frame (I will discuss this in more detail in the next chapter).

- You will use different lintels for timber frames / SIPS than you would for traditional build. They only need to hold the brickwork up, not the brick *and* blockwork. They are simpler and cheaper to buy and should be detailed on your building regs specification.
- You won't need to make dummy window and door frames as the SIPS / timber frames have all the openings built in. Just remember to double check all the openings for position and size.
  Over the years when I was buying timber frames for my own projects, I generally found one or two mistakes on most houses (with the main culprits being window / door openings missing or made to the wrong size). The good thing with timber framed homes is that if there is a problem of this nature, it is generally quickly and easily fixable on site.

Timber cladding / rendering with timber frame or SIPS

If you have chosen to go for the single skin external wall option, you'll find things a lot quicker and easier than if you are using a brick or block external skin.

Your specification will give you details of the exact construction, but basically, you will be fixing battens to the outside of the timber frame or the SIPS panels over a breather paper which is fitted at the factory. Then you will simply fix either the timber cladding or possibly a cement board to the battens, followed by the render.

These operations (the battening / cladding / boarding but not the rendering) are tasks, that with a bit of experience or practice, that you could possibly consider doing yourself. However, my advice would be, unless you think you can come up with a finished job that is just as good as a professional joiner, to leave it to the experts.

The rendering should always be done by a professional company. This is the first part of the house that anyone will see and you want it to look good.

Mortgage Payments with Timber Frame / SIPS

Using a timber frame / SIPS will usually bring significant advantages over traditional build when it comes to your stage mortgage payments.

The speed of the build with either timber frame or SIPS will mean that you get from your *floor slab complete* payment to your *roofed in* payment far faster than you would do with traditional build.

This can prove to be a very important factor in helping your cash flow to stay positive and can, in some circumstances be the difference between a project succeeding or failing.

Things to think about:

As with traditional construction, whether you are using timber frame or SIPS, as your frame is being erected, you will still need to be considering the following activities:

Joiners: You won't usually need these for the roof structure, but you might need them to come in to fit the fascias and soffits (depending on whether or not this is included in your frame package).

You will certainly need to have them lined up and ready to go to work either on your cladding / render, or first fixes inside the building (or both), as soon as the roof is covered.

External windows and doors: With either timber frame or SIPS, you generally won't need to be worried about the openings being out of plumb, however, as with traditional build, when you order window and doors, always remember to deduct 10mm off the structural size for the size of the window itself.

Felt / battens / roof tiling: This will be pretty much the same process as if you were building in brick and blockwork.

Electricians & plumbers: You will need to keep in touch with the electricians and plumbers whilst the shell of the house is going up to make sure they are programmed in to start their section of the work as soon as it is ready for them.

Conclusion on building the shell with timber frame / SIPS:

I think that, even if you weren't sure before, after reading this chapter so far, you should now be more aware of how much simpler the timber build option is for you as a project manager.

For self-builders with family and other commitments, the time you save between organising all the activities and actually doing the building works for a traditional house, compared to the much reduced level of commitment for a timber frame or SIPS, is something you should seriously look into.

As with every self-build project, you will usually be under both financial and practical pressures to get the job finished quickly, starting from the day you start on site.

These two systems should help you to make that day arrive much sooner!

4) Closed panel

As you are well aware by now, this is the system I would recommend for your self-build project. I have detailed many of its benefits previously, but the actual use of it on site is where it can come in to its own.

There are a number of closed panel systems available. A bit like with SIPS, all of them have their own individual features and idiosyncrasies. For simplicity, I will use the system I used to manufacture to describe how everything generally works and how using this system affects your input as a project manager.

As with timber frame or SIPS, the closed panel system takes the place of the inside skin of the cavity wall. It can also be used as a stand-alone skin in a single skin wall.

Just as with any other type of external wall, it carries the load from the structure and passes it down to the foundations.

Where closed panels differ from timber frame and SIPS is that there is a lot more work done at the factory with closed panels and the panels are more often made in large sections, so the erection time is usually shorter with closed panel construction.

In my opinion, closed panels only really only become the obvious best choice for self-build when the large panels are used (up to 12m long).

Where the small panels are used, I still see it as a better option generally than *most* of the other main building methods. However, because of the significant difference in speed between the large and small closed panel construction times, it is possible that (although still being significantly slower to build), taking other factors in to account such as price, standard timber frame could potentially offer a better overall package.

Due to the fact that the closed panels system is highly bespoke, the suppliers are often able to give you a bit more flexibility when it comes to specification than you can generally expect with timber frame.

From my own experience, a lot of timber frame companies are set up to do *one* type of frame, to *one* specification (*it is what they are used to doing and it is the only option they offer. Anything else would just confuse them!*). However, you may find that some of the larger companies can offer more design and spec choices.

Closed panel companies (and, it has to be said, SIPS companies), tend to be a bit more forward thinking. They realise that there is a market out there full of people who all want different things. They are also aware that, at this time, their sector of the market would still be classed as "niche". Most people are aware of timber frame as a build method, but not many are aware of SIPS, or closed panel.

Therefore, the people who offer the closed panel system have to work that bit harder to get the business.

As an example, with a good closed panel company, you should be able to make the following choices (SIPS companies may offer some, but not all of the same choices):

i. Choose the thickness, types of insulation and insulation values of your external walls.
ii. Choose whether or not to have the internal walls insulated.
iii. Design your electrical layout and have all the conduits and back boxes pre-built in to the panels.
iv. Have plumbing conduits built into the panels.
v. Include ducting for alarm wiring / automated house wiring / built in hifi cables, etc. within the panel.
vi. Add a structural OSB board behind the plasterboard to allow you to hang heavy objects on walls anywhere in the house (or optionally change the plasterboards to a cement board, which would give you both strength and extra fireproofing at the same time)
vii. Choose the thickness of your floor boards (which are then made into floor cassettes in the factory and brought to site complete)
viii. Choose to have rooms in the roof and a structural attic floor at little or no extra cost (depending on the style of your roof design).
ix. Include dormer roof features as part of the design, which are then brought to site ready assembled.

With a closed panel system, you get significantly more of your house brought to you complete, compared to timber frame and noticeably more than if you were to use SIPS.

As a project manager, this would obviously make your life much easier, by virtue of the fact that it could save you weeks, or even months of:

- Supervision
- Finding materials
- Measuring materials
- Pricing
- Ordering
- Coordinating trades, deliveries and activities.

A few things to bear in mind when using closed panel systems:

- Due to the speed of erection of the frame there will be no time to get the scaffolders back to alter the scaffolding between erecting the ground floor, first floor and roof, so you will need them to do the whole lot in one go. All around the house, to full height (including any hop ups you may need).
- You will need to be able to fit a crane on site, or immediately adjacent to it, in order to offload and position the panels.
- Again, due to the speed of erection, you will need to get the follow on activities such as roof tiling, window fitting, brickwork electrical, plumbing and joinery first fixes all organised at the same time as organising the erection of the frame itself (a 5 bedroomed, 3 storey house would take us around 4 - 5 days to fully erect, from slab to weathertight).

Theoretically, once the ground floor wall panels and floor cassettes are on, because it is not difficult at that stage to make the ground floor of the building weathertight and as long as it is safe to do so, your bricklayers, electrician, plumbers and joiners could potentially all start work with their first fixes.

This could be as soon as day 2 or 3 after the frame erectors arrive on site. The main thing to be aware of, if the bricklayers are starting work, is to make sure that they are protected from anything falling from above (from the crane, the scaffolding, or the building itself).

- Often, the closed panel frame company will also be able to supply the windows and possibly the external doors, but if your frame supplier doesn't include them as part of the package, you'll need to get them organised to come as soon as the wall panels are in place so the building can be made weathertight and secure asap.

Here's one we made earlier:

Here is a quick look at the diary of a closed panel frame for a 5 bed detached house that we supplied and erected a couple of years ago:

Day 1: Ground floor, floor cassettes and part of the first floor complete. The plastic sheeting was used to protect the plasterboard wall finish. Shortly after that we started using cement boards instead of plasterboards. These were waterproof and much stronger than plasterboards.

Day 2: Complete the first-floor walls, fit second floor cassettes and start third floor walls.

Day 3: Complete third floor walls, roof cassettes and dormers (building weathertight).

Brickwork for closed panels

All the options for brickwork, blockwork, single skin construction, cladding etc. are almost identical to how they are with traditional build, standard timber frames or SIPS.

The only real practical difference is that you can generally start work on both the outside and the inside, sooner.

Follow on trades

All the follow-on trades work will follow the same general path to how it would be if you were using traditional build, timber frame, or SIPS. The main differences to you, as project manager will be that:

- You need to get them all organised much earlier in the project.
- The electricians and the plumbers should be finished much faster as part of their work has already been incorporated in to the panels (the ducting / back boxes etc.)
- There should be far less for you to do as a project manager, due to the fact that, because things like sockets and switches are already in place, there are fewer opportunities for errors to creep in. This also means that there will be less for you to check up on as work progresses.

Conclusion on building the shell with closed panels

To me, as a site manager and self-builder, this product and system just makes *so much* sense, especially for the self-build market.

After building houses for around 30 years and having been around closed panel construction in recent years, I have not yet found any other product or system that would tempt me to change my mind on that fact.

If anyone says to you "Oh, they will be more expensive to buy" point them to the fact that by building much faster, you can save a lot of money in prelims and off costs (see earlier chapters). Yes, they may not be the cheapest to buy, but if you utilize the benefits and opportunities they give you to get the job completed much quicker, the cost savings of doing so could (and should) more than cancel out the extra cost of the buying the system. The financial savings could also potentially pretty much pay for you to hire a professional project manager to run the whole thing for you!

Shop around

There are quite a few variations of closed panels available, so as usual, shop around the different companies and weigh up the pros and cons of each system before you choose the best for you and your project.

Due to the fact that there is a lot of work to do in designing and manufacturing these kits, you will need to get the frame ordered **at least** 2 – 3 months before you need it.

5) ICF (insulated concrete formwork).

As I mentioned earlier, the methods used for this form of construction are quite different to any of the other methods I have covered in this book.

When I speak to ICF sales people at the shows, they generally give the impression that it is a fast, easy, sustainable building product that anyone with a bit of practical skill can construct on their own. I must admit that I am yet to be convinced of that.

Personally, from having seen a few ICF projects being undertaken in my local area over the years and also after watching the odd television programme following the progress of someone actually building an ICF house, I think it is possibly a bit slower, more difficult and more complicated than the we are led to believe.

Anyway, this chapter is dealing with how to build it, not whether or not you should believe the hype, so let's get on with it!

Personally, although the marketing info says you should be able to, I would not recommend trying to build the house from ICF yourself (whether or not you have a good level of practical skill. However, also from what I hear, it is reasonably difficult to find tradespeople who know about and who can construct ICF buildings. For this reason, if you need to find someone who can erect the kit for you, it may be necessary to search quite a distance away from your site in order to find someone suitable.

I would also recommend that you don't take on any builder to build this kit, who says something like: *"How hard can it be? I'll give it a go"*. From what I have seen and heard, I think you need to bring in trained and experienced people if you want to make sure that everything is done right, first time.

Note: Most ICF companies offer training for anyone thinking of building the houses themselves.

As project manager, you can provide a valuable service (and will be kept quite busy) making sure everything is delivered when it should be and sorting out / organising all the bits and pieces that will be needed to keep the whole process running smoothly.

Whether or not you are going to erect the kit yourself, it may be a good idea for you to get a bit of training on the basics of how the whole thing works, before you start. That way, as the house is being built, you will be abler to monitor and comment on the operation and at least ask the right questions if something is not quite looking right (*check out the self-build centre in Swindon to see if there are any courses running there, or contact the ICF companies and see if they can point you in the direction of a decent training course somewhere near you.*

The practicalities:

The relationship between the foundations and the walls is slightly different with ICF to how it is with traditional or timber build, so, as well as finding a team who can use the ICF system itself, you will also need to employ a ground worker who is either familiar with the system or who is capable of learning what its implications are on the foundations. You need them to be able to complete their work, with no errors, first time. If they don't get their bit of the job right before the delivery of all the main materials and if that results in you not being ready to start when you should be, you could find yourselves losing the ICF erection team to another job for a lengthy period of time.

On a practical note, you will need a lot of storage room on site for the ICF units themselves (which come in various different shapes and sizes) and the ancillary products you will need to put it all together. They are rather bulky and you will need to have a good stock of them sorted out and ready to go on day one, so that you don't have to keep stopping work to wait for more units to be delivered.

Also, bear in mind that the polystyrene *forms* that you will be using to create the walls, have all been designed for a specific location in the building, so not only will you need to have them all stored safely, you will also need to be able to locate the correct pieces easily and quickly as work proceeds. You won't be very popular if, every time the builders need another form, they have to go rooting through huge great piles of the things to find the right one!

Steel

An important part of this system is the reinforcing steel which is built into each wall, so as well as getting all the kit you will need to site on time and in the right quantities, you will also need to order the steel.

The ICF designs should include the specification for the steel, so if it is not coming to site as part of the kit, you should just be able to send the schedules out to local steel stockists to price up and deliver whatever you need. Make sure you get all the spacers, tie wire and anything else the spec may list in the small print and again, make sure you get it all there on day 1.

Scaffold:

Scaffolding for ICF will normally be built as you go along (similar to traditional build).

As with the other types of build we have looked at, you will need to discuss with the ICF suppliers / installers, the numbers of lifts required for the scaffolding and the heights at which each platform will need to be set at (an average height for a lift of ICF is around 1.4m, so you may find you need up to 4 lifts for the main walls and up to another 3 hop ups for gables or any irregular roof shapes.

As project manager, just as with the other construction methods, you will usually be responsible for organising this and making sure the scaffolders arrive when they are needed (which, in theory could be every couple of days while you build the shell). Also make sure the warranty and building inspectors are geared up to call whenever they need to, in order to check on and approve progress.

Structural floors: With the ICF system, you can choose to use either of the following floor constructions for, not only the ground floor, but also usually also for the upper floors:

a) **Concrete slab or beam and block floor**

From my own experience of talking to people who are either considering, or who have used ICF, this is often the floor construction of choice.

Two of the main reasons people opt for this method of construction are that 1) It is very strong and 2) Theoretically it should also create a building that is very quiet to live in. Part of achieving that strength and quietness is to include concrete intermediate floors, as well as a concrete ground floor slab.

If this is the option you have chosen, you will need a crane, you will possibly need to bring in some extra reinforcing steelwork and you might find that you even need some steel RSJs (depending on the spans between supporting walls).

To find a suitable supplier for the beams, just do a search on "beam and block flooring" and add your postcode, to see if there is anyone around you manufacturing or supplying what you need.

None of this is likely to be particularly fast or cheap!

b) **Timber floor**

This will usually be a much quicker and cheaper option than the concrete floor. However, unless you really go to town on the soundproofing side of things, it won't generally give you the same levels of strength or quietness as the concrete floor option.

To install a timber joisted floor, once the concrete is poured to form the ground floor walls, you will usually need to cut slices of the polystyrene away at the external walls and bolt joist trimmers directly to the concrete. You can then fix joist hangers and slot the joists into position.

It might be possible to get the building designed so that the joists can be built *into* the concrete wall itself. If this is an option which interests you, talk to the supplier / designer.

Again, with the ICF system you will usually have to organise all the timber flooring works yourself, getting the joiners in at the right time and making sure that they know how to do what they need to do (*many joiners will never have worked on an ICF project before, so you may have to gather some information together for them on how the whole thing works and goes together*).

Most of the information you need for the follow-on trades should be either supplied directly by the ICF supplier or they should give you details of where to go in order to find out what you (and everybody else) needs to know.

Openings

These are not too complicated as long as you follow the instructions, but they need building accurately and carefully.

If the formwork does not form a good seal all around every opening, you could find that when the concrete is actually being poured into the formwork, that the fluids in the mix may leak out. This could not only create empty voids in the walls, but also decrease its insulation and strength. It will also, once the concrete has set, leave lumps of dried cement on the surface of the walls which have to removed.

Good quality seals are especially important for the lintels at the tops of the openings, where all the weight is acting downwards from the building structure above and where it is therefore important that all the concrete is in the right place and that it is doing its job properly.

Roof

For the roof construction of an ICF house, you can usually use any of the normal roofing options:

- Trusses
- Attic trusses
- Traditional hand cut roof
- SIPS (*this may be an expensive option if you are not buying the walls from the same manufacturer, as they will incur a lot of design / manufacture and transport costs just to get the roof to you*).

The detailing between the walls and the roof structure will be different from most of the other options we have looked at for the construction of the shell of the house, but the differences should not cause too much problem to experienced joiners.

Whichever style of roof structure you choose, you will again need to organise the materials supply and its construction *separately* from the ICF kit itself (you may find that you also need a crane for a couple of days to install the bulk of the roof).

Remember also, that (*theoretically at least*) the shell can go up pretty quickly, so make sure the speed of construction doesn't catch you out when getting materials delivered for the roof and for getting the roofers and follow on trades organised.

External wall finishes

The options for the finishes to the external walls for an ICF house are a little different to those available for most of the other build options. The finished appearance will often be pretty much the same, but the methods of creating the finish are slightly different because of the nature of the construction of the walls themselves. Your standard choices will generally be:

- Brick slips
- Render
- Patterned concrete

By the time you get to the point of building the house, you should already be well aware of your choices, but also make sure you are aware of all the associated costs and how they compare (like-for-like) to the other available build options, remembering to take in to account speed of build in your figures.

Conclusion on building the shell with ICF

This system has been around for many years and has managed to get a decent niche market with self-builders in the UK. It gives you a very solid, soundproofed house, with exceptional levels of thermal mass and thus good insulating qualities and very good airtightness.

It has never really taken off with the commercial house builders and there must be a reason for that.

I have never used it, so I can't really comment on how good or bad it really is in practice.

As I said earlier, all I would say to you, is that if you are considering using the ICF system; make sure you speak to a few people who have already built with it.

The main questions to ask are:

I. "Was it as fast and easy as you thought it was going to be?"
II. "Was it good value for money?"
III. "Do you still think it is a sustainable product?"
IV. "Would you use it again next time?"

Chapter 13
The internal fit out

Introduction

As with the previous chapter, there are so many different ways to approach the internal fit out that it is not going to be possible for me to cover them all in this book. So, what I am going to do is to take the stand point of a project manager who is organising and overseeing the project, who needs to know a bit about everything but doesn't need to have an in depth knowledge of anything.

I will be using a simply designed 4 bed detached house as a sample build and I will run through all the different options for the same build methods as I did in the last chapter, namely:

1. Traditional brick / block
2. Timber frame
3. SIPS
4. Closed panel
5. ICF

Probably an important thing for me to repeat here, is what I have already said a few times earlier in the book and that is:

> **There is no definitive right or wrong way to go about the internal fit out of the house.**
>
> **A lot of it comes down to personal choices, timescales and budget.**

Having said that, there is usually a sensible route through the process, whichever build method you have decided to use. There may even be *more than one* sensible route.

By this stage of the job you may start to find yourself getting tight on cash flow. If you are, don't ignore the problem, or it will just get worse.

If money is getting a bit tight you should (if you have taken note of the early chapters) have a decent financial buffer to fall back on. If not, you need to start to work on a Plan B as soon as you realise there is a problem. Go and see the mortgage lender or your bank manager to see if you can free up more funds sooner, but just as importantly, don't just carry on spending as if there were no tomorrow.

It is very tempting at this stage of the job to start to look at the luxuries. The posh kitchens, bathrooms, tiles, flooring, fittings and furniture. The tendency of many self-builders is to say: "Lets buy it, we'll find the money somewhere". ***Really*** try to restrain yourself from doing this, or it may end up in tears.

You should have been keeping in regular touch with each sub-contractor whilst you have been constructing the foundations and the shell of the house, discussing start and finish dates for their sections of the work. If that is the case, all the guys who are going to be needed for the internal works should know when you will want them to start on site.

Many self-builders tend to like to get one job done at a time. I take a different view, mainly because I want to get the house finished as quickly as possible.

So, as long as everyone working within the building can do so without getting in each other's way and as long as the quality of the work remains high, I like to cram as may tradespeople in to the building as possible.

This fast tracking obviously requires a lot more organisational skill and you may not fancy the idea if this is your first project, but if you can manage it, it offers a significant benefit to the job advantages *over and above simply finishing faster.* That benefit is that, with different trades on site at the same time, they can stand in the same room and talk to each other, in order to solve the problems that occur from hour to hour and day to day on every new build project.

Left on their own, tradespeople will tend to do it their own way, which may be fine, but sometimes this approach can cause problems for other follow on trades. If everyone is there together, they will tend to notice things being done by the other trades which could potentially be going to cause them problems with their part of the project. If these problems are picked up early, they can usually be fixed in a way that keeps everybody happy.

There is one exception to the pile them high theory when it comes to tradespeople and that is where the decorators are concerned.

Where possible you need to give the decorators the *whole house* to themselves and leave that job until as late in the project as possible in the programme, when all the *dirty* trades have pretty much finished their work. This will hopefully minimise the chances of your lovely new clean walls getting grubby marks all over them!

You should leave the tradespeople, wherever possible, to get on with their work without you constantly staring over their shoulders and if you notice anything you are not sure of, don't just march in and accuse them of poor work (as a poke in the eye often offends!)

It *is* however important that you keep your eyes open for shoddy looking work. The way to do this is (as I have mentioned before), from the first day a new trade arrives on site, to wait until the guys have gone home and then have a good look round at what they have done. If you see something you are not happy with, make a note of it, but don't necessarily say anything just yet (*unless it is something which could be dangerous either to people or to the job*). They may be in the middle of something which may look dodgy at the moment, but that will be fine when they have finished the job. If, when the job is finished, you still don't feel happy about it, *then* is the best time to say something.

If you do have to speak to any trades person about their work, especially when they are new on site, be fairly inflexible and let them know that they will have to put it right or do it again (and not get paid for doing so). By approaching the matter this way, you will be doing yourself two favours:

a) The person / company responsible for the shoddy work will realise that you have a reasonable level of knowledge of what you are doing, so they won't easily be able to pull the wool.
b) They will also know that they can't get away with poor quality work, so will tend to at least try make sure there is nothing else for you to pull them up on.

First fixing

First fixing a traditional build:

This is where you will usually find yourself at this point in the project:

- Roof structure complete, roof at least felt and battened (weatherproof), preferably tiled.
- External doors and windows in, but if you plan to install anything special or expensive, you may decide to put temporary doors or windows wherever there is a chance of damage occurring to anything which would cost a lot to repair or replace.
- The house needs to be lockable and secure.

- Scaffolding probably still up whilst the outside bits and pieces are finished.
- Drainage and services not installed (but with the under slab drains and ducting in place ready for them).
- Concrete ground floor not screeded yet.
- Joists fitted, but possibly not the floor boards.
- Internal blockwork walls built, internal timber walls not built.
- No stairs fitted

Job 1: Floor boards

The joiners will need to get this job done first so that people can walk about upstairs to get the other jobs done. It is part of what is called "the joinery first fix".

When you fix floor joists, you should leave a 10mm gap around wherever they meet the external walls to allow for expansion and contraction as the house heats up and cools down.

Unfortunately, this 10mm gap is where a lot of the sound between floors gets through and leaves you with the house much noisier to live in.

This weakness is exacerbated if the plasterboard joints between the ceiling and the walls downstairs have not been cut and fitted accurately. All you need are tiny gaps between adjacent boards and sound will sneak through.

I have a potential cure for these two problems: 1) Where you have the gap around the floor boards, insert something like 15mm thick x 25mm thick neoprene (which works best when it has to be squeezed in to the gap). Then mastic right around the wall / ceiling joints downstairs and plan to use ceiling covings in each room. This should help to solve the problem.

(Note: If you apply mastic to the wall to ceiling joint, the plasterers may complain that their plaster skim does not stick to the mastic, which it won't! Covings solve this problem at the same time as further reducing sound transmittance between rooms and floors).

The additional benefit of fitting ceiling covings is that when the joists and the plastering work dries out, after a few months, you often get minor cracking in walls. One of the main areas these will appear is at this wall to ceiling joint. So, if you install covings to all rooms, it could save you from having to fill in and paint over these cracks, just when you think you have finished all the building works and have started to get the house looking tidy!

Back to floor boards

There are many types of floor boards available, however, my preferred option for all new housing would be:

22mm thick, moisture resistant chipboard with a plastic coated top surface

I like these because:

- They are (obviously) thicker than the standard 18mm board so are less prone to move and creak.
- The moisture resistance means that if you get a water leak anywhere, there is less chance of there being serious damage done to the floor.
- They are better for soundproofing between floors.
- They look nicer than standard boards.
- They are easier to keep clean whilst building works are going on.

As I said earlier, I suggest that you glue and screw or glue and nail the floor boards down (using ring shank nails if nailing). This further reduces the likelihood of creaks once the heating is on and the floor starts drying / shrinking.

Don't throw floor board offcuts away, they will come in handy for a lot of the bits and pieces that need doing from now until the end of the project.

Floor board laying for a 2000 sq ft house should be about a day's work for 2 joiners.

Job 2: Internal stud walls

Whilst the floor boards are being laid, you need to be making sure you are ready to move straight on to constructing any timber internal walls.

For this job, my chosen material would be:

Ex 4" x2" softwood CLS

CLS tends to offer a more consistent quality than standard sawn timber. It is usually pretty straight and doesn't tend to twist like a lot of standard sawn timber. It also has slightly rounded corners which make it less prone to giving you splinters!

If you buy it in full packs, you should get decent prices on it.

The chippies should be well versed in how to knock up the timber stud walls. If not, then the drawings and specifications should have the relevant details on them.

Generally, for a standard internal stud wall the spec would be:

- A base plate and a head plate.
- Studs at generally 600mm centres (so they take standard 1200mm plasterboards).
- A strengthening timber nogging half way up the wall (see right hand wall in the next image).
- OSB backing boards, fixed to noggings wherever there is to be any structural load on the wall (e.g. TVs / radiators, shelving etc. to be hung later).
- More OSB on noggings wherever there is an electrical socket or switch (to fix the back boxes to).

If the timber stud wall is to be load bearing, then the construction of it may need to be more sturdy (how to construct the load bearing timber walls should be detailed on drawings and specifications).

I always like to insulate timber internal walls with 100mm of fibreglass insulation to reduce sound transference between rooms. The easiest time to install this is once the first fix plumbing and electrical work has been completed and when one side has been plaster boarded. If you install it before that stage, it could get in the way of the work the different trades need to do.

The other joinery jobs which will usually be done at this stage include:

- Fitting door linings.
- Fitting window boards (cills).
- Fitting the staircases (but not the handrails, spindles, newels etc.)
- Fixing loft access frame.

Job 3: First fix plumbing & electrics

These two trades can usually run simultaneously, as long as they are not getting in each other's way. Talk to both trades before programming them in, to make sure they are happy to work alongside each other *(to keep progress moving swiftly, you need to get multiple trades working in the building at the same time wherever you can)*.

Plumbing first fix

If you are installing ground source / air source / solar heating / log burners / underfloor heating or any other specialist system related to the plumbing / heating installation, in order to find out how and what you need to do for each item, you should have been talking to the supplier / installer well before starting the internal fit out.

Once you know what is needed for each activity, you will be able to programme the work in to your first fix schedule.

It is important that you don't miss anything at this stage because trying to add missing bits (for example), for the solar panelling or the underfloor heating later, could be both time consuming and expensive.

The standard first fix plumbing works will normally include:

- Pipework required for mains connection.
- Hot / cold water pipework.
- Heating pipework.
- Ventilation ducts through walls.
- Waste pipes for sinks / toilets / baths / showers.
- Guttering / downpipes (if the external walls are ready for them), however these can be done at any time.

Underfloor heating: If you are going to install underfloor heating, now is the time that the pipework is usually installed.

This operation can slow the main progress of the job for a week or so, as it entails clearing everyone and everything out of any areas of the building where it is going to be fitted. The installers (either your plumbers or a specialist company) will then come in and lay the insulation and pipework, before you bring in a floor screeder to lay a sand and cement floor screed over the whole area. Once the screed has been laid it will need to be left for up to a week to gain strength, before you can allow the other tradespeople back into the building to carry on their work.

Project manager input:

As project manager, you probably won't need to have a lot to do with the main plumbing installation. It will normally be done on a supply and fit basis. This is a sensible approach on a self-build project as there are literally hundreds of bits and pieces which, if you took on the job of supplying the materials, you would find a nightmare to list and order. The plumbers deal with this stuff every day and will probably get better prices, simply by knowing where to go for everything and being a regular customer. They will also usually prefer to be in charge of getting the materials, so that they know that they have everything they need, in the right quantities, when they need it.

The information they will require to order materials should all come from the drawings and specifications, which you will have marked up with the positions of all the main plumbing equipment (such as baths, sinks, toilets, showers, radiators etc.) and any additional information on items that you included in the tender documents.

Things to watch out for during the plumbing installation:

- **The positioning of the boiler:** You should always try to design your plumbing system so that the length of pipework between the boiler and the fittings is kept to a minimum. The longer the run, the more water you will waste waiting for hot water to come through when you turn the hot taps on. Bathrooms above the boiler are ideal, but wherever they are, just make sure the plumber is routing the pipework as directly as possible from boiler to fitting.
- **Care being taken with the jointing of the copper or plastic pipes.** If they get this wrong, you could end up with leaks all over the house when the water is turned on. Finding and fixing leaks can prove to be very difficult as the leak will not necessarily show on the walls or ceilings in exactly the same place that it is escaping from the pipe. To actually find it and get to it to fix it can mean cutting floors up or making holes in ceilings (which are then difficult to "make good"). This is something you want to avoid if at all possible.

If you want to reduce the potential for leaking pipes to a minimum, I would suggest the following:
Use plastic (not copper) piping. This comes in long rolls and can therefore be fitted in very long runs. The advantages of this are: 1) Speed of fixing, 2) fewer soldered joints.

If you can fit one single length of pipework from a fitting (tap or radiator), to a central manifold (a brass fitting to which a lot of pipework lengths can be attached), the chances of leaks along the length of the pipe will all but be removed (unless you stick a nail through a pipe). The only other places for leaks to occur, would usually be at either end of the pipe. You should therefore quickly be able to locate any leaks at fittings (taps, radiators etc.)

If you have an accessible manifold at the opposite end of the pipe run (under the floor boards with a screw down cover), to which all the lengths of pipes run from the individual fittings, you should also be able to quickly find any leaks there. Being able to find leaks so easily, could potentially save you a lot of repair work, cost and time, both during the build period and in the future.

- **Holes being cut in the wrong places, or too large.** The main areas where problems occur with holes, are in walls, joists and floor boards. Oversized holes cut in external walls can reduce the airtightness of the building and cause it to fail the airtightness test. They can also reduce the overall insulation value of the house.
  If holes are cut too large or in the wrong place in joists, the building inspector can either condemn the joists or ask for them to be reinforced by fixing extra timbers adjacent to the holes to add strength. All holes in joists should be just large enough to take the pipe passing through, plus a few millimetres all round for expansion, or for some sort of wadding to be wrapped round the pipe to stop it from moving. Holes should be located either in the top half or at half way up the joist (see your project's building regs spec for details).
  Holes in floor boards will reduce the strength of the board and, if oversized, could allow sound transmittance between floors.
- **Copper pipes lying on joists** can cause creaking and clicking when the system is heating up and cooling down. They should all be packed up on a special wadding which stops them from directly touching and moving across the joists as they expand and contract. This reduces (and potentially removes) the possibility of noisy central heating. Using plastic piping for the central heating also helps to make the system a lot quieter.
- **Cold water pipes touching or running very close to hot water pipes:** This can cause heat transference between the pipes and also potentially creates further (creaking) noise as the cold water pipe heats up.
- **Make sure that lagging is fitted to any pipes on the outside of the building** and if required, in the loft space.
- **Mark up a drawing with the locations of pipework** in walls and in the floors, then copy the drawing and keep the copies for future reference, in case of future leaks or other problems. Also mark the floors with a permanent marker to show where the pipe runs are (it is best to ask the plumbers or joiners to do this as they proceed with their work).
- **If you are going to need a water supply taking outside** the building for whatever reason (to an annex for example), make sure that the plumber, when he is installing the first fix, does what he needs to do so that there is an accessible fitting ready to pick up later in the job to extend it to wherever it is needed.

For an average 4 bed detached 2000 sq ft traditionally built house over 2 floors, the first fix plumbing work should take around 4 - 7 man days, depending on the number of bathrooms, utility room etc.

Electrical first fix

As with the plumbing first fix, if you are installing alarm systems or some of the more specialist systems such as automated or smart house, built in hi-fi or cinema etc. you will need to coordinate the first fix works so that the suppliers or installers of these systems come in at the right time and are able to do what they need to do without holding any of the other trades up.

The electrical first fix will normally include:

- All the electrical wiring (but not fittings).
- Fixing socket and switch back boxes.
- Earthing cables.
- Built in hi-fi or automatic house systems.
- Alarm cabling.
- Anything else that needs doing before the walls are plastered and the ceilings boarded.
- Any special systems you have built in to your plans such as solar panels, ground source or air source heating, automatic gates, wiring to sheds or other outbuildings etc.

Project manager input

As with the plumbing first fix, as a project manager you should not need to have much to do with this work. It will normally be set up on a supply and fit contract, mainly because there are so many bits and pieces that need to be thought about and ordered.

So, theoretically you shouldn't need to worry about trying to work out how much of what materials to buy. Just leave it to the experts who can probably get better prices than you anyway.

The things to watch out for during the electrical first fix will include:

- **Holes through walls, joists and floor boards** (for the same reasons as for the plumbing).
- **You want to see wiring from fittings running straight up and down the walls** where possible (as opposed to diagonally or in multiple directions). If you are drilling a hole in a wall in a few years' time, it is normal assume that the original wiring was installed vertically. If it wasn't, then you, or future occupants of the house risk drilling through any cables which have been unusually routed.
- **Wiring which is to be embedded in plaster should be fitted inside a duct** to protect it from any potential chemical reaction with the plaster (which could rot the plastic coating and expose bare wires).
- **Good quality jointing** (you don't want to see any bits of bare wire at joints, anywhere in the house).
- **Missing cables:** It can often happen that a cable is missed by the electricians. If that happens, it can be a time consuming and costly exercise to install it later in the job. If you take a copy of the electrical layout and walk around the house, one room at a time, you should be able to pick up missing or misplaced sockets or switches, allowing you to notify the electrician to put them in.
- **Allow for any external wiring or cabling** to feed other locations (annexes / landscaping features etc.)
- **Mark up a drawing** with as much electrical information as possible and keep a couple of copies for future reference.

For an average 4 bed detached 2000 sq ft house the first fix electrical work should take around 6 – 8 man days depending on the complexity of the installation.

Job 4: Plaster boarding / plastering

Once all the first fixes are complete, the next task will usually be to either plaster or dry line the solid external walls and to fit the plasterboard to any timber walls and to the ceilings. I'll run briefly through both options, but if you are not familiar with the process of plastering, I also suggest that you have a look at some of the plastering videos on YouTube. A lot of the best videos on there are American (so the terminology will be different), but there are a few British ones worth watching too.

Plastering (or wet plastering as it is sometimes referred to) will usually be carried out by professional plasterers, who will normally provide their own tools and any plant they need. Check this with them before they arrive at site, in case there is anything they need you to provide for them. They will normally ask you to supply the materials.

The first job will usually be the plastering of the solid walls. On new houses, this will consist of two coats:

1) The render coat, which is a fairly roughly finished coat that gives a good bonding surface to the next coat

2) The skim coat, which is given a smooth finish ready for painting.

Dry lining work can be done by the plasterers, the joiners, or a specialist dry lining company. On the external walls this involves sticking plasterboards to the blockwork internal skin using a specialist bonding adhesive.

The next job will be to plate any timber stud walls with plasterboards (or cement boards – see later).

Again, this job can either be done by the plasterers, the joiners or dry liners (it is worth getting prices from all of them if possible).

The boards should be fixed to the studs using plasterboard screws, with the length of the screw being at least 2.5 x the thickness of the board. Screws should be fixed at around 300mm centres (max) generally and 150mm centres around all openings.

With dry lining, once the boards are fitted to both the external and internal walls, you then have a choice of finishes:

I. **Taping and skimming:**
    This involves using a material called scrim tape (normally self-adhesive), which is applied to all the plasterboard joints on all walls and ceilings. A plasterer then finishes the wall by applying a thin coat of skim plaster (around 2mm thick) and as the skim sets, they continually work the surface with finishing trowels to give a very smooth surface, ready for decorating.
    NOTE: If you are planning on using a skim to finish the walls, you will tend to use **Square edged** boards. These are readily available at any builders' merchant.

II. **Taping and jointing:** This task will normally be carried out by a specialist taping and jointing company (rather than by a plasterer). The process involves applying three coats of a tape and slurry mix to the joints of the plasterboards, usually using a special applicator device and a slurry mix that sets to a give a fairly smooth surface, that can then be sanded, ready for decoration.
    It is normal for the tapers and jointers to supply their own tools and materials. **Note:** You will use **tapered edge** boards for this method of installation.

It is well worth while you taking a look at some YouTube videos for both these systems. Once you have seen the work being done properly, you will be in a better position to be able to keep your eyes open for checking the quality of the job that your own guys are producing.

Materials

If the walls are being plastered (as opposed to dry lined), you will normally buy the materials, so remember to shop around for the best prices. None of the materials involved are particularly difficult to find or order and are quite cheap.

The standard materials include:

- **Plasterboards / cement boards:** We are all familiar with plasterboards, but not many people know about cement boards. They are worth looking at as an option for your internal walls.

   Cement boards are basically a sheet of concrete. They are much stronger than plasterboard, so may reduce the need for extra support behind the boards where loads are to be applied to the walls. They offer far better fire resistance. They are water resistant to a much greater extent than plasterboard (better if you have leaks). They cost more, but I think the extra is worth paying, especially for walls between habitable rooms.

   I normally do a rough measurement of the area of the walls and ceilings, then simply order one or two pallets of boards (at around 56 boards per pallet) to get the plasterers going and order more pallets as they are needed, until the job is nearing completion.

   As the end of the job is nearing, I will then do a more accurate measure and try to order the exact number of boards required to finish (plus 5% waste).

- **Sand:** Normally in the 1-ton bags. Order full bags until the job is nearing completion, then maybe think about getting the 25kg bags to finish the last bits.
- **Cement**: If there are a lot of walls to plaster, I'll buy cement by the pallet load and get more delivered as it is needed.
- **Admixture:** In 25 litre containers (this helps to make the plaster mix more workable for applying to the walls).
- **Skim**: This comes in bags and I buy it by the pallet load, then top up as required.
- **Render and skim beads** (to fix to external corners and around openings to form straight and plumb edges and corners).
- **Adhesive.** To fix the plaster beads to the walls with, you will only normally need a few bags of this.
- **Scrim tape** (self-adhesive): This is quite cheap, so buy at least half a dozen rolls and get more when you need it.

The things you'll need to watch out for with the plastering include:

- **The thickness of the coats:** It should be around ½" (around 11mm – 12mm) for the render coat and 2mm for the skim. If the walls are out of plumb (which often happens with blockwork walls), the render coat may have to be thickened in some areas so that the finished wall surface can be made plumb. This process is known as dubbing out and the problem with it is that it has the effect of thickening the finished wall. When this happens, it can cause problems with the fitting of the door linings (which are usually bought to suit an _exact_ thickness of wall). If there are just one or two walls which have had to be dubbed out, the joiner will probably suggest getting a couple of wider standard door linings, which they will then plane down to the required width to suit the wall. If the blockwork is poor and most of the walls have had to be dubbed out, then you would be advised to survey each wall and buy the correct width lining for each one (_possibly getting them made to measure for each location_).
- **The finish to the skim:** This is the surface which will be decorated so it needs to be completely smooth. If there are trowel lines, rough areas or humps and bumps in the surface, they will show through the paint finish. Try to monitor the first couple of walls that are skimmed and see if you are happy with them. If not, get on to the plasterers straight away and tell them you need a better finish than what they produced so far.
- **Badly fitted screws:** If the screws or nails used for fixing the plasterboards on to the timber studs are over-tightened or hammered in too far, they can break the paper surface of the board (_this does not happen with cement boards, for which you need special hardened screws just to get through the board in the first place_). If the surface of the plasterboard is broken, then after you have finished the skim coat and it has set, there is every chance that at some time in the future the plaster will pop, leaving the unsightly blemish of a hole and a screw or nail head on the surface of your wall. This popping can happen if the wall is knocked with something heavy like furniture, or when you are trying to nail something into the wall with a hammer.

- **If the screws are under tightened or the nails are not hammered in far enough** so that they don't quite touch the plasterboard, the same sort of thing can happen.
- **Wasted boards:** Try to make sure the dry liners use up the smaller bits of board where possible, to avoid excessive waste. It is easy for them to continually pick up new boards for each section of work, but any waste left at the end of the job will have to be disposed of by you, usually in a skip, which can get expensive these days (*especially as plasterboard now often needs to be segregated from normal builders' waste*).

Ceiling covings:

I mentioned this earlier, but it is worth just repeating here. Over the years, I have got in to the habit of coving every ceiling in new houses. Why? Well, they can look quite nice, and also they can help to hide the annoying drying out cracks that all new homes tend to get after a few months. When timber dries it shrinks. So does plaster (to a minimal extent). This results in hairline cracks appearing around the building.

Cracks always find the easiest places to appear. The places where the structure is weakest. - In the case of drying out cracks, the most common places for them to appear are:

1) The joints between the walls and ceilings.
2) Between ground floor and first floor windows and doors (*on a 2-storey house, this is normally a much shorter distance than it is from the ground floor to the roof*).
3) Around window and door frames.

Coving all the wall to ceiling joints basically hides any cracks, which may or may not appear and saves you having to go back, rub down and re-paint after 6 months and again possibly after 12 months.

The cracks between openings on different floors only tend to happen on traditionally built houses and I am afraid you are stuck with them.

The cracks around the door frames tend to be hidden by the architraves and the cracks around window frames can be hidden with a fine mastic joint, or even sometimes, a thick coat of paint. These cracks therefore don't tend to cause much of a problem.

The plastering will usually be the last operation of the first fix phase of the job. Once it has been completed, you will be ready to move on to the second fixes.

First fixing for a 200 sq ft, simple 4 bed traditionally built house should take between 3 – 7 weeks, depending on how well organised you are.

We will look at the second fixes for traditionally built houses after we have run through the first fixes for the other common build options.

First fixing a timber framed house:

The first fix for a timber framed house follows the same lines as for a traditionally built house, so reading the previous section will give you a good idea of what it entails. There are, however a few differences which I will detail below:

Timber frame kits normally include the floor boarding, so that's one job you won't usually have to worry about getting all the materials for.

Job 1: Insulation

The first job, once the building is weathertight, is normally to install the insulation to the external walls and wherever you need or want it in the internal walls

If it rained while the frame was being erected, there will be a good chance that the frame will still be wet when you come to install the insulation. This could potentially cause longer term problems.

The most common type of insulation to install in timber framed houses if fibreglass. The problem with using fibreglass is that if it gets wet, the weight of the moisture can make it sag and if this happens, it can significantly reduce its insulating qualities by uninsulated gaps being created at the top of the wall.

Another potential problem with fitting insulation into wet walls is that once everything is sealed in, there is the possibility of mould forming over time within the insulation. Obviously, this is something you need to avoid.

If the walls are very wet when you are ready to start fixing the insulation, there are two things you could do:

1. Wait until the frame dries out before fitting the insulation (you might find that there are a few dry areas you can get on with while you wait).
2. Use rigid foam insulation instead of fibreglass. The rigid foam doesn't absorb moisture and won't sag. It is also a much more efficient insulator than fibreglass, so you won't need the same thickness of rigid foam to give you the same U values. Rigid foam, however is significantly more expensive than fibreglass, so make sure you are aware of any cost implications if you decide to swap.

It is usual for the joiners to fit the insulation in to the frame. Your job as project manager will be to make sure the materials are there in the right quantities and to make sure that it is being installed correctly. The main thing you need to watch out for are gaps around the insulation, often found if the joiners are not taking enough care when cutting and fitting it.

Also, watch out for waste. There will be lots of areas around the house where small amounts of insulation are required, so make sure that the leftover bits from the large areas of wall are not just thrown away. Put them in to plastic bags and use them to do the bits and bobs.

Job 2: Noggings / door linings / window boards / stairs / loft access

As with timber walls in traditionally built houses, once the insulation has been fitted, the next jobs will usually to be fit the any additional first fix joinery items such as noggings (see previous section).

Job 3: First fix plumbing and electricals

The first fix plumbing and electrical installations for a timber framed house pretty much follow the same process as for a traditionally built house (see previous section).

Job 4: Vapour barrier

The job of a vapour barrier in a timber framed building is to stop moisture from being able to get through the plasterboard and into the frame, where it can get trapped, reducing the walls insulating properties and causing the insulation to sag (leaving uninsulated areas).

In most timber frame homes, the vapour barrier normally takes the form of a plastic sheet, covering the whole of the area of inside face of the external walls (plastic sheeting tends to be the cheapest option, but there are also various other specialist options on the market).

It is not generally required for internal walls, because any moisture which gets into the walls will usually dry out pretty quickly by having a natural airflow passing the faces of the walls either side of it.

The joiner will normally fit the vapour barrier, stapling it to the studs of the frame and taping all the joints. Passive house enthusiasts don't tend to like the idea of the barrier being stapled to the frame as theoretically, the process of stapling is creating hundreds of tiny holes in the plastic sheeting. Personally, I don't worry too much about this, as the staples should all be going in to timber studs, so they won't be creating access points for either air, or moisture to get through to the voids within the panels.

Your building regs specification will detail the type of vapour barrier to use and you will be able to order the most commonly used products from any builders' merchant.

Job 5: Plaster boarding & finishing

One area where the choices available for timber frames differ from traditionally built houses, is the list of options for finishing the internal face of both the external and internal walls. You cannot wet plaster a timber framed house. They need to be dry boarded, using plasterboards (or cement boards)". The reason for this is simply that, to apply wet plaster you need a solid wall (either brick or concrete).

Apart from that, the choices for finishing the walls in a timber framed house are pretty much identical to those for finishing the stud walls to a traditionally built house (i.e. boarding / taping / skimming, or boarding / taping / jointing – see previous section for details).

First fixing a SIPS house

The main difference between timber frame and SIPS related to the fact that more work is done in the factory, which will obviously mean that there is less for you to do on site.

Here is a reminder of what a SIPS panel looks like:

When it comes to first fixing SIPS frames, there are two options:

1) Conduit holes (pre-drilled in the factory) within the panel itself.
2) Create a Service void inside the frame.

SIPS panels offer a built in advantage over standard timber framed houses, in that they are manufactured with an OSB board on both sides. On the inside face, this means that every SIPS wall will have a load bearing ability that is not achieved using standard timber frame stud walls (without noggings). Fixings attached to any finished wall of a SIPS house, will go through the plasterboard and in to the OSB.

1) Conduit holes

Around 15 years ago, this was the preferred option for most self-builders using the SIPS system, but it has since been replaced in popularity by the service void option. The way the conduit system works, is that when the panels are designed (using your own drawings for the panel designs), the clients will sit down, usually with the manufacturer and together plan out both the plumbing and electrical layouts for the whole house.

The SIPS manufacturer will then drill holes either down from the top or up from the bottom of the panels to the locations where sockets, switches etc. are required. At those locations, holes will be cut in the OSB board on the internal face of the walls to allow cables and / or pipes to be fed up inside the panel and pulled out of the top (or bottom), by the electricians or plumbers, as part of the overall wiring or plumbing installation.

Once the plumbing and electrical first fix installation has been completed, a vapour barrier will be fitted to the internal face of the external walls (just the same as for timber framed houses).

Holes will need to be cut through the vapour barrier where there are any plumbing or electrical fittings, so to make sure you don't reduce its performance, make sure you tape around each fitting to re-create the vapour barrier seal.

The problem with the conduit option is that if you miss anything in your plumbing or electrical design, once the first fix has been completed, it is very difficult to add in any extra fittings later.

If you found that, once the frame was up, you needed to add an extra socket, switch or pipe run, you would usually need to cut a chase through the OSB and into the insulation in order to do so. Once the extra service was installed, you would then need to make good both the chase and the wall finish, which would be a fiddly, time consuming (and therefore costly) thing to have to do.

2) Service voids

This, to my mind is the better of the two options for SIPS first fix installations (although it reduces your room width by a few inches). This is how it works:

i. Fit the vapour barrier.
ii. Attach a framework of timber battens (preferably 2" x 1") to all the walls, generally at 600mm centres, with the individual battens running vertically. These battens will be used to fix the plaster / cement boarding to later, so they must be accurately positioned to match plasterboard sizes (*for this reason, I suggest that whoever fixes the battens also fixes the boards, - that way they will try to make sure they get all the batten positions correct first time*).
iii. Run all the plumbing and electrical services to complete the first fix works, within this newly formed service area.
iv. Fix noggings where required to take heavy objects which will be fixed to the finished walls. This is the weak bit of this option, - you are now not going to be using the OSB board which forms part of the SIPS panel, to fix your heavy items to, instead you are having to buy and fix more OSB between the battening and behind the plasterboard.
v. Board the walls with plasterboard or cement board.

If you are using standard plasterboards, I suggest that, rather than fixing noggings in between the timber battens just where you know you are going to need them, you consider boarding the **whole of the house** with OSB before fixing the plasterboards. That way you will be futureproofing the house if you want to fix additional heavy items anywhere.

Alternatively, use cement boards for the finished wall surface instead of OSB, as I suggested in the "First fixing a traditional build" section of this chapter. This should do away with the need for any additional support.

Other first fix works for SIPS houses

Once the plumbing and electrical work are completed, you will then carry on with installing all the other first fix joinery items as detailed earlier in this chapter, followed by the plasterboards or cement boards.

First fixing a closed panel framed house

As there are presently a few different types of closed panel system available, each with its own characteristics, it is a bit difficult to list the first fix process in any definitive order. However, the two things you can be fairly sure of as a project manager are:

1) There will less work for you to organise.
2) The first fix process should be completed in a shorter time than it would take for any of the other main build methods.

Basic closed panels:

Some closed panels come in a similar state to a SIPS panel, with insulation built in to the panel and simply an OSB board on each face (no plasterboard / cement board). This is its most basic form and the first fix operations for this type of panel will be pretty much the same as they are for SIPS panels which use the service void option for first fixing.

These panels would not be my first choice as they don't really take advantage of all the benefits that are available to the closed panel system.

Panels with service ducting built in

We looked at these panels in earlier chapters, so I won't go into detail about what they offer here, but suffice to say that these are the panels I would make my first choice as long as spec and the insulation levels are high, the build quality was good and the price was right.

The installation of the service ducting and the pre-fixing (in the factory) of all the back boxes for the sockets and switches within the panels just makes the whole first fix process so much faster, simpler, less stressful and less prone to error.

Add in a cement board finish, fitted in the factory (rather than plasterboard with either OSB noggings, or full OSB boarding to all walls) and you should be able to achieve not only a very fast first fix, but one which costs less, creates much less waste and where everything is exactly in the right place - first time!

Panels with all services pre-installed

This is the method we are used to seeing with the German and Scandinavian kit houses. There is nothing wrong with it. It is extremely quick and usually offers a very high quality finished product, but it is also very expensive and outside the financial reach of many self-builders.

The process

Depending on which closed panel system you use, the first fix works will obviously vary somewhat, but as a basic rule of thumb, follow the same processes for the first fix overall as if you were building a traditionally built or timber framed house, knowing that *some* of the work will already have been done at the factory, so:

- There should be very little or no work to do with insulation.
- The vapour barrier may already be fitted.
- You may or may not need to create a service void.
- The sockets and switch boxes (etc.) may already be in place.

- You may or may not need to fit noggings.
- Door linings and even the doors themselves, may already be fitted (in the factory).
- Windows may already be fitted.
- The plaster boarding or cement boarding may have been completed.
- You will still need to complete the wall ready for decorating, with either a plaster skim or tape and joint finish.

The rest of the first fix jobs detailed in the previous sections of this chapter will all usually need doing, as they would for any of the other build options (door linings/ stairs / window boards etc.)

First fixing an ICF house

This is the only major building system which varies in the method of first fixing from the others covered so far in this chapter. The differences are not huge, but you do need to be aware of them.

- Firstly, you may still have some timber internal walls in the house. If so, you will treat those as you would any of the other first fixes detailed above.
- You will need to create routes for the cables and pipes to run in. This involves creating chases in the polystyrene concrete shutters. This is done using a hot blade (a blade which melts the polystyrene). You need to be careful when marking out for all the piping and wiring, as moving wrongly positioned services is going to be difficult, time consuming and costly once the wall surface has been applied.
- Once the services have been installed you will usually apply plasterboards to the face of the wall using an approved adhesive.

If you are going to be fixing heavy objects to the wall, you will have to drill through the plasterboard and polystyrene and into the concrete before you achieve a strong fixing point. This will involve some pretty long screws, even for minor items.

It would be a good idea to consider using a cement board finish to the wall rather than plasterboard. That way the cement board would give you the strength to hang a lot of the more standard heavy items, without you needing to drill right through to the concrete. However, remember that the board will only be glued to the polystyrene so won't be a strong as if it were screwed to a timber stud.

All the other first fix items will be installed in a similar manner to the other main build options.

Second fixing

Introduction:

Once you have completed the first fixes, whichever build method you have used, you will have basically levelled the playing field.

Whether you built traditionally, timber frame, SIPS, closed panel or ICF, once the services have been installed and the walls have been given their specified finish (plasterboard / cement board / skim), you will end up with a house full of empty spaces all waiting to be given a personality and turned from spaces in to personalised, finished rooms.

This is where all the stressful work should start to diminish and the fun bit starts. You now have a blank canvas on which to create something brand new and exciting.

A few things to watch out for at this stage of the project are:

1) **Your budget:** The chances are that you will now be starting to get towards the end of your available finances, unfortunately, this is also the time that you start to buy the nice things that you have had your eyes on since you drew the first lines of your design on a bit of paper! Just don't go mad! Remember there are still a lot of jobs to be done and a lot of bills to be paid. You don't want to end up overspending and putting stress back on yourself by making rash decisions on spending at this stage.

2) **Consider each room carefully:** Once you are physically able to stand in a room, you can get a feel for it that you can't get from a drawing. So, before you start to spend money on your second fixes, decoration and furniture, just take some time standing in each room and trying to envisage how you would like it to end up. Think about paint colours, finishes to skirtings and architraves and any other features that will make the most of the space.

3) **Monitor the quality:** This is the bit of the job that everyone is going to see when you move in. Stuff that is hidden inside walls, under the floors or in the roof doesn't have to be particularly pretty, but the things you are going to be looking at every day, **does!**

    So, from day one of the second fix installation, keep your eyes peeled for poor or untidy workmanship and where you find it, jump on whoever is responsible straight away, getting them to put right what is wrong. By doing so, you will set the tone, not only for them, but for everyone else working on the job.

4) **Pile 'em high:** As I have said before, self-builders tend to do one job at a time, possibly because that way the whole process is easier to control. However, there is no reason why joiners, plumbers, electricians and any other specialist installers can't all be working in the house together, as long as they are not tripping each other up. You could have joiners hanging doors, fixing skirtings and architraves and fitting kitchens, plumbers fixing radiators and bathrooms and electricians fixing sockets and switches all over the house. If you can pull this off, you could save weeks on your programme.

5) **Leave the decorating till last:** As I have said before, it is always advisable to leave the decorating until everyone else has pretty much finished making a mess. If you get the walls painted and then they get dirty, you are going to have some pretty irate decorators giving you some severe earache and who may be demanding that they are paid again for the extra work involved in re-painting.

    If you can zone the second fix works to get certain areas finished, you might be able to get the decorators going a bit sooner, but if not, try to have everyone else out of the building before you bring them in.

    If you are really tight on time, you could possibly apply the primer paint coats to the woodwork and the first coats of emulsion to the walls and ceilings, but, just remember, you may still have to pay for any marks to be made good as a consequence, unless you repair the damage yourself. That's ok, especially if it gets you in the house a couple of weeks' sooner.

I won't be using the "Job 1 / Job 2" indexing system I used for the first fixes in this section. The order of the works for second fix does not generally need to be as rigid as it needs to be for the first fix and it will depend on each set of circumstances, on each project, as to what and when things can be done.

As a rule, as I have just said, try to get as many jobs going concurrently as possible without overloading the house with people.

So, instead of "Job 1 / Job 2" I will just bullet point each item, leaving you to discuss the programme with your sub-contractors to decide the best time to programme in each activity.

Second fixing a traditional build

- **Joinery**

Hanging doors / ironmongery: This will usually be one of the first jobs of the second fix phase. Doors can be bought from £15 upwards, but I would suggest that as long as your budget is ok, that you spend at least £60 to £100 per door, so that you get something that is going to create a high quality finished appearance.

Bear in mind also, that sound passes through doors (so solid doors are better than hollow doors) and it also gets through any gaps around the doors edge. Consider using fire door linings which have an intumescent strip in the frame. This not only helps prevent the spread of fire and smoke, but it also reduces sound transmittance around the door edges.

Door hinges and handles are a personal choice, but they do add a certain something to the room if they look right (yes - even the hinges!). Go to the trade ironmongery companies. They are usually a lot cheaper than the DIY stores. Personally I like a nice chrome finished hinge with matching handles.

Some doors might need to be fire doors whether you want them or not. Check the building regs spec to find out which.

Skirtings / architraves: As with the doors, your choice of skirtings and architraves will go a long way to creating a feel in the room. You don't need to keep the same style all the way through the house. You may go for solid wood downstairs and painted upstairs. Take a bit of time to go and look at some developers houses to get some ideas.

Skirtings start at the cheaper end with *4-inch pencil round*. Don't bother with these, or your house will look like a cheaply finished office. The minimum spec suitable for a self-build would be something like a 6-inch Torus or lambs tongue in softwood, which would then be painted and can give quite a nice finish. However, for a bit more money you could be looking at a pre-finished veneered MDF skirting with a natural wood finish. These are a fraction of the price of solid hardwood skirtings, but many people would not be able to tell them apart.

All the same choices are available for the architraves, but one modern idea is to contrast the architrave with the skirting. A pre-finished veneered skirting with a white painted architrave can look very nice, especially if you carry the mix and match theme through to the stairs and any other timber features you have in the building.

Kitchens / utility rooms: I will be covering this subject in a bit of detail in the next chapter, but I just need to say here that you will be looking at fitting the kitchen / utility rooms at this stage of the project. Both the plumbers and the electricians will need these jobs done in order to be able to complete their own second fix works.

Stair handrails: As with the doors / skirtings / architraves, the stairs can be used to create a feel to the finished house. They are usually the first thing you will see when you come in through the front door, so a bit of thought should be given to how they look. The usual stair treatment is simply to paint or stain all the spindles, stringers, handrails and newels and carpet the treads. However, with a bit more thought, you can easily create something which catches the attention and gives the house more of a feeling of quality. Here is an example:

Possibly window boards? The question mark does not mean I am not sure when the window boards (or window cills as many people call them) should be fitted, it just means that there are two trains of thought on when to fit them. One method is to fix them with the first fix so the plasterboard is fitted around them, possibly giving a tidier finish. The other option is to fit them as a second fix item.

My thoughts on this subject would be:

1. Fit them as a first fix item if you are going to paint them (any dirt or other marks will be rubbed down and covered by the paint).
2. Fit them as a second fix item if you are installing them pre-finished or if you are going to stain them. In other words, if the finished appearance can be damaged during the ongoing building works, fit them as late as possible.

A thick window board can add to the quality feel of a room and may be worth paying a bit extra for. Something maybe 1.5" thick (as opposed to less than an inch for some of the cheaper options) often gives a nice appearance.

Loft insulation: Loft insulation requirements are getting more and more stringent (which is a good thing), but they have resulted in us making a standard trussed roof attic pretty much useless for storage or for anything else.

Fitting fibreglass loft insulation under a sloping roof is a real pain in the backside! You need overalls, gloves and goggles to protect yourselves from being damaged by the glass fibres. It also needs to be laid carefully, so that you keep the required ventilation through the roof space (normally from eaves through to eaves) and you need to make sure you don't leave any gaps for heat to escape through.

Check your building regs spec for how much insulation you will need to install and how to lay it.

One option to make the job a bit easier and keep your attic a bit more usable, would be to swap the fibreglass for rigid foam insulation. This will generally be a bit easier to fit (as long as you cut it to the right sizes and accurately so you don't end up with gaps) and it will also take up less space, possibly allowing you to put a "light duty" floor down to utilise the attic space as we have always done in the past, for storage.

Built in furniture / wardrobes etc. One weakness with new homes in the UK is that we don't tend to allow enough storage space within the design. Building your own home allows you to do so.

There are no rules here. Everyone has their own ideas on what sort of storage spaces they would like, just bear in mind that often the pre-manufactured stuff can often turn out to give you a better quality, lower cost finished job.

A lot of people think that buying a load of timber, getting the joiners to build the wardrobes and then getting them painted and varnished will be a good way to save money. Although there are times when that is the right choice, it is not usually the case. The time and labour involved can make hand built furniture a lot more expensive than shop bought and unfortunately it can also end up looking very cheap, detracting from the overall quality of the finished house.

Bear in mind also that speed of build is very important in keeping your costs down (as I detailed in the early chapters), so for every day that you have a chippy working on building your furniture and wardrobes, you will be paying out for a number of other running costs for the rest of the job.

I would suggest looking around at the pre-finished options before you make up your mind on which way to go with this.

Shelving: The same general thought applies to shelving as to built-in furniture, however, shelving can sometimes offer a quick and cheap option for storage, so is possibly something to think about, as long as you consider where you are putting the shelves and the visual and practical impact they will have on the finished job.

- **Plumbing**

Water mains connection: The mains water connection will normally be fitted within the kitchen units, often under the sink. Where this is the case, the plumbers need to fit the main basic components of the water supply pipework before the kitchen units are fitted. There will usually be welding to be done at floor level and insulation to be fitted in to the entry ducting before it is sealed (to stop any unwanted critters from sneaking into the house up the ducting!)

A stop tap will be fitted inside the building and once that has been done, you can think about getting the mains water supply connected to the house.

Gas main connection: You will normally have fitted a metre box to one of the external walls of the house. The gas main will be installed in a trench up to that box and your plumber will run your internal gas pipework from the metre box to the boiler, gas fires etc. Usually, once your gas system has been fully tested and you are ready for the final connection to be made, the supplier will install the metre itself (this final connection method can vary from region to region, but basically you test the completed installation, then you get it turned on).

Boiler: I suggest that you spend a bit of time researching boilers. There are so many types out there now. Most new boilers are very energy efficient, so that is not something you should need to lose sleep over, but you do need to make sure it is up to the job.

You need to give some thought to how it will be used on a day to day, or hour to hour basis. Consider this:

It is winter, you have a family of two adults and three children. Both adults work and all the kids are at school. In the morning rush, over a period of less than an hour, and during the evening, you will need the central heating on and probably baths or showers for numerous people. The boiler needs to be able to cope with the demand without putting it under permanent strain or with it simply not supplying enough hot water for everyone's needs.

Talk to your plumbing contractor to make sure you choose your boiler wisely and don't shy away from paying out over £1500 for a decent one.

My favoured system would be a big combi boiler (giving at least 3.5 / 4.5 gallons of good hot water per minute), possibly linked to a well-insulated cylinder. That way, when there is a surge of demand for hot water, there will be a good supply already hot in the cylinder, so the boiler has less work to do over that period.

I am seeing some good deals for boilers on line these days, so it may be worth you stating in your tender package that you will supply the boiler, but leave the rest of the basic plumbing installation materials for the plumbers to source.

Kitchens / bathrooms: I'll be looking at these in the next chapter, but they both form part of the standard plumbing second fix installation works.

Radiators / underfloor heating: If you are installing underfloor heating you will usually have installed the pipework for the system as part of the first fix. The pipes themselves will usually now be sticking up through the floor screed ready to be trimmed and fitted to a manifold and the water supply.

The best place to position the manifold is under the stairs or in a cupboard that you won't need to access regularly. You need to make sure you can access all the controls and valves quickly in case there are any leaks and for servicing / maintaining the system.

Specialist plumbing equipment: The second fix works will usually encompass the finals works for everything involved with gas, oil or water. That will include things like oil tanks / gas tanks / garden irrigation fittings / water features etc.

Your job:

The main thing that you (as project manager) need to think about with regard to the second fix plumbing, is the way it combines with the other ongoing works. You need to keep in regular conversation with the other trades, to make sure that the things that need doing to allow the plumbers to do their job are all completed by the time the plumbers are ready for them. – This is quite a complicated task that will require a lot of thought and planning on your part, especially if it is your first project.

- **Electrical**

Mains connection: As with the gas supply, you will usually have fitted an electrical metre box to the external wall of the house, the mains supply will be brought underground to the metre box and your electricians will run the cables to a fuse box. Once the electrical installation has been completed and tested, you can request the supply connection.

Fuse board: The fuse board will usually be located close to the metre box, high up on an internal wall. Each fuse box will contain a number of fuses, each of which is connected to a different part of the installation (downstairs sockets/ upstairs sockets / downstairs lights / upstairs light / cooker / boiler etc.) These days, all fuse boxes are fitted with sensitive trip switches which will cut off the power to any part of the system which starts to show signs of being faulty.

A thick cable then runs from the fuse box to the metre box where it connects to the metre itself.

Sockets / switches / light fittings: As with the doors / architraves etc., socket and light switches, perhaps surprisingly, can have a significant visual impact on the appearance of the finished room.

There is no problem with fitting the basic white sockets and switches. We are all used to them and they are found in some quite expensive house, however, paying a bit extra for something a bit nice can just give each room that little bit of extra something.

By the way: Chrome fittings are a pain to keep clean! Everyone who touches them will leave a finger mark and kids with dirty fingers will give you a never-ending cleaning job if they can reach them.

Brass fittings are not quite as bad in this respect, but are a bit old fashioned these days.

There are however, lots of nice looking modern options which you will find in the catalogues of the electrical wholesalers, including remote controlled dimming switches which don't cost very much at all. I have used these and can strongly recommend them. Just make sure before you go buying them for every room, that the wiring system is suitable for them. Some of them don't work where there are two or more switches for the same light fitting.

Also, watch out for one of the booby traps when it comes to light fittings. Standard room height in the UK are around 2.4m from floor level. Large, fancy light fittings can often hang around 0.5m – 0.6m+ from the ceiling to their lowest point. If like me, you are over 6' (1.8m) tall, this can present a problem and a hazard to the head! Bear this in mind when you are choosing your fittings.

Earthing to fittings: These are a standard part of the electrical installation, but I just thought I'd mention them briefly, partly so you'll know what they are when you see them, and partly so you can make sure they are not forgotten.

You need to supply an earthing strip to certain appliances and fittings around the house. Check on the building regs spec and just do a visual check to make sure they are not forgotten. Earthing strips are normally seen as a thick green and yellow cable running from an appliance or fitting into the floor or wall.

Other specialist fittings: These would include all the items mentioned in the first fix section that you may have included in your project.

Be warned: This is where your remaining dribs and drabs of money could start to disappear in large chunks if you are not careful.

A lot of the items which would come under the heading specialist could also usually be described as luxuries. Don't get caught in the trap of getting carried away buying lots of expensive toys at this stage unless you are sure that your finances can stand the stress.

Shop around on line for the best deals. There can be literally £1,000's difference in the cost of different systems that basically do the same thing. If your budget could risk becoming a bit tight by buying new, check out sites like E-Bay and Gum Tree to try to find some of the luxuries you would like to get hold of, second-hand. You might be surprised at what you come across.

External fittings: There are a few electrical additions and fixtures you may be fitting to the outside of the house, including:

- **Solar panels:** Make sure you not only shop around for these, but also do your homework on them. Solar panels have advanced in leaps and bounds over the past few years and are continuing to do so. If you researched them a year or so ago, don't just go ahead and buy what you originally liked, without checking to see if there is now something better and cheaper. The chances are that there will be.
- **Security lighting:** Most new self-build houses will have some sort of external security lighting. The best ones will have movement / heat sensors, will only operate after dusk and will have an override switch so you can put them on to act as permanent flood lights if you are doing something outside at night.
- **External sockets:** It is useful to have two or more of these dotted around the perimeter of the building, especially if your house is quite big. Make sure you get good quality weatherproof ones and mastic seal all-round the box where it meets the wall to make sure water can't get in to the house.
- **Patio heaters:** These are not very green things to be fitting to your energy conscious house, as they will eat electricity, but if you want to be able to stay outside on your patio to prolong an evening in the garden, they are useful to have.

Tiling

The approach to floor and wall tiling in new homes has changed a lot in the past few years. 20 years ago, it was seen as something to stop the plaster and the floor boards getting wet, but around 10 or so years ago, when interior design became a fashionable concept, people started to include tiling as an integral and important part of any home, new or old.

There are no particular rules. If you like a particular tile and if it suits the room you are going to use it in and if the cost of it doesn't break the bank, then that is the right tile for you.

There are, however a few things to bear in mind when it comes to choosing and fixing both floor and wall tiles, these include:

➤ **Tiling is actually quite a complicated job and costs a lot more than the price of the tiles themselves**
  It is easy to look at a nice tile in a show room and think that it is reasonably priced, however just be aware that the tile is only part of the full kit you will need to do the job. You are also going to need:

  - Edging strips (costing from £3 to £20 for a 2.4m length)
  - Corner beads (£3 to £20 for a 2.4m length)
  - Adhesive (up to £20 / tub or bag)
  - Grout (up to £20 / bag)
  - Feature tiles (such as borders, mosaics etc.)
  - Sealant (if the tiles are not pre-glazed)

- Hardboard (if the sub floor is likely to move / shrink / expand)
- Spacers
- Labour costs (from around £12 to £40 / sq metre depending on the amount of work involved.

> **Don't try to do the tiling yourself unless you are confident of achieving a high quality finish**
> A poor tiling job can spoil the whole effect of a room. The tiling is pretty much the first thing you notice when you walk into a bathroom. Make a mess of it and all the effort and cost of trying to create a visually attractive room, could end up being a waste of time and money.

> **Very big tiles are hard to fix and can look a mess if not fixed properly**
> Big tiles, properly fixed can look very impressive. Big tiles with corners not quite meeting properly (either in level or line), can not only look like a dog's dinner, but can actually create trip hazards on floors, catch the dirt and end up with their corners getting chipped. Only experienced tilers should attempt to lay large tiles.

> **Small tiles cost more to fix**
> Small, individual tiles will be a lot more labour intensive to fix. Common sense says that if there are 12 tiles to a square metre, then they will usually be fixed much faster than if there are 30. Grouting will also take longer. So, expect to pay up to twice as much per square metre (or more) for fixing 4" square tiles as you would for fixing 12" square tiles.

> **Floor tiles on timber floors need special attention**
> If you are fixing tiles to upstairs rooms, you need to bear in mind that timber floors will move. Normal tile adhesive and grout is not flexible, so you need to use a special flexible adhesive in these areas. It is also normal to use a hardboard intermediate layer between the structural floor and the tiles. Hardboard doesn't tend to shrink or expand in the same way as a chipboard floor or joisted floor, so movement cracks are less likely to appear where you use it.

> **Some tiles need sealing before grouting**
> There are a few tiles which are sold without a sealer / glaze. These tiles will need to be sealed after being fixed. Be careful if you use this type of tile. If you apply the grout before the sealer, it can permanently stain the surface of the tile. A tiler forgot to seal this type of tile one of my jobs a few years ago, and we ended up having to take the whole lot up, bin them and re-lay new ones.

> **Tiling upper storey floors can cause problems if you have water or gas leaks:**
> If you tile over upper floors (most commonly bathrooms) and then at some time in the future, you find you have leak on a water or gas pipe joint underneath the tiles, it could be a fairly major task to try to get to the problem area in order to fix it.
> If you used plastic piping for your first fix (as suggested earlier in this chapter), the chances of this problem occurring are going to be much lower, but you still need to bear it in mind as a possibility when choosing your floor finishes.

> *Seriously* **think about not tiling anything that you may need to access later**
> That same thinking needs to be applied to *anything and everything* else that you might consider tiling over which you may need to access in the future, such as toilet cisterns, sink waste pipes, boxing in around pipework or cabling, etc.

> **If you are going to tile over areas which are being boxed in, use thick timber for the actual boxing in**
> Bear in mind that thin timber boarding is more likely to move than thick timber boarding. So, if you are going to be tiling over any boxed in areas, use at least ½" thick (or preferably ¾") plywood or chipboard for the job and use the flexible adhesives / grouts.

> **Shop around**

Prices of tiles and all the ancillary materials needed to complete the job vary enormously. It is well worth spending a bit of time shopping around before you buy. Try to get trade prices where possible, either by telling them that you are building a full house and will need a lot of tiles, or get your tile fitters to try to get better deals for you by using their trade status. Spending a bit of time on sourcing bargains could well save hundreds of pounds.

> **Good tiling can add considerable value to your home:**
One good thing about tiling these days it that, if done properly, it can make your house much more desirable to potential future buyers and can therefore increase its market value by a noticeable amount. You may not be thinking about this at the moment, but if you catch the self-build bug, the chances are that you will end up building at least one more, if not a couple more houses before you settle. So, bear in mind that one day you may be wanting to sell up quickly for the best price achievable. Try therefore, to make the appearance and quality of your tiling work for you when that day comes.

Decorating

This is one of the jobs a lot of self-builders will consider taking on themselves (after all, you don't need a high level of skill to chuck some paint onto a wall, do you? Well yes you do!)

Over the years, I have seen many examples of self-build projects which have been spoilt by the owners deciding to have a go at the decorating and making a complete pig's ear of it!

Paint on the window and door frames, uneven coats, rough joint lines between different colours, heavy brush marks visible in the finished walls etc.

I am not saying don't have a go at the decorating yourselves, but only do so if you are pretty sure you can achieve a high standard finish. If you mess up the decorating, you could devalue your new home significantly and just as it is with the tiling, even if you have spent a fortune on all the other finishing items, it can still look like the whole thing has been built by a gang of chimpanzees!

Don't think that you can save money by buying cheap paints. It doesn't work that way. Cheap paints are almost invariably thinner paints. Thinner paints don't cover the walls as well and take more coats to achieve a decent finished job. For each coat of paint across a full new 4 bed house, you might pay up to £1,000 in labour and materials, so an extra coat being needed because you use thin paint, could make the few quid saving you made by buying it in the first place look a bit pathetic!

One of my tricks when it comes to painting is to use the very thick **obliterating paint** *for new plaster throughout the whole house.*

By doing so and by not thinning the first coat, I find that I can usually perfectly adequately cover the walls with two coats rather than the usual three. This will save time and money, whether you are doing the work yourselves or you bring in a professional decorator.

However, persuading a professional decorator not to use a thin first coat (a mist coat) and to only apply two coats of thick paint will sometimes not be an easy thing to do. They "like to do it the way they have always done it", so you might only be able to use this trick if you do the decorating yourself.

Final fixes

As with the second fixes, once you reach the final fix stage, no matter which of the main build methods you have used, you will be doing pretty much the same things.

Final fixes are basically all the tidying-up bits. The bits you couldn't do in the second fix because there are still things that someone else needs to do before the final finishing work can be done. They usually includes some or all the following:

- **Boxing in:** These are fitted in such places as around waste pipes in bathrooms and around downpipes which run from ceiling to floor inside the building.

  Basically, anything which is going to look unsightly when everything is finished, can get boxed in to hide it. The boxing in frame will usually be made out of either a 2" x 1" or 2" x 2" timber framework, with plywood or chipboard fitted over it. This can then either be painted, tiled or carpeted. Boxing ins on the floor can often make good low level shelves.

- **Flooring:** Leave the fitting of flooring until as late as possible, especially in the areas where furniture is going to be brought in to the house (e.g. through halls etc.)

  You really need all the decorating and final snagging to have been completed before laying any flooring (floor tiles can usually be protected by plastic sheeting and are easier to clean than carpet or timber floors if they get any marks on them, so laying them a little earlier shouldn't usually be a problem).

  To save a bit of time at the end of the job, it may be possible to completely finish all the works in a number of rooms, then lay the flooring and close those rooms off from access by anyone working in the house.

- **Custom built furniture**

  This includes things like fitted wardrobes, shelving, TV units etc. Just bear in mind that when considering the best time to build these items, that you may wish to fix skirting boards to them. If so, you may want to do some or all the work on them during the second fix stage.

  (Left: A part built lounge unit that I built in one of my own self builds & the same unit complete).

Mastic (internal / external)

As part of the process of making your new home as airtight as possible, the job of mastic treating any potential leak points has become more important over the past few years. Your house will be tested for airtightness when it is complete and if it fails you will need to find out why and fix it.

Bringing in a professional company to go around the whole house to mastic all vulnerable areas will be, to my mind, money well spent. The job only takes a few hours, so isn't usually expensive. At the same time as treating any potential air leak areas, the mastic treatment process will also seal everything else that needs it against water damage (things like showers, baths, worktops, window frames etc.)

I would suggest that you consider mastic treating (or at least caulking) skirting boards, both top and bottom on all external walls. This will help to stop air leaking through poorly fitted plasterboards into the wall structure and potentially through to the outside of the building, via any small gaps in the blockwork or timber frame.

Mastic treating the ceiling / wall joints (or the tops and bottom of any fitted covings) can provide a potential double benefit of reducing both air leakage and sound transmittance between floors.

- **Checking for airtightness**

  As part of your preparation for the airtightness test, you should spend some time carefully looking round each room to see if there are any areas which could be seen as weak points. The mastic treatment will catch a lot of these, but there may be some glaring weak spots such as badly fitted loft access hatches, poorly cut holes in external walls where pipework passes through, gaps *under* door frames (easy to miss because they are not naturally in your line of eye sight). Make good any weak points before the air test.

> **Re-fixing fittings**

During the second fix stage of the project, your tradespeople will have fitted things like door handles, light and socket switches, light fittings etc. However, what often happens next is that when the decorators arrive, they unscrew most of those fittings for the paint to be able to go slightly behind them and to reduce the chances of paint getting on to the fittings themselves. Someone then has to go back around to refix everything that has been loosened.

I would normally get the decorator to do this job. Just make sure that all the sockets and switches are level when they are re fixed. There is a bit of tolerance in most plastic fittings which allows them to go back on slightly out of level. This can look horrible to anyone with a keen eye.

> **Snagging**

Pretty much at the end of the job comes the snagging. When everyone has finished or nearly finished their work, you need to present them with their own snagging list.

The way I go about drawing up all the separate lists is to first of all, pick a time when there is no one on site. Preferably at the end of a day very close to the end of the job. I then take a note pad and pen and go in to every room one at a time and simply stand and look at every detail within each room.

By slowly moving your eyes around the room, the ceiling, the walls and the floor, you will tend to naturally see any faults, blemishes or errors. Make lists of all the items in each room (hopefully there won't be many if everyone has been doing their jobs properly).

Do the same around the outside of the building (and if there has been any landscaping work done, check that over too).

Check garages and outhouses, manhole covers, garden walls, fencing. In other words, check **everything** that has been constructed, either as part of your own project or where your own project affects other properties around it (e.g. fencing / walls etc.)

Once you have compiled your list, you need to transfer the relevant items for each trade on to a new sheet, which you will give to the tradesmen to work through and put right.

DO NOT pay anyone their final payment until the snagging has been done.

If you have agreed retentions with everyone, that can take the some of the stress of the snagging works, as you will be keeping a sum of money from the final payment for a period of normally six months. This sum of money can then be used, if necessary, to cover any remedial works that need doing, which, for whatever reason, the guys who did the job originally couldn't or wouldn't come back to put right.

Nearly there!

We're getting near the time for you to move in now. Another few days and you should be able to start bringing your furniture in.

However, before you do, you need to get your final certificates sorted and make sure everything is working properly and safely. We'll look at these items in the final chapter, but once you reach this stage, all the hard work should have been completed and you can start to plan a moving in date.

Chapter 14
Kitchens & bathrooms

These two subjects could easily have been included as part of the first and second fix chapters, but taking into consideration the amount of money spent on these rooms these days, I thought it would be worthwhile giving them a bit more attention and a chapter of their own.

As with many parts of the self-build process, there are no real rights and wrongs when it comes to kitchen and bathroom installation, but because of the large sums of money involved, it is a good idea to be aware of the implications of the choices you are going to be making.

Most self-builders will be building on limited budgets and will be looking for ways to maximise the bang for their buck. Trying to create rooms which have the wow factor and which look like they have cost a fortune, but have actually been bought for a reasonably modest outlay.

Over the years, I have picked up a few tricks when it comes to designing and buying kitchens and bathrooms and these are what I will be concentrating on in this chapter. If you bear what I am going to say in mind when you start to look at your own kitchen and bathroom installations, you could save thousands (and potentially tens of thousands) of pounds on your overall build budget.

Let's start with kitchens and utility rooms. We'll be looking at:

- What is a sensible budget for your project?
- Do you need the same style of units in both rooms?
- Design your own kitchen.
- Design your own utility room.
- Finding a supplier.
- Who will fit your kitchen?

1) What is a sensible budget for your project?

Take a trip to any of the self-build shows and you could be forgiven for coming away thinking that, to get a nice kitchen, you need to plan on paying out £50,000 upwards. Some of the kitchens displayed (which don't actually look that special to me) have price tags attached approaching £100,000, with the display models being shipped out at bargain prices as low as £35,000!

I have been fitting kitchens for the past twenty odd years, both for my own self-build projects and for the commercial housing I have built. I have never yet gone above the £10,000 mark for a single kitchen (maybe just over that for kitchen and utility room together).

I may not have installed anything as grand as the show kitchens, but generally when people have come to look, they have liked what they see. Below is an example of a self-build kitchen I did, on a very tight budget, in one of my own houses, about 7 years ago. It may not have the look of some of the latest kitchens, but at the time, it was one of the most popular styles:

The units (solid oak fronted), worktops, sink and tap cost me less than £4,000. The range cooker cost around £800. I bought a basic extractor unit and got the joiner to knock up the hood, which we then coated with an "artexy" type of covering to give a rough textured finish.

The wall tiles behind the range cooker and above the worktops were in a shiny gold finish, which seemed to work at the time (not sure about them now though). I only needed about 2 – 3 sq metres of these, at around £20 / sq m (I fitted them myself).

The floor tiles are natural "elephant skin" slate which was quite cheap as I remember (at around £15 - £20 / sq m) and again I laid the floor myself.

I left a bin space (I always do), as (*surprise, surprise*) it gives you somewhere to put a decent sized bin! (Which is something a lot of kitchen designers don't do) and I used a bit of coordinated colour with the furnishings. There was a 30-inch TV hung on the wall to the left of the photo (which you can't see) with a TV Arial and BT socket concealed behind it.

The most expensive features of the kitchen units themselves were, believe it or not, the two open end units which cost more than a base unit each!

The chairs were around £40 each and I put a little coffee table in so that whilst people were cooking, others could be sitting in the same room, chatting. The downlights were £20 for a set of six in B & Q and were on a dimmer switch.

The whole room, as you see it in the photo, complete with the TV, cost somewhere in the region of £6,300 (including VAT, which I later got back on a lot of the stuff)

Colour wise, I used an obliterating paint in "Country cream" for the walls then mixed a separate 10 Litre tub with some white paint to lighten the colour up (whilst keeping the general hue of the colour) and used that for the ceiling. Finally, I mixed another small tub with some more white paint to give the lightest version of the colour to the ceiling covings.

When I came to sell the house, the two rooms which got the most positive comment were the kitchen and the living / dining room (which I showed a few pages ago).

Kitchens have changed a lot in the past few years. The kitchen is now not just the room for cooking in. It is often the social centre of the house. People don't close the kitchen doors when they have guests, they put furniture in them to encourage everyone to head there!

Home owners want to show off their shiny posh kitchen units with slow closing drawers, curved cupboard doors, their posh appliances, ice makers, boiling water taps, LED lighting, their smooth slide out racking in room height cupboards, American freezers etc. The number of toys now available, means that when a new kitchen is installed into a house these days, it bears little or no resemblance to the pleasant but functional rooms we have been used to.

The two main problems with that fact are:

1) As the number of toys and the choices of styles of units has increased, so has the cost.

2) We poor self-builders, who are often trying to build Buckingham Palace for a fiver, have now got to either find the money to install a kitchen that keeps up with the Joneses, or we have to find a way to cheat, to make it look like we have spent a lot of money when we haven't!

So, how much should you, potentially a cash-strapped self-builder, allow in your budget for the fitting out of your kitchen and utility rooms?

The money you can afford to set aside will be strongly linked to your overall build budget and your build spec for the rest of the house. Different people have different priority areas for where they want to spend their money. So, what I'll do here is give you a rough guide to the minimums and maximums that I personally reckon you need to be looking to spend on your kitchens. If you want to go above these figures, that's fine, but you may have to lower your goals in other parts of the house if you do.

If your aim is to spend a lot lower amounts than I show below, again that is fine, just make sure you don't spoil the overall look of the house just to be able to tell your friends *"We paid tuppence for the whole kitchen"*!

(Figures are "net", after allowing for your VAT refund, but include fitting and appliances)

BUILD COST (INC LAND)	APPROX HOUSE VALUE	MIN SPEND	MAX SPEND
£100,000	£130,000 to £160,000	£3,500	£6,500
£150,000	£180,000 - £220,000	£6,000	£10,000
£200,000	£240,000 - £300,000	£8,000	£12,000
£250,000	£290,000 - £350,000	£9,000	£15,000
£300,000	£350,000 - £420,000	£10,000	£17,000
£300,000+	Up to £1,000,000	£15,000	£35,000

2) Do you need the same style of units in both rooms?

The answer to that question is "No, but it helps".

Most utility rooms tend to be adjacent to the kitchen and as such, if the door is left open, you will be able to see through to the utility room from the kitchen. If you spend most of your budget in your kitchen and only get a few cheap units and worktops in the utility room, when you see the two together, if you are not careful, the utility room can shout out: *"I was done as cheaply as possible, we had no money left!"* That is fine while you are living in the house and as long as you keep the utility room door closed when you have visitors, but can have a negative impact, if and when you come to sell the house.

The trick here, to my mind is to spend as little as possible on the utility room, but make it look as nice for a quick glance as the kitchen. How do you do this? It is not difficult and I'll show you how it works in practice in the design section below, but basically:

- Use the same unit doors, but if there is a cheaper carcass available, use it.
- Use as few units as possible and try to use the 1000mm standard width units where possible.
- High-line (without drawers) units are cheaper than draw line (with drawers). So, if you don't need drawers in this room, don't put any in.
- Don't use fancy features such as pull out racking, carousels etc.
- If you have expensive worktops in the kitchen, try to find a laminate worktop with the same finish for the utility.
- Leave spaces for the washing machine and tumble drier (*rather than building them in to units. You only really need to do that if they are in the kitchen*).
- Think about leaving spaces under the worktop area for all the different recycling bins, then buy nice looking, large modern bins. This could save you hundreds of pounds when compared to the cost of housing the bins inside base units.
- If you need wall units, try to line them up with the floor units (to keep a high quality visual aspect) but try to use 1000mm units if possible.
- Use your boiler to take up the space of one floor or wall unit (depending on the size of the boiler).
- Use the same flooring as you use in the kitchen, this will help to blend the two rooms together.
- Think about using one or two full height units. They don't tend to be too expensive but give you something that replaces one floor unit plus one wall unit and are very useful for storing ironing boards, sweeping brushes, vacuum cleaners etc.
- Install a good sized single sink in the utility room. You don't usually need a draining board in here, but a good bowl for washing clothes and other stuff that you don't want to take into the kitchen is a good idea and will be a good selling point if you want to move in a few years. Belfast sinks are still very popular for utility rooms.
- Don't bother fitting special lighting to the utility room units. People won't be in there long enough to notice or appreciate it. Keep that sort of thing for the main kitchen.
- Do use the same plinths, cornices and covings as you used in the main kitchen, unless it is very expensive stuff. If that is the case, a similar but simpler, cheaper style will usually be ok in the utility room as long as it doesn't stand out like a sore thumb.

3) Design your own kitchen

Before I start this section I would like to apologise in advance to any kitchen designers who are reading it. I don't mean to offend you with what I am going to write, I am just giving the readers my own view on how it is possible to design what I think is a perfectly good kitchen without it costing an arm and a leg.

I know you will always recommend using design methods and formulas when designing kitchens and utility rooms, I am simply giving an alternative way of doing it. It is a way I have been doing it for years and I haven't come unstuck using it yet!

Where to start

When you go to a kitchen supplier, if you can take along a design of your own, you stand a much better chance of getting what you want and not what they want to sell you. So, spending a few hours learning how to design a simple kitchen and then coming up with the basics of something that you would be happy with, would be, to my mind a very good use of your time.

By imposing your own ideas onto a designer, who may be on a percentage commission from the total cost of each sale made, you will stand a much better chance of keeping both them and the budget under control.

It would be handy if you could download a simple kitchen design app on to your computer. If you can't do that, or if you are not comfortable trying to use computers for this sort of thing, then get hold of a pad of graph paper (A3 is ideal, A4 will normally be adequate), a scale rule, a 3H pencil and a rubber.

- Either on the computer, or on paper, draw your room layout as accurately as possible. If you are using paper, pick as large a scale as possible to fill as much of the page as possible with the room (it is handy to draw in the wall thickness on your drawing. – It just looks a bit more professional).
- Include in your drawing, the positions and sizes of windows, doors and any other feature that could have an effect on your design. For the windows, add information on the height of the window cill from finished floor level.
- If you have already designed the electrical layout, mark all the socket and switch positions on the drawings and their height from the floor. Where possible you should design your kitchen / utility *before* designing your kitchens electrical layout.
- Mark up any other features in the room which could affect your design. Things like the water entry point, beams protruding from the ceiling, pillars etc.

Basic design criteria

For any kitchen design, you will need to know some of the basic information about unit widths, depths and heights, plus some other bits and pieces.

Here are some the most important ones to help you to come up with a simple design (I am only giving you the information you will need to be able to draw up **simple** kitchen designs here. I am not going to get technical and start detailing all the different types of doors and worktops, - there are far too many of them. I'll leave that job to the professional designers to sort out when you take them your simple designs):

- **A standard base unit** is around 600mm deep (front to back) and is manufactured so that when it has a worktop fixed to it, the top of the worktop is about 910mm from the finished floor level.
- **Standard widths of base and wall units** are generally 300mm, 400mm, 500mm, 600mm, 800mm and 1000mm. Some manufacturers go up to a 1200mm unit or more.
- **Single door units** go up to 600mm wide. Single draw units go a lot wider these days. Up to around 3m.
- **The main types of doors are:**
    - Draw-line (with a drawer at the top).
    - High-line (with just a full height door).
    - Draw units with a number of drawers (there are many permutations of this style of door, – check the manufacturers catalogues to see what each of them can supply).
    - Curved (usually high-line).
    - Glazed (usually only found on wall units).

- **Worktops** are usually 600mm wide as standard and come in a number of lengths (generally 1m, 2m, 3m and occasionally 4m), They come with a variety of edge trims and details.
- **Fridge cabinets, freezer cabinets, oven housing cabinets, dishwasher cabinets and microwave cabinets** are normally 600mm wide externally, so built-in appliances are made narrower to fit inside all standard housing units (about 560mm wide).
- **You can buy range style ovens and hobs** in all sorts of widths with any number of oven, pan drawers, rings etc. Have a look around at the sort of thing you like before you design your kitchen and allow a space the right size to take it.
- **You will need to run a vent pipe** from the hob to and through the external wall, so consider the positioning of your oven hob combination.
- **You can fit a hob in a different location in the room, away from an oven.** Ovens don't usually need their own ventilation to the external wall.
- **Extractor hoods** come in all sorts of sizes and styles. When you are preparing your design, just draw a simple extractor shape at the width of the oven or hob and then decide what sort of fitting you want later when you are having the detailed design done.
- **Sinks are normally positioned** under windows. I am not sure why this is, maybe it is so we can day dream of being somewhere else when we are washing up!
- **Sinks generally come as:** Single bowl, 1.5 bowl and double bowl. Some have left or right hand drainers, some have double drainers and some have no drainers.
- **Sinks** will take up a big chunk of the top shelf of the base unit wherever you position them. If you situate them in the middle of an 800mm or 100mm unit, the space either side will be just about useless. Try to get them to fit to one end of the unit, so you can still use the top shelf at the other end.
- **You can get waste disposal units** for under the sink, but these are not all they are cracked up to be and cost quite a lot to buy, fit and maintain.
- **There are various types of taps,** but all are usually either individual hot and cold pillars, or mixer taps with just one pillar. There are now very elaborate taps available which can add a touch of luxury to the kitchen without adding too much to the price. These include a tap that provides both boiling and chilled water, instantly. Check the catalogues yourselves before having your taps chosen for you by the designer.

Minimise the flowery stuff

If you go to a professional kitchen designer, the chances are that they will be telling you all about the design criteria that you need to take on board, in order to create a well-thought-out design, which *"minimises foot travel and maximises efficiency of movement whilst creating a flow through design, whilst also using the natural available light and which is pleasing to the eye"*. Great, but common sense and a bit of thought can often tell you pretty much the same stuff and can often save you a lot of money!

Here are a few of the design rules that I try impose on myself and my own designs. Sometimes they have to be compromised because of other factors, but in general, the closer to these rules you can keep, the better the finished kitchen will look and perform and the less it will cost.

- ➢ **Keep walking distances to a minimum:** Think about the activities that will be taking place in the kitchen and try to make allowances for them to reduce the distances you will have to carry things.
- ➢ **Make sure there are adequate worktops near to ovens and hobs.**
- ➢ **Keep pan drawers under or close to the hob.**
- ➢ **Keep the oven and hob near to the sink.**
- ➢ **Position a bin or bin space** near to where most of the food preparation works will be carried out.
- ➢ **Plan for the kettle to be near both the bin and the place the cups, mugs, tea and coffee will be stored.**

- **Keep the fridge near to where food is going to be prepared**, but the freezer can go further away as access to it will be needed less often.
- **Positioning the sink under a window** feels better than having it with a wall behind it.
- **Draw-line units** (with single drawers at the top and a cupboard door underneath) make using the drawers easier than having to bend to almost floor level to access the drawers in a multi drawer unit.
- **The new style long deep drawers are very useful when it comes to see what is inside.** They make it much easier to see what is stored at the back than it is when you have either high-line or draw-line units.
- **Special worktops can be very expensive**, but don't scrimp by getting the cheapest laminate finished worktops. They are what you will notice immediately on entering the room. Talk to your supplier or designer about the options available and prices. As a rule, don't let your worktops cost more than your kitchen units (which they easily can if you aren't careful).
- **Try to line up the base and wall units**. Units out of line can make the design look tatty.
- **Try to balance out units either side of the hob / extractor**. If this is not possible, try to keep some sort of basic theme either side (see the image of one of my self-build kitchens earlier in this chapter).
- **Put plenty of double electrical sockets in**. Think about the best places for them to go. Make sure you put the required sockets in for appliances (some of which will be at low level *behind* units).
- **Keep the extractor as near to an external wall as possible** to allow an easy route for the extractor fan to blow air to the outside of the building.
- **Try to design the room to allow for a sitting area** / coffee table / breakfast bar (if space allows). This helps turn the room in to more of a socialising area rather than just a work room.
- **Design your lighting to complement the unit design.** Don't put ceiling lights too close to the walls where there are going to be units positioned. Remember that a base unit is 600mm deep, so lighting needs to be at least 1000mm from these walls. Balance your lighting across the ceiling so it doesn't look lop-sided.
- **Hanging lights above breakfast bars creates a nice feature**.
- **Dimming lights can create a nice atmosphere**, preferably remote controlled (these systems start at around £40 in some of the trade suppliers).
- **Think about installing BT and TV points**. I also usually take a TV feed from the living room to the kitchen and various other rooms. I link this with remote controls, so any channel can be watched in any room (make sure you pick a system that allows multi-channel viewing or there will be arguments!)
- **For appliances in the kitchen** (rather than the utility room), where possible, get them built-in (which means they have a door front which match the rest of the kitchen). A bright white dishwasher / washing machine can detract from the overall appearance.
- **Be careful with the fancy bits.** They are where the suppliers tend to make most of their profits. Anything non-standard is normally expensive.
- **Try to see the whole kitchen as a *single concept*.** The units, worktops, appliances, tiling, wall colours, ceiling, lighting etc. all need to come together to create a look that works.
- **Check out the new toys** available now for kitchen which weren't around a few years ago. Some of them are gimmicks, but some are good ideas, things like:
    - **Fold-out worktop extensions.**
    - **Fold-out ironing boards.**
    - **Boiling / chilled water taps.**
    - **Single ovens with doors which disappear under the unit.**
    - **Full height slim units, with full pull out racking** (allowing you to see everything inside the cupboard at a glance as you pull it out)
    - **Low cost LED lighting** for the kickboards (the bottom plinth under the cupboard), plinth lighting (under the wall units), lighting designed for the tops of the wall units to take the place of the cornices

- ❖ **Hidden lighting**, which gives a subtle glow rather than providing room illumination.
- ❖ **Worktop upstands**: These have been around for quite a while but have only recently become popular. A 6" upstand to the worktops and a splash back of some sort for the hob can do away with the need to for wall tiles in some cases, saving money and time on the overall project.

4) Design your own utility room.

The utility room is usually looked upon as just being "*the other room*" and is generally given less importance and attention than the kitchen when it comes to creating a look for the whole room. I don't really have a problem with that thinking, but seeing as it is usually positioned right next to the kitchen, if you can carry the kitchen theme on into the utility room, that's no bad thing either.

I tend to design utility rooms which are only around 1.5m - 1.7m wide but try to make them quite long. The minimal width is not normally a problem that you will only tend to use the room to go to, go through, or come out from. To be able to walk comfortably past the units, you only need 900mm – 1000mm of floor width.

You won't often stand in the utility room chatting, therefore, a narrow walkway giving access to all the units and appliances, which does not rob too much floor space from the kitchen or other rooms, is usually perfectly adequate.

The utility room is there to do a job, so what do you need it to do?

- House the washing machine.
- House the tumble drier.
- Give you somewhere to wash things you don't want to wash in the kitchen sink.
- Store all the stuff you don't really want hanging round the kitchen.
- Give you somewhere to put the laundry, pre and post washing.
- Somewhere to store the ironing board / vacuum cleaner / sweeping brushes / mops etc.
- Somewhere to take off dirty / wet clothes and boots.
- Lots of other bits and pieces.

I don't normally go far from a standard simple design for a utility room. It goes something like:

- The same units as used in the kitchen.
- One long row of base and wall cabinets along the full length of one wall.
- Spaces for the washing machine and tumble drier.
- At least one full height unit for storing tall things.
- A sink with a draining board and a fairly functional basic mixer tap.
- A low to mid-price range worktop.
- A 6" upstand to save having to tile the wall area between the base and wall units.
- At least two double electrical sockets above the worktop, plus low level sockets behind the units (for appliances). Plus at least one double socket low down on the empty wall for general use.
- I tend to keep the same flooring as the kitchen.
- Don't bother with fancy lighting. It won't be noticed.

Depending on the value of your kitchen, you shouldn't need to spend much more than £4,000 on your utility room units / worktops. Without the cost of the washing machine and drier, really a target of more like £2,000 for a house valued at up to £250,000 would be about right.

5) Finding a kitchen supplier

Wherever you live, you won't need to look very hard to find kitchen suppliers. There are literally thousands of small and large companies selling kitchens, dotted around all the major towns and cities in the UK. So how do you find the right one?

As a rule of thumb, the small shops that you will find on high streets, tend to be set up to attract the remodellers and refurbishers. The people who have lived in a house for a number of years and fancy a change. The small guys tend to offer a highly-personalised service. They will come and survey your existing kitchen, spend time with you discussing your options for replacements. They will then take out your old kitchen, make any alteration required to the plumbing and electrics and finally fit your new kitchen.

That's great if that is what you need, but for you as a self-builder, that probably is not the best or most cost effective option.

The type of suppliers you would normally be best trying to source would be the ones who deal with the building trade on a regular basis. Whether you realise it or not, as a self-builder, you are also a builder or developer. You are a builder of houses! As such you should be entitled to the advantages that that position offers. One of those advantages is that you get stuff cheaper. In this case, where Mr and Mrs Smith from Acacia Grove would be paying £25,000 for their replacement kitchen, you would expect to be able to buy pretty much everything they bought for about half that price

Once you begin to find the right sort of suppliers *(search "trade kitchen suppliers" and add your post code to get you started)*, you could maybe make appointments with 2 or 3 designers, to discuss your ideas. You will need to take a scaled drawing (preferably 1:50) showing as many measurements as possible and you sit down and try to describe what you are hoping to achieve. The designer will take your drawing (and the notes they write whilst talking to you) and should, within a few days be sending you their initial designs.

You will usually find quite a variation in the designs from the different companies, even after you have given them the same basic information. Each kitchen design is a personal thing and every designer will see the room differently when it comes to utilising the space it provides. The chances are that out of, say 4 designs you look at, you'll think two of them are nice and you won't like the other two. If you don't like any of them (which won't happen very often), don't waste your time flogging a dead horse, instead start the process all over again, find a new set of suppliers and get a new set of designs done.

Once you get to a position where you have maybe one or two favourite designs from companies that you think seem to be professional and competitive, you can start to look at the overall package that they offer.

If possible try to visit the factory to see the units being built, ask for references, compare the prices and see if you are tending towards one supplier. If you are, then you may be best to go with them. If you are not quite sure, don't just give up hunting for the right one, you could be spending a lot of money on this one item. Your kitchen will possibly be more expensive than any other single item in the whole project and you want to make sure you get what you want, from the right people, at the right price.

6) Who will fit your kitchen?

You have two sensible choices and one not so sensible choice here:

1) **Sensible:** Get the supplier to fit it
2) **Sensible:** Get the joiners on site to fit it.
3) **Not so sensible:** Try fitting it yourself (only sensible if you know how to do it!)

1) **Get the supplier to fit it:** This will usually be the more expensive of the two sensible options, simply because the supplier will have to organise everything and everyone needed for your specific project and they won't know exactly what they are going to find when they get to your site, so they will normally add some contingencies to their price.

    You will usually get a good quality job with this option, as the guys doing the job will be fitting this type of kitchen every day of the week. You will usually also have the peace of mind that if anything is found to be wrong with anything to do with the installation at any time in the next year or so, they will normally be quite easy to get back to put things right.

2) **Get the joiners on site to fit it:** This will normally be the best overall option if you are happy that the guys who will be fitting it are genuine, experienced kitchen fitters. The fact that they will already be working on site will tend to help them to keep their prices down.

    Try to get them to give you a price per unit, which includes *all the ancillary works*. This is the easiest way to price and pay for the job.

    The fitting price will vary depending on whether the units are pre-assembled or flat pack. By far the biggest part of fitting a unit is putting the thing together in the first place. So you can expect your fitting price to double if this needs doing. I always tend to go for the pre-assembled units.

3) **Try fitting it yourself:** Unless you are a skilled joiner, don't even try to fit the kitchen yourselves if it has cost you more than a few hundred pounds to buy (which would mean it would either be second hand or something you create rather than buying it from a supplier).

    Ok, if you buy flat pack units and can read instructions, you could knock the units up ready for a joiner to take over to do the difficult bits, but the kitchen is usually something you will be paying a lot of money for. Something which makes a statement about the house and something which will affect the end value of the finished job. So it needs to be done properly. There is a lot to know about fixing kitchen units if the job is to be done correctly and there are special tools needed for fixing worktops (especially the more expensive ones). So, unless you are supremely confident of your abilities, let the people who are trained to do the job, do it.

Bathrooms

I don't really need to go in to a lot of details here. Bathrooms have not varied that much over the past few decades. Everyone knows pretty much what they want and need from a new bathroom, so I'll just go through a few thoughts and ideas, to give you some things to consider as you plan and make your own decisions.

My biggest problem with modern bathrooms is that many of them tend to concentrate on form over function. Badly designed equipment, toilets that are uncomfortable to sit on, with seats which will cost a fortune to replace (if they still make them in a couple of years), baths that are cramped and uncomfortable to lie in, sinks that don't drain properly and splash water everywhere, fancy plugs that either don't seal the waste hole properly, or stop operating properly after a few months, whirlpool baths that are all but useless. I am sure you will have come across at least some of these.

So, what *should* you be looking for when thinking about bathroom equipment? Here are a few pointers which may help you to make the right decisions when choosing bathroom equipment:

- **Baths:**

    - **Standard baths** are normally around 1700mm x 700mm (heights can vary)
    - **Slightly oversized baths** (1800mm x 800mm) are ideal for taller people.
    - **Baths with square ends** are usually uncomfortable. Rounded ends are better.

- **Sloping ends** mean there is less room at the bottom of the bath for your body to stretch out, but ends that are *too* steep can be uncomfortable.
- **"Double ended" baths** with taps halfway along the side (*instead of being at one end*), are good for saving water. They allow two people to bathe in comfort and both can reach the taps.
- **Steel baths** are a lot colder than fibreglass baths. They can feel cold to the touch when you get in and the water tends to cool faster.
- **If you buy fibreglass baths**, don't get the 3mm thick ones. They won't generally last long. 5mm thick is better.
- **Stand-alone baths** (the ones that have the fancy feet) are nice to look at, but can be impractical and are awkward to keep clean underneath.
- **Boxing in** the sides of the baths and possibly tiling the boxing in can look very nice, but make sure you think about getting access to fix any problems under the bath in the future, without having to take the tiles off.
- **Boxing in** a bath is a good way to form ledges on which to store your bits and pieces (soaps / shampoos etc.) They tend to keep things tidy and also make it easy to reach whatever you need while you are using the bath.
- **Watch out for fancy plugs** which stick up from the base of the bath. They can be uncomfortable and you can end up inadvertently pulling them out when you move whilst bathing. Pop up plugs, in my experience often cause problems by either not popping up enough to let the water out quickly, or not seating down properly to enable them to make a good seal (only allowing the water to trickle slowly away).
- **A good position for the taps** is mid-way along the side nearest the wall. This saves you having to lean the whole length of the bath to turn them on.
- **Waterfall taps** are a nice addition to the tap range. Worth having a look at.
- **A shower hose adjacent to your main taps** is a good idea for rinsing your hair whilst you are bathing.
- **Jetted water bath systems** are ok, but they need maintenance, or they can become a health hazard. If you just get the basic ones in a small bath they don't tend to be very effective. You really need a larger bath for them to come in to their own. I have had them in small baths in a few houses and after the first few weeks they never tend to get used again.
- **If you install a shower over the bath,** make sure that the shower screen is capable of stopping the water from splashing on to the floor.
- **Sunken baths** are something a lot of people like the idea of, but they don't really work practically in modern houses, as they would usually end up sticking down into the room below, resulting in you having a big boxing in having to be built in the ceiling! – Not particularly pretty or practical!
  If this is something you like the idea of, consider using a boxing in with steps *up* to the bath instead of *down* to it.

- **Toilets:**

- **Standard style toilets are generally a good choice.** You will always be able to get replacement fittings (such as seats, internal flushing equipment etc.)
- **Unusual shapes normally mean expensive,** but often also mean uncomfortable.
- **If you build a toilet cistern in to a boxing in of any sort**, make sure you can access it for repairs or replacement without having to take tiles off to do so.
- **Watch out for seats which don't stand up.** Believe it or not, some toilet designs don't consider the fact that the seat needs to remain in an upright position for some of the time. Just check before you buy.
- **Seats coming loose** is very common. Ask the sales person how easy it is to tighten them, if and when this is required.

- **Watch out for seat lids which hide the flush mechanism.** Quite often (especially with built in toilets), the flush mechanism can be situated behind the seat lid. This can be a nuisance as it means you having to lower the lid before you can flush the cistern.
- **Very modern styled toilets could date quickly.** Remember avocado and pink baths? You don't want your loo to be an embarrassment to you in the future! I tend to think simple is good.
- **Toilets with small bowls tend to get dirty quickly.** Large bowls with steeply sloping sides tend to stay cleaner for longer and are easier to clean.
- **Make sure you get a dual-flush water saving cistern.** These can save a lot of water, but some of the cheaper toilets (especially imports) may not have the dual-flushing mechanism.
- **You can link your toilet to a grey water system.** If you are installing one of these systems, talk to your plumber about it.

Showers

- **Showers come in all shapes and sizes.** The fashion at the moment is to try to minimise the physical / visual impact of the shower, by doing away with the tray, keeping it at floor level and having a walk-through design. This is fine but watch the cost. The fittings you need to make your shower disappear can be very expensive.
- **Small showers can be impractical.** The smallest standard shower cubicle tends to be 750mm x 750mm. This is getting a bit small for an adult to be able to move round in. 850mm x 850mm can be just about ok, 900mm x 900mm or 900mm x 1200mm gives a much more pleasant experience when showering.
- **Corner showers can be good space savers.** The 45-degree angle of the front of a corner shower can come in useful in small rooms, leaving a bit more floor area to move about on. Folding doors which open inwards can further help to maximise the manoeuvring area in the room.
- **Shower fittings and associated pipework can be surface mounted or recessed.** If they are recessed and they develop a fault, it can be difficult and costly to get at the pipework and fittings, in order to fix them.
- **Fixed head (showers fixed so that they simply send the water vertically downwards)** can look nice, but are a bit impractical when you want to wash all your nooks and crannies. If you go for one of these, also consider having a hand-held hose shower head as well.
- **Running the showers directly from a combi boiler** will usually tend to give you a very good power shower experience. In some areas where there is low water pressure, the feed to the shower can be *a bit wimpy*, so won't give that same effect without some sort of pump fed boost (which a combi will give you).
- **Make sure you seal properly around shower trays and side panels.** If they are not applied correctly, over time, the seals around the shower unit can fail, forming tiny cracks and gaps where the unit attaches to the wall.
Water will get through these cracks and can cause damage to the floors and walls. Make sure that whoever does the mastic sealing (when the unit is installed) does a good job and keep your eyes open for any cracks appearing over the years.
- **Watch the tile fixing and joints:** You need to use waterproof adhesive and grout for tiling showers. Flexible adhesive and grouts are also a good idea, especially if the shower is being fixed to a timber stud wall.

Sinks

- **As with a lot of the new bathroom equipment, sinks are tending to suffer from the form over function problem.** Have a good look at any sink before you buy. Are they a functional shape (do they drain easily and quickly, taking dirt and soap scum with the water)? Are they deep enough (or would they potentially allow water to splash out over the top)? Is there a flat area around the bowl, where you can store soap and other bits and pieces without having to have a separate shelf?

- **Watch the size of the sink.** Bathrooms in new homes are often fairly small. Make sure you don't order a sink which is impractically large so that it gets in the way of movement around the room. Also make sure that it is big enough to have a decent wash in. Small sinks can lead to a lot of water ending up on the floor.
- **Try to keep the fittings under the sink hidden.** The water and waste pipes to a wall mounted sink can look unsightly if they are not dealt with properly. Plinths or columns which run from the floor to the underside of the sink are one way to solve this problem. Another is to use chrome plated water and waste fittings to improve the appearance.
- **Try to keep taps as unobtrusive as possible.** Taps which protrude too far over the sink can end up getting covered in soap and toothpaste. Small mixer taps which just extend over the sink by a couple of inches will be easier to keep clean. Waterfall taps are a nice feature, but on a sink, they can end up getting messy quite quickly.

Moving on to the rooms themselves

A general rule: Keep pipework for the water supplies as short as possible

With all new homes being fitted with water meters now and water supply costs constantly rising, it is important not to waste water.

The location of your bathrooms and their various fittings is important when it comes to both wasting water and energy.

Every time you turn on a hot tap to draw water from either a boiler or a cylinder, you have to run off all the cold water that is already in the pipes, before the hot water can reach the place where it is needed. Bathrooms on a different floor and at the other end of the house to the boiler or cylinder can not only waste a lot of water, but also will mean that the energy used to heat the water that is in the pipes when you turn off the tap, will have been wasted too.

Keeping frequently used bathrooms / en-suites / shower rooms as close to the location of the boiler / cylinder as possible could have a significantly positive effect on your fuel bills. However, balance this out with making sure that to save energy, you don't end up with a room and house layout that is impractical.

I. **Main (family) bathrooms:**
These rooms will usually take most of the wear and tear and therefore need the most rugged types of fixtures and fittings. It is worth spending a bit extra on the equipment in this room in order to make sure that everything is up to the job it is going to be asked to do.
Having both a shower and a bath is a good idea (where room permits). Separate showers are best (min 850mm square), but over the bath is fine if you are tight on floor space. Storage is a good thing to provide in the main bathroom. Cupboards for towels, toilet rolls and cleaning materials, shelving for all the bits and bobs etc. Make sure you give some thought at the design stage to how this room is going to be used.

II. **En-suites**
En-suites to a main bedroom or a kid's room can also often get quite a bit of a hammering, so again bear this in mind when choosing the equipment. An en-suite to a guest bedroom will probably only get light usage and as such may only need a small amount of money spending on it.

III. **Jack and Jill bathrooms:**
These are useful rooms that are situated between two bedrooms, to give each room a shared en-suite. A lockable door is fitted from the bathroom to each bedroom and whoever is using it simply locks the door to the other bedroom (remembering to unlock it as they leave).

Soundproof doors are a good idea for these rooms. If there is at least one other bathroom which has a bath or shower on the same floor as the Jack and Jill room, it is not usually important to provide a shower in the Jack and Jill room. Just a toilet and a sink will normally suffice.

IV. **Shower rooms:**

These are normally located on the ground floor, but may also be found where the attic is being utilised as living space (to save people from having to move between floors to use a toilet and for guests as an en-suite). Shower rooms to the ground floor can provide an ideal place for anyone to clean up, without having to walk through the house, if they come in with muddy / dirty clothes on.

Downstairs shower rooms are also good for people with disabilities and if you are trying to make your new home Lifetime Homes compliant. As you get older, getting upstairs to use the bathroom / toilet could get more difficult, so having a shower on the ground floor may prove to have been a very good move (at some time in the future).

V. **Wc's**

In recent years, these little rooms have started to receive more attention. They do tend to get well used, especially if you are going to be doing a lot of entertaining.

I would suggest that you always try to position these rooms near to the front door (so that they are easily accessible as soon as you enter the house). I would not recommend that they go adjacent to the utility room (where your guests may be treated to viewing your dirty laundry) when they wish to use them.

It is a good idea to make sure the walls to any ground floor wc's are strong enough to bear significant weight in case you need to fix fittings to assist people with disabilities (hand rails etc.)

Chapter 15
External works

Introduction

In this chapter, we will be looking at some of the basic jobs involved in connecting your new home up to the various services, and getting the outside areas ready for you to move in.

I am not going to try to teach you how to design your landscaping, or look too much in detail at all the options for how you can treat your garden space. There are hundreds of other books which specialize in those subjects. What this chapter aims to do, is to simply take you through the processes to get from the stage where the inside of your house is pretty much complete, to where you can move in and start to use the house, keep it clean and start to think about how it will look in a few years' time.

We will be looking at:

1) **Service connections**

    The four service connections you will usually need to organise are:
    - Water
    - Gas
    - Electricity
    - Telecoms

Depending on where you are located in the country, you may find that one or more of these is not available. If so the solutions include:

- **Water:** Drill a well down below the water table and install a pump which connects to your plumbing system. Water is usually found fairly close to the surface of the ground in the UK, so this doesn't have to be a particularly expensive exercise.
- **Gas:** Use Calor gas or something similar. You can buy the large portable cylinders and exchange them as and when you need to, or you can permanently install the very large bulk gas tanks, which you will locate somewhere in the garden, or possibly underground. These can be refilled as required by a gas supply company using specialised delivery vehicles. This type of gas is more expensive than a standard gas supply but will suit some people. Your boiler may need a slight adjustment to be able to run on Calor gas, but this is not usually a problem.
- **Electricity:** Solar panels (either just generating electricity or both electricity and hot water). The price of solar energy has come down a lot in the past few years and you can now get a decent system fully installed for around £5,000 - £6,000. Solar panels on their own will probably not generate enough power to keep everything going in the house all of the time, so you may need to think about installing some sort of back up. A generator would then be my first choice. I wouldn't think of using wind turbines as, like solar, they only generate power intermittently.
- **Telecoms:** With all the mobile technology now available, we are getting less dependent on having a permanent telecoms connection. You may be able to use your phones and other devices to give you everything you need.

If not, as far as I am aware at the time of writing (*unless you have a poor credit rating, or there could be fraud involved*), BT have an obligation to provide a service to *any* property that requests it, no matter how far off grid it is.

2) Drainage and Drainage connections:

There are three common types of mains drainage:

1. Foul water (for all the nasty stuff).
2. Surface water (for rainwater and the cleaner stuff).
3. Combined foul and surface water.

If any of these are available close to your project, you will usually be looking to connect to them.

The process involves making an application to your local drainage authority, getting and accepting a quote and programming in the work. You (or rather your ground worker) will install the main part of the system around the house and run a 4" plastic or clay pipe to a position close to the main drain. From there, the final connection *must* be made by a drainage contractor who has been approved by the authority. **You are not allowed to make your own connection to a main drain.**

If you are lucky, the main drains will run close to your plot boundary, on your side of the road. If you are less lucky, they could run either in the road itself, or on the opposite side of the road. If so, the connection job becomes more complicated, potentially involving closing part or all of the road and in some cases (usually where the road is very busy) a night-time connection.

If a road must be partially or fully closed, your connections costs can rise significantly, due to the amount of work involved and the need to hire in traffic control equipment and extra fees that become payable to the Highways Authority.

If there are no main drains close to you, you have various other options, including:

1. **Soakaways** (for surface water only): These are a simple system which involves excavating a large deep hole, at least 5m away from the building, filling it with large (4"+) clean stone, covering the top of the stone with a waterproof layer (so the soil cannot wash down into the stone and reduce its effectiveness) and covering the excavation over to form up your garden or driveway.
You can then run your surface water waste, usually in 4" pipes, from the house or other drainage points, to the soakaway.
When it rains, the water fills all the voids formed by the stone and slowly then drains away in to the surrounding ground.
Before you construct soakaways, you will need to test the surrounding ground to see how well water will drain in to it. Clay soils don't allow easy drainage, whilst some sand and peats can be very good at absorbing water. The size, depth and number of soakaways will be determined by the porosity of the surrounding ground.
2. **Septic tanks** (for foul water only): We have all heard of septic tanks. They are big containers buried underground, in to which the foul waste water is drained. There is usually a filtration system built in to the unit, which allows the liquids to be separated from the solids. The liquids then usually leave the tank and drain into the ground around the tank via a system of irrigation pipework.
You will need to get the system you intend using approved by the authority, because, as you can imagine, the stuff you are draining into the ground may not be very pleasant! – If your plot is located near to a watercourse (stream / river etc.) you may have to find alternative solutions for dealing with the foul waste. If so, you will

probably need to hire the services of a professional drainage engineer, who will be able to identify the best options for your particular site.

3. **Irrigation** (for surface water only). This is another simple idea for dealing with the surface water. If you have a large plot, you can install a network of pipework, usually fairly close to the surface of the ground, into which you can feed all your surface water connections. The pipework is called land drainage and it has hundreds of small holes along its length, which allow the water to seep out into the surrounding ground. A drainage engineer will usually be involved to work out the length of pipework you will need and to make sure that the water entering the ground does not cause problems such as boggy patches.

Low level plots

If the lowest point of a new building is lower than the mains drain, you may need to install a pump, to pump either or both types of waste up to the level where they can enter the main drains effectively. This would require a chamber to be designed and installed in the ground, at a convenient location. A suitable pump will then be installed in to the chamber. A power connection will also need to be supplied, to run the pump.

To get the waste to the chamber you can either gravity feed it (install it on a downwards slope) from the building, or you can install a macerator (a system which grinds down all the solids to form a slurry which can be pumped through a small diameter pipe). Either way, this is again something you will need the input of a drainage engineer to help you with.

When and how to install the drainage

Some builders will install the drainage at the start of the job. I tend to do it at the end, after the scaffolding has been taken down. My reasoning being that, if things don't go completely smoothly with the installation at the start of the job, it can slow the overall progress, whereas, by doing the drainage work at the end of the job, all the other important tasks will already have been completed, so won't be negatively affected by any installation problems.

The drainage installation is a very important and technically complicated job, which needs to be carried out by professional people. I would not recommend trying to lay the drains yourself unless you have been taught to do so professionally.

A lot of people will use clay drainage because they think it is a better-quality product. Some designers (especially the older ones) will specify clay drainage simply out of habit. I have always used plastic, which is a fraction of the price of clay and I have never had any problem with it. Plastic manholes are ok to a certain depth (about 4'). If my drains are deeper than this, I would tend to change to concrete rings or brickwork for the manholes (a drainage engineer can sort all these decisions out for you).

You need to detail everything in relation to the drainage works on your building regs specification, so you have to get it all designed correctly before you will be allowed to start work.

3) Driveways

The driveway will often need to do up to four jobs, including.

1) Linking the house to the road.
2) Providing parking spaces for occupants and visitors.
3) Providing a turning area to allow vehicles to drive on to the site in a forward gear, turn around on site and then be able to exit in a forward gear (this is to avoid the necessity to have to back out onto a main road).
4) Providing a solid surface for people with movement disabilities to be able to access the property and the house.

You will already be aware of some, or all of the choices for driveway finishes, most of them have been around for a long time, but I'll run through a bit about the construction and some of the finishes, just to clarify a few things and introduce a couple of the newer or more sustainable options.

Constructing the drive sub base: You will usually have removed the topsoil from the driveway area at an early stage of the project and the chances are that you will have formed up some sort of stone surface in order to give you access for delivery vehicles to access and exit the site.

Common sense says that you should form up a temporary drive in the same place as your permanent drive, so that you avoid doing the job twice, possibly wasting stone in doing so.

If you have done the job properly, you will have laid a good thickness of stone (as detailed in your building regs specification) to the driveway area and the constant back and forth effect of all the vehicles coming to site will have compacted the stone nicely by this late stage of the project.

What you need to do next is to get an excavator back to form up the surface of the drive to all the levels and slopes that are required on the drawings. The finished drive will need to have slopes built in to its design, to allow natural drainage. The proposed levels will be shown on your drawings and the ground worker or drive layer should know how to make sure the stone is formed up so that it doesn't allow puddling anywhere on the finished driveway.

As well as creating natural drainage, the slopes of the driveway need to be such that they allow people with disabilities to use it to access the house, without problems. This involves restricting the maximum slope of the drive to an angle which allows a wheelchair to be pushed up it without problem. At the time of writing the maximum slope in the area where I live is 1 in 12. Check the regulations in your area (just in case there are regional variations or in case things have changed between me writing this and you doing the job).

To avoid puddling occurring, before the final finish is given to the drive, the ground worker's / drive layers will usually use string lines, pulled between kerbs, to make sure all the slopes are falling the right way.

Around the edge of the driveway, depending on what finish you intend to use, you may choose to install edgings. These can be in the form of treated timber (3" x 1" or 4" x 1") or they can be made up of concrete edging kerbs (either 6" x 2" or something larger if required).

You may need to build drainage into the driveway area if there are unavoidable areas which could potentially hold water. If your drive slopes towards the house, you may need to install drainage channels along the whole of the front of the house / garage to catch all the water that runs towards it, to stop it reaching anywhere it could potentially cause damage.

The level of the top of the sub base stone will depend on the type of driveway finish you propose to use.

Types of finish:

I. **Gravel:** This is the cheapest, quickest and easiest way to create a presentable driveway. You will simply buy bulk loads of your chosen gravel (and there are many to choose from), tip it on the drive and rake it out.
    I like this finish, but it needs a bit of maintaining. If any soil has been mixed in with the stone used to form up the drive, weeds can quickly grow though, making it look tatty very quickly. One way to combat this is to week kill the driveway and lay a sheet of thick plastic over the whole area before you lay the stone, making sure that you take the plastic right up to the edges. If you leave even small areas without any sheeting, small amounts of weed could still come through and spoil the overall appearance.
    Whatever measures you take to stop the weeds, you will find over time that some do start to appear. The easiest thing to do when that happens is just to weed kill them.

Gravel is not a suitable surface where you are constructing a disabled access. It is more difficult to walk on generally than a hard surface and wheel chairs also have difficulties on it (the wheel tend to sink in to the stone).

You may be able to mix and match gravel areas and hardstanding areas around your disabled access, to both create the proper access and to save you some money.

Gravel driveways are naturally porous, which will help to minimise the surface water drainage you need to install.

II. **Brick or clay paving:** There are many different types of brick / block paving finishes, but they all basically do the same job. They create a very strong hard finished surface that should last a long time (if laid correctly). If the stone or sand under the paved area is not compacted properly, you can get some areas settling more than others, which over time can result in an uneven driveway surface.

Brick paving has become perhaps the drive finish of choice for most self-builders over the past 20 years. The choices of colour, shape and finish give the user infinite possibilities to create a high quality and unique appearance to one of the main feature areas of the house (and usually pretty much the first thing anyone sees when they approach the property).

The latest trend for brick paved drives is to make the driveway area porous. In other words, the bricks are made (and / or laid) to a slightly different shape or pattern which leaves gaps between each brick. This method allows water to drain through the paved area without weakening the structure as a whole.

The main reason porous paving is becoming popular is because of the fact that as a country, we are paving over vast areas of ground, with varying types of coverings, most of which have to have a drainage system incorporated, which takes the water away to somewhere else to be dealt with.

Porous paving allows water to get access through the paved area, down in to the substructure (the ground) *close to where it lands*, thus reducing the need to have an artificial network of pipes to deal with its disposal. Many planning offices are now insisting on new developments adopting porous paving, by adding it as an imposed planning condition.

Overall, I would say that this is a good choice for driveways for self-builders, but not necessarily the best choice for footpaths or other areas of the landscaping.

III. **Macadam:** This is the age-old driveway finish that we are all used to seeing on both older and many new houses. It is getting less popular now we have all the new and different alternatives, however, it remains a good value for money and offers a fast-to-lay option when and where it is needed.

Housing developers still tend to opt for macadam on driveways for mid-sized new homes, but often use brick pavings on their top-end developments.

Laying macadam driveways is a quick and simple operation, usually incorporating a specialist laying machine, a few men with shovels and rakes and a sit on vibrating roller. The delivery vehicle will tip the macadam into a hopper on the front of the laying or spreading machine, from where it will be fed through to the back, spread out and laid in an even thickness. The vehicle has sliding feeders fitted, which allow the width of the strip being laid, to be varied from around 6' up to around 12' wide.

Once the main ribbon of macadam had been laid, the guys with the shovels will tidy up the edges and then the roller will come in and start to compact the whole area to give a finished job. A large driveway area can be completed in just a few hours.

IV. **Imprinted or patterned concrete (both names mean the same thing):** This form of paving for driveways became popular about 10 years ago. It was a new way to achieve a high-quality finish which looks better than tarmac and would compete with brick paving. It has never really become a major competitor to brick paving and from what I understand does seem to have a few inherent problems, such as:

- You may need to get planning permission for it as it is classed as non-porous
- It can change colour as it dries out and can fade in areas of high use.
- It can chip if something sharp / heavy it dropped on it.
- If expansion joints are not included as part of the construction it can expand and crack.
- It can also crack if the sub-base has not been laid and compacted correctly or if it is not laid to an adequate thickness.
- The surface may need to be treated fairly regularly in order to maintain the shiny finished appearance that it had when it was initially laid.

The choice of finishes is varied and the appearance of the finished job is quite attractive (however, some people don't like the overly shiny look).

Price wise, although I have never used it, I understand it is in the same sort of price range as standard brick paving, but bear in mind that there are fewer contractors who can lay imprinted concrete than there are who can lay brick paving, so you may get a more competitive price if you go for the brick option.
If you choose to use this product, make sure you get some sort of warranty which will cover you if construction faults are found within the first few years (once everything has had time to settle, shrink or expand).

V. **Resin:** Resin driveways have only just started to become popular with self-builders. You may have seen this product used quite widely by councils in town centres, where they often create attractive features surrounding individual trees or colourful footpaths.

The product itself is not very strong, so needs to be laid on to an existing surface such as concrete or macadam. The stone can either be premixed with the resin and laid with a trowel to a smooth finish, or the resin can be laid first, with the stone then being scattered by hand into the wet resin mix and trowelled smooth to give the final surface appearance.

The choice of finished appearances is very varied. There is a wide range of colours and types of gravel available and you can use more than one colour on a single driveway. It is also easy to create features such as writing or pictorial shapes in the finished surface.

Price wise, it tends to be more expensive than most of the other options, mainly due to the fact that it needs an existing hard surface to either be created or to exist already, for it to lie on. Also, although the resin itself can be fairly porous, the fact that it needs to have either concrete or macadam underneath it (neither of which is porous), to give it its strength, you may need to apply for planning permission before laying it.

Who should lay your driveway?

Unless you are simply going to be raking out gravel, it is always sensible to get a professional in to lay your drive. Your main access to vehicular traffic is something that needs to stay in good condition for a long time and you don't want it looking a mess within a couple of years because you have tried to save a few bob along the way.

Look at your driveway as an investment. If you come to sell the house a few years down the line, it will be part of your shop window, one of the bits that everyone will see first, before they get inside the house to see what you have done there. If they don't like the outside, there is a good chance they will never bother to come to look at the inside!

4) Footpaths

All the same basic finishes are available to you for footpaths as are available for driveways. However, as footpaths don't tend to get the same sort of constant heavy traffic use, they don't normally need to be anything like as strong as driveways, normally only needing to cope with foot and light plant or machinery traffic such as lawnmowers etc.

Because they don't need to be as strong, footpaths can be created using a few other products which will possibly look just as nice or nicer than the driveway options, but should also work out as a low-cost alternative.

Other options include:

I. **Standard concrete paving slabs:** I want to separate these out from the next option decorative stone or decorative concrete slabs, so I can say that I don't think these are a good choice for self-builders. Why? They look naff!
    They are functional, they do a job, they do it cheaply and they form a footpath, but they generally won't improve the look of your landscaping or the value of your property one bit!
    By all means use them if your budget is getting tight and you need something just to tidy up and / or finish the job, but think about changing them when you can afford to!
    Here, for your delectation is a picture of a stack of standard concrete slabs, ready to be laid!

(See what I mean?)

II. **Decorative stone or decorative concrete slabs:** For a very small extra cost over and above the standard concrete slab, you can start to find a huge range of attractive and colourful products which will give you a far better finished job. Just pop into your local builder's merchants or landscaping / gardening centre and you will be able to pick up catalogues with hundreds of different types, colours and shapes, which are mostly reasonably priced and can be delivered to you within a few days.

    The only advice I would give on choosing any of the available products, is to shop around. If you go to some of the outlets which aim to attract the retail customers, you can find yourselves paying up to twice as much for pretty much the same product as you will if you go to a builders' merchant and haggle over the price.

III. **Timber decking:** Timber has never really taken off as a product for creating footpaths, especially around the house itself. It is, however fairly popular if you are building on a slope and it can be a cheaper option to form steps rather than using concrete.

Who should lay footpaths?

You could, theoretically lay the footpaths yourselves (especially if you are just fixing a weed barrier, a timber edging and raking out gravel). The quality of laying is (slightly) less important than for driveways, which are going to have cars and vans driving over them for the next few decades. However, don't try to lay them unless you know *what you are doing* and are sure you can come up with a decent finished job. You'll need to know how much soil to dig out, what depth of sub base to use, how to treat and weed kill the excavated ground surface, compact it and blind it. You will also need to know how to set the slabs out, how to cut them and what mix to lay them on (*usually a sand / cement semi dry mix gives the best finished job*).

5) Patios

All the same choices are available for patios as are available for drives and footpaths, however two of the choices tend to be the most popular: 1) Stone / concrete paving and 2) decking. There is a good reason for this, both these products can allow you to simply and quickly create an attractive outside sitting / entertaining area at low cost.

Why are these two options popular?

1) **Stone or concrete paving slabs:** For the same reasons I gave a few paragraphs ago.
2) **Timber decking:** This product comes in to its own when used for decking. It allows you to create any shape or style, at different levels, with or without steps, with or without fencing and railings (which can usually be fixed to the main framework which forms the decking itself).

    You can form up planted areas within the decking and even build in water features, benches or anything else that takes your fancy.

    Timber decking gives you a firm, even flat surface on which to place tables and chairs, without them rocking when you sit at them. The decking can also be set at the same level as the finished floor of your home, to give the effect of extending your inside living space, to the outside, with just a small gap left between your wall and the decking to allow for drainage, making sure water doesn't have a chance of getting across from the timber to the main structure of the house itself.

    There are one or two downsides with decking:

    i. **Maintenance:** You will need to treat the decking timbers before you fit them, then as you are fitting you will need to re treat any "cut ends". The whole decking will then need to be re-treated every couple of years to keep it looking pristine.

ii. **Danger of slipping:** Decking does have a tendency to get slippy, especially if it is left untreated for a while. Mould can grow on its surface, and when wet, this can create a dangerous slip hazard. It can also become more slippy than many of the other surface options in icy conditions.

If you are considering using decking, think about looking at the plastic or wood / plastic options. They are often made from recycled materials and give just the same amount of flexibility of use, but could potentially remain in a good condition for longer. They are pre coloured (coloured in the factory) and their colour doesn't tend to fade like it does with painted on stain. They also often have more grip designed in to their upper surface and won't allow mould to grow on their surface, so are less dangerous in wet or icy conditions.

Price wise, plastic / timber decking tends to work out more expensive than standard timber decking but this extra cost is saved over the years with the reduced amount of maintenance needed and the potentially longer lifespan of the product.

Here is an image of composite plastic decking. Different products tend to have different surface features, but all tend to look fairly similar to timber decking:

6) Lawns

There is not a huge amount I can say about lawns in a book like this. A lawn is a simply a lawn. It's not something technical, you either want one or you don't. If you are looking for a low maintenance garden you probably won't. If you like to spend time getting your hands dirty during the summer months, you probably will.

There are three main options when it comes to laying a lawn to a new home: seed / turf / artificial grass. I'll quickly run through them in a minute, but first it is worth just touching on what you need to do to get the garden ready to receive whichever option you choose.

Garden preparation:

During the building process, it is tempting to chuck some of the rubbish that the building process generates on to the garden area and then at the end of the job, cover it over with a few inches of topsoil and turf to hide it. Unfortunately, that method often leads to a very uneven lawn, with stones, bricks and other detritus slowly appearing at the surface over the coming years (presenting a hazard to lawnmower blades).

If you need to bury rubble and other building waste, as long as you are actually *allowed* to bury what you intend to bury, you would be advised to do the job properly:

i. Excavate a hole a few feet deep, as big as it needs to be.
ii. Put the waste in and spread it level so that it does not come within 2' or so of the surface. As you put the waste in, use the back of the bucket of the excavating machine to compact it down as much as possible. If the hole is not too deep (less than 3') and as long as the sides are pretty solid and don't stand any chance of caving in whilst you are working within the hole, it is a good idea to compact the waste with a whacker plate every 6" or so as you fill. This will minimise the chance of any settlement over the coming years
iii. Once you have reached a level which is going to be around 6" – 10" below the proposed surface level, cover the waste with thick plastic sheeting to stop the soil from being washed down in to the rest of the rubble and other waste below it.

By taking the time to carry out this fairly small job, as long as you have done it properly, once you have prepared and laid the lawn, you should find that the surface stays nice and level and does not start to form ups and down across its surface.

The area over the hole, together with the rest of the area to be lawned should now be prepared so that the whole garden area comes about level with the top of the waste hole formation. Once that has been done, a good quality topsoil should be laid evenly across the whole area, preferably about 6" – 10" deep.

Before laying the final surface, this topsoil then needs to be compacted using either a vibrating roller or a water-filled roller. As you compact the soil, you will see uneven areas appearing. Where this happens, spread out more topsoil to bring the area back level with the rest of the proposed lawned area (a 6' long straight edge is a good tool to help you to do this. Something like a piece of 3" x 1" planed piece of timber).

Repeat this process until you are happy that the whole garden is level. Once this operation has been completed, you should end up with around 5" – 7" thickness of compacted topsoil. You are now ready to apply your lawn finish. Your choices are:

➢ **Seed:** There is nothing wrong with seeding a lawn, however, for some reason most self-builders tend to go for the turf option. This is probably with the aim of getting a low cost, instantaneous garden, or possibly because you can lay turf all year round (*note: you should only seed at certain times of the year, either late Summer to mid-Autumn, or possibly mid spring if you give it plenty of water*).
Seeding is a cheap option which can give you a lawn *to look at* in a few weeks and a lawn *to walk on* soon after that. It is also a good option on sloping ground where turf may tend to slide and have difficulty rooting properly. The instructions on the seed bag or box are all you need to spread the seed correctly. If you are covering a large area it might be a good idea to get hold of a mechanical seeder (hire shops will usually stock these).
Once you have seeded the whole area, if possible, it is a good idea to cover everything with fine mesh netting to stop the birds from eating the seed.
There are numerous types of grass seed. Try to pick the best one for the area you are going to be using it. For a hard-wearing family lawn, seed with some rye grass in it is a good idea.
One thing to watch out for: Some seeds say "fast growing" on the box. Many years ago, I bought some of this thinking that it would produce a nice lawn quickly. It did, but then carried on growing quickly from then on! This meant that during the summer months, the lawn cutting was almost a full-time job! Not one of my best ideas!

➢ **Turf:** As I just mentioned, turfing is probably the most commonly chosen option when it comes to creating a lawn for self-builders. It is cheap, it creates an attractive finished job fast and it can be laid at any time of year (some suppliers recommend winter laying rather than summer laying). Two people can usually turf a decent sized lawn in a few hours.

Preparation of the ground to take the turf is pretty much the same as for seeding. If you don't prepare properly and leave stones and brick in the ground, the chances are you will end up with an uneven, stony lawn after a few months.

Turf will usually be delivered to site in rolls of approximately 1 sq m. These can be lifted by hand and rolled out in position. To cut the turf, you can either rip it or cut it with a spade.

The laying process goes like this:

- Start at in one corner and work across to the opposite corner, facing the bare soil.
- Stand on timber boards rather than the soil (to avoid indentations).
- Stagger the joints so they look like brick wall. Avoid gaps.
- If you find a hollow or bumpy area, level it out with some sand.
- Once you have laid the whole area, lightly roll it with a garden roller or "tamp" it with a flat piece of timber nailed to a brush handle.
- Leave the turf undisturbed for a few days. This time is critical for root development.

Cost wise. Turf can be bought in bulk from around £1.25 per sq m. High quality turf will cost up to £5.00 per sq m.

Try to make the time to go to the supplier's yard to have a look at the different types of turf available. Different types can give very different finished appearances to your lawn.

➢ **Artificial grass:** I have seen this stuff appearing more and more over the past few years, in builders' merchants and at trade and self-build shows. The sellers of artificial grass seem to be saying to us:

"Want more time to yourselves? Fed up with mowing the lawn in during the summer months? Well, why not just cover it with green plastic and be done with it?"

Ok, that may be a little harsh, but wherever I see either stands with samples of this type of lawn on them, or I see an actual lawn covered over by it, I immediately think: "That's plastic!" It just looks wrong to me (that is a purely personal opinion). You can usually see the joints and where there are any uneven areas, they stand out like a sore thumb because the light catches them differently, showing up any imperfections. The blades are too standard and not grass blade shaped. The blade colours are obviously trying to copy the natural colours, but they don't quite manage it. Even from a distance, it is obvious where a lawn is artificial because it simply looks artificial!

Don't take my word for it, if you need to lay a lawn and you are considering this product as an option, get some samples or go to a builders' merchant who sell it and see if you agree or not. If you like it, just ignore my ranting!

Cost wise, it is more expensive than turf or seeding and you need to prepare differently before you lay it. The process involves getting the sub surface pretty level, then laying and compacting sand at about 35mm thick. Any unevenness in this layer will be visible through the turf. I would suggest that you then apply a good weedkiller to the whole area. The next job is to lay a good quality weed barrier over the whole area (which will probably cost more than turf on its own), leaving it a couple of inches short all around the edges of the proposed lawn area.

Lay the artificial turf in a similar manner to laying natural turf, but make sure you lay each piece with the grain sloping in the same direction. Cut the ends where required with a sharp blade to get a good straight joint.

Once the turf has been laid, you then need to go around with special tape and joint every piece of turf together, by fixing the tape facing upwards to the underside of all edges. You then need to add an adhesive to each joint. The advice is then to "fluff up" the joints to try to disguise them.

Around the edges, you need to stick pins through the turf at about 8" apart to hold it down and again, fluff up the turf around each pin.

I don't know about you, but to my mind, all that just says *nightmare!* Not only while you are laying it, but imagine a few years down the line when weeds have started growing through the mat, the edges have all frayed, the lawn has settled with wear and pulled some of the joints apart, showing bare ground where they do and allowing weeds to grow.

Ok, I'll stop! Can someone out there prove me wrong? If so, get on touch and I'll update this bit and apologise to the artificial turfing industry!

7) External fixtures and fittings

I am only going to touch lightly on this subject. There are literally thousands of external fixtures and fittings that you can choose from, to finish and enhance the external areas of your new home.

All I am going to do is look at the subject more broadly as part of your overall project and make a few comments which you might wish to consider as you go about choosing all your finishing bits and bobs.

1) Cost

You may be short of money by now, so you need to bear in mind that some of the things listed below can make a big dent in your overall budget without necessarily giving you value for money. However, some of the items listed are cheap, useful and will add to the end value of your finished home.

- **Conservatories** can cost well over £10,000, take a big chunk of your garden away and may add little to the value of the house. Building a garden or sun room into the original design, which has a lot of glazed area to do pretty much the same job as a conservatory, could be a much better option.
- **Planting:** As I said earlier, I am not going to go into landscaping or landscaping design in any detail in this book, however it is worth me just mentioning how a small amount of careful planting can be used to turn a building site into a garden in a short time and at low cost. In my business as a housing developer, I have created a couple of show homes to help me to sell the houses I have been building.
Any show house needs to have kerb appeal in order to get people through the door. A nice house with a tatty front garden loses a lot of its appeal, so about ten years ago, I decided I needed to come up with a simple and quick way to turn the front garden of one of the houses I built into something which looked nice, so that it didn't put anyone off coming to have a look inside.
The property already had a brick paved driveway, but the garden (which was a fair size) either side of the drive was a mess.
All I did to turn the area into something that looked reasonable, was to level the whole area, spread a few inches of topsoil out, buy 2 dozen evergreen bushes, each around 18" high and plant them around the length and curves of the driveway. I then added a few feature bushes, dotted around the main area of the garden. Finally, I laid a good quality weed barrier and bought about 3 tonnes of forest bark to cover the whole area. The result looked really impressive and even got comments from viewers (potential buyers) to the house.
The cost? About £350 - £400.
There is no reason why you could not do something similar on your project to get yourselves a tidy looking garden in a short time and on a low budget. Anything more would be a bonus.

- **External lighting** can add that bit of glitz and luxury. Driveway lighting, decking lighting, floodlighting etc. can all be built in to your initial plans without costing the earth.
- **External heating** is getting popular for patio / decking / barbeque areas. Heaters attached to the wall can extend your options when it comes to sitting out late in to the evenings. They don't cost a lot to install, however, they are expensive to use and are not at all sustainable. A log fire-pit built into, or close to your patio or decking (watch out for fire risks) can be a much more visually attractive option, whilst also being classed as sustainable and not costing much to install.
- **Ponds / water features** can create an attractive feature but the more elaborate ones can eat significantly in to your budget. The sound of running water is a very relaxing sound and is a good feature to include where you may be sitting outside to relax. If cash is tight, consider stand-alone equipment rather than permanent fixtures. They will usually cost a lot less and you have the option of taking them with you when you move.
- **Boundary security / cameras** may be a good idea on the top end of the housing range, but generally, for thee and me, the bunch of folk who don't have Bentleys sitting on the drive, just some simple security will usually suffice. Gravel drives and paths make a noise when they are trodden on and are a great security feature. External floodlighting is cheap to install and is also a very good security device. 500 watt floodlights on each corner of the house and possibly somewhere near the gate can be a good security investment.
- **Outside audio-visual entertainment equipment** is generally quite expensive to install and you may not get the benefit from it unless you live in a remote location where the noise it creates is not going to disturb the neighbours. It may seem like a great idea, but after you have had the police around a couple of time after complaints from the neighbours, it may be consigned to sit unused, going rusty from then on.
- **Hot tubs** are the dream of many self-builders. The thought of having your own hot tub in the back garden is an enticing one. However, hot tubs are a bit like Marmite. You either love them or hate them.

  Just bear in mind before you go paying out between £5,000 - £10,000 to buy and install a decent one (especially if there is a chance that you may move within the next few years and even more so if you are going to build some sort of housing for the tub), that other people may not think the same as you do on this subject. Having a permanently situated hot tub in the garden could be something that puts some potential buyers off buying the house. They are also expensive to run, need constant maintenance and after the initial excitement of having one wears off, can sit for months on end without being used.
- **Insect resistant areas** are something not a lot of people think about but, from my own experience, insects can spoil a good evening in the garden.

  On my next self-build, I am going to incorporate a sheltered area which has a very fine mesh netting curtain designed in to it, which can be dropped around the sitting area to stop insects getting at us while we sit and relax (without impeding the view of the garden or the sunset).

  A simple door opening flap can be built in to the mesh to allow the next round of drinks to be delivered from the kitchen!

2) Longevity:

A lot of the external features you will see online or at the shows are a bit gimmicky. They can seem like a good idea at the time, but they can just be something that has suddenly become fashionable and will only be around for a short time.

If you see new products which catch your eye that you are considering incorporating in to your project, before buying them, just ask yourself the question: "Am I going to still be getting regular use out of this in 10 years' time?". If not, then give it some more thought before buying.

3) Simplicity

As you plan your external finishes, just remember that *simple* usually tends to offer good value, whilst *complicated* tends to be more expensive and not necessarily be worth the money you pay for it.

As a self-builder, you will normally have a finite budget and it is easy to persuade yourself that something is a great idea when in fact it is a complicated and expensive gimmick.

For example, a very nice quality set of patio furniture may set you back £1,000+ and it could give you and the family pleasure for years, whereas installing a powered awning above your patio, which has to be permanently wired in to your main electrics and will probably need regular maintenance, could cost up to five time that amount and only be used very intermittently.

4) Blending in with the rest of the job:

A simple example of what I mean by blending in, would be the inclusion of Roman style pillars at the front entrance of the house, to try to give the message that "This house is a Roman mansion, lifted brick by brick from Rome and re built here in Swindon". I have seen lots of examples of this around the country and, unless it is done properly and as part of a significantly large building, it can just look silly.

Similarly, trying to incorporate other features you see on other houses which you like and want to add in to your own project can be something that can seriously backfire and cost you a lot of money at the same time. Things like:

- Grand automatic gates on little houses.
- Full height lamp posts on short drives.
- Swimming pools / hot tubs in tiny back gardens.
- Artificial turf around traditional cottage style buildings.
- Grand water features, various statues, concrete lions on top of gate posts (which will turn in to strange gargoyles a few years later after a few harsh winters have caused them to lose some of their features)

8) Garden walls / fencing:

We Brits *do* like our garden walls, our fencing and our gates!

Using these features around our homes is something that is bred in to us from a young age, with the old saying: "An Englishman's house is his castle" still being just as relevant today as it was 50 years ago.

I have no problem with walls, gates or fences. I think that in the right place and if they are done properly, they enhance the overall development, whilst increasing privacy and security and not necessarily costing a fortune.

In case you are planning on installing fences and / or gates, I'll just run through some of the things you might want to think about:

9) Brick / block garden walls

This option is, is far and away the most expensive way to create a perimeter boundary to your garden. It is also the most permanent, the strongest and needs the least maintenance.

Whether you build the wall in brick, or block with a rendered finish, you are going to need to undertake some or all the following operations:

- **Clear the whole perimeter** of debris and topsoil
- **Excavate a foundation** around 300mm (12") wider than the wall itself (bearing in mind that you may need to get permission from your neighbour to pour the foundation a few inches inside his garden so that the face of the wall itself will sit exactly on the boundary. You may also need planning permission).

- **Pour concrete** to the full length of the foundation. This can involve barrowing concrete a long way from the delivery wagon, which may have to stay at the front boundary. You need to make sure that the top of the foundation is level along its whole length (allowing for steps ups and step downs) and that it is at the right level for the brickwork, so that the wall can be built using full thickness bricks (which don't need to be cut to reach an exact level for the top of the wall).
- **Get all materials / plant delivered** and spread around the job, trying to minimise the amount of labour required to then carry everything from A to B from where you have left them, to where they are needed when the brickies arrive (this is called double handling and wastes time and money).
- **Get the brickies in to build the wall,** again remembering that you may need to work on your neighbour's garden to be able to build it, for which you may need to get their permission (possibly disturbing some of their landscaping to do so).
- **Bring scaffolding in if and when required.**
- **Possibly source special coping stones** to "top off" the fully built wall.

From that list of jobs, it is easy to see where the high cost arises, but if you choose this option and you are using decent brickies, you should end up with a finished product that will enhances your home and increase its value.

Fencing

For people with limited or even reasonably good budgets, there is normally a fencing option which will suit your project and you pocket. If you are good at DIY and you do a bit of homework on how to erect fencing, you could think about taking on this task yourself.

There are two main types of garden fencing: 1) **Pre-made panels** and 2) **In-situ** fencing.

1) **Pre-made panels:** we have all seen the array of fencing panels in the garden centres. There are dozens of styles to choose from. Standard panels are 8ft long and come in heights from 2'6" to 8".
Costs for pre-made panels range from around £10 for a simple waney lap style and go up to £80+ for fancy style panels with curves, trellis or other features built into them.
To erect this type of fence you will need to buy the panels, fence posts and fixing materials. The supplier will show you your options.

You will also need to decide how you are going to bed the fence posts. Your choices are to concrete them in, or to use metal spikes, which you first hammer in to the ground at exact centres (calculated to match the width of the fence panel). Once you have checked their positioning, you can then slot the posts in to the top of the spike and tighten the spike around the post.

The spikes generally look like this

If you decide to concrete the posts in, you need to excavate holes at centres which match the length of the panels, usually allowing for at least 4" of concrete around the post. Carefully locating the post within the hole for level, plumb, height and line, you can then concrete it into its final position.

You will need to support the post whilst the concrete sets, to stop it from moving.

Once the concrete has set, or the spike has been driven, you can then fix your panels between the posts.

2) **In situ fencing:** The fixing of the posts for erecting an in situ fence, follows pretty much the same steps as the panel method, however, instead of fixing the panels between the posts, two or three timber rails (depending on the height of the fence) are fixed horizontally between the post. To these rails are then fixed lengths of timber to form up the finished fence, as shown here:

Extras / options to consider:

- **Think about using a concrete base panel** below the timber fence. These can prolong the life of the fence by raising the timber above the soil or grass and reducing its tendency to rot from the bottom up.
- **Concrete posts** can also prolong the life of fencing. Timber posts can often rot near the base due to touching the soil or grass. After a few years of being hammered by strong winds, this is where they tend to fail. Concrete posts solve this problem.
- **Good quality treatments:** The better the quality of the stain / treatment given to the fence, the longer it will last. Also make sure you treat all cut ends of both posts and panels, as this is where a lot of the moisture does its damages (especially via the end grain of the posts).

Chapter 16
Final certificates / snagging / moving in / vat refunds

Introduction

Well, here we are! The last chapter.

You should, by now be putting into place, the final few pieces of the jigsaw that has been your long-time dream and more recent adventure:

The mission to create your own dream home, your own Grand Design.

With a bit of luck, hopefully all you need to do now is to dot a few i's and cross a few t's and you'll literally be home and dry.

It has probably been hard work, stressful and a strain on you and your family, but if things have gone anything like to plan, once the dust has settled and you have had time to take a breath and recover, I bet you'll be thinking about having another go at some time in the future. If that is the case, that's great, but first you just need to get this project finished properly.

At this stage of the job it is very easy to wind everything down and just concentrate on getting yourself and your family in to the house. Don't do that! Just *hang fire* for a bit longer and get all the loose ends tied up, otherwise they will be hanging around for months.

Before you move in you need to get your final certificates from both the warranty company and Building Control. The house is not passed as being fit for habitation until you have done so.

If you move in too early and something goes wrong, which can be associated with you living in the property, you may find it difficult to make an insurance claim. You may also find yourself getting phone calls from the warranty inspectors saying *"OI! - What are you playing at? The house isn't finished!"*

In this chapter I am going to run through the final bits of the jigsaw, the bits that should only take you a few days to sort out, but are just as important as the rest of the build. Once you get these done, *then* is the time to move in and to start to enjoy your shiny, fantastic, brand new home!

So, here is your final check list of *to do's* for the practical works:

1. Plan a moving in date but don't start moving in

The worst thing you can do at this stage of the project is to start to bring your furniture and belongings in to the building, before all the final finishing works and snagging have been completed. If you do, you will forever be moving them from room to room, as you find they are in the way of the plumber, or decorator, or whoever needs to get to the bit of the room where you have stored your stuff!

By all means, provisionally book your removals company for a date in a few days or a couple of weeks' time from now.

Start to pack (leaving out just what you will need for the next few days) and plan where everything is going to go when you do start to move it in to the new house.

Sort out the kids change of school, re-direct the post from a couple of weeks' time, start to get your utility bills sorted out at the *old* end and your utility suppliers at the *new* end, but if at all possible leave the new house completely empty of all your personal baggage until the appropriate time.

What often happens when you move in too early, is that you take one enormous sigh of relief and you start to think "*Well that's it, we're pretty much done. We'll do the odds and ends in the next few weeks when we have had time to recover*". Don't fool yourself, you won't. You will be too busy enjoying all the rooms that are finished and usable, to go back to the hard work of getting builders in for the little bits that are left.

Just restrain yourself for a few more days and keep up the momentum that you have (hopefully) managed to build up over the past few months, to get to yourself over the finishing line before you start to think that the race has been run.

2. **Check all the finishing works and make sure there is nothing that has been missed or needs attention:**

This is an important job and getting it done properly it is another reason for keeping the house as clear of your things as possible.

Get yourself an A4 pad and pen and go slowly round the whole job, looking for problems. This is a surprisingly easy thing to do. When everything is clean, new and shiny, blemishes tend to stick out like a sore thumb.

- Run your hands over the paintwork. Is it a good finish?
- Are the skirtings, architraves and window boards all properly fitted? Are they caulked (*a thin line of filler around their edges, between them and the wall, applied by tube and mastic gun*).
- Are the sockets and switches level? Are there any screws missing?
- Are there cracks in floor or wall tiles? Or any missing grout? Are the edging strips fitted neatly?
- Are floor tiles laid so that there are no corners sticking up to catch the dirt, trip you up or just to look bad?
- Are the bare floors smooth, without cracks and ready to receive whatever finish they are going to take?
- Are the ceiling coving joints smooth and pretty much invisible?
- Is there paint on the windows? Do the windows open and close properly? Have the window lock keys been supplied?
- Do all the electrical and plumbing fittings work properly? Are there any bare cables anywhere?
- Is there any sign of leaking pipes on the ceilings, under radiators or anywhere else the pipework runs?
- Are worktops jointed properly? Do kitchen doors and drawers work smoothly?
- Do doors open and close properly (and do they catch the latches)? Is there paint on the handles or hinges? Do they squeak?
- Do fire doors operate correctly? Has the intumescent strip been fitted in to the fire door frames?
- Are there any creaks in the floor boards?
- Are there any blow holes in the plasterboards (where nails or screws have "popped" the surface of the plasterboard and blown a bit of the skim off, leaving a circular indent)?
- Are there any cracks in the plaster? If you have used dry lining, are any joints visible or rough?
- Has all the mastic work been done properly?
- Is the attic insulated correctly? Is there clear ventilation through the attic? (Check your building regs spec).
- Anything else?

Once you have thoroughly checked the inside of the building, go outside and do the same. Look for:

- Poor jointing in brickwork.
- Cracks or rough finishes to render.
- Poor painting or staining.
- Paint on windows and doors.
- Have all the gutters and downpipes been fitted correctly? Are there any signs of leaks?
- Have all holes through the walls been made good properly and tidily?
- Has all the mastic work been done properly?
- Has anyone left their mess on site?
- Do manhole covers fit correctly?
- Do any patio slabs wobble? Are the joints all done properly?
- Does any fencing feel loose?
- Are there any cracked brick pavings? Are there any cracks in an imprinted concrete drive?
- Does the driveway puddle when it rains?
- Anything else?

3. Look for potential air leaks

This is just a snagging item, but I have separated it from the rest because it is quite an important one when it comes to getting your final certificates.

Before the warranty and building control inspectors sign the job off as complete, you will need to carry out an air test on the structure. To my mind this is a complete waste of time, however, you are stuck with having to do it, so you need to be ready for it.

Basically, what you need to do is to identify any places around the exterior walls or roof of the house, where, if the building were to be pressurised, air could leak out to the outside. If you find any, you need to seal them.

You are looking for any poor joints, poor seals around doors and windows, poorly fitted loft hatches, anything where even the tiniest bit of air could escape.

You may think to yourself: "Hang on, I have a letter plate here that will let air out and vents in the kitchen, utility room and bathrooms and I have a fireplace with a chimney. Won't they let loads of air out?"

Yup! They will, but in their infinite wisdom, whoever writes the building regulations, decided that these areas are not important and they have concentrated on the bits of the house where the tiny leaks you may get, could cost you upwards of about 5p a year! (The test costs about £300 – £350!)

4. Get anyone you need, to come back and attend to whatever they need to

Make sure you do this before you pay the final invoices (preferably keeping the 5% retentions we discussed in an earlier chapter).

Use your snagging list (mentioned above), to list all the different jobs by trad" and, as quickly as possible, get everyone back you need, to tidy up their bits and pieces.

5. Re-check all the snagging to make sure you are happy with it

Take all your snagging lists (preferably whilst the people responsible for it are still on site) and go through all the items once they have (theoretically) been attended to. If you are still not 100% happy with the finished job, get whoever is responsible back on it, to get it right.

6. Clean up the outside / drive / cabins etc.

There is usually no reason why you can't be doing this at the same time as the snagging checks Once you start to bring your furniture, belongings and the whole family in to the house, you don't want them treading mud and other debris in to the house. So get everything outside as tidy as possible.

Off hire anything you have not yet off-hired (assuming you don't need it anymore). Pressure wash the drive to get rid of oil, mortar or anything else which may have landed on it and just get the whole of the outside (especially the entrance) looking as tidy and finished as possible.

7. Call in the airtightness testers

Once the snagging has been completed and you think you have caught all the potential air leaks, you can call in the airtightness testers.

When they arrive, they will require a house completely empty of people for the time they are there. No-one will be allowed in to the building.

What they do is seal up all the holes in the external walls and pressurise the whole building, then wait to see if it loses air or not. The amount it loses will determine whether or not it passes.

As part of the process, they will seal up your letter plate, all vents through walls, your fireplace and any other significant holes that will allow air to escape.

As I said earlier, what I find daft about this whole process is that once they have finished, they take off all the seals and reinstate all the original big holes such as a huge great gaping fireplace (which has an 9" hollow tube up and out through the roof), and either pass or fail you on the tiniest of other leaks in other places around the house.

Is this just me or is that daft?

8. Call in the warranty and building control inspectors

Assuming you have passed the air test (you will need the certificate), you can now call in the warranty and building control inspectors to check the house over one last time and hopefully pass it as complete.

Once you have this certificate you can legally move in. You can also claim your final payment on your stage mortgage and claim your VAT back.

The final inspection is always a bit of a nervy time. You may be just about standing at the front door with your suitcases when the inspectors call and if, for any reason the building fails the inspection, you might have to bring people and tools back in to start ripping things out or fixing things, basically making a mess of your nice clean home!

By the time you reach this stage, the inspectors will have carried out numerous inspections whilst the house is being built and they will have passed it at all those stages, so really, this inspection is only to cover the work that has been done since the last inspection (usually around the plastering stage). So as long as you have not dropped any major clangers, there should only be minor issues that need tending to after this final inspection.

If your house passes, the inspector will normally contact their office and they will post out your completion certificate within a few days. If you need it quickly (so you can claim your final stage payment, for example), they may be able to give you a provisional certificate whilst they are on site. If this is something that you want or need, mention it when you book the visit, so they remember to bring the certificate book with them.

9. Make the claim for your final mortgage stage payment

Once you have either your official final, or your provisional completion certificate from either one of the inspectors, you can contact your lender to ask them to free up the final stage mortgage payment.

They don't normally need to send anyone out to check and re-value the house at this stage, but if they do require that to happen, just get it organised as quickly as possible.

10. Move in:

At last! – Your big day has arrived. Get moved in and get as much as you can, sorted as quickly as possible. You are going to need to relax and have a good rest after all your efforts, so just try to make sure you are not looking at piles of unpacked stuff in every room you walk into.

The chances are that the first thing you will want to do is to invite family and friends over, to marvel at what you have created, so when sorting all your "stuff" out, it can be a good idea to concentrate first on the entertaining rooms.

Try and make this operation as quick, as complete and as final as possible so that you aren't having to constantly trek back and forth to your old home, to get bits and pieces you need.

11. Sort out the paperwork for and make your VAT refund claim:

By this point, whether you are a potential, or actual self-builder, you already know that new build self-build housing is zero rated for VAT (*funnily enough, that doesn't mean it is VAT free. – Oh no! - It is actually **eligible** for VAT, but it has been **set** at a rate of 0%. That makes it easier to change if the government fancy doing so at any time in the future*).

You can only make one VAT claim on a new build and that claim can only be made at the end of the project, once you have received your final certificates.

Assuming you have not delegated the whole project to one VAT registered contractor. you will have been paying VAT on most, if not all your materials and labour purchases for the duration of the build. It doesn't matter how long your build takes to complete, you only need to make your claim at the end of the job.

If you employ anyone on a supply and fit basis, they should not charge you VAT, however some of them will either try to, or even *insist* on doing so, saying you can claim the VAT back yourself at the end of the job. I have tried to argue with these people and they tend to simply say "Our accountant has told us to charge it". As long as they are the cheapest and best option, I would usually *just shut up and put up* when I am in that position!

To make a claim, you can go to hmrc.gov.uk and make your way to the VAT section, then drill down to the right pages to find a form "431NB". You can get an explanatory leaflet from the same place.

Alternatively, if you are reading this on your kindle reader on a computer, at the time of writing this, you can copy the link below and paste it in your browser:

https://www.gov.uk/government/uploads/system/uploads/attachment_data/file/487894/VAT431NB_form_and_notes.pdf

(The explanatory notes are included with the form from this link)

The refund claim you can make is for most of the building **materials**, including (this is not a comprehensive list):

Stone / concrete / cement / sand / additives / bricks / blocks / timber / timber Frame kits / lintels / insulation / roof trusses / roof coverings / windows / doors / ironmongery / plasterboards / plaster / electrical fittings / plumbing fittings / boiler / fitted kitchen units (not free standing units) / fitted bathroom equipment / paint / fitted wood flooring / fitted bedroom furniture (i.e. it fixed in to walls / floors, as opposed to free standing) / burglar alarms / solar panels. (and lots more).

There are also a lot of exceptions where VAT is charged, but is not reclaimable.

Use the VAT explanatory leaflet to check that you are completely clear about what you can claim and what you can't. If your claim is found to be faulty, it could be returned to be altered, which could waste time for you if you need the money quickly.

Make sure you keep good financial records during the project. If you lose just one invoice it could cost you dearly. Imagine losing the invoice for a load of bricks and not realising you had done so, for example:

10,000 bricks @ £400 / 100 + VAT = £4,000 + £800 = £4,800

You could just have lost £800 of your refund!

A good idea is to not only collect invoices, but also to collect delivery notes. Delivery notes are often lost on site. You may not be there when a delivery arrives and one of the guys will chuck the delivery note in the cabin or worse, in the skip!

Tell everyone on site that delivery notes are to be collected and give them a clip board to attach them to in the cabin so you can collect them regularly. Once you have all the delivery notes, you can easily and quickly reconcile them to the invoices when they arrive.

Another thing to watch out for, is being charged for non-deliveries. Sometimes the supplier will be short of something you have ordered and will scribble on the delivery note "not in stock". Theoretically, the copy of this note should be picked up by the admin department and a relevant deduction made to your full invoice, however, all too often, the alteration is missed and you may be charged for the full delivery, *including* the bits that were missing.

The VAT claim form is notoriously difficult to fill in, but it has got a bit easier in recent years. If you think you are going to struggle with it, just go on line and search "Self-build VAT refunds" and you should find a number of companies who will do it for you for a few hundred pounds

You will need to include the following with your claim:

- Originals of all invoices.
- Your claim calculations.
- The Completion certificate issued by building control.
- A copy of the planning permission.
- A full set plans for all the building and other works related to the claim.

Once you have submitted your claim, you should get an acknowledgement within a couple of weeks. If there are any problems with it, you will also be notified.

Depending on how busy the claims department is, the process may take three months or more before you get the money in your bank account.

Well that's about it!

If you are reading the book for the first time, hopefully you will now be *fired up and raring to go*, but whether you are or not, even if you are just thinking a bit more seriously about taking on your own self-build project, if you have the time and if you have found the book useful, I suggest that, when you are ready, you read it right through again, but next time, just concentrate on small sections at a time.

Hopefully, you have been making notes as you have been reading, so if you start again at the beginning, you will be able to mix what I have been saying, with your own thoughts to come up with a sensible plan that will suit you, your family and your own situation.

It's a bit like revising (but hopefully a bit more interesting!). By re-reading, with what you have learnt from the first read through and by adding your own thoughts in to the mix, you should start to become clearer on which of the myriad of choices you have in front of you that you like the look of and how everything would need to work for **you.**

As I said at the start, this is not a manual, it is a guide. Use it as such. Let it help you to do things in the right order, to research what you need and ignore what you don't need. Let it help you to make decisions at the right time, with the knowledge and confidence that if you make a wrong choice, there are always other options, either to fix what you messed up on, or to go back a step and head off down another, more appropriate route.

Although this is a substantial book, it has only touched on the overall subject of self-building. I have no doubt that some of you will have read it and will now be saying: "Well that was great, but I wanted to know more about specialist foundations, or extensions / refurbs / retaining walls / sustainability / straw bales / ground source heating / balconies / kitchens / bathroom fittings, or community build. – Ok, I hold my hands up. – Guilty as charged! There is not a lot of information on those subjects (and many others) within these pages. If there had been, you would need to buy a wheelbarrow just to carry the book! However, what I hope I have done here is to show you simple ways to work out what all the other stuff is that is not in the book, for yourself.

I hope I have helped to enable you to make your own choices, with just a bit of a nudge in the right direction and a bit of an explanation of what to expect and how to deal with it, whichever route you take.

If I have managed to do that, I have done my job here.

Over the past few years whilst I have been acting as Self-build expert for Grand Designs Live (*the show with the TV programme's ethos*) and Homebuilding & Renovating Magazine's live shows, I have spoken to literally hundreds of people who would love to take on a self-build project, but for one reason or another have not had the confidence to do so.

If this book has one overall aim, it is to give people the confidence, the nerve and the will to have a go, with the knowledge that as they do so, they are aware of what they need to do and how and when they need to do it.

So, what are you waiting for? Get off your chair and get on with it! (and let me know if I have been of any help when it is all done and dusted).

Good luck!

Printed in Great Britain
by Amazon